De Gruyter Handbook of Sustainable Entrepreneurship Research

De Gruyter Handbook of Sustainable Entrepreneurship Research

Edited by
Gjalt de Jong, Niels Faber, Emma Folmer, Thomas B. Long
and Berfu Ünal

DE GRUYTER

ISBN 978-3-11-221397-1
e-ISBN (PDF) 978-3-11-075615-9
e-ISBN (EPUB) 978-3-11-075620-3
ISSN 2748-016X
e-ISSN 2748-0178

Library of Congress Control Number: 2023937426

Bibliographic information published by the Deutsche Nationalbibliothek
The Deutsche Nationalbibliothek lists this publication in the Deutsche Nationalbibliografie;
detailed bibliographic data are available on the internet at http://dnb.dnb.de.

Typesetting: Integra Software Services Pvt. Ltd.
Printing and binding: CPI books GmbH, Leck

www.degruyter.com

De Gruyter Handbooks in Business, Economics and Finance

De Gruyter Handbook of Personal Finance
Edited by: John E. Grable and Swarn Chatterjee

De Gruyter Handbook of Entrepreneurial Finance
Edited by: David Lingelbach

De Gruyter Handbook of Organizational Conflict Management
Edited by: LaVena Wilkin and Yashwant Pathak

De Gruyter Handbook of Sustainable Development and Finance
Edited by: Timothy Cadman and Tapan Sarker

De Gruyter Handbook of Responsible Project Management
Edited by: Beverly L. Pasian and Nigel Williams

De Gruyter Handbook of Business Families
Edited by: Michael Carney and Marleen Dieleman

De Gruyter Handbook of Disability and Management
Edited by: Joy E. Beatty, Sophie Hennekam and Mukta Kulkarni

For more information, scan QR code below or visit https://www.degruyter.com/serial/dghbef-b/html

Contents

Part III: **Sustainable Entrepreneurship and Context**
Thomas B. Long

Part IV: **Business Models**
Niels Faber

Part V: **Performance and Impact**
Emma Folmer, Valerija Golubic

List of Contributors

Shatabdi Acharjee is an ex-MS student at the Rural Sociology Department at Bangladesh Agricultural University. Her MS thesis focuses on the challenges and opportunities of women's online businesses in Bangladesh. She holds a Bachelor of Science degree in Agricultural Economics from Bangabandhu Sheikh Mujibur Rahman Agricultural University, Bangladesh. Music is her special interest. She loves painting, cycling and travelling.

Wee Chan Au is Lecturer in Management Practice at Newcastle University Business School (NUBS). She received her PhD in Human Resource Management from Monash University. Her research interest lies in work, health and well-being. She has published her work in edited books and in leading scholarly journals such as the *Journal of Business Ethics*, *Career Development International*, *Human Resource Development International*, *Journal of Social Entrepreneurship* and *Personnel Review*. Wee Chan is interested in supporting young people to engage in social innovation and social entrepreneurship activities. In addition, she engages young people to take active roles in sustainability and addressing social issues through various educational endeavours.

Frank Berkers, MSc, is a senior scientist at TNO Strategic Business Analysis where he is, since 2008, the lead scientist for business modelling and value network analysis. He developed several methods to support collaborative and sustainable business modelling and analysis, including the Value Case Methodology. He has founded and is a trainer in TNO's strategic initiative Orchestrating Innovation, which trains leaders of large open societal impact focused innovation hubs and networks. He is currently pursuing a PhD on 'strategic decision making for platform business models'. Frank holds a master's degree in Econometrics from Maastricht University. Before joining TNO, he has held positions at ABN AMRO as a marketing/consumer intelligence analyst and at market research agency SKIM as a senior methodologist where he set up preferred suppliers, with McKinsey and Monitor, in the field of computer-aided choice experiments.

Vincent Blok is Associate Professor in Philosophy of Technology and Responsible Innovation at the Philosophy Group, Wageningen University (the Netherlands). He is also Director of the 4TU. Ethics Graduate School in the Netherlands. In 2005, he received his PhD in philosophy at Leiden University with a specialisation in philosophy of technology. Together with seven PhD candidates and four post-docs, he reflects on the meaning of disruptive technologies for the human condition and its environment from a continental philosophical perspective. His books include *Ernst Jünger's Philosophy of Technology: Heidegger and the Poetics of the Anthropocene* (Routledge, 2017), *Heidegger's Concept of Philosophical Method* (Routledge, 2020) and *The Critique of Management* (Routledge, 2022). Blok has published over a hundred articles in high-ranked philosophy journals like *Environmental Values*, *Business Ethics Quarterly*, *Synthese* and *Philosophy & Technology*, and in multi-disciplinary journals like *Science*, *Journal of Cleaner Production*, *Public Understanding of Science* and *Journal of Responsible Innovation*. See www.vincentblok.nl for more information about his current research.

Alain Daou is Associate Professor of Entrepreneurship at the Olayan School of Business (OSB) and Director of the Nature Conservation Center at the American University of Beirut. Through his research, Alain looks at how social enterprises innovate, scale up and have a positive impact, with a particular focus on extreme contexts. In 2020, he was chosen as part of the #thinklist of racialised thinkers in responsible business by the University of Bath's Centre for Business, Organisation and Society (CBOS). In 2021 the SME impact initiative at Khaddit Beirut that he chairs was recognised as an AACSB International Innovation That Inspires.

Hellen Dawo is a Kenyan researcher, now based in the Netherlands. She obtained her Bachelor of Science degree from Moi University, Kenya. For over five years she worked in manufacturing and

https://doi.org/10.1515/9783110756159-203

agricultural research in western Kenya. In 2016 she embarked on a master's in Environmental and Energy management at the University of Twente in the Netherlands, graduating with a cum laude distinction. Her PhD studies commenced in November 2018, after completing a year as a trainee at Phillips, Amsterdam office. Given her expertise in environmental issues and governance, Hellen's current research focuses on understanding the influence of contexts such as regulatory institutions, incumbent enterprises, local authorities, and local community on creation and growth of sustainable enterprises. She has presented her preliminary findings at various influential European and American conference meetings in her study area. Between 2019 and 2020, she also worked with the Global Center on Adaptation to develop an online introductory course on climate adaptation governance. Hellen is currently a lecturer at Utrecht University.

Milou Derks is a senior programme coordinator at Orange Corners where she focuses on stimulating entrepreneurship and employment for women and youth in low- and middle-income countries. She is also a PhD student at the Department of Industrial Engineering and Innovation Sciences at the Eindhoven University of Technology (TU/e). Her research interests focus on ecosystem- and business model-thinking for scaling sustainable and circular innovations in the Global South. Her research results are regularly published in journals and conference proceedings.

Andreana Drencheva is Senior Lecturer (Associate Professor) in Entrepreneurship at King's College London (UK). Her research interests focus on why and how individuals and communities engage in (social) entrepreneurship in their local, often under-researched, context and with what intended and unintended impact. Her research has appeared in journals such as *Business & Society, Entrepreneurship Theory and Practice, Journal of Business Ethics, Journal of Business Venturing, Journal of Small Business Management* and *Journal of Social Entrepreneurship*. She collaborates with support organisations to co-create services, programmes and tools that help (aspiring) social entrepreneurs to develop their ventures, while maintaining their well-being.

Manon Eikelenboom is a postdoctoral researcher at the Organization Sciences department of the Vrije Universiteit Amsterdam (VU). She obtained her PhD from the Centre for Sustainable Entrepreneurship at the Faculty Campus Fryslân, University of Groningen, and her Master of Science in Global Economics and Management (research master) from the University of Groningen. Her research focus is on the transition towards a circular economy in the building sector, paying attention to organisational change and multi-party collaboration including topics such as trust, role divisions and power dynamics. In her research, she actively engages with practitioners through focus group discussions and action research methodologies.

Margo Enthoven is a postdoctoral researcher at the Department of Entrepreneurship, Innovation and Technology of the Stockholm School of Economics. She obtained her PhD from the Centre for Sustainable Entrepreneurship at the Faculty Campus Fryslân, University of Groningen. Her research focuses on the role of opportunity recognition in sustainable entrepreneurship, and how individual values and social networks come into play to explain the processes behind sustainable opportunity recognition.

Philipp Eppe is a research associate and PhD student at the Department of Resilient Energy Systems at the University of Bremen. He obtained his Master of Science in Environmental Psychology at the University of Groningen. His research focus is on investigating socio-technical transformation pathways. He is developing an interactive, agent-based modelling platform by linking socio-technical and participatory methods and by developing and integrating suitable methods in the field of complex decision-making.

Fatima Zannat Esha received a Master of Science in Rural Sociology degree with the highest CGPA in her class from Bangladesh Agricultural University. In her MS thesis, she researched women's entrepreneurship, empowerment and psychological well-being. She graduated with a Bachelor of Science degree in Agricultural Economics from Bangabandhu Sheikh Mujibur Rahman Agricultural University. She is a research fellow of the COVID-19 and Climate Change project funded by IORA-GIZ. She appreciates contributing her skills to research which addresses different socio-economic challenges. She aspires to be a full-time researcher in the socio-economic arena.

Niels Faber is Assistant Professor at the University of Groningen (Faculty Campus Fryslan) and researcher/lecturer at Hanze University of Applied Sciences. His research focuses on the organisational aspects of sustainability and the circular economy. This translates into such themes as sustainable and circular business models, and the ensuing transition and assessment of the progress made towards a circular economy. He has produced numerous academic and professional publications and is co-editor of a series of online columns on the circular economy and the triple transition (climate challenge, energy transition and circular economy). Recently, he co-edited the book *Organizing for Sustainability* (Open Access publication at Palgrave-MacMillan).

K. S. Farid is a Professor in the Department of Rural Sociology of the Bangladesh Agricultural University, Bangladesh. He is a social demographer and a qualitative researcher by training and practice. 'Neo-Marxist perspective on international migration and how migration creates inequality' is the main focus of his academic research. He is interested in studying the dynamics and underpinnings of political history and political economy and how diplomatic practices affect them. He has published research articles and project reports on various socio-economic issues including migration.

Emma Folmer is Assistant Professor of Sustainable Entrepreneurship at the Faculty Campus Fryslân, University of Groningen, the Netherlands. Her research focuses on the spatial and institutional context of conventional and social entrepreneurship. She is also interested in community and collective entrepreneurship and creating impact in local communities. Emma is currently researching this in the context of community energy groups through the CREDs funded project 'Social Entrepreneurship at the Grid Edge: Understanding the Opportunities for Community Led DSR and Collective Self-Consumption' with Dr Charlotte Johnson, Dr Anna Rebmann and Ms Alexandra Schneiders.

Rick Gilsing is a business consultant/scientist at TNO Strategic Business Analysis (the Netherlands) as well as holds a position as a researcher in the Department of Industrial Engineering and Innovation Sciences at the Eindhoven University of Technology (TU/e). His research interests relate to topics on business engineering and innovation, particularly in the context of service-dominant business and collaborative, networked ecosystems. Currently, he focuses on supporting the evaluation and innovation of collaborative business models through design science-based research, developing techniques and methods in supporting decision making on the innovation of such business models. His research results are regularly published in IS journals and conference proceedings.

Valerija Golubic is a PhD student at the Centre for Sustainable Entrepreneurship at the Faculty Campus Fryslân, University of Groningen, where she also obtained her Master of Science degree in Sustainable Entrepreneurship. Her research focuses on social entrepreneurship. More specifically, she investigates the trade-offs between social and financial performance and the role of social enterprises' business models in this relationship, stakeholder-induced tensions in social enterprises, and the legitimation strategies undertaken in order to deal with the tensions.

Angela Greco is a scientist at the Strategic Analysis and Policy department of TNO, the Netherlands Organisation for Applied Scientific Research, and a research affiliate at the University of Groningen. She is one of the recipients of the 'Top female Technology Fellowship' granted by the Delft University of Technology, where she has been appointed as Assistant Professor. Prior to these positions, she was a postdoctoral fellow at the Ivey Business School at Western University. She obtained her PhD from the Centre for Sustainable Entrepreneurship at the University of Groningen and her Master of Science in Civil Engineering from Delft University of Technology. Her theoretical focus is on the role of organisational hybridity in sustainability transitions and on participatory approaches for systemic design. Most of her work is dedicated to connecting academic research with urgent sustainability challenges.

Bart van Hoof is Associate Professor at the School of Management, Universidad de los Andes in Bogotá, Colombia. He holds a PhD in Industrial Ecology from Erasmus University in Rotterdam. His research and teaching interests are focused on dissemination of environmental management practices in industrial and agri-food systems in emerging markets. He has served as senior advisor of the National Strategies on Circular Economy of the Colombian and Peruvian governments, as the environmental director of Eco-petrol and worked as a consultant in the design and implementation of diffusion mechanisms for environmental management in Colombia, Peru, Paraguay, Panama and Mexico.

Alexandra Ioan is a practitioner and researcher focused on developing effective civil society organisations and governance processes. She has held various research and leadership positions in international organisations and academic settings which have shaped her strong commitment towards a constructive exchange between research and practice. She completed her PhD in Governance at the Hertie School in Berlin and has collaborated with, among others, the Stanford Center on Philanthropy and Civil Society, the Competence Center for Nonprofit Organizations and Social Entrepreneurship at Vienna University, Ashoka, the German Marshall Fund of the United States, and the EU Presidency Project of CONCORD Europe.

Mona Itani is Assistant Professor at the Suliman S. Olayan School of Business at the American University of Beirut since 2021. Prior to this role, she was appointed as the coordinator of the Entrepreneurship Initiative at the Maroun Semaan Faculty of Engineering and Architecture from 2018 to 2021 where she was driving the faculty's mission to become a leading entrepreneurship and innovation school in Lebanon and the Middle East. She is a published author on entrepreneurship, women, ethics and education. She founded Riyada for Social Innovation SAL in 2017 and in 2020, she co-founded Shabab Lab, the first social innovation e-learning platform in the region. She is a renowned public speaker, award-winner and expert on entrepreneurship and social innovation in the Arab world.

Charlotte Johnson is head of research programmes at the Centre for Sustainable Energy. Her research focuses on domestic energy use and community engagement in urban transition. She is currently providing social research support to community energy groups through a knowledge exchange grant, including Repowering London who are trialling a P2P electricity market in a London housing estate. Previously, she worked as the social researcher on Energywise, a DNO-led randomised control trial of smart meters in 500 low-income homes. She has published on the gender impacts of Demand Side Response based on this trial.

Gjalt de Jong is Professor of Sustainable Entrepreneurship in a Circular Economy at the Faculty Campus Fryslân, University of Groningen. Professor de Jong builds on more than 30 years of experience in academia, business and management. He holds a Master of Science in Economics and a PhD in Business Administration from the University of Groningen. He is the chair and head of the Sustainable Entrepreneurship in a Circular Economy department, founder-former director of the Master of Science programme Sustainable Entrepreneurship, founder-director of the Centre for Sustainable Entrepreneurship, founder of the Sustainable Start-up Academy and chair of the board of the faculty's research institute. He currently also serves as the strategy advisor for the president of the University of Groningen, concerning systemic transitions in agriculture. Prior to his current position, he served as Associate Professor at the Faculty of Economics and Business, University of Groningen, and as senior management consultant for KPMG and PricewaterhouseCoopers.

Jan Jonker is Emeritus Professor of Sustainable Entrepreneurship at Radboud University, Nijmegen (the Netherlands), appointed to his chair for life. His work focuses on activist contributions to shaping a different economy, based on new concepts of value creation around sustainability, social inclusion and circularity. The basis of his work are the 'slow' trends that shape the economy as well as society. He specialises in sustainable and circular business models and strategy, and in particular looks at how change, transition and transformation present key challenges, and what concepts and tools are available to address them. He works at home and abroad and is an enthusiastic public speaker in four languages (Dutch, French, English and [rusty] German).

Geo Kocheril studied Applied Systems Science (MSc) at the University of Osnabruck. He worked at the Wuppertal Institute for Climate, Energy and Environment, where he was part of an interdisciplinary team developing a computational model of energy systems. As a research associate at the Department of Resilient Energy Systems at the University of Bremen, he focuses his research on modelling socio-technical energy systems and transdisciplinary decision support systems. He is trained as a 'Peace and Conflict Consultant' at the Academy for Conflict Transformation (forumZFD, Cologne). He is also interested in applying socio-psychological research in models of conflict transformation in the context of energy systems.

Thomas B. Long is Assistant Professor of Sustainable Entrepreneurship at the Faculty Campus Fryslân, University of Groningen, and a member of the university's Centre for Sustainable Entrepreneurship. Tom's research interests focus on responsible innovation in contexts of sustainable entrepreneurship, success factors for sustainable business models and the role of entrepreneurship in postgrowth economies. Tom's PhD, completed at the University of Leeds (UK) in 2013, focused on management of supply chain greenhouse gas emissions by public and private focal organisations in the UK.

Jacob Lundberg, MSc in Entrepreneurial Engineering, is the Incubation Manager of the Start-up Incubator at Aalborg University (Copenhagen), Denmark. He has his academic roots in software and is a former tech entrepreneur. Jacob has been part of several start-ups, often responsible for business development and management. He supports and coaches entrepreneurs with various perspectives on sustainability from early concept development to scaling the business and connecting with investors.

Alyssa Matteucci has spent the past decade working to improve the social sector. She started her career at the Duckworth Lab at the University of Pennsylvania, where she studied psychological determinants of success. She wanted to understand what helps individuals to persevere through hardship and reach their full potential. This experience opened her eyes to the systemic barriers that threaten individuals' success. Since then, she's held research positions at the Wharton Social Impact Initiative, Ashoka, and ImpactED, an impact-evaluation consultancy serving non-profits. In each of these roles, Alyssa used research to help organisations to provide greater opportunity to their constituents.

Laviu Mozumdar is Professor of Rural Sociology at Bangladesh Agricultural University. He holds a PhD in entrepreneurship from Wageningen University, the Netherlands. He teaches graduate-level rural entrepreneurship and innovation and quantitative research methods, and supervises MS and PhD students. He has 14 years of research experience, including more than 8 years in entrepreneurship. He runs research projects financed by Nuffic-Niche, USAID, and GIZ. He has published research articles in Clarivate- and Scopus-indexed journals. He is the Associate Editor of the *Bangladesh Journal of Agricultural Economics* (2022–2024) and an editorial board member of the *Journal of Developmental Entrepreneurship*. Currently, his research interests extend to digital entrepreneurship in emerging countries.

Rikke Kristine Nielsen, PhD in management and organisation studies, holds a position as Associate Professor at the Department of Communication and Psychology, Aalborg University (Copenhagen), Denmark, where she is affiliated with the Environmental Humanities research cluster. Nielsen's research is focused on leadership paradoxes and organisational transformation, particularly in global/international settings. Nielsen pursues these research interests through collaborative and co-creational forms of research such as action research and action learning with a view to creation of knowledge with both academic and practical/societal impact (https://vbn.aau.dk/da/persons/136386).

Onno Omta defended his PhD thesis at the University of Groningen on the Management of Innovation in the pharmaceutical industry in 1995. From 2000 to 2018, he was Chaired Professor in Business Administration at Wageningen University (the Netherlands). During his professorship, 50 of his PhD students defended their PhD theses successfully. He is (co-)author of many scientific articles on innovation management. His research interests encompass entrepreneurship and innovation in chains and networks in the life sciences.

Stefano Pascucci is Professor of Sustainability and Circular Economy at Exeter University. He is a social scientist interested in sustainability connected to organisation theories, innovation management, entrepreneurship and value chain analysis. His research focuses on agribusiness, sustainability and circular economy. He is particularly concerned about how to analyse the interplay between sustainability, innovation and value chain configurations. Prior to joining the University of Exeter Business School, in September 2016, Pascucci was Associate Professor of Innovation and Organisation of Agribusiness at the Management Studies Group of Wageningen University. From 2009 to 2011, he was post-doc Marie Curie Fellow at the Agricultural Economics group of Wageningen University. He holds a PhD in Agricultural Economics and Policy from the University of Naples Federico II (Italy). He is member of the Institutional and Organizational Economics Academy and alumnus of the Ronald Coase Institute.

Bartjan Pennink is Assistant Professor at the Department of Global Economics and Management, University of Groningen (RUG). The focus of his research is on modelling the process of Local Economic Development which is closely related with sustainable business models. He is involved in courses on Corporate Social Responsibility (MSc) and on Organizational Theory (BSc). From 2015, he has held a Visiting Lecturer position in the field of Research Methodology at the Institute of Finance Management in Tanzania (Dar es Salaam). He also contributes to the honours master's programmes of the RUG by Masterclasses on Ubuntu and on New (Sustainable) Economic Business Models. Besides his regular work, he is also a city guide (together with a team) that shows tourists how interesting Appingedam, the city where he lives, is. He is also a member of the choir, Toonkunst koor Delfzijl, and a chair of the workgroup, The Green Nicolai Church (working on sustainability).

Anna Rebmann is Lecturer in Social Entrepreneurship at King's Business School, King's College London. Her research focuses on comparative entrepreneurship – how the institutional and cultural context impacts both social and commercial entrepreneurship. She is also interested in how community-based social enterprises find opportunities and create change in their local communities. Anna is currently researching this in the context of community energy groups through the CREDs-funded project 'Social Entrepreneurship at the Grid Edge: Understanding the Opportunities for Community-Led DSR and Collective Self-Consumption' with Dr Charlotte Johnson, Dr Emma Folmer and Ms Alexandra Schneiders.

Arne Remmen is Professor of Technology, Environment and Society at the Department of Development and Planning, Aalborg University, and holds a PhD in Constructive Technology Assessment. Since 1980 he has done research in the relations between technological and social change and especially on the innovation dynamics within cleaner production, environmental management and cleaner products in industries as well as on the incentives and policy instruments to support this. The research has been action-oriented and conducted in close collaboration with both enterprises and governmental agencies in order to facilitate a transition towards circular economy and sustainable development.

Dana Schadenberg is a researcher in sustainability and identity. Departing from critical social theory, she investigates the systemic societal structures that underlie anthropogenic climate change and (un)sustainable behaviour in relation to identity formation. She is especially interested in how the Western-European understanding of autonomy characterises the relation of the self to (non)human others, and constructing an alternative understanding based on an appreciation of (bio)diversity, empathy and connection. Her interests brought her to research the role of education in developing environmental ethics. She has a background in identities and cultures of Europe, sustainable entrepreneurship, ethical and environmental philosophy, and international relations.

Alexandra Schneiders is Senior Research Associate at the University College London (UCL) Energy Institute and the Task Leader of the Global Observatory on Peer-to-Peer, Community Self-Consumption and Transactive Energy Models (GO-P2P), a Task of the User-Centred Technology Collaboration Programme by the International Energy Agency (IEA). Her research focuses on the policy and regulatory enablers/obstacles of rolling out peer-to-peer and community self-consumption models, including those using distributed ledger technologies (DLTs) such as blockchain, at UK and EU levels. Prior to joining the UCL Energy Institute in 2018, she was working in Brussels in political and legal consultancies, advising corporate and public sector clients, such as the European Commission, on energy and financial services-related topics. Her background is in law and politics, and she holds degrees from the University of Amsterdam as well as the College of Europe.

Mmapatla Precious Senyolo is Associate Professor of Agricultural Economics and Social Scientist Researcher at the School of Agricultural and Environmental Sciences, University of Limpopo (UL), South Africa. He obtained a PhD and MSc from Wageningen University and a BSc in Agricultural Economics from the UL. Her recent research includes studying how the characteristics of innovations impact their adoption; exploring climate-smart agricultural innovations in South Africa; enhancing the adoption of climate-smart technologies using public–private partnerships; and lessons from WEMA case in South Africa. Her research interests include the intersection of agricultural economics and development, policy and environmental economics, socio-economics of climate change and food security.

Denise Speck is a passionate change-maker. A graduate of the University of Groningen's Sustainable Entrepreneurship master's programme, Denise is now an independent sustainable entrepreneur who innovatively combines transdisciplinary research skills and the art of digital storytelling to support responsible businesses in creating long-term, sustainable impact.

Dr. rer. nat. Torben Stührmann received his PhD in 2009 from the Max-Planck-Institute for Marine Microbiology on microbial detoxification mechanisms in marine oxygen minimum zones. He then worked as a post-doctoral researcher at the Helmholtz Zentrum in Munich. In the context of his molecular biology work, he has made research visits to the USA and Israel. Since 2012 he has been working at the University of Bremen, focusing on socio-technical transformation research and resilience in different transdisciplinary energy and sustainability research projects. Since mid of 2018, he has been acting team leader of the Department of Resilient Energy Systems at the University of Bremen.

Hendrik Thelken works at an integrated utility company, which is a driving player in the German energy transition. He obtained his PhD from the Centre for Sustainable Entrepreneurship at the Faculty Campus Fryslân, University of Groningen, and his MSc in International Business and Finance from the University of Groningen. In his PhD research he focused on individual drivers of sustainable entrepreneurial intent and how sustainable entrepreneurs find ways to deal with (paradoxical) tensions between triple bottom-line goals.

Berfu Ünal is Assistant Professor of Social Psychology at the Department of Sustainable Entrepreneurship in a Circular Economy at the Faculty Campus Fryslân, University of Groningen. Her research focuses on understanding the psychological roots of pro-environmental actions and using theory-based interventions to change unsustainable behaviours. She leads several projects investigating the adoption and acceptability of sustainable innovations and solutions. She focuses on diverse stakeholders in her research such as citizens, sustainable entrepreneurs and businesses.

Walter Vermeulen is based at the Copernicus Institute of Sustainable Development of Utrecht University (the Netherlands) and has long-standing experience in analysing progress in implementing sustainability practices in business in many different countries, both inside companies and in their socio-economic networks. He is especially focusing on new forms of private governance in (international) supply chains and on practices of circular economy, both in Europe and in supplier countries worldwide. Assessing the performance of these forms of value chain collaboration is enabled with the Oiconomy Pricing approach, revealing the hidden costs of unsustainability. He also published articles on the essence of the concept of sustainable development and the social dimension and the need for transdisciplinary research. Vermeulen is former President of the International Sustainable Development Research Society (isdrs.org). He has also been programme leader of the International Master Sustainable Development at Utrecht University. His list of publications can be found at https://www.researchgate.net/profile/Walter_Vermeulen.

Esther van der Waal is a postdoctoral researcher based at the University of Groningen. She has a background in spatial sciences as well as science and technology studies. Her work focuses on the transformative potential of local energy initiatives as innovators in the energy transition. Her research interests include local energy initiatives, socio-technical innovation, social impact analysis, social studies of energy sustainability, local embedding of technology, energy policy, and interactive and participative planning as well as governance.

Lennart Winkeler studied Engineering and Management and Production Engineering (MSc) at the University of Bremen. As a research associate at the Department of Resilient Energy Systems at the University of Bremen, he focuses his research on agent-based models for socio-technical systems and the support of a resilient energy transition by interactive decision support tools.

Sjors Witjes is Associate Professor at Radboud University, the Netherlands. Sjors has been part of corporate sustainability and innovation processes in Europe, Latin America, and the USA and he has supported the United Nations, national governments and standardisation organisations to enhance corporate sustainability. Through his academic work, Sjors supports organisations by reflecting on their contribution to a more sustainable society.

Jian Li Yew envisions a world where principles and resources complement, and she dedicates her career to impact investment. She is the Chief Executive Officer of Citrine Capital, an asset management firm committed to the generation of both financial returns and positive developmental outcomes through principled and practical investment activities backed by sound research. Previously, Jian was involved in several impact-orientated institutions, including non-profit entities, social enterprises and research centres. She has a bachelor's degree in Biochemistry from the University of Melbourne and a master's in International Development from King's College London.

Gjalt de Jong

1 Introduction

A General Model of Sustainable Entrepreneurship in a Circular
Economy

Abstract: Many countries and regions face unprecedented social and environmental
crises and disruptive events. The impact of these crises and disruptive events can no
longer be ignored and require fundamental changes to our economic systems. The
current linear economies are unsustainable and need to be replaced by circular systems. Sustainable entrepreneurs solve the grand challenges and balance social, environmental and economic goals simultaneously in order to safeguard social welfare
for current and future generations. Sustainable entrepreneurship research is innovative with a convergence of principles and practices. This chapter presents a general
model of sustainable entrepreneurship in a circular economy. The general model integrates the individual level with the internal and external environment of the organisation and relates these to triple bottom line performance and eventually the circular
economy and social welfare in regions and nation states. In doing so, it offers a coherent and systemic perspective for sustainable start-ups and for incumbent for-profit
firms aiming for transitions and it presents a wide range of opportunities for new research agendas.

Keywords: sustainable entrepreneurship, circular economy, social welfare, radical innovations, paradigm changes

Gjalt de Jong, University of Groningen, Faculty Campus Fryslân

https://doi.org/10.1515/9783110756159-001

1 Introduction

As the world's population continues to increase, the per capita gross domestic product (GDP) is projected to result in a doubling of global material consumption.[1,2] This is problematic because natural resources are limited and the societal costs of unbridled consumption and production in terms of pollution and climate change are already rapidly increasing and crossing the points of no return (Chen et al., 2022; Steffen et al., 2015; Steffen & Morgan, 2021). Many countries and regions already face unprecedented social and environmental crises and disruptive events. The United Nations (UN) Sustainable Development Goals (SDGs) identify 17 critical grand challenges for the twenty-first century that urgently need to be solved, including climate change, access to clean water and sanitation, democratisation, access to healthcare, clean energy and the elimination of poverty (https://sdgs.un/goals.html). The impact of these crises and disruptive events can no longer be ignored and require fundamental changes to our economic systems. The current 'take–make–waste'-based economies are unsustainable and need to be replaced by circular systems and attitudes that balance social, environmental and economic goals simultaneously in order to safeguard social welfare for current and future generations (Cosme, Santos, & O'Neill, 2017; Macekura, 2020).

Sustainable entrepreneurs aim to solve the grand challenges and are therefore key in the transition towards circular economies and sustainable societies (Eikelenboom &

---

1 This chapter did not appear overnight – it is the outcome of a 30-year process of trying, discarding and starting again. During the past three decades, I have developed and exploited all opportunities to develop all aspects of the modern and sustainable academic profession: designing, implementing and supervising international educational programmes and educational institutions; supervising junior and senior researchers in bachelor's, master's and PhD programmes; presenting and lecturing regularly at international conferences and other discussion venues; advising public and private companies, network organisations and government agencies facing strategic sustainability challenges; and joining public debates about sustainability in the media. In the course of all this experience, I developed the transdisciplinary, interdisciplinary, multi-level and multi-method research programme of sustainable entrepreneurship in a circular economy presented in this chapter.

2 This chapter is the outcome of inspiring alliances formed with the colleagues who acted as co-authors in the publications this work brings together (for updated overviews, see: https//www.rug.nl/cf/cse). I include key references for this chapter leaving in-depth literature reviews and analyses for specific elements of the general model to the Parts included in this *De Gruyter Handbook of Sustainable Entrepreneurship Research*. The reader is also referred to the various PhD theses that study specific (combinations of) elements discussed in this chapter and that have been published at the Centre for Sustainable Entrepreneurship (Faculty Campus Fryslân, University of Groningen). I feel privileged to have worked with four of the most renowned statesmen of academic science. Angus Maddison showed the benefit of historical and quantitative methods of analysing wicked problems such as endemic poverty. Bart Nooteboom showed the benefit of interdisciplinary research paradigms and Arjen van Witteloostuijn of transdisciplinary research paradigms. Jouke de Vries challenged to integrate all new paradigms into the radically new scientific discipline of sustainable entrepreneurship in a circular economy, which is now presented in its entirety in this chapter.

de Jong, 2021). Sustainable entrepreneurs are here defined as sustainable opportunity-oriented individuals who generate new sustainable products, services and production processes, with new sustainable business models that simultaneously balance ecological, social and economic goals, which result in sustainable welfare for current and future generations. Sustainable entrepreneurship is the field of research that studies the causes and consequences of sustainable entrepreneurship.

Sustainable entrepreneurship started in 1972 when the Club of Rome published its first major report, 'The Limits to Growth', calling for scientific assessments of the impact of human behaviour and the use of resources (Meadows et al., 1972). The Club of Rome challenged the mainstream paradigm of continuous material growth and the pursuit of unlimited economic expansion (for economic growth theories see, for example, Maddison, 1995 or Acemoglu & Robertson, 2012). Already in 1972, the Club of Rome highlighted the need for business to radically reconsider its role and its legitimacy in society, urging a transformation from maximising profits at all costs for a limited number of stakeholders to adapt to the limits of natural resources.

This wake-up call for society and business has been echoed in various international summits and reports of the United Nations, including the United Nations Conference on Environment and Development (UNCED) (Earth Summit) in Rio de Janeiro (1992) and the yearly Climate Change Conferences with the notable editions in Kyoto (1997), Paris (2015) and Glasgow (2021) introducing radically new policy agendas in terms of ambitions, protocols and plans (https://www.un.org/development/desa/en/about/conferences.html). Simultaneously, a large number of scientific studies in many different domains have been published that all point in the same direction: the behaviour of human beings in general and of for-profit business in particular destroy many of the precious ecological and social resources on the Earth. The decisive influence of human behaviour and for-profit business on climate change has been a subject of ongoing debates for decades.

This debate has been settled by the most recent report of the Intergovernmental Panel on Climate Change (IPCC, 2021). Based on sophisticated scientific methods and large-scale and fine-grained observational data, the IPCC now unequivocally concludes that human-caused emissions are responsible for global warming. The IPCC shows that if the world continues to take the current carbon-intensive pathway, global warming could climb to 3.3–5.7 °C higher than pre-industrial levels by the end of the century. The IPCC argues that if the world takes very ambitious actions to curb emissions in the 2020s, global warming can still be limited to 1.5 °C by the end of the century. The effects of human-made climate change will be universal for all regions in the world. Many consequences of climate change will soon become irreversible over time, including rising seas and the loss of species. The time to take measures to prevent even more serious consequences is running out. The IPCC therefore calls for radical new ways of using and producing energy and of making and consuming goods and services in new economic systems.

It is in this context that sustainable entrepreneurship has developed in the past four decades (for reviews of the literature see, for example, Terán-Yépez, 2020; Muñoz & Cohen, 2018). The phenomenon of sustainable entrepreneurship as doing business in society and as a new research paradigm perfectly aligns with the general laws of evolution (Greco & de Jong, 2017). Sustainable entrepreneurship gained foothold with a limited number of start-ups and first-movers in the early years followed by early adopters and an early majority. The same pattern holds for sustainable entrepreneurship as an independent field of research. The first publications arrived in the beginning of this century in specialist field journals with a rapid increase in recent years, including special issues in leading journals such as *Journal of Cleaner Production, Sustainability* and *Journal of International Council for Small Businesses*. Whether or not sustainable entrepreneurship will become the dominant paradigm in business and in science is still an open question to date. Nevertheless, it is understood that sustainable entrepreneurship successfully survived its infancy stages (for updated overviews of sustainable start-ups in Europe, see: https://digital-strategy.ec.europa.eu/en/policies/startup-europe). It is more likely to mature than to break down and disappear again, both in business and in science.

The *De Gruyter Handbook of Sustainable Entrepreneurship Research* offers state-of-the-art insights for the new field of research that is developing in tandem with practice. The field of research is innovative, developing in many different directions with a convergence on principles and practices. The aim of this chapter is to offer an overview of the main perspectives and opportunities. For this, it presents a general model of sustainable entrepreneurship in a circular economy. The general model integrates the individual level with the internal and external environment of the organisation and relates these to triple bottom line performance and eventually the circular economy and social welfare in regions and nation states. In doing so, it offers a coherent and systemic perspective for sustainable start-ups and for incumbent firms aiming for transitions. It also offers opportunities for coherent and new research agendas.

The outline of this chapter is as follows. Section 2 reviews the need and legitimacy for sustainable entrepreneurship as a new field of research. Section 3 presents the general model for sustainable entrepreneurship in a circular economy. The general model also offers the structure of the *De Gruyter Handbook of Sustainable Entrepreneurship Research*, which is addressed in Section 4. Finally, Section 5 concludes this chapter with an appraisal highlighting the added value of the *De Gruyter Handbook of Sustainable Entrepreneurship Research* for students, scholars and practice.

2 The Legitimacy of Sustainable Development

Sustainable entrepreneurship is a radical innovation that supplants existing for-profit business paradigms and business models.[3] In doing so, it actively replaces economic growth systems with something entirely new, namely a system based on a circular economy with social welfare for all. Sustainable entrepreneurship is the modern-world best practice version of Schumpeter's original theory. Schumpeter (1934) highlighted the crucial role that entrepreneurs play in breaking up old structures and creating new ones in processes of creative destruction. Schumpeter (1934, p. 66) coined the term 'enterprise' for actions, which carry out radical innovations and 'entrepreneurs' for individuals who do so. According to Schumpeter, entrepreneurs are the only individuals who eventually foster long-term economic growth because entrepreneurs strive for individual profit and challenge established paradigms and practices. Entrepreneurs bring the continuous dynamics needed for the survival of systems.

In a similar vein, sustainable entrepreneurs challenge the taken-for-granted paradigms of economic growth and maximising profits at all costs by presenting radical new solutions. Sustainable entrepreneurs purposely develop new circular and social systems. This raison d'être of sustainable entrepreneurship requires a complete renovation of Schumpeter's original perspectives and of all mainstream economic, business, management and entrepreneurship theories, insights and applications. Sustainable entrepreneurship argues that all existing economic, business, management and entrepreneurship theories and research paradigms have no legitimacy and very often even a negative benefit for economies and for societies. All mainstream paradigms are fundamentally rooted in the perspectives of maximising economic growth and economic value of enterprises. Students from day 1 onwards in economic, business, management and entrepreneurship academic degree programmes use textbooks that learn that firms only exist to maximise profits for a limited number of stakeholders.

Neither the grand challenges – as formulated by the United Nations – nor the survival of species on the Earth can be meaningfully addressed by these mainstream paradigms, the more so because mainstream paradigms are the root causes of the grand challenges in the first place. In the modern world economy, the mainstream paradigms of maximising economic growth and profits are no longer valid. These mainstream paradigms block progress and therefore need to be replaced with the completely new paradigm of sustainable entrepreneurship.

This also applies to the so-called new economic perspectives such as green growth or ecological economics and the business equivalents such as corporate social responsibility, corporate philanthropy or green washing. Economists, entrepreneurs and

---

3 The legitimacy question applies to scientists as well. Scientists are no longer drawn from the nobility. However, they do have the privilege of gaining unique knowledge, knowledge that is the entitlement of modern society in the broad sense of the word. To mangle the proverb, it is not nobility, but scientific knowledge that is socially obliged to serve: *episteme oblige.*

managers attempting to maintain the legitimacy of mainstream paradigms claiming that adjusted versions thereof are also able to analyse and solve grand challenges have introduced these perspectives. However, it is impossible to meaningfully relate sustainability to mainstream economics, business, management and entrepreneurship other than to conclude that for centuries these mainstream paradigms have unbridled, in tandem and without any sense of morality only served the interests of the individual at staggering and ever-increasing costs of societies.

In a similar vein, mainstream paradigms have attempted to downsize the need for radical paradigm shifts, claiming that new technologies will solve negative externalities of existing business models or that these negative externalities are a responsibility of governments, that is, should be paid by governments and taxes. The reality is that despite some successful efforts, the rate of technical innovations is lagging far behind in solving grand challenges. Equally so, many governments have largely failed to solve the mounting ecological and social challenges; otherwise, these crises would no longer exist (or at least not at the breadth and depth we observe today).

Hence, we therefore not only need a new paradigm, that is, a radical new way of thinking and doing business in society, but we need it faster than ever before given that many ecological, social and economic disasters are now getting beyond points of no return as the IPCC so convincingly argues and reports.

3 A General Model of Sustainable Entrepreneurship in a Circular Economy

3.1 Points of Departure and Design Principles

The general model of sustainable entrepreneurship presented here builds on three points of departure that serve as the design principles. These three design principles result either in a general model that is different from other models and approaches that focus on sustainable entrepreneurs' self or on one or a limited number of sustainable entrepreneurship features. The general model that is presented here explicitly reflects the goal of sustainable entrepreneurship, its multi-level and therefore interdisciplinary and transdisciplinary nature and its resilience.

First, sustainable entrepreneurs are key in the transition from the linear to a circular economy and to achieve social welfare for all. Therefore, these two main and interrelated system objectives are the explicit end goal of the general model. Without social or environmental considerations in entrepreneurship, social welfare will become unsustainable. These goals differentiate mainstream entrepreneurship from sustainable entrepreneurship and mainstream public policies from sustainable public policies. Sustainable entrepreneurs are centre stage in transition from the linear and profit-maximising economies to the circular and social welfare societies. The implication is that sustainable entrepreneurship is systemic: only when all elements in the entire system change, success will arrive and can be maintained. The general model includes the butterfly principle, allowing for the observation that a minor change by one individual may result in ever-increasing changes in the entire system.

Second, sustainable entrepreneurship is inherently a multi-level phenomenon. Sustainable entrepreneurs are opportunity oriented and generate new products, services, production processes, techniques and organisation models that substantially reduce negative social and environmental impact, while simultaneously improving the circular economy and social welfare for all. The general model combines individual features with organisational, contextual and macro-level characteristics. The DNA of sustainable individuals eventually determines the social welfare of countries. In doing so, it also relates interdisciplinary with transdisciplinary perspectives given that new theories, methods and impact depend on the different units of analyses that the general model accounts for. With this in mind, the research paradigm and legitimacy are fundamentally different from mainstream entrepreneurship and its equivalents. Mainstream entrepreneurship scholars consider themselves as rational machines who observe and analyse reality with hindsight. Sustainable entrepreneurship builds on intrinsic motivation to save the planet Earth for future generations and considers the creation of new products, services and solutions for the grand challenges as a joint and collaborative effort of academic scholars and practitioners.

Third, sustainable entrepreneurship is universal and consistent and offers opportunities for expansion in the future. The general model presented here therefore is resilient and can be adapted in the future. By adapting the general model, sustainable entrepreneurship as a scientific discipline will continue to fulfil its social responsibility and retain its legitimacy. The legitimacy of some scientific disciplines is often maintained by pointing to its historical value. An appeal to historical value often provides no more than a temporary continuation of an outdated legitimacy. Scientific disciplines in their original condition last about 10 years. The general model seems well able to yield meaningful insights in the future. It is difficult to foresee all future contingencies but there are meaningful trends indicating that the quest for sustainable entrepreneurship will continue.

3.2 A General Model of Sustainable Entrepreneurship in a Circular Economy

Sustainable entrepreneurship is multi-faceted – it is related to individual leadership as much as it is to internal and external organisation, alliances, context and public policies. The general model uniquely enables us to disentangle the causes and consequences of sustainable entrepreneurship at each of these levels (see Figure 1.1). It presents a rigorous approach to everyday sustainable entrepreneurship challenges, offering both scholars and practitioners guidance for the design, implementation and management of sustainable entrepreneurship, which has true benefit for our modern world societies. This is relevant for directors, managers, employees, policymakers, consultants, researchers and students who search for new inspiration to think fundamentally about all dimensions of sustainable entrepreneurship in order to solve grand challenges.

The latter is not as logical as it seems. Many enterprises have no or a very outdated sustainability perspective. In times of crisis, there is neither time nor financial resources to come up with new ones. In times of economic prosperity enterprises lose interest to think about the shadow of a greying future. This makes the design, implementation, management and impact of sustainable entrepreneurship among the most challenging activities of leadership in the modern world economy for which the general model offers important guidelines.

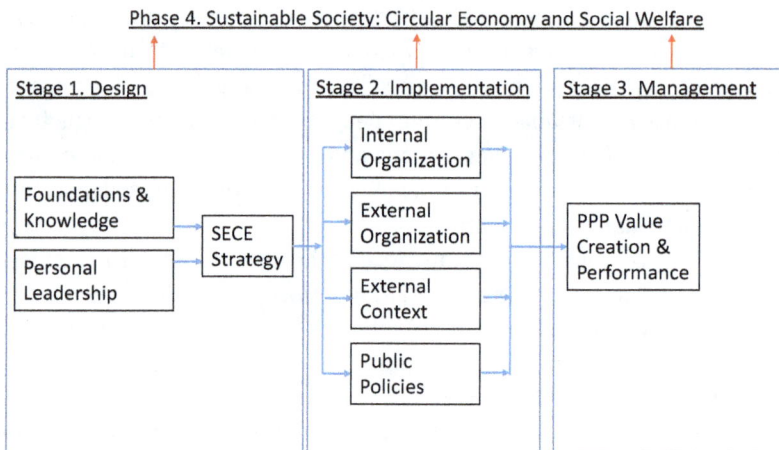

Figure 1.1: A general model of sustainable entrepreneurship.

The general model is divided into four distinct phases, namely the design, implementation, management and societal impact of sustainable entrepreneurship. The general model is among the first that explicitly integrates these four phases into one coherent framework. In doing so, the general model is much more refined than mainstream for-profit entrepreneurship models such as the standard 'strategy–structure–performance' paradigm.

The general model is generic and applies to all types of organisations, is resilient in its content and structure, offers a wide range of opportunities to design new research agendas and serves as a best-practice example for initiating new sustainable enterprises or transforming existing ones. A description of the main characteristics for each of the four stages in the general model follows including comparisons between mainstream for-profit firms versus sustainable enterprises.

3.2.1 Designing Sustainable Enterprises

Sustainable enterprises can be designed from scratch or can result from transforming existing (for-profit) enterprises. In either case, strategy is among the most important features of the design phase. Strategies are plans, actions and decisions that are taken in order to achieve goals (specified in missions, visions and values), so an enterprise can survive the external environmental changes (in markets, politics and technologies) that are enabled as well as constrained by the resources of the enterprise. Since there are enterprises, strategy is an issue. The word 'strategy' derives from the Greek word *strategos*: the art of the general leading an army to victory. Strategy is the generic way of thinking and of working, which allows complex issues to be reduced to manageable proportions and for which the general model is essential.

The key issue here is that sustainable enterprises have a completely different end goal in mind than mainstream firms. The strategy of sustainable enterprises is not to differentiate from peers in order to become a monopolist, determine prices and therefore maximise profits. The strategy is to find solutions for grand challenges in order to save the planet Earth for future generations – requiring a unique set of plans, actions and decisions for the specific enterprise in question. Hence, sustainable enterprises are dedicated to cooperation and not to competition. The sustainable strategy of an enterprise determines the products, services, prices, market position, triple bottom line performance and, eventually, its contribution to the circular economy and social welfare.

The strategy of sustainable entrepreneurship does not drop out of heaven like manna. It is craftsmanship and has two important determinants. Although teams, groups or entire organisations can determine strategies, most often they are the result of an individual decision-making process: sustainable leadership. Sustainable leadership is altruistic and captures individual sustainability norms, values, motivation, vision, knowledge, experience, authority to act, access to resources and social capital. The recognition of societal problems and solutions is what differs sustainable leadership from mainstream management. The discovery and exploitation of sustainable problems and solutions is the creative process, which is part of each new or incumbent sustainable entrepreneur. Sustainable leadership also relates to individual events and experience that offers specific intrinsic motivation and drivers to start sustainable enterprise in order to solve societal challenges. For-profit leadership is egoistic and aims to maximise individual or company income at all costs irrespective of the societal impact.

A second determinant of making sustainable strategic decisions concerns in-depth sustainability knowledge and expertise in general and of sustainable entrepreneurship in particular. These foundations are a *sine qua non* for sustainable strategy among others because of the inherent complexity, triple bottom line ambitions and ambiguity of sustainable strategies. Mainstream entrepreneurship 'only' focuses on maximising profits for a few individuals. The maximisation of profits serves as a relatively simple benchmark and motivates for-profit enterprises to take any measure needed to capture financial growth ambitions (including financial misconduct, tax avoidance, the use of child labour, expropriation of public resources such as clean air, soil and water, pollution and grease money, corruption or bribes). Mainstream entrepreneurs receive their knowledge and expertise from mainstream university programmes that are rooted in neoclassical economics and that are the dominant paradigm of doing for-profit business. In a similar vein, sustainable entrepreneurs need to be well informed about the causes and consequences of sustainable strategic choices. Put differently, a lack of in-depth sustainability knowledge and expertise (or sustainable leadership) will never result in a sustainable strategy.

3.2.2 Implementing Sustainable Enterprises

Phase 2 concerns the implementation of the sustainable strategy. A sustainable strategy cannot do without a sustainable internal organisation. Sustainable strategies and sustainable internal organisation need to be aligned in order to make the sustainable enterprise successful, which is reflected in sustainable business models and innovations.

Mainstream enterprises are driven by efficiency, productivity and top-down hierarchical bureaucratic 'command-and-control' governance structures. Such features of the internal organisation and related business models do not match with the strategic choice to be a sustainable enterprise. Sustainable enterprises thrive by principles of democracy and shared decision-making structures, by human resource policies that foster sustainable leadership and organisational culture of employees and organisational members, by sustainable financial management reporting authentic financial results and choices, by sustainable logistics identifying the ecological footprint of traffic and transport and by sustainable marketing sharing the authentic narrative of the sustainable enterprise. These internal company-specific features create the company-specific sustainable business models. Sustainable business models need to be renewed and innovated over time. Note that efficiency and productivity are part of sustainable business models but from a different perspective. Sustainable business models include financial performance and robustness but as one of the means (and hence, not the goal) to solve grand challenges.

A second element of the implementation of a sustainable enterprise concerns the external organisation including horizontal and vertical strategic alliances, networks and ecosystems. Sustainable enterprises are to a significant extent open systems for which high-trust alliances with a wide variety of external stakeholders are important. Sustainable alliances, networks and ecosystems need to be designed, implemented and managed in continuous cycles of open collaboration.

Mainstream enterprises mainly collaborate with external partners and their suppliers in order to share costs and as a tool to increase company profits. Sustainable enterprises collaborate from a learning perspective based on shared sustainable strategies. Learning is a crucial competence for which different perspectives outside the organisation are a requirement. Without differences new knowledge and expertise cannot be developed. Radical new solutions to solve grand challenges need combinations of different sets of knowledge and expertise that a single sustainable enterprise cannot develop individually. Radical new solutions require sustainable alliances, networks and ecosystems of sustainable enterprise in order to identify and capitalise sustainability opportunities for the benefit of the society. The management of horizontal and vertical sustainable alliances, networks and ecosystems requires competencies that are completely different from the management of for-profit alliances.

A third element of the implementation of a sustainable enterprise concerns the positioning of the sustainable enterprise in its external regional, industrial, national and international contexts. Sustainable enterprises operate in hyper-dynamic contexts. The modern world in which sustainable entrepreneurs position themselves is extremely heterogeneous. Sustainable entrepreneurs continuously need to optimally position themselves in these heterogeneous, globalising and changing contexts. Country borders, for example, become increasingly permeable, making the composition of the country environments in which an international sustainable enterprise operates one of its success factors.

Sustainable entrepreneurship is inherently about context. Sustainable entrepreneurs want to redesign the context and introduce new business models, services and products in order to successfully solve ecological or societal challenges. At the same time, sustainable enterprises are subject to evolutionary laws and need to survive competition from incumbent for-profit firms, new market entrants and new market technologies. Where mainstream enterprises take the external context as a given, sustainable enterprises aim to change it. Although this seems impossible at first sight – over the past decades, industry structures and formal and informal institutions have developed that serve the maximisation of profits and economic growth of nation states – sustainable entrepreneurs see opportunities. This also applies to the context of less developed countries that often report remarkable numbers of new sustainable start-ups. The grand challenges offer sustainable enterprises competitive advantages over mainstream for-profit enterprises that not only lack the skills, expertise and intrinsic motivation but also the resilience needed to survive grand challenges. For-profit entrepreneurship might very well be a failing organisational paradigm in external environments that are increasingly dangerous for the survival of human beings (and other species) and that require a completely new organisational paradigm that sustainable enterprises are developing and implementing.

A fourth element of the implementation of sustainable enterprises concerns government policies and public governance. Over the past decades, public policies at almost all levels have become 'professionalised', implying that the number and size of rules, regulations and instruments not only have increased at dazzling speeds but also that the institutional contexts are dedicated to maintaining for-profit entrepreneurship and economic growth at all costs. Conventional policy paradigms prevail despite the increasingly acknowledged importance of sustainability and the need for fundamental and systemic economic change in the European Union.

Sustainable entrepreneurs are radical innovators and want to introduce new products and services that very often do not align with the existing rules and regulations that have been designed for the linear economy, for economic growth and for maximising company profits. They also need to compete with for-profit incumbent entrepreneurs who benefit from subsidy and tax havens resulting in substantial price differentials. Sustainable entrepreneurs need competencies and expertise in order to amend or innovate the formal institutional infrastructure. Public–private partnerships enable sustainable entrepreneurs to overcome legal obstacles for the introduction of new sustainable solutions, including sharing information, creating and fostering new policy instruments and motivating public servants at all levels to innovate their organisations. A sustainable enterprise is not a product that can be bought on a market. Sustainable entrepreneurs need to design, implement and manage the sustainable enterprises themselves and this relates to public policies. It is worthwhile highlighting that democratic and election systems often favour conservatism rather than the innovation in policies needed for sustainable entrepreneurship.

3.2.3 Managing Sustainable Enterprises

Phase 3 concerns the management of the triple bottom line of sustainable enterprises. This performance feature differentiates mainstream from sustainable enterprises. The management of triple bottom line performance highlights the need for radically new academic research including new research questions, aims, theories and new research methods. Mainstream entrepreneurship research paradigms have never been designed in order to understand the causes and consequences of profit maximisation. Adding sustainability to mainstream theories fails among others because mainstream theories drive on egoism, whereas sustainable entrepreneurship drives on altruism. The failure of mainstream theories to address triple bottom line performance is also reflected in the unreliable strategies of green washing and corporate social responsibility. Stakeholders require transparent and consistent information from companies for their investment decisions and reject ambiguous and unreliable company ambitions and profiles (resulting also in successful lawsuits initiated by activists).

Starting a new sustainable enterprise is essentially about the management of the triple bottom line performance. Sequential management approaches offer opportunities to solve conflicts that may arise when sustainable entrepreneurs aim to optimise all three dimensions at the same time. New sustainable enterprise may, for example, first combine financial with social performance adding ecological performance in a later stage. In either case, the triple bottom line performance induces many new questions that cannot be answered with mainstream research paradigms and for which the new field of sustainable entrepreneurship is designed.

3.2.4 The Circular Economy and Social Welfare

Phase 4 concerns the creation of and transition towards a circular economy with social welfare for all citizens by means of sustainable entrepreneurship. This ambition is opposite to mainstream paradigms and highlights the need for the new field of sustainable entrepreneurship.

The mantra of economic growth is challenged by the limits of planet Earth. Neoclassical economists – and their proponents in business and public governance – consider economic growth measures such as GDP per capita as the only relevant focus and guideline for business and public policy. Mainstream scholars have attempted to adjust the economic growth paradigm in perspectives such as green growth. These new perspectives equally fail to address the grand challenges because they still consider growth as viable and needed for nation states. This contradicts the limitations of the Earth and the negative externalities of any growth perspective, whether it is green or not.

Sustainable entrepreneurs are intrinsically motivated to establish circular economies and social welfare. De-growth is the point of departure, and economic and social systems need to be adapted to the limits of resources as soon as possible. Sustainable entrepreneurs univocally accept the evidence from decades of academic research that has recently been integrated into the latest report from the IPCC. There is no discussion that current for-profit business and economic growth paradigms are among the most important determinants of the grand challenges as formulated by the United Nations.

Sustainable entrepreneurship has benefits for new sustainable societies that are based on the principles of the circular economy and social welfare. In recent years, a wide variety of circular economy and social welfare measures have been developed by national offices of statistics and international organisations such as the Organisation for Economic Co-operation and Development (OECD) (https://www.oecd.org/wise/measuring-well-being-and-progress.html). In doing so, they address the comment of neoclassical economists that sustainable societies with the new principles of the circular economy and social welfare cannot be measured and are therefore not relevant. This comment no longer holds. The statistical achievements also enable us to measure circular economy and social welfare at regional levels.

It is among the most important features of the general model that the strategic decisions of sustainable entrepreneurs eventually result in a circular economy and social welfare. As Viederman (2011) already argued, a sustainable society on the principles of the circular economy and social welfare

> ensures the health and vitality of human life and nature's capital for present and for future generations. A sustainable society stops activities that destroy human life and nature's capital. It encourages those activities that serve to conserve what exists, restore what has been damaged, and prevent future harm. (Viederman 2011)

Which is precisely what the Brundtland Committee voiced when defining a sustainable society as one that meets the needs of the present without compromising the ability of future generations.

The clash between the neo-classical and the sustainable entrepreneurship paradigms is about the clash between egoism versus altruism. It is about ethics, morality and taking responsibility for behaviour; features are all completely neglected in neo-classical and economic growth theories and paradigms. The economic growth paradigm ignores global warming, ozone depletion, loss of biodiversity and the uneven distribution of wealth simply because this paradigm cannot include ethics and morality in the models. Egoism and maximising profits are not only necessary but also essential requirements for neo-classical economics and economic growth models.

Sustainable entrepreneurship shows that ethical and responsible business is not only viable but also successful in establishing a circular economy with social welfare. Essentially, it simply is a matter of choice.

3.3 Evidence and Applications of the General Model

Evidence for sustainable entrepreneurship in general and for the general model in particular increasingly becomes available. First, *The De Gruyter Handbook of Sustainable Entrepreneurship Research* presents state-of-the-art knowledge and insights for almost all dimensions of the general model with a particular focus on foundations, leadership, business models, innovation and performance and impact. Second, research developed at the Department of Sustainable Entrepreneurship in a Circular Economy (Faculty Campus Fryslân, University of Groningen) systematically studies research questions for specific dimensions or combinations of dimensions reflected among others in journal publications (e.g., Dawo, Long, & de Jong, 2022; Greco, Long, & de Jong, 2021; Eikelenboom & de Jong, 2021; Eikelenboom, Long, & de Jong, 2021; Thelken & de Jong, 2020), a substantial number of PhD research projects (e.g., Dawo, 2023; Eikelenboom, 2022; Thelken, 2021; Enthoven, 2021; Greco, 2020; de Ritter, 2019) and community reports (e.g., Dawo et al., 2021). The general model offers guidelines for future research adding, among others, complexities and opportunities for new data collection. For example, it is well known that radical innovations are often complex, involving interdependencies, dynamics and feedback mechanisms among all dimensions of the general model. More research that is recent develops advanced projects aiming to disentangle and understand underlying complexities and causalities of radical innovations in detail.

Third, the general model offers guidelines for systemic national transitions such as the transition from industrial to nature inclusive farming in the Netherlands and elsewhere. Such transitions are often hampered by a lack of oversight and overview. The general model offers roadmaps for transitions in the entire value chains ranging from the care of soils and new nature-inclusive business models of farmers to their suppliers, cooperatives, clients and eventually consumers with relationships to health and biodiversity challenges in nation states as well.

A fourth application of the general model concerns the master's programme in sustainable entrepreneurship at the University of Groningen (de Jong, 2019). The structure and content of the master's programme is identical to the general model and now successfully completed five editions. The master's programme offers a unique real-world problem-solving programme that crosses the boundaries of business functions, disciplines and stakeholders. Mainstream business programmes are rooted in neo-classical economics. It has been suggested that financial scandals are a reflection of how business school programmes are conducive to creating managers who are prone to immoral behaviours. Even economists now indicate the detrimental effect of mainstream MBA education programmes on managerial behaviour later in their career. Acemoglu, He, and le Maire (2022), for example, study newly appointed chief executive officers in the United States and Denmark. They find that those with an MBA increase return on assets in the first 5 years of their new appointment. However, this increase in financial firm performance is not the result of traditional economic determinants such as higher sales, increased investments or higher productivity. The financial superior performance results from suppressing workers' wages. The shareholder value is increased by cutting costs rather than by growing the company. Acemoglu, He, and le Maire (2022) relate this to MBA programmes that are focused on maximising shareholder value and teach new managers to primarily reduce unnecessary costs in general and that of worker salaries in particular. Employees are costs rather than human capital.

New academic programmes are needed to learn students' new ways of doing business with new sets of leadership, entrepreneurship and academic competencies. The aforementioned master's programme in sustainable entrepreneurship at the University of Groningen offers transdisciplinary and interdisciplinary teaching methods offering students to develop all knowledge and competencies needed for successful sustainable entrepreneurship, which is also now evidenced by the alumni of the programme.

3.4 Future-Proof Resilience of the General Model

A logical question, which emerges because of the considerations addressed so far, concerns the future-proof resilience of the general model. The foundations, content and structure of the general model are universal, consistent and offer good opportunities for expansion in the future. In a sense, many of the elements of the general model are timeless. Whatever the future looks like, sustainable entrepreneurship requires a balance between all elements specified in the general model including leadership, structure, cooperation, timely responses to changes in the global and local environment, adaptations to new government policies and ethical considerations.

The general model presented here will be adapted in the future. By adapting the general model, sustainable entrepreneurship as a scientific discipline will continue to fulfil its social responsibility and retain its legitimacy. The legitimacy of some scientific disciplines is often maintained by pointing to its historical value. An appeal to historical value often provides no more than a temporary continuation of an outdated legitimacy. Scientific disciplines in their original condition last about 10 years. The current general model seems well able to yield meaningful insights in the future. It is difficult to foresee all future contingencies but there are meaningful trends indicating that the quest for successful sustainable entrepreneurship will continue.

A first trend is technological progress and new scientific revolutions. Sustainable entrepreneurs today operate in an information technology (IT)/artificial intelligence (AI) version 2.0 world. This has already led to dramatic changes relevant for sustainable entrepreneurship, for example, the systematic shift in consumer behaviour away from local stores to the Internet. There is little doubt that IT/AI will be further re-versioned in the future. Overall, the IT/AI revolution has been gradual, and sustainable entrepreneurs have had the time to redesign their strategies or adapt them to the new IT/AI reality. The IT/AI revolution does, however, also move partly in spurts and will, for example, skip some stages. Technology will be directly connected to sustainable entrepreneurship in many ways. Scientific revolutions will play a role here in product development – such as the role the new biotechnology played in medicine – and also in controlling and directing human behaviour in terms of eating habits and social connections.

New IT/AI capabilities will lead to self-reinforcing scientific revolutions. For instance, IT/AI capabilities in neuroscience have rendered the neurophysiological structure of the human brain open to study and insight. This raises fascinating questions about how we view ourselves as human beings (such as the extent to which people independently make decisions and whether decision-making processes occur autonomously outside consciousness), but also whether and how a company's 'brain' can be 'technologised', and how this relates to sustainable entrepreneurship. Sustainable entrepreneurs, which can quickly realise this type of new scientific knowledge, will have new opportunities to solve the grand challenges.

A second trend involves changes in the world order, including current national boundaries, the ownership of companies and their financial and human capital. To some extent, a country is a sliding analysis unit. Most countries have relatively short histories, and the borders of many countries are often arbitrary and liable to change. Border changes carry with them a new world order, with China as an economic leader making its mark on the world. China's entry to the modern world economy was delayed by environmental and population factors, but China will create new strategic issues for the rest of the world. The coming dominance of China casts current sustainable business models and strategic choices in a different light, offering both opportunities and threats. The current industrial distribution and the corresponding distribution of wealth along current national lines of specialisation and regional infrastructure will be brought into question by Chinese dominance. That said, China is also a country where sustainability challenges are most prominent and where solutions are scaled in order to address these successfully.

The trends demonstrate the legitimacy of sustainable entrepreneurship as a scientific discipline in the future. They reveal a future proofing of the general model presented in this chapter. These trends will make new demands on sustainable entrepreneurs of the future: they will all need to be IT/AI perceptive and aware of the changes in the global business environment. There will be a greater urgency to solve the social issues surrounding sustainability, ageing and energy and the strategic decisions needed to address them.

4 The *De Gruyter Handbook of Sustainable Entrepreneurship Research*

4.1 Structure and Overview

The general model explains how sustainable entrepreneurs address grand challenges and are therefore key in the transition towards sustainable societies. They are defined as sustainable opportunity-oriented individuals who generate new sustainable products, services and production processes, with new business models that simultaneously balance ecological, social and economic goals, which result in a circular economy with sustainable welfare for current and future generations. The general model and this definition highlight the important features that taken together define sustainable entrepreneurship as a new research domain.

The *De Gruyter Handbook* consists of five main themes each presenting state-of-the-art thinking: foundations, leadership, innovation, business models, performance and impact. Each part consists of four chapters that together offer in-depth perspectives, taking stock and offering new avenues for future research. The introductions of each of the five parts explain the general aim, content and relationships between the chapters of a particular part. The chapters can also be read as stand-alone sources of information. Taken together, the chapters analyse and discuss important elements of the general model in detail.

Part I on Foundations departs from the perspective that liberal market economic systems adapted in many advanced nation states create new crises at ever-increasing rates. Sustainable entrepreneurship is a radical innovation that supplants existing for-profit business paradigms and business models. The chapters in Part I discuss the evolution of sustainable entrepreneurship as a science and the particular research, teaching and consultancy paradigms of sustainable entrepreneurship.

Part II on Leadership highlights the importance of leadership reflected among others in the sustainable opportunity recognition process related to the start of new sustainable enterprises. The chapters in Part II discuss values, opportunity threats, opportunity recognition and sectoral transitions.

Part III on Innovation highlights the importance of innovation. Sustainable entrepreneurs do or invent something new to solve a particular grand challenge. Such sustainable innovations can be incremental or radical in the way that they introduce solutions. Radical solutions are game changers and challenge the legitimacy of incumbent firms. The chapters in Part III discuss innovation diffusion and the role of females, story-telling and fragile environments.

Part IV highlights the importance of business models to support the triple bottom line performance of sustainable entrepreneurship, simultaneously balancing the interests of people, planet and profit. New business models imply a systemic new design for sustainable ventures that use the triple bottom line as the benchmark for how they add value, approach strategy and organisation, utilise networking, build alliances and position themselves in the market. These issues are discussed in the chapters in Part IV.

Part V on Performance and Impact highlights the crucially important role of sustainable entrepreneurs to generate sustainable performance and impact and their decisive importance in the systemic transition towards sustainable societies. The term 'sustainable' here reflects the inherent sustainable performance and impact of the (combination of) sustainable leadership, sustainable innovation and sustainable business models. The chapters in Part V discuss community entrepreneurship, impact investments, social entrepreneurship and the relationships between theory and practice.

4.2 Added Value of the *De Gruyter Handbook*

Sustainable entrepreneurship as a new field of research represents an emerging area of interest that is benefiting from the co-evolution of sustainable entrepreneurship as a new field of science in conjunction with sustainable entrepreneurship as a new standard of doing business and designing public policy. This is reflected in the growth of sustainable entrepreneurship start-up ventures, the increasing integration of sustainability in small- and medium-sized enterprises as well as in incumbent corporations and the increasing interest of policymakers in the transition towards sustainable societies, gross domestic welfare and the circular economy.

To date, the important role of business in the transformation from linear to circular and sustainable societies is seldom discussed by national and international business and policymaking organisations such as the United Nations and the World Economic Forum. However, academic research universities and universities of applied sciences are increasingly incorporating sustainable entrepreneurship into their master's and MBA programmes, benefiting from the growth of state-of-the-art, new and innovative fundamental research as well as the growing number of case studies, practitioner action plans and the increasingly heard need to have better and more up-to-date knowledge and competencies.

The *De Gruyter Handbook of Sustainable Entrepreneurship Research* serves different academic communities and incorporates examples and guidelines that will inspire leaders who are making progress towards sustainable entrepreneurship or are keen to engage with these ideas. The content and chapter design will suit the needs of multiple audiences from around the world. First, junior and senior undergraduate students will benefit from Part I on foundations offering in-depth overviews of the legitimacy of sustainable entrepreneurship, its role in science and the implications for research, education and consultancy. They will also find value in other parts offering academic and practical examples including research (methodological) elements for undergraduate theses on sustainable entrepreneurship or capstone projects with organisations taking a more responsible view of business and entrepreneurship.

Second, graduate students in economics, business, management and entrepreneurship (either in full degree programmes or for electives) will benefit from all chapters as developing researchers or advanced practitioners. Of particular value will be the foundation sections where they will find guidance on research design for novel sustainable entrepreneurship projects in terms of interdisciplinary, action research, grounded theory, transdisciplinary and multi-method approaches.

Third, instructors will benefit from the ability to add state-of-the-art research to ongoing discussions on sustainability, sustainable entrepreneurship and societal transitions. The specific structure of the handbook offers first foundations (urgently needed at the start of courses for students new to these subjects and/or for students who already have some knowledge) that are complemented with subsequent parts that focus on the key elements of sustainable entrepreneurship. The handbook is therefore likely to be used for undergraduate, graduate, MBA and applied managerial courses and programmes.

All audiences will benefit from the end-of-chapter content that provides discussion points, research guidance and opportunities for managerial applications. Furthermore, both established and emergent researchers in different domains will benefit from highly contemporary, industry- and region-specific situations that provide both methodological guidance and topic richness to reinforce their research proposals and/or thesis development.

The success of sustainable entrepreneurship as a new paradigm and field of research is reflected in an increase in the number of publications and special issues in leading journals and the publication of handbooks (e.g., Kyriö, 2018; Pinna, 2020). These handbooks also offer overviews often based on advanced literature reviews. The *De Gruyter Handbook of Sustainable Entrepreneurship Research* complements existing publications in its coverage of topics, in the explicit identification of different paradigms and in its generic ambition and structure that offers end-to-end reviews of contemporaneous state-of-the-art insights.

4.3 Conclusions

Sustainable entrepreneurship has a history in Europe and elsewhere. In the 1950s and 1960s, sustainable entrepreneurs aimed at fostering the position of employees. In the 1970–2000 period, the Club of Rome, the Brundtland Committee and the UN summits voiced concerns about economic growth rates. During the early years of the twenty-first century, the importance of entrepreneurs in the transition towards a sustainable society was first identified in policy advisory boards and much later in cabinet visions and new regulations. Business networks such as the World Business Council for Sustainable Development highlight the need for entrepreneurs to challenge the neoclassical paradigm and to fundamentally redesign business models using sustainability as the benchmark.

The efforts have not been without results. Sustainability in business is changing from a marketing tool that greenwashes company reports or is based on the need to align practices with new regulations to a fundamental driver of doing business. Companies are not only looking for eco-efficiencies (such as energy conservation or waste reduction) but also how to be of benefit to a broad range of stakeholders. Companies now disclose governance, social and environmental information and change their profit-oriented focus to sustainability by means of sustainable accounting standard boards, chief sustainability officers and global reporting initiatives.

Despite all efforts, however, sustainable entrepreneurship is not yet the default. The transition process would benefit from knowledge that is more academic and experience demonstrating that sustainable entrepreneurship can save the planet Earth and can be financially successful. This precisely is the aim of the *De Gruyter Handbook of Sustainable Entrepreneurship Research*.

References

Acemoglu, D., He, A. X., & le Maire, D. (2022). *Eclipse of rent-sharing: The effects of managers' business education on wages and the labour share in the US and Denmark*. Working Paper 29874, National Bureau of Economic Research. http://dx.doi.org/10.2139/ssrn.4059303

Acemoglu, D., & Robertson, J. (2012). *Why Nations Fail: The Origins of Power, Prosperity and Poverty*. New York: Crown Publishing.

Chen, S., Chen, D., Tan, Z., Chen, M., & Han, J. (2022). Knowledge mapping of planetary boundaries based on bibliometric analysis. *Environmental Science and Pollution Research, 29*, 67728–67750. https://doi.org/10.1007/s11356-022-22292-6

Cosme, I., Santos, R., & O'Neill, D. W. (2017). Assessing the degrowth discourse: A review and analysis of academic degrowth policy proposals. *Journal of Cleaner Production, 149*, 321–334. https://doi.org/10.1016/j.jclepro.2017.02.016

Dawo, H. L. A. (2023). *Sustainable entrepreneurship in protected areas. Drivers, challenges, strategies and opportunities*. Doctoral Thesis, University of Groningen, Faculty Campus Fryslân.

Dawo, H. L. A., Long, T., & de Jong, G. (2022). Sustainable entrepreneurship and legitimacy building in protected areas: Overcoming distinctive barriers through activism. *Business Strategy and the Environment*. https://doi.org/10.1002/bse.3118

Dawo, H. L. A., Long, T., Ragni Yttredal, E., Wilde Tippett, A., & de Jong, G. (2021). *Sustainable Entrepreneurship in the North Sea Region: A Guide Book of Best Practice Examples*. Report Interreg North Sea Region Prowad Link.

de Jong, G. (2019). Educating sustainable entrepreneurship. The case of the University of Groningen. In A. Fayolle, D. Kariv & H. Matlay (Eds.), *The Role and Impact of Entrepreneurship Education. Methods, Teachers and Innovative Programmes* (pp. 319–331). Cheltenham: Edward Elgar.

de Ritter, M. (2019). *Mission-driven entrepreneurs for ecosystems in sustainable systems change*. Doctoral Thesis. University of Groningen, Faculty Campus Fryslân.

Eikelenboom, M. (2022). *Achieving sustainability together. Stakeholder collaboration for corporate sustainability and the circular economy*. Doctoral Thesis. University of Groningen, Faculty Campus Fryslân.

Eikelenboom, M., & de Jong, G. (2021). The impact of managers and network interactions on the integration of circularity in business strategy. *Journal of Organization and Environment, 35*(3), 365–393. https://doi.org/10.1177/1086026621994635

Eikelenboom, M., Long, T., & de Jong, G. (2021). Circular strategies for social housing associations: Lessons of a Dutch case. *Journal of Cleaner Production, 292*, 1–14. https://doi.org/10.1016/j.jclepro.2021.126024

Enthoven, M. P. P. (2021). *Unpacking opportunity recognition for sustainable entrepreneurship*. Doctoral Thesis. University of Groningen, Faculty Campus Fryslân.

Greco, A. (2020). *Changing for good: Transforming existing businesses in sustainable enterprises*. Doctoral Thesis. University of Groningen, Faculty Campus Fryslân.

Greco, A., & de Jong, G. (2017). *Sustainable entrepreneurship: Definitions, themes and research gaps*. Working Paper No. 6, Centre for Sustainable Entrepreneurship, University of Groningen, Campus Fryslân.

Greco, A., Long, T., & de Jong, G. (2021). Identity reflexivity: A framework of heuristics for strategy change in social organisations. *Management Decision, 59*(7), 1684–1705. https://doi.org/10.1108/MD-10-2019-1369

Intergovernmental Panel on Climate Change (IPCC). (2021). *Climate Change 2021: The Physical Science Basis. Contribution of Working Group I to the Sixth Assessment Report of the Intergovernmental Panel on Climate Change* In V. Masson-Delmotte, P. Zhai, A. Pirani, S. L. Connors, C. Péan, S. Berger, N. Caud, Y. Chen, L. Goldfarb, M. I. Gomis, M. Huang, K. Leitzell, E. Lonnoy, J. B. R. Matthews, T. K. Maycock, T. Waterfield, O. Yelekçi, R. Yu & B. Zhou (Eds.). Cambridge: Cambridge University Press. https://doi.org/10.1017/9781009157896

Kyrö, P. (Ed.). (2018). *Handbook of Entrepreneurship and Sustainable Development Research*. Cheltenham: Edward Elgar.

Macekura, S. (2020). *The Mismeasure of Progress: Economic Growth and Its Critics*. Chicago: The University of Chicago Press.

Maddison, A. (1995). *Monitoring the World Economy 1820–1992*. Paris: Organization for Economic Cooperation and Development.

Meadows, D. H., Meadows, D. L., Randers, J., & Behrens III, W. W. (1972). *The Limits to Growth: A Report for the Club of Rome's Project on the Predicament of Mankind*. New York: Universe Books.

Muñoz, P., & Cohen, B. (2018). Sustainable entrepreneurship research: Taking stock and looking ahead. *Business Strategy and the Environment, 27*(3), 300–322. https://doi.org/10.1002/bse.2000

Pinna, M. (Ed.). (2020). *Sustainable Entrepreneurship. A Systematic Review of Academic Research*. New York: Springer.

Schumpeter, J. A. (1934). *The Theory of Economic Development: An Inquiry into Profits, Capital, Credits, Interest, and the Business Cycle*. Piscataway: Transaction Publishers.

Steffen, W., et al. (2015). Planetary boundaries: Guiding human development on a changing planet. *Science, 347*(6223), 736–746. https://doi.or/10.1126/science.1259855

Steffen, W., & Morgan, J. (2021). From the Paris agreement to the anthropocene and planet boundaries framework: An interview with Will Steffen. *Globalizations, 18*, 1289–1310. https://do.org/10.1080/14747731.2021.1940070

Terán-Yépez, E., Marín-Carrillo, G. M., Del Pilar Casado-Belmonte, M., & de las Mercedes Capobianco-Uriarte, M. (2020). Sustainable entrepreneurship: Review of its evolution and new trends. *Journal of Cleaner Production, 252*. https://doi.org/10.1016/j.jclepro.2019.119742

Thelken, H. (2021). *Thinking apart and together. The role of cognition in managing multiple goals in sustainable enterprises*. Doctoral Thesis. University of Groningen, Faculty Campus Fryslân.

Thelken, H., & de Jong, G. (2020). The impact of values and future orientation on intention formation within sustainable entrepreneurship. *Journal of Cleaner Production, 266*. https://doi.org/10.1016/j.jclepro.2020.122052

Viederman, S. (2011). A sustainable society: What is it? How do we get there? *The George Wright Forum*, 34–47. http://www.jstor.org/stable/43597318

Part I: **Foundations**
Gjalt de Jong

The chapters in Part I address the evolution of the sustainable entrepreneurship field of research and the new paradigms in research, teaching and consultancy that have been developed in the past decades. Sustainable entrepreneurship research does not develop in isolation. It is the interaction between research, teaching and consultancy paradigms in co-evolutionary processes that constructs sustainable entrepreneurship as a new field of research. This tandem of research–teaching–consultancy is what differentiates sustainable entrepreneurship from for-profit business, management and economics in general and from for-profit entrepreneurship in particular. Part I therefore offers four chapters that allow the reader to come to grips with state-of-the-art paradigms and insights in each of these foundational elements of sustainable entrepreneurship.

The foundations and the characteristics define sustainable entrepreneurship as a field of research that – with a delay of a few decades after the first business and policy practices in the 1970s – began to emerge in the first academic publications in the 2000s. In a period of about 10 years, at least two generations of sustainable entrepreneurship research have been developed.

The early and first generation of sustainable entrepreneurship research from 2000 to 2010 implicitly or explicitly used mainstream economic, business and entrepreneurship paradigms to assess the role of sustainability on the financial performance of for-profit firms, predominantly using quantitative research methods that have long been mainstream in economics, business and entrepreneurship. This first generation developed sub-fields such as corporate social responsibility or philanthropy, blending entrepreneurship and sustainability with insights from the fields of science such as biology and ecology.

This first generation of sustainable entrepreneurship research has much in common with the marketing approach of for-profit firms that use sustainability jargon in company reports, and have stand-alone sustainability departments or sustainability managers to communicate their societal relevance and legitimacy in a new world of ongoing globalising crises while fundamental changes in leadership, innovation, business models and societal outcomes are left unchanged.

The first generation received some attention in leading journals though the number of sustainable entrepreneurship publications and domain-specific journals remain rare. The first generation is characterised by desktop research with relatively low levels of scholar–practitioner interactions. Taken together, the above also explains the relatively low take-up of sustainable entrepreneurship research and teaching in mainstream economic, business and management faculties of academic research institutes.

The second generation of sustainable entrepreneurship as an independent field of research gained a foothold and early momentum from 2010. This second generation of research decisively breaks with the first generation and fundamentally challenges the role and legitimacy of sustainable entrepreneurship as an academic science in the context of global crises and grand challenges. In doing so, it mimics the complete end-

https://doi.org/10.1515/9783110756159-002

to-end process of sustainable entrepreneurship as a completely new and increasingly successful category of business.

The second generation questions the design and identification of fundamental and society-relevant research aims and questions, and proposes radically new and appropriate research methods and theories. The need for transdisciplinary and for action-based (grounded theory) research is identified and embraced over the instrumental use of causation. In doing so, the radical newness of the second generation of sustainable entrepreneurship research also questions the content and methods of academic teaching content, and fosters the need to actively engage with (regional) stakeholders in all phases of research. The aim is to design, implement and sustain radical new solutions that solve grand challenges through the development of new joint collaborations. This approach breaks with the desktop and default publication-oriented attitudes of conventional scholarship typical of the first generation of sustainable entrepreneurship research.

Stefano Pascucci reflects on the evolution of sustainable entrepreneurship as a field of research and critical insights and questions that emerge from this. He introduces two narratives and fields of enquiry. A first narrative perceives sustainability as a business opportunity. A second narrative challenges the former and discusses whether entrepreneurs have a role to play in meaningfully addressing social and ecological issues at all. It questions whether businesses and entrepreneurs can act as change agents and whether 'entrepreneurship-ism' can develop solutions to the grand challenges of sustainability. In doing so, Pascucci highlights a number of critical tensions that result from these debates between the two narratives. The chapter offers thought-provocative and in-depth perspectives on the key concepts of sustainability, entrepreneurship and the business–society–nature relationships.

Angela Greco, Rikke Kristine Nielsen and Manon Eikelenboom reflect on the evolution of research paradigms in the field of sustainable entrepreneurship. This is important because in the mainstream business, management and entrepreneurship, the paradigm of positivism dominates. Although positivism has had its merits in research, it also excludes the identification of many new research questions, aims and hence findings that are outside the domain of positivism. In their chapter, Greco, Nielsen and Eikelenboom offer unique and very thorough overviews of knowledge production and problem solving in academic research. They make a strong case for action research and position action research as tools to navigate through dynamic, ambiguous and uncertain processes of sustainable entrepreneurship. Sustainable entrepreneurship is characterised by these features and therefore requires ditto action research tools in order to design, formulate and answer research questions that are relevant for sustainable entrepreneurship. Greco, Nielsen and Eikelenboom offer detailed discussions for crucial aspects and dimensions of action research as well as case examples that help scholars who are, or soon will be, involved in this research paradigm.

Dana Schadenberg, Emma Folmer and Thomas B. Long reflect on the evolution of teaching paradigms in the field of sustainable entrepreneurship. Mainstream business, management and entrepreneurship faculties, schools and departments in research universities generally offer generic teaching content focusing on the neo-classical for-profit maximising role of businesses and entrepreneurship in society using conventional teaching and examination methods. Schadenberg, Folmer and Long build on a recent systematic literature review showing that teaching paradigms for sustainable entrepreneurship are maturing. Based on their review of the literature, they present and discuss five key elements of sustainable entrepreneurship education, namely competencies, teaching approaches, the role of the university and the university ecosystem, assessment and attitudes. In doing so, Schadenberg, Folmer and Long argue that the new and innovative teaching methods that focus on creating competencies rather than knowledge are experiential, collaborative and reflective. The chapter offers valuable insights for those who are, or soon will be, involved in teaching sustainable entrepreneurship in the modern world economy.

Rikke Kristine Nielsen, Arne Remmen and Jacob Lundberg reflect on the evolution of consultancy paradigms. This feature is perhaps among the most important that differentiates mainstream and conventional research from sustainable entrepreneurship scholarship. Sustainable entrepreneurship scholars are eager to actively and collaboratively engage with stakeholders outside the boundaries of the university in order to design, implement and manage co-created solutions for ongoing sustainability challenges. Mainstream scholars consider consultancy not their realm and therefore not part and parcel of academic research universities – where scholarship is best perceived as rational machines that with desktop research pursue advanced quantitative projects to be published in high-ranked journals irrespective of whether or not such research has societal value and impact or addresses audiences other than the few readers of the articles. Nielsen, Remmen and Lundberg show that consultancy paradigms have matured and nowadays offer solutions for complex and so-called wicked problems: problems that are difficult to solve because of incomplete, contradictory, and changing requirements are often difficult to recognise. They present and discuss pre-conditions and outcomes of relevant conversations between sets of varied stakeholders and why such conversations are essential for successful outcomes. Nielsen, Remmen and Lundberg present various case studies that support their perspective. They offer important lessons learned including the productive consultancy matrix that portrays consultation as a combination of the ability to facilitate trustful knowledge sharing and engagement. Again, this chapter offers valuable and state-of-the-art insights relevant for scholars who are, or who soon will be, exploring consulting as part of their research activities in sustainable entrepreneurship.

Stefano Pascucci

2 Sustainable Entrepreneurship Research: Narratives, Tensions and Future Agendas

Abstract: Sustainable entrepreneurship research is a fast-rising field of enquiry in the management and organisation literature, signalling an emerging interest for understanding how societies respond to ever-increasing environmental degradation and detrimental impact on socio-ecological processes in contemporary economies. Within this scholarship, we recognise the co-existence of two narratives and fields of enquiry: on the one hand, we have scholars interested in looking at sustainability as a business opportunity. On the other hand, an emerging community of scholars is challenging this assumption and questioning the role of entrepreneurship to produce and reproduce social and ecological struggles. This coexistence reflects on a number of critical tensions affecting business studies in more general terms, and the wider conversation on sustainable development goals. In this chapter, we have attempted to unearth and discuss these tensions, particularly looking at how scholars and practitioners position themselves in their understanding of sustainable entrepreneurship. Looking at this literature, we have distilled three conceptual dimensions to map sustainable entrepreneurship research. First, we discuss *sustainability* as a concept gathering notions and principles from different schools of thought and worldviews. Second, we interpret *entrepreneurship* as a field of (business) practices but also evoking the notion of activism in socio-technical transitions, for example mobilising the idea of social entrepreneurship for sustainability, pro-social or community-based entrepreneurship. Finally, we look at *business–society–nature relations* through multiple worldviews, and mobilise different combinations of environmental and socio-economic perspectives.

Keywords: sustainable development, business case for sustainability, socio-ecological transitions, business–society–nature relations

1 Introduction

Sustainable entrepreneurship scholarship is a fast-rising field of enquiry in the management and organisation literature (Muñoz & Cohen, 2018; Terán-Yépez et al., 2020). It describes an emerging interest for understanding how societies respond to ever-increasing environmental degradation and detrimental impact on socio-ecological processes in contemporary economies. It also indicates that we have entered an era of 'entrepreneurship-ism', where scholars and practitioners identify in 'entrepreneurial activities, entities and

---

Stefano Pascucci, Exeter University, UK

https://doi.org/10.1515/9783110756159-003

orientation' the answer to their quest for solutions to twenty-first-century grand challenges, and a way to operationalise sustainable development goals (SDGs), through creativity, ingenuity and innovative processes. There is a 'warm feeling' about entrepreneurs and entrepreneurship inside and outside academia, and the change they can bring about. Why is that so? What does entrepreneurship bring into our conversations on climate change, biodiversity loss, planetary boundaries and SDGs? This is a key point to define in order to clarify how we position the current debate on sustainable entrepreneurship research.

One way to look at it is to link this field of enquiry to the wider conversation about the role of businesses, and the economy, in shaping socio-ecological crises. For some scholars (and practitioners), the early twenty-first century is a landscape of global challenges, in which humanity is networked in a globalised market economy that is operating at a geological scale and disrupting planetary systems and cycles (Whiteman, Walker, & Perego, 2013). This globalised market economy creates relations of exploitation and over-consumption leading to over-use of resources in existing ecosystems, over-using natural capital embedded in a worldwide network of economically driven relations. In this landscape, economic growth is still fundamentally coupled with resource consumption, resulting in overwhelmingly negative societal and environmental impacts. In this narrative, creating a 'business case' for tackling these challenges is the way forward to identify solutions (Belz & Binder, 2017; Shepherd & Patzelt, 2011). From this perspective, entrepreneurs become the key actor to stimulate change, and entrepreneurial activities and orientation are the enabling elements to trigger and support change-making processes in the economy, and therefore to begin a process of re-thinking and re-designing use and consumption of natural capital (Muñoz & Cohen, 2018; Terán-Yépez et al., 2020). This narrative is germane to research fields such as responsible innovation, corporate social responsibility, responsible and sustainable business models, and circular economy (Ergene, Banerjee, & Hoffman, 2021). In this scholarship the *business case for sustainable entrepreneurship* is related to the idea of incremental changes, transitions that tackle the contradictions of globalised market economy 'from within', as in the case of sustainable or circular business models (Fischer, Pascucci, & Dolfsma, 2022; Kennedy & Bocken, 2020). In the circular entrepreneurship discourse, for instance, the narrative has shifted more decisively in this direction, indicating to support the emergence of an 'industrial economy that is restorative by intention and design' (EMF, 2012: 14), to support business models that utilise 'ecosystem cycles in economic cycles by respecting their natural reproduction rates' (Korhonen et al., 2018: 547). Similarly, the business case for sustainable entrepreneurship focuses on strategic business responses to issues of social and environmental sustainability, creating a 'worldview' and collective narrative essential for transforming the twenty-first-century market and consumption-driven economies (Muñoz & Cohen, 2018). In this narrative, redesigning a globalised market economy entails profound social and ecological changes, as well as transforming political systems and institutional regimes, in which business activities are the drivers for changing social norms, political processes and institutions, shaping how an economy functions at any point in time. Fundamentally, this narrative evokes the emergence of a globalised market economy able to maintain economic forces and tensions 'within' the boundaries of socio-ecological systems, the planetary cycles that support life on the planet Earth and the social conditions to ensure a just and safe space for humanity (Whiteman, Walker, & Perego, 2013). The evidence for this narrative is that over the years, particular ways in which a global market economy operates within these boundaries have timidly emerged, within and between countries and economies (Raworth, 2017). They have been informed by initiatives like the SDGs, for example, or the UN Global compact, or taken the form of 'sustainability-driven', 'one planet' strategies or 'just' socio-economic activity, referencing constructs such as 'triple bottom line' evaluations or socio-economic and eco-environmental life-cycle analyses (Muñoz & Cohen, 2018).

In our view, the narrative based on a 'business case for sustainable entrepreneurship' has been challenged, and to various extents contrasted, by an alternative approach. Some scholars, in fact, have strongly opposed the idea of positioning businesses, and entrepreneurs, as change actors. Moreover, and perhaps more importantly, they have challenged the idea of 'entrepreneurship-ism' as a way to find solutions to what they recognise as structural problems created by an over-exploitative globalised economy. In this narrative, it highlights the fundamental contradictions of modern capitalism and neo- or post-liberal systems as unresolvable 'from within' (Ergene, Banerjee, & Hoffman, 2021). The exploitative nature of the twenty-first-century economy cannot be 'fixed' by mobilising incremental change processes using business strategies and entrepreneurial endeavours that replicate the same logics and structures that have led to over-depleting natural resources and disrupted planetary systems and cycles. Moreover, this scholarship rejects the idea that socio-ecological crises are 'experienced' by humanity as one entity. Instead, they indicate the need for understanding socio-ecological struggles through power relations and inequality lenses. In fact, they are more interested in developing a socio-ecological case for sustainable entrepreneurship as an agenda for socio-ecological transformations, requiring novel and more disruptive frameworks and practices to emerge. According to this view, sustainable entrepreneurship can be seen as an emerging interdisciplinary and multi-faceted field of practice and enquiry, characterised by a critical stand on the role of businesses. It is engaged in opening conversations on potential frames and perspectives on how we should rethink and (re-)organise production, consumption and exchange of resources, and how we can create a more participative and distributive economy at all scales. This scholarship seems to indicate the need to adopt an engaged and participatory approach, acknowledging the role of research and practices in indigenous, gender, feminist, community, grassroots and social movement studies, as an integral part of its context of enquiry. Moreover, this scholarship attempts to define a radical agenda, and after almost a decade of sustained effort is now emerging as an alternative field of enquiry and practice in the area of sustainable business and management (Ergene, Banerjee, & Hoffman, 2021).

The presence of these two agendas and fields of enquiry in the sustainability entrepreneurship scholarship is of particular relevance for what we present in this chapter. It reflects a number of critical tensions affecting business studies in more general terms, and the wider conversation on SDGs. Recently, few scholars have attempted to navigate these tensions and identify how sustainable entrepreneurship studies emerged, while mapping what this field of enquiry is about (see, for example, Muñoz & Cohen, 2018). We have unearthed and discussed these tensions, particularly looking at how scholars and practitioners position themselves in their understanding of sustainable entrepreneurship (Table 2.1). Looking at this literature, scholars seem to propose to distinguish between a business and social ecological agenda through three key dimensions: first, to understand sustainability as a concept gathering notions and principles from different schools of thought and practices. Second, interpreting *entrepreneurship* as a field of business practices, or otherwise evoking activism in socio-technical transitions, for example, mobilising the idea of social entrepreneurship for sustainability, pro-social or community-based entrepreneurship. Finally, looking at *business–society–nature relations* through multiple worldviews, and mobilising different combinations of environmental and socio-economic perspectives.

Table 2.1: Positioning sustainable entrepreneurship research.

Key dimensions	Business case perspective	Socio-ecological perspective
Worldview	Entrepreneurs are relevant actors to be mobilised in order to trigger economic, social, technological and ecological change(s) and as such to identify solutions to socio-ecological crises must engage with them primarily.	Entrepreneurs produce and reproduce historical and structural socio-ecological crises and therefore solutions need to engage with them by re-thinking their role in wider business–society–nature relations.
Scope	Sustainable development goals form an integral part of sustainable entrepreneurial strategies and practices.	Environmental and social justice form an integral part of the entrepreneurial strategies and practices.
Context	Sustainable entrepreneurship manifests in the emergence of novel business models, through the actions of innovative individuals or teams, within established organisations as well as in innovation ecosystems. Social and environmental entrepreneurship is combined with business-focused entrepreneurship.	Sustainable entrepreneurship manifests in the emergence of alternative, collective forms of socio-ecological change. Social and environmental activism and contestation are contexts for sustainable entrepreneurship. Indigenous communities, social movements, collectives, cooperatives form contexts of sustainable entrepreneurship.

In the following sections of this chapter, we discuss these perspectives in further detail; using them to explain how sustainable entrepreneurship research has contributed to a better understanding of the complexity and contradictions of contemporary economies and societies. We start by looking into *sustainability* as a source of inspiring narratives and worldviews to frame sustainable entrepreneurship. We then move into discussing *sustainable entrepreneurship* as an expanding field of theory and practice, involving researchers engaged with businesses, social actors and communities. In the third section, we look into how *business–society–nature relations* have been addressed in the sustainability entrepreneurship scholarship, as an opportunity for understanding socio-ecological transitions, innovation and a more sustainable future, economically, socially and environmentally. Our final considerations refer to the unresolved tensions in this emerging field, as well as future development and agendas.

2 Making Sense of Sustainability in Sustainable Entrepreneurship Research

The first analytical and conceptual dimension delineating sustainability entrepreneurship research refers to how scholars make sense and engage with the notion of sustainability. Disentangling the meaning of sustainability from the one related to entrepreneurship is not an easy task when reviewing the literature in this area. However, the key analytical and conceptual differentiation seems to occur in relation to whether sustainability is used to refer to a set of means to achieve a set of goals, or rather an end goal in itself, for which mobilising entrepreneurial actions or practices is key.

When sustainability is associated with a set of means to achieve a set of goals, scholars tend to confine the entrepreneurial activities in the 'business-as-usual' realm, and therefore highlight that considerations for social and environmental aspects of the entrepreneurial activities can enhance the success of these activities. It is the standard argument of scholars interested in business success, innovation and new venture creation in which social and environmental dimensions are considered. For instance, Shepherd and Patzelt (2011) argue that if entrepreneurs want to create a successful business that contributes to (sustainable) development, they must include and adapt sustainability within their business strategy. Accordingly, in the last decade interest from companies and entrepreneurs to understand the real impact of their business on the environment and society has increased. Because of this, the traditional concept of entrepreneurship focusing on value creation in terms of economic results has been extended to address non-economic benefits, such as social and environmental ones (Shepherd & Patzelt, 2011; Urbaniec, 2018). This approach portrays *sustainability* and *sustainable development* as business as usual augmented by incremental environmental or social initiatives (Roome, 2012), creating opportunities to mitigate or reduce risk (and/or costs), increasing revenues and/or enhancing reputation (Carroll & Shabana, 2010). According to Schaefer, Corner, and Kearins (2015), these entrepreneurial initiatives are merely oriented to decreasing *unsustainability*, rather than supporting/enhancing sustainability (Cohen & Winn, 2007; Ehrenfeld & Hoffman, 2013). In this approach, sustainability becomes the context for seeking new opportunities for value creation, delivery and capture. As such, sustainability opportunities become a key aspect of sustainability entrepreneurship practice and research. According to Muñoz and Cohen (2018), sustainability opportunities enable entrepreneurs' pursuit of new ventures and activities to *simultaneously* achieve economic, environmental and social outcomes. As such, sustainability opportunities enable entrepreneurs to sustain the natural environment as well as provide (social) development gain for the entrepreneur(s) and others (Patzelt & Shepherd, 2011). For these scholars, sustainability opportunities re-enforce the 'business case for sustainability' approach (Dyllick & Hockerts, 2002; Young & Tilley, 2006), aiming primarily at improving the efficiency of businesses by reducing their negative impact on nature, communities and people (Munoz & Cohen, 2017).

A different take to sustainability and its meanings is reflected when scholars focus on sustainability as a set of end goals, or state of the world. In this conceptualisation, entrepreneurs and entrepreneurial activities are the means to achieve a much larger or more relevant end. The notion of sustainability-as-flourishing recently highlighted by Schaefer, Corner, and Kearins (2015) captures this approach quite fruitfully. They particularly refer to the idea that sustainability is about the possibility that humans and other life will flourish on the Earth forever (Cooperrider & Fry, 2012). Based on this broader notion, they emphasise how sustainability is about dynamic systems constructs (Berkes et al., 2003), and an aspirational ideal future state that goes beyond surviving (Ehrenfeld & Hoffman, 2013). This scholarship sees sustainability achieved by businesses in need to create transformational, not incremental, change, involving fundamental transitions in society, as a process that may contribute to bringing about socio-ecological transformations. This approach focuses on entrepreneurship that creates social and/or environmental value beyond private economic benefits, as a process that has the potential to transform economies, institutions and societies (Pacheco, Dean, & Payne, 2010). Existing literature has already explored entrepreneurship as a process for achieving sustainability and, particularly, focused on typologies of entrepreneurship considered to be more suitable for tackling social and environmental challenges (Hall, Daneke, & Lenox, 2010). These types include social, environmental and sustainable entrepreneurship (Binder & Belz, 2015). Taken together, these types of entrepreneurship are proposed to not only reduce unsustainability but also to create social and environmental value, and to bring about transformational change. Based on both strands of research, the way scholars understand, frame and engage with sustainability influence the second analytical and conceptual dimension of sustainability entrepreneurship research, leading to the question of what do we understand as entrepreneurship in sustainability-oriented research contexts? Who is the sustainable entrepreneur in this scholarship? How does that differ from other approaches to entrepreneurship research? We address these questions in the next section of this chapter.

3 Sustainable Entrepreneurship: Antecedents and Archetypes

Despite the discussion on what is sustainability, scholars have also been preoccupied to identify the key features of entrepreneurship (and entrepreneurs) when related with sustainability or sustainable development (Muñoz & Cohen, 2018). As mentioned above, part of this scholarship revolves around the tension of whether entrepreneurship works as a means to achieve sustainability, or vice versa. Regardless, scholarship in this area has been unfolding around three lines of enquiry that investigate the *conditions* or *antecedents*, and the *typologies* of sustainable entrepreneurship.

When looking at conditions or antecedents associated with the emergence of sustainable entrepreneurship, researchers tend to focus on features of the entrepreneur(s), the entrepreneurial process and/or the organisational setting in which the entrepreneurial activities emerge. For example, Muñoz and Cohen (2018) reviewed literature to distil some key features of sustainable entrepreneurship, for instance related to (i) the type of knowledge and skills of the entrepreneurs, (ii) entrepreneurial self-efficacy, (iii) motivation and intention and (iv) values and attitudes. What emerges from their analysis is a set of antecedents based on the entrepreneurs' capacity to recognise opportunities related to sustainability or sustainable development, and develop entrepreneurial intention and orientation towards more radical and structural changes.

According to this perspective, opportunities are more likely to be recognised if the entrepreneur(s) can build on a set of skills, knowledge and competences, including prior experience, related to social and ecological issues (Muñoz & Cohen, 2018). Teams and individuals who are familiar with socio-ecological processes and struggles more likely understand their entrepreneurial agency as connected with aspects of sustainability or sustainable development. Patzelt and Shepherd (2011) indicate that these conditions are conducive to the definition of an entrepreneurial model in which sustainable development opportunities are recognised based on the individual's prior knowledge and motivation. This model suggests interconnection with the definition of beliefs or motivations that trigger the entrepreneur's realisation of their capacity to act and enact upon socio-ecological struggles, and not only to seek economic opportunities or pursue economic outcomes, in what scholars have associated with a socio-ecologically oriented *self-efficacy* (Muñoz & Cohen, 2018). The relevance of self-efficacy in sustainable entrepreneurial processes is recognised particularly by acknowledging the complexity of skills, knowledge and competencies needed by entrepreneurs to deal with socio-ecological processes, and to enact sustainability-oriented actions (Shepherd & Patzelt, 2011). According to this view, a critical condition to develop an agency for promoting sustainable changes or transformations is defined by the entrepreneur's belief in their capability to perform a task aligned with socio-ecological struggles they are dealing with, and by developing a set of cognitive, social, linguistic and/or physical skills, and through experience (Muñoz & Cohen, 2018). Particularly, Shepherd and

Patzelt (2011) have emphasised how self-efficacy is a key antecedent of sustainable entrepreneurial action, since the set of skills, knowledge and experience needed to recognise and eventually exploit a sustainability opportunity may differ from the evaluation involving personal economic gain. This view also emphasises that self-efficacy for sustainable entrepreneurs is more complex than of purely commercial entrepreneurs, because understanding and navigating through ecological and social environments entail a higher degree of complexity. This is also reflected in what scholars recognise as another condition for emergence of sustainable entrepreneurship processes, and namely the motivations and intentions of the entrepreneurs. This scholarship emphasises the relevance of how 'business with a purpose' is often a key aspect associated with sustainable entrepreneurship. Some scholars identify the variety and diversity of purposes as the key condition for the emergence of sustainable businesses (De Clercq & Voronov, 2011). As such, entrepreneurs interested in sustainability, and sustainable development, not only build their entrepreneurial orientation and purpose by mobilising more complex skills and competences but also by engaging with a wider set of motivations (Schaltegger & Wagner, 2011). Scholars have also indicated this process as acquiring an entrepreneurial transformative mind-set to make decisions and take actions (Walley & Taylor, 2002). From this perspective, sustainable entrepreneurs act upon, react and/or resist socio-ecological challenges by developing a vision of different futures, and with the intention to trigger wider and broader changes: they elaborate a vision of a sustainable future that envisages structural changes in society. This intention, although actualised in a variety of entrepreneurial strategies, entails a willingness or intention to combine and balance the desire to change the world with the desire to make money (Muñoz & Cohen, 2018).

Leiserowitz, Kates, and Parris (2005) have indicated that more than intentions or motivations, scholars should focus on values and worldviews of the entrepreneurs in order to better understand their interest for sustainability. They mobilise the idea that these entrepreneurs deal with a wide set of values, such as equality, solidarity, freedom, tolerance, respect for nature and shared responsibility, which guide their ambitions and frame their attitudes and behaviours. This scholarship suggests that sustainable entrepreneurship can emerge only as an alternative to the more standard business orientation, as a new way of doing business and organising by combining principles of economic, ecological and social–ethical sustainability (Walley & Taylor, 2002).

Related to the debate on conditions and antecedents, another strand of literature has investigated more direct forms or typologies of sustainable entrepreneurship, and related definitions. We can distinguish between two approaches within this strand of literature, with relevance for understanding how research in sustainable entrepreneurship is unfolding. On the one hand, we have scholars, particularly in the early stage of emergence of sustainable entrepreneurship research, who have distilled typologies based on the idea that sustainable entrepreneurship emerges as an expanded domain of entrepreneurship and incorporates traits of social and environmental business logics or practices. This is aligned with the idea of adding to economic gains social and ecological considerations or outcomes. Cohen and Winn (2007: 35), for instance, suggest to 'define sustainable entrepreneurship as the examination of how opportunities to bring into existence "future" goods and services are discovered, created, and exploited, by whom, and with what economic, psychological, social, and environmental consequences'. Pacheco and colleagues (2010: 471) also define sustainable entrepreneurship in relation to future goods and services, namely 'as the discovery, creation, evaluation, and exploitation of opportunities to create future goods and services that are consistent with sustainable development goals'. Similarly, Patzelt and Shepherd (2011: 632) underline that 'sustainable entrepreneurship is the discovery, creation, and exploitation of opportunities to create future goods and services that sustain the natural and/or communal environment and provide development gain for others'.

Dean and McMullen (2007: 58) offer a complementary view, stressing the relevance of market failures as a source of opportunities to the emergence of sustainable entrepreneurship. They indicate that scholars should see this emergence as 'the process of discovering, evaluating, and exploiting economic opportunities that are present in market failures which detract from sustainability, including those that are environmentally relevant'. All these approaches emphasise the emergence of sustainable entrepreneurial activities in relation to 'market failures', thus recognising the limitation of market-based mechanisms to tackle socio-ecological challenges, but also signalling that solutions might be found in 'future' goods and services, as a consequence of the expansion of market-based activities. Lans, Blok, and Wesselink (2014: 37) capture this view in their definition by stating that 'sustainable entrepreneurship is seen as a way of generating competitive advantage by identifying sustainability as new business opportunities, resulting in new and sustainable products, methods of production or ways of organising business processes in a sustainable way'. There is indeed a sense of predominant economic logics in these definitions, as highlighted by Hockerts and Wüstenhagen (2010: 482), who indicate 'sustainable entrepreneurship as the discovery and exploitation of economic opportunities through the generation of market disequilibria that initiate the transformation of a sector towards an environmentally and socially more sustainable state'. This last definition stresses the connection between sustainable entrepreneurial processes and transformations, and bridges towards the scholarship that has engaged with the conceptualisation of sustainable entrepreneurship more decisively as an alternative to market-based mechanisms or processes, and connected to social and institutional changes. Muñoz and Cohen (2018) have been among the first to highlight the relevance of this approach to investigate sustainable entrepreneurship. They emphasise particularly that sustainable entrepreneurship needs changes in the dominant institutional context to emerge and eventually succeed (Hall et al., 2010), for example a shift in cultural and social norms (Pacheco, Dean, & Payne, 2010), which is key to generate recognition of forms of entrepreneurial values, beyond profit- and market-based mechanisms or logics (O'Neill, Hershauer, & Golden, 2009). Similarly, Muñoz and Dimov (2015) have pointed out the relevance of supportive social and institutional contexts, the wider set of formal and informal rules and norms in society, as triggering factors to facilitate (or hamper) the emergence of sustainability-oriented business ideas. This scholarship brings to attention the role of the 'context' to understand how entrepreneurial activities relate to sustainability and sustainable development. In so doing, it triggers the point of considering sustainability in context, and equally the context of sustainable entrepreneurship. We recognise that business–society–nature relations, and how scholars have positioned sustainability, sustainable development and entrepreneurship in these relations represent this context. This is the focus of the next section of this chapter.

4 Sustainable Entrepreneurship in Context: Questioning Business–Society–Nature Relations

The interest of extant scholarship for investigating the context of sustainable entrepreneurship can be seen from two interconnected but complementary perspectives (Table 2.2).

Table 2.2: Views of the role of context in sustainable entrepreneurship research.

Conceptual and analytical dimensions	Context of sustainable entrepreneurship	Sustainable entrepreneurship in context
Logic/main approach	Sustainable entrepreneurship emerges in the wider context of business–society–nature relations	Sustainable entrepreneurship is a form of entrepreneurship that is context specific, embedded and/or place-based
Behavioural assumptions	Sustainable entrepreneurship emerges primarily out of prosocial behaviours (e.g. environmental- and/or social-oriented actions)	Sustainable entrepreneurship emerges primarily out of collaborative actions but instilled by still self-interested actors
Role of context	As a wider conceptual framework to understand the role of entrepreneurship in socio-ecological transformations	As a place, site, geography, web of economic, social and ecological relations
Purpose or scope	To tackle social inequalities and/or ecological crises	To enhance socio-economic and ecological conditions conducive to entrepreneurial activities

First, the context of sustainable entrepreneurship is understood through the wider investigation of business–society–nature relations. It positioned entrepreneurship within a larger set of social and economic mechanisms and processes shaping our different societies and economies that are related or embedded within ecologies and the 'natural world'. As pointed out by Schaefer, Corner, and Kearins (2015: 397), this strand of scholarship emphasises that 'life on Earth cannot flourish until society recognizes and enables the best rather than the worst of human nature'. This scholarship promotes an idea of business–society–nature relations based on 'reconciliation', an idea of humankind fostering compassionate behaviour rather than opportunism and selfishness, and reflects an awareness of human interconnectedness (Ehrenfeld & Hoffman, 2013; Scharmer & Kaufer, 2013). This perspective would challenge the idea of sustainability as a business opportunity in the classical sense of value creation and capturing and based only on the actions of self-interested actors, and instead looking for entrepreneurial actions inspired by prosocial behaviour and positive feelings (Harré, 2011). In this literature, pro-social behaviour is associated with creativity and leading to the generation of ideas that are both novel and useful – particularly for others (Polman & Emich, 2011). Moreover, in this literature there is a sense of effectiveness associated with creative, inclusive and participating solutions needed to tackle socio-ecological struggles affecting humanity. This view emphasises humanity's capacity to care, a process that would see business–society–nature relations based on a human behaviour that involves *caring for others and for nature*. In this literature, scholars also highlight how social equity and justice should be enacted in order to ensure sustainable futures for humanity on the Earth (Raworth, 2013). The source of socio-ecological challenges is seen to be connected to increased social inequalities in the form of extreme human deprivation, social exclusion and vulnerability. This view suggests a context for sustainable entrepreneurship in which business–society–nature relations are oriented to enhance social equity and justice, thus emphasising the role of business–society as a context for entrepreneurial activities and related impacts.

The second perspective for investigating the context of sustainable entrepreneurship does not mobilise a reconceptualisation of business–society–nature relations, but instead uses contexts or contextualisation to understand the nature and purpose of the entrepreneurial actions. It builds upon the notion of *entrepreneurship in context*, a place-based view of what entrepreneurship does or does not. For instance, this scholarship highlights the relevance of the interaction between the different actors animating the context where entrepreneurial activities take place. These interactions are often systemic, involving multiple stakeholders, including competitors, suppliers, local government, civil society and non-governmental organisations (NGOs) (Gibb & Adhikary, 2000). This entails a notion of sustainable entrepreneurship as an expression or product of an innovation ecosystem, or part of a collective – multi-actors and sector-oriented actions, rather than stemming out of individual actions. Moreover, this scholarship acknowledges that the context of sustainable entrepreneurs is embedded in a web of economic and social relations and geographies (Steyaert & Katz, 2004). In this domain, scholars explore how entrepreneurs are embedded in markets, social systems and territories, what factors influence priorities for the entrepreneur embedded in multiple contexts and how the embeddedness influences the venturing process (Cohen & Muñoz, 2015; Kibler et al., 2015; Shrivastava & Kennelly, 2013).

5 Emerging Themes and Unsolved Tensions in Sustainable Entrepreneurship Research

The different views on the role of context are not the only conceptual and analytical dimension creating debate and diversity in the wider field of sustainable entrepreneurship research. As indicated in the introduction of this chapter, this scholarship is not separated but actually deeply embedded in the wider discussion on the role of businesses in society, and as we framed it, whether scholars adopt a worldview where there is a business case for sustainability or rather it is prevailing a socio-ecological case for sustainability (Ergene, Banerjee, & Hoffman, 2021). Understanding these different 'worldviews' is key for mapping the emergent themes and unsolved tensions in this scholarship. Among several debates and emerging conversations, we have selected two that seem conducive to a wider theoretical development and contribution, within and beyond entrepreneurship research. The first one refers to the investigation of new contexts for sustainable entrepreneurship, adopting a system thinking and design perspective. More than the context in itself, what seems of relevance is the sustainable entrepreneurial ecosystem where a number of actors co-exist and form complex interactions. They indicate that sustainable entrepreneurial activities emerge not only in the so-called market dynamics but also in social and ecological systems (Steyaert & Katz, 2004). Understanding the emergence of entrepreneurial ecosystems in response to, or because of, socio-ecological struggles seems to mobilise research strands that are crossing over disciplinary boundaries and embrace views stemming from complexity science, ecology and system thinking. Sustainable entrepreneurship research can benefit from these views in order to explore how entrepreneurs are embedded in markets, social systems and territories, and how embeddedness influences entrepreneurial processes (Muñoz & Cohen, 2018). This is a key aspect of how the scholarship in this field will develop, particularly given the strong relationship between sustainability and local development. As Muñoz and Cohen (2017) highlight the embeddedness of sustainable entrepreneurs not just in economies but also in social and ecological systems that could give rise to new insights regarding the formation of sustainable entrepreneurial opportunities in relation to socio-ecological challenges and struggles. Scholars following a 'business case for sustainability approach' would see this as an opportunity to investigate how sustainable entrepreneurs develop new businesses focused primarily on social, economic and environmental response to or recovery from socio-ecological challenges. Vice versa, scholars inspired by a socio-ecological case for sustainability would look at the complex interactions between the ecological and social domains to question structural factors determining the struggles and the challenges. Equally, this scholarship is more likely to broaden the field and open up to a wider understanding of what 'entrepreneurship' means, and where it materialises and by whom.

This constitutes the second area where a promising debate is forging the future agenda of sustainable entrepreneurship research. Recently, scholars have more seriously considered the role of grassroots collectives, social movements and communities as change-makers and entrepreneurial actors in socio-ecological struggles (Bacq, Hertel, & Lumpkin, 2022; Pascucci et al., 2021). These studies bring entrepreneurship into a critical socio-scientific dimension, and engage with the key questions of why, when and how social and ecological changes happen, and the key role of entrepreneurial actions, identities and outcomes (Dentoni et al., 2018). Moreover, this agenda opens up to non-Western and de- or post-colonial interpretation and understanding of entrepreneurship, for instance engaging with the notion of indigenous entrepreneurship (Peredo et al., 2004). In indigenous entrepreneurship scholarship, the key aspect is indeed the relations between people and the ancestral territories and the natural resources in them. As indicated by Peredo and colleagues (2004), the purpose of many indigenous peoples is the recovery of access to, and use of, their traditional lands, including re-establishing a connection with the indigenous patrimony, as the basis for their capacity to engage in entrepreneurship and development. Moreover, indigenous entrepreneurship research often engages with the notions of community-based economic and local development (Peredo, 2014). A community and place-based perspective seems to be the key emerging dimension for the burgeoning interest to understand how structural factors that have triggered the twenty-first-socio-ecological crises can be reverted and deeply challenged. As Bacq, Hertel, and Lumpkin (2022: 2) recently mentioned, 'most societal challenges, such as poverty, climate change, and inequality, manifest in communities, and solutions need to be developed for, in, with, and by the members of communities'. However, and despite this increased recognition, the key question revolves around the scale and the magnitude of the diffused socio-ecological devastation that humanity is currently facing. As pointed out by Ergene, Banerjee, and Hoffman (2021), we are experiencing social and environmental problems of a very different type compared to those we have faced in the past. These problems are generated 'by a systemic failure of our dominant political economy supporting the conditions for unlimited raw material extraction, energy use, material consumption, and waste releases in a continuous pursuit of profits and economic growth' (Ergene, Banerjee, & Hoffman, 2021: 1324). Whether a more engaged scholarship will be able to support the mobilisation of community and place-based entrepreneurial approaches, as well as to create post-colonial and non-Westernised views to entrepreneurship for socio-ecological impacts and changes, remains an unresolved question.

References

Bacq, S., Hertel, C., & Lumpkin, G. T. (2022). Communities at the nexus of entrepreneurship and societal impact: A cross-disciplinary literature review. *Journal of Business Venturing*, *37*(5), 106231.

Belz, F. M., & Binder, J. K. (2017). Sustainable entrepreneurship: A convergent process model. *Business Strategy and the Environment*, *26*(1), 1–17.

Berkes, F., Colding, J., & Folke, C. (2003). *Navigating Social-ecological Systems: Building Resilience for Complexity and Change*. Cambridge, UK: Cambridge University Press.

Binder, J. K., & Belz, F. M. (2015). Sustainable entrepreneurship: What it is. In P. Kyrö (Ed.), *Handbook of Entrepreneurship and Sustainable Development Research* (pp. 30–72). Cheltenham (UK): Edward Elgar Publishing.

Carroll, A. B., & Shabana, K. M. (2010). The business case for corporate social responsibility: A review of concepts, research and practice. *International Journal of Management Reviews, 12*(1), 85–105.

Cohen, B., & Muñoz, P. (2015). Toward a theory of purpose-driven urban entrepreneurship. *Organization & Environment, 28*(3), 264–285.

Cohen, B., & Winn, M. I. (2007). Market imperfections, opportunity and sustainable entrepreneurship. *Journal of Business Venturing, 22*(1), 29–49.

Cooperrider, D., & Fry, R. (2012). Mirror flourishing and the positive psychology of sustainability. *Journal of Corporate Citizenship, 46*, 3–12.

De Clercq, D., & Voronov, M. (2011). Sustainability in entrepreneurship: A tale of two logics. *International Small Business Journal, 29*(4), 322–344.

Dean, T. J., & McMullen, J. S. (2007). Toward a theory of sustainable entrepreneurship: Reducing environmental degradation through entrepreneurial action. *Journal of Business Venturing, 22*(1), 50–76.

Dentoni, D., Pascucci, S., Poldner, K., & Gartner, W. B. (2018). Learning 'who we are' by doing: Processes of co-constructing prosocial identities in community-based enterprises. *Journal of Business Venturing, 33*(5), 603–622.

Dyllick, T., & Hockerts, K. (2002). Beyond the business case for corporate sustainability. *Business Strategy and the Environment, 11*, 130–141.

Ehrenfeld, J. R., & Hoffman, A. J. (2013). *Flourishing: A Frank Conversation about Sustainability*. Redwood City, CA: Stanford University Press.

EMF – Ellen MacArthur Foundation. (2012). *Towards the Circular Economy Volume 1: An Economic and Business Rationale for an Accelerated Transition*. Cowes, UK: Ellen MacArthur Foundation.

Ergene, S., Banerjee, S. B., & Hoffman, A. J. (2021). (Un)sustainability and organisation studies: Towards a radical engagement. *Organization Studies, 42*(8), 1319–1335.

Fischer, A., Pascucci, S., & Dolfsma, W. (2022). Designing a circular contract Template: Insights from the Fairphone-as-a-Service project. *Journal of Cleaner Production, 364*, 132487.

Folke, C., Colding, J., & Berkes, F. (2003). Synthesis: Building resilience and adaptive capacity in social-ecological systems. *Navigating Social-Ecological Systems: Building Resilience for Complexity and Change, 9*(1), 352–387.

Gibb, A., & Adhikary, D. (2000). Strategies for local and regional NGO development: Combining sustainable outcomes with sustainable organisations. *Entrepreneurship & Regional Development, 12*(2), 137–161.

Hall, J. K., Daneke, G. A., & Lenox, M. J. (2010). Sustainable development and entrepreneurship: Past contributions and future directions. *Journal of Business Venturing, 25*(5), 439–448.

Harré, N. (2011). *Psychology for a Better World: Strategies to Inspire Sustainability*. Department of Psychology, University of Auckland.

Hockerts, K., & Wüstenhagen, R. (2010). Greening Goliaths versus emerging Davids – Theorising about the role of incumbents and new entrants in sustainable entrepreneurship. *Journal of Business Venturing, 25*(5), 481–492.

Kennedy, S., & Bocken, N. (2020). Innovating business models for sustainability: An essential practice for responsible managers. In O. Laasch, R. Suddaby, R. E. Freeman, & D. Jamali (Eds.), *Research Handbook of Responsible Management* (pp. 640–653). Cheltenham (UK): Edward Elgar Publishing.

Kibler, E., Fink, M., Lang, R., & Muñoz, P. (2015). Place attachment and social legitimacy: Revisiting the sustainable entrepreneurship journey. *Journal of Business Venturing Insights, 3*, 24–29.

Korhonen, J., Nuur, C., Feldmann, A., & Birkie, S. E. (2018). Circular economy as an essentially contested concept. *Journal of Cleaner Production, 175*, 544–552.

Lans, T., Blok, V., & Wesselink, R. (2014). Learning apart and together: Towards an integrated competence framework for sustainable entrepreneurship in higher education. *Journal of Cleaner Production, 62,* 37–47.

Leiserowitz, A. A., Kates, R. W., & Parris, T. M. (2005). Do global attitudes and behaviours support sustainable development? *Environment: Science and Policy for Sustainable Development, 47*(9), 22–38.

Muñoz, P., & Cohen, B. (2017). Towards a social-ecological understanding of sustainable venturing. *Journal of Business Venturing Insights, 7,* 1–8.

Muñoz, P., & Cohen, B. (2018). Sustainable entrepreneurship research: Taking stock and looking ahead. *Business Strategy and the Environment, 27*(3), 300–322.

Muñoz, P., & Dimov, D. (2015). The call of the whole in understanding the development of sustainable ventures. *Journal of Business Venturing, 30*(4), 632–654.

O'Neill Jr, G. D., Hershauer, J. C., & Golden, J. S. (2009). The cultural context of sustainability entrepreneurship. *Greener Management International, 55,* 33–46.

Pacheco, D. F., Dean, T. J., & Payne, D. S. (2010). Escaping the green prison: Entrepreneurship and the creation of opportunities for sustainable development. *Journal of Business Venturing, 25*(5), 464–480.

Pascucci, S., Dentoni, D., Clements, J., Poldner, K., & Gartner, W. B. (2021). Forging forms of authority through the sociomateriality of food in partial organisations. *Organization Studies, 42*(2), 301–326.

Patzelt, H., & Shepherd, D. A. (2011). Recognizing opportunities for sustainable development. *Entrepreneurship Theory and Practice, 35*(4), 631–652.

Peredo, A. M. (2014). Poverty, reciprocity and community-based entrepreneurship: Enlarging the discussion. In *The Routledge Companion to Entrepreneurship* (pp. 287–304). Abingdon: Routledge.

Peredo, A. M., Anderson, R. B., Galbraith, C., Honig, B., & Dana, L. P. (2004). Towards a theory of indigenous entrepreneurship. *International Journal of Entrepreneurship and Small Business, 1*(1), 1–20.

Polman, E., & Emich, K. J. (2011). Decisions for others are more creative than decisions for the self. *Personality and Social Psychology Bulletin, 37*(4), 492–501.

Raworth, K. (2013). Defining a safe and just space for humanity. In *State of the World 2013* (pp. 28–38). Washington, DC: Island Press.

Raworth, K. (2017). *Doughnut Economics: Seven Ways to Think like a 21st-Century Economist.* Vermont, US: Chelsea Green Publishing.

Roome, N. (2012). Looking back, thinking forward: Distinguishing between weak and strong sustainability. In P. Bansal & A. J. Hoffmann (Eds.), *The Oxford Handbook of Business and the Natural Environment* (pp. 620–629). Oxford: Oxford University Press.

Schaefer, K., Corner, P. D., & Kearins, K. (2015). Social, environmental and sustainable entrepreneurship research: What is needed for sustainability-as-flourishing? *Organization & Environment, 28*(4), 394–413.

Schaltegger, S., & Wagner, M. (2011). Sustainable entrepreneurship and sustainability innovation: Categories and interactions. *Business Strategy and the Environment, 20*(4), 222–237.

Scharmer, C. O., & Kaufer, K. (2013). *Leading from the Emerging Future: From Ego-system to Eco-system Economies.* Oakland, CA: Berrett-Koehler Publishers.

Shepherd, D. A., & Patzelt, H. (2011). The new field of sustainable entrepreneurship: Studying entrepreneurial action linking 'what is to be sustained' with 'what is to be developed'. *Entrepreneurship Theory and Practice, 35*(1), 137–163.

Shrivastava, P., & Kennelly, J. (2013). Sustainability and place-based enterprise. *Organization & Environment, 26*(1), 83–101.

Steyaert, C., & Katz, J. (2004). Reclaiming the space of entrepreneurship in society: Geographical, discursive and social dimensions. *Entrepreneurship & Regional Development, 16*(3), 179–196.

Terán-Yépez, E., Marín-Carrillo, G. M., Del Pilar Casado-Belmonte, M., & De Las Mercedes Capobianco-Uriarte, M. (2020). Sustainable entrepreneurship: Review of its evolution and new trends. *Journal of Cleaner Production, 252,* 119742.

Urbaniec, M. (2018). Sustainable entrepreneurship: Innovation-related activities in European enterprises. *Polish Journal of Environmental Studies, 27*(4), 1773–1779.

Walley, E. E., & Taylor, D. W. (2002). Opportunists, champions, mavericks . . .? A typology of green entrepreneurs. *Greener Management International, 38*, 31–43.

Whiteman, G., Walker, B., & Perego, P. (2013). Planetary boundaries: Ecological foundations for corporate sustainability. *Journal of Management Studies, 50*(2), 307–336.

Young, W., & Tilley, F. (2006). Can businesses move beyond efficiency? The shift toward effectiveness and equity in the corporate sustainability debate. *Business Strategy and the Environment, 15*(6), 402–415.

Angela Greco, Rikke Kristine Nielsen, Manon Eikelenboom

3 Fostering Sustainability and Entrepreneurship Through Action Research: The Role of Value Reciprocity and Impact Temporality

Abstract: The fields of sustainability and entrepreneurship share their dynamic processes, their high degree of uncertainty and complexity and their endeavour on systemic impact. These inherent characteristics call researchers to engage in action research (AR). Action research equips researchers with unique tools to navigate the volatility and complexity of sustainable entrepreneurship while simultaneously fostering its purpose and uncovering new theoretical insights. Yet, action research efforts fostering sustainable entrepreneurship are still emergent. The mutual affinity between sustainable entrepreneurship and action research is still seldom addressed in the literature and often confused with other forms of collaborative knowledge production and problem-solving such as co-creation and consulting. In this chapter, we discuss the central principles of this form of academic knowledge production, their practices and implications for sustainable entrepreneurship. We begin by defining action research and its unique methodological features. We then highlight research practices to address two fundamental, but overlooked, aspects of action research: value reciprocity and impact temporality. We illustrate these aspects by providing two cases of action research in a sustainable entrepreneurship context. This chapter offers directions for the researcher embarking on action research journeys aimed at fostering sustainable entrepreneurship.

Keywords: action research, sustainable entrepreneurship, academic impact, value reciprocity

1 Introduction

Many of the sustainability challenges society faces today, such as climate change, income inequality and biodiversity loss, are caused by the unintended consequences of

Angela Greco, The Netherlands Organisation for Applied Scientific Research, Radarweg 60, 1043NT Amsterdam, The Netherlands
Rikke Kristine Nielsen, Department of Communication and Psychology, Aalborg University (Copenhagen), Denmark
Manon Eikelenboom, Faculty of Social Sciences, Vrije Universiteit Amsterdam (Amsterdam), The Netherlands

https://doi.org/10.1515/9783110756159-004

businesses' pursuit of profit (Bansal, Grewatsch, & Sharma, 2021). In the past decades, entrepreneurs have responded to these challenges by shifting their focus from the sole pursuit of profit to environmental and social value by creating products, processes and services that serve both society and the environment simultaneously. Researchers have theorised this phenomenon, referring to it as 'sustainable entrepreneurship' (e.g., Muñoz & Cohen, 2018). In response to this emerging practice, researchers are increasingly seeking to understand the underlying causes, motivations and characteristics of sustainable entrepreneurship. However, by doing so, researchers are confronted with two important challenges. On the one hand, sustainable entrepreneurship cannot be understood by simply looking at past data, as traditionally seen in (positivistic) science, since this approach to entrepreneurship is unprecedented: the business models, approaches and solutions pertinent to sustainable entrepreneurship are new and emergent (Gast, Gundolf, & Cesinger, 2017). On the other hand, researchers are increasingly confronted with passively witnessing urgent – at times catastrophic – matters with little to no influence on them (Williams & Whiteman, 2021). These two challenges might constitute the motives behind the increased popularity of action research (AR) among sustainability scholars, besides the methodological benefits of this complex research method (Wittmayer et al., 2014).

Sustainability and entrepreneurship present problems that are ill-defined, with dynamic processes and moving targets, characterised by volatility and a strive to accelerate transitions (Keahey, 2021). These characteristics require a careful yet flexible research design and input of many different actors. In this light, AR is a promising research method to address complex sustainability challenges, which are systemic in nature (Loorbach et al., 2010). By implementing AR, researchers can exert greater and real-time impact on today's pressing sustainability challenges. Instead of passively following phenomena, they can be at the forefront of societal and organisational change by translating, co-creating and performing new knowledge (Bansal & Sharma, 2021). Additionally, sustainability challenges suffer from the knowledge–practice gap (Bansal et al., 2012). It is our assertion that AR can bridge this gap through close interaction between researchers and practitioners. In fact, addressing sustainability challenges requires a quadruple–helix collaboration (Carayannis, Barth, & Campbell, 2012), in which academia, businesses, governments and civil society can collaboratively and responsibly innovate to tackle systems challenges. AR is an important means through which researchers can orchestrate quadruple–helix collaborative forms of innovation and effectively tackle sustainability challenges, by tapping from the wisdom of the crowd and across multiple disciplines (e.g., Greco, Eikelenboom, & Long, 2021). In this way, AR allows us to know what you do not know and address our blind spots (Senge & Scharmer, 2008).

Despite all these benefits, AR remains a challenging method. Researchers can find it challenging to simultaneously contribute to practical and theoretical challenges. Pursuing both types of contributions can inadvertently result in unintended consequences on practitioners, leading to negative as opposed to positive research impacts.

Additionally, AR impacts can be challenging to trace and monitor and can take a long time to occur. In this chapter we highlight these two challenges by introducing the concepts of 'value reciprocity' and 'impact temporality'. Before doing so, we briefly introduce the definition of action research and its evolution. We then differentiate AR from similar practical and academic practices, such as co-creation, and consultancy. Going forward, we highlight the intrinsic link between the field of sustainable entrepreneurship and AR. Subsequently, we illustrate the concept of impact reciprocity and temporality through two examples of AR in the context of sustainable entrepreneurship. We conclude this chapter by highlighting the limitations of AR for sustainable entrepreneurship and offering a future outlook.

2 Action Research: Background, Central Principles and Connection to Sustainable Entrepreneurship

2.1 What Is Action Research?

Action research (AR) is a form of systematic investigation that typically entails attempts to solve practical problems in real-world settings through the involvement of stakeholders who work or live in those settings (Willis & Edwards, 2014). It combines research – developing new knowledge – with action – seeking to change a social system. AR was first introduced by the social psychologist Kurt Lewin in 1947 as a democratic way of improving professional practice in response to the massive social changes of World War II (Kemmis, McTaggart, & Nixon, 2013). Lewin's approach to AR involved two basic assumptions. The first is that changing 'social practice' is a sociocultural process and not an individual process. The second is that the focus must be on 'action': if research produces 'nothing but books' it will not be enough (Willis & Edwards, 2014).

In the 1950s there was growing criticism of AR (Levin, 2012). (Positivistic) researchers critiqued the scientific rigour of the method, arguing that practitioners lacked the competencies to actively contribute to research insights. This contributed to the replacement of AR models following Lewin's traditions with models that were more confined to scientific experts and less participatory (Willis & Edwards, 2014). However, from 1970 onwards, as the dominant positivistic paradigm was challenged by interpretive and critical theory, many more models of AR, building on the ideas of Lewin, have been used in diverse fields including indigenous rights, environmental conservation and education (e.g., Gutberlet, 2008). This led to the development of diverse approaches to AR with different methods, aspirations and procedures including action science, action learning and critical AR (see Table 3.1).

Despite their differences, most AR approaches share several key features (Kemmis, McTaggart, & Nixon, 2013). First, AR is collaborative. It recognises the capacity of

Table 3.1: Different action research approaches.

Approach	Main aims	Characteristics
Industrial action research	Changing social systems in organisations	– Consultant-driven – Strong focus on collaboration – Use of reflection
Action science	Studying practices in organisational settings as a source of new understandings and improved practices	– Distinction between espoused theory and theories in use – Focus on gaps between theory and practice
Action learning	Studying one's own situation, clarifying what the individual/organisation is trying to achieve and removing obstacles.	– Task-oriented – Bringing individuals together to learn from one another's experiences
Participatory action research	The researcher is a tool (rather than the owner) for facilitating change and social transformation	– Shared ownership – Community-based analysis of social problems – Researcher is embedded in the organisation
Critical action research	Focuses on the emancipation and transformation of individuals in order to improve social practice	– Strong commitment to participation – Fit in the critical social science tradition – Communicative action and space

people living and working in particular settings to participate actively in all aspects of the research process. AR approaches thus reject the idea that an external expert enters a setting to record and theorise about what is happening. Second, it is future-oriented, as the research conducted is intended to improve practices and create a more desirable future (Gümüsay & Reinecke, 2021). Third, it implies systems development, as it aims to build appropriate structures and modify the relationships in a system to create change. Fourth, it generates theory grounded in action, where theory often provides a guide for the AR process. Fifth, it is agnostic, as the objectives, problem and method of AR must be generated from the process itself. Finally, it is situational, as the relationships between people, events and things are a function of the situation as relevant actors define it at that specific point in time.

Given its dynamic ontology, it can be challenging to univocally define the AR research process. In his seminal work, Lewin (1947) describes the AR process as a spiral of steps. Each of the steps constitutes a circle of planning, action and evaluation concerning the result of the action. Various frameworks have been developed to practically support scholars in developing AR (see Figure 3.1 for an example). The conscious enactment of the AR cycle steps is a central feature of AR and essential for its success (Maestrini et al., 2016). It is important to note that AR projects are emergent; the second step will follow as a consequence of the first step and can therefore not be planned in advance.

Context & purpose

Data Gathering

Data Feedback

Evaluation

Monitoring

Implementation

Data Analysis

Action Planning

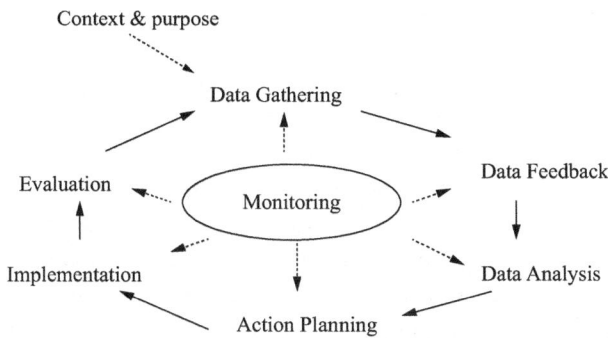

Figure 3.1: Action research cycle (adapted from Coughlan & Coghlan, 2002).

Despite the clear methodological features pertinent to the different AR approaches, AR is often confused with researchers' consultancy-driven endeavours or knowledge co-creations. Therefore, in the following section we differentiate AR from similar 'action-driven' academic and non-academic activities.

2.2 What Is Not Action Research?

Collaborative and participatory pathways for practical/societal impact of research come in many forms and guises of which AR is but one. Many different methodologies have been suggested to capture collaboration between researchers and actors from practice such as insider/outsider research (Gioia et al., 2010; Louis & Bartunek, 1992), engaged scholarship (Van de Ven, 2007), alongsider research (Wickins & Crossley, 2016), enactive research (Johannisson, 2020) or action ethnography (Erickson, 2006). A common denominator for all these approaches is 'double-hurdle research', i.e., research characterised by both rigour and relevance (Pettigrew, 1997) with the ambition of 'double-impact', academic and practical impact at the same time.

It is essential to clearly differentiate AR research approaches from other approaches to academia–practitioner engagement that may involve collaboration, practical value-added and actionable research outcomes (Pearce & Huang, 2012) yet should not be understood as research more generally or AR specifically. According to Greenwood and Levin, 'Action research refers to the conjunction of three elements: action, research and participation. Unless all three elements are present, the process may be useful, but it is not AR' (Greenwood & Levin, 2007: 5). It follows from this assessment that AR must be distinguished from, for instance, consultation, although AR often involves consultation. Process consultation defined as a 'a set of activities on the part of the consultant that help the client to perceive, understand, and act upon the process event that occur in the client's environment in order to improve the situation as defined by the client' (Schein, 1988: 11) or (organisational) consultation in which 'a third-party (other than those directly in and responsible for the system) engages with a system for the purpose of helping it improve or change' (Jamieson, Barnett, & Buono, 2016: vii) does not necessarily involve the goal of producing research and practice outcomes. Although the collaboration may be helpful and positively impact non-academics partners or clients, it is not AR.

Similarly, AR should be pro-actively framed as (potentially) distinct from co-creation, a concept originating in the marketing discipline (e.g., Prahalad & Ramaswamy, 2004; Torfing & Ansell, 2021), yet recently often used to signify collaborative knowledge production between diverse groups of stakeholders for solving wicked problems of societal importance more generally (Degnegaard, 2014). By way of illustration, an EU Horizon 2020-funded project exploring impact in social science and humanities research defines co-creation as 'collaborations in which various actors actively join forces to tackle a shared challenge. Participants can belong to any sector of society, such as industry, government, civil society and academia', also sometimes referred to as the 'quadruple helix' (Vandael et al., 2018: 3). Co-creation is an elusive concept that is used generously in public discourse and points to a very broad and highly diverse spectrum of knowledge producing collaborations (Sharma & Bansal, 2020) that may or may not involve research. AR offers a specific methodology that is co-creational in its nature, yet unlike (some) understandings of co-creation does involve a clear research ambition in addition to the creation of societal impact and practical problem-solving with stakeholders outside academia.

Because of its explicit research and societal impact ambition, AR is ideally positioned to fill the numerous research and practice gaps still present in the field of sustainable entrepreneurship, as discussed in the following section.

3 Action Research and Sustainable Entrepreneurship

Sustainable entrepreneurship is a developing field, which is reflected in the methodologies adopted. Reviews of the field (Gast, Gundolf, & Cesinger, 2017; Muñoz & Cohen, 2018) have shown that a large share of the articles in sustainable entrepreneurship is conceptual in nature. Researchers are increasingly adopting qualitative research designs (Muñoz & Cohen, 2018), relying mostly on insights from case studies and semi-structured interviews (Gast, Gundolf, & Cesinger, 2017; Miles et al., 2014). While acknowledging the importance of inductive theorising at these first stages, researchers have called for an advancement of empirical research in sustainable entrepreneurship (Gast, Gundolf, & Cesinger, 2017; Muñoz & Cohen, 2018). Novel methodological approaches are needed due to the complexity and uniqueness of the sustainable entrepreneurship phenomenon (Muñoz & Cohen, 2018). Furthermore, it is important that sustainable entrepreneurship research becomes more relevant to practice, where researchers can, for example, play an active role in advancing opportunity-based sustainable entrepreneurship, enabling entrepreneurs to better meet market and financial challenges and successfully re-designing business models to focus on sustainability (Gast, Gundolf, & Cesinger, 2017).

AR approaches could offer a valuable contribution; however, these approaches have only rarely been applied in the context of sustainable entrepreneurship (Tasker, Westberg, & Seymour, 2010). The benefits of AR methodologies have been emphasised in both the entrepreneurship and sustainable development literature. For example, entrepreneurship researchers have argued that AR allows for both the development of a holistic perspective of complex situations and the inclusion of the needs of practising managers (Leitch, 2007). Furthermore, sustainable development literature has shown that AR methodologies can help integrate scientific and grassroots knowledge, empower marginalised communities and enable the development of practical solutions to sustainability problems (Keahey, 2021). AR approaches can offer a space in which alternative ideas, practices and social relations can emerge, which is crucial to advance sustainable development, as there are no silver-bullet solutions and fundamental societal changes are required (Wittmayer et al., 2014). In addition, examples from closely related fields, such as social entrepreneurship, show promising results. For example, the AR study of Berglund and Wigren-Kristoferson (2012), regarding a think-and-do-tank with diverse actors, enabled the identification of new real-world actions that involved complex and multi-faceted solutions to pave the way for social entrepreneurs to address the unsatisfactory state of local areas in Swedish municipalities.

As sustainable entrepreneurship comprises a research environment that is rich in complexity, it provides an opportunity for learning and can benefit from the active participation of academics and their meaningful interaction with multiple stakeholders. Therefore, in what follows we will refer to AR focusing on participatory AR (PAR). PAR is defined as

> a participatory process concerned with developing practical knowing in the pursuit of worthwhile human purposes, which seeks to bring together action and reflection, theory and practice, in participation with others, in the pursuit of practical solutions to issues of pressing concern to people, and more generally the flourishing of individual persons and their communities. (Reason & Bradbury, 2008a: 4)

In the experience of the authors this type of AR is important in the sustainable entrepreneurship context as this context requires the participation of multiple stakeholders. Sustainable entrepreneurs often have to deal with complex societal problems, where multiple, and oftentimes conflicting, perceptions of both the problems and solutions exist (Hassan, 2014). Therefore, there is no general rule on how these problems can be addressed and what 'sustainable' is, as this is highly dependent on the context, the different stakeholders involved and their perspectives (Eikelenboom, 2022). The involvement of multiple different stakeholders in participatory processes is therefore essential. Despite its benefits, adopting AR methodologies in sustainable entrepreneurship research may also come with several challenges, which will be outlined in the next section.

4 Challenges and Limitations of Action Research

AR is deemed to be particularly promising for producing societal/practical impact while also producing academic impact (Simsek et al., 2018), yet it presents many challenges. Creating useful practice-oriented research requires scholars to bridge or productively inhabit a challenging interface – the 'in-between' landscape of the academic–practitioner gap. Indeed, it has been suggested that 'the reason why the research–practice gap endures is that bridging it is beyond the capabilities and scope of most individuals' (Bansal et al., 2012). Below we highlight some of the most occurring challenges in AR.

First and foremost, impact (academic as well as societal/practical) need not be positive. Indeed, negative impact may also be the result of AR (Derrick et al., 2018), and an underlying danger in exploring a problem is the potential to exacerbate that problem. Assessing the real risk for all involved stakeholders in an AR project involves getting as much information as possible about the participants and their organisation as well as enquiring into the cost–benefit relationship of stakeholders.

Second, impact and 'solutions' to the explored challenges may take many shapes and forms. Focusing on the research process caters to the fact that the impact experienced by non-academic stakeholders is likely to be just as much in the process of conducting the research as receiving the results ex-post (e.g., Newell, 2005). It is central to assessing the risk of AR that the ability to frame academic problems in a way suited for actions and negotiating access to and committing practitioners to engage in such collaborative relationships are competences in their own right.

Third, an AR collaboration rests on mutuality and reciprocity; it has to be a mutually beneficial situation and not a zero-sum game. At the same time, it is necessary to engage in open dialogue about the fact that not all practitioner problems or views can be addressed, just as not all research gaps can be covered. Practitioners will need to embrace the fact that researchers are engaging with them with a view to producing knowledge that is desirable and relevant outside the unique organisational context, fulfilling their responsibility to add to the scientific pool of knowledge.

Fourth, an additional source of risk for researchers is that the AR project may demand that the researcher is knowledgeable about a broad range of methodologies, leading the researcher into new and potentially unchartered territory (Nielsen, 2014, 2016). Therefore, a risk assessment also involves mutual examination of the necessary competences involved, for example, whether the researcher is capable of producing the desired results and if all parties possess sufficient 'absorptive capacity' for mutual learning (Cohen & Levinthal, 1990).

Finally, AR assumes equality between the parties consistent with a view of academic and practical knowledge – there is 'no reason to see one [form of knowledge] as superior to the other; instead, knowledge production may be strengthened by using the different sources and methods of knowledge production in cooperation' (Löwsted & Stjernberg, 2006: 5). AR breaks with the common perception of the subject/object relationship between researcher and field of research in that the action researcher him/herself is an active part of his/her own field of research. The action researcher needs to be able to work with not only epistemological approaches suited for such a knowledge production situation but also ontological frames allowing for close contact between researcher and field as a hallmark of quality rather than 'field pollution'.

In the remainder of this chapter, we will focus on two often overlooked challenges and strengths of AR: the temporality of impact – i.e., planning impact as an ex-ante purposeful ingredient of the research – and value reciprocity – i.e., the on-going process of exchange with the aim of establishing and maintaining equality and mutual benefits for researchers and practitioners.

4.1 Temporality of Impact

I do not have good experiences working with researchers. Every time it gets interesting, they leave.

This quote is part of a conversation one of the authors had with a manager discussing research–practice collaborations. A challenge of this collaborative method is that the impact AR strives for can often require a long time to materialise. Yet, researchers are usually driven by a specific research question that might be bound to a certain time frame and (scarce) resources. These might not necessarily match their stakeholders' temporal needs, as illustrated by the quote above. This is a challenging issue for the action researcher who should, on the one hand, manage the short-term AR goals, and on the other, be open to long-term changes of the AR projects that might emerge as the impact of the collaboration begins to manifest. Failing to account for impact emergence in AR will likely result in replicating the problem expressed by the manager through the quote reported above. We refer to this problem as the Cinderella metaphor: when the party gets interesting, Cinderella (researcher) runs away from the castle. All that is left is a shoe (a theoretical paper) and a prince (practitioner) hunting for the lost princess. Others try to fit the shoe (theoretical paper) to different girls of the town (multiple contexts). But the shoe does not fit any other girl (each context is unique). How can Cinderella keep dancing after midnight (how can researchers keep on contributing to impact beyond theoretical contribution and beyond the specific time of that specific context)?

This challenge is particularly salient to sustainability problems like those tackled by sustainable entrepreneurs. Sustainability problems are urgent, yet solutions to these problems need to have long-term systems effects (Bansal, Grewatsch, & Sharma, 2021). In 2018, the IPCC report estimated that only 12 years were left to figure out how to act on the climate crisis. Yet, transitions do take a long time. This aspect should push sustainable entrepreneurship researchers to strive for both immediate and long-term impact, which is one of the main opportunities provided by the AR method. Just like a doctor is deemed responsible to act in medical emergencies around her, so are sustainability scholars responsible to share their knowledge when faced with questions on climate change and crisis. In this light, AR collaborations can serve as a vehicle for uncovering blind spots and research gaps, innovation and accelerating sustainability transitions. It is the experience of the authors that action researchers addressing those challenges can sometimes be addressed, or critiqued, as researcher activists (Apple, 2010). In this context, they might be regarded as climate activists (Kirchherr, 2022). This view is an additional trigger to the relevance–rigour debate. The action researcher studying sustainable entrepreneurship should not be discouraged by those critiques. Recent work on research philosophy has proven that researchers exert impact (whether positive or negative) on their environment irrespective of their effort not to do so. For example, the idea of a fly on the wall supported by positivist ethnography is utopian in sustainability research since the researcher will impact stakeholders' cognition, knowledge and possibly practices, already by introducing their research goal (Greco, 2020). Instead of framing impact as an undesired side-effect of research efforts, AR advocates for purposeful and intentional impact. Action researchers aiming for impact on sustainability practice can leverage the temporal aspect of impact by seeking learning and change in the past, present and future (Reinecke & Ansari, 2017 [1988]). They can do so by carefully planning their data collection upfront, seeing impact rather than an ex-post consequence, as an ex-ante purposeful ingredient of research.

The example in the following section shows how short- and long-term sustainability impact can be an integral part of AR design and outcomes.

4.1.1 Case Example: Impact Temporality Behind the Building and Technology Innovation Centre

The Building and Technology Innovation Centre () is a Dutch initiative in which researchers work together with public and private entities to align the most updated knowledge on design, technology and innovation for the sustainability transitions of the built environment. This initiative includes several entrepreneurs looking to launch a breakthrough technology on the market. The researchers work towards creating an extensive inventory to map, for example, users' needs working with promising energy communities, and they experiment with fit-for-purpose new forms of collaborations. These research efforts result in the bridging of innovations of more experienced businesses with those of the nascent ones, connecting sectors and disciplines throughout the process.

'Temporality' is in the BTIC programme one of the main challenges, an opportunity and a focus because it strives for long-term societal impact through short-term stakeholders' benefits. Throughout the process, researchers and organisations navigate the complexity of multiple societal transitions: climate adaptation, circularity, energy transition, digitalisation and urban transformations (e.g., infrastructures and mobility). The ambition is to scale up this knowledge so as to apply the innovations needed to reach the national sustainability targets by 2030.

For example, this programme included a project on sensible thermal energy storage (TES). TES is a technology that stocks thermal energy by heating or cooling a storage medium so that the stored energy can be used at a later time for heating and cooling applications and power generations. TES can increase the reliability of renewable energy sources, increase the business case of sustainable energy technologies and reduce carbon dioxide emissions. However, TES is still largely absent in the building landscape. Households have little to no incentive to install TES, and entrepreneurs attempting to enter this market are struggling to survive. The sustainable entrepreneurs developing TES needed both short-term solutions to develop the technologies as well as long-term institutional changes accelerating the energy transition to facilitate the market uptake of TES. Therefore, a team of researchers within the BTIC consortium decided to research the following question: how can sensible TES align with the interests of stakeholders from an energy perspective, a financial perspective and from the perspective of a building owner and users?

To address this question, the researchers partnered with grid operators, installation companies and two entrepreneurs who were developing an innovative solution for tensile TES that could be installed in the backyard family houses. The entrepreneurs installed a prototype of the technology at a field lab of Delft University of Technology monitored by the researchers of the BTIC programme. Potential users, policymakers and other companies could interact with the entrepreneurs and see the prototype being tested in real time. This research enabled this enterprise to survive in the short term since the institutional environment will unlikely enable this technology to scale up before 2024 while enhancing knowledge on TES and contributing to the energy transition in the long term.

It is important to note that short and long-term impacts will only be possible if all the stakeholders nourish a genuine interest in the goal and process of the AR endeavours as discussed in the following section.

4.2 Value Reciprocity

AR is a timely response to the demands for double-impact (Tihanyi, 2020), yet creation and extraction of mutual value added are not a built-in property or guaranteed outcome of AR collaborations. Throughout the AR process, your role as researcher is to 'serve as a resource to those being studied' (Babbie, 2015: 341). Pursuing this double objective of acting as a resource to participants and studying participants at the same time will inevitably lead to contradicting tensions that must be navigated by the action researcher. Academic as well as practical impact can be created or destroyed at any given point in the process, and changes in priorities, staffing or available resources in an AR consortium often give rise to re-negotiations or re-calibration of the impact and activities planned as part of the research design.

An overlooked aspect of AR is that AR not only presupposes capable and professional action researchers but also capable and engaged stakeholders. Action researchers Greenwood and Levin observe that '[a]ction research is social research carried out by a team that encompasses a professional action researcher and the members of an organisation, community, or network ("stakeholders") who are seeking to improve the participant's situation' (Greenwood & Levin, 2007: 3). In an *ideal* world:

- A sustainable entrepreneur or enterprise is actively seeking out the help of action researchers in response to an identified need for solutions and new knowledge.
- The researcher has a fortunate combination of availability and expertise to design and engage in a research project.
- The researcher manages to study the problem and identify solutions in cooperation with stakeholders in a time that suits the participants' needs.
- Participants appreciate the outcomes and are ready to implement the insights resulting from this collaboration.

While such a scenario might be what transpires from a scientific article depicting a wonderful story of AR, such a linear process is utopian or extremely rare in practice. Researchers are rarely the first go-to person when a sustainable enterprise or entrepreneur is facing a problem. Unless they know you from bestselling publications or through their proximate network, it is unlikely they will think of your expertise as a solution to their problem. Consequently, the responsibility for starting an AR collaboration lies with the researchers who have their own expertise, interests and research agenda that may only partially match the interest of stakeholders. Therefore, a more likely scenario than the 'ideal world' scenario outlined above is that the researchers are de facto the ones in need of help. You will have a desire – or a need, driven by academic goals – for data, insights and exploration. You are hoping to find 'someone to help', yet it is important to critically evaluate if participants really want to be helped by you. If not, you may have to leave them alone.

When you attract and assemble an AR consortium, you will realise that participants' time and attention is going to be your scarcest resource, and that your research design and outcome depend upon your ability to make participants prioritise collaborating with you. Researchers must create a platform of common enquiry and gain the attention of stakeholders before, during and after the process. 'Political entrepreneurship', defined as 'the exploitation of opportunities in order to allocate scarce resources to outcomes and preferences' (Björkman & Sundgren, 2005: 403), is a precondition for academic and practical impact realisation. The action researcher must act as a political entrepreneur in order to create and focus attention, resources and interest for the project among participants.

Aligning research interests and expertise to participant needs is a creative process of compromises. Researchers will have to adjust their research questions, making time and space for messy processes that might not necessarily lead to new theoretical insights. Simultaneously, participants will need to appreciate that research collaborations are long-term endeavours, quite different from their fast-paced businesses. The collaborations will seldom lead to silver-bullet solutions, but will eventually yield valuable learnings, illuminate new worthwhile perspectives and positively impact sustainability practices.

4.2.1 Case Example: Value Reciprocity in the Circular Neighbourhood Initiative

We will now turn to illustrating challenges related to value reciprocity in the context of a three-year AR project of an entrepreneurial initiative of a social housing association to involve the local community, next to other stakeholders (including the local municipality and local businesses), in the design and implementation of circular economy approaches in a low-income neighbourhood in the Netherlands, called the Circular Neighbour (CN) initiative. The researchers joined the housing association with the objective to collaboratively design, execute and evaluate the CN initiative. The AR project involved several phases including diagnosing, action planning, action taking and evaluation.

A main challenge in the AR project was to ensure that the topic being studied was truly one that the practitioners wanted to investigate. The lead researcher had previous working relationships with the housing association, exploring the challenges the housing association was facing regarding the involvement of community members in the energy transition and circular economy. The involvement of the researchers in the CN initiative was welcomed by several members of the housing association who had collaborated with the researcher before. In initial discussions with the involved stakeholders the purpose of the initiative was discussed as well as the opportunities for collaboration and reciprocal benefits. However, in these discussions it became apparent that the practitioners interpreted circularity in a broader way compared to the traditional environmental and economic focus of the concept (Murray et al., 2017), which is illustrated in the following quote.

> I think very differently about circularity than you might assume, I see the circular economy as a social practice, revaluing the talents of people in the neighbourhood. We have to find out what people want and can do and make use of these talents, instead of leaving people without a job at home. (Interview: owner community space)

In several instances, the practitioners pushed the researchers to define 'circularity', assuming a technical explanation and arguing that it may not be a useful concept in the neighbourhood. Therefore, some practitioners, especially those who had not previously worked with the researcher, were not sure of the benefits of the project:

> I don't know if this project is interesting for us. Will a focus on such a technical topic provide support to the work we do in this neighbourhood? (Conversation between the researcher and a member of the social team)

In response to this, the researchers were clear that the practitioners could define circularity in the way that was most appropriate for the CN initiative. This led to a change in the dynamics of the project as the practitioners recognised that they were seen as experts on the topic within the neighbourhood and able to share this expertise with the researchers and consequently shape the scope of the CN initiative. Furthermore, practitioners had to adjust their action-oriented way of working, as extra time had to be incorporated to examine different perspectives on circularity to shape the initiative before action could be taken. It also required a change in the perspectives of the researchers, as they had to incorporate a broader understanding of circularity in their study compared to the understanding that is generally adopted in the scientific literature by including environmental, economic and social considerations. This example highlights that value reciprocity requires time for relationship building and maintenance, where both researchers and practitioners may have to adjust their perspectives to ensure that the AR project is valuable for both parties.

5 Future Outlook

Due to its novelty, and the wickedness of the challenges it addresses, the field of sustainable entrepreneurship can greatly benefit from AR. An AR research design can deal with knowledge production for sustainable entrepreneurship in ways that more traditional research methodologies cannot. Also, AR can exert positive impacts both before and during research, not only after. However, the practice of AR is a challenging one and unfortunately still somewhat under-appreciated depending on the type of scholarly environment the researcher is confronted with. The degree to which a more theoretical or applied impact is pursued as well as the geographical location – in the extent to which a geo-political environment is pushing research impact for scholarly success, as increasingly seen in the EU – are important factors in favouring or hampering AR efforts (e.g., George et al., 2016; MacIntosh et al., 2021; Pettigrew & Starkey, 2016).

Irrespective of their specific scholarly environment, we invite researchers working in the different fields of sustainability sciences to benefit from the potentials of AR in underpinning new knowledge to address the pressing sustainability challenges of our time. Such assertion can be implemented in many forms, but there are a few developments that are needed for this to materialise.

First, academia should educate young and senior scholars in AR. Just like a person who has never studied statistics would probably not dare to perform a causal analysis without educating him/herself beforehand, the same should be the case for a person attempting to perform AR. While this might sound logical, it is our experience that given the common misunderstanding on what the AR method entails – often mistaken for co-creation and/or consultancy – it is often performed by inexperienced researchers. This might inadvertently not only result in poor theoretical insights as a result of the research – as data collection and analysis are challenging, especially when going solo – but might also result in negative unintended consequences in practice, and paradoxically create more harm than good on stakeholders. Proper AR training in doctoral programmes should be developed in sustainability-driven universities.

Second, and related to the previous, the purposeful combination of AR and action learning in sustainable entrepreneurship should be explored further. Academic institutions are being critiqued about their disputable contribution to society in general (Tourish, 2020) and to sustainability transitions in particular (Kirchherr, 2022) through both their research and teaching activities. For example, it appears that business schools inadequately prepare students to understand and address the complexity of wicked problems (Parker, 2018). Such reductionism can negatively impact students' sense of responsibility, as they narrow their focus on the problem at hand and not the broader context in which the current problem may sit (Blasco, 2021). One way to overcome this challenge is for business pedagogy to move outside of the institutional walls of a classroom in experimental (action) research settings.

Third, sustainable entrepreneurship research should be designed to address forward-looking inquiry (Sharma et al., forthcoming) for which AR is suitable. Theorising what does not yet exist is not only possible and worthwhile, but should be a priority of our times (Gümüsay & Reinecke, 2021). In the midst of an unprecedented climate and human crisis rapidly unfolding, researchers should focus on possible, probable and desirable futures to shape our present-day actions. The current research paradigms largely grounded on past data, and current experiences fall short in researching wicked problems that are dynamic and complex, for which the past and present may be inadequate in responding to what is to come. Future research should explore ways in which AR can harmonise forward-looking enquiry.

In conclusion, sustainable entrepreneurship and researchers have a collective role to play and responsibility in addressing wicked problems. We describe one way to do this. We hope that scholars can orchestrate similar research approaches to foster thinking and actions around future possibilities to address wicked problems and foster resilient and thriving societies.

References

Apple, M. W. (2010). Theory, research, and the critical scholar/activist. *Educational Researcher, 39*, 152–155.

Babbie, E. (2015). *Observing Ourselves: Essays in Social Research*. Illinois: Waveland Press.

Bansal, P., Bertels, S., Ewart, T., MacConnachie, P., & O'Brien, J. (2012). Bridging the research–practice gap. *Academy of Management Perspectives, 26*(1), 73–92.

Bansal, P., Grewatsch, S., & Sharma, G. (2021). How COVID-19 informs business sustainability research: It's time for a systems perspective. *Journal of Management Studies, 58*(2), 602–606.

Bansal, P., & Sharma, G. (2021). Three different approaches to impact: Translating, cocreating, and performing. *Business & Society, 61*(4), 827–832.

Berglund, K. A. E., & Wigren-Kristoferson, C. (2012). Using pictures and artefacts in a PAR process to disclose new wor(l)ds of entrepreneurship. *Action Research, 10*(3), 276–292.

Björkman, H., & Sundgren, M. (2005). Political entrepreneurship in action research: Learning from two cases. *Journal of Organisational Change Management, 18*(5), 399–415.

Blasco, M. (2021). 'We're Just Geeks': Disciplinary identifications among business students and their implications for personal responsibility. *Journal of Business Ethics, 178*(1), 1–24.

Carayannis, E. G., Barth, T. D., & Campbell, D. F. (2012). The quintuple helix innovation model: Global warming as a challenge and driver for innovation. *Journal of Innovation and Entrepreneurship, 1*(1), 1–12.

Cohen, W. M., & Levinthal, D. A. (1990). Absorptive capacity: A new perspective on learning and innovation. *Administrative Science Quarterly, 35*(1), 128–152.

Coughlan, P., & Coghlan, D. (2002). Action research for operations management. *International Journal of Operations & Production Management, 22*, 220–240.

Degnegaard, R. (2014). Co-creation, prevailing streams and a future design trajectory. *CoDesign, 10*(2), 96–111.

Derrick, G. E., Faria, R., Benneworth, P., Pedersen, D. B., & Sivertsen, G. (2018). Towards characterising negative impact: Introducing Grimpact. In *23rd International Conference on Science and Technology Indicators* (pp. 1199–1213). Leiden University, CWTS, November 2018.

Eikelenboom, M. (2022). *Achieving sustainability together: Stakeholder collaboration for corporate sustainability and the circular economy*. Doctoral Thesis. University of Groningen, Faculty Campus Fryslân.

Erickson, F. (2006). Studying side by side: Collaborative action ethnography in educational research. In G. Spindler & L. Hammond (Eds.), *Innovations in Educational Ethnography: Theory, Methods and Results* (pp. 235–257). London: Psychology Press.

Gast, J., Gundolf, K., & Cesinger, B. (2017). Doing business in a green way: A systematic review of the ecological sustainability entrepreneurship literature and future research directions. *Journal of Cleaner Production, 147*, 44–56.

George, G., Howard-Grenville, J., Joshi, A., & Tihanyi, L. (2016). Understanding and tackling societal grand challenges through management research. *Academy of Management Journal, 59*(6), 1880–1895.

Gioia, D. A., Price, K. N., Hamilton, A. L., & Thomas, J. B. (2010). Forging an identity: An insider–outsider study of processes involved in the formation of organisational identity. *Administrative Science Quarterly, 55*(1), 1–46.

Greco, A. (2020). *Changing for Good: Transforming Existing Organisations into Sustainable Enterprises*. Doctoral dissertation. University of Groningen, Faculty Campus Fryslân.

Greco, A., Eikelenboom, M., & Long, T. B. (2021). Innovating for sustainability through collaborative innovation contests. *Journal of Cleaner Production, 311*, 127628.

Greenwood, D. J., & Levin, M. (2007). *Introduction to Action Research: Social Research for Social Change* (2nd edition). Thousand Oaks, CA: SAGE Publications.

Gümüsay, A. A., & Reinecke, J. (2021). Researching for desirable futures: From real utopias to imagining alternatives. *Journal of Management Studies, 59*(1), 236–242.

Gutberlet, J. (2008). Empowering collective recycling initiatives: Video documentation and action research with a recycling co-op in Brazil. *Resource Conservation and Recycling*, *52*(4), 659–670.

Hassan, Z. (2014). *The Social Labs Revolution: A New Approach to Solving Our Most Complex Challenges*. Oakland, CA: Berrett-Koehler Publishers.

Jamieson, D. W., Barnett, R. C., & Buono, A. F. (Eds.). (2016). *Consultation for Organisational Change Revisited*. Charlotte, NC: IAP.

Johannisson, B. (2020). Searching for the roots of entrepreneuring as practice: Introducing the enactive approach. In W. B. Gartner & B. T. Teague (Eds.), *Research Handbook on Entrepreneurial Behavior, Practice and Process* (pp. 138–167). Cheltenham: Edward Elgar Publishing.

Keahey, J. (2021). Sustainable development and participatory action research: A systematic review. *Systemic Practice and Action Research*, *34*(3), 291–306.

Kemmis, S., McTaggart, R., & Nixon, R. (2013). *The Action Research Planner: Doing Critical Participatory Action Research*. Singapore: Springer Verlag.

Kirchherr, J. (2022). Bullshit in the sustainability and transitions literature: A provocation. *Circular Economy and Sustainability*, 1–6.

Leitch, C. (2007). An action research approach to entrepreneurship. In H. Neergaard & J. P. Ulhøi (Eds.), *Handbook of Research Methods in Entrepreneurship* (pp. 144–169). Cheltenham: Edward Elgar.

Levin, M. (2012). Academic integrity in action research. *Action Research*, *10*(2), 133–149.

Lewin, K. (1947). Frontiers in group dynamics: II. Channels of group life; social planning and action research. *Human Relations*, *1*(2), 143–153.

Loorbach, D., Van Bakel, J. C., Whiteman, G., & Rotmans, J. (2010). Business strategies for transitions towards sustainable systems. *Business Strategy and the Environment*, *19*(2), 133–146.

Louis, M. R., & Bartunek, J. M. (1992). Insider/outsider research teams: Collaboration across diverse perspectives. *Journal of Management Inquiry*, *1*(2), 101–110.

Löwstedt, J., & Stjernberg, T. (Eds.). (2006). *Producing Management Knowledge*. Abingdon: Routledge.

MacIntosh, R., Mason, K., Beech, N., & Bartunek, J. M. (2021). *Delivering Impact in Management Research: When Does It Really Happen?*. Oxfordshire: Routledge.

Maestrini, V., Luzzini, D., Shani, A. B. R., & Canterino, F. (2016). The action research cycle reloaded: Conducting action research across buyer–supplier relationships. *Journal of Purchasing and Supply Management*, *22*(4), 289–298.

Miles, M. B., Huberman, A. M., & Saldana, J. (2014). *Qualitative Data Analysis: A Methods Sourcebook*. London: Sage.

Muñoz, P., & Cohen, B. (2018). Sustainable entrepreneurship research: Taking stock and looking ahead. *Business Strategy and the Environment*, *27*(3), 300–322.

Murray, A., Skene, K., & Haynes, K. (2017). The circular economy: An interdisciplinary exploration of the concept and application in a global context. *Journal of Business Ethics*, *140*(3), 369–380.

Newell, S. (2005). The fallacy of simplistic notions of the transfer of 'best practice'. In A. F. Buono & F. Poulfelt (Eds.), *Challenges and Issues in Knowledge Management* (pp. 51–68). Charlotte, NC: Information Age Publishing.

Nielsen, R. K. (2014). *Global mindset as managerial meta-competence and organisational capability: Boundary-crossing leadership cooperation in the MNC. The case of 'group mindset' in Solar A/S*. PhD series No. 24.2014. The PhD School in Economics & Management, Copenhagen Business School. https://research.cbs.dk/en/publications/global-mindset-as-managerial-meta-competence-and-organizational-c

Nielsen, R. K. (2016). *Industrial PhDs in EM: A stakeholder approach to the potentials and pitfalls of industrial PhD projects*. The PhD School in Economics & Management, Copenhagen Business School.

Parker, M. (2018). *Shut down the Business School: What's Wrong with Management Education*. London: Pluto Press.

Pearce, J. L., & Huang, L. (2012). Toward an understanding of what actionable research is. *Academy of Management Learning & Education, 11*(2), 300–301.

Pettigrew, A., & Starkey, K. (2016). From the guest editors: The legitimacy and impact of business schools – Key issues and a research agenda. *Academy of Management Learning & Education, 15*(4), 649–664.

Pettigrew, A. M. (1997). The double hurdles for management research. In T. Clark (Ed.), *Advancement in Organisational Behaviour: Essays in Honour of Derek S. Pugh* (pp. 277–296). London: Dartmouth Press.

Prahalad, C. K., & Ramaswamy, V. (2004). Co-creation experiences: The next practice in value creation. *Journal of Interactive Marketing, 18*(3), 5–14.

Reason, P., & Bradbury, H. (2008a). Introduction. In P. Reason & H. Bradbury (Eds.), *The Sage Handbook of Action Research* (pp. 1–11). Newbury Park, CA: Sage Publishing.

Reason, P., & Bradbury, H. (2008b). Concluding reflections: Whither action research. In P. Reason & H. Bradbury (Eds.), *The Sage Handbook of Action Research* (pp. 695–707). Newbury Park, CA: Sage Publishing.

Reinecke, J., & Ansari, S. (2017 [1988]). Time, temporality and process studies. In: A. Langeley & H. Tsoukas (Eds). *The Sage Handbook of Process Organization Studies* (pp. 402–416). Newbury Park: Sage. Schein, E. H. (1988). *Process Consultation – Its Role in Organisational Development.* Reading, MA: Addison-Wesley.

Schein, E. H. (1988). What are the lessons of the OD fable? *Group & Organization Studies, 13*(1), 29–32.

Senge, P. M., & Scharmer, C. O. (2008). Community action research: Learning as a community of practitioners, consultants and researchers. Handbook of action research: The concise paperback edition, 195–206.

Sharma, G., & Bansal, P. (2020). Cocreating rigorous and relevant knowledge. *Academy of Management Journal, 63*(2), 386–410.

Sharma, G., Greco, A., Grewatsch, S., & Bansal, P. (forthcoming). Cocreating forward: How researchers and managers can address wicked problems together. *Academy of Management Learning & Education.*

Simsek, Z., Bansal, P., Shaw, J. D., Heugens, P., & Smith, W. K. (2018). From the editors – Seeing practice impact in new ways. *Academy of Management Journal, 61*(6), 2021–2025.

Tasker, M., Westberg, L., & Seymour, R. G. (2010). Action research in social entrepreneurship: A framework for involvement. *International Journal of Action Research, 6*(2–3), 223–255.

Tihanyi, L. (2020). From 'that's interesting' to 'that's important'. *Academy of Management Journal, 63*(2), 329–331.

Torfing, J., & Ansell, C. (2021). Co-creation: The new kid on the block in public governance. *Policy and Politics, 49*(2), 211–230.

Tourish, D. (2020). The triumph of nonsense in management studies. *Academy of Management Learning & Education, 19*(1), 99–109.

Vandael, K., Dewaele, A., Buysse, A., & Westerduin, S. (2018). *Guide to Co-creation.* Ghent: Ghent University & Ministry of Makers.

Van de Ven, A. H. (2007). Engaged scholarship: A guide for organizational and social research. Oxford University Press on Demand.

Wickins, E., & Crossley, M. (2016). Coming alongside in the co-construction of professional knowledge: A fluid approach to researcher positioning on the insider-outsider continuum. In M. Crossley, L. Arthur & E. McNess (Eds.), *Revisiting Insider–Outsider Research in Comparative and International Education* (pp. 225–240). Oxford: Symposium Books.

Williams, A., & Whiteman, G. (2021). A call for deep engagement for impact: Addressing the planetary emergency. *Strategic Organization, 19*(3), 526–537.

Willis, J. W., & Edwards, C. (Eds.). (2014). *Action Research: Models, Methods, and Examples.* Charlotte, NC: Information Age Publisher.

Wittmayer, J. M., Schäpke, N., Van Steenbergen, F., & Omann, I. (2014). Making sense of sustainability transitions locally: How action research contributes to addressing societal challenges. *Critical Policy Studies, 8*(4), 465–485.

Dana Schadenberg, Emma Folmer*, Thomas B. Long

4 Sustainable Entrepreneurship Education

Abstract: This chapter will give a state-of-the-art and integrated understanding of sustainable entrepreneurship education. It will examine its main components including competences, attitude, teaching approaches, the university ecosystem and assessment. The chapter draws on the results of a systematic literature review conducted for the Erasmus + Teaching Entrepreneurship for Sustainability project. The chapter highlights the importance of sustainable entrepreneurship competencies in creating a mindset for change. The need for sustainable entrepreneurs and so-called 'change makers' highlights the importance of sustainable entrepreneurship education, which empowers students through collaborative, experiential and reflective learning to better our world.

Keywords: sustainable entrepreneurship, education, sustainability, change makers

1 Introduction

This chapter presents the content and methods of teaching core competencies relevant for successful sustainable entrepreneurship (from here often abbreviated to SE). SE is a relatively new field of research and business practice that can be seen as both a critique on our current economic system and as an answer to the societal needs of today.

The concept of sustainable entrepreneurship consists of two parts: sustainability and entrepreneurship. The academic and professional use of sustainability dates back to the end of the former century. Elkington (1997) was among the first to introduce the world to the idea of the triple bottom line. The triple bottom line highlighted the need to balance the interests of People, Planet and Profit. It is now widely used by sustainable development organisations, entrepreneurs and academic scholars in part due to its simplicity, which is also a source of critique. The triple bottom line combines well with entrepreneurship. It intuitively conveys the need for enterprises to foster the interests of people and of the natural environment, while making the necessary profit in the process to sustain themselves, so they can keep on creating social and/or environmental value in the future. The economic profit does not only refer to

*Corresponding author: **Emma Folmer,** University of Groningen, Campus Fryslân, Wirdumerdijk 34, 8911CE, Leeuwarden, The Netherlands
Dana Schadenberg, Student-partner researcher in sustainability and identity, Trinity College, Dublin, Green 2, DO2PN40 Ireland
Thomas B. Long, University of Groningen, Campus Fryslân, Wirdumerdijk 34, 8911CE, Leeuwarden, The Netherlands

https://doi.org/10.1515/9783110756159-005

the profit for the enterprise itself but also the real economic benefits enjoyed by the society.

The triple bottom line inherently includes entrepreneurship, that is, the creation of an enterprise capable of producing sustainable value. Entrepreneurship has in business and management education conventionally been understood as the art of starting up a new enterprise (Kent, Sexton, & Vesper, 1982). But entrepreneurship is more than that. One of the earliest and well-known definitions of entrepreneurship derives from Schumpeter (1934), who defined entrepreneurship as the process of creative destruction. Creative destruction originates from disrupting innovations like Ford's moving assembly line or Netflix's business model move from renting out videos to streaming subscriptions.

Entrepreneurs find or make opportunities, on which they then *undertake* action. While entrepreneurship often culminates in starting up a new venture, it can also take place within existing enterprises and organisations. Entrepreneurship is just as much about opportunity recognition and exploitation as it is about the process of starting up a venture, maybe even more so. To be an entrepreneur is first and foremost to have a certain mentality or way of looking at the world and second about knowing how to start and to run a new business.

Sustainability and entrepreneurship, long thought to have come from the opposing worlds of not-for-profit charity and profit-seeking business, are actually two sides of the same coin. Persons engaged in sustainable development are persons who aim to foster systemic changes. Like entrepreneurs they are disruptors. They envision a world where social welfare is not equated with monetary revenues, which historically spurs the exploitation of people and places. They define social welfare in terms of well-being (O'Mahony, 2022; Taylor, 2011). Making the well-being of people and of our planet as the most important societal goal (rather than maximising profits and economic growth) is nothing short of a fundamental transformation of contemporaneous mainstream paradigms.

A crucial driver of change is education and the teaching programmes that aim to create a better world and put sustainability and entrepreneurship at the centre. This chapter will elaborate on such teaching programmes and explore the current state of the art of the field of sustainable entrepreneurship education (from here on, often abbreviated to SEE). The outline of this chapter is as follows. Section 2 examines how sustainability and entrepreneurship relate to each other and what sustainable entrepreneurship is. Section 3 reviews five key components of SEE. These key components derive from a systematic literature review conducted for the Erasmus + Teaching Entrepreneurship for Sustainability project. The chapter concludes with a discussion of the main insights presented in this chapter offering avenues for future research.

2 Education on Sustainability and Entrepreneurship

Sustainability has been firmly rooted in different programmes of the United Nations Educational, Scientific and Cultural Organization (UNESCO) since 1945. According to UNESCO, education for sustainable development has the ability to 'empower learners with knowledge, skills, values and attitudes to take informed decisions and make responsible actions for environmental integrity, economic viability and a just society' (UNESCO, 2020: 30). UNESCO's programmes dedicated to education for sustainable development are an intrinsic part of the fourth Sustainable Development Goal concerning the quality of education. The European Union embraces the SDGs given that sustainable development is a core principle of the Treaty on European Union. The European Union is also very much aware that we live in a 'rapid changing society where it is essential that everyone has the capacity to act upon opportunities and ideas, to . . . shape the future for the common good' (European Commission, n.d.). The European Union therefore created the European Entrepreneurship Competence Framework consisting of 15 competences including ethical and sustainable thinking (Bacigalupo et al., 2016) The EEC framework increasingly is embedded in other international organisations including the OECD (2018) who refers to the EEC framework in their policy notes on entrepreneurship competences.

Education for Sustainable Development (from here on referred to as ESD) and Entrepreneurship Education (from here on referred to as EE) have much in common and are both important topics for international policy-making institutes. That said, SE is relatively new and not yet the dominant paradigm in teaching. Sustainability principles are often provided as 'add-on' aspects to entrepreneurship education, not yet integrating the two concepts (Lans, Blok, Wesselink, 2014; Ploum et al., 2018). Nonetheless, notable exceptions exist and the number of sustainability teaching programmes that incorporate entrepreneurship education is increasing.

To identify these programmes and their best practices, the Teaching Entrepreneurship for Sustainability project was initiated (from here on referred to as TES). This Erasmus + project is a collaboration between Uppsala University, University of Groningen and Nord University. It aims to improve our understanding of how entrepreneurship and sustainability can be successfully integrated in teaching. As part of the project, a systematic literature review of current practices in sustainable entrepreneurship education and teaching was conducted. This chapter draws on the findings of this literature review to give an account of the current status of SEE.

An important question concerns the definition or conceptualisation of SE. Entrepreneurs and sustainable value makers are in Schumpeter's term creative destructors and disruptive innovators. There is an on-going nature or nurture debate on sustainability competences in general and for SE skills in particular. Can the capacity to enact change be taught or is it a personality trait? Can individuals learn to see opportunities where others see problems? These questions are central to the field of SEE in general and for twenty-first-century education in particular. Research shows that young adults feel helpless and powerless in the face of anthropogenic climate change (Marks et al., 2021). According to a survey of 10,000 young persons in 10 countries, 75% of the respondents think that 'the future is frightening' (Marks et al., 2021: 863). These are young adults indicating that they do not feel prepared for the future. It has thus never been more important to design and implement educational programmes that make young adults feel confident in their abilities to make a change and to enable them to take transformative actions. In other words, we need sustainable entrepreneurs as change agents of the future. How can we teach these sustainable entrepreneurial attitudes? And likewise, how can we teach young adults to value sustainability? This chapter answers these questions and in doing so reflects the current state of debate concerning the added value of teaching.

There are many different definitions of SE (see, for example, Hockerts & Wüstenhagen, 2010; Pacheco et al., 2010; Shepherd & Patzelt, 2011). This chapter aligns with the definition of Greco and de Jong (2017: 14) who define SE as 'the discovery, creation, and exploitation of entrepreneurial opportunities that contribute to sustainability by generating social and environmental gains for others in society'. This definition captures the key elements of SE. It also relates to on-going debates including what 'generating social *and* environmental gains' precisely means. For example, does it mean that work integration social enterprises are not sustainable enterprises because they are only engaging in the social dimensions of entrepreneurship? Are ecopreneurs, that is, entrepreneurs aiming to generate environmental value, not sustainable entrepreneurs? The on-going debate on definitions resonates in the literature on SE and in the education programmes that are identified and reviewed for this chapter. For example, many courses that are reviewed for this chapter initially concern social entrepreneurship. The reviews show that they also classify as SE given that these courses generate societal impact and encompass social and ecological value creation, thus involving the three sustainability pillars (Calvo et al., 2020; Halberstadt, Timm et al., 2019; Kim et al., 2020).

The growing interest for sustainability in the field of entrepreneurship comprises social entrepreneurship and ethical entrepreneurship more broadly (Fellnhofer, 2019; Vallaster et al., 2019). Our review only includes articles on SEE, which meant that the reviewed programmes covered both social *and* environmental value creation, regardless of whether or not the course was named 'social entrepreneurship' or 'ecopreneurship' (ecological entrepreneurship). In business practice, it is often the case that a company business model either aims at generating social *or* environmental value. Ideally, an entrepreneur is sustainable if he/she accounts for both, meaning that if the business model is wired towards generating social gains, the entrepreneur does not disregard its environmental impact and aims at least to mitigate and/or compensate for any of the potential environmental costs. The same logic holds for an ecopreneur. In sum, a sustainable entrepreneur is not a 'one issue' entrepreneur. They create social *and/or* environmental value, *while generally aiming to do both simultaneously.*

The integration of sustainability and entrepreneurship started with the latter, when business programmes saw a need to incorporate more sustainability thinking into their entrepreneurship programmes (Pinna, 2020). To date, this is the most dominant logic that can be identified in the SEE literature, although in recent years the second pathway, where entrepreneurship is integrated into sustainability education, increased. This is possibly due to a broader recognised need for tools in sustainability education with which to enable students to make a change (Brundiers, Barth, & Cebrián, 2021). The idea that entrepreneurship is a specific action – that is, starting a company – has changed into a broader perspective of the entrepreneur as a 'change maker', that is, someone who takes action to create change. This shift in perspective as seeing the entrepreneur as business maker to change maker is an important step in the field of sustainable education, where sustainability-makers have long been conceptualised as change-makers.

The overlap of ESD and EE shows most clearly in the competences that are formulated for entrepreneurs and change-makers more broadly. Although the competences for ESD and EE have different names, Lans, Blok, and Wesselink (2014) noticed overlap and developed a new framework that integrated the two into one set of SE competences. The Erasmus + CASE (Competencies for A Sustainable Socio-Economic Development) project (2015–2018) validated and developed this framework with teaching approaches and teaching tools that allow teachers to teach these competences to students. The Erasmus + CASE project conducted a systematic literature review of teaching and learning methods used in the educational fields of entrepreneurship and sustainable development, covering 110 articles in the 2015–2018 period (Biberhofer et al., 2016).

The Erasmus + TES project continues from the CASE project and includes the original set of competences and teaching approaches. The Erasmus + TES project conducted a systematic literature review of all academic articles published about SEE from January 2015 to February 2021. A careful review of 1126 initial articles resulted in a first selection of 169 articles that eventually resulted in a final set of 52 articles that are used for the review in this chapter. The literature review shows that SE is a rapidly growing field of interest, with most of the articles that are reviewed here published in 2019 and 2020.

The systematic literature review presented in this chapter resulted in five key elements of SEE: competences and (corresponding) teaching approaches, the role of the university and the university ecosystem in SEE and an assessment of the competences. Figure 4.1 presents the theoretical framework of this chapter that integrates the five key elements of contemporaneous SE teaching.

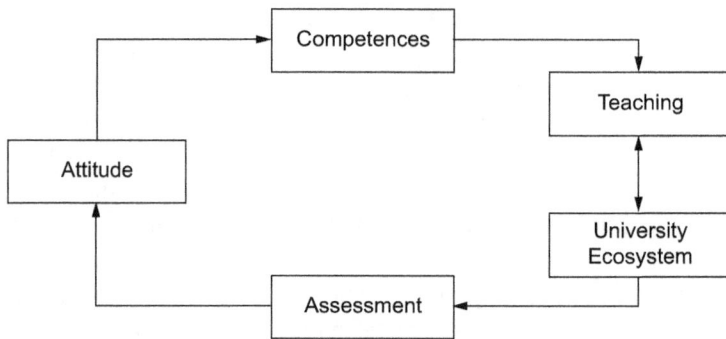

Figure 4.1: Teaching sustainable entrepreneurship.

3 Key Elements of Sustainable Entrepreneurship Education Explored

This section presents the key elements of sustainable entrepreneurship education that have been identified in the literature: competences, attitudes, teaching approaches, the university and ecosystem, and assessment.

3.1 Sustainable Entrepreneurship Competences

This section presents the SE competences and teaching approaches that derived from the systematic literature review. The five most important SE competencies are system thinking competence, anticipatory thinking competence, normative competence, strategic competence and interpersonal competence. Of these five competences system thinking and anticipatory thinking have been found to be the least contested in literature. A brief discussion of each of the five competences is follows.

System thinking is 'the ability to identify and analyse all relevant (sub)systems across different domains (people, planet, profit) and disciplines, including their boundaries' (Ploum et al., 2018: 119). It is one of the core competencies for sustainable entrepreneurs and particularly important in the beginning of the sustainable entrepreneurial process (Foucrier & Wiek, 2019).

Anticipatory thinking is 'the ability to collectively analyse, evaluate, and craft "pictures" of the future in which the impact of local and/or short-term decisions on environmental, social, and economic issues is viewed on a global/cosmopolitan scale and in the long term' (Ploum et al., 2018: 119). Put differently, it concerns the ability to think long term (intergenerational), about social/political developments and to be able to deal with risks and uncertainty (Biberhofer et al., 2019). Note that system thinking and anticipatory thinking in part overlap. System thinking is the thinking of different levels of space (local, regional, global), while anticipatory thinking deals with the thinking of different levels of time (past, present, future). They both deal with thinking beyond there and now and about venturing into more complex and uncertain considerations.

Normative competence concerns the ability to define sustainability values as the centre of entrepreneurial decisions (cf. Ploum et al., 2019). 'Doing the right thing' is the main driver for the actions that sustainable entrepreneurs undertake. It is therefore closely related to values and worldviews that underlie SE competences (Biberhofer et al., 2019). As such the normative competence can be seen as the most fundamental or 'first' competence for SE. It also comprises negotiation and the reconciliation of norms, as one's own norms will inevitably at some point clash with others, especially with SE. It is therefore inherently related to the ability to think critically and being open to diversity to enter into discussion with others.

Strategic competence 'is regarded as a set of skills that includes the ability to recognize and analyse problems, see new opportunities and possible solutions, and to bring sometimes highly idealistic visions, ideas and solutions of SDE "down to earth"' (Biberhofer et al., 2019: 8). Some see creativity and innovativeness as crucial parts of the strategic competency, while others describe strategic competency as comprising only default managerial skills that are devoid of any ingenuity. The strategic competency can therefore be viewed as a jacket that can be put on in two ways. Students might have to learn that running a successful business demands leadership skills such as innovativeness, having a vision and thinking long term by 'using and constantly reworking strategies to remain competitive on the social entrepreneurial market' (Halberstadt, Schank et al., 2019: 2; Halberstadt, Timm et al., 2019) as well as managerial skills such as organisation, planning and controlling or 'how to identify a target customer segment, propose a relevant value, identify distribution methods, locate key resources, ensure adequate revenue streams' (Serhan & Yannou-Lebris, 2020: 22). This differentiation between the leadership and the managerial side of the strategic competences aligns with the difference between the strategic and the action competency that are often highlighted in SEE literature. Ploum et al. (2018) found that these competencies cannot be distinguished enough and should be seen as one competency, namely strategic action competence. Hence in the TES project we have renamed strategic competence to strategic action competence.

The last competence of the CASE framework concerns interpersonal competencies and is especially important for SE because sustainable entrepreneurship calls for more dialogue than mainstream business and often involves a more diverse set of stakeholders to engage with. It underlies all other competences and is important throughout the entire entrepreneurial process (Foucrier & Wiek, 2019). Characteristics of this competency are the ability to communicate in a transdisciplinary way with multi-stakeholder networks and engage in participative teamwork and show integrative leadership (Biberhofer et al., 2019). Note that the ability to think and work interdisciplinary and transdisciplinary is also conceptualised as the competency of embracing diversity and interdisciplinarity in the framework of Lans (Biberhofer et al., 2019). In the CASE framework of competences, 'coping with diversity' and 'intercultural competencies' are both viewed as expressions of interpersonal competence. Overall, there is an inclination in literature to view dealing with diverse stakeholders as an important expression of interpersonal competence, which suggests embracing diversity and interdisciplinarity as part of the interpersonal competence.

The TES literature review resulted in two additional competencies that are not included in the CASE competency framework, namely, opportunity recognition competence and industry-specific knowledge.

First, opportunity recognition competence is often identified as a competence for conventional entrepreneurs but not included in the competence framework of Lans, Blok, and Wesselink (2014) or the CASE framework. We highlight the competency here given that it is an important competence for any type of entrepreneur needed to be able to recognise opportunities. It is unclear whether opportunity recognition can be developed through teaching although there are examples in the literature where opportunity recognition is trained by analysing sustainability problems and defining possible (business) solutions (Baggen et al., 2018; Ploum et al., 2019). Yet, opportunity recognition might be better fostered through other competences, for example, through the systemic and anticipatory competence, as they allow for a better than average understanding of where developments in the world are heading, which should help in spotting opportunities for SE.

Second, industry-specific knowledge is also not listed in the original SE competence frameworks as a competence for sustainable entrepreneurship. However, the TES literature review has shown that previous knowledge is important to come up with a business idea (Baggen et al., 2018). Especially students with different disciplinary or cultural knowledge backgrounds develop innovative business ideas together when successfully bridging diversity and cultural difference gaps.

3.2 Sustainable Entrepreneurship Attitudes

Competences function as building blocks that make up the sustainable and entrepreneurial attitude and abilities a sustainable entrepreneur ought to have. In the SEE literature, attitudes, values, worldviews, orientations, intentions and drivers (from here on referred to as attitudinal subjects or, shortened, attitudes) are also self-standing subjects of research. These attitudes are harder to grasp than the comparatively concrete competences, but not less important. They are an inherent part of SE and most obviously linked to the normative competence. Concretely entrepreneurial intention, self-efficacy, sustainability orientation and how these are related, are recurring themes for research.

For entrepreneurial intention the main question in the literature concerns its drivers (e.g., self-efficacy) and how these can be measured. Interestingly there is not much literature on sustainability intentions with the notable exception of Vuorio, Puumalainen, and Fellnhofer (2018) that studies sustainability oriented entrepreneurial intentions. The role of self-efficacy for SE is an on-going debate. Self-efficacy, that is, believing in yourself and in your capabilities, is important for an entrepreneur. Yet its role in the entrepreneurial process is not yet clear (Baggen et al., 2018; Ploum et al., 2019).

Research on attitudinal subjects is characterised by its inconclusiveness about the underlying relationships and relative importance vis-à-vis the subjects. This relates to a question that still seems largely unanswered in the SEE literature, namely what is the place of attitudes in education?

One way of understanding the function of attitudes in SE is through the AMO (Abilities, Motivation, Opportunities) framework, which holds that the (work) performance of sustainable entrepreneurs depends on three interacting dimensions: (1) ability, which is defined in terms of competencies; (2) motivation, meaning attitudinal subjects; and (3) opportunity (Biberhofer et al., 2019). The more these elements are present, the more sustainability-driven entrepreneurs are successful. These three elements are interrelated, meaning that if one has ability and motivation but no context for opportunity for action, SE is not successful.

Students can learn competences and can also learn about opportunities. However, it is not within a teacher's purview to prescribe students which values to believe in. At the most they can teach students to talk and think about values to question them and develop them. This brings to the fore three other competences seen as crucial for sustainable entrepreneurs, namely creativity, critical thinking and (critical) reflection. Halberstadt, Timm, and colleagues (2019) view creativity as a sub-competence of interpersonal competence, but most articles mention creativity as an important skill for SE in every aspect, unrelated to a specific competence. The same goes for critical thinking, which can be viewed as a basic competence that is a 'prerequisite to foster competencies in sustainability' (Biberhofer et al., 2019: 57). Last, (critical) reflection is an important ability for sustainable entrepreneurs and can be seen as a key skill as well as a tool to be used to further SE competence development.

3.3 Sustainable Entrepreneurship Teaching Approaches

Our review of the SEE literature indicates convergence on the competences necessary for a sustainable entrepreneur. Yet, the debate about the role of opportunity recognition, (previous) disciplinary knowledge, attitudinal subjects and, more generally but equally crucial, about the abilities of creativity and critical thinking/reflection in the sustainable entrepreneurship process continues. Nonetheless, there is increasing agreement that all these elements, ranging from values and intentions to visionary and managerial aptitudes, are important for SE and therefore ideally should also be included in the content of a sustainable entrepreneurship teaching programme. The next question concerns the teaching methods, that is, how to teach the competences, skills and abilities.

Since sustainable entrepreneurs rely more on a wide range of abilities than on a specialised knowledge, sustainable entrepreneurship education aims to be as experiential as possible. Unlike conventional education known for top-down and instructional teaching methods, SEE involves students in 'learning by doing'. A key theme in SEE literature is the transition from traditional teacher-centred teaching to a more learner-centred teaching approach. Learner-centred learning in the view of Biberhofer and Rammels (2017: 73) is a form of experience-based learning, in the sense that 'the experience of the learner occupies central place in all considerations of teaching and learning'. Experience-based learning, also referred to as active or experiential learning, is a core characteristic of SEE, with the most often used forms being challenge-based or problem-based learning. The challenges or problems are often based on real-life sustainable entrepreneurial problems and situations and are usually designed as a project or a competition. Such solution-oriented teaching approaches have a collaborative character, while often also being competitive, with teams of students striving to have the best sustainable business model or prototype.

Learning by doing is more than dealing with problems and challenges only. Participating in entrepreneurship programmes or in placement opportunities is also important teaching approach in SEE (Manning et al., 2020). The latter often takes the form of service-learning, which Halberstadt, Schank and colleague (2019: 2) define as encompassing 'volunteer and community service projects, field studies and internship programs'. It contrasts with the more mainstream form of an internship as students rather than working for a business or an organisation, 'try to find solutions cooperating with partners such as communities, NGOs [non-governmental organisations] and companies' (Biberhofer, & Rammel, 2017: 73). The concept of 'service' learning might therefore not do the approach complete justice, as students are not simply in service, but rather engage in reciprocal relationships with their partners to generate social/sustainable value (Metha et al., 2016). Service learning is a valuable way to improve commitment to society and is therefore also an opportunity to engage in transformative learning (Martínez-Campillo, Sierra-Fernández, & Fernández-Santos, 2019). 'Transformative learning is characterised by a quality shift in perception and meaning-making, which brings the learner to the crucial point of questioning and reframing his/her world views, assumptions and habits' (Biberhofer & Rammels, 2017: 66). Service learning allows for transformative learning because it helps students to develop and apply values. It makes them aware of societal problems and sparks critical reflection and opinions about the state of the world, and how it should be (Halberstadt, Schank et al., 2019). Transformative learning is not solely enabled by service learning. It can also take place in the classroom, for example, through discussion that enables critical (self-)reflection.

In most cases problem-based or challenge-based learning is combined with inter- and transdisciplinary learning. Interdisciplinary learning means students from different cultural and/or disciplinary backgrounds work together, while transdisciplinary learning refers to students working with people from outside the university, such as businesses and other communities of society, as partners/stakeholders. Multiculturalism, interdisciplinarity and transdisciplinarity often overlap. Most learning in SEE is collaborative and the teams are usually interdisciplinary given that SE often is an elective or a master's programme. This means that SE programmes mostly incorporate graduate students who already have a particular disciplinary background such as an undergraduate degree in business or in engineering. Students from different disciplinary backgrounds come together in an SE class due to their shared interest in sustainability or entrepreneurial matters and bring different forms of knowledge and experiences, which is beneficial for creating innovative ideas (Biberhofer & Rammels, 2017; Karlusch, Sachsenhofer, & Reinsberger, 2018). Last, most of the teamwork in SEE is transdisciplinary, meaning that the teams work with external partners/stakeholders. Figure 5.2 shows how experiential the most often used teaching approaches in SEE are. The teaching approaches are organised from teacher-centred (top) to learner-centred (bottom), starting with the traditional lecture that puts the teacher at the centre of the educational experience and ending with teaching approaches such as service learning, the sustainability challenge and the business model competition, which put the learner at the centre. This categorisation corresponds largely with the inter- and transdisciplinarity of the teaching approaches. It must be noted that the categorisation of teaching approaches as experiential and teacher- or learner-centred is highly dependent on the teacher and the educational context. A discussion, for example, can be teacher-led or student-led, and there are workshops where students work in teams (interdisciplinary) and with external partners (transdisciplinary) as well as workshops where students work on their own. The organisation of the teaching approaches from teacher-centred to learner-centred and their categorization as low, intermediate or highly experiential is based on how the teaching approaches were described in the articles that were reviewed in the systematic literature review (see Table 4.1).

Within each of the teaching approaches particular tools are used. Frequently used tools during seminars are case studies, a quite conventional way to engage the student. In recent years student games have become more and more accepted to use in the classroom. With the rise of serious gaming there are now various games available to teach students certain skills. Other often used tools are the sustainable development goals from the United Nations that are often used as a point of departure for challenges that students need to find an (entrepreneurial) solution for. When the solution of such a problem or challenge has the form of a business case, the (sustainable) business model canvas is a helpful tool. This helps students to understand all stakeholder interests they have to take into account and all the steps they need to go through to set up a start-up.

Table 4.1: Teaching approaches and experiential learning.

Teaching approach	Level of experiential learning
Traditional lecture	Low
Guest lecture	Low
Discussion	Low/intermediate
Flipped classroom	Intermediate
Conference/Café dialogue	Intermediate
Fieldtrip	Intermediate
Workshop	Intermediate
Simulation/role play	Intermediate/high
Field study	Intermediate/high
Internship	High
Service learning	High
(Sustainability) challenge	High
Hackathon	High
Pitching contest	Intermediate/high
Business model competition	High

A good example of how both service-learning and challenge-based learning combine with inter- and transdisciplinary learning is the sustainability challenge (Biberhofer & Rammels, 2017). In this programme, students can choose a service-learning or an entrepreneurship (business start-up) track for the duration of one semester. The course is centred on transdisciplinary learning and teaching, which is exemplified by the use of a kick-off event to start the course where students, practitioners and teachers meet. The students then work in interdisciplinary teams of four to five students on a service-learning project or a start-up project.

Often external partners provide the challenges for the student teams (e.g., Grega & Pikoń, 2018; Hermann, Bossle, & Amaral, 2020) and act as business partners and helplines to the students in a business model competition or hackathon (Brekken et al., 2018; Serhan & Yannou-Lebris, 2020). An interesting example for this approach is the affordable design and entrepreneurship (ADE) programme (Noyes & Linder, 2015). In this programme students aim to create social ventures in coordination with external stakeholders. The programme has an international transdisciplinary aspect, as the stakeholders are from non-Western contexts such as Ghana. Students work in interdisciplinary teams, coming from an engineering or entrepreneurship background, and are introduced to opportunity briefs in which social challenges are presented from which they select one to work on with local partners. Moreover, the students select which opportunities to pursue in the ADE product-venture incubation pipeline, hence, students decide which venture ideas to prioritise. In these programmes students learn how to interact with external stakeholders and bridge cultural differences.

It is worthwhile mentioning that interdisciplinary and intercultural teams have more barriers than disciplinary and mono-cultural teams (Karlusch, Sachsenhofer, & Reinsberger, 2018). For the success of inter- and transdisciplinary teaching formats it is therefore important that students have sufficient time for the team development process ranging from trying out, failing and reflecting on their actions (Biberhofer & Rammels, 2017).

3.4 The University and the Ecosystem

Transdisciplinary learning is a key aspect of active and experiential teaching methods including the engagement with communities outside the university. These communities can include many different types of stakeholders; they can refer to specific (local) communities but also to businesses or industries, public institutions, associations or non-governmental organisations (Hermann & Bossle, 2020). For real-world teaching, partnerships with communities play a key role with partners being, for example, from industry (Jennings et al., 2015), regional centres of expertise (Biberhofer & Rammels, 2017) or investors (Kim et al., 2020). These partners can also be active within the teaching programmes of the university, for example, offering guest lectures or helping, monitoring and evaluating students (Kim et al., 2020). By incorporating these different stakeholders as partners in SEE, a study programme can achieve co-creation of innovative solutions for a wide range of sustainability problems. Needs from communities are then combined with the expertise and knowledge gained in the study programme to allow for the emergence of successful and sustainable student-led start-ups (Serhan & Yannou-Lebris, 2020).

The university can play a key role in establishing and fostering the connections between communities and students. When universities become a support system for (sustainable) entrepreneurship, they often denote themselves as an entrepreneurial university (Kim et al., 2020; Tiemann, Fichter, & Geier, 2018). This means that the university actively supports entrepreneurial activities, deviating from its original function as a knowledge production site (Kim et al., 2020; Tiemann, Fichter, & Geier, 2018). The closely related concept of a sustainable university aims to support societal change through actively combining and engaging in university, research, teaching and management in order to solve sustainability challenges (Biberhofer & Rammels, 2017). In the next step, the university goes beyond its role as an education platform and becomes an innovation hub that fosters sustainable entrepreneurs by providing real-life environments and multi-actor engagement tools that help realise entrepreneurial solutions for sustainability problems (Manning et al., 2020; Kim et al., 2020). The university develops into a living lab, which often also includes incubators that support students with, for example, patent applications, the transfer of spin-offs into new companies, research–industry collaborations and entrepreneurial training on management best practices (Daub et al., 2020; Noyes & Linder, 2015). In a living lab context the university has integrated and institutionalised (transdisciplinary) SEE, as opposed to considering SEE as a mere add-on to methods and programmes in the university (Biberhofer & Rammels, 2017).

A sustainable entrepreneurial university as the centre of a web of relations with external partners in a university ecosystem is essential to foster experiential learning (Torres et al., 2019). Very often, however, the institutional framework in universities poses a barrier to an integrated implementation of SEE and its respective support systems. These barriers, consisting of university rules, regulations and institutions, result from insufficient resources, a lack of international cooperation or a paucity of sustainable entrepreneurship intentions (Fichter & Tiemann, 2018). The SEE literature indicates that a top-down approach, often resulting from the initiatives of a few key individuals, is the most important factor in creating a sustainable and entrepreneurial university. To date, few examples of collective efforts exist to establish a sustainable entrepreneurial university (Wakkee et al., 2019).

3.5 Assessment

Assessment is perhaps the most neglected part of sustainable entrepreneurship education. The articles covered in the TES review often do not mention assessment or only in a few sentences. Assessment is addressed in more detail in only 10 of the publications including one overview of assessment criteria (Castro & Zermeno, 2020; Silva et al., 2018). One explanation for such sparse coverage of assessment in SEE can be found in the experiential character of the teaching approaches in SEE which complicate assessment. The experiential and active teaching approaches used in SEE call for a different form of assessment than conventional methods such as exams (Burden & Sprei, 2020; Parris & McInnis-Bowers, 2017). Assessment often takes the form of project or reflection reports (Biberhofer & Rammels, 2017; Brekken et al., 2018; Burden & Sprei, 2020; Silva et al., 2018), journals/diaries and portfolios, (Jennings et al., 2015; Parris & McInnis-Bowers, 2017; Silvia et al., 2018) or presentations (Castro & Zermeno, 2020; Herman, Bossle, & Amaral, 2020; Parris & McInnis-Bowers, 2017). Conventional assessment tools aim to measure individual student knowledge, while in SEE the most important aim is to generate competences, skills and attitudes. This incompatibility of conventional assessment forms and experiential teaching approaches call for flexibility in the curricular formats to allow for suitable assessment methods for appraising business models and plans, presentations, journals, diaries and reflections (Halberstadt et al., 2019). Reflections are often used as assessment tools in SEE combining peer and tutor feedback with individual self-assessment (e.g., Brekken et al., 2018; Burden & Sprei, 2020; Hermann, Bossle, & Amaral, 2020).

Institutional barriers often block the assessment formats that would benefit, align and foster sustainable entrepreneurship education, forcing teachers to use conventional assessment methods such as written (essay) exams that are inadequate to measuring SE competencies and students' progress (Halberstadt et al., 2019). This highlights the importance of embedding SEE and its character of experiential learning in the institutional framework of the university. Experiential inter- and transdisciplinary learning requires appropriate university institutional environments given that it is of a completely different character from conventional learning and teaching methods. It requires adapting grading procedures, which usually is outside the scope of individual teachers and educational programme directors. The success of SEE requires the institutionalisation of experiential inter- and transdisciplinary learning and assessment methods within the university.

4 Discussion and Conclusions

This chapter started with demonstrating the similarities between entrepreneurs and sustainable value makers. They are both creative destroyers and disrupting innovators. Consequently, the question arose whether it is possible to teach students to become a change-maker. This chapter has demonstrated that it is possible and that the success of such endeavour depends on *how* you teach. Being a change agent is challenging and opposite mainstream thinking. The essence of sustainable entrepreneurship education and its much needed potential, therefore, is its ability to empower students; to enable students to reflect on the world, their place in it and how they want the world to be. Conventional teaching methods are not focused on developing the capacity to reflect and act. We should therefore turn to new innovative teaching methods that are (1) focused on creating competences, not knowledge; (2) that are experiential; (3) collaborative; and (4) reflective.

The SEE literature has established the five competences that are essential for a sustainable entrepreneur. However, these five competences might not be an exhaustive list. Opportunity recognition, creativity, critical thinking and (critical) reflection are also crucial abilities for a sustainable entrepreneur, yet they are not regarded as core competences in the SEE literature. The competences and teaching methods are not set in stone – they progress, and more research is needed to understand the abilities, competences and attitudes of sustainable entrepreneurs.

Sustainable entrepreneurship education is more than a study programme because it engages with the outside world. Interactions with different communities, from businesses to local citizens, can be facilitated by the programme coordinators and teachers of the SE programme. An active role on the part of the university is important for connecting with the 'real world'. Due to the transdisciplinary and experiential nature of SEE, a successful SE programme requires a level of institutionalisation throughout the university in general and for the assessment of student progress in particular.

In conclusion, this chapter introduced the importance of sustainable entrepreneurship competencies, teaching methods and assessment. It is worthwhile to highlight two final conclusions. First, sustainable entrepreneurship cannot simply be treated as an add-on, meaning adding sustainability to an entrepreneurship course, or vice versa, or adding a sustainable entrepreneurship programme to the university's list of courses without making the necessary adjustments within the university's (institutional) setting. The transdisciplinary and experiential nature of sustainable entrepreneurship education requires an unconventional way of teaching. One that is more challenging for both teachers and students but also more rewarding if done right because new sustainable ways of teaching can enact real change, tackle real challenges and create real value in cooperation with external communities. This does not mean that SE can only be taught as a full-fledged program; however, rather the opposite. The TES research has found that having a disciplinary background is important for students to generate entrepreneurial ideas. This suggests that it might be better to teach SE as a master's programme or to integrate SEE in an existing programme rather than offer it as a bachelor programme. But whether it is taught as an elective module or a master's programme, teaching sustainable entrepreneurship requires a holistic teaching approach that accommodates experiential, collaborative and reflective learning. Second, real-world learning of SE allows the student to try, fail, learn and to try again in a safe space, which will develop self-confidence of students needed in changing careers. By learning how to work together with students from different disciplinary or cultural backgrounds, students can create collective solutions to global problems. By learning how to critically reflect on yourself and the world, to question assumptions and get to know yourself, you come to understand what you can contribute to in life. SEE is not just about venture creation, it is about the creation of a sustainable mindset. The added value of SEE lies in giving students the tools to help realise a different world and, most importantly, the realisation and self-confidence that they can change the world themselves.

References

Bacigalupo, M., Kampylis, P., Punie, Y., & Van den Brande, G. (2016). *EntreComp: The Entrepreneurship Competence Framework*. Luxembourg: Publication Office of the European Union; EUR 27939 EN. doi: 10.2791/593884.

Baggen, Y., Kampen, J. K., Naia, A., Biemans, H. J. A., Lans, T., & Mulder, M. (2018). Development and application of the opportunity identification competence assessment test (OICAT) in higher education. *Innovations in Education and Teaching International, 55*(6), 735–745.

Biberhofer, P., Lintner, C., Bernhardt, J., & Rieckmann, M. (2019). Facilitating work performance of sustainability-driven entrepreneurs through higher education: The relevance of competencies, values, worldviews and opportunities. *International Journal of Entrepreneurship and Innovation, 20*(1), 21–38.

Biberhofer, P., & Rammel, C. (2017). Transdisciplinary learning and teaching as answers to urban sustainability challenges. *International Journal of Sustainability in Higher Education, 18*(1), 63–83.

Biberhofer, P., Bockwoldt, L., Rieckmann, M., Ambros, M., Rammel, C., Lintner, C., Bernhardt, J., Činčera, J., Bernatíková, P., Binka, B., Fraňková, E., Boman, J., Olsson, M., Lundgren, E., Brunner, K., & Medek, M. (2016). *Joint CASE Report on Content and Methods for the Joint Master Program on Sustainability-Driven Entrepreneurship*. Germany: Vienna University of Economics and Business Austria, University of Vechta.

Brekken, C. A., Peterson, H. H., King, R. P., & Conner, D. (2018). Writing a recipe for teaching sustainable food systems: Lessons from three university courses. *Sustainability, 10*(6), 1–19.

Brundiers, K., Barth, M., & Cebrián, G. (2021). Key competencies in sustainability in higher education – Toward an agreed-upon reference framework. *Sustainability Science, 16*, 13–29.

Burden, H., & Sprei, F. (2020). Teaching sustainable development through entrepreneurial experiences. *International Journal of Sustainability in Higher Education, 22*(1), 142–156.

Calvo, S., Lyon, F., Morales, A., & Wade, J. (2020). Educating at scale for sustainable development and social enterprise growth: The impact of online learning and a massive open online course (MOOC). *Sustainability, 12*(8), 1–15.

Castro, M. P., & Zermeno, M. G. G. (2020). Challenge based learning: Innovative pedagogy for sustainability through e-learning in higher education. *Sustainability, 12*(10), 1–15.

Daub, C. H., Hasler, M., Verkuil, A. H., & Milow, U. (2020). Universities talk, students walk: Promoting innovative sustainability projects. *International Journal of Sustainability in Higher Education, 21*(1), 97–111.

Elkington, J. (1997). The triple bottom line. *Environmental Management: Readings and Cases, 2*, 49–66.

European Commission, E. (n.d.). *The European Entrepreneurship Competence Framework (EntreComp)*. https://ec.europa.eu/social/main.jsp?catId=1317&langId=en

Fellnhofer, K. (2019). Toward a taxonomy of entrepreneurship education research literature: A bibliometric mapping and visualisation. *Educational Research Review, 27*, 28–55.

Fichter, K., & Tiemann, I. (2018). Factors influencing university support for sustainable entrepreneurship: Insights from explorative case studies. *Journal of Cleaner Production, 175*, 512–524.

Foucrier, T., & Wiek, A. (2019). A process-oriented framework of competencies for sustainability entrepreneurship. *Sustainability, 11*(24), 1–18.

Greco, A., & de Jong, G. (2017). Sustainable entrepreneurship: definitions, themes and research gaps. Centre for Sustainable Entrepreneurship: Working Paper Series No. 6. University of Groningen, Campus Fryslân.

Grega, W., & Pikoń, K. (2018). A new education model in sustainable energy. *International Journal of Innovation and Sustainable Development, 12*(1–2), 13–27.

Halberstadt, J., Schank, C., Euler, M., & Harms, R. (2019). Learning sustainability entrepreneurship by doing: Providing a lecturer-oriented service learning framework. *Sustainability, 11*(5), 1–22.

Halberstadt, J., Timm, J. M., Kraus, S., & Gundolf, K. (2019). Skills and knowledge management in higher education: How service learning can contribute to social entrepreneurial competence development, *Journal of Knowledge Management, 23*(10), 1925–1948.

Hermann, R. R., & Bossle, M. B. (2020). Bringing an entrepreneurial focus to sustainability education: A teaching framework based on content analysis. *Journal of Cleaner Production, 246*.

Hermann, R. R., Bossle, M. B., & Amaral, M. (2020). Lenses on the post-oil economy: Integrating entrepreneurship into sustainability education through problem-based learning. *Educational Action Research, 30*(3), 480–506.

Hockerts, K., & Wüstenhagen, R. (2010). Greening Goliaths versus emerging Davids – Theorizing about the role of incumbents and new entrants in sustainable entrepreneurship. *Journal of Business Venturing, 25*(5), 481–492.

Jennings, G., Cater, C. I., Hales, R., Kensbock, S., & Hornby, G. (2015). Partnering for real world learning, sustainability, tourism education. *Quality Assurance in Education, 23*(4), 378–394.

Karlusch, A., Sachsenhofer, W., & Reinsberger, K. (2018). Educating for the development of sustainable business models: Designing and delivering a course to foster creativity. *Journal of Cleaner Production, 179*, 169–179.

Kent, C. A., Sexton, D. L., & Vesper, K. H. (1982). *Encyclopaedia of Entrepreneurship*. University of Illinois at Urbana-Champaign's Academy for Entrepreneurial Leadership Historical Research Reference in Entrepreneurship. SSRN: https://ssrn.com/abstract=1496225

Kim, M. G., Lee, J. H., Roh, T., & Son, H. (2020). Social entrepreneurship education as an innovation hub for building an entrepreneurial ecosystem: The case of the KAIST social entrepreneurship mba program. *Sustainability*, *12*(22), 1–23.

Lans, T., Blok, V., & Wesselink, R. (2014). Learning apart and together: Towards an integrated competence framework for sustainable entrepreneurship in higher education. *Journal of Cleaner Production*, *62*, 37–47.

Manning, L., Smith, R., Conley, G., & Halsey, L. (2020). Ecopreneurial education and support: Developing the innovators of today and tomorrow. *Sustainability*, *12*(21), 1–19.

Marks, E., Hickman, C. M., Pihkala, P., Clayton, S., Lewandowski, E., Mayall, E. E., Wray, B., Mellor, C., & Susteren, L. V. (2021). Young people's voices on climate anxiety, government betrayal and moral injury: A global phenomenon. *SSRN Electronic Journal*, 863–873.

Martínez-Campillo, A., Sierra-Fernández, M. P., & Fernández-Santos, Y. (2019). Service-learning for sustainability entrepreneurship in rural areas: What is its global impact on business university students? *Sustainability*, *11*, 19.

Mehta, K., Zappe, S., Brannon, M. L., & Zhao, Y. (2016). An educational and entrepreneurial ecosystem to actualize technology-based social ventures. *Advances in Engineering, Education*, *5*(1), 1–38.

Noyes, E., & Linder, B. (2015). Developing undergraduate entrepreneurial capacity for social venture creation. *Journal of Entrepreneurship Education*, *18*(2), 113–124.

Organisation for Economic Co-operation and Development (OECD). (2018). *Developing entrepreneurship competencies*. Policy note. SME Ministerial Conference, Mexico.

O'Mahony, T. (2022). Toward sustainable wellbeing: Advances in contemporary concepts. *Frontiers in Sustainability*, *3*. doi: 10.3389/frsus.2022.807984

Pacheco, D. F., Dean, T., & Payne, S. P. (2010). Escaping the green prison: Entrepreneurship and the creation of opportunities for sustainable development. *Journal of Business Venturing*, *25*(5), 464–480.

Parris, D. L., & McInnis-Bowers, C. (2017). Business not as usual: Developing socially conscious entrepreneurs and intrapreneurs. *Journal of Management Education*, *41*(5), 687–726.

Pinna, M. (2020). *Sustainable Entrepreneurship, A Systematic Review of Academic Research*. Springer Cham. https://doi.org/10.1007/978-3-030-57818-3

Ploum, L., Blok, V., Lans, T., & Omta, O. (2018). Toward a validated competence framework for sustainable entrepreneurship. *Organization and Environment*, *31*(2), 113–132.

Ploum, L., Blok, V., Lans, T., & Omta, O. (2019). Educating for self-interest or -transcendence? An empirical approach to investigating the role of moral competencies in opportunity recognition for sustainable development. *Business Ethics*, *28*(2), 243–260.

Serhan, H., & Yannou-Lebris, G. (2020). The engineering of food with sustainable development goals: Policies, curriculums, business models, and practices. *International Journal of Sustainable Engineering*, *14*(1), 12–25.

Schumpeter, J. A. (1934). *The Theory of Economic Development*. Cambridge, MA: Harvard University Press.

Shepherd, D. A., & Patzelt, H. (2011). The new field of sustainable entrepreneurship: Studying entrepreneurial action linking "what is to be sustained" with "what is to be developed." *Entrepreneurship Theory and Practice*, *35*(1), 137–163.

Silva, M. F., Malheiro, B., Guedes, P., Duarte, A., & Ferreira, P. (2018). Collaborative learning with sustainability-driven projects: A summary of the EPS@ISEP programme. *International Journal of Engineering Pedagogy*, *8*(4), 106–130.

Taylor, D. (2011). Wellbeing and welfare: A psychosocial analysis of being well and doing well enough. *Journal of Social Policy*, *40*(4), 777–794.

Tiemann, I., Fichter, K., & Geier, J. (2018). University support systems for sustainable entrepreneurship: Insights from explorative case studies. *International Journal of Entrepreneurial Venturing*, *10*(1), 83–110.

Torres Valdés, R. M., Lorenzo Álvarez, C., Castro Spila, J., & Santa Soriano, A. (2019). Relational university, learning and entrepreneurship ecosystems for sustainable tourism. *Journal of Science and Technology Policy Management, 10*(4), 905–926.

United Nations Educational, Scientific and Cultural Organization (UNESCO). (2020). *Education for Sustainable Development: A Roadmap.* Paris: UNESCO.

Vallaster, C., Kraus, S. M., Lindahl, J. M., & Nielsen, A. (2019). Ethics and entrepreneurship: A bibliometric study and literature review. *Journal of Business Research, 99*, 226–237.

Vuorio, A. M., Puumalainen, K., & Fellnhofer, K. (2018). Drivers of entrepreneurial intentions in sustainable entrepreneurship. *International Journal of Entrepreneurial Behaviour & Research, 24*(2), 359–381.

Wakkee, I., Van der Sijde, P., Vaupell, C., & Ghuman, K. (2019). The university's role in sustainable development: Activating entrepreneurial scholars as agents of change. *Technological Forecasting and Social Change, 141*, 195–205.

Rikke Kristine Nielsen, Arne Remmen, Jacob Lundberg

5 Consultation: Building Social Relations with Productive Benefits

Abstract: Like other contemporary challenges grand and small, sustainability has been understood as paradoxical (Smith & Lewis, 2011), "wicked" problems (Starik & Kanashiro, 2013) characterized by multiple stakeholders, disputed values, complex interconnectedness, foggy problem definition, limited or contested knowledge and ongoing change (McMillan & Overall, 2016). This chapter presents consultation as a precondition for sustainable entrepreneurship (research) since the ability to identify, cultivate and engage relevant conversation partners is essential for facilitating productive entrepreneurial (inter-)action. First, we discuss aspects of sustainable entrepreneurship that call for stakeholder consultation and involvement. Next, the concept of advice-seeking consultation/consulting is discussed as the pursuit of knowledge from relevant others for professional purposes. We go on to present the Productive Consultation Matrix portraying consultation as a combination of ability to facilitate trustful knowledge sharing and engagement. Throughout the chapter, we present cases from consultation practice. The chapter concludes with a discussion of consultation potentials and pitfalls.

Keywords: consultation, stakeholder engagement, productive interactions, facilitation, knowledge sharing

1 Introduction

Sustainable entrepreneurs can be defined as sustainable opportunity-oriented individuals that design and develop more sustainable products, services, and production processes, combined with sustainable business models that simultaneously balance ecological, social, and economic goals (also see Chapter 1). Sustainable entrepreneurs are actors that leverage and operate in a context of problems and opportunities that are ill-defined, dynamic, and involve multiple stakeholders (Greco, 2020) by facilitating concerted action among different groups of stakeholders. To generate, maintain and develop stakeholder engagement and willingness to invest resources (e.g., knowledge, attention, capital, time)

Rikke Kristine Nielsen, Department of Communication and Psychology, Aalborg University (Copenhagen), Denmark
Arne Remmen, Department of Development and Planning, Aalborg University, Denmark
Jacob Lundberg, Department of Innovation and Research Support, Aalborg University (Copenhagen), Denmark

https://doi.org/10.1515/9783110756159-006

sustainable entrepreneurs need to be skilled at consultation. For researchers to engage with sustainable entrepreneurial settings, the sustainable entrepreneurship researcher needs to identify and connect with stakeholders, negotiate access, and secure engagement through a (research) project.

For the sustainable entrepreneur, the unique selling proposition lies in the integration of environmental, social, and economic outcomes (Benkert, 2021) sometimes framed as a simultaneous consideration of "people, planet, profit" or the "triple bottom line" pursuing "development that meets the needs of the present without compromising the ability of future generations to meet their own needs" (World Commission on Environment and Development, 1987: 16). As such, sustainability is a question of engagement with sustainability in plural, sustainabilities, in that the individual and collective aspects of sustainability are interconnected in a myriad of ways, where advancement of one dimension may create both negative as well as positive synergies to other dimensions of sustainability or groups of stakeholders (Gao & Bansal, 2013; Hahn et al., 2018; Jay, Soderstrom, & Grant, 2017).

Operating in this context places a premium on the ability to mobilize resources, optimize knowledge sharing, accessing networks, ecosystems, and relevant communities of practice (e.g., Birley, 1985; Bacq et al., 2015; Clough et al., 2019; Jenkins, 1983; Murray, Kotha, & Fisher, 2020). One avenue for achieving this is through consultation with the aim of facilitating "productive interactions" (Spaapen & Van Drooge, 2011) with relevant conversation partners and (current or future) stakeholders.

The outline of the chapter is as follows: in Section 1, we define and discuss the concept of advice-seeking consultation/consulting as the pursuit of advice or insights from relevant others for professional purposes. In Section 2, we present the first of three consultation case studies exemplifying the value of external consultation in sustainable entrepreneurship incubation within the Aalborg University Student Incubator's start-up program. In Section 3, we discuss motivations and characteristics of consultation, highlighting that consultation not only takes place with stakeholders but also within a larger circle of conversation partners, or with potential future stakeholders. Section 4 presents our second consultation case study illustrating how reaching out to stay connected in the sustainable entrepreneurship ecosystem is central to sustainable entrepreneurship research in practice. Section 5 presents the Productive Consultation Matrix, portraying consultation as a combination of ability to facilitate trustful knowledge sharing and engagement, where different potential outcomes of the consultation processes can be seen a result of the sustainable entrepreneur's or sustainable entrepreneurship researcher's competencies (or lack thereof) for handling the building blocks of productive consultation. Section 6 presents a third consultation case study illustrating how PhD students from the Danish Industrial PhD Program work with and experience consultation as part of their PhD education. The final section concludes the chapter by discussing the potentials and pitfalls of consultation as well as the need for a conscious strategy for keeping the ear to the ground through consultation.

2 Creating and Leveraging Productive Interactions

Consultation is a multifaceted concept that can be seen as an umbrella term for a variety of practices and research approaches. For example, consultation is a central aspect of research paradigms such as action research (Greenwood & Levin, 2007; also see Chapter 4 of this volume), phronetic social science (Flyvbjerg, Landman, & Schram, 2012), or citizen science (Bonney et al., 2016). Consultation is also a methodology for exploring and facilitating topics such as organizational change (Jamieson, Barnett, & Buono, 2016) or community change (Senge & Scharmer, 2008) as well as a research design and genre, "a stakeholder consultation," in its own right (e.g., Van Ginkel et al., 2020). Consultation can also, however, be considered a (research) practice undertaken unrelated to a specific research project or particular purpose with the aim of fostering general connectivity with relevant conversation partners and keeping an ear to the ground – a practice that may over time result in new research projects or collaborations, but without having defined an explicit purpose up-front.

On a general level, the *Cambridge Dictionary* informs us that consultation is "a meeting to discuss something or to get advice" (Consultation, 2022). So, to consult is to seek advice or information, conferring and discussing with others to access their knowledge pools and presupposes an advice seeker and an advice giver who engage in the act of consultation together. Google's *English Dictionary* (provided by Oxford Languages) adds an additional layer to consultation by defining it both as "the action or process of formally consulting or discussing" as well as "a meeting with an expert, such as a medical doctor, in order to seek advice" (Consultation, n.d.). This dual understanding of the word is a source of considerable confusion so consultation can not only be understood as general advice seeking and information exchange, but also as advice seeking with a formally recognized expert such as an accountant, doctor, or researcher. Yet, the kind of "experts" we will think about in this chapter are not limited to formally designated experts, but rather conversation partners who are "experts" in the sense that they possess detailed knowledge about a phenomenon or practice that the sustainable entrepreneur or sustainable entrepreneurship researcher are interested in knowing more about. An "expert" in this sense of the word could be a potential user of a product or service, a member of a community affected by a situation, a competitor, or a research informant in addition to formal experts in a particular field. So, consultation is information exchange with "experts" who often distinguish themselves from the kind of experts who would usually give rise to conducting expert interviews for research purposes (Bogner, Littig, & Menz, 2009) and could take place informally and emergently as knowledge-sharing opportunity arises and develops, not necessarily as result of following a research protocol, program or pre-booked appointment.

Although researchers themselves are often called upon in their capacity as experts for media interviews, policy advice (Pedersen, 2014), or (management) consulting purposes, it also follows from the understanding of consultation outlined above that the sustainable entrepreneur or researcher is cast as the *advice seeker*, not the *advice giver* in possession of expertise. This also involves a distinction between consulting as "the act of doing consultation" (present participle of the verb "to consult") and professional/expert consulting where a consultant (for instance, a researcher) intervene in a situation through process consultation defined as a "a set of activities on the part of the consultant that help the client to perceive, understand, and act upon the process event that occur in the client's environment in order to improve the situation as defined by the client" (Schein, 1988: 11) or (organizational) consultation in which "a third-party (other than those directly responsible for the system) engages with a system for the purpose of helping it improve or change" (Jamieson, Barnett, & Buono, 2016: vii; also see Kubr, 2002). Our point of departure in this chapter is that to consult or do consultation from an advice-seeking point of view is *not* synonymous with being a consultant engaged in (professional or management) consulting. Rather, to consult and engage in advice-seeking consulting and consultation is to seek and exchange advice or information from relevant others for professional purposes related to sustainable entrepreneurship research or practice. In the following first of three case studies, we shall explore consultation as an activity central to the Aalborg University Student Incubator's start-up program.

3 Consultation Case Study #1: Aalborg University Student Incubator – The AAU Startup Program

The Aalborg University Incubator (where the third author is employed) is an initiative divided into two elements: a physical workspace with basic office facilities and entrepreneurship programs that take place in this workspace. The primary objective of the incubator is to help student-founded start-ups succeed in the early stage of the journey. The main program in the incubator is the AAU Startup Program, which accepts applications from students from all disciplines and all levels of university education. The students bring an idea or concept with them, and they get up to 18 months to build a company around the idea. Over the 18 months, the program is divided into three phases that get increasingly customized the further a start-up goes. The first phase focuses on basic entrepreneurship workshops, the second phase includes a dedicated mentor from a relevant industry for each start-up and phase three focuses on fundraising and settling on the right business model.

The AAU Startup Program is designed to deliver general knowledge to the broader population of entrepreneurs, but the individual consultation with a start-up coach is where each start-up feels a sense of progression in their daily challenges. Since all entrepreneurial journeys are different, the consultation meetings differ in nature and in focus, but common for practically all entrepreneurs is the key role of consultation in the early stage of developing a company. Consultation is integral to the entrepreneurship incubator in several ways: first, all student entrepreneurs are part of a formalized consultation framework, with their start-up coach contributing with process know-how but also an external mentor from industry contributing with domain-specific knowledge. In addition, the very first part of the entrepreneurship program requires entrepreneurs to consult with external conversation partners. This is done to validate and seek out challenges to their basic assumptions about the core problem that they plan to offer a solution to as well as reality test the solutions they have in mind.

Many start-ups with sustainability as a core focus find out early in their process just how complex the concept can be. An example in case of the value of consultative validation from the AAU Incubator is a team developing a reusable ovulation test. During the validation process supported by a process-oriented start-up coach, the team's first objective was to figure out whether they were correct in assuming that people would pay a higher price for a reusable ovulation test and that people acknowledge the problem in the single use of already existing ovulation tests. Another perspective for the team to work on was validation of the construction of the product itself. The sustainable aspect provided a clear purpose and motivation for the entrepreneurs but ended up adding a new layer of complexity to the already intricate process of entrepreneurship in which consultation was central to navigating this complexity.

An additional example of the use of entrepreneurial consultation is a wastewater initiative at the AAU Incubator by four engineering students that managed to bring many perspectives on sustainability in-house from an early stage. A key to their early stage success was an advisory board assembled from the university environment including both active and retired researchers and similar domain experts. At the AAU Incubator, sustainability-focused start-ups, compared to start-ups without this focus, have an easier time assembling high-quality advisory boards. Potential candidates for the advisor roles seem to be attracted to entrepreneurial projects with a strong purpose besides profit and especially to the potential societal or environmental impact. So, consultation can be a first step towards forming advisory boards. In the start-up program student entrepreneurs choose the conversation partners they wish to seek out, and often they choose partners that are already part of the conversation or business they are entering, for instance professional associations or business networks. Helpful as this may be, an important learning point is that eye-openers often come from consulting "complete strangers" only peripherally connected to the business idea and unique selling proposition.

In recent years, the growing focus on sustainable start-ups has almost created parallel reality for funding, and a common saying among the start-ups at the Aalborg University incubator is that "it is just easier to get funded if you work with sustainability." Although this experience is not necessarily indicative of the actual funding situation, it is a potential risk that some sustainable start-ups are awarded so much soft funding and awards that they postpone the development of a feasible business model, and risk being too late when they run out of funding. Going outside to include unlikely conversation partners can be a sobering, needed experience to secure the long-term viability of the venture.

4 Motivations and Characteristics of Consultation

As demonstrated in the consultation case study from the Aalborg University Student Incubator, key characteristics of consultation include its indirect and problem-solving emphasis, collegial and voluntary nature, and attention to both the interaction process as well as the outcome of the interaction (Dickert & Sugarman, 2005). Consultation is an activity undertaken to build and sustain productive interactions and beneficial (external) relationships over time. Motivations for consulting internal or external conversation partners in the ecosystem surrounding a project or venture include (but are not limited to):

–   identification and monitoring of trends, "next practice," and challenges of conversation partners with a view to understanding and tracking the needs and perceptions over time
–   scouting (Burke, 1994: 72), generating, and cultivating stakeholders (Alvarez & Sachs, 2021; Brown & Bylund, 2022) for current or future projects
–   insight into the way in which your knowledge and services are experienced as value-creating (or not) from relevant others outside the study/business environment
–   collection and elicitation of information, ideas, opinions, criticism, suggestions, and insights from a wide range of (current or future) stakeholders as a way of conducting reality check and due diligence for your ideas
–   keeping ears on the ground and connected to informal grape-vine communication in relevant fora and conversations
–   leveraging existing networks and connections
–   fostering participation and engagement of networks and communities of conversation partners

Conversation partners from whom advice is sought may or may not represent groups that you would naturally consider stakeholders. A stakeholder is a member of those groups that make a difference, or more formally "any group or individual who can affect or is affected by the achievement of the organization's objectives" (Freeman, 1984: 46). Consultation is different from stakeholder communication (Foster & Jonker, 2005) in that stakeholder communication would tend to focus on individuals or groups who are already stakeholders in your project or venture. Although some of your conversation partners may be your stakeholders, consultation often takes place within a larger circle of conversation partners, or with partners that are potential future stakeholders. Soliciting insights from persons or groups that are outside your immediate perception of your stakeholder landscape or relevant conversation partners may give rise to surprising insights from your blind spots. The research literature on science communication, for instance, points to interviewing persons who are foreign to your field, so-called tricksters (Horst & Michael, 2011) as a way of connecting with opinions and perspectives outside your "echo chamber."

Consultation is an open-ended two-way, process of dialog between the conversation partners. Communication researchers Grunig and Grunig (2013) distinguish between asymmetrical dialog, where the aim of the interaction is to manipulate or persuade, even though it may involve two-way interaction and symmetrical dialog – a form of communication where two-way communication is not simply designed to ensure that an audience has received the message accurately or as intended. Rather, this form of communication is where both parties are involved in a "conversation" – a dynamic form of communication with no external agenda and no demand of delivery (Trench, 2008). Although conversation parties may have a notion of the overall purpose of interacting, the outcome of the consultation is not established up-front. It is therefore also important to note that consultation does not include asking for approval or permission. The goal of consultation is not consent or agreement, but open two-way exchange of ideas focusing on the insights of conversation partners.

The distinction we have made between advice-seeking and advice-seeking in consultation may seem artificial in that advice-seeking and advice-giving consultation both can be mutually beneficial for all parties involved and often co-occur in practice. Yet, it is our assertion that it is helpful to separate the two forms from each other in that the purposes and competence needed involved in each of the two different approaches to consultation are different: is interaction taking place as a platform for dissemination of the researcher' or entrepreneur' existing knowledge to somebody? Or with a view to expanding the researcher's current understandings by soliciting inputs from conversation partners? Also, the power relation between the helping advice giver and the advice-seeking help recipient is different regarding who takes the role of the advice giver (Schein, 2009): the person seeking advice is likely to experience "1 downness" related to displaying vulnerability in asking for help and advice, while the helper is likely to experience "1 upness" related to being a person that others come to for advice. Awareness of potential power asymmetries as well as taking actions to dismantle them is central to consulting that yields trustworthy insights.

In the following consultation case study, we will explore how sustainable entrepreneurship researchers may benefit from consultation with the sustainable entrepreneurship ecosystem as an avenue for staying connected and informed about current trends, future possibilities, and potential collaborators.

5 Consultation Case Study #2: Consultation in Sustainable Entrepreneurship Research Practice

Our focal point in this case is consultation as an integrated part of research practice in the form of formalized research projects, a series of workshops, and/or by forming a triple helix network. The research on sustainable entrepreneurship was carried out in several ways related to specific projects with single entrepreneurs, together with groups of, for example, designers or companies, and by creating formalized networks. These three different examples will be described briefly in the following.

Consultation may be part of action research projects such as was the case in a project involving sustainable entrepreneurs and companies engaged in a journey towards creating more sustainable product designs and business models. The role of the researcher is here to engage in critical and constructive dialogs about different potentials and pathways, as well as challenging the company with new knowledge and perspectives. This can be related to generating specific knowledge based on a life-cycle assessment of a product to more general discussions and sparring concerning how a circular business model can be set up and implemented. In a specific case with a manufacturer of school furniture, the researchers took part in discussing sustainable properties of the products and in outlining how the company could change from "just" producing furniture towards delivering services-related maintenance and repair thus prolonging product lifetime. The owner of the company envisioned flexible learning environments that gave space for more physical activities during the school day. In the same period, Aalborg Municipality was engaged with researchers in a European project on Circular Public Procurement, and it was decided to investigate how a public tender could be made asking for both high-quality school furniture and flexible learning environments. This turned out to be an example of sustainable product–service–system, where the system perspective was not just about creating an infrastructure for take-back of old products but in fact created a new value proposition for the company and customers. Instead of a competition on the price of the furniture from a central procurement department, direct relations and dialogs were established between the supplier and the schools concerned to identify suitable sustainable solutions. From a research perspective, the case study added a new dimension to understanding product–service–system, since the detailed case study illustrated that the system aspect could be seen as a new paradigm, where the learning environment and the engaged stakeholders were determining the school furniture and the lay-out of the spaces – instead of the other way around (described in detail in Kristensen & Remmen, 2019).

In more recent research collaborations with enterprises, at least four different types of dialog have taken place at different stages, but not necessarily in a specific order:
– dialog around the principles of sustainability and circular economy
– screening of current products, services, and business models of the company
– assessment of potentials of a change in current product designs and business strategies
– development of a road map or action plan for the company

Discussions have centred on how sustainability principles could relate to the specific company and the trade. Often, a brainstorm has generated ideas for new initiatives followed by a discussion of how current activities in the company relate to these principles and circular strategies, such as regenerate, slowing, narrowing, and closing. A screening of products, competitors, upcoming regulations, market trends, etc. have given a platform for considering changes in current products and business models, and for making experiments regarding, for example, using materials with a high-recycled content or improving the durability of the products. Finally, the collaboration is often resulting in a road map or action plan related to how the company can improve their initiatives. Some of these research collaborations have lasted for three to five meetings over half a year, while in other cases the collaboration is extended over several years also involving students writing master's theses, and new research projects. In the case of a textile company, the collaboration has been ongoing for 30 years with a change in focus from employee participation in implementing an environmental management system over life cycle assessment (LCA) and eco-design of products to circular business models.

On several occasions, the consultation has had the format of a series of workshops, where companies with a common interest have met. This was applied for the first time back in the mid-1990s, where companies met with an interest in implementing an environmental management system. Here they got presentations from more experienced companies and researchers, and worked on specific tasks such as formulating an environmental policy, setting up targets, and making an action plan. "Homework" was also involved, and the participants should discuss the specific task back in the company, and then at the next workshop present their environmental policy, and so on. This learning process and knowledge sharing turned out to be effective both related to costs and to outcome for the companies since the management system got adapted to the company and its culture and traditions. For the researchers, this gave insight into the difficulties and possibilities in implementing management systems for continuous improvements in especially small- and medium-sized companies without any former experience within this field.

Nearly 15 years ago, several enterprises, a municipality and the university researchers took the initiative to create Network for Sustainable Business Development in Northern Denmark as a triple helix partnership around thematic seminars, company visits, common projects, etc. Today, the network includes more than 140 companies, most municipalities in Northern Denmark, and several departments at the university. The network is centred on the same areas of interests as mentioned above – with special focus on the sustainability screening and the plan for sustainable business development.

The enterprises especially highlight two benefits: they have got access to university researchers, and the municipalities have changed their role from control and enforcement towards being a more proactive dialog around facilitating changes within areas of common concern and interest. The benefits for the researchers are easy access to the enterprises and municipalities, and creation of mutual trust in the collaboration and increasing knowledge about common interests related to sustainable entrepreneurship and innovations. Further, this type of long-term relations creates an in-depth knowledge about the company that could not be reached through single case studies; and for students it is a huge benefit related to doing their problem-based semester projects, for doing internships, and for writing the final master's thesis.

6 Productive Consultation: Facilitating Engagement and Trusting Knowledge Sharing

Identification, access negotiation, and ongoing relationship management is key to forming productive relationships in consultation such as is outlined in the consultation case study from sustainable entrepreneurship research. For consultation to take place, you need conversation partners to consult with. Yet not all relationships with conversation partners are per default productive or beneficial. Encouraging present and potential conversation partners to participate and commit to consultation processes is a competency and activity in and of itself. Conversation partners need to spend time and resources consulting with you. Also, the relationship must be characterized by trust for conversation partners to share real needs, wants, and opinions. In the following section, we will outline productive consultation as an achievement resulting from the ability to foster engagement and trustful knowledge sharing.

The enabling conditions necessary for productive consultation interactions in a context characterized by transdisciplinarity, stakeholder multitude, and conversation partner diversity can be captured using the building blocks of co-creation as inspiration. In the following, we expand Prahalad and Ramaswamy's (2002, 2004) DART-framework outlining the building blocks of Dialog, Access, Risk, and Transparency as preconditions for productive consultation. We extend the use of the DART model from its initial focus on business–consumer innovation (such as sustainable entrepreneurship), broadening the framework to also include academia–practitioner innovation (researchers and practitioners sharing and gaining insights on topics such as sustainable entrepreneurship).

The first building block of the DART-framework, Dialog, "implies interaction, deep engagement and the ability and willingness to act on both sides" (Prahalad & Ramaswamy, 2004: 9). This in turn is facilitated through the building block of "Access," gaining and giving access to relevant fora and conversation partners. The building block of "Risk" involves an open and trusting risk–benefits assessment, where all participants understand the potential for positive, negative, or no impact of interacting. Finally, "Transparency" refers to information sharing and dismantling of information asymmetry between participants, including how the information will be used. A central point here is that you need to facilitate a productive setting vis-à-vis dialog, access, risk, and transparency at the same time. Productive consultation involves simultaneous mastery of all the building blocks. Figure 5.1, the Productive Consultation Matrix, portrays different potential outcomes of the consultation processes, where the process is a result of the sustainable entrepreneur's or sustainable entrepreneurship researcher's competencies

(or lack thereof) for handling the building blocks of consultation. The two main dimensions of the matrix are:
1) engagement (combining the building blocks of dialog and access), reflecting ability to gain access to and facilitate genuine, active involvement of conversation partners
2) knowledge sharing (combining the building blocks of transparency and risk), capturing the ability to foster a high degree of informed and trustful mutual self-disclosure and knowledge sharing

Both dimensions can be cast as high or low, creating different conditions for productive consultation (see Figure 5.1).

Trusting knowledge sharing

(Transparency + Risk)

	Low	High
High	**HIGH ENGAGEMENT/ LOW TRUST:** **Limited consultation potential**	**HIGH ENGAGEMENT/ HIGH KNOWLEDGE SHARING:** **Valuable consultation potential**
Engagement (Dialogue + Access) **Low**	**LOW KNOWLEDGE SHARING/ LOW ENGAGEMENT:** **Little or no consultation potential**	**HIGH TRUST/LOW ENGAGEMENT:** **Random consultation potential**

Figure 5.1: The Productive Consultation Matrix. Developed from Nielsen, Buono, and Poulfelt (2017).

In the upper left-hand corner of the matrix, conversation partners are characterized by high engagement, but low trust. This combination should lead advice seekers to consider if consultation is tantamount to superficial networking that fails to generate productive benefits due to conversation partners' unwillingness to disclose actual problems. Conversation partners that could be placed in this quadrant could be "dangerous friends" that may come across as very interested but share little and therefore have limited consultation potential, unless action is taken to create a more trusting and psychologically safe dialog environment.

In the lower left-hand quadrant of the matrix, conversation partners are characterized by low knowledge sharing and low engagement. Conversation partners in this quadrant are unlikely to spend the necessary time or resources on consultation as well as to share their knowledge. They therefore present little or no consultation potential. If insights from conversation partners that an advice seeker evaluates to be in this quadrant is deemed central to the venture or project, action must be taken to increase commitment and trust.

In the lower right-hand quadrant of the matrix, conversation partners are characterized by high trust, but low engagement. These conversation partners are interesting in that they are willing to share but may prove difficult to commit to consultation. This does not necessarily present a problem for one-time consultation, but if an ongoing exchange of ideas is in demand a more stable engagement is needed when random consultation potential does not suffice.

In the upper right-hand quadrant of the matrix, conversation partners are characterized by high engagement as well as high knowledge sharing. These are valuable conversation partners, particularly if a long-term relationship is the goal. Conversation partners are willing and able to give access and insight into relevant problems including both tacit and formalized pools of knowledge. This group of conversation partners present the opportunity for an ongoing relationship of productive consultation and interactions over time.

The Productive Consultation Matrix can be used to evaluate and develop consultation relationships. The first step, of course, is to be able to form an opinion of different groups of conversation partners. Initial ideas about conversation partners may not hold up in reality and should be reality tested in practice. Conversation partners may change preferences and relevance over time, and each conversation partner/ groups of conversation partners may be in-between quadrants. Thinking about relevant conversation partners with the matrix is a starting point for considering the value of different conversation partners, forming informed opinions about their importance as well as formulating working hypotheses of the development potential of different groups – evaluations that will all be subject to ongoing (re-)calibration.

In the following consultation case study from the Danish Industrial PhD Program, we will demonstrate how development of competency for handling the building blocks of productive consultation can be facilitated as part of PhD education.

7 Consultation Case Study #3: Consultation in the Industrial PhD Program

I wish to broaden my view of stakeholders as resources and look beyond just university and company.

I will put more focus on aligning with different stakeholders including quick initial meetings with more distant, but still relevant parties.

Anonymous industrial PhD students reflecting on the value of consultation, cohort of spring 2019

The Danish Industrial PhD Program is a funding scheme where a corporation (private or public) in collaboration with a research institution applies for a PhD subsidy from the Danish Innovation Fund based on a research project application. This application and project plan must address both academic impact as well as practical and societal impact of the PhD project, and students divide their funding, time, and physical presence between a university and a corporation for the duration of the PhD study (three years). Except for the fact that industrial PhDs have a knowledge dissemination obligation throughout their PhD project instead of a teaching obligation at the university, the PhD education and assessment criteria are the same as for any other PhD, and the title conferred upon successful completion of the thesis is simply PhD. The attention paid to consultation throughout the process is, however, a distinguishing feature.

This practitioner-focused doctoral education can be considered a "double-impact degree," where traditional PhD education is supplemented by additional requirements for practical and societal impact. The program covers all disciplines including science, technology, engineering, and mathematics (STEM), health as well as social science and humanities, and host organizations are both small- and medium-sized enterprises (some with a recent past as start-ups) as well as larger, more established corporations. The Industrial PhD Program focuses on grand challenges research, particularly green transition, technology innovation, life science, health and welfare technology as well as strategic and challenge-driven research and innovation in new technologies (Innovation Fund Denmark, n.d.b). Consequently, many industrial PhD projects focus on sustainable transformation and innovation in corporations or society at large. A certain variation can be observed across cohorts, but typically a minority of Industrial PhD students enter the program with an explicit ambition to become entrepreneurs (approximately five to ten per cent); most students pursue a career goal of intrapreneurial research in established corporations (approximately 75 to 80%); while some five to ten per cent foresee a career in a university or other public research institution (Nielsen, 2022a).

Consultation is part and parcel of the set-up of the program as well as the educational activities offered to this group of knowledge entrepreneurs. First and foremost, an industrial PhD has a minimum of two supervisors – one at the host university and one at the host company. While the university supervisor is a researcher, the company supervisor need not hold a PhD or a research position in the host organization and is often particularly focused on the practical and societal impact of the project. Throughout the research project, this trio confers and deliberates on the progress of the project in what is often termed "trilemma meetings," hinting at the fact that these consultations balance commercial and practical demands with academic considerations and individual career wishes.

Consultation competency is part of the T-skill profile (Bierema, 2019) that a tailor-made PhD course for industrial PhDs seeks to facilitate as a competence among the industrial PhD students. The industrial PhDs are part of the same PhD education as all other PhDs, but this course is an obligatory PhD course for all industrial PhDs (five European Credit Transfer and Accumulation System [ECTS]) offered by the funding body in collaboration with universities about the opportunities and challenges involved in conducting research in-between academia and practice. The first module, coordinated by the first author, entitled "The Best of Both Worlds – the Potentials and Pitfalls of Mutual Value Co-Creation in-between Academia and Practice," requires students to collect insights (through informal interviews or "coffee meetings") from relevant conversation partners in and outside their immediate stakeholder circle.

During the course, participants are invited to share and discuss the insights gathered as well as reflecting on the value of prioritizing time for consultation going forward in their project. As also suggested by the opening quotes, this typically leads industrial PhD students to engage in "more communication with both coworkers and end-users" and place higher value on "stepping out of the comfort zone," "create networks," and "have constant interaction with stakeholders allowing for a better understanding on the ongoing situation" in addition to receiving adequate feedback (Nielsen, 2022a). This focus on consultation with conversation partners and stakeholders continues through the course's modules 2 and 3, where students further develop and update their stakeholder analysis and plan for continued interaction with conversation partners.

8 Conclusions: Keep Your Ears to the Ground

> Starting to see every situation – and particularly, every conversation – as an opportunity to experience serendipity is an active decision (Busch, 2022: 67).

When time and (social) change is of the essence, "inside–out"-thinking gives way to "outside–in"-thinking. The urgency of grand challenges and the accelerated pace of change in society suggests that many more companies and researchers are working with an open style of collaboration and inclusion to force necessary change. Different forms and degrees of user involvement are widespread, including innovation and development strategies such as user-driven innovation, co-production, co-creation, co-innovation, and co-design and crowdsourcing. Similarly, researchers have been encouraged to supplement an academic conceptualization of what is interesting (Davis, 1971) with a more societal view of what is important (Tihanyi, 2020) as guiding principles for their research. Researchers have been invited to see practice impact in new ways, where "concurrent pathways" of conducting research with practitioners in reciprocal and co-productive collaborations is evaluated as "perhaps the most undervalued in current considerations" of practical impact (Simsek et al., 2018: 2024).

Notwithstanding, consultation with conversations partners and stakeholders is a complex process. It is a balancing act between being able to reap the benefits while anticipating the costs of stakeholder involvement; between making oneself vulnerable to new risks, while at the same time building resilience from being "in touch with reality." Consultation is a double-edged sword, a paradoxical situation: should entrepreneurs and researchers keep their good ideas to themselves and work them through before involving the world? Or should they involve stakeholders such as customers, suppliers, and colleagues in the machine room, exposing themselves to unexpected feedback that shakes the core competency or idea itself, but at the same time may provide break-through insights (Hjalager, 2018)? In this chapter, we have erred on the side of answering, "Yes, you should take the chance and run the risk" given that the topic of this handbook is *sustainable* entrepreneurship (research) emphasizing social change, concerted action, and inclusivity.

We have presented the Productive Consultation Matrix as one avenue for consciously and strategically working with consultation and presented examples of the ways in which consultation takes place in practice through our three consultation case studies. One central point is that not all consultation is equally beneficial. Three pitfalls seem particularly pertinent in this regard.

Advice seekers are unlikely to be able to know up-front which groups of conversations partners will be more productive and for how long. It has been proposed that there might be diminishing returns of collaborating and consulting with practice after a certain level of critical mass has been obtained (Larsen, 2011; Norn, Wohlert, & Anthonsen, 2014), but such level is undefined. The individual entrepreneur and researcher will need to evaluate the value of interaction on an ongoing basis, yet also be prepared to experiment and take chances.

Chance encounters and serendipitous meetings may be time consuming and denying of planning yet yield invaluable insights. Serendipity, the occurrence and development of events by chance in a beneficial way, however, is consistently associated with unexpected and positive personal, scholarly, scientific, organizational, and societal events and discoveries (Busch, 2022; McCay-Peet & Toms, 2015). Staying alert and open for opportunity requires a flexible mind, but also a courageous mind that new input can result in both new challenges as well as opportunities.

Expectation management is critical in that some conversation partners may believe that being consulted is tantamount to having control or co-decision-making power. Unwarranted or misguided beliefs among conversation partners about their level of influence (or lack there-of) may leave partners with the experience that seeking their advice is mere involvement tokenism (Arnstein, 1969, 2019). Consequently, ongoing psychological contracting explicating the terms of the exchange and open communication (Clutterbuck, 2005) about the purpose and privileges involved is essential for sustaining productive relationships over time.

These challenges, however, do not do away with the fact that "showing up" and stepping outside the comfort zone by initiating the dialog is a first necessary step. Consultation processes require a conscious strategy and leadership to work – at times because funding bodies demand the formulation and evaluation of a consultation strategy throughout a research project, but more broadly speaking to develop and maintain productive, beneficial, and healthy relationships over time needed to produce sustainable knowledge, products, and services. Cultivating a consultation mindset involves a conscious effort to develop an ecosystem of conversation partners and a dedication to developing absorptive capacity (Cohen & Levinthal, 1990) for capitalizing on consultation with conversation partners from both stakeholders as well as the wider ecosystem.

References

Alvarez, S., & Sachs, S. (2021). Where do stakeholders come from? *Academy of Management Review*, https://doi.org/10.5465/amr.2019.0077

Arnstein, S. R. (1969). A ladder of citizen participation. *Journal of the American Planning Association*, *35*(4), 216–224.

Arnstein, S. R. (2019). A ladder of citizen participation. *Journal of the American Planning Association*, *85*(1), 24–34.

Bacq, S., Ofstein, L. F., Kickul, J. R., & Gundry, L. K. (2015). Bricolage in social entrepreneurship: How creative resource mobilization fosters greater social impact. *The International Journal of Entrepreneurship and Innovation*, *16*(4), 283–289.

Benkert, J. (2021). Reframing business sustainability decision-making with value-focused thinking. *Journal of Business Ethics*, *174*(2), 441–456.

Bierema, L. L. (2019). Enhancing employability through developing T-shaped professionals. *New Directions for Adult and Continuing Education*, *2019* (163), 67–81.

Birley, S. (1985). The role of networks in the entrepreneurial process. *Journal of Business Venturing*, *1*(1), 107–117.

Bogner, A., Littig, B., & Menz, W. (Eds.) (2009). *Interviewing Experts*. New York: Springer.

Bonney, R., Phillips, T. B., Ballard, H. L., & Enck, J. W. (2016). Can citizen science enhance public understanding of science? *Public Understanding of Science*, *25*(1), 2–16.

Brown, L., & Bylund, P. L. (2022). Where do stakeholders come from? Entrepreneurial choice as the genesis of stakeholder emergence. *Academy of Management Review*, https://doi.org/10.5465/amr.2021.0503

Burke, R. J. (1994). Organizational factors influencing work habits. *Perceptual and Motor Skills*, *79*(1), 273–274.

Busch, C. (2022). *Connect the Dots: The Art and Science of Creating Good Luck*. London: Random House.

Clough, D. R., Fang, T. P., Vissa, B., & Wu, A. (2019). Turning lead into gold: How do entrepreneurs mobilize resources to exploit opportunities? *Academy of Management Annals*, *13*(1), 240–271.

Clutterbuck, D. (2005). Communication and the psychological contract. *Journal of Communication Management*, *9*(4), 359–364.

Cohen, W. M., & Levinthal, D. A. (1990). Absorptive capacity: A new perspective on learning and innovation. *Administrative Science Quarterly*, *35*(1), 128–152.

Consultation (n.d.). Google Dictionary, retrieved on 7 October 2022, https://tinyurl.com/yftxeu2r

Consultation (2022). Cambridge Dictionary, retrieved on 7 October 2022, https://dictionary.cambridge.org/dictionary/english/consultation

Davis, M. S. (1971). That's interesting! Towards a phenomenology of sociology and a sociology of phenomenology. *Philosophy of the Social Sciences*, *1*(2), 309–344.

Dickert, N., & Sugarman, J. (2005). Ethical goals of community consultation in research. *American Journal of Public Health*, *95*(7), 1123–1127.

Flyvbjerg, B., Landman, T., & Schram, S. (2012). *Real Social Sciences: Applied Phronesis*. Cambridge: Cambridge University Press.

Foster, D., & Jonker, J. (2005). Stakeholder relationships: The dialogue of engagement. *Corporate Governance: The International Journal of Business in Society*, *5*(5), 51–57.

Freeman, R. E. (1984). *Strategic Management: A Stakeholder Approach*. Boston, MA: Pitman.

Gao, J., & Bansal, P. (2013). Instrumental and integrative logics in business sustainability. *Journal of Business Ethics, 112*(2), 241–255.

Greco, A. (2020). Combining SDGs: The need for a responsive approach to manage sustainability paradoxes, In *Academy of Management Proceedings* (Vol. 2020, No. 1, p. 21826 Briarcliff Manor, NY 10510: Academy of Management.

Greenwood, D. J., & Levin, M. (2007). *Introduction to Action Research: Social Research for Social Change* (2nd edition). Thousand Oaks, CA: SAGE Publications.

Grunig, J. E., & Grunig, L. A. (2013). Models of public relations and communication. In J. E. Grunig (Ed.), *Excellence in Public Relations and Communication Management* 285–325. Oxfordshire: Routledge.

Hahn, T., Figge, F., Pinkse, J., & Preuss, L. (2018). A paradox perspective on corporate sustainability: Descriptive, instrumental, and normative aspects. *Journal of Business Ethics, 148*(2), 235–248.

Hjalager, A. M. (2018). Indefra-ud kontra udefra-ind. Åbne og lukkede videnflows. In R. K. Nielsen, A. M. Hjalager, H. H. Larsen, F. Bévort, T. D. Henriksen & S. Vikkelsø (Eds.), *Ledelsesdilemmaer – og kunsten at navigere i moderne ledelse* (pp. 43–54). Copenhagen: Djøf Publishing.

Horst, M., & Michael, M. (2011). On the shoulders of idiots: Re-thinking science communication as "event." *Science as Culture, 20*(3), 283–306.

Innovation Fund Denmark (n.d.a.). *Industrial Researcher*, retrieved on 7 October 2022, https://innovationsfonden.dk/en/p/industrial-researcher

Innovation Fund Denmark (n.d.b.). *New Course for Industrial PhD Students*, retrieved on 7 October 2022, https://innovationsfonden.dk/da/nyhed/new-course-industrial-phd-students

Jamieson, D. W., Barnett, R. C., & Buono, A. F. (Eds.). (2016). *Consultation for Organizational Change Revisited*. Charlotte, NC: IAP.

Jay, J., Soderstrom, S., & Grant, G. (2017). Navigating the paradox of sustainability. In W. K. Smith, M. W. Lewis, P. Jarzabkowski & A. Langley (Eds.), *The Oxford Handbook of Organizational Paradox* (pp. 357–372. Oxford: Oxford University Press.

Jenkins, J. C. (1983). Resource mobilization theory and the study of social movements. *Annual Review of Sociology, 9*(1), 527–553.

Kristensen, H. S., & Remmen, A. (2019). A framework for sustainable value propositions in product-service systems. *Journal of Cleaner Production, 223*, 25–35.

Kubr, M. (Ed.) (2002). *Management Consulting: A Guide to the Profession*. Geneva, CH: International Labour Organization.

Larsen, M. T. (2011). The implications of academic enterprise for public science: An overview of the empirical evidence. *Research Policy, 40*(1), 6–19.

McCay-Peet, L., & Toms, E. G. (2015). Investigating serendipity: How it unfolds and what may influence it. *Journal of the Association for Information Science and Technology, 66*(7), 1463–1476.

McMillan, C., & Overall, J. (2016). Wicked problems: Turning strategic management upside down. *Journal of Business Strategy, 37*(1), 34–43.

Murray, A., Kotha, S., & Fisher, G. (2020). Community-based resource mobilization: How entrepreneurs acquire resources from distributed non-professionals via crowdfunding. *Organization Science, 31*(4), 960–989.

Nielsen, R. K. (2022a). *Collective Wisdom #3*. Industrial PhD course module 1, The Best of Both Worlds – the Potentials and Pitfalls of Mutual Value Co-Creation in-between Academia and Practice, Cohorts of 2019 and 2020. CBS Executive, Denmark

Nielsen, R. K. (2022b). *Pre-module Student Surveys 2018–2022*. Industrial PhD course module 1, The Best of Both Worlds – the Potentials and Pitfalls of Mutual Value Co-Creation in-between Academia and Practice, CBS Executive, Denmark.

Nielsen, R. K., Buono, A. F., & Poulfelt, F. 2017. At the knowledge interface: Developing co-created research competency. In *Academy of Management Proceedings* (Vol. 2017, No. 1, p. 11156). Briarcliff Manor, NY 10510: Academy of Management.

Norn, M. T., Wohlert, J., & Anthonsen, M. (2014). *University Researchers' Collaboration with Industry and the Public Sector – A Survey of University Researchers in Denmark.* Copenhagen: DEA.

Pedersen, D. B. (2014). The political epistemology of science-based policy-making. *Society, 51*(5), 547–551.

Prahalad, C. K., & Ramaswamy, V. (2002). The co-creation connection. *Strategy and Business, 27,* 50–61.

Prahalad, C. K., & Ramaswamy, V. (2004). Co-creating unique value with customers. *Strategy & Leadership, 32*(3), 4–9.

Schein, E. H. (1988). *Process Consultation – Its Role in Organizational Development.* Reading, MA: Addison-Wesley.

Schein, E. H. (2009). *Helping. How to Offer, Give, and Receive Help. Understanding Effective Dynamics in One-to-One, Group, and Organizational Relationships.* San Francisco, LA: Berrett-Koehler Publishers.

Senge, P. M., & Scharmer, C. O. (2008). Community action research: Learning as a community of practitioners, consultants and researchers. In P. Reason & H. Bradbury (Eds.), *Handbook of Action Research: The Concise Paperback Edition* pp 195–206. Thousand Oaks, CA: Sage.

Simsek, Z., Bansal, P., Shaw, J. D., Heugens, P., & Smith, W. K. (2018). From the editors – seeing practice impact in new ways. *Academy of Management Journal, 61*(6), 2021–2025.

Smith, W. K., & Lewis, M. W. (2011). Toward a theory of paradox: A dynamic equilibrium model of organizing. *Academy of Management Review, 36*(2), 381–403.

Spaapen, J., & Van Drooge, L. (2011). Introducing 'productive interactions' in social impact assessment. *Research Evaluation, 20*(3), 211–218.

Starik, M., & Kanashiro, P. (2013). Toward a theory of sustainability management: Uncovering and integrating the nearly obvious. *Organization & Environment, 26*(1), 7–30.

Tihanyi, L. (2020). From "that's interesting" to "that's important." *Academy of Management Journal, 63*(2), 329–331.

Trench, B. (2008). Towards an analytical framework of science communication models. In D. Cheng, M. Claessens, T. Gascoigne, J. Metcalfe, B. Schiele & S. Shi (Eds.), *Communicating Science in Social Contexts – New Models, New Practices* 119–135. New York City, NY: Springer.

Van Ginkel, K. C., Botzen, W. W., Haasnoot, M., Bachner, G., Steininger, K. W., Hinkel, J., Watkiss, P., Boere, E., Jeuken, A., Sainz de Murieta, E., & Bosello, F. (2020). Climate change induced socio-economic tipping points: Review and stakeholder consultation for policy relevant research. *Environmental Research Letters, 15*(2), 023001.

World Commission on Environment and Development. (1987). *Report of the World Commission on Environment and Development: Our Common Future.* United Nations through Oxford: Oxford University Press.

Part II: **Leadership**
A. Berfu Ünal

In Part II, we focus on sustainable entrepreneurs as leaders of change and innovation in the market. Sustainable entrepreneurs develop solutions, services and products that are not only novel and innovative but also impactful in terms of environmental and societal benefits. They lead market dynamics by creating niche domains that serve the greater public and environmental good, and by setting examples for how businesses can be both profitable and sustainable. They can radically disrupt conventional approaches, bring in fresh and new perspectives and can play a key role in transitioning into a green economy. The chapters in Part II dive into the process behind how sustainable entrepreneurs become leaders of change and innovation by using theories from different disciplines such as social psychology, environmental psychology, organisational psychology, business, management and entrepreneurship. Viewing sustainable entrepreneurs as leaders of change and innovation begs important questions to be answered from a research point of view: are there some stable characteristics or traits that make up sustainable leaders? Would certain characteristics increase the likelihood for some people to lead as sustainable entrepreneurs? How can sustainable entrepreneurs lead and support societal transitions that are sustainable? We use insights from previous literature on leadership in order to discuss the role of sustainable entrepreneurs as leaders.

Leadership, as a study field, comprises several eras where the focus has changed from the study of stable trait factors in leaders to the study of behavioural patterns existing in different leadership styles and how they can lead to different outcomes (Derue et al., 2011). Trait theories in leadership are used to explain leadership behaviour with reference to certain stable personality characteristics, such as being assertive, self-confident, determined and creative (Judge et al., 2002). As such, trait theories are used to predict what kind of people are more likely to succeed in becoming a leader. While trait theories are useful to sketch a general profile of a leader, they are also criticised to be somewhat restrictive and categorical. In addition, trait theories do not necessarily cover the process of becoming a leader and why a personality factor or a stable individual difference factor can be more enabling than another, and via which processes, as we will discuss both in Chapters 6 and 7.

Indeed, not only stable individual difference factors but also situational factors and the context (see Part III) play a role in the emergence of sustainable entrepreneurs as leaders. For instance, in contexts where there is a strong emphasis on societal and systemic transitions towards more environmentally sustainable operations and markets, sustainable entrepreneurs would flourish more easily. Such contexts would make problems around sustainability more salient as well, thereby triggering sustainable entrepreneurs to recognise opportunities to address these problems (Chapter 8). On a larger scale, sustainable entrepreneurs could also help with changing the context for the better by leading sustainability efforts in regions and cities. An example is the electric or hydrogen transition in cities to make our mobility, logistics and industries greener. Sustainable entrepreneurs could lead these transitions, by, for instance, transforming public opinion on sustainability issues with their sustainable solutions and businesses or by

https://doi.org/10.1515/9783110756159-007

creating a clear vision (see Chapter 9). This is also in line with a recent and most accepted theory on leadership, the transformational leadership theory (Bass, 1990). The theory posits that transformational leaders can potentially induce positive change in their followers by enabling them to work towards a shared vision and by being an inspiring role model. Sustainable entrepreneurship inherently calls for such a transformational leadership style that is associated with intrinsic changes in the behaviour of other stakeholders and a long-lasting societal change.

Part II on leadership covers both individual and contextual factors that might explain sustainable entrepreneurship endeavours, outcomes and processes, as well as their interaction. We cover a range of methods too, from literature reviews to opinion papers and an empirical study. In addition, we contribute to the need to have more interdisciplinary research in sustainable entrepreneurship by combining theories and approaches from psychology, entrepreneurship and business.

In Chapter 6, Berfu Ünal discusses the role of personal values in predicting the intention to become a sustainable entrepreneur. Values are stable individual difference factors that are developed early on in life, and that serve as guiding principles in life (Schwartz, 1992). Taking sustainable entrepreneurship as an environmental action to create positive impact, Ünal introduces four types of values that have been particularly a focus of interest in environmental psychology to study pro-environmental actions (Steg et al., 2014): biospheric, altruistic, egoistic and hedonic values. After giving a summary of the values research, she zooms into the direct and indirect influence of values on pro-environmental intentions and behaviours, and she draws conclusions for the study of sustainable entrepreneurship. Ünal also provides us a reflection on future research needs in this domain and how theories from environmental psychology could be used to test and develop theory in studying sustainable entrepreneurship.

In Chapter 7, Hendrik Thelken and Gjalt de Jong take an alternative approach to study individual difference factors in becoming a leader in sustainable entrepreneurship. They use the infamous Big-Five personality inventory (Costa & McCrae, 1992) as a basis for the mapping of personality factors. They investigate which personality factors are more strongly related to the consideration of future consequences, which can be defined as being aware of the possible outcomes of one's behaviours and therefore considering the future consequences before taking action (Strahman et al., 1994). Thelken and de Jong argue that consideration of future consequences is a relevant factor in studying sustainable entrepreneurship as one might expect that sustainable entrepreneurs are those with potentially a higher awareness of unsustainable actions for the future of our planet. They empirically test the relationships between the Big-Five personality factors and consideration of future consequences, and advance our understanding on how the different personality characteristics of sustainable entrepreneurs could make them focus on future environmental consequences, which might serve as a trigger to engage in sustainable entrepreneurship.

Chapter 8 follows from the previous two chapters by zooming in on opportunity recognition, which is defined as a first step to start a business (Short et al., 2010). In this chapter, Margo Enthoven first gives us a historical account of how the concept of opportunity recognition has evolved, what kind of definitions were used and how these definitions differ in critical aspects explaining the process behind opportunity recognition. In addition, Enthoven presents us with her own typology of opportunity recognition by linking opportunity recognition to identity theory, arguing that depending on the different identities entrepreneurs might use to define themselves, they might recognise opportunities differently. Notably she makes a distinction between opportunity recognition following from the recognition of problems or following from the recognition of solutions. As such, Enthoven also aims at providing guidelines for aspiring sustainable entrepreneurs in how to recognise opportunities by focusing on existing problems or solutions.

In the last chapter, Philipp Eppe, Lennart Winkeler, Geo Kocheril and Torben Stührmannin focus on the role of sustainable entrepreneurs as leaders of a transition to a hydrogen economy. Indeed, not much is known about how sustainable entrepreneurs could help with the transition to a hydrogen economy as the field of hydrogen economy is only recently emerging. The authors have a particular focus on three questions: how can we learn from the past about the different types of socio-technical innovations that sustainable entrepreneurs could pioneer? What are the types of leadership needed by entrepreneurs to make the transition to a hydrogen economy successful? What are the guiding principles needed for resilient leadership in hydrogen economy? In light of the final question, the authors provide an extensive guideline as a toolkit for sustainable entrepreneurs, which can be used to lead hydrogen economy transitions.

References

Bass, B. M. (1990) From transactional to transformational leadership: Learning to share the vision. *Organizational Dynamics*, *18*(3), 19–31.

Costa, P., & McCrae, R. (1992). Four ways five factors are basic. *Personality and Individual Differences*, *13*, 653–665.

Derue, D. S., Nahrgang, J. D., Wellman, N. E., & Humphrey, S. E. (2011). Trait and behavioral theories of leadership: An integration and meta-analytic test of their relative validity. *Personnel Psychology*, *64*(1), 7–52.

Judge, T. A., Bono, J. E., Ilies, R., & Gerhardt, M. W. (2002). Personality and leadership: A qualitative and quantitative review. *Journal of Applied Psychology*, *87*(4), 765–780.

Schwartz, S. H. 1992. Universals in the content and structure of values: Theoretical advances and empirical tests in 20 countries. *Advances in Experimental Social Psychology*, *25*, 1–65.

Short, J. C., Ketchen, D. J., Shook, C. L., & Ireland, R. D. (2010). The concept of 'opportunity' in entrepreneurship research: Past accomplishments and future challenges. *Journal of Management, 36*(1), 40–65.

Steg, L., Bolderdijk, J. W., Keizer, K., & Perlaviciute, G. (2014). An integrated framework for encouraging pro-environmental behaviour: The role of values, situational factors and goals. *Journal of Environmental Psychology, 38*, 104–115.

Strathman, A., Gleicher, F., Boninger, D. S., & Edwards, C. S. (1994). The consideration of future consequences: Weighing immediate and distant outcomes of behavior. *Journal of Personality and Social Psychology, 66*(4), 742–752.

A. Berfu Ünal

6 Value-Driven Leadership in Sustainable Entrepreneurship

Abstract: Values, serving as key principles in life, can predict entrepreneurial intentions and behaviours. Research identified self-enhancement values (e.g., competence) as particularly relevant in predicting entrepreneurship endeavours. Interestingly, new evidence suggests that values that are not related to self-enhancement but self-transcendence (e.g., biospheric values) could be equally, if not more relevant when the focus is on starting a sustainable enterprise rather than a conventional enterprise. In the current chapter, we first explain the value theory with reference to key conceptualisations. Next, we discuss the process of how values predict environmental actions like sustainable entrepreneurship, by using insights from the field of environmental psychology. Finally, we draw conclusions for sustainable entrepreneurship research, and identify current gaps in our knowledge and future research needs on this topic.

Keywords: values, self-transcendence values, self-enhancement values, value–belief–norm theory

1 Introduction

It is expected that our planet Earth will warm up by 2 °C by the year 2100 if CO_2 emissions are not drastically reduced in the coming decades (IPCC, 2022). Such an increase in temperature is associated with irreversible effects, including biodiversity loss, extreme climate hazards, loss of life and ecosystems and loss of resources that are key to our survival. Mitigation and climate adaptation strategies are estimated to be effective if we manage to keep global warming below 1.5 °C (IPCC, 2022). As such, it is of utmost importance to reduce our CO_2 emissions and reach a steady state where global warming is kept below 1.5 °C. Unsustainable businesses, industries and sectors are a major threat to strategies aimed at mitigating the adverse effects of climate change and global warming. We need radical systemic transitions in all sectors whereby unsustainable practices are replaced by sustainable ones with minimal negative impact on the environment. Sustainable entrepreneurs can play a major role in these much-needed systemic transitions by introducing CO_2 neutral solutions in the market and by innovating and greening the way sectors and businesses operate. An important question is what kind of characteristics distinguish sustainable entrepreneurs from conventional entrepreneurs. Knowing this

A. Berfu Ünal, Department of Sustainable Entrepreneurship in a Circular Economy, Faculty Campus Fryslân, University of Groningen, Groningen, the Netherlands

https://doi.org/10.1515/9783110756159-008

would help create a context allowing for sustainable entrepreneurs to flourish, thereby helping to mitigate environmental problems.

In their definition of sustainable entrepreneurship, Shepherd and Patzelt (2011) argue that sustainable entrepreneurs can be distinguished by looking at what they prioritise in their businesses. More specifically, while conventional entrepreneurs prioritise economic profitability over other goals, sustainable entrepreneurs prioritise environmental goals as well while engaging in some form of business innovation. As such, sustainable entrepreneurs do not only focus on aspects to be developed (e.g., economic and non-economic gains) but also on aspects to be preserved, such as the environment, resources and communities (see Shepherd & Patzelt, 2011, for an overview). The definition departs from the traditional understanding of entrepreneurship as being mainly interested in the 'Profit' component of the triple P, and brings forward the importance of considering the 'People' and 'Planet' components as well. Indeed, sustainable entrepreneurs strive to find a balance to manage the so-called triple bottom line (Elkington, 2004) of being economically, socially and environmentally resilient (Kuckertz & Wagner, 2010). Therefore, another major distinction of sustainable entrepreneurs from conventional entrepreneurs is having a strong motivation to protect the environment. What kind of factors determine whether an entrepreneur has such motivation? And who are more likely to lead in sustainable entrepreneurship endeavours? In the current chapter, we will introduce values as a psychological factor with a motivational influence in affecting not only decisional outcomes to become a sustainable entrepreneur but also related processes and drivers of sustainable entrepreneurship, such as opportunity or problem recognition. In that, we aim at bridging the fields of environmental psychology and sustainable entrepreneurship, and discuss how we can gain insights from environmental psychology to use and develop theory in sustainable entrepreneurship research.

2 Value Theory

Entrepreneurship is a value-driven process (Muñoz, 2017), meaning that certain values might guide and motivate individuals to pursue entrepreneurship. Values are defined as leading principles in life that serve as a compass and remind us about what we deem important (Schwartz, 1992; Steg, Bolderdijk et al., 2014). A prominent, widely accepted and cross-culturally valid approach to study values is Schwartz's (1992) conceptualisation of basic values (also see Schwartz & Bardi, 2001). Schwartz's (1992) value theory comprises four quadrants that are depictive of a continuum of value clusters (motivational goals) in a circular structure, on which ten distinct value types are mapped (see Figure 6.1). These four value clusters are openness to change, conservatism, self-enhancement and self-transcendence. Openness to change refers to having a key interest in novelty and innovation as well as enjoying life. Conservatism, on the other hand, refers to having a key interest in preserving tradition, conforming to social expectations and keeping the status quo. The third value cluster is self-enhancement, which puts the emphasis on competence, power and self-achievement. Finally the fourth cluster, self-transcendence, puts the emphasis on the well-being of others and shying away from acting in line with self-interests.

Schwartz (1992, 2012) identifies six characteristics that are inherent to values. First, values motivate people to act in a certain way because they are goals that are desirable for the individual. Therefore, they guide and predict behaviour and decisions. As an example, values related to the motivation of openness to change would lead someone to look for novel and pleasurable experiences in any given situation. Second, values are related to affective outcomes. For instance, when we encounter a situation that is against our core set of values, we would feel threatened, and our affective response would be negative. At times, these emotions also inform us in a top-down manner, making us categorically against options that are in seeming contradiction with our values (Perlaviciute et al., 2018). Third, values are difficult to change once formed; they are stable over situations and time. This indicates that the same set of values motivate similar actions in different settings, such as in the private sphere and work sphere. Fourth, values determine which consequences of behaviours are more important for the individual and whether there would be a conflict with one's core values if acted in a certain way. For instance, someone with the key value of benevolence would consider the consequences of their actions on other people's well-being, and if there is a possible threat to the well-being of others, they might refrain from executing that particular action. Fifth, people hold various values but some values are more important than others. Hence, the prioritisation of values differs from individual to individual, making it a stable individual difference factor. This means that, for example, for some people values that are under self-transcendence might be of key importance while for some others these values might be further down in priority. Sixth and final, values might conflict with one another. More specifically, Schwartz posits that when two values on the four quadrants are proximal to each other, then they are more similar or at least positively related. For example, achievement and power or achievement and hedonism as neighbouring values are expected to have a positive correlation. On the contrary, when two values are distal to each other, they might be negatively related and they might even conflict with each other. For example, self-direction, which is a value signifying independence and action-orientedness, is distal to the value conformity, which signifies the importance of acting in line with the expectations of others and restraining self-interest. As a result, these two values might oppose each other. When such conflict arises, action follows from considering the relative importance of different values for the individual, and whether the context supports the activation of these values.

Applications of Schwartz's values to entrepreneurship were mostly focused on openness to change and self-enhancement values as the most relevant motivators behind entrepreneurship endeavours and intentions (Gorgievski, Ascalon, & Stephan, 2011; Morales et al., 2019; Kirkley, 2016). Indeed, entrepreneurs have traditionally been associated with features such as being innovative, ambitious, creative and independent, willing to pioneer, having self-direction and having clear individual goals to achieve (Fayolle, Liñán, & Moriano, 2014; Kirkley, 2016). Therefore, values on the left side of the circular value conceptualisation (Figure 6.1), which reflect a motivation for self-enhancement and openness to change, have been in general associated with entrepreneurship. Values on the right side of the circular value conceptualisation, on the other hand, were somewhat negatively associated with entrepreneurship (Hueso et al., 2020). This might be because entrepreneurs are generally viewed as risk-takers and opportunity seekers (McGrath, MacMillan, & Scheinberg, 1992; Shane & Venkataraman, 2000), which might oppose values such as conformity, tradition or security that are nested on the right side and that are related to avoiding risks and maintaining the status quo (Schwartz & Bardi, 2001). In addition, values that put the emphasis on prioritising the well-being of others (i.e., universalism and benevolence) nested under self-transcendence were thought to discourage people from being entrepreneurs as entrepreneurship might require an egoistic focus in the process of starting a new business, where personal time needs to be dedicated to work rather than others (Hueso et al., 2020). Are the same set of values applicable to understand what would predict sustainable entrepreneurship intentions and behaviours?

As discussed, we argue that sustainable entrepreneurship differs from classical entrepreneurship in the sense that it inherently puts the emphasis on aspects to be protected as well as to be developed (Shepherd & Patzelt, 2011). Following from that, if we were to map what type of values would put the emphasis on aspects to be sustained and aspects to be developed, we could argue that self-enhancement and openness to change would be more related to aspects to be developed, while self-transcendence and conservatism would be more related to aspects to be sustained. This means that not only the left side of the circular value conceptualisation might be relevant to study sustainable entrepreneurship but also the right side (see Figure 6.1), opening new avenues for research in the field of sustainable entrepreneurship. Indeed, the findings of Santos and colleagues (2021) already demonstrated links between values nested under conservatism and self-transcendence and the decision to become self-employed, as one of the proxies to becoming an entrepreneur. However, new research is needed that specifically looks into intentions to become a sustainable entrepreneur and how values other than the ones nested under self-enhancement and openness to change can be relevant. In addition, we reason that perhaps a value conceptualisation that is more predictive of sustainable behaviours and actions could better explain the outcomes and processes involved in sustainable entrepreneurship. Below we will discuss such value conceptualisation that is adapted from the value scale of Schwartz (1973) and that is specifically relevant to understand involvement and interest in pro-environmental actions and endeavours like sustainable entrepreneurship.

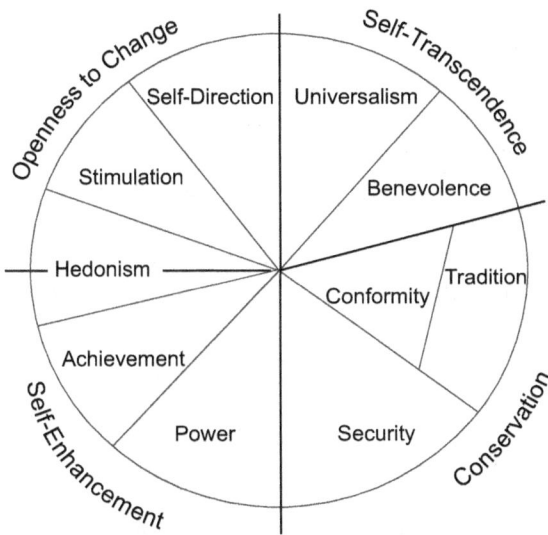

Figure 6.1: The theoretical structure behind the value-conceptualisation of Schwartz (retrieved from Schwartz, 2012).

3 Values That Are Particularly Related to Sustainable Behaviours

Sustainable entrepreneurship can be regarded as a pro-environmental endeavour, and therefore values literature from environmental psychology could help us understand which values are more relevant to predict the behaviour of sustainable entrepreneurs. With the emergence of environmental problems such as global warming and ozone depletion, scholars were interested in studying whether attitudes towards environmental issues were rooted in people's values (Stern, Dietz, & Guagnano, 1998). However, as Schwartz's value measure was lengthy to administer with 56 items and as it did not include a dedicated value for the preservation of the environment, scholars came up with an alternative measure that is brief and easier to administer (please see Bouman, Steg, & Kiers, 2018; De Groot & Steg, 2008; Stern, Dietz, & Guagnano, 1998; Steg et al., 2014b, to read more about the process of developing the brief value measure). Particularly, four types of values are distinguished in environmental psychology based on Schwartz's value theory and are used to explain people's pro-environmental intentions and actions: biospheric, altruistic, egoistic and hedonic values. Among these four values, biospheric and altruistic values are nested under self-transcendence values, meaning they put the emphasis away from the self. More specifically, people who strongly endorse biospheric values find it of utmost importance to protect the environment while people who strongly endorse altruistic values find it of utmost importance to protect the well-being of others. Hence, both biospheric and altruistic values make one focus on aspects that transcend the self. The other two values, egoistic and hedonic, are nested under self-enhancement values, meaning they put the emphasis on maximising benefits for the self. In line with that, people who strongly endorse egoistic values find it of utmost importance to increase their personal gain, profit or status, while people who strongly endorse hedonic values find it of utmost importance to increase pleasure and convenience at any given time. As we will discuss in more detail below, the four values exert their influence on sustainable actions either directly or indirectly via inter-mediate variables. As such, different processes might be at play in explaining the influ-ence of values on sustainable actions.

3.1 Direct Effect of Values on Sustainable Actions

Research shows that biospheric and altruistic values are positively related to pro-environmental behaviours and intentions as well as awareness of environmental prob-lems and feeling a moral responsibility to act on these problems (De Groot & Steg, 2008; Jakovcevic & Steg, 2013; Nordlund & Garvill, 2003; Ünal, Steg, & Granskaya, 2019; Ünal, Steg, & Gorsira, 2018; Steg, Dreijerink, & Abrahamse, 2005; Stern, 2000). Indeed, biospheric people in particular consider the consequences of their actions for the environment, they act pro-environmentally consistently and simply for the sake of protecting the environment. Biospheric people are therefore less likely to be discouraged when pro-environmental behaviours are costly or effortful. Altruistic values are also posi-tively related to pro-environmental actions (Steg et al., 2014a) unless they are in con-flict with biospheric values. For instance, when people had to choose between donating to a pro-environmental versus pro-social cause, altruistic values predicted donating to a pro-social cause positively and biospheric values predicted donating to a pro-environmental cause negatively: a strong endorsement of biospheric values was associated with preferring to donate to a pro-environmental cause over pro-social cause (De Groot & Steg, 2008). Yet, when there is no such goal conflict, altruis-tic and biospheric values are both related to pro-environmental choices and actions.

As mentioned, many pro-environmental actions can be costly (time-wise or finan-cially) or effortful, such as consuming organic produce or having to walk to a nearby waste separation facility instead of throwing your recyclable waste in the residual bin. Such costly pro-environmental actions might be discouraging for people who strongly endorse egoistic and hedonic values. Supporting this argument, egoistic and hedonic values are mostly found to be either not related to pro-environmental actions or negatively related (De Groot & Steg, 2008; Jakovcevic & Steg, 2013; Thøgersen & Ölander, 2002; Ünal, Steg, & Granskaya, 2019; Ünal, Steg, & Gorsira, 2018). This has been a pattern that was confirmed in various pro-environmental domains, such as car-use reduction, recycling, adoption of sustainable innovations or acceptability of pro-environmental policies. It needs to be noted that egoistic and hedonic values could also facilitate pro-environmental actions depending on the domain (Steg et al., 2014b). For example, when the pro-environmental behaviour is financially or status-wise beneficial for the person, people who strongly endorse egoistic values might consider executing the behaviour. An example could be the adoption and sustainable use of solar panels in anticipation of saving money by producing energy (Namazkhan, 2022). Similarly, when executing the behaviour is pleasurable, people who strongly endorse hedonic values might consider doing it. An example is, for instance, commuting to work by bike rather than by car on a sunny day for the fun of it rather than being concerned about traffic-related CO_2 emissions.

Hence, the abundance of research from environmental psychology points out that biospheric values in particular and altruistic values are more likely to steer a person towards sustainability while egoistic and hedonic values are more likely to steer a person away from sustainability, except when the execution of the behaviour might fulfil the motivation of self-enhancement. Interestingly, there has not been a thorough investigation of whether and how the four values (Steg et al., 2014a) are related to the undertaking of sustainable entrepreneurship. Can we observe the same pattern of relationships in the pro-environmental domain of sustainable entrepreneurship?

Indeed, one might expect that having a key concern for the protection of the environment (i.e., biospheric values) or others in a community (i.e., altruistic values) would have a direct relationship with looking for opportunities to improve the quality of the environment or well-being of others, respectively. Hence, biospheric values in particular as well as altruistic values are expected to predict sustainable entrepreneurship intentions and behaviours. In addition, undertaking the endeavour of sustainable entrepreneurship could also be appealing to people who strongly endorse egoistic values, if starting up a sustainable business is associated with personal gains such as financial profit or recognition. Similarly, if starting up a sustainable business is associated with having pleasure and fun, such as the pleasure of starting a new venture, one can imagine that people who strongly endorse hedonic values might also be interested in this endeavour. As such, different motivations might be at play to predict the intention and behaviour of sustainable entrepreneurship. An interesting question is whether sustainable entrepreneurs could strongly endorse two seemingly contradicting values, such as biospheric and egoistic values or whether two seemingly contradicting values could equally strongly and positively predict their behaviours. That is because according to Schwartz, values that are nested under opposing motivations, such as the motivation to self-enhance and self-transcendence, would be in conflict. In other words, biospheric and egoistic values, for example, should be in conflict with each other, leading to different choices and actions. Yet, sustainable entrepreneurship involves starting up a business, and characteristics such as independence and autonomy might facilitate this process despite being mainly associated with an egoistic self-concern. In addition, starting up a sustainable business inherently needs some form of financial gain in order for the enterprise to exist over time. This means that having an egoistic motivation to make revenue might be crucial for the achievement of the normative biospheric goal of the enterprise. Hence, co-endorsement of egoistic and biospheric values could be important for starting, as well as for the success and scaling up of sustainable enterprises. This is an assumption that is yet to be investigated. In addition, it is also curious to investigate whether sustainable entrepreneurs are able to balance this seeming conflict of both doing good for the environment while being profitable, which we will discuss further.

3.2 Indirect Effect of Values via Intermediate Factors

Values are regarded as distal predictors of behaviour. As such, they are also thought to affect behaviour and intentions via some other intermediate variables. One theory that aims at explaining the indirect influence of values on behaviours is the value–belief–norm theory (VBN) (see Figure 6.2) by Stern (2000). The theory builds on the norm–activation model (NAM) (Schwartz, 1973) which argues that pro-environmental actions result from a moral normative process, whereby feeling a moral obligation to act pro-environmentally (i.e., personal norm) has a direct and strong influence on behaviour. This moral obligation stems from the belief that one can change the adverse environmental outcomes by changing their behaviour (i.e., outcome efficacy), which is a consequence of having awareness of environmental problems resulting from one's individual behaviour (i.e., problem awareness). The VBN model explains what would ignite this process of norm activation to act pro-environmentally.

More specifically, Stern (2000) argues that values fuel this norm–activation process. Values colour beliefs and perceptions indeed (Steg et al., 2014a), meaning they make us think and reason in a certain way that is in line with our key values. According to the VBN theory, biospheric values specifically and altruistic values colour beliefs such that more importance is given to environmental problems, which increases awareness about these problems and the felt responsibility that one can help with the solution of these problems by changing unsustainable behaviours. This process results in feeling a strong moral obligation to act and change behaviour. The VBN, however, predicts that egoistic and hedonic values would either have no influence on the norm–activation process or a negative influence. For instance, it is expected that a strong concern for one's personal benefits and pleasure (i.e., egoistic and hedonic values) might have a negative impact on problem awareness and outcome efficacy, as pro-environmental actions can be costly in terms of time or effort (Steg et al., 2014a), thereby having negative implications for the fulfilment of egoistic and hedonic values.

There has not been a full replication of the VBN theory yet to predict sustainable entrepreneurship intentions or related processes such as opportunity recognition. In a recent study, we tested whether values predict sustainable opportunity recognition via problem recognition, which we defined similar to problem awareness in VBN and

NAM (Enthoven, 2021). Findings revealed that biospheric values were positively related to both problem and opportunity recognition for sustainable entrepreneurship whereas egoistic values were negatively related. In addition, problem recognition mediated the effect of biospheric values on sustainable opportunity recognition (please see Enthoven, 2021 for a detailed account of the findings). As the recognition of sustainable opportunities is a first step to start a sustainable business, it is crucial to find factors that predict this process. Based on our study, we conclude that having a key concern for the environment (i.e., biospheric values) would fuel this process of opportunity recognition both directly but also indirectly by means of making the person aware of environmental problems (i.e., problem recognition). Hence, biospheric values seem to work as a general motivating factor for sustainable entrepreneurship processes.

Evidence from the study of Thelken and de Jong (2020) further supports the premise that biospheric values would have a positive relationship to sustainable entrepreneurship endeavours. Notably, it was found that intention to start a sustainable entrepreneurship endeavour was predicted by positive attitudes towards sustainable entrepreneurship, which had a strong relationship with holding biospheric values. The finding indicates that a strong concern for the environment not only colours beliefs as cognitive estimations but also attitudinal evaluations about what is favourable and unfavourable. A positive evaluation of sustainable entrepreneurship is then related to being more willing to start a sustainable business. Thelken and de Jong (2020) also found a weak albeit positive relationship with altruistic values and attitudes towards sustainable entrepreneurship as well as with hedonic values and attitudes towards sustainable entrepreneurship. As altruistic values are also a type of self-transcendence value, it is not surprising that altruistic values predict sustainable entrepreneurship processes positively. However, the finding on hedonic values might come as a surprise when one compares it to findings from environmental psychology literature, as mainly negative or no effects of hedonic values were shown in the literature (Jakovcevic & Steg, 2013; De Groot & Steg, 2008). It could be argued that a positive relationship with hedonic values gives support to the conceptualisation of Shepherd and Patzelt (2011) that entrepreneurship also focuses on aspects to be developed, such as personal outcomes like pleasure, which is a premise that needs to be investigated further.

In a similar vein, one could expect a positive relationship between egoistic values and attitudes towards sustainable entrepreneurship as egoistic values also put the emphasis on aspects to be developed, such as maximising positive outcomes for the self, in the form of making money or profit as well as in the form of gaining reputation. As argued by Dean and McMullen (2007), sustainable entrepreneurs could play a key role in changing market dynamics by finding sustainable and environmental solutions that are also profitable. In other words, sustainability and profitability need not exclude each other in sustainable entrepreneurship endeavours but can rather be used to support each other. If sustainable entrepreneurs are then those who value both sustainability and profitability, one might assume they would endorse both biospheric and egoistic values or that egoistic values would also be related to sustainable entrepreneurship intentions, as discussed before. While such a relationship was not revealed in the study of Thelken and de Jong (2020), it is of interest for future research to look into whether egoistic values and biospheric values could go hand in hand in supporting sustainable entrepreneurship. This is an important question both on a theoretical level as well as practice level and it will also help with the previous call of having the need to do more research to understand which values drive sustainable entrepreneurship (Rajasekaran, 2013) and via which processes.

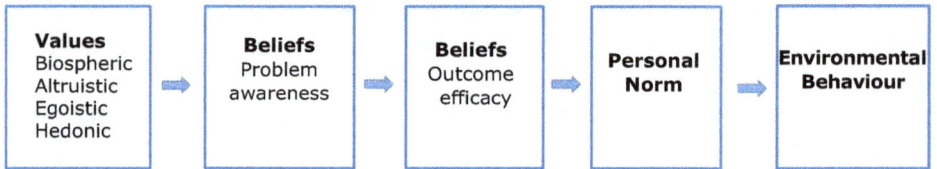

| **Values** Biospheric Altruistic Egoistic Hedonic | ⇨ | **Beliefs** Problem awareness | ⇨ | **Beliefs** Outcome efficacy | ⇨ | **Personal Norm** | ⇨ | **Environmental Behaviour** |

Figure 6.2: Value–belief–norm theory. Adapted from Stern (2000).

3.3 Indirect Effect of Values as a Moderator

Values as general motivating factors do not only predict behaviour indirectly via intermediate mediators like in the VBN model. Values could also interact with contextual factors in predicting sustainable actions and behaviours. In other words, values moderate the effect of contextual factors in predicting sustainable behaviours. For instance, in one study researchers investigated how cultural context interacts with entrepreneurship values in predicting owning an enterprise (Morales et al., 2019). They used two values from Schwartz's value conceptualisation that are most conventionally associated with entrepreneurship: self-enhancement and openness to change. Cultural context was measured with two dimensions from Schwartz's cultural classification, mastery and egalitarianism, which reflected expectations about how members of that country should behave (Schwartz, 1999) and that were found to be positively related to early stage entrepreneurial activity (Liñán, Fernández-Serrano, & Romero, 2013). As an example, in cultures that score high on mastery as opposed to harmony, people are expected to act independently, be assertive and make use of their skills to achieve goals. In cultures that value egalitarianism as opposed to hierarchy, people are considered equal and are encouraged to change the status quo rather than being confined in their social roles. Morales and colleagues (2019) found that values of openness to change and self-enhancement moderated the relationship between cultural context and having an enterprise. More specifically, a cultural context that values mastery and egalitarianism was found to be particularly stimulating for people with somewhat lower entrepreneurship values. When people had high entrepreneurship values then the cultural context did not matter as people with high entrepreneurship values would pursue their goal irrespective of contextual support. In countries where sustainable entrepreneurship is not desired or supported, context might inhibit the flourishing of sustainable entrepreneurship. Values play a key role in motivating individuals to pursue sustainable entrepreneurship where contextual support is missing.

The supporting function of context has also been investigated in other studies in relation to different contextual factors. For instance, Ruepert, Keizer and Steg (2017) looked at perceived Corporate Environmental Responsibility (CER) among employees and how it affects pro-environmental actions at work. A positive perception of CER would be indicative of employees thinking that they are working in a context that prioritises environmental goals and that follows a roadmap and strategy to implement these goals. Findings revealed that perceived CER was positively related to pro-environmental actions at work, particularly for employees with weak to moderate biospheric values. This indicates that for those who are very strongly biospheric, contextual factors such as CER do not need to be in place. People with a very strong biospheric concern would carry out the desired actions anyway irrespective of contextual reminders or support. However, for those with a somewhat lower concern for the environment (weak or moderate biospheric values), contextual support would be needed to remind them about the right behaviour. Therefore, findings of Ruepert and colleagues suggest that CER could act like a contextual reminder for employees, motivating them to do the right thing even though they normally have a lower concern for the environment.

Perceptions about a sustainable entrepreneur at the workplace could act like a contextual factor as well. Sustainable entrepreneurs might have a transformational influence over their colleagues and employees by being a good role model with their own sustainable behaviour at work as well as with their sustainable business goals for the enterprise. This is an important leadership role given that employee pro-environmental behaviour at work could help with the reduction of CO_2 emissions. In a recent replication of this theorisation of Ruepert and colleagues (2017), we investigated whether perceived environmental transformational leadership would indeed positively impact pro-environmental intentions at work (Saral, Ünal, & De Jong, forthcoming). Environmental transformational leadership is defined as being able to create a concrete environmental vision at work and inspiring employees to follow that vision without being coercive, but rather by being an inspiring role model (Graves, Sarkis, & Zhu, 2013). We found that perceived environmental transformational leadership is related to acting pro-environmentally at work, particularly among those with a lower concern for the environment (weak biospheric values). Similarly, environmental transformational leadership was related to a higher intrinsic motivation to act pro-environmentally at work, particularly among those who are normally not concerned for the environment. Our findings, therefore, support the theoretical reasoning of Ruepert and colleagues (2017) by showing that environmental transformational leadership could also act like a contextual factor supporting employee pro-environmental behaviour.

As sustainable entrepreneurs are usually those with a strong focus on protecting the environment and sustaining natural resources, they can be regarded as environmental leaders as well. Therefore, they could act like transformational leaders in the workplace who are capable of having an influence on daily pro-environmental decisions of their employees. On top of the positive impact they can create with a sustainable business, they could also impact employee behaviours at work positively, which would be another way to help reduce CO_2 emissions resulting from unsustainable businesses and practices.

4 Conclusions

Sustainable entrepreneurship is a field that is rapidly growing but still in its infancy. We need theories that are particularly relevant for research and applications in the field. We argue that existing theories from environmental psychology can be used and replicated in the field of sustainable entrepreneurship in order to test whether they are readily applicable. That is because sustainable entrepreneurship is a domain that involves various actions and intentions that are pro-environmental. In addition, new theories can be developed based on insights from environmental psychology that can explain not only sustainable entrepreneurship intentions and behaviours but also related processes, such as sustainable problem and opportunity recognition.

The current chapter had the aim to introduce an alternative value conceptualisation adapted from Schwartz's value theory, that is specific to the study of pro-environmental actions, and that is currently the prominent approach to study the motivational roots of pro-environmental actions (Steg et al., 2014a). We provided a summary of the literature on how values might directly or indirectly influence pro-environmental intentions and actions, and which theories, like the value–belief–norm theory, are applicable to understand the process behind value-driven decisions for sustainable behaviours. Next, we discussed how this specific value conceptualisation could predict sustainable entrepreneurship intentions and behaviours, and via which processes. Finally, we also mentioned new avenues for research in sustainable entrepreneurship, which we will elaborate on.

One line of research that is currently missing is whether self-transcendence values drive intentions and actions to become a sustainable entrepreneur or not. While self-enhancement values have been conventionally put together with entrepreneurship, we reason that self-transcendence values could be equally, if not more, related to sustainable entrepreneurship intentions and behaviours. As scholars nested different values under the dimension of self-transcendence (De Groot & Steg, 2008; Schwartz; 2012; Stern et al., 1998; Steg et al., 2014a), we propose to particularly focus on biospheric and altruistic values as these were found to provide a stable basis for pro-environmental actions in general (De Groot & Steg, 2009). How would biospheric and altruistic values uniquely contribute to the prediction of sustainable entrepreneurship intentions? How are they related to the processes involved in sustainable entrepreneurship such as problem recognition? As biospheric and altruistic values might also be in conflict when the person needs to choose between engaging in an environmental versus pro-social action, a related research question is whether different forms of sustainable entrepreneurship (i.e., focusing on preserving the well-being of the environment versus well-being of communities and others) are rooted in different values. In line with this argument, one might expect altruistic values to be more strongly associated with social entrepreneurship than sustainable entrepreneurship for instance, as this would put the emphasis on improving the well-being of communities and others, which needs to be tested by future research.

A second line of research follows from the first one and concerns whether the seemingly contradicting values under self-enhancement and self-transcendence could actually be less conflicting in the domain of sustainable entrepreneurship. This can be studied by asking for value prioritisations and linking these to sustainable entrepreneurship intentions and processes, such as sustainable problem and opportunity recognition. For instance: do biospheric and egoistic values predict sustainable entrepreneurship intentions positively and equally strongly? And how are these values prioritised by sustainable entrepreneurs?

A third line of research is to study how sustainable entrepreneurs would deal with sustainability challenges in the face of scaling up. Indeed, a fast scaling up of enterprises associated with economic growth might pose dangers to sustainability, which might threaten the fulfilment of biospheric motivations. How would sustainable entrepreneurs deal with such challenges and how would they ensure to safeguard sustainability in the face of high profitability? In a similar vein, prioritising sustainability at the start-up phase could jeopardise profitability, leaving the sustainable entrepreneur with the danger of ceasing their business ventures (Thelken, Ünal, & Enthoven, 2021). As such, it is important to study how sustainable entrepreneurs find a balance between the fulfilment of sustainability and economic goals, and whether these goals are directly related to their strongly endorsed values.

A final and fourth line of research concerns the study of cultural context and how it might facilitate or impair the emergence of sustainable entrepreneurs. The dominant view of cultural context having a strong and direct influence on entrepreneurship likelihood is already challenged (Stephan & Pathak, 2016). Indeed, cultural context, described by using aggregate values as representing the context, is shown to be a distal and mainly an indirect predictor of entrepreneurship endeavours (Stephan & Uhlaner, 2010; Stephan & Pathak, 2016). How does cultural context exert its influence? What are some relevant mediating and moderating factors that can explain the influence of cultural context particularly for sustainable entrepreneurship likelihood?

The field of sustainable entrepreneurship will be strengthened when research is more theory based and where applications come from theory. We invite scholars to explore the potential of other theories from environmental psychology to be used in sustainable entrepreneurship research.

References

Bouman, T., Steg, L., & Kiers, H. A. (2018). Measuring values in environmental research: A test of an environmental portrait value questionnaire. *Frontiers in Psychology, 9*, 564.

Dean, T. J., & McMullen, J. S. (2007). Toward a theory of sustainable entrepreneurship: Reducing environmental degradation through entrepreneurial action. *Journal of Business Venturing, 22*(1), 50–76.

De Groot, J. I., & Steg, L. (2008). Value orientations to explain beliefs related to environmental significant behavior: How to measure egoistic, altruistic, and biospheric value orientations. *Environment and Behavior, 40*(3), 330–354.

De Groot, J. I., & Steg, L. (2009). Mean or green: Which values can promote stable pro-environmental behavior? *Conservation Letters, 2*(2), 61–66.

Elkington, J. (2004) Enter the triple bottom line. In A. Henriques & J. Richardson (Eds.), *The Triple Bottom Line, Does It All Add Up? Assessing the Sustainability of Business and CSR* pp. 1–16. London: Earthscan Publications Ltd.

Enthoven, M. (2021). *Unpacking opportunity recognition for sustainable entrepreneurship.* Doctoral Dissertation. University of Groningen.

Fayolle, A., Liñán, F., & Moriano, J. A. (2014). Beyond entrepreneurial intentions: Values and motivations in entrepreneurship. *International Entrepreneurship and Management Journal, 10*(4), 679–689.

Gorgievski, M. J., Ascalon, M. E., & Stephan, U. (2011). Small business owners' success criteria, a values approach to personal differences. *Journal of Small Business Management, 49*(2), 207–232.

Graves, L. M., Sarkis, J., & Zhu, Q. (2013). How transformational leadership and employee motivation combine to predict employee proenvironmental behaviors in China. *Journal of Environmental Psychology, 35*, 81–91.

Hueso, J. A., Jaén, I., Liñán, F., & Basuki, W. (2020). The influence of collectivistic personal values on the formation of entrepreneurial intentions. *International Small Business Journal, 38*(5), 449–473.

Intergovernmental Panel on Climate Change (IPCC) (2022). Summary for policymakers. In H.-O. Pörtner, D. C. Roberts, E. S. Poloczanska, K. Mintenbeck, M. Tignor, A. Alegría, M. Craig, S. Langsdorf, S. Löschke, V. Möller & A. Okem (Eds.), *Climate Change 2022: Impacts, Adaptation, and Vulnerability. Contribution of Working Group II to the Sixth Assessment Report of the Intergovernmental Panel on Climate Change* Cambridge: Cambridge University Press.

Jakovcevic, A., & Steg, L. (2013). Sustainable transportation in Argentina: Values, beliefs, norms and car use reduction. *Transportation Research Part F: Traffic Psychology and Behaviour, 20*, 70–79.

Kirkley, W. W. (2016). Entrepreneurial behaviour: The role of values. *International Journal of Entrepreneurial Behavior & Research, 22*(3), 290–328.

Kuckertz, A., & Wagner, M. (2010). The influence of sustainability orientation on entrepreneurial intentions – Investigating the role of business experience. *Journal of Business Venturing, 25*(5), 524–539.

Liñán, F., Fernández Serrano, J., & Romero, I. (2013). Necessity and opportunity entrepreneurship: The mediating effect of culture. *Revista de Economía Mundial, 33*, 21–47.

McGrath, R. G., MacMillan, I. C., & Scheinberg, S. (1992). Elitists, risk-takers, and rugged individualists? An exploratory analysis of cultural differences between entrepreneurs and non-entrepreneurs. *Journal of Business Venturing, 7*(2), 115–135.

Morales, C., Holtschlag, C., Masuda, A. D., & Marquina, P. (2019). In which cultural contexts do individual values explain entrepreneurship? An integrative values framework using Schwartz's theories. *International Small Business Journal, 37*(3), 241–267.

Muñoz, P. (2017). A cognitive map of sustainable decision-making in entrepreneurship: A configurational approach. *International Journal of Entrepreneurial Behavior & Research, 24*(3), 787–813.

Namazkhan, M. (2022). Modeling household energy consumption to understand sustainable energy behaviour: An integrated approach. Doctoral Dissertation. University of Groningen.

Nordlund, A. M., & Garvill, J. (2003). Effects of values, problem awareness, and personal norm on willingness to reduce personal car use. *Journal of Environmental Psychology, 23*(4), 339–347.

Perlaviciute, G., Steg, L., Contzen, N., Roeser, S., & Huijts, N. (2018). Emotional responses to energy projects: Insights for responsible decision making in a sustainable energy transition. *Sustainability, 10* (7), 2526.

Rajasekaran, B. (2013). Sustainable entrepreneurship: Past researches and future directions. *Journal of Entrepreneurship and Management, 2*(1), 20.

Ruepert, A. M., Keizer, K., & Steg, L. (2017). The relationship between corporate environmental responsibility, employees' biospheric values and pro-environmental behaviour at work. *Journal of Environmental Psychology, 54*, 65–78.

Santos, S. C., Neumeyer, X., Caetano, A., & Liñán, F. (2021). Understanding how and when personal values foster entrepreneurial behavior: A humane perspective. *Journal of Small Business Management, 59*(3), 373–396.

Saral, H. C., Unal, A. B., & De Jong, G. (forthcoming). Exploring the direct and indirect mechanisms behind the influence of environmental transformational leadership on employee green behaviors.

Schwartz, S. H. (1973). Normative explanations of helping behavior: A critique, proposal, and empirical test. *Journal of Experimental Social Psychology, 9*(4), 349–364.

Schwartz, S. H. (1992). Universals in the content and structure of values: Theoretical advances and empirical tests in 20 countries. *Advances in Experimental Social Psychology, 25*, 1–65.

Schwartz, S. H. (2012). An overview of the Schwartz theory of basic values. *Online Readings in Psychology and Culture, 2*(1), 2307–2919.

Schwartz, S. H., & Bardi, A. (2001). Value hierarchies across cultures: Taking a similarities perspective. *Journal of Cross-cultural Psychology, 32*(3), 268–290.

Schwartz, S. H. (1999). A theory of cultural values and some implications for work. *Applied Psychology, 48*(1), 23–47.

Shane, S., & Venkataraman, S. (2000). The promise of entrepreneurship as a field of research. *Academy of Management Review, 25*(1), 217–226.

Shepherd, D. A., & Patzelt, H. (2011). The new field of sustainable entrepreneurship: Studying entrepreneurial action linking 'what is to be sustained' with 'what is to be developed'. *Entrepreneurship Theory and Practice, 35*(1), 137–163.

Steg, L., Bolderdijk, J. W., Keizer, K., & Perlaviciute, G. (2014a). An integrated framework for encouraging pro-environmental behaviour: The role of values, situational factors and goals. *Journal of Environmental Psychology, 38*, 104–115.

Steg, L., Dreijerink, L., & Abrahamse, W. (2005). Factors influencing the acceptability of energy policies: A test of VBN theory. *Journal of Environmental Psychology, 25*(4), 415–425.

Steg, L., Perlaviciute, G., Van der Werff, E., & Lurvink, J. (2014b) The significance of hedonic values for environmentally relevant attitudes, preferences, and actions. *Environment and Behavior, 46*(2), 163–192.

Stephan, U., & Pathak, S. (2016). Beyond cultural values? Cultural leadership ideals and entrepreneurship. *Journal of Business Venturing, 31*(5), 505–523.

Stephan, U., & Uhlaner, L. M. (2010). Performance-based vs socially supportive culture: A cross-national study of descriptive norms and entrepreneurship. *Journal of International Business Studies, 41*(8), 1347–1364.

Stern, P. C., Dietz, T., & Guagnano, G. A. (1998). A brief inventory of values. *Educational and Psychological Measurement, 58*(6), 984–1001.

Stern, P. C. (2000). New environmental theories: Toward a coherent theory of environmentally significant behavior. *Journal of Social Issues, 56*(3), 407–424.

Thelken, H. N., & de Jong, G. (2020). The impact of values and future orientation on intention formation within sustainable entrepreneurship. *Journal of Cleaner Production*, *266*, 122052.

Thelken, H. N., Ünal, A. B., & Enthoven, M. P. M. (2021). Individual resolution of (paradoxical) tensions between economic and sustainable goals in growing sustainable enterprises. Working paper. Included in the *Academy of Management Proceedings* as Cognitive Strategies to Resolve Paradoxical Tensions in Sustainable Enterprises.

Thøgersen, J., & Ölander, F. (2002). Human values and the emergence of a sustainable consumption pattern: A panel study. *Journal of Economic Psychology*, *23*(5), 605–630.

Ünal, A. B., Steg, L., & Gorsira, M. (2018). Values versus environmental knowledge as triggers of a process of activation of personal norms for eco-driving. *Environment and Behavior*, *50*(10), 1092–1118.

Ünal, A. B., Steg, L., & Granskaya, J. (2019). 'To support or not to support, that is the question'. Testing the VBN theory in predicting support for car use reduction policies in Russia. *Transportation Research Part A: Policy and Practice*, *119*, 73–81.

Hendrik Thelken, Gjalt de Jong

7 Back to the Sustainable Future: The Influence of the Big Five Personality Traits on Consideration of Future Consequences

Abstract: Despite consideration of future consequences as key for sustainability, the literature has not explained why individual variations in consideration of future consequences exist. Future consequences of decisions are important for sustainability because the benefits of sustainability goals might only be capitalized in the future, while their costs are incurred in the present. The aim of this study is to investigate the impact of the Big Five personality traits on individual variations of consideration of future consequences. This study is among the first to analyze this causal relationship using longitudinal data of 3,444 Dutch individuals. The empirical results highlight the importance of all Big Five personality traits either for short-term or for long-term consideration of future consequences. These findings contribute to the debate on the role of the future in sustainability decision-making by integrating psychology and future orientation literature.

Keywords: consideration of future consequences, Big Five personality traits, sustainability, sustainable entrepreneurship

1 Introduction

The survival of the global society and planet Earth are under threat. In the social sphere persistent poverty of billions of people, rising inequalities among countries in terms of wealth, opportunity, unemployment as well as various humanitarian crises such as terrorism or other forms of violent extremism threaten to reverse the progress made in the last decades. These threats make the need to consider future consequences of contemporaneous behavior and decisions more relevant than ever. The key role of the future in sustainability directly derives from the definition of sustainable development defined by the Brundtland Commission as "the development that meets the needs of the present without compromising the ability of future generations to meet their own needs" (Brundtland, 1987: 43). Sustainability cannot do without a consideration of future consequences. Consideration of future consequences (CFC) concerns "the extent to which individuals consider the potential outcomes of their

---

Hendrik Thelken, Gjalt de Jong, Faculty Campus Fryslân, University of Groningen, Groningen, the Netherlands

https://doi.org/10.1515/9783110756159-009

current behaviors and the extent to which they are influenced by these potential outcomes" (Strathman et al., 1994: 743). Research has acknowledged the intertemporal and intergenerational dimensions of sustainability (Arnocky, Milfont, & Nicol, 2014); however, these approaches lack explanations as to why individual variation in consideration of future consequences exist (Joireman & King, 2016; Strathman et al., 1994). Individual variation in the consideration of future consequences arguably exists. Some individuals do consider future consequences and others do not.

Research on the individual-level resolution of intertemporal dilemmas has gained momentum but is mainly concerned about the outcomes or consequences of future orientation. Consideration of future consequences has been valuable to explain intertemporal dilemmas in economics (Webley & Nyhus, 2006), pro-environmental action (Arnocky, Milfont, & Nicol, 2014), individual differences in sustainability (Joireman et al., 2001) and in sustainable entrepreneurship (Thelken & de Jong, 2020). Sustainable entrepreneurs contribute to the transition toward a more circular economy in the future through the integration of external dynamic capabilities into their enterprises (Eikelenboom & de Jong, 2019). Sustainable entrepreneurs need the cognitive ability of future orientation for forward thinking (Lans, Blok, & Wesselink, 2014) or backward induction (Hahn & Knight, 2021). In a recent study, Thelken and de Jong (2020) find that consideration of future consequences positively influences the intention to become a sustainable entrepreneur.

With few exceptions, however, most studies have not explained variations in consideration of future consequences. The first contribution of this study concerns understanding how individuals develop their consideration of future consequences. In addressing this issue, this research responds to the calls for more individual-level research on the determinants of future consequences (Strathman et al., 1994; Joireman & King, 2016). We argue that personality traits determine variations in consequences of future consideration because personality traits are shaped by life experience, learning, and family backgrounds (Trommsdorff, 1983; Strathman et al., 1994). We use the Neuroticism-Extraversion-Openness (NEO) five-factor Inventory of the Big Five personality traits to explain variations in consideration of future consequences, which is a well-established and consistent measurement of personality traits (Costa & McCrae, 1992b). The theoretical mechanisms that explain the causal relationships between the Big Five personality traits and an individual's consideration of future consequences is the first main contribution of this study.

The second contribution consists of testing our hypothesized relationships with a longitudinal panel data set of 3,444 Dutch individuals (Dutch Household Surveys, CentERdata, Tilburg University, http://centerdata.nl/en/). These longitudinal data enable us to test our hypotheses using advanced quantitative methods that simultaneously solve two methodological issues in the literature. First, existing CFC studies predominantly used small-scale and laboratory samples with students as the unit of analysis. Such cross-sectional data impede an in-depth analysis of causal mechanisms. Moreover, although students may offer a relevant empirical context, it is also well-known that students can behave differently from non-student individuals. Also, the results of different small-scale and cross-sectional samples are difficult to compare due to heterogeneity in research design and research contexts. The DHS dataset that is employed in this study is large, longitudinal, and incorporates (Dutch) citizens; it therefore addresses the aforementioned limitations. Second, our dataset enables us to address possible time-dependent dynamics in consideration of future consequences (Toepoel, 2010) and in personality traits. Our study is among the first to test the time-varying causal relationships between personality traits and consideration of future consequences.

The outline of this paper is as follows. We begin by formulating our hypotheses about the effects of the Big Five personality traits on CFC. Then, we introduce this paper's research methodology addressing issues related to the collection of our data and our measures of the variables. Following that, we present our empirical evidence. Finally, we conclude with an appraisal, discussing the study limitations and offering reflections on opportunities for future research.

2 Theory and Hypotheses

2.1 Theoretical Foundations

On a cognitive level, future oriented individuals extend personal considerations into the future, which include the future consequences of their behavior. They are therefore better able to cognitively structure future events into a causal order (Trommsdorff, 1983). This perspective is rooted in the foundational work of Strathman et al. (1994) who developed the CFC measurement instrument. The CFC measurement instrument consists of items measuring consideration of future consequences and of items measuring consideration of immediate consequences. Individuals can have a long-term or a short-term future orientation. The CFC measurement instrument explicitly accounts for this. The original work of Strathman et al. (1994) has led to a substantial number of studies aiming to explain behavior in intertemporal trade-off settings using an individual's CFC scores (for a review, see Thelken, 2021). These studies have found that individuals scoring high on CFC are more likely to eat healthy, exercise more, and sleep better. In the field of economics, high CFC scores have been associated with lower levels of impulsive buying behavior, temporal discounting and higher savings levels. Ethical studies report that those high in CFC show more rigorous moral reasoning, have higher moral character and are more considerate of social responsibility. These relationships are reflected in a greater likelihood of environmentally conscious behavior, a greater general concern for the environment, a higher engagement in pro-environmental political actions and more positive attitudes toward sustainable entrepreneurship.

Taking the above into account, CFC is very valuable to explain future oriented behavior including sustainability and sustainable entrepreneurship where intergenerational and intertemporal dimensions are center stage (Thelken & de Jong, 2020). However, it remains unclear which factors determine variations in CFC. Without understanding why variations in CFC exist, the use and change of CFC in sustainability and sustainable entrepreneurship is challenging. For this, we use the personality trait literature.

Strathman et al. (1994) concluded that most individuals will have developed consideration for future consequences by the time they reach their adulthood, which is in line with similar findings on future orientation and age development (Steinberg et al., 2009). Strathman et al. argue that this might be due to events in the early stages of life or family-specific contexts. In a similar vein, it is argued that by the time of adolescence, individuals have developed a relatively stable set of personality traits (Costa & McCrae, 1992b). Personality traits are defined as "relatively enduring patterns of thoughts, feelings, and behaviors that reflect the tendency to respond in certain ways under certain circumstances" (Roberts, 2009: 140). Personality traits therefore determine how individuals respond in situations where they have to consider the future consequences of their behavior. We use the revised version of the NEO Big Five personality trait inventory measuring conscientiousness, agreeableness, extraversion, openness, and neuroticism, which are the most important of all personality traits (Costa & McCrae, 1992a). The underlying mechanisms of our hypotheses relate to arguments presented in intertemporal choice theories. Temporal discounting theories build on the utility theory and the discounted-utility models (Frederick, Loewenstein, & O'Donoghue, 2002). The main proposition is that, ceteris paribus, receiving a reward today is valued more than receiving the reward in the (near) future (Hirsh, Morisano, & Peterson, 2008). In a similar vein, neuropsychological studies show that a delay of gratification is closely related to stimuli in the dopaminergic incentive-reward circuits in the ventral striatum (Hirsh et al., 2008). These stimuli within the ventral striatum are moderated through cognitive abilities and through personality (Shamosh et al., 2008). Below, we hypothesize that similar discounting and neuropsychological mechanisms explain the impact of personality traits on CFC (Steinberg et al., 2009).

2.2 Hypotheses

2.2.1 Conscientiousness

Conscientiousness is the first personality trait that we relate to CFC. Conscientiousness captures a person's discipline and control. Conscientious individuals are organized, self-disciplined, and dutiful (Costa & McCrae, 1992b). These underlying dimensions of this personality trait explain the hypothesized positive effect of conscientiousness on CFC (Nurmi, 1991; Strathman et al., 1994). This manifests itself in behaviors that are beneficial only in the long term, such as the greater tendency to save for the future (Nyhus & Webley, 2001), greater health concerns (Jerram & Coleman, 1999) or environmental preservation (Hirsh, 2014). These examples show that more conscientious individuals are able to delay the reward of their behaviors and hence can be expected to use a lower discount rate when it comes to intertemporal choices.

Interestingly, recent research has found that conscientiousness and cognitive abilities are mutually reinforcing. This also refutes the initial argument that intelligence and conscientiousness are negatively correlated and that the latter compensates for a lack of the former (Murray, McCabe, & Ballard, 2014). Additionally, an advanced cognitive ability of an individual has been related to better anterior prefrontal cortical functions. In other words, more conscientious individuals can be expected to have greater cognitive resources to make controlled decisions, which in turn suppress short-term stimuli from the mid-brain dopaminergic incentive reward system (Hirsh et al., 2008). We thus hypothesize:

Hypothesis 1. High scores in conscientiousness lead to higher CFC.

2.2.2 Agreeableness

Agreeableness is the second personality trait that we relate to CFC. Agreeableness can be described as the tendency of an individual to be willing to comply with and trust other people. Accordingly, more agreeable persons show greater concern and more compassion for society (Hirsh, 2014). In a similar vein, Trommsdorff (1983) already found that socialization determines a person's future orientation. Therefore, the more agreeable a person, the greater his/her social intelligence and moral reasoning resulting from an outward thinking, altruistic personality. A more optimistic outlook of the future could be the result. Indeed, research shows that future-oriented people are more optimistic, which is a key facet of agreeableness (Sharpe, Martin, & Roth, 2011). Optimism could lead to individuals expecting a positive environment in the future, which would lead to flatter temporal discounting curves (Hirsh et al., 2008).

We therefore argue that more agreeable persons have higher considerations of the future consequences of their actions because they are concerned about the social structure of the future. This is due to their greater optimism about the future, the resulting lower discount rates for future gains, and therefore the greater acceptance of delayed rewards. We thus hypothesize:

Hypothesis 2. High scores in agreeableness lead to higher CFC.

2.2.3 Extraversion

Extraversion is the third personality trait that we relate to CFC. Extravert individuals are outgoing, assertive, and talkative, and enjoy human interaction (Costa & McCrae, 1992b). Previous research has related extraversion to high sensational needs (Zuckerman, 1994).

High sensational needs can lead to risk-seeking behavior, which indicates short-termism. Examples are a higher probability of substance abuse (Keough, Zimbardo, & Boyd, 1999) or excessive financial risk taking (Zuckerman, 1994). Accordingly, extravert individuals favor immediate rewards and hence also have a higher discount rate for intertemporal choices and a lower tolerance of delayed gratification (Hirsh et al., 2008).

Neuropsychological studies suggest that heightened sensational needs arise from a stronger mid-brain dopaminergic incentive reward system and that extravert individuals therefore receive larger phasic bursts of dopamine (Hirsh et al., 2008). Considering that mid-brain structures are more receptive to immediate rewards (McClure et al., 2004), extraverts are more receptive to immediate gratifications. These stronger stimuli also reduce the mediating influence of the cognitive ability to develop higher-order mental models to suppress these stimuli. We thus hypothesize:

Hypothesis 3. High scores in extraversion lead to lower CFC.

2.2.4 Openness to Experience

Openness to experience is the fourth personality trait that we relate to CFC. Openness is related to a person's cultural habitat. It describes how open people are to new experiences at a cultural or an intellectual level. Openness to experience manifests itself in a person's ideas and ethical understandings. Individuals scoring high on openness to experience are more inquisitive and value the novelty of new experiences (Nga & Shamuganathan, 2010). Such curiosity and inquisitiveness leads to a stronger motivation for intellectual and educational activities (Moutafi, Furnham, & Paltiel, 2004). This leads to higher crystallized intelligence, that is, the increasing accumulation of knowledge, skills, and information. In addition, open individuals have higher fluid intelligence (Moutafi, Furnham, & Paltiel, 2004). Individuals with high fluid intelligence are quick thinkers, they relate concepts in novel ways, and discover novel approaches to problems.

Previous research provides evidence that more open individuals show higher cognitive abilities and are better able to develop higher cognitive resources to make controlled decisions that suppress the short-term motivated stimuli from the mid-brain dopaminergic incentive reward system (Hirsh et al., 2008). In terms of intertemporal decision-making, more open individuals apply lower temporal discount rates, are more tolerant of delayed gratifications, and are therefore likely to have a higher CFC. We thus hypothesize:

Hypothesis 4. High scores in openness lead to higher CFC.

2.2.5 Neuroticism

Neuroticism is the fifth personality trait that we relate to CFC. Neuroticism describes chronic emotional instability and a tendency toward psychological distress. It represents the opposite of an emotionally stable person, who is predictable and consistent in his/her emotional reactions and overall mood. Previous studies have shown that neurotic individuals are unable to demonstrate the discipline and cognitive stability required for future orientation (Hirsh et al., 2008). Neuroticism thus relates to lower cognitive abilities. This negative relationship to cognitive abilities is mainly determined by the anxiety facet, which impairs cognitive functioning (Moutafi, Furnham, & Paltiel, 2004). Therefore, individuals with lower emotional stability apply higher discount rates (Hirsh et al., 2008). This implies that they derive a greater subjective utility from immediate rewards and behavioral consequences than from future rewards.

Laboratory experiments have shown that neuroticism is negatively related to risk taking. The reason for this is that people scoring high on neuroticism tend to display high levels of harm avoidance and therefore risk aversion (Paulus et al., 2003). In other words, more neurotic individuals try to reduce ambiguity for the long term and try to avoid harm by securing their well-being for as long as possible. This leads to a longer time horizon in their future planning. We thus hypothesize:

Hypothesis 5. High scores in neuroticism lead to higher CFC.

3 Method

3.1 Data and Sample

Our data derives from the Dutch DNB Household Survey (DHS) (CentERdata, Tilburg University, http://www.centerdata.nl/en/). The DHS surveys have been conducted annually since 1993 and they offer representative samples of the Dutch population aged 16 years and older. The yearly DHS survey is a panel survey consisting of six questionnaires, covering approximately 2,000 households from different socioeconomic areas. The DHS survey is conducted online. Participants without Internet access are provided with appropriate equipment, which enables them to complete the survey either via a telephone or via their television set.

We selected DHS surveys that enabled us to measure consideration of future consequences and the Big Five personality traits in the same year. That is, we matched personality trait measures with CFC data based on a unique indicator for the individual and the household. This selection criterion enabled us to use the DHS surveys for 2005, 2009, 2013, 2014, and 2015. We deleted cases with missing observations. We also deleted cases with inadequate answers for one of our control variables, namely education (individuals who either indicated the option "other" or "no education yet," as their educational information was not included in our sample). This selection process resulted in an unbalanced panel dataset for 3,444 individuals corresponding to 5,246 observations (approximately 1.52 observations per individual). Our database provides unique individual-level and longitudinal data for an individual's personality traits, consideration of future consequences, and various sets of control variables for the years 2005, 2009, 2013, 2014, and 2015. The unique features of our database allow us to measure our constructs and to test all our hypothesized causal relationships.

3.2 Measures

3.2.1 Consideration of Future Consequences

The DHS surveys that we selected for our study include the original items of Strathman et al.'s (1994) measure of consideration of future consequences. The size and the longitudinal nature of our database enables us to address and solve the general concern of sampling errors and replicability. In a series of exploratory and confirmatory factor analyses, and using the benefits of our large-scale and longitudinal panel dataset, we developed different measures for consideration of future consequences that are used in the regression analyses (an advanced statistical appendix with econometric details, fit indices, and a comparison of our measures with CFC measures in the literature is available upon request). We developed our measure for CFC in two steps.

In the first step, we used an exploratory principal components analysis with promax rotation to identify the initial CFC factor in our dataset following the recommendation of Matsunaga (2010). Given the size and the longitudinal nature of our database, this approach is appropriate because promax rotation will result in uncorrelated factors. In the second step, following the recommendation of Watkins (2013), we re-tested the initial outcomes of the principal component analysis in the first step by applying a Monte Carlo Principal Component Statistical Analysis (PCSA) parallel simulation with 1,000 replications in the second step.

The outcome of these two steps resulted in two different factors. The first factor is identified as "CFC-Future" (with an eigenvalue 3.23, 29.39 percent of variance explained, $n = 5$, $M = 4.04$, $SD = 1.05$). This factor consists of five items, namely (1) "I think about how things can change in the future, and try to influence those things in my everyday life"; (2) "I often work on things that will only pay off in a couple of years"; (3) "I am willing to sacrifice my well-being in the present to achieve certain goals in the future"; (4) "I think it is important to take warnings about negative consequences of my acts seriously, even if these negative consequences would only occur in the distant future"; and (5) "I think it is more important to work on things that have important consequences in the future, than to work on things that have immediate but less important consequences." All items are measured on a five-point Likert scale ranging from 1 = "Very inaccurate" to 5 = "Very accurate." Negatively formulated items are reversed prior to using them in the factor analyses. The CFC-F scale includes positively formulated items and measures an individual's long-term future orientation. The Cronbach's alpha coefficient of 0.77 for CFC-F is well above the threshold value.

The second factor is identified as "CFC-Immediate" (eigenvalue 2.18, 19.83 percent of variance explained, $n = 3$, $M = 4.46$, $SD = 1.14$). This factor consists of three items, namely (1) "In general, I ignore warnings about future problems because I think these problems will be solved before they get critical"; (2) "I think there is no need to sacrifice things now for problems that lie in the future, because it will always be possible to solve these future problems later"; and (3) "I only respond to urgent problems, trusting that problems that come up later can be solved in a later stage." Negatively formulated items are reversed prior to using them in the factor analyses. This factor measures the susceptibility of an individual to act on considerations of immediate future consequences. The Cronbach's alpha of 0.74 for this factor is satisfactory. Note that the Pearson correlation coefficient between the two factors is 0.22, which justifies the promax rotation. The fact that we identified two different factors indicates that no issues with common-method variance in our database exist. We used the additive scales of the items for each of the two factors as the measure for CFC-F and CFC-I in the regression analysis.

In the regression study, we also included an overall measure of consideration of future consequences. For this overall measure, we added the aforementioned items and used this as the measure for overall CFC. This overall CFC measure is very similar to the ones used in other CFC studies (Strathman et al., 1994; Hevey et al., 2010). It therefore serves as an additional benchmark to test the hypothesized causal relations between the different personality traits and consideration of future consequences.

3.2.2 Big Five Personality Traits

Our database enables us to use the NEO inventory of the Big Five personality traits using ten items per personality trait (for a detailed overview of the Big Five personality trait items, see Costa & McCrae, 1992a, 1992b). All the items for each of the five personality traits were measured on a five-point Likert scale ranging from 1 = "Very inaccurate" to 5 = "Very accurate." All negatively formulated items were reversed prior to using them in our analyses. We used the averaged summed scales of items per personality trait in the regression analyses. The Cronbach's alphas for each of the five personality traits range from 0.76 to 0.87 and exceed the threshold values.

3.2.3 Control Variables

Several sets of variables were included to control for alternative explanations of the predicted relationships. First, this study included four socioeconomic variables and controlled for intelligence and environmental stability (Dunkel & Weber, 2010; Nurmi, 1991; Toepoel, 2010): education (measured on a 7-point scale, with 1 = the lowest level of education and 7 = the highest level of education), having children (measured with a dummy variable with 1 = if the individual has one or more children and 0 = when an individual does not have children), marital status (measured with a dummy variable with 1 = if the individual is married and 0 = if the individual is not married), and employment (measured with a dummy variable with 1 = if the individual is employed and 0 = if the individual is not employed). Second, this study controlled for the potential ex ante positive effects of higher income on future orientation and planning (Webley & Nyhus, 2006). We measure the natural logarithm of individual income in constant prices using 2015 as the benchmark year. Third, we controlled for demographic influences and included the individual's age and gender (measured with a dummy variable that 1 = for males and 0 = for females). Fourth, in line With Strathman et al. (1994), we controlled for the potential positive ex ante effect of better health on CFC (health status is measured on a 5-point Likert scale with 1 = "Excellent health" and 5 = "Poor health"). Fifth, we controlled for time effects and included year dummies for 2005, 2009, 2013, 2014, and 2015.

3.3 Estimation Procedure

The size and longitudinal nature of our database enabled us to use advanced and appropriate estimation techniques. We estimated the influence of each of the five personality traits on overall CFC, CFC-F, and CFC-I using two-way generalized least squares random effects models including Mundlak fixed effects. The advantage of the Mundlak specification is that it enables including time-invariant variables such as gender within the model (Mundlak, 1978). Furthermore, we controlled for entity-fixed effects that would indicate individual changes in personality scores (for the plasticity hypothesis see, e.g., Roberts & Mroczek, 2008). Model 1 specifies our estimation techniques:

$$CFC_{it} = \alpha + \sum_{i=1}^{5} \beta T_{it} + \delta X_{it} + \gamma \underline{Z}_{it} + \tau_t + \theta_i + \vartheta_{it} \tag{7.1}$$

CFC_{it} is measured as the loading item average of consideration of future consequences of individual i at time t. T_{it} is the vector of the five personality trait variables, X_{it} a vector of covariates of control variables, $\underline{Z}_{it}$ is the mean of all time-varying variables as specified by Mundlak (1978), τ_t are the time dummies for each year, θ_i is the random effects for individual i, and ϑ_{it} is the zero-mean residual. In all models, one time dummy is omitted to avoid perfect multicollinearity.

4 Results

In our dataset, CFC-I and CFC-F show significant within-variation degrees of approximately 0.40 to 0.50 scale points in the 2005–2015 period. This indicates that the two CFC scales are not stable over longer periods and confirms the need to analyze consideration of future consequences longitudinally as is reported in this study. The same conclusion applies to the Big Five personality trait measures (a statistical appendix with details is available upon request). Overall, our data for the personality traits supports the plasticity hypothesis (Roberts & Mroczek, 2008).

Prior to the regression analyses, we performed the usual diagnostic tests for multicollinearity. The diagnostic tests indicated no multicollinearity problems within the two-way random effects models, including those with Mundlak fixed effects (with condition indices below 30, variance inflation factors lower than ten and all correlation coefficients significantly below absolute values of 0.50). A summary of the standardized estimation results is presented in Table 7.1. A discussion of the main findings follows (with significant control variables in line with expectations).

Table 7.1: Summary of the study results.

	Overall CFC		CFC-Future		CFC-Immediate	
	β	t-Stat	β	t-Stat	β	t-Stat
Panel A: Big Five						
Openness	0.62	(1.27)	0.10	(1.55)	0.07	(0.87)
Conscientiousness	1.05***	(2.63)	0.11**	(2.11)	0.15**	(2.17)
Extraversion	−1.06***	(2.54)	−0.00	(0.01)	−0.24***	(3.31)
Agreeableness	0.98**	(2.22)	0.12**	(2.08)	0.04	(0.48)
Neuroticism	0.39	(1.03)	0.16***	(3.14)	−0.07	(1.17)
Panel B: Controls						
Gender	1.01***	(3.30)	0.21***	(5.37)	0.04	(0.95)
Marital status	1.39**	(2.22)	0.26***	(3.04)	0.03	(0.31)
Children	0.72	(1.23)	0.07	(0.93)	0.08	(0.76)
Health	−0.61**	(2.07)	−0.03	(0.80)	−0.06	(1.12)
Employment	0.07	(0.14)	0.02	(0.22)	0.05	(0.57)
Education	−0.06	(0.14)	0.00	(0.01)	−0.06	(0.77)
Income	−0.05	(0.76)	0.02	(0.27)	−0.01	(0.84)
Year dummy 2005	−0.78	(1.35)	0.03	(0.35)	−0.15	(1.57)
Year dummy 2009	−1.65***	(2.95)	−0.16***	(2.11)	−0.12	(1.26)
Year dummy 2015	−1.23***	(2.49)	−0.08	(1.21)	−0.19**	(2.29)
χ^2(time)	18.06***	[0.00]	31.00***	[0.00]	7.68*	[0.05]
χ^2(Mundlak)	36.01***	[0.00]	41.66***	[0.00]	22.49*	[0.07]
Pseudo R^2	0.10		0.12		0.04	
No. observations	5,246		5,246		5,246	

Hypothesis 1 predicted a positive impact of conscientiousness on CFC. Table 7.1 shows this hypothesis is supported: a one unit increase on the conscientiousness score leads to a significant 1.05 unit increase on the overall CFC scale ($p < 0.01$). Panels B and C of Table 7.1 show that a one unit increase on the conscientiousness scale leads to a significant 0.11 unit increase for CFC-Future and a significant 0.15 unit increase for CFC-Immediate, respectively (both with $p < 0.05$). Conscientiousness therefore is important for both, the buffer and the susceptibility hypotheses. This result indicates that higher conscientiousness leads to higher CFC-Future and CFC-Immediate, which buffers the effects of temptations of immediate rewards and leads to less susceptibility to act on the immediate consequences of activities.

Hypothesis 2 predicted that agreeableness is positively related to CFC. Table 7.1 reports that Hypothesis 2 is supported: agreeableness is significantly and positively related to overall CFC ($\beta = 0.98$, $p < 0.05$). Table 7.1 also shows that a one unit increase on the agreeableness scale leads to a significant 0.12 unit increase in CFC-Future. However, no significant effects of agreeableness on CFC-Immediate was found. This illustrates the relative importance of the social intelligence and optimism facets as crucial mechanisms in the relationship between an individual's future orientation and agreeableness. The results show that individuals with higher agreeability scores are more considerate of the consequences of their behavior for the long-term future (CFC-F) than for the immediate future (CFC-I).

Hypothesis 3 predicted a negative relationship between extraversion and CFC. Table 1 reports that this hypothesis is supported. Extraversion is strongly significant and negatively related to overall CFC ($\beta = -1.06$, $p < 0.05$). The analyses for the two sub-dimensions of future consequences shows this effect is driven by the negative effect of extraversion on CFC-Immediate ($\beta = -0.24$, $p < 0.001$). Individuals scoring high in extraversion are more susceptible to the benefits of prioritizing the immediate future consequences of their actions over the long-term consequences.

Hypothesis 4 predicted a positive relationship between openness and CFC. Table 7.1 shows that this hypothesis is not supported. The effect of openness on overall CFC, CFC-Future, and CFC-Immediate is positive but not significant for all of these relationships. This implies that openness to experience does not offer a significant explanation for individual differences in CFC.

Hypothesis 5 predicated a negative relationship between neuroticism and CFC. Table 7.1 shows that this hypothesis is not supported. Neuroticism does not have a significant effect on overall CFC. Furthermore, Table 7.1 shows that a unit increase on the neuroticism scale leads to a strongly significant 0.16 unit increase in CFC-Future ($p < 0.01$). This positive effect is not in line with our hypothesis and with previous research that suggested that more neurotic individuals do not display the discipline and cognitive ability for any orientation on the future consequences of their behavior and actions (Hirsh et al., 2008).

4.1 Robustness Tests

Several additional analyses were performed to test for robustness. First, the regression study was repeated using different measurements for CFC. We found that using averaged or factor scores for overall CFC, CFC-Future, and CFC-Immediate instead of the additive scores reported in Table 7.1, did not change the results in terms of the signs or the significance levels of the estimated parameter coefficients.

Second, we tested for potential censored effects. The CFC-Future and CFC-Immediate measures might be biased due to left or right censoring of the measures. We therefore employed a series of Tobit regression models to test for bias due to left or right censoring. The Tobit regression results are similar to the ones reported in Table 7.1 further confirming the robustness of our findings.

Third, the possibility of non-linear relationships between the variables of interest was investigated by using interaction terms with two-way Generalized Least Square specifications of our models. Individuals might have a tendency to provide mean-centered responses on Likert-scales. Therefore, in theory it is possible that the marginal effect of a one unit increase for extreme score changes of overall CFC, CFC-Future, and CFC-Immediate is higher than for average scores, where individuals are relatively indifferent about the future consequences of their behavior. In a test of robustness, we therefore included polynomial variables for each of the personality traits. The estimation results for this test of robustness with polynomial variables did not indicate any statistically significant non-linear relationship between personality traits and overall CFC, CFC-Future, or CFC-Immediate.

5 Discussion

This study investigated the relationships between the Big Five personality traits and an individual's considerations of future consequences – which is key to the understanding of sustainable entrepreneurship. In the Dutch context and in our window of observation, we found strong support for the general hypothesis that personality traits determine individual differences in consideration of future consequences. The results advance the debate about the role of the future in individual decision-making processes in significant ways.

First, this study addressed the debate in the individual decision-making literature regarding the reasons why some individuals do consider the future consequences of their decisions and others do not. We contribute to the decision-making literature by, theoretically and empirically, showing that personality traits determine decisions in which time plays an important role (Costa & McCrae, 1992b; Strathman et al., 1994). This study offers a fine-grained and nuanced perspective by explaining personality trait differences between individuals that consider the short-term versus those that consider the long-term future consequences of their decisions. In doing so, this study adds new dimensions to the ongoing debate concerning the buffering and the susceptibility hypothesis (Joireman & King, 2016). The results of our study also offer important guidelines for the awareness of future consequences, which is an important first step toward changing considerations of future consequences. In a similar vein, we offer inspiration concerning the influence of ambiguity about future consequences and rewards (Strathman et al., 1994). The more ambiguous future consequences of behavior and decisions are, the more an individual's attitude toward such risks could come into play.

Second, this study is among the first to test the validity of the different latent factors of CFC with the use of a large-scale longitudinal dataset that includes more than 5,000 observations (Hevey et al., 2010). Our study complements laboratory, small-scale, and cross-sectional research settings. The DHS dataset includes "real-world" citizens, is a representative sample of the entire Dutch population and enables to take important individual characteristics such as diversity in socioeconomic situations, education, age, (perceived) health, and income into account. Our study shows that previously used CFC measures may need to be reconsidered (Strathman et al., 1994; McKay et al., 2015; Petrocelli, 2003). We offer important guidelines for unraveling CFC structures using a large-scale and socio-demographically diverse dataset.

Third, the DHS dataset enabled us to study the stability of CFC and personality traits over a period of ten years. Our study is unique in showing that both variables significantly change over time. This confirms the need to use longitudinal data for CFC and personality traits. It also highlights the importance of the plasticity versus the plaster theory concerning the stability of personality traits. Cross-sectional data lacks the opportunity to include variations of personality traits over time and could therefore bias estimators (Brown & Taylor, 2014). Our study informs scholars to consider CFC and personality traits as dynamic constructs and therefore to employ longitudinal data in order to appropriately test causality that control for changes of these constructs over time. Our distinction between the dynamics of CFC-F and CFC-I on the one hand and the relationship with the dynamics of personality traits on the other also informs practitioners and policymakers. They should take these dynamics into account when making strategic decisions or when designing policy intervention targeted at fostering the future orientation of individuals.

Fourth, although our unit of analysis concerns Dutch citizens and CFC in general, the insights of our study offer three important insights for sustainable entrepreneurship. A first insight concerns explicitly accounting for the role of the future. Consideration of future consequences is key in sustainability because intergenerational equity, that is, the need to consider the interests of future generations, is one of the crucial pillars of sustainable development (Brundtland, 1987). It therefore is a fundamental requirement for individuals who design and implement sustainable enterprises (Geissdoerfer et al., 2018). Individual differences in CFC could therefore be an important predictor of sustainable entrepreneurship intentions. Individuals who do consider the future consequences of their behavior might be more willing to forego personal interests on behalf of future generations (Arnocky, Milfont, & Nicol, 2014; Thelken & de Jong, 2020). Previous research argued that personality traits are poor direct predictors of entrepreneurial intentions. Our study shows the indirect importance of personality traits for sustainable entrepreneurship via its decisive impact on short-term and long-term considerations of future consequences that, in turn, determine the intention formation process of sustainable entrepreneurship.

A second insight concerns the contributions of our research to the susceptibility and the buffering hypotheses (Joireman & King, 2016). The distinction between these two hypotheses directly relates to our differentiation between immediate and future consequences. This distinction has important implications for the process of fostering sustainable entrepreneurship intentions (Kuckertz & Wagner, 2010). On the one hand, in line with the buffering hypothesis, sustainable entrepreneurship education needs to focus on increasing an individual's CFC. On the other hand, if the susceptibility hypothesis prevails, education has to lower concerns for immediate consequences. Our study shows the importance of testing the personality traits of nascent sustainable entrepreneurs. It helps in determining if an individual is cognitively able to buffer short-term needs (when, for example, they have a conscientious personality trait) or if an individual is more likely to be susceptible to short-term needs (when, for example, they have an extravert personality trait).

A third and final insight relates to the psychological aspects of sustainable entrepreneurship action (Muñoz, 2018; Vuorio, Puumalainen, & Fellnhofer, 2018). Individuals need to have sustainability knowledge and motivation as well as entrepreneurship competencies in order to recognize sustainable business opportunities. Personality traits may have opposing effects on sustainability and entrepreneurship. On the one hand, extravert individuals, for example, are better able to take risks, be assertive, and enjoy human interaction (Leutner et al., 2014). This helps to form teams and networks, which are important determinants of entrepreneurship (Unger et al., 2011). On the other hand, our study shows that extravert individuals are also more susceptible to the rewards of short-term gratification, which might hamper their ability to consider intergenerational equity and therefore might reduce their success in terms of sustainability. For these and other personality traits, our study offers insights to explain and foster the success of sustainable entrepreneurship.

5.1 Limitations and Future Research

There were several limitations within this study, which point to potential areas for future research. First, the measures used were constrained by the information that could be obtained from the DHS surveys. Although the data and measures offered unique opportunities to test the impact of personality traits on consideration of future consequences accounting for dynamics, new data with more observations per individual in a balanced panel dataset would offer new opportunities to test the validity and robustness of our findings. The strongly significant results that confirm our hypothesized relationships derive from the unique data that is relevant to the research aim of this paper and can be re-tested with samples from different national contexts. Another issue pertains to a potential method effect due to our unit of analysis. Our study controlled for a method effect using a two-factor model in the context of Dutch citizens. Although the use of citizens as a unit of analysis complements the use of students as a unit of analysis in other studies, future research may include other entities such as sustainable entrepreneurs or sustainable policy-makers. Such future studies would offer a direct test of the importance of personality traits and consideration of future consequences in sustainability settings. Third, driven by theory, we investigated the impact of personality traits on consideration of future consequences. Although our research is nuanced and fine-grained, including the tests of non-linear relationships, future research may analyze feedback relationships and use integrative approaches. Such integrative approaches can study how different cognitive determinants – such as life events, personality traits, and mental processes – act as mediators between CFC and actual behavior (Joireman & King, 2016). Our research offers guidelines for structural equation models that offer opportunities to incorporate feedback loops between personality traits, CFC, and other socio-economic characteristics that are presented in this paper.

6 Conclusions

This study addresses the debate in the recent literature concerning the considerations of future consequences by individuals. Due to the conflicting nature of short-term benefits for individuals and long-term benefits for others, individuals might not be able to appropriately address sustainability challenges. Recent evidence has shown that consideration of future consequences is important to start new sustainable enterprises. The contribution of this study is that it investigated whether and how personality traits explain individual differences in consideration of future consequences. This study theoretically advanced the literature by presenting new hypotheses and applying insights from psychology and decision-making perspectives. Evidence was found for personality traits that determine immediate or future consequences with an important role for conscientiousness, extraversion, and neuroticism. These personality traits explain why some individuals do consider future consequences and others not.

References

Arnocky, S., Milfont, T. L., & Nicol, J. R. (2014). Time perspective and sustainable behavior: Evidence for the distinction between consideration of immediate and future consequences. *Environment and Behavior, 46*(5), 556–582.

Brown, S., & Taylor, K. (2014). Household finances and the "Big Five" personality traits. *Journal of Economic Psychology,* 45, 197–212.

Brundtland, G. H. (1987). *Report of the World Commission on Environment and Development: Our Common Future (The Brundtland Report).* https://sustainabledevelopment.un.org/content/documents/5987our-common-future.pdf

Costa, P., & McCrae, R. (1992a). Four ways five factors are basic. *Personality and Individual Differences, 13,* 653–665.

Costa, P. & McCrae, R. (1992b). *Revised NEO Personality Inventory (NEO PI-R) and NEO Five-Factor Inventory (NEO-FFI): Professional Manual.* Odessa, FL: Psychological Assessment Resources.

Dunkel, C. S. & Weber, J. L. (2010). Using three levels of personality to predict time perspective. *Current Psychology, 29*(2), 95–103.

Eikelenboom, M., & de Jong, G. (2019). The impact of dynamic capabilities on the sustainability performance of SMEs. *Journal of Cleaner Production, 235,* 1360–1370.

Frederick, S., Loewenstein, G., & O'Donoghue, T. (2002). Time discounting and time preference: A critical review. *Journal of Economic Literature, 40*(2), 351–401.

Geissdoerfer, M., Morioka, S. N., De Carvalho, M. M., &Evans, S. (2018). Business models and supply chains for the circular economy. *Journal of Cleaner Production, 190,* 712–721.

Hahn, T. & Knight, E. (2021). The ontology of organizational paradox: a quantum approach. *Academy of Management Review.*

Hevey, D., Pertl, M., Thomas, K., Maher, L., Craig, A., & Chuinneagain, S. N. (2010). Consideration of future consequences scale: Confirmatory factor analysis. *Personality and Individual Differences, 48*(5), 654–657.

Hirsh, J. B. (2014). Environmental sustainability and national personality. *Journal of Environmental Psychology, 38,* 233–240.

Hirsh, J. B., Morisano, D., & Peterson, J. B. (2008). Delay discounting: Interactions between personality and cognitive ability. *Journal of Research in Personality,* 42(6), 1646–1650.

Jerram, K. L., & Coleman, P. G. (1999). The big five personality traits and reporting of health problems and health behaviour in old age. *British Journal of Health Psychology, 4*(2), 181–192.

Joireman, J., & King, S. (2016). Individual differences in the consideration of future and (more) immediate consequences: A review and directions for future research. *Social and Personality Psychology Compass, 10*(5), 313–326.

Joireman, J. A., Lasane, T. P., Bennett, J., Richards, D., & Solaimani, S. (2001). Integrating social value orientation and the consideration of future consequences within the extended norm activation model of proenvironmental behaviour. *British Journal of Social Psychology, 40*(1), 133–155.

Keough, K. A., Zimbardo, P. G., & Boyd, J. N. (1999). Who's smoking, drinking, and using drugs? Time perspective as a predictor of substance use. B*asic and Applied Social Psychology, 21*(2), 149–164.

Kuckertz, A. & Wagner, M. (2010). The influence of sustainability orientation on entrepreneurial intentions – Investigating the role of business experience. *Journal of Business Venturing,* 25, 524–539.

Lans, T., Blok, V., & Wesselink, R. (2014). Learning apart and together: Towards an integrated competence framework for sustainable entrepreneurship in higher education. *Journal of Cleaner Production, 62,* 37–47.

Leutner, F., Ahmetoglu, G., Akhtar, R., & Chamorro-Premuzic, T. (2014). The relationship between the entrepreneurial personality and the Big Five personality traits. *Personality and Individual Differences, 63,* 58–63.

Matsunaga, M. (2010). How to factor-analyze your data right: Do's, don'ts, and how-to's. *International Journal of Psychological Research*, 3, 97–110.

McClure, S. M., Damon, J. L., Kim, L., Cypert, S., Montague, M., & Montague, P. (2014). Neural correlates of behavioral preferences for culturally familiar drinks. *Neuron, 44*(2), 379–387.

McKay, M. T., Cole, J. C., & Percy, A. (2015). Further evidence for a bifactor solution for the Consideration of Future Consequences Scale: Measurement and conceptual implications. *Personality and Individual Differences, 83*, 219–222.

Moutafi, J., Furnham, J., & Paltiel, L. (2004). Why is conscientiousness negatively correlated with intelligence? *Personality and Individual Differences, 37*, 1013–1022.

Mundlak, Y. (1978). On the pooling of time series and cross section data. *Econometrica, 46*, 69–85.

Muñoz, P. (2018). A cognitive map of sustainable decision-making in entrepreneurship: A configurational approach. *International Journal of Entrepreneurial Behavior & Research, 24*(3), 787–813.

Murray, E., McCabe, P., & Ballard, K. J. (2014). A systematic review of treatment outcomes for children with childhood apraxia of speech. *American Journal of Speech-Language Pathology, 23*(3), 486–509.

Nga, J. K. H., & Shamuganathan, G. (2010). The influence of personality traits and demographic factors on social entrepreneurship start up intentions. *Journal of Business Ethics, 95*(2), 259–282.

Nurmi, J. E. (1991). How do adolescents see their future? A review of the development of future orientation and planning. *Developmental Review, 11*(1), 1–59.

Nurmi, J. E. (1992). Age differences in adult life goals, concerns, and their temporal extension: A life course approach to future-oriented motivation. *International Journal of Behavioral Development, 15*(4), 487–508.

Nyhus, E. & Webley, P. (2001). The role of personality in household saving and borrowing behaviour. *European Journal of Personality, 15*, 85–103.

Paulus, M. P., Rogalsky, C., Simmons, A., Feinstein, J. S., & Stein, M. B. (2003). Increased activation in the right insula during risk-taking decision making is related to harm avoidance and neuroticism. *Neuroimage, 19*(4), 1439–1448.

Petrocelli, J. V. (2003). Factor validation of the consideration of future consequences scale: Evidence for a short version. *The Journal of Social Psychology,* 143(4), 405–413.

Roberts, B. & Mroczek, D. (2008). Personality trait change in adulthood. *Current Directions in Psychological Science,* 17, 31–35.

Roberts, B. W. (2009). Back to the future: Personality and assessment and personality development. *Journal of Research in Personality, 43*(2), 137–145.

Shamosh, N. A., DeYoung, C. G., Green, A. E., Reis, D. L., & Johnson, M. R. (2008). Individual differences in delay discounting: Relation to intelligence, working memory, and anterior prefrontal cortex. *Psychology Science, 19*(9), 509–615.

Sharpe, J. P., Martin, N. R., & Roth, K. A. (2011). Optimism and the Big Five factors of personality: Beyond neuroticism and extraversion. *Personality and Individual Differences, 51*(8), 946–951.

Steinberg, L., Graham, S., O'brien, L., Woolard, J., Cauffman, E., & Banich, M. (2009). Age differences in future orientation and delay discounting. *Child Development, 80*(1), 28–44.

Strathman, A., Gleicher, F., Boninger, D. S., & Edwards, C. S. (1994). The consideration of future consequences: Weighing immediate and distant outcomes of behavior. *Journal of Personality and Social Psychology, 66*(4), 742–752.

Thelken, H. N. (2021). *Thinking apart and together: The role of cognition in managing multiple goals in sustainable enterprises*. PhD Thesis. University of Groningen.

Thelken, H. N., & de Jong, G. (2020). The impact of values and future orientation on intention formation within sustainable entrepreneurship. *Journal of Cleaner Production, 266*, 122052.

Toepoel, V. (2010). Is consideration of future consequences a changeable construct? *Personality and Individual Differences, 48*(8), 951–956.

Trommsdorff, G. (1983). Future orientation and socialization. *International Journal of Psychology, 18*(1–4), 381–406.

Unger, J. M., Rauch, A., Frese, M., & Rosenbusch, N. (2011). Human capital and entrepreneurial success: A meta-analytical review. *Journal of Business Venturing, 26*(3), 341–358.

Vuorio, A. M., Puumalainen, K., & Fellnhofer, K. (2018). Drivers of entrepreneurial intentions in sustainable entrepreneurship. *International Journal of Entrepreneurial Behavior & Research, 24*(2), 359–381.

Webley, P., & Nyhus, E. K. (2006). Parents' influence on children's future orientation and saving. *Journal of Economic Psychology, 27*(1), 140–164.

Zuckerman, M. (1994). *Behavioral Expressions and Biosocial Bases of Sensation Seeking*. London: Cambridge University Press.

Margo Enthoven

8 Unpacking Opportunity Recognition for Sustainable Entrepreneurship

Abstract: Opportunity recognition is one of the first steps to start a sustainable business. Interestingly, there has been a huge debate regarding the definition of this concept as well as how sustainable entrepreneurs recognise opportunities. This chapter gives a focused overview of the concept of opportunity recognition. We first provide a historical description, summarising how the concept evolved over the years. We follow by discussing how the process of opportunity recognition for sustainable entrepreneurship is different from opportunity recognition in conventional entrepreneurship. We finalise the chapter with a new typology of opportunity recognition in sustainable entrepreneurship, where the different types of opportunities that have been discussed are mapped as problem or solution-led opportunities. As such, the chapter introduces a novel tool to help aspiring entrepreneurs with identifying what type of opportunity is best fitting their sustainability endeavours, depending on their focus.

Keywords: opportunity recognition, sustainability problems, sustainable entrepreneurship

1 Introduction

Society has become increasingly critical of business practice, and specifically of businesses' pursuit of economic growth regardless of potential societal and environmental costs. Critics point to the correlation between economic growth and environmental degradation (Fischer-Kowalski & Swilling, 2011; OECD, 2002), and to the regular failure of markets to account for the true costs of social and environmental degradation (Austin, Stevenson, & Wei-Skillern, 2006; Cohen & Winn, 2007). Therefore, the view that business needs to become more sustainable is now accepted among policymakers, management scholars and entrepreneurs alike (Markman et al., 2019). While it has become increasingly recognised that entrepreneurs can play a central role in the transition to a more sustainable society, how such a transition might be realised is still the topic of ongoing debate (Markman et al., 2019; Schaefer, Corner, & Kearins, 2015).

In response to this situation, this chapter addresses how and why entrepreneurs start a business with the aim to create sustainable change. Entrepreneurs cannot start a business without first recognising an entrepreneurial opportunity (Short et al.,

Margo Enthoven, Department of Entrepreneurship, Innovation and Technology, Stockholm School of Economics, Stockholm, Sweden

https://doi.org/10.1515/9783110756159-010

2010). An entrepreneur recognises an opportunity by creating a fit between a market need, interest, or want, and resources in the form of a new venture idea (Ardichvili, Cardozo, & Ray, 2003; Davidsson, 2015). This fit is an opportunity if it creates new or superior value for customers. This results in the introduction of products or services with superior value for customers (Belz & Binder, 2017). The discovery, development and exploitation of new opportunities are necessary to transform 'business as usual' into 'sustainable business' (Emas, 2015).

Entrepreneurship scholarship has for many years assumed that opportunities exist in the interaction between the entrepreneur and their environment, partially in the entrepreneur's mind, and partially in the existence of an enabler in the environment of the entrepreneur. Whether an opportunity can be recognised and exploited by an entrepreneur is dependent on the entrepreneur's skills and confidence (Davidsson, 2015). Therefore, the entrepreneurship field revolves around the individuals and processes that lead to the discovery, evaluation, and exploitation of opportunities, as well as the effects of these efforts (Shane & Venkataraman, 2000). Additionally, the entrepreneurship literature emphasises that opportunities may be recognised in relation to problems, but that this is not always the case (Vogel, 2017). Instead, opportunities based on problems represent only one of multiple types of opportunity (Chandler, DeTienne, & Lyon, 2003). As such, opportunities in relation to grand challenges represent a specific type of opportunity, because they exist in relation to one or more problems that constitute a grand challenge. The sustainable entrepreneurship literature therefore emphasises that a sustainable entrepreneur need first recognise a social or environmental problem before recognising an opportunity (Belz & Binder, 2017; Eller et al., 2020; Santos, 2012).

In this chapter, I aim to answer the question: *what is different about the process of opportunity recognition when entrepreneurs recognise opportunities for sustainable development?* I therefore first discuss what opportunity recognition is and how our understanding of the concept has evolved over the years. In the first part of this chapter, I will review the evolution of opportunity recognition as a concept and which theories have shaped our current understanding of opportunity recognition. In the second part of this chapter, I discuss the role of opportunity in relation to sustainability problems, and the extent to which the main opportunity theories shape our understanding of sustainable entrepreneurship. I will also develop a typology of opportunity recognition for sustainable entrepreneurship, and the different ways in which (aspiring) sustainable entrepreneurs may act if they wish to discover opportunities for sustainable entrepreneurship.

2 A Brief History of the Opportunity Concept

2.1 The Schumpeterian View: A Neoclassical Approach

Schumpeter is seen as the forefather of entrepreneurship and opportunity literature. In his view on entrepreneurship, he is different from the economists of his time (Gaglio, 1997). What is important to understand about this time is that macro theories of the market were dominant, and the agency of individuals was hardly recognised within these macro theories. Schumpeter, however, theorises about what causes the *individual* entrepreneur to exploit an opportunity, rather than his contemporary peers who were more interested in explaining the macro movements of the market. Schumpeter argues that entrepreneurs are the agents who create change in otherwise stagnant markets, which makes them different from all the other market actors (Schumpeter, 1934). Entrepreneurs are theorised to create new combinations of existing means, which causes markets to evolve. The new combinations that these entrepreneurs introduce create greater value for the market than other combinations that were already existing in the market. Schumpeter's conceptualisation was important, because it emphasised the agency of the entrepreneur in the introduction of new goods and services into the market, rather than his contemporaries who only discussed entrepreneurship as a function of the workings of the market at large (Gaglio, 1997).

2.2 The Entrepreneurship-as-Problem-Solving Approach

While Schumpeter opened the stage for discussion of the agency of entrepreneurs, only a few scholars discussed opportunity recognition until the 1990s (Buttner & Gryskiewicz, 1993). Before the 1990s, the opportunity literature evolved from contributions in the strategy literature and the psychology literature, with a focus on organisational and individual problem solving and learning (Isenberg, 1986; Newell & Simon, 1972; Pounds, 1969; Tversky & Kahneman, 1981). While these literatures have generated important insights into opportunity recognition, both literatures typically deal more with problem solving than with the generation of new opportunities (Buttner & Gryskiewicz, 1993; Kiesler & Sproull, 1982; Nutt, 1984). On the one hand, the strategy literature was designed to capture dynamics within an existing organisation, rather than the process that individuals or teams go through when starting new ventures. The psychology literature, on the other hand, focused on individual learning and decision making, but did not capture the dynamic between opportunities in the market and the entrepreneur. The literature on opportunity recognition was built heavily on these two literatures that have a strong problem orientation, but this changed in 1997 with Gaglio's seminal work on opportunity recognition. Her work caused a revolution, as she argued that the creativity of entrepreneurs is not confined to the problem spaces of the problems presented to entrepreneurs. Instead, entrepreneurial opportunity can go beyond mere problem solving and can even generate new economic activity without having recognised or defined a problem (Gaglio, 1997). She also highlighted that managers and entrepreneurs are distinctly different, as managers are more concerned about solving current organisational problems, whereas entrepreneurs are more prone to observe and react to market change. As such, the seminal work of Gaglio also points out that not all business actors should be regarded as entrepreneurs as the mere solving of problems is not a sufficient condition to be recognised as an entrepreneur.

2.3 The Opportunity Wars

As a response to this renewed focus on the entrepreneur as an agent of change in markets, a new wave of literature appeared (Shane, 2000, 2003; Venkataraman, 1997; Shane & Venkataraman, 2000). This literature goes beyond both macro market theories and the problem-solving theories of the twentieth century, as the notion that opportunity exists partially in the market, and partially in the head of the entrepreneur, gave rise to a new understanding of opportunity recognition. Opportunity recognition does not just occur in the entrepreneur's head, and neither do new opportunities 'appear' in the market of themselves. Instead, lucrative opportunities need to be present both in the environment and in the mind of the entrepreneur. As such, the concept of opportunity exists on the nexus between individual and environment (Shane, 2003). This theoretical angle led to a new generation of entrepreneurship research, focusing on the ways in which entrepreneurs recognise opportunities.

This new wave of literature also argues that opportunities can be recognised solution-first, rather than problem-first. Opportunities can, for instance, be recognised as the application of a new technology in a different market, without necessarily first recognising a problem in that market. Shane (2000) shows how entrepreneurs in the 3D printing space first learned about the new three-dimensional (3D) printing technology after it was developed at Massachusetts Institute of Technology (MIT), after which they introduced new applications of 3D printing in a range of different markets. To illustrate, while 3D printing was initially introduced to print prototypes such as architectural models, entrepreneurs in the medical sector found that it could print prostheses in medical applications, and thereby provide a much more efficient way of creating personally tailored medical devices. These entrepreneurs first learned about the technology, without recognising a problem with current prostheses making practices. The recognition that 3D printing could optimise the making of prostheses came after careful investigation of the technology, rather than from defining and redefining a problem in the medical sector. As such, these entrepreneurs needed to 'create' a demand for their new application of 3D printing for medical prostheses. This opportunity thus arose without an explicitly defined or recognised problem. With the recognition that opportunities can arise without a connection to problems, this paper ended the focus on opportunity recognition as a problem-solving process (Shane, 2000).

From 2003 to 2020, the opportunity literature expanded vastly, and an episode that became known as 'the opportunity wars' occurred (Wood & McKinley, 2020; Wood, 2017; Wright & Phan, 2020). In these dramatically named 'wars', scholars debated whether opportunities exist objectively in the market and can be recognised by individuals with the right information and motivation (Grégoire & Shepherd, 2012), or whether they are created and unique, and therefore only exist in the mind of the entrepreneur until they are enacted in the market (Alvarez & Barney, 2007). This back-and-forth debate caused major frustration in the field of entrepreneurship, with several scholars considering the concept of opportunity to be unproductive in the advancement of the entrepreneurship field. Several scholars proposed to dislodge the concept of opportunity altogether and replace it with something else. Foss and Klein (2015) argued that the concept could simply be an application of entrepreneurial judgement to an investment situation. Davidsson (2015) on the other hand replaced the opportunity construct by introducing several new concepts, including external enablers, new venture ideas and opportunity confidence. In this re-conceptualisation, external enablers are the market circumstances that influence the attempts of an entrepreneur to actualise a new opportunity. These external enablers can, for instance, be demographic and regulatory changes that create space for new economic activity. New venture ideas are the new offerings and the configuration of means to actualise these offerings in the market, which exist in the mind of the entrepreneur. Finally, opportunity confidence refers to the entrepreneur's judgement on the attractiveness of the new venture idea. It is the main stimulus for the entrepreneur to bring their new venture idea to the market.

The re-conceptualisations of opportunity differ in the extent to which they depart from the use of the concept of opportunity, yet these re-conceptualisations still consider the same event: the gestation of new combinations of means to meet customer needs (McBride & Wuebker, 2022). Eventually, it became recognised that the abovementioned re-conceptualisations, as well as opportunity recognition and creation views, could coexist in the entrepreneurship field under the wider umbrella of opportunity, with some scholars arguing that opportunities are partially discovered, and partially created (Renko, Shrader, & Simon, 2012; Wood & McKinley, 2020). The field has now moved on to new discussions on opportunity recognition (Ramoglou & Gartner, 2022).

2.4 Post-opportunity Wars: Alternative Theories

With the coming and going of the opportunity wars, new views on opportunity arrived. Some scholars view opportunity as a design process (Ding, 2020) involving three main steps: first, an opportunity needs to be discovered, and second, recognised by an entrepreneur, and third it needs to be accepted and acknowledged by others so that its importance is taken up by the market. Following this design process, guidelines were offered as to how to navigate the opportunity recognition process (Ding, 2019). Some others argue that the opportunity recognition process has been too much focused on the entrepreneur, and too little on those who the entrepreneur serves: the consumers (Ramoglou, Zyglidopoulos, & Papadopoulou, 2021). They argue that, while there is no opportunity without an entrepreneur, there is also no opportunity without consumers. The realisation dawned that scholars have predominantly theorised that opportunities in the market exist without recognising that consumers are behind these market opportunities, and that these opportunities are based on the consumers' needs (Ramoglou, 2021). Arguably, the opportunities lie in the demand side with the consumers, while entrepreneurs only create supply. In that sense, opportunities are actualised in collaboration with consumers, who create the boundaries for the opportunity space, and the extent to which an opportunity is allowed to be pursued by the wider society.

3 Opportunity in Sustainable Entrepreneurship

To answer the question, '*What is different when entrepreneurs recognise opportunities for sustainable development?*', I will outline the efforts made in the opportunity and sustainable entrepreneurship field based on the above discussion of the history of entrepreneurial opportunity. In a final section, I will develop a typology of opportunities for sustainable entrepreneurship.

3.1 Sustainability, Market Failures and Market Imperfections

Some of the first influential efforts to theorise about sustainable entrepreneurship and opportunity, have been developed based on the notion that opportunities for sustainable entrepreneurship arise from imperfections or failures in a market (Cohen & Winn, 2007; Dean & McMullen, 2007). This literature builds on environmental and welfare economics, which pose that social and environmental problems arise from inherent inefficiencies in the economic system. While neoclassical economists uphold that markets efficiently organise the exchange of resources to provide most utility for all actors, environmental and welfare economics pose that markets inherently fail to do so, thereby causing social and environmental problems (Dean & McMullen, 2007). Entrepreneurship scholars have subsequently argued that these market failures provide opportunities for sustainable entrepreneurs to pursue new ventures that may resolve this market failure (Cohen & Winn, 2007; Dean & McMullen, 2007).

One of the main differences between opportunity recognition in the general entrepreneurship literature and opportunity recognition in the sustainable entrepreneurship literature, is its focus on problem recognition. While the literature on entrepreneurial opportunity had previously abandoned its focus on problems, the rise of social and sustainable entrepreneurship has called the attention of researchers back to the problem focused approach (Belz & Binder, 2017; Żur, 2015). This is due to the increasing framing of sustainability issues as wicked problems and grand challenges (Markman et al., 2019). Sustainability literature has called upon society to address these problems and challenges, and the entrepreneurship literature has answered. Entrepreneurship is recognised as a way to address the problems and challenges that have been raised by the sustainability field, and the need of opportunities to be recognised in relation to these problems and challenges has been made prevalent by numerous entrepreneurship scholars (Belz & Binder, 2017; Cohen & Winn, 2007; Hu et al., 2020).

3.2 Opportunity Based on Sustainability Problems

Considering the significant focus of sustainable entrepreneurship on addressing sustainability problems, it is important to understand how sustainable entrepreneurs recognise opportunities based on sustainability problems. As such, we need to understand what a problem is, how it is recognised and why some individuals recognise sustainability problems and subsequent opportunities while others do not. A problem refers to a significantly undesirable situation, which may be solvable by someone, although probably with some difficulty (Smith, 1989). When an individual recognises a problem, they become uncomfortable, because the problem signals that reality is not as they would like it to be (Baer et al., 2013; Jonassen, 2000). The result is that the individual will devote attention to the problem, and put effort into looking for solutions (Cowan, 1986; Pedersen, 2009). The following example illustrates how problems are recognised: when an individual watches the news and sees that a drought in an underdeveloped region leads to hunger and infant mortality, the individual is aware of the situation and the children's need for food and water. However, this situation only becomes a recognised problem once the individual considers the children's suffering to be undesirable. If the individual does not care, decides to ignore the information, or does not receive the message, then it is unlikely that they recognise a problem (Pedersen, 2009; Tversky & Kahneman, 1981).

In the previous example, a judgement on the desirability of a situation needed to be made by the individual to recognise a problem. Hence, what defines problem recognition is a judgement on an external situation (Cowan, 1986; Pedersen, 2009). How individuals judge situations based on desirability has been a crucial topic in management and economics since the very genesis of these fields (Smith, 1776, 1759). Two dominant assumptions on individuals' judgements of situations that still inform the current literature on entrepreneurship are grounded in economic sociology and neoclassical economics, which both assert that behaviour is motivated by a central goal. In neoclassical economics, this goal is utility, whereas in economic sociology the goal is power (Fligstein, 2018). Although these assumptions are valid and helpful to the literatures from which they originate, one of the key features of (sustainable) entrepreneurship is the presence of multiple, oftentimes conflicting, goals (Harmeling et al., 2009; Mitzinneck & Besharov, 2019; Sarasvathy & Ramesh, 2019). While motivations of power or utility may be present, and sometimes even central to the behaviour of sustainable entrepreneurs, sustainable entrepreneurs have a range of motivations that are not exclusively related to power or utility, as discussed in Chapter 6. What stems from the above is that the entrepreneurial opportunity literature has mostly built on assumptions that emphasises certain entrepreneurial motivations over others. However, more recent literature on entrepreneurial opportunity questions the assumptions that entrepreneurship is solely motivated by certain values, and not by others. While the reasons to engage in sustainable entrepreneurship may differ across individuals and cultures, it commonly results from a mix of values, including but not limited to power, personal gain and environmental and social sustainability (see Chapter 6).

3.3 Wicked Problems and Non-opportunity Beliefs

The opportunity wars and the discussions on addressing wicked problems through entrepreneurship have sparked discussion about the occurrence of non-opportunity. Non-opportunity is a situation in which an individual perceives an opportunity while there isn't one (Gras et al., 2020; Ramoglou & Gartner, 2022; Renko, Shrader, & Simon, 2012). This can occur in many situations, for instance when an opportunity may exist for privileged individuals, but not for individuals with resource constraints (Ramoglou & Gartner, 2022). It also occurs when there may be a customer base for a new opportunity, but where other stakeholders do not show support for the opportunity and thereby limit the opportunity space (Ramoglou, Zyglidopoulos, & Papadopoulou, 2021). Non-opportunity in the context of sustainability has also been discussed in relation to wicked problems, which are problems that are complex in nature, that can span regional and national boundaries and that are prone to contestation (Dorado & Ventresca, 2013; Gras et al., 2020). These problems have many interactions, associations and non-linear dynamics (Ferraro, Etzion, & Gehman, 2015). The wicked problem literature argues that wicked problems cross the boundaries of industries, nations and public–private distinctions. As such, wicked problems need to be addressed by a collective. In addition, multiple parties often believe that they know the solution to the wicked problem, while the proposed solutions conflict and the conflicts seem irreconcilable (Dorado & Ventresca, 2013), leading to failing to solve the problem.

Indeed, some scholars doubt that an individual alone in a venture has the potential to solve a wicked problem, without significant communal effort (Gras et al., 2020). Others warn that entrepreneurship might make matters worse, if not pursued in a way that acknowledges institutional circumstances and processes (Dorado & Ventresca, 2013; Rittel & Webber, 1973). Both streams argue that the opportunity literature is too individual oriented, whereas wicked problems need to be addressed collectively by a group of actors across society (Gras et al., 2020; Head, 2008). When entrepreneurs pursue entrepreneurship to address a wicked problem in a solo effort, this is conceptualised to fail due to the nature of the problem as spanning the boundary between public and private (Gras et al., 2020). Other authors assert that entrepreneurs may lead efforts to address wicked problems, but that they cannot do so in an isolated effort in the market. Entrepreneurs may also need to change institutions and work with stakeholders to address wicked problems. Additionally, they emphasise that wicked problems can never be terminally solved, but only temporarily re-solved over and over again (Dorado & Ventresca, 2013).

In relation to this, research emerged that advocates that opportunities for sustainable development can only successfully be recognised when a wide range of stakeholders are involved. Therefore, some researchers have conceptualised sustainable entrepreneurship entirely as a collective effort, in which communities or networks of actors conjointly create opportunities to address sustainability issues.

4 A Typology for Sustainable Entrepreneurship

To answer the question of what is different about opportunity recognition for sustainable entrepreneurship, it is helpful to discuss a typology of opportunities (see Table 8.1). While I have discussed above that sustainable entrepreneurship literature has revitalised the opportunity-as-solution view because sustainable entrepreneurs often aim to address grand challenges, other entrepreneurs may also pursue opportunities based on problems, such as consumer problems. In addition, sustainable entrepreneurs may also find a solution first, and a problem second. It is thus important to understand where traditional and sustainable entrepreneurs stand in relation to the problem–solution dichotomy.

While a focus on problems serves as a theoretical perspective on the environmental side of the entrepreneur–environment nexus (Shane, 2003), a typology on opportunity also needs to consider the entrepreneur as an individual. Numerous theories and approaches exist that explain why an entrepreneur as an individual recognises an opportunity, one of which is the identity theory. Identity reflects how one defines themselves (van der Werff, Steg, & Keizer, 2014), which is a motivated process depending on the context as well as key values people endorse (Bouman et al., 2021). It is widely known that identity is crucial in opportunity recognition, as it determines which motivations and considerations come to the fore when entrepreneurs evaluate an opportunity (Mathias & Williams, 2017). Identity is also a concept that includes or predicts some of the other predictors of opportunity recognition. For instance, identity is linked to motivation, and identity includes other important concepts such as values and beliefs, all of which have been used to explain opportunity recognition. Identity theory also recognises that entrepreneurs are individuals who are embedded in their social environment, whereas other theories consider the entrepreneur as a solo entity. In the above discussion on creation versus discovery, we concluded that opportunities exist partially in the brain of the entrepreneur, and partially in the environment. As such, it is important to discuss the individual from a perspective that allows us to consider their environment.

In this section, I will develop a typology of opportunity based on the above-mentioned theoretical perspectives. First, I will build on the opportunity literature and the problem-first versus solution-first dichotomy. This dichotomy represents the question of whether opportunities are based on the recognition of a problem first or based on the search for the new application of an existing solution. Second, I will build on the identity literature, which describes which opportunities entrepreneurs recognise and pursue based on their identity.

There are multiple identity theories, but there is one type that considers how the entrepreneur relates to their social environment, called social identity theory (Tajfel & Turner, 1979). This theory from social psychology can be used to relate to an entrepreneur's social relationships and to understand how an entrepreneur relates themselves to different groups and categories in society. The literature on entrepreneurial identity posits that how an individual identifies strongly influences whether they will find an entrepreneurial opportunity attractive, and which entrepreneurial opportunities they select (Fauchart & Gruber, 2011; Mathias & Williams, 2017, 2018).

Fauchart and Gruber (2011) discuss three types of entrepreneurs, based on their social identity. The first type, called Darwinian entrepreneurs, includes entrepreneurs who are more sensitive to opportunities that will lead to the highest potential monetary gain. A second type of entrepreneur looks for opportunities that will help them to support their community, and that will help them to gain support from their community. A third type of entrepreneur seeks to advance a social or environmental mission, and therefore mainly pursues opportunities that they believe to have a positive societal impact (Fauchart & Gruber, 2011). These three types of entrepreneurs pursue three different types of opportunities: 1) opportunities that serve the motivation of the entrepreneur to make money for themselves, 2) opportunities that serve the motivation of the entrepreneur to be a meaningful part of their (local) community and 3) opportunities that serve the motivation of the entrepreneur to solve a larger societal problem, or to contribute to the common good.

Considering that entrepreneur and opportunity are interconnected, we can argue that there are certain types of opportunity that fit with certain types of entrepreneurs. Therefore, I develop a typology of opportunity below, based on literature on the identity of entrepreneurs and the literature on opportunity. These types are: the Darwinian opportunity, the community-oriented opportunity and the mission-driven opportunity. These three categories include opportunities based on problems and those based on solutions.

In this framework, I reframe the definition of opportunity as a means–ends combination brought together by an entrepreneur into a product or a service (Ardichvili, Cardozo, & Ray, 2003; Schumpeter, 1934). Instead, I view opportunity as a problem–solution pair, brought together by an entrepreneur into a product or a service (Hippel & Krogh, 2016; Hsieh, Nickerson, & Zenger, 2007). This definition stems from the above discussion and allows us to view opportunity from both a creation and a discovery view.

Dividing opportunities into problem-led and solution-led helps to understand how the opportunity recognition process can be broken down according to the two most important components of opportunity: problem and solution. Additionally, the division of opportunities into Darwinian, community, and mission oriented reflect the different lenses through which entrepreneurs evaluate problems in their environments. Table 8.1 includes a description and explanation of the different opportunity

Table 8.1: A typology of opportunities.

Type of opportunity	Problem-led	Solution-led
Darwinian: motivated by personal monetary gain for the entrepreneur	Problem-led Darwinian opportunity	Solution-led Darwinian opportunity
	Typically led by a customer problem; a potential market for a 'solution' to the problem is envisioned	Typically, a systematic search and application of an existing solution (business model, technology, process) to a different market than where it was originally introduced
	Example: medical innovations specifically aimed towards relieving a specific condition	Example: the smartphone was a combination of existing technologies into a new product that no one knew that they needed
Community: motivated by the desire to add value and be a valuable part of a specific community	Problem-led community opportunity	Solution-led community opportunity
	Led by a social problem of a specific social group of which the entrepreneur is a part	Led by a solution that they realised could add value to their community
	Example: farmers' collectives, a rock climber developing a new training tool geared specifically for the climbing community	Example: 'diaspora' entrepreneurs who moved away from their local community but move back to add value to their community with a specific solution that they found elsewhere
Mission: motivated by the desire to contribute to solving a large societal problem, including environmental and social problems	Problem-led mission opportunity	Solution-led mission opportunity
	Led by a social or environmental problem that exists on a 'larger than local' scale	Led by a solution that is later applied to a specific societal problem
	Example: the search for plant-based leather alternatives with the goal to provide a more environmentally friendly alternative to leather	Example: medical technology for lab-growing organs applied to the meat industry and the potential to eliminate animal suffering behind meat

types based on the type of identity of the entrepreneur and whether they are problem-first or solution-first.

As a result of the discussion above, I arrive at six different opportunity types based on three types of motivations (see table 8.1). First, mission-oriented opportunities are archetypical opportunities for sustainable development and come from the motivation to contribute to solving a large societal problem. While problem-solving is central to this opportunity type, it can also be solution-led, when aspiring entrepreneurs are aware of a promising solution but have not yet found the problem that this solution can address. Second, Darwinian opportunities are opportunities motivated by monetary gain. While this opportunity is not intended to contribute to sustainable development, it may become a sustainable opportunity when sustainability is profitable. Third, community-oriented opportunities are not necessarily aimed at contributing to sustainable development but can do so inadvertently through the strengthening of local communities and local natural resources.

I realise that in many cases these types of opportunities overlap. For instance, an entrepreneur may recognise an opportunity that serves both a monetary motivation and the motivation to contribute to the public good. Additionally, there are instances in which problems and solutions are recognised as an inseparable whole, a so-called problem–solution pair (Hippel & Krogh, 2016). As such, I consider these types of opportunities to be 'archetypes' or 'ideal types', with opportunities in practice oftentimes showing elements of more than one archetype.

5 Conclusions

In this chapter, I have attempted to answer the question: *what is different about the process of opportunity recognition when entrepreneurs recognise opportunities for sustainable development?* For this purpose, I have included a brief history of opportunity recognition and discussed how opportunity is viewed in sustainable entrepreneurship. In my discussion of sustainable entrepreneurship, I have at several instances referred back to the history of opportunity, and specifically the discussion of problems in opportunity and the assumptions on entrepreneurs' motivations behind recognising an opportunity.

The sustainable entrepreneurship literature has added value to the entrepreneurship and opportunity discussion by challenging the assumption that opportunities are recognised out of desire for personal monetary gain and by revitalising the discussion on problems in opportunity recognition with new perspectives. The problem–solution discussion was revitalised by the discussion on sustainable entrepreneurship in response to grand challenges and wicked problems. Early perspectives on sustainable entrepreneurship have fed into this discussion by describing how sustainable entrepreneurship can address market failures, or, in other words, solve the sustainability problems that stem from the inability of the market system to operate in a way that maximises the public good (Cohen & Winn, 2007; Dean & McMullen, 2007). As such, what changes for the concept of 'opportunity' when we add 'sustainable', is that sustainable entrepreneurship always addresses a sustainability problem. This problem recognition, however, does not have to occur before opportunity recognition. It can occur simultaneously, or after the recognition of a solution to the problem. It is the problem–solution pairing in response to a grand challenge or wicked problem that makes an opportunity for sustainable entrepreneurship.

Additionally, I highlight how the discussion on sustainable entrepreneurship has challenged classic views on economic activity, as it occurs that the motivations for entrepreneurship go beyond the assumed motivations that inform our classic economic theories. Instead of assuming that entrepreneurship stems from a desire for personal monetary gain or power only, sustainable entrepreneurship research shows that entrepreneurs can have a whole range of motivations to recognise something as an opportunity (see Chapter 6), and that it follows that the entrepreneurial identity is more complicated than assumed. Considering that motivations and identity are crucial in the recognition of opportunities, sustainable entrepreneurship research and its contributions to our knowledge on entrepreneurial motivations and identity have opened space for alternative explanations of opportunity recognition, based on alternative motivations.

References

Alvarez, S. A., & Barney, J. B. (2007). Discovery and creation: Alternative theories of entrepreneurial action. *Strategic Entrepreneurship Journal, 1*(1), 11–26.

Ardichvili, A., Cardozo, R., & Ray, S. (2003). A theory of entrepreneurial opportunity identification and development. *Journal of Business Venturing, 18*(1), 105–123.

Austin, J., Stevenson, H., & Wei-Skillern, J. (2006). Social and commercial entrepreneurship: Same, different or both. *Entrepreneurship Theory & Practice, 30*(1), 1–22.

Baer, M., Dirks, K. T., & Nickerson, J. A. (2013). Microfoundations of strategic problem formulation. *Strategic Management Journal, 34*(2), 197–214.

Belz, F. M., & Binder, J. K. (2017). Sustainable entrepreneurship: A convergent process model. *Business Strategy and the Environment, 26*(1), 1–17.

Bouman, T., van der Werff, E., Perlaviciute, G., & Steg, L. (2021). Environmental values and identities at the personal and group level. *Current Opinion in Behavioral Sciences, 42*, 47–53.

Buttner, E. H., & Gryskiewicz, N. (1993). Entrepreneurs' problem-solving styles: An empirical study using the Kirton adaption/innovation theory. *Journal of Small Business Management, 31*(1), 22–31.

Chandler, G. N., DeTienne, D., & Lyon, D. W. (2003). Outcome implications of opportunity creation/discovery processes. *Frontiers of Entrepreneurship Research, January*, 398–409.

Cohen, B., & Winn, M. I. (2007). Market imperfections, opportunity and sustainable entrepreneurship. *Journal of Business Venturing, 22*(1), 29–49.

Cowan, D. A. (1986). Developing a process model of problem recognition. *Academy of Management Review, 11*(4), 763–776.

Davidsson, P. (2015). Entrepreneurial opportunities and the entrepreneurship nexus: A re-conceptualization. *Journal of Business Venturing*, *30*(5), 674–695.

Dean, T. J., & McMullen, J. S. (2007). Toward a theory of sustainable entrepreneurship: Reducing environmental degradation through entrepreneurial action. *Journal of Business Venturing*, *22*(1), 50–76.

Ding, T. (2019). Understanding the design of opportunities: Re-evaluating the agent-opportunity nexus through a design lens. *Journal of Business Venturing Insights*, *11*, e00108.

Ding, T. (2020). What if opportunities are conceived as design artifacts? A rejoinder to foss and klein. *Academy of Management Perspectives*.

Dorado, S., & Ventresca, M. J. (2013). Crescive entrepreneurship in complex social problems: Institutional conditions for entrepreneurial engagement. *Journal of Business Venturing*, *28*(1), 69–82.

Eller, F. J., Gielnik, M. M., Wimmer, H., Thölke, C., Holzapfel, S., Tegtmeier, S., & Halberstadt, J. (2020). Identifying business opportunities for sustainable development: Longitudinal and experimental evidence contributing to the field of sustainable entrepreneurship. *Business Strategy and the Environment*, *29*(3), 1387–1403.

Emas, R. (2015). The concept of sustainable development: Definition and defining principles. In *Brief for GSDR* (pp. 10–13140). https://sustainabledevelopment.un.org/content/documents/5839GSDR% 202015_SD_concept_definiton_rev.pdf

Fauchart, E., & Gruber, M. (2011). Darwinians, communitarians, and missionaries: The role of founder identity in entrepreneurship. *Academy of Management Journal*, *54*(5), 935–957.

Ferraro, F., Etzion, D., & Gehman, J. (2015). Tackling grand challenges pragmatically: Robust action revisited. *Organization Studies*, *36*(3), 363–390.

Fischer-Kowalski, M., & Swilling, M. (2011). Decoupling natural resource use and environmental impacts from economic growth. *United Nations Environment Programme*. UNEP/Earthprint.

Fligstein, N. (2018). *The Architecture of Markets*. Princeton University Press.

Foss, N. J., & Klein, P. G. (2015). Introduction to a forum on the judgement-based approach to entrepreneurship: Accomplishments, challenges, new directions. *Journal of Institutional Economics*, *11*(3), 585–599.

Gaglio, C. M. (1997). Opportunity identification: Review, critique, and suggested research directions. *Advances in Entrepreneurship, Firm Emergence and Growth*, *3*, 139–202.

Gras, D., Conger, M., Jenkins, A., & Gras, M. (2020). Wicked problems, reductive tendency, and the formation of (non-)opportunity beliefs. *Journal of Business Venturing*, *35*(3), 1–15.

Grégoire, D. A., & Shepherd, D. A. (2012). Technology-market combinations and the identification of entrepreneurial opportunities: An investigation of the opportunity-individual nexus. *Academy of Management Journal*, *55*(4), 753–785.

Harmeling, S. S., Sarasvathy, S. D., & Freeman, R. E. (2009). Related debates in ethics and entrepreneurship: Values, opportunities, and contingency. *Journal of Business Ethics*, *84*, 341–365.

Head, B. (2008). Wicked problems in public policy. *Public Policy*, *3*(2), 101.

Hippel, E. V., & Krogh, G. V. (2016). Problem solving without problem formulation. *Organization Science*, *27*(1), 207–221.

Hsieh, C., Nickerson, J. A., & Zenger, T. R. (2007). Opportunity discovery, problem solving and a theory of the entrepreneurial firm. *Journal of Management Studies*, *44*(7), 1255–1277.

Hu, X., Marlow, S., Zimmermann, A., Martin, L., & Frank, R. (2020). Understanding opportunities in social entrepreneurship: A critical realist abstraction. *Entrepreneurship: Theory and Practice*, *44*(5), 1032–1056.

Isenberg, D. J. (1986). Thinking and managing: A verbal protocol analysis of managerial problem solving. *Academy of Management Journal*, *29*(4), 775–788.

Jonassen, D. H. (2000). Toward a design theory of problem solving. *Educational Technology Research and Development*, *48*(4), 63–85.

Kiesler, S., & Sproull, L. (1982). Managerial response to changing environments: Perspectives on problem sensing from social cognition. *Administrative Science Quarterly*, *27*(4), 548–570.

Markman, G. D., Waldron, T. L., Gianiodis, P. T., & Espina, M. I. (2019). E pluribus unum: Impact entrepreneurship as a solution to grand challenges. *Academy of Management Perspectives*, *33*(4), 371–382.

Mathias, B. D., & Williams, D. W. (2017). The impact of role identities on entrepreneurs' evaluation and selection of opportunities. *Journal of Management*, *43*(3), 892–918.

Mathias, B. D., & Williams, D. W. (2018). Giving up the hats? Entrepreneurs' role transitions and venture growth. *Journal of Business Venturing*, *33*(3), 261–277.

McBride, R., & Wuebker, R. (2022). Social objectivity and entrepreneurial opportunities. *Academy of Management Review*, *47*(1), 75–92.

Mitzinneck, B. C., & Besharov, M. L. (2019). Managing value tensions in collective social entrepreneurship: The role of temporal, structural, and collaborative compromise. *Journal of Business Ethics*, *159*, 381–400.

Newell, A., & Simon, H. A. (1972). *Human Problem Solving*. Engelwood Cliffs, NJ: Prentice-Hall.

Nutt, P. C. (1984). Types of organisational decision processes. *Administrative Science Quarterly*, *29*(3), 414–450.

Organisation for Economic Co-operation and Development (OECD) (2002). Sustainable development: Indicators to measure decoupling of environmental pressure from economic growth. *OECD Report*, 1.

Pedersen, L. J. T. (2009). See no evil: Moral sensitivity in the formulation of business problems. *Business Ethics: A European Review*, *18*(4), 335–348.

Pounds, W. F. (1969). The process of problem finding. *Industrial Management Review*, *11*(1), 1–19.

Ramoglou, S. (2021). Knowable opportunities in an unknowable future? On the epistemological paradoxes of entrepreneurship theory. *Journal of Business Venturing*, *36*(2), 106090.

Ramoglou, S., & Gartner, W. B. (2022). A historical intervention in the 'opportunity wars': forgotten scholarship, the discovery/creation disruption, and moving forward by looking backward. *Entrepreneurship: Theory and Practice*, *0*(0), 1–18.

Ramoglou, S., Zyglidopoulos, S., & Papadopoulou, F. (2021). Is there opportunity without stakeholders? A stakeholder critique and development of opportunity-actualization. *Entrepreneurship Theory and Practice*, *0*(0), 1–29.

Renko, M., Shrader, R. C., & Simon, M. (2012). Perception of entrepreneurial opportunity: A general framework. *Management Decision*, *50*(7), 1233–1251.

Rittel, H. W. J., & Webber, M. M. (1973). Dilemmas in a general theory of planning. *Policy Sciences*, *4*(2), 155–169.

Santos, F. M. (2012). A positive theory of social entrepreneurship. *Journal of Business Ethics*, *111*(3), 335–351.

Sarasvathy, S. D., & Ramesh, A. (2019). An effectual model of collective action for addressing sustainability challenges. *Academy of Management Perspectives*, *33*(4), 405–424.

Schaefer, K., Corner, P. D., & Kearins, K. (2015). Social, environmental and sustainable entrepreneurship research: What is needed for sustainability-as-flourishing? *Organization & Environment*, *28*(4), 394–413.

Schumpeter, J. A. (1934). *The Theory of Economic Development*. Cambridge, MA: Harvard University Press.

Shane, S. (2000). Prior knowledge and the discovery of entrepreneurial opportunities. *Organization Science*, *11*(4), 448–469.

Shane, S. (2003). *A General Theory of Entrepreneurship: The Individual-Opportunity Nexus*. Cheltenham, UK: Edward Elgar Publishing Limited.

Shane, S., & Venkataraman, S. (2000). The promise of entrepreneurship as a field of research. *Academy of Management Review*, *25*(1), 217–226.

Short, J. C., Ketchen, D. J., Shook, C. L., & Ireland, R. D. (2010). The concept of 'opportunity' in entrepreneurship research: Past accomplishments and future challenges. *Journal of Management, 36*(1), 40–65.

Smith, G. (1989). Managerial problem identification. *Omega, 17*, 27–36.

Smith, A. (1759). *The Theory of Moral Sentiments* (2002nd ed.) Cambridge: Cambridge University Press.

Smith, A. (1776). *An Inquiry into the Nature and Causes of the Wealth of Nations* (2007th edition). Petersfield: Harriman House.

Tajfel, H., & Turner, J. C. (1979). An integrative theory of intergroup conflict. In W. G. Austin & S. Worchel (Eds.), *The Social Psychology of Intergroup Relations* (pp. 7–24). Monterey, CA: Brooks/Cole.

Tversky, A., & Kahneman, D. (1981). The framing of decisions and the psychology of choice. *Science, 211*, 453–458.

Venkataraman, S. (1997). The distinctive domain of entrepreneurship research: An editor's perspective. In J. Katz & R. Brockhaus (Eds.), *Advances in Entrepreneurship, Firm Emergence and Growth* (Vol. 3. pp. 119–138). Greenwich, CT: JAI Press.

Van der Werff, E., Steg, L., & Keizer, K. (2014). I am what I am, by looking past the present: The influence of biospheric values and past behavior on environmental self-identity. *Environment and Behavior, 46*(5), 626–657.

Vogel, P. (2017). From venture idea to venture opportunity. *Entrepreneurship: Theory and Practice, 41*(6), 943–971.

Wood, M. S. (2017). Misgivings about dismantling the opportunity construct. *Journal of Business Venturing Insights, 7*, 21–25.

Wood, M. S., & McKinley, W. (2020). The entrepreneurial opportunity construct: Dislodge or leverage? *Academy of Management Perspectives, 34*(3), 352–365.

Wright, M., & Phan, P. H. (2020). The opportunity wars in entrepreneurship. *Academy of Management Perspectives*, https://spiral.imperial.ac.uk/handle/10044/1/66009

Żur, A. (2015). Social problems as sources of opportunity: Antecedents of social entrepreneurship opportunities. *Entrepreneurial Business and Economics Review, 3*(4), 73–87.

Philipp S. Eppe*, Lennart Winkeler, Geo Kocheril, Torben Stührmann

9 Leadership in Transitions: The Case of Hydrogen

Abstract: Hydrogen from renewable energies (green hydrogen) plays a central role in achieving the goals of the Paris Climate Agreement. The development of hydrogen economies within the energy transition will pressure existing technical regimes, break up market structures and create new power relations. However, due to its disruptive nature, this early transformation phase is characterised by significant uncertainties and questions about the right transformation path. Hence, supply, demand and infrastructure challenges – a three-sided chicken-and-egg problem – are emerging, and the usual first-mover advantage does not exist in the local hydrogen economy. Therefore, developing approaches as isolated technical applications will not be sufficient to address these complex challenges with much-needed solutions. Against this background, this chapter provides guidance to sustainable entrepreneurs seeking to establish themselves in the evolving hydrogen economy to minimise entrepreneurial, strategic investment and business risks. First, we describe the specifics of transformations and apply theoretical approaches to the current hydrogen situation. Subsequently, leadership styles and decision criteria are described and examined for applicability in the current hydrogen situation. Based on this, we formulate a six-step guide for sustainable entrepreneurs. The six components of the guide include: developing a vision, understanding and reflecting on the environment, communicating, building a network, building trust and aiming for transdisciplinarity. For each of these points, we describe benefits and necessities. Finally, we present two methodological approaches (decision support systems and participatory modelling) that can be used to implement the recommended actions based on resilience criteria.

Keywords: transformations, leadership, sustainable entrepreneurs, resilience, hydrogen

1 Leadership in Transitions: The Case of Hydrogen

The latest Intergovernmental Panel on Climate Change (IPCC) report again highlights humanity's influence on the emergence and rapid progress of the climate crisis, with greenhouse gases, especially carbon dioxide, playing a central role (IPCC, 2022). To mitigate the crisis, the United Nations agreed to limit global warming to a maximum of 2 °C compared to the pre-industrial era in 2015 as part of the Paris Climate Agreement (UNFCC, 2015). In

*Corresponding author: Philipp S. Eppe, Fachgebiet Resiliente Energiesysteme, SFG 2230, Enrique-Schmidt-Str. 7, 28359 Bremen, Germany, e-mail: eppe@uni-bremen.de
Lennart Winkeler, Geo Kocheril, Torben Stührmann, Department of Resilient Energy Systems, University of Bremen, Bremen, Germany

https://doi.org/10.1515/9783110756159-011

order to achieve the goals of the Paris Climate Agreement and thus prevent irreversible climate impacts, tipping points and resulting economic damage, emissions must be avoided as early as possible (Cai, Lenton, & Lontzek, 2016).

Hydrogen produced using renewable energy (green hydrogen) plays a pivotal role in achieving the described goals. It is envisaged that green hydrogen will foster large-scale integration of renewable energies and power generation (Flis & Deutsch, 2021). By distributing energy across sectors and regions, green hydrogen can decarbonise transportation and industrial energy use and assist in decarbonising building and heat power while serving as renewable feedstock (European Clean Hydrogen Alliance, 2021). Green hydrogen will, for example, be crucial as a primary material and energy carrier for climate-neutral production in the chemical, cement and steel industries, replacing fossil fuels and avoiding CO_2 emissions. Since hydrogen can be transported and stored, it can also contribute to the resilient security of supply.

However, climate-neutral hydrogen production is not yet competitively priced at this stage. Furthermore, due to technical and physical limitations of climate-neutral hydrogen production, the direct use of green electricity is often more energy-efficient, climate-friendly and cost-effective (Joas et al., 2020). Therefore, and due to limited hydrogen availability, there are differences between sectors regarding applicability and feasibility. In some sectors, hydrogen is considered uncontroversial (e.g., steel production and long-haul aviation) (Deutsch & Schimmel, 2021). However, it is unlikely to be utilised by individuals or smaller sectors because the economies of scale (e.g., cost advantages due to scale of operation) will not be achieved (Kader & Kaya, 2021; Schimmel et al., 2021).

As hydrogen gains momentum in the global energy transition, a fundamental shift in transport, industry and power generation is in the offing. Developing local hydrogen economies will pressure existing technical regimes, breaking up market structures and establishing new power arrangements. However, the disruptive nature of this early phase of transformation is characterised by significant uncertainties and questions about the appropriate transformation path.

Additionally, and despite the ambitious goals and investments, green hydrogen, while being necessary and feasible, could continue to be a scarce resource in the future due to distributional conflicts and possibly political, economic or technical barriers to its expansion (Schimmel et al., 2021; Schlund, Schulte, & Sprenger, 2022). Supply, demand and infrastructure challenges, a three-sided chicken-and-egg problem, emerge (Schlund, Schulte, & Sprenger, 2022), and the usual 'first mover' advantage does not exist in local emerging hydrogen economies. Entrepreneurs in volatile markets with an insufficient hydrogen supply may not survive (Astiaso Garcia, 2017). At the same time, a constant and predictable demand for hydrogen is necessary for manufacturers to advance their technology and increase their production (Schimmel et al., 2021). Lastly, a hydrogen-compatible infrastructure, without which spatially distributed trade is impossible, must be in place to create competitive market conditions (Schlund, Schulte, & Sprenger, 2022).

These non-linear transformation paths and the related path dependencies, uncertainties and risks of lock-in technology, infrastructure and product developments pose a significant entrepreneurial, strategic investment and business risk. Many questions and challenges arise, and priorities and expectations vary considerably. Relevant actors, which need to adapt in many ways, have different potentials and constraints, and different hydrogen production technologies are currently in different maturity phases (Dehghanimadvar et al., 2020).

Developing approaches as isolated technical applications will not be sufficient to address these complex challenges with much-needed solutions. Potential industry leaders need a holistic view of its facets to navigate this change optimally. Cross-sector processes require a resilience approach considering the entire hydrogen value chain. Stakeholders should consider processes in the context of the overall system from a socio-technical perspective. The transition from carbon-intensive technologies to those based on renewable energy sources has already produced a discernible socio-technical shift (Chappin, 2011). The right balance between societal readiness and technology development is critical for a successful hydrogen diffusion, as these influence implementation options and technology trust (Yun & Lee, 2015).

Against the background described, this chapter attempts to guide entrepreneurs who want to establish themselves in the developing hydrogen economy. Entrepreneurs are critical change agents and often play an essential role in introducing disruptive sustainable energy innovations (Hockerts & Wüstenhagen, 2010; Reddy, 2015). Nevertheless, they tend to be overlooked in the hydrogen literature. At the same time, entrepreneurial businesses have higher failure rates than new subsidiaries of incumbent firms (Neffke et al., 2018). To provide guidance, we will attempt to answer the following questions:
– What are socio-technical transformations, and what can we learn from the past?
– Which entrepreneurial decisions and leadership are needed to succeed in the developing hydrogen economy?
– Which tools and approaches can help to realise these actions resiliently?

We will base the structure of the chapter on the formulated questions, followed by a final remark. Then, by answering the second question, we formulate guiding principles for entrepreneurs who want to establish themselves in the emerging hydrogen economy.

2 Socio-technical Transformations

Authors often use the terms 'transformation' and 'transition' interchangeably and research communities with shared and differing perspectives exist around both terminologies (Chappin & Ligtvoet, 2014; Hölscher, Wittmayer, & Loorbach, 2018). However, differentiating the terms 'transformation' and 'transition' can give insights into the dynamics of change and guide practical decisions in the emerging green hydrogen economy. We, therefore, distinguish between these terms following the multi-level perspective of Geels and Schot (2007), which defines a transformation as one possible transition pathway.

Socio-technical transitions describe changes to a system that, according to Geels and Schot (2007), consists of a landscape level, a regime level and a niche level. The socio-technical landscape represents a slow-changing overarching environment, such as macroeconomics, deep cultural patterns and macro-political developments that cannot be directly influenced by niche and regime actors. The socio-technical regime describes shared cognitive routines in a community of engineers, scientists, policy-makers, users and stakeholders that contribute to structuring technological development. Examples of these routines are stabilising existing development paths through regulations and standards and adapting lifestyles to technical systems, infrastructures and competencies. Technological niches, in contrast, form the micro-level where radical innovations emerge that are initially unstable low-power socio-technical configurations supported and developed by small networks of committed actors. Transformations, as one possible transition path, occur when regime actors respond to a moderate landscape pressure, which occurs when niche innovations are not yet advanced enough, by changing development paths and innovation activities. This process distinguishes transformation from other transition processes such as reconfiguration, technological substitution and de- and re-alignment (see Geels & Schot, 2007).

Applied to the current hydrogen situation, we observe that landscape pressure emerges from progressive environmental degradation, climate change, the finite nature of natural resources and societal pressure demanding solutions to these problems. Further, with all its associated agreements, visions and objectives, the agreed energy transition creates additional landscape pressure. Niche innovations have not yet been sufficiently developed to counter the landscape pressure, as green hydrogen technologies are either not mature enough, not cost-competitive or not sufficiently expanded. Relevant regime actors respond to this situation by promoting and incorporating hydrogen technologies and researching possible transformation scenarios. These actors include political stakeholders influencing the direction of development paths and innovation activities and industrial stakeholders influencing policy through lobbying. For niche actors, such as entrepreneurs, this creates the opportunity to act as pioneers to develop alternative practices or technologies that can gradually change the regime level, thus transforming the system towards a hydrogen-based economy.

As can be seen, transformation processes are characterised by discontinuity and socio-technical change. Several transformations have taken place in the past. Historical examples of socio-technical transformations are the introduction of piped water supply, the conversion of cesspools into sewage systems or the automobile and its associated infrastructure (Farla et al., 2012). Also, the iron and steel industry transformed once before in the nineteenth century, when it switched from using bio-fuels to coal as part of the energy transition (Madureira, 2012).

The envisaged transformation to a hydrogen economy is purpose-driven in addressing the problem of climate change. It thus differs from historical transformations, which were largely emergent, with entrepreneurs taking advantage of the commercial opportunities of new technologies (Geels et al., 2017). Nevertheless, some features between past transformations and a possible hydrogen transformation can be observed, and the transformation to a green hydrogen economy faces similar complexities and uncertainties about the appropriate transformation path as other multi-level sustainability challenges such as water–energy–food security of supply (Pahl-Wostl, 2019). In these uncertainties, existing knowledge and practices are often no longer sufficient, and there is a higher demand for innovation to drive recovery (Anderson & Li, 2014).

However, transformation processes are usually slow and take several decades (Farla et al., 2012). Moreover, it is often challenging to change broad institutional structures, mainly because they are a valuable asset for some actors who benefit from an existing system. Change then becomes a question of conflicts of interest and power struggles (Farla et al., 2012). Further, transformations cannot be reduced to technical implementation and are not only driven by financial incentives, regulations and information provision. Instead, they also include social, political and cultural processes and changes in consumer habits (Geels et al., 2017). Nevertheless, rapid action is required to mitigate environmental degradation and climate change. A quick shift towards a hydrogen economy is needed to reduce emissions, and obstacles and setbacks on this path should be avoided as far as possible.

To overcome the described uncertainties and to deal with the complexity of socio-technical transformations, the concept of resilience can act as a guiding principle. Resilience can be understood as 'the ability of an entity – e.g., asset, organisation, community, region – to anticipate, resist, absorb, respond to, adapt to, and recover from a disturbance' (Carlson et al., 2012). Hydrogen itself can increase system resilience by increasing energy flexibility and decentralisation and providing energy storage (European Clean Hydrogen Alliance, 2021; Schlund, Schulte, & Sprenger, 2022). However, the resilience concept is also essential for all those who want to play a part in the developing hydrogen economy, for existing market players who are under pressure to transform themselves and for new market players who have yet to establish themselves. Both are facing the uncertainty of positioning themselves in a highly dynamic environment. Therefore, especially in such systems under transformation, it is essential to strengthen all relevant stakeholders' adaptive capacity along the supply chain.

As can be noted, the transformational features described require strategic decisions from all actors involved. These decisions can have long-term and far-reaching effects, and many critical decisions, such as mission definition and resource allocation, require strategic leadership. For entrepreneurs who want to establish themselves in the emerging hydrogen economy, it is therefore vital to understand the decisions and leadership required for success in the evolving hydrogen economy.

3 Entrepreneurial Decisions and Leadership

There are several definitions of the term leadership, but there is still a lack of consensus on its meaning (Harrison et al., 2020). We will use an understanding of entrepreneurial leadership that focuses on social processes based on group activities changing the actions and behaviour of others to achieve desired goals, objectives and visions (Mokhtar et al., 2019). Entrepreneurship itself can be understood as a variant of leadership, and leadership directly influences organisational performance and is critical for meeting the challenges described above (Lin & Yi, 2021; Uhl-Bien, Marion, & McKelvey, 2007; Vecchio, 2003). We deliberately do not refer to governance but exclusively to leadership aspects related to entrepreneurship. Further, as entrepreneurs who will be part of the transformation towards a green hydrogen economy are likely to have a central concern for the environment, they will be called sustainable entrepreneurs from this point onward.

Any leadership must always be applied appropriately to the given situation (Mokhtar et al., 2019). Concerning the hydrogen transformation, the question arises as to which leadership style is best suited to establish oneself successfully and one's own company in the evolving hydrogen economy. Previous leadership literature has identified diverse leadership styles. The latest fundamental leadership approach is the transformational-transactional leadership theory (Burns, 1978). This theory distinguishes between transactional leadership, which describes a working relationship of 'give and take', where the relationship between leader and followers builds on an exchange, for example, through a system of rewards for achieving specific goals, and transformational leadership, where the leader displays charisma and a shared vision with his/her followers and inspires others to exceptional performance (Lai, 2011). However, as this approach focuses on the interpersonal level, it is not sufficiently applicable for the focus of this book chapter. We aim to identify leadership styles and decision-making practices that can be applied to inter-organisational settings and go beyond the typical leader–follower relationship.

One of the theories describing inter-organisational leadership is the concept of supply chain leadership. Supply chain leadership is 'a set of behaviours exhibited by one (or more) firm(s) in influencing and orchestrating the actions and behaviours of supply chain partners' (Mokhtar et al., 2019: 7). However, inter-organisational networks in the emerging hydrogen economy are likely to go beyond buyer–supplier relationships and are potentially non-hierarchical. According to Endres and Weibler (2019), this specific context could foster leaderless cooperation or shared leadership. Given the current state of the hydrogen economy and current trends, it is likely that the inevitably emerging networks will share a common network identity and motivation to drive the hydrogen economy. Therefore, a move towards shared leadership seems more likely (Endres & Weibler, 2019). Shared leadership, also called collective leadership, cannot be limited to one individual but is a plural form of leadership where leadership is collectively shared by different people and built in interaction. This kind of collaborative, cross-organisational and network leadership is one of the most important new topics in leadership research. Many scholars see it as necessary to meet the challenges of far-reaching societal, economic and technical changes (Endres & Weibler, 2019). Shared leadership is positively associated with creativity, diffusion of innovation and organisational resilience and therefore is likely to be beneficial in inter-organisational network exchanges (Ali, Wang, & Johnson, 2020; Currie & Spyridonidis, 2019; Gichuhi, 2021; Hoch, 2013).

Further, and beyond network efforts and inter-organisational exchanges, entrepreneurial leaders also require specific competencies to seize opportunities while overcoming challenges (Harrison, Burnard, & Paul, 2018). In light of the described transformational context and identifying the best hydrogen leadership style(s), it is vital to understand the specific competencies needed. Some of the following competencies are part of existing leadership theories, either going beyond the competencies any sustainable entrepreneur should possess (e.g., Simba & Thai, 2019) or seeming particularly relevant in the hydrogen context. Relevant competencies include vision and trust creation, opportunity identification (see Chapter 8), foresight capacity, critical reflection, flexibility, communication and network development. The section on guiding principles for resilient leadership in transformative systems will translate these competencies into strategic actions for successful hydrogen leadership. First, however, it is essential to understand how decision-making, as part of leadership, works and how it can affect sustainable entrepreneurial hydrogen leadership.

Homo economicus as a concept is an essential pillar of the neoclassical economics approach, and associated with it are, in particular, the core assumptions of rational decisions and the maximisation of utility. However, the completeness and validity of these assumptions were already criticised in 1979 based on empirical social psychological experiments (e.g., Kahnemann & Tversky, 1979). In contrast to the normative approach of homo economicus, various theories have been developed in behavioural economics to describe individual decision-making, such as prospect theory (Kahneman & Tversky, 1979), bounded rationality (Sent, 2018) and the theory of planned behaviour (Ajzen, 1991). These theories illustrate that it is beyond human capabilities to always make entirely rational decisions. Instead, humans often rely on so-called heuristics, which describe rules of thumb or mental shortcuts, to simplify the process of decision-making (Cossette, 2014). Under great uncertainty and complexity, as in the current hydrogen situation, these heuristics can theoretically be an effective and efficient aid to decision-making (Busenitz & Barney, 1997; Zhang, Bij, & Song, 2020). However, heuristics can also lead to biases (errors in prediction or estimation) and, therefore, to costly mistakes and catastrophic decisions (Cossette, 2014).

Entrepreneurs tend to be more prone to decision-making biases and heuristics than managers of larger enterprises, as they often lack general and situational knowledge (Busenitz & Barney, 1997; Zhang, Bij, & Song, 2020). This susceptibility is why it is crucial to keep biases like over-confidence and over-optimism in mind when following the strategic actions formulated in the next section. Later, this chapter will also present methodologies that can reduce the use of heuristics and the vulnerability to biases (i.e., decision support systems and participatory modelling).

4 Specific Entrepreneurial Conditions

Incumbent firms are forced by disruptive innovations, such as hydrogen technology, to renew their capabilities and competencies, albeit often reluctantly, to remain viable in a changing environment (Geels, 2014; Kivimaa et al., 2021). The oil and gas industry, for example, has the potential to act as a producer, supplier or pipeline operator of low-carbon hydrogen (Schlund, Schulte, & Sprenger, 2022). This renewal might also include upskilling and reskilling of the workforce.

Sustainable entrepreneurs do not have to change but can reinvent themselves and their business idea and possibly create more sustainable alternatives as innovative solutions for tomorrow's markets. They might even be more credible in their claim to be part of the solution and not the problem (Hockerts & Wüstenhagen, 2010). This particular position brings both opportunities and challenges. For example, opportunities for new business models such as energy suppliers, renewable energy producers and hydrogen technology providers can be expected (Schlund, Schulte, & Sprenger, 2022).

Nevertheless, sustainable entrepreneurs are at a disadvantage compared to established companies that want to enter the hydrogen economy or have already established themselves in areas of the value chain. Not only are they less politically influential, have fewer resources and lack market presence compared to the prominent established players in the sectors affected by the hydrogen transformation, but they also lack technical manufacturing capacity, experience with large-scale pilot testing, existing distribution channels and service networks (Geels, 2014; Hockerts & Wüstenhagen, 2010; Johnstone et al., 2020; Rothaermel, 2001). Furthermore, sustainable entrepreneurs often have to spend a lot of time upfront building relationships with market actors, explaining how developed technologies work and gaining the trust of potential customers and partners (Reddy, 2015). Larger established companies are often already organised in networks like the International Hydrogen Council (Hydrogen Council, 2017).

5 Guiding Principles for Resilient Leadership in Transformative Systems

Despite the uncertainties and potential obstacles and disadvantages described, the time seems good for sustainable entrepreneurs who want to enter the hydrogen economy, as costs for electricity from renewable energies and electrolyser costs are expected to decrease significantly, while electrolyser capacities are likely to increase (International Energy Agency, 2021; Nuñez-Jimenez & De Blasio, 2022). In addition, a market for hydrogen and hydrogen technologies with a turnover of more than 2.5 trillion dollars annually and jobs for more than 30 million people worldwide have been forecast (Hydrogen Council, 2017). These conditions create a unique window of opportunity. First, however, sustainable entrepreneurs must know which strategic actions can help establish themselves in the emerging hydrogen economy to stand out from the competition. The following section describes the six guiding principles for resilient leadership in transformative systems.

1. Developing a vision

Developing a vision is the first crucial step for any sustainable entrepreneur trying to establish their business in the emerging hydrogen economy. A good vision is practical and plausible, and entrepreneurial leaders should have a vision for a year or more that they want to realise to be successful in the long term (Pauceanu et al., 2021). Furthermore, developing a vision and effectively communicating it, which is also an essential part of the transformational leadership style (Lai, 2011), is crucial to gain public and follower support for one's hydrogen business model. Vision support can be gained not only by emphasising the urgency of the problems and thus the need for more sustainable technologies and processes but also (and perhaps even more so) by communicating one's own business as part of an attractive vision of an alternative future (Turnheim & Geels, 2012). However, it is essential to remember that this does not mean that short-term, measurable results are not crucial for sustainable entrepreneurial leadership (Connelly, 2007), and leaders must balance long-term and short-term needs (Alblooshi, Shamsuzzaman, & Haridy, 2021).

Furthermore, a vision always needs monitoring to verify its success. Socio-technical systems in transformation processes are very dynamic and require good monitoring. Results can then be analysed and reflected upon to make necessary adjustments. The decision support approaches presented later can help with monitoring. This approach is essential to making value chains more flexible and resilient (Kagermann et al., 2021), which we will explain in more detail in the next section.

2. Understanding and reflecting on the environment

To develop, recognise and realise visions and short-term results resiliently, sustainable entrepreneurs must be able to identify opportunities, act with foresight and critically reflect on situations while remaining flexible. Therefore, it is crucial to understand the socio-technical system in which the respective sustainable entrepreneur moves and becomes aware of existing dependencies. This understanding also includes a more profound comprehension of possible risks that could jeopardise the entrepreneurial project's success and risks that limit the effectiveness and stability of the emerging supply chains.

While a willingness to take risks is necessary for any entrepreneurial leader (Harrison et al., 2020), sustainable entrepreneurs must be careful not to fall for over-confidence and over-optimism biases. Sustainable entrepreneurs should build supply chains transparently to identify risks and vulnerabilities to external shocks, and continuous risk management should occur among members of strategic alliances. Several methodological approaches can be derived from the resilience approach to avoid emerging unsustainable and linear path dependencies and vulnerable supply chains. To gain a more holistic understanding of one's products, a prospective life-cycle assessment (Thonemann, Schulte, & Maga, 2020) and thorough market analysis to identify symbiotic companies that allow diversification and multiple sourcing (preferably with several suppliers for each component) might be helpful.

3. Communicating

As others need to become aware of a vision for it to be implemented, the vision needs to be communicated. Therefore, communication is essential for hydrogen entrepreneurs. Successful communication, as part of, for example, the collective leadership theory, is a precondition for understanding potential problems, setting common goals, identifying where and which expertise lies within a network, building up trust and sharing any leadership role (Friedrich et al., 2009; Friedrich, Griffith, & Mumford, 2016; Meier et al., 2016). Using their charisma and expertise, entrepreneurial leaders can communicate shared values and vision, enabling network members to deal with the uncertainties and risks associated with implementing new ideas while gaining their acceptance and trust (Alblooshi, Shamsuzzaman, & Haridy, 2021). This communication also involves knowledge and idea-sharing to facilitate collective decision-making (Friedrich et al., 2009; Friederich, Griffith, & Mumford, 2016). In this context, an informal atmosphere can facilitate an open and unbiased exchange and go beyond a rational and purely instrumentalist attitude towards the developing network (Endres & Weibler, 2019). According to Kantabutra (2020), visions that are short, clear, future-oriented, stable, challenging, abstract, desirable and contain content that increases stakeholder satisfaction are easier to communicate.

4. Building a network

Building formal and informal networks will be necessary to implement the described visions successfully. An active social strategy for networking and cross-collaborative network efforts are part of sustainable entrepreneurial success (Kerr, Kerr, & Xu, 2018). This link seems especially true for a successful market ramp-up of hydrogen technologies. Network development and the corresponding network awareness create trust-based contacts and support structures from which innovations can emerge, thus enabling change and improved resilience (Brown, 2021; Farla et al., 2012; Friedrich, Griffith, & Mumford, 2016). These networks can further help build social capital, discover more entrepreneurial opportunities and find new potential suppliers and customers.

Sustainable entrepreneurs should aim to form strategic alliances to achieve these benefits. These strategic alliances should go beyond buyer–supplier relationships and involve a long-term perspective, high levels of partner commitment and mutual integration, specific investments in assets and governance mechanisms and sharing of strategic resources such as information, routines, knowledge and skills (Hudnurkar, Jakhar, & Rathod, 2014; Meier et al., 2016). Sustainable entrepreneurs should synthesise knowledge by collaborating, connecting and combining their diverse knowledge (Anderson & Li, 2014). Increased actor and knowledge diversity and long-term commitment can foster co-creation and promote social sustainability and the achievement of environmental targets (Johnstone et al., 2020). Since it is unlikely and unrealistic for an individual to be a well-resourced leader in all situations, this collective diversity approach should be applied to inter-organisational alliances and corporate teams, respectively (Friedrich et al., 2009).

Moreover, to strengthen their impact, these alliances should go beyond an individual's career or an organisation's success and aim for shared network identity. Through collective action and cooperation, actors can significantly shape and coordinate the building process of an emerging field (Musiolik & Markard, 2011). It is also critical to share risks and rewards and promote interactive organisational learning to facilitate knowledge spillovers and thus reduce competitive disadvantages vis-à-vis incumbents while increasing the system's resilience. To avoid costly hydrogen transport over long distances, these strategic alliances can help organise the value chains so that hydrogen is predominantly produced close to consumption (Schlund, Schulte, & Sprenger, 2022). However, alliances should not only focus on national actors but should also be embedded internationally and at the European level, as this allows the exploitation of the full potential of hydrogen (Schlund, Schulte, & Sprenger, 2022; Wang et al., 2020).

5. Building trust

Trust, which can be understood as a 'psychological state comprising the intention to accept vulnerability based upon positive expectations of the intentions or behaviour of another' (Rousseau et al., 1998: 395), plays a vital role within these networks. It is one of the critical factors in relationships between organisations and alliance performance and, therefore, an essential determinant for an alliance's success (Meier et al., 2016). Building inter-organisational trust based on reciprocal interactions is not a one-off task but one to work on continuously. Sustainable entrepreneurial leaders must take trust-building measures, such as communication or alliance-specific investments (Meier et al., 2016). These measures can mean consciously investing time and energy to get to know one another and openly stating intentions and plans to increase transparency (Connelly, 2007). It is also important to create mutual, trust-based agreements between actors in the developing hydrogen economy about what investments will be made and what could help overcome the three-sided chicken-and-egg problem. However, building and maintaining trust also means that the benefits of collaboration should outweigh the costs, such as disclosing information that gave sustainable entrepreneurs a competitive advantage and loss of autonomy (Connelly, 2007).

6. Aiming for transdisciplinarity

The uncertainties associated with the necessary change do not only affect individual areas, disciplines or industries. They cannot be considered from a single perspective. Therefore, there is a need for transdisciplinary approaches in addition to creating trust between stakeholders. Creating transdisciplinarity, which is 'the ongoing process of inquiry-driven interaction, engagement of knowledge, and informative action that can assist in addressing the complexities of the world' (Heidkamp, Garland, & Krak, 2021: 4), by integrating different political and industrial stakeholders, citizens and experts within these alliances, enables a co-creation of the upcoming transformation. For sustainable entrepreneurs, this also means actively pursuing research and development on novel solutions of the value creation operated by the company concerning a possible positioning in hydrogen applications, that is, through methodical product development and optimisation or the introduction of innovation management. Where possible, it can be beneficial to join already existing transdisciplinary networks.

Sustainable entrepreneurs should, for example, seek to participate in publicly funded integrated demonstration projects. These offer unique opportunities that contribute to better coordination between different research and development directions, create opportunities for small and medium-sized enterprises, provide training and education and better assess costs and benefits (Zubaryeva, Dilara, & Maineri, 2015). Additionally, support platforms can help sustainable entrepreneurs to get the assistance needed (e.g., International Energy Agency, 2022).

6 Design Principles and Approaches Improving Resilience

As described above, the uncertainties and interdependencies associated with the transformative market introduction of hydrogen technologies and the increasing frequency of natural and human-made disasters, the strategic actions formulated require technology and business assessment that follows concepts of resilience and the associated guideline principles. Resilience aspects must be considered to promote a sustainable transformation, mitigate the impact of future stressors on the system and ensure a secure and robust infrastructure and supply. However, resilience is not only crucial regarding infrastructure but might be an additional helpful code of practice for sustainable entrepreneurial leaders and their business aspirations. Likewise, resilience should be considered a potential competitive advantage and not just a tool to mitigate risk (Klibi, Martel, & Guitouni, 2010). Goessling-Reisemann and Their (2019) proposed the following resilience-enhancing design principles, which are also applicable to potential entrepreneurial leaders in the emerging hydrogen economy:

- diversity
- redundancy

- geographical dispersion
- balance of feedback mechanisms
- flexible coupling
- modularity
- subsidiarity
- buffer and Storage
- unallocated resources
- flexible system requirements

These design principles can be applied to organise processes and to build infrastructures to be resilient against a wide range of possible stressors (Goessling-Reisemann & Thier, 2019). Translated for sustainable entrepreneurs, diversity can mean that, for example, electricity generation should be diversified to avoid path dependencies. The various elements of the system to be built should be as disparate, varied and balanced as possible. Redundancy, on the other hand, means that elements of the system (e.g., required resources or technologies) should be available as often as possible and beyond the actual need, whether by sheer number or specific functions. Thus, if one of the system's elements fails, the system's functionality (e.g., the supply chain) can be maintained.

Geographic dispersion contrasts with the stated recommendation to build hydrogen supply chains locally. This design principle encourages system elements to be geographically dispersed to minimise vulnerability to stressors such as extreme weather events or terrorist attacks. Entrepreneurial leaders must weigh any additional costs associated with transportation routes against greater resilience.

Feedback mechanisms address the monitoring of processes and long- and short-term goals. In addition to technical monitoring, the described open communication structures can contribute to better monitoring of processes and thus enable rapid action. To avoid cascading failures, for example, in the supply or production chain, a flexible or optional coupling can enable the functioning or partial functioning of elements and subsystems. Buffering and storing material, decentralised organisation and shared leadership can all contribute to optional coupling. In addition, certain modularity of the emerging system, that is, the existence of subdivided fully functioning sub-segments, is necessary to ensure reparability and reduce downtime.

In the context of shared leadership, subsidiarity is especially crucial. Applied to sustainable entrepreneurs and their networks, it suggests that, where possible, problems should be solved where they arise. Therefore, problems at lower organisational levels should be able to be solved independently of decisions at higher levels. These structures enable innovation, trust and the achievement of goals and visions. Again, successful communication plays a crucial role in this.

One of the problems that could need to be solved could be, for example, the sudden limitation of resources. Again, buffers and storage can help to maintain system function by providing additional capacity. In doing so, they can not only decouple subsystems but also allow the actors more time to react to the resource shortage. In the medium term, hydrogen will be able to contribute to renewable energy storage but should also be stored to react in case of possible hydrogen scarcity.

Taking this idea further, it also makes sense to build up additional resources (personnel, machines, time) that are not tied to specific tasks but are used variably as needed. These additional resources increase the flexibility of processes and, thus, the ability of the socio-technical system to deliver its service, even under stressful conditions. For hydrogen consumers, this could mean, for example, not using the total capacity of hydrogen in day-to-day business from the outset.

These resilience criteria described may seem like luxury issues to some entrepreneurs, but they are critical to the long-term success of the company and the hydrogen economy. Therefore, entrepreneurial leaders should base their decisions on these resilience criteria as they promote the long-term implementation of the hydrogen economy.

Further, it is helpful to consider transformations and strategic decisions under STEEP criteria (Social, Technological, Economic, Ecological, Political). However, research into implementing novel technologies mainly focuses on techno-economic studies to examine possibilities for integrating inventions into the existing system. For the successful transition from invention to innovation, it is essential to consider other perspectives besides the classic technical and economic dimensions to gain a holistic view of the transformation. For example, social interventions often hinder the speed of transformation and implementation.

Originally consisting of four components – Political, Economic, Social, Technological, (PEST) – the acronym STEEP is frequently used in analyses for strategic corporate planning and goes hand in hand with SWOT (Strengths, Weaknesses, Opportunities, Threats) analyses (e.g., Sammut-Bonnici & Galea, 2014). The PEST or STEEP analysis can serve as a tool for creating technology road maps, that is, considering possible future scenarios for one or more technologies (Szigeti et al., 2011). Adding the ecological perspective broadens the perspective to relevant areas of the energy transition. Complex interrelationships of energy systems are processed, observed and communicated so that new impressions, perspectives and insights can be gained by and from those involved (Fiukowski, Müller, & Gaudchau, 2017).

Under STEEP considerations, several tools and approaches are available to study and improve resilience, assist decision-making, and moderate, integrate and monitor processes. We present two: Decision Support Systems (DSS) and participatory modelling.

6.1 Decision Support Systems

The term Decision Support Systems (Power, 2002) describes tools that serve the exploration and simulation of complex processes and systems. Processing and visualising data and dynamics lowers barriers and empowers non-specialist stakeholders, policymakers and administrators (Deckert et al., 2020). As modern digital media offer a broad set of possibilities to enhance the experience, John et al. (2020) suggest broadening the terminology to Decision Visualisation Environment (DVE). Direct interaction with digital media can support better grasping of abstract concepts and simplify access to complex problems (Jacob et al., 2008; Shneiderman, 1982). Furthermore, it enables the exploration of different transformation scenarios and simplifies the identification of appropriate transformation pathways.

Therefore, applying these visualisation environments can support multi-criteria leadership decision-making (e.g., reducing biases), enhance communication and monitoring processes, and create a joint discussion base for networking and trust-building. Interactive participation and modelling effectively use these tools to bring stakeholders together and organise information about complex systems (Tuler et al., 2017). Therefore, these tools can empower stakeholders to solve energy sustainability problems (Siksnelyte et al., 2018), improving the considered system's resilience. Furthermore, the foresight capacity mentioned above, which is necessary for any resilient system to deal with uncertainties and the relativity of future conditions, can be enhanced by thoroughly analysing future scenarios (Sharifi & Yamagata, 2016). Incorporating STEEP dimensions into these decision-making processes can help deepen the understanding of the system and therefore improve long-term performance and alleviate risks.

6.2 Participatory Modelling

Participatory modelling, on the other hand, is considered an experiential and transdisciplinary learning process that combines stakeholders' attention, knowledge, motivation and vision to co-create and discuss scenarios supported by modelling tools and experts (Voinov et al., 2018). These modelling approaches are established methods for optimising operational planning decisions and the exploratory utilisation of world models (Dantzig, 1963; Meadows et al., 1972). Using computer models and model-based strategic analysis to make better strategic far-reaching decisions has a long tradition.

In energy system analysis, optimisation models play an essential role, with the model focusing on 'prescriptive' analysis of energy systems to make (cost-)optimal decisions (Brown, Hörsch, & Schlachtberger, 2018; Davenport & Harris, 2007; Gurobi, 2021; Hilpert et al., 2018). However, there are questions and concerns about these approaches regarding the adequate representation of societal actors and the socio-technical transformation dynamics of the complex energy transition (Li, Trutnevyte, & Strachan, 2015). In the scientific debate, different modelling approaches are compared for their strengths and gaps and how they can be combined synergetically and consistently (Kocheril et al., 2021; Köhler et al., 2018; Robinson et al., 2018). Selecting the appropriate modelling tool as a DSS is equally crucial as clarifying the appropriate model purpose and the associated opportunities and risks of predictive, descriptive, explorative and learning model tools (Edmonds et al., 2019).

However, in model development and model-tool usage of complex emerging socio-technical transformation pathways and markets, such as the hydrogen economy, risks arise from blind spots of the subjective mental models of the modeller or the organisation. In order to reduce these risks of biased assumptions and models through a shared learning process, the approach of participatory and companion modelling or decision theatre can be helpful both internally and externally with stakeholders from politics, non-government organisations (NGOs) and other affected groups (ASU, 2020; Étienne, 2014; Lumosi, Pahl-Wostl, & Scholz, 2019; Scholz, Dewulf, & Pahl-Wostl, 2014; Worrapimphong et al., 2010). These approaches provide a low-threshold way to communicate and understand the complexity of future sustainable systems (Beers et al., 2010; Mößner, 2018). Moreover, this collective and social learning environment can improve community resilience and adaptivity (Henly-Shepard, Gray, & Cox, 2015).

The presented approaches can promote cooperation by building trust and facilitating fruitful relationships. However, their success depends largely on sustainable communication and the functionality of the described transdisciplinary trust networks.

7 Final Remarks

The topic of hydrogen has repeatedly aroused interest in the past but has not yet been able to make a breakthrough. Now, the rapid decline in the cost of renewable energy, technological developments and the need to drastically reduce greenhouse gas emissions are unlocking new possibilities (European Commission, 2020).

This chapter aims to guide sustainable entrepreneurs who want to establish their businesses in the developing hydrogen economy. Sustainable entrepreneurs often work under uncertain, dynamic and changing conditions (Harrison et al., 2020). However, due to the three-sided chicken-and-egg problem and political and economic ambiguities regarding future developments (e.g., lack of uniform regulations and policies), the current hydrogen situation is particularly marked by uncertainties.

By providing six-step guiding principles, we aim to support sustainable entrepreneurs, proposing that developing a vision, understanding and reflecting on the environment, communicating, building a network, building trust, and transdisciplinary are essential for entrepreneurial success in the developing hydrogen economy. We argue that coordinated, intensive collaboration within the private sector will be necessary for a successful ramp-up of hydrogen technologies (Kearney Energy Transition Institute, 2020) and that coupled, orchestrated transformation processes and trust networks will be needed. Furthermore, we recommend using tools such as decision support systems or participatory modelling to support the implementation of these steps and carry out sustainable monitoring processes. These tools can help entrepreneurial leaders consider the described resilience principles when making decisions.

Furthermore, according to the European Clean Hydrogen Alliance (2021), integration, synchronisation and visibility are the keystones of hydrogen introduction and diffusion throughout the value chain. Integrating the hydrogen infrastructure based on enhanced coordination and communication between electricity, gas, district heating and hydrogen sectors is essential for a successful supply chain. This integration requires a well-organised planning process to develop a cost-effective, secure energy system that enables timely carbon neutrality. Further, a synchronisation of the hydrogen value chain is needed to lower the transformation costs. A massive expansion of power generation capacities from renewable energies must coincide with investments in hydrogen production (development of electrolysers and procurement of green hydrogen), hydrogen-compatible infrastructures and hydrogen end-use devices. Additionally, increasing the visibility of ongoing hydrogen projects and the communication of industrial actors planning to deploy hydrogen and related technologies can increase the acceptance of further actors, also concerning additional costs associated with introducing hydrogen technologies (European Clean Hydrogen Alliance, 2021). Lastly, hydrogen visibility can enhance decision-making, response-ability and supply chain efficiency, positively impacting supply chain resilience (Negri et al., 2021).

Considering and engaging various stakeholders offers practical ways to support integration, synchronisation and visibility within socio-technical transformations (Chilvers, Pallet, & Hargreaves, 2018). Collective and shared leadership is needed, which rapidly and effectively integrates the expertise of the entire actor-network to address these uncertainties and complexities in the business domain. Exemplary methods of collective leadership and large group facilitation, like future search, may be helpful here (Endres & Weibler, 2019; Weisbord & Janoff, 2005). To achieve the integration, synchronisation and visibility mentioned above, sustainable business leaders need to develop a shared vision based on a comprehensive picture of the current conditions, opportunities and potential obstacles. This vision should be communicated to policymakers and civil society through transdisciplinary trust-based alliances. Further, learning from successful local projects and transferring the generated insights to the national and European levels is also essential.

To avoid risky path dependencies and 'sunk costs,' the hydrogen market will most likely focus on 'safe' no-regret transformation and technology paths, such as in material hydrogen use, long-distance transport (air and ship) or long-term energy storage. Due to the broad range of possible applications and the resulting growth of new potential niches, however, players are also pursuing riskier hydrogen paths. These dynamics indicate the disruptive nature of the hydrogen case and highlight the need for sustainable entrepreneurs to proceed systematically and prudently. Technological innovations are expected in the upcoming market ramp-up or scaling of the pilot and demonstration facilities and technologies developed so far, enabling a fast-learning curve and cost reduction. Nevertheless, hydrogen will be a scarce commodity, especially at the beginning of the energy transition, with developments towards the middle end of the century assuming a more relaxed situation.

However, it cannot go unmentioned that speeding up the transformation and making renewable hydrogen cost-competitive will require extra incentives, political communication and policy support to create a supportive and expedient legal framework (Grubler, Wilson, & Nemet, 2016). Good policy governance can reduce risks of stranded assets and encourage opportunities for new value chains in the emergence phase of new green hydrogen markets by providing clear regulatory frameworks and prioritising incentives for (infra-)structures applicable to the energy system as a whole. The further expansion of renewable energy sources and power grids, sustained low renewable electricity prices and a decrease in the cost of electrolysis across Europe are the preconditions for a succeeding hydrogen economy (Sadik-Zada, 2021; Schlund, Schulte, & Sprenger, 2022). The private sector cannot achieve these conditions alone.

In doing so, it may be beneficial to consider the specific strengths and weaknesses of incumbents and sustainable entrepreneurs and to pursue a portfolio that provides balanced incentives (Hockerts & Wüstenhagen, 2010). However, it is also important to note that incumbent actors may not change their practices fast enough to bring about system-wide change and are likely to create resistance through lobbying that could ultimately hinder the low-carbon transformation process (Johnstone et al., 2020; Turnheim & Geels, 2012). For the natural gas infrastructure, for example, the current hydrogen situation means its business model's upcoming end or transformation push.

Finally, we would like to add a few caveats regarding our recommendations. We know that many of the topics covered in this chapter have only been touched upon and that they involve much more depth from a scientific point of view. In this chapter, however, we do not claim to describe all areas in depth. Instead, we want to give sustainable entrepreneurs an overview of their interrelationships and formulate application-oriented recommendations, including guiding principles for resilient leadership in transformative systems. We think that it is vital to identify and scientifically prepare application-oriented practices. In some cases, however, this goes against the spirit of entrepreneurship as sometimes a fail-fast-fail-often approach might be more effective.

We are also aware that there is not a single leadership formula or set of competencies and decision-making practices that will automatically make someone a good leader, that every leader is different and that no two leaders display their leadership qualities in the same way (Friedrich et al., 2009; Glover & Quisenberry, 2021). In addition, the collaborative, inter-organisational framework is a challenging one for traditional leaders, as single leadership, as the still dominant and widespread understanding of leadership in the corporate and organisational context, does not seem to be the kind of leadership that fits this context (Endres & Weibler, 2019). Nevertheless, emerging leaders in the hydrogen economy face similar problems and uncertainties that may better be solved by sharing leadership responsibility between individuals with different capabilities and qualities. Furthermore, shared leadership is positively associated with team creativity, innovation and diffusion of innovation, and organisational resilience (Ali, Wang, & Johnson, 2020; Currie & Spyridonidis, 2019; Gichuhi, 2021; Hoch, 2013). Entrepreneurial leaders in inter-organisational networks can benefit from these insights by sharing their knowledge, ideas and perspectives, increasing network performance, facilitating complex problem solving and achieving goals (Gichuhi, 2021). This process is essential, as the current hydrogen situation requires a shared vision and jointly planned efforts and actions to overcome the hurdles described in this chapter and ultimately create a resilient hydrogen economy. Further, by working together in networks, additional leadership skills can be learned and passed on, further strengthening the network efforts' effectiveness.

Lastly, our chapter deals mainly with the European area and cannot be applied to the global hydrogen economy. Specific national and cultural differences and conditions may influence the strategic actions needed for sustainable entrepreneurs. Nevertheless, we advocate a transformation towards a hydrogen economy that is prospectively based only on renewable energies, as this is the only way to reduce emissions effectively. The course must be set today in politics and business to achieve this reduction.

References

Ajzen, I. (1991). The theory of planned behaviour. *Organisational Behaviour and Human Decision Processes, 50*(2), 179–211.

Alblooshi, M., Shamsuzzaman, M., & Haridy, S. (2021). The relationship between leadership styles and organisational innovation. *European Journal of Innovation Management, 24*(2), 338–370.

Ali, A., Wang, H., & Johnson, R. E. (2020). Empirical analysis of shared leadership promotion and team creativity: An adaptive leadership perspective. *Journal of Organizational Behavior, 41*(5), 405–423.

Anderson, A., & Li, J. (2014). Entrepreneurship and networked collaboration; synergetic innovation, knowledge and uncertainty. *Journal of General Management, 40*(1), 7–21.

Astiaso Garcia, D. (2017). Analysis of non-economic barriers for the deployment of hydrogen technologies and infrastructures in European countries. *International Journal of Hydrogen Energy, 42*(10), 6435–6447.

Arizona State University (ASU). (2020). *Decision Theater Collaborative Research Methodology*. Arizona State University. https://dt.asu.edu/sites/default/files/2020-07/Collaborative%20Research%20Methodology.pdf

Beers, P. J., Veldkamp, A., Hermans, F., Van Apeldoorn, D., Vervoort, J. M., & Kok, K. (2010). Future sustainability and images. *Futures, 42*(7), 723–732.

Brown, B. C. (2021). Sane leadership in a crazy world: Essentials of complexity leadership. *Metaintegral Associates. Viitattu, 18,*

Brown, T., Hörsch, J., & Schlachtberger, D. (2018). PyPSA: Python for power system analysis. *Journal of Open Research Software, 6*(3), 1–15.

Burns, J. M. (1978). *Leadership*. Harper & Row. https://www.worldcat.org/title/leadership/oclc/3632001

Busenitz, L. W., & Barney, J. B. (1997). Differences between entrepreneurs and managers in large organisations: Biases and heuristics in strategic decision-making. *Journal of Business Venturing, 12*(1), 9–30.

Cai, Y., Lenton, T. M., & Lontzek, T. S. (2016). Risk of multiple interacting tipping points should encourage rapid CO_2 emission reduction. *Nature Climate Change, 6*(5), 520–525.

Carlson, J. L., Haffenden, R. A., Bassett, G. W., Buehring, W. A., Collins, M. J., III, Folga, S. M., & Whitfield, R. G. (2012). *Resilience: Theory and Application* (No. ANL/DIS-12-1). Argonne National Lab.(ANL), Argonne, IL (United States). Retrieved from web: https://www.osti.gov/servlets/purl/1044521

Chappin, É. J. L. (2011). *Simulating Energy Transitions*. The Netherlands: Next Generation Infrastructures Foundation Delft.

Chappin, E. J., & Ligtvoet, A. (2014). Transition and transformation: A bibliometric analysis of two scientific networks researching socio-technical change. *Renewable and Sustainable Energy Reviews, 30*, 715–723.

Chilvers, J., Pallett, H., & Hargreaves, T. (2018). Ecologies of participation in socio-technical change: The case of energy system transitions. *Energy Research & Social Science*, *42*, 199–210.

Connelly, D. R. (2007). Leadership in the collaborative interorganizational domain. *International Journal of Public Administration*, *30*(11), 1231–1262.

Cossette, P. (2014). Heuristics and cognitive biases in entrepreneurs: A review of the research. *Journal of Small Business and Entrepreneurship*, *27*(5), 471–496.

Currie, G., & Spyridonidis, D. (2019). Sharing leadership for diffusion of innovation in professionalised settings. *Human Relations (New York)*, *72*(7), 1209–1233.

Dantzig, G. B. (1963). *Linear Programming and Extensions*. Princeton, New Jersey: Princeton University Press.

Davenport, T. H., & Harris, J. G. (2007). Competing on analytics: The new science of winning. *Harvard Business Review Press, Language*, *15*(217), 24.

Deckert, A., Dembski, F., Ulmer, F., Ruddat, M., & Wössner, U. (2020). Digital tools in stakeholder participation for the German Energy Transition. Can digital tools improve participation and its outcome? In *The Role of Public Participation in Energy Transitions* (pp. 161–177). London, UK: Elsevier.

Dehghanimadvar, M., Shirmohammadi, R., Sadeghzadeh, M., Aslani, A., & Ghasempour, R. (2020). Hydrogen production technologies: Attractiveness and future perspective. *International Journal of Energy Research*, *44*(11), 8233–8254.

Deutsch, M., & Schimmel, M. (2021). *Making Renewable Hydrogen Cost-competitive: Policy Instruments for Supporting Green H2*. Agora Energiewende & Guidehouse. Retrieved from web: https://static.agora-energiewende.de/fileadmin/Projekte/2020/2020_11_EU_H2-Instruments/A-EW_223_H2-Instruments_WEB.pdf

Edmonds, B., Le Page, C., Bithell, M., Chattoe-Brown, E., Grimm, V., Meyer, R., Montañola-Sales, C., Ormerod, P., Root, H., & Squazzoni, F. (2019). Different modelling purposes. *Journal of Artificial Societies and Social Simulation*, *22*(3), 1–6.

Endres, S., & Weibler, J. (2019). Understanding (non)leadership phenomena in collaborative interorganizational networks and advancing shared leadership theory: An interpretive grounded theory study. *Business Research*, *13*(1), 275–309.

Étienne, M. (2014). *Companion Modelling: A Participatory Approach to Support Sustainable Development*. Versailles, France: Springer.

European Clean Hydrogen Alliance. (2021). *Reports of the Alliance Roundtables on Barriers and Mitigation Measures*. Retrieved from web: https://ec.europa.eu/growth/system/files/2021-11/ECH2A%20RTs%20reports%20on%20barriers%20and%20mitigation%20measures_FINAL.pdf

European Commission. (2020). *Communication from the Commission to the European Parliament, the Council, the European Economic and Social Committee and the Committee of the Regions – A hydrogen strategy for a climate-neutral Europe*. European Commission.

Farla, J., Markard, J., Raven, R., & Coenen, L. (2012). Sustainability transitions in the making: A closer look at actors, strategies and resources. *Technological Forecasting & Social Change*, *79*(6), 991–998.

Fiukowski, J., Müller, B., & Gaudchau, E. (2017). *Stakeholder Empowerment in Participatory Processes of the Energy Transition – An Evaluation of Impacts of Simulation Tools*. Retrieved from web: https://reiner-lemoine-institut.de/wp-content/publications/2017ENavi/Fiukowski_Stemp_Tools.pdf

Flis, G., & Deutsch, M. (2021). *12 Insights on Hydrogen*. Agora Industry. https://static.agora-energiewende.de/fileadmin/Projekte/2021/2021_11_H2_Insights/A-EW_245_H2_Insights_WEB.pdf

Friedrich, T. L., Griffith, J. A., & Mumford, M. D. (2016). Collective leadership behaviors: Evaluating the leader, team network, and problem situation characteristics that influence their use. *The Leadership Quarterly*, *27*(2), 312–333.

Friedrich, T. L., Vessey, W. B., Schuelke, M. J., Ruark, G. A., & Mumford, M. D. (2009). A framework for understanding collective leadership: The selective utilisation of leader and team expertise within networks. *The Leadership Quarterly*, *20*(6), 933–958.

Geels, F. W. (2014). Reconceptualising the co-evolution of firms-in-industries and their environments: Developing an inter-disciplinary Triple Embeddedness Framework. *Research Policy*, *43*(2), 261–277.

Geels, F. W., & Schot, J. (2007). Typology of socio-technical transition pathways. *Research Policy, 36*(3), 399–417.

Geels, F. W., Sovacool, B. K., Schwanen, T., & Sorrell, S. (2017). The socio-technical dynamics of low-carbon transitions. *Joule, 1*(3), 463–479.

Gichuhi, J. M. (2021). Shared leadership and organizational resilience: A systematic literature review. *International Journal of Organizational Leadership, 10*(SI), 67.

Glover, J., & Quisenberry, W. (2021). Leadership perspectives – A nascent's journey. *Academia Letters.* Retrieved from web: 10.20935/AL3511

Goessling-Reisemann, S., & Thier, P. (2019). On the difference between risk management and resilience management for critical infrastructures. In M. Ruth & S. Goessling-Reisemann (Eds.), *Handbook on Resilience of Socio-Technical Systems* (pp. 117–135). Cheltenham, UK: Edward Elgar Publishing.

Grubler, A., Wilson, C., & Nemet, G. (2016). Apples, oranges, and consistent comparisons of the temporal dynamics of energy transitions. *Energy Research & Social Science, 22*, 18–25.

Gurobi. (2021). *Prescriptive Analytics: The Data Science Master Key Discover how Companies like Uber, Air France, SAP, and the NFL use Prescriptive Analytics to Solve Their Most Complex Challenges.* https://cdn.gurobi.com/wp-content/uploads/2021/11/V2_1897_GUR_Prescriptive-Analytics_WhitePaper.pdf

Harrison, C., Burnard, K., & Paul, S. (2018). Entrepreneurial leadership in a developing economy: A skill-based analysis. *Journal of Small Business and Enterprise Development, 25*(3), 521–548.

Harrison, C., Omeihe, I., Simba, A., & Omeihe, K. (2020). Leading the way: The entrepreneur or the leader? *Journal of Small Business and Entrepreneurship*, 1–17.

Heidkamp, C. P., Garland, M., & Krak, L. (2021). Enacting a just and sustainable blue economy through transdisciplinary action research. *The Geographical Journal.* doi: 10.1111/geoj.12410.

Henly-Shepard, S., Gray, S. A., & Cox, L. J. (2015). The use of participatory modeling to promote social learning and facilitate community disaster planning. *Environmental Science & Policy, 45*, 109–122.

Hilpert, S., Kaldemeyer, C., Krien, U., Günther, S., Wingenbach, C., & Plessmann, G. (2018). The open energy modelling framework (oemof) – A new approach to facilitate open science in energy system modelling. *Energy Strategy Reviews, 22*, 16–25.

Hoch, J. E. (2013). Shared leadership and innovation: The role of vertical leadership and employee integrity. *Journal of Business and Psychology, 28*(2), 159–174.

Hockerts, K., & Wüstenhagen, R. (2010). Greening Goliaths versus emerging Davids – Theorising about the role of incumbents and new entrants in sustainable entrepreneurship. *Journal of Business Venturing, 25*(5), 481–492.

Hölscher, K., Wittmayer, J. M., & Loorbach, D. (2018). Transition versus transformation: What's the difference? *Environmental Innovation and Societal Transitions, 27*, 1–3.

Hudnurkar, M., Jakhar, S., & Rathod, U. (2014). Factors affecting collaboration in supply chain: A literature review. *Procedia – Social and Behavioral Sciences, 133*, 189–202.

Hydrogen Council. (2017). *Hydrogen Scaling up – A Sustainable Pathway for the Global Energy Transition.* Belgium: Hydrogen Council. https://hydrogencouncil.com/wp-content/uploads/2017/11/Hydrogen-scaling-up-Hydrogen-Council.pdf

International Energy Agency. (2021). *Could the Green Hydrogen Boom Lead to Additional Renewable Capacity by 2026?* https://www.iea.org/articles/could-the-green-hydrogen-boom-lead-to-additional-renewable-capacity-by-2026

International Energy Agency. (2022). *How Governments Support Clean Energy Start-ups – Insights from selected approaches around the world.* https://iea.blob.core.windows.net/assets/c0efd465-a914-4fe6-b3cf-cbbf96a9d8c6/Howgovernmentssupportcleanenergystart-ups.pdf

Intergovernmental Panel on Climate Change (IPCC) (2022). *Climate Change 2022: Impacts, Adaptation, and Vulnerability. Contribution of Working Group II to the Sixth Assessment Report of the Intergovernmental Panel on Climate Change.* Cambridge: Cambridge University Press.

Jacob, R. J., Girouard, A., Hirshfield, L. M., Horn, M. S., Shaer, O., Solovey, E. T., & Zigelbaum, J. (2008). Reality-based interaction: A framework for post-WIMP interfaces. *Paper presented at the Proceedings of the SIGCHI Conference on Human Factors in Computing Systems* (pp. 201–210).

Joas, F., Witecka, W., Lenck, T., Peter, F., Seiler, F., Samadi, S., Schneider, C., Holtz, G., Kobiela, G., & Lechtenböhmer, S. (2020). *Klimaneutrale Industrie: Schlüsseltechnologien Und Politikoptionen Für Stahl, Chemie Und Zement; Studie*. Agora Energiewende. https://epub.wupperinst.org/frontdoor/deliver/index/docId/7675/file/7675_Klimaneutrale_Industrie.pdf

John, B., Lang, D. J., Von Wehrden, H., John, R., & Wiek, A. (2020). Advancing decision-visualisation environments – empirically informed design recommendations. *Futures, 123*, 102614.

Johnstone, P., Rogge, K. S., Kivimaa, P., Fratini, C. F., Primmer, E., & Stirling, A. (2020). Waves of disruption in clean energy transitions: Socio-technical dimensions of system disruption in Germany and the United Kingdom. *Energy Research & Social Science, 59*, 101287.

Kader, R., & Kaya, F. (2021). *Overcoming Lock-In and Path Dependency: Hydrogen Energy Transitions*. https://www.diva-portal.org/smash/get/diva2:1562005/FULLTEXT01.pdf

Kagermann, H., Süssenguth, F., Körner, J., Liepold, A., & Behrens, J. H. (2021). *Resilience as a Goal for Economic and Innovation Policy*. Munich: Acatech.

Kahneman, D., & Tversky, A. (1979). Prospect theory: An analysis of decision under risk. *Econometrica, 47*(2), 263–291.

Kantabutra, S. (2020). Toward an organizational theory of sustainability vision. *Sustainability, 12*(3), 1125.

Kearney Energy Transition Institute. (2020). *Hydrogen Applications and Business Models: Going Blue and Green?* https://www.kearney.com/documents/17779499/18269679/Hydrogen+FactBook+Final+-+June+2020.pdf/01ae498b-3d38-deca-2a61-6f107699dde1?t=1592252815706

Kerr, S. P., Kerr, W. R., & Xu, T. (2018). Personality traits of entrepreneurs. *Foundations and Trends in Entrepreneurship, 14*(3), 279–356.

Kivimaa, P., Laakso, S., Lonkila, A., & Kaljonen, M. (2021). Moving beyond disruptive innovation: A review of disruption in sustainability transitions. *Environmental Innovation and Societal Transitions, 38*, 110–126.

Klibi, W., Martel, A., & Guitouni, A. (2010). The design of robust value-creating supply chain networks: A critical review. *European Journal of Operational Research, 203*(2), 283–293.

Kocheril, G., Krebs, F., Nacken, L., & Holzhauer, S. (2019, September). Open and integrative modelling in energy system transitions – Conceptual discussion about model reusability, framework requirements and features. In *Conference of the European Social Simulation Association* (pp. 499–505). Cham: Springer.

Kocheril, G., Krebs, F., Nacken, L., & Holzhauer, S. (2021, April). Open and Integrative Modelling in Energy System Transitions—Conceptual Discussion About Model Reusability, Framework Requirements and Features. In Advances in Social Simulation: Proceedings of the 15th Social Simulation Conference: 23–27 September 2019 (pp. 499–505). Cham: Springer International Publishing.

Köhler, J., De Haan, F., Holtz, G., Kubeczko, K., Moallemi, E., Papachristos, G., & Chappin, E. J. L. (2018). Modelling sustainability transitions: An assessment of approaches and challenges. *Journal of Artificial Societies and Social Simulation, 21*(1), 8.

Lai, A. (2011). Transformational-transactional leadership theory. AHS Capstone Projects. Paper 17. http://digitalcommons.olin.edu/ahs_capstone_2011/17

Li, F. G. N., Trutnevyte, E., & Strachan, N. (2015). A review of socio-technical energy transition (STET) models. *Technological Forecasting & Social Change, 100*, 290–305.

Lin, Q., & Yi, L. (2021). The multi-level effectiveness of entrepreneurial leadership: A meta-analysis. *Journal of Management & Organization*, 1–19.

Lumosi, C. K., Pahl-Wostl, C., & Scholz, G. (2019). Can 'learning spaces' shape transboundary management processes? Evaluating emergent social learning processes in the zambezi basin. *Environmental Science & Policy, 97*, 67–77.

Madureira, N. L. (2012). The iron industry energy transition. *Energy Policy, 50*(1), 24–34.

Meadows, D. H., Meadows, D. L., Randers, J., & Behrens, W. W. I. (1972). *The Limits to Growth: A Report for The Club of Rome's Project on the Predicament of Mankind*. Club of Rome. doi: 10.1349/ddlp.1

Meier, M., Lütkewitte, M., Mellewigt, T., & Decker, C. (2016). How managers can build trust in strategic alliances: A meta-analysis on the central trust-building mechanisms. *Journal of Business Economics*, *86*(3), 229–257.

Mokhtar, A. R. M., Genovese, A., Brint, A., & Kumar, N. (2019). Supply chain leadership: A systematic literature review and a research agenda. *International Journal of Production Economics*, *216*, 255–273.

Mößner, N. (2018). *Visual Representations in Science: Conceptual Epistemology*. London: Routledge.

Musiolik, J., & Markard, J. (2011). Creating and shaping innovation systems: Formal networks in the innovation system for stationary fuel cells in Germany. *Energy Policy*, *39*(4), 1909–1922.

Neffke, F., Hartog, M., Boschma, R., & Henning, M. (2018). Agents of structural change: The role of firms and entrepreneurs in regional diversification. *Economic Geography*, *94*(1), 23–48.

Negri, M., Cagno, E., Colicchia, C., & Sarkis, J. (2021). Integrating sustainability and resilience in the supply chain: A systematic literature review and a research agenda. *Business Strategy and the Environment*, *30*(7), 2858–2886.

Nuñez-Jimenez, A., & De Blasio, N. (2022). *The Future of Renewable Hydrogen in the European Union*. Harvard Kennedy School. https://www.belfercenter.org/sites/default/files/files/publication/Report_EU%20Hydrogen_FINAL.pdf

Pahl-Wostl, C. (2019). Governance of the water-energy-food security nexus: A multi-level coordination challenge. *Environmental Science & Policy*, *92*, 356–367.

Pauceanu, A. M., Rabie, N., Moustafa, A., & Jiroveanu, D. C. (2021). Entrepreneurial leadership and sustainable development – A systematic literature review. *Sustainability*, *13*(21), 11695.

Power, D. J. (2002). *Decision Support Systems: Concepts and Resources for Managers*. Greenwood Publishing Group. https://scholarworks.uni.edu/facbook/67/?utm_source=scholarworks.uni.edu%2Ffacbook%2F67&utm_medium=PDF&utm_campaign=PDFCoverPages

Reddy, B. S. (2015). Access to modern energy services: An economic and policy framework. *Renewable & Sustainable Energy Reviews*, *47*, 198–212.

Robinson, D. T., Di Vittorio, A., Alexander, P., Arneth, A., Michael Barton, C., Brown, D. G., Kettner, A., Lemmen, C., O'Neill, B. C., Janssen, M., Pugh, T. A. M., Rabin, S. S., Rounsevell, M., Syvitski, J. P., Ullah, I., & Verburg, P. H. (2018). Modelling feedbacks between human and natural processes in the land system. *Earth System Dynamics*, *9*(2), 895–914.

Rothaermel, F. T. (2001). Incumbent's advantage through exploiting complementary assets via interfirm cooperation. *Strategic Management Journal*, *22*(6–7), 687–699.

Rousseau, D. M., Sitkin, S. B., Burt, R. S., & Camerer, C. (1998). Introduction to special topic forum: Not so different after all: A cross-discipline view of trust. *The Academy of Management Review*, *23*(3), 393–404.

Sadik-Zada, E. R. (2021). Political economy of green hydrogen rollout: A global perspective. *Sustainability*, *13*(23), 13464.

Sammut-Bonnici, T., & Galea, D. (2014). PEST analysis. https://www.um.edu.mt/library/oar/bitstream/123456789/21816/1/sammut-bonnici%20pest.pdf

Schimmel, M., Kerres, P., Jörling, K., Klessmann, C., Schröder, J., Altrock, M., Kliem, C., Maiworm, C., Hillmann, S., Deutsch, M., Hauser, P. D., & Sartor, O. (2021). *Making Renewable Hydrogen Cost-competitive: Policy Instruments for Supporting Green H_2. Guidehouse Energy Germany*. GmbH. https://static.agora-energiewende.de/fileadmin/Projekte/2020/2020_11_EU_H2-Instruments/A-EW_223_H2-Instruments_WEB.pdf

Schlund, D., Schulte, S., & Sprenger, T. (2022). The who's who of a hydrogen market ramp-up: A stakeholder analysis for Germany. *Renewable & Sustainable Energy Reviews*, *154*, 111810.

Scholz, G., Dewulf, A., & Pahl-Wostl, C. (2014). An analytical framework of social learning facilitated by participatory methods. *Systemic Practice and Action Research*, *27*(6), 575–591.

Sent, E. (2018). Rationality and bounded rationality: You can't have one without the other. *The European Journal of the History of Economic Thought, 25*(6), 1370–1386.

Sharifi, A., & Yamagata, Y. (2016). Principles and criteria for assessing urban energy resilience: A literature review. *Renewable & Sustainable Energy Reviews, 60*, 1654–1677.

Shneiderman, B. (1982). The future of interactive systems and the emergence of direct manipulation. *Behaviour & Information Technology, 1*(3), 237–256.

Siksnelyte, I., Zavadskas, E. K., Streimikiene, D., & Sharma, D. (2018). An overview of multi-criteria decision-making methods in dealing with sustainable energy development issues. *Energies, 11*(10), 2754.

Simba, A., & Thai, M. T. T. (2019). Advancing entrepreneurial leadership as a practice in MSME management and development. *Journal of Small Business Management, 57*(S2), 397–416.

Szigeti, H., Messaadia, M., Majumdar, A., & Eynard, B. (2011). Steep analysis as a tool for building technology roadmaps. In *Proceedings of the Conference: eChallenges e-2011, Florence, Italy* (Vol. 28). https://www.researchgate.net/profile/Mourad-Messaadia/publication/301295850_STEEP_analysis_as_a_tool_for_building_technology_roadmaps/links/5710af4808aefb6cadaabdd9/STEEP-analysis-as-a-tool-for-building-technology-roadmaps.pdf

Thonemann, N., Schulte, A., & Maga, D. (2020). How to conduct prospective life cycle assessment for emerging technologies? A systematic review and methodological guidance. *Sustainability, 12*(3), 1192.

Tuler, S. P., Dow, K., Webler, T., & Whitehead, J. (2017). Learning through participatory modeling: Reflections on what it means and how it is measured. In B. Gray (Ed.), *Environmental Modeling with Stakeholders* (pp. 25–45). Cham: Springer.

Turnheim, B., & Geels, F. W. (2012). Regime destabilisation as the flipside of energy transitions: Lessons from the history of the British coal industry (1913–1997). *Energy Policy, 50*(1), 35–49.

Uhl-Bien, M., Marion, R., & McKelvey, B. (2007). Complexity leadership theory: Shifting leadership from the industrial age to the knowledge era. *The Leadership Quarterly, 18*(4), 298–318.

United Nations Framework Convention on Climate Change (UNFCC). (2015). *The Paris Agreement.* https://unfccc.int/sites/default/files/english_paris_agreement.pdf

Vecchio, R. P. (2003). *Entrepreneurship and Leadership: Common Trends and Common Threads.* Elsevier Inc. doi: 10.1016/S1053-4822(03)00019-6

Voinov, A., Jenni, K., Gray, S., Kolagani, N., Glynn, P. D., Bommel, P., Prell, C., Zellner, M., Paolisso, M., & Jordan, R. (2018). Tools and methods in participatory modeling: Selecting the right tool for the job. *Environmental Modelling & Software, 109*, 232–255.

Wang, A., Van der Leun, K., Peters, D., & Buseman, M. (2020). *European Hydrogen Backbone.* Guidehouse. https://gasforclimate2050.eu/wp-content/uploads/2020/07/2020_European-Hydrogen-Backbone_Report.pdf

Weisbord, M., & Janoff, S. (2005). Faster, shorter, cheaper may be simple; It's never easy. *The Journal of Applied Behavioral Science, 41*(1), 70–82.

Worrapimphong, K., Gajaseni, N., Le Page, C., & Bousquet, F. (2010). A companion modeling approach applied to fishery management. *Environmental Modelling & Software: With Environment Data News, 25*(11), 1334–1344.

Yun, S., & Lee, J. (2015). Advancing societal readiness toward renewable energy system adoption with a socio-technical perspective. *Technological Forecasting and Social Change, 95*, 170–181.

Zhang, H., Bij, H. V. D., & Song, M. (2020). Can cognitive biases be good for entrepreneurs? *International Journal of Entrepreneurial Behaviour & Research, 26*(4), 793–813.

Zubaryeva, A., Dilara, P., & Maineri, L. (2015). Publicly funded research, development and demonstration projects on electric and plug-in vehicles in Europe. http://bookshop.europa.eu/uri?target=EUB:NOTICE:LDNA27149:EN:HTML

Part III: **Sustainable Entrepreneurship and Context**
Thomas B. Long

The chapters in this section explore context and how it interacts with sustainable entrepreneurship. Recent reviews have demonstrated that context has only emerged as a distinct theme and key factor in sustainable entrepreneurship scholarship after an early focus on change-agents and the individuals who become sustainable entrepreneurs (Pacheco, Dean, & Payne, 2010), as well as on the processes lying behind sustainable entrepreneurship (Belz & Binder, 2017).

There are a number of ways in which context interacts with sustainable entrepreneurship. For instance, we often see that sustainable products and services face challenges in the market, and can struggle to achieve high adoption rates, even where they are technologically or financially advantageous, and do not externalise costs in the same way as other products do. Think of the recent success of electric vehicles (EVs): it is only thanks to huge government support that EVs have become a small success and a relatively common sight on the streets. It took external influences and changes in the wider context for EVs to advance. This example illustrates how context shapes the sustainable entrepreneurial process and its outcomes. In a different context, there may not have been governmental support, nor enough consumer interest in EVs, and so ultimately no success for this alternative, more sustainable product (Pinkse & Groot, 2015). This illustrates how context influences the potential success of sustainable entrepreneurship and how sustainable entrepreneurs are subject to context and, in some ways, even hostage to it.

Fortunately, sustainable entrepreneurs can shape, and even radically alter their contexts. In order to tackle the comparative disadvantage sustainable products and services have in the market, we find examples where sustainable entrepreneurs change beliefs, norms and standards, as well as the rules and regulations – the institutions – that combine to form context (Alvarez, Young, & Woolley, 2015). Indeed, for sustainable entrepreneurs to succeed, we often see that it is a requirement to actively change context, often through processes of collective action (Pacheco, Dean, & Payne, 2010).

In our exploration of context, we can see 'tangible' contextual effects, for instance how the entrepreneurial ecosystem facilitates (or not) the development of sustainable innovations, such as EVs. And we can see the tangible impacts of shaping context, for instance, through market creation and institutional changes. Here, the dominant focus is often still on wealth creation, technological innovation and venture capital financing to boost growth and achieve the win–win of sustainable value creation and profits.

This focus on the tangible also 'narrows' our perspective, however. By exploring different contexts, we can open new understandings, broaden our lens, observe heterogeneity, and so provide new insights into sustainable entrepreneurship. For example, by taking a context lens, we can consider how location affects the sustainable entrepreneurship process, and even what we consider to be sustainable entrepreneurship and who we see as sustainable entrepreneurs. This can include how people, history and changes in social, economic and political power shape environments and communities

https://doi.org/10.1515/9783110756159-012

and so also the motivations, processes and outcomes of sustainable entrepreneurship. A clear example of this is the dominance in our perception of Western perspectives on what entrepreneurship is, what it looks like, who does it and how. When we investigate non-Western and often non-urban and less technological context, often in the Global South, we see more diversity and less homogeneity, which enables new insights and new opportunities for theorising.

The chapters that follow all tackle context. They do so, either head-on, as seen in Chapter 3, or by documenting cases of sustainable entrepreneurship in 'unusual' and often non-Western, Global South contexts (Sections 2.5, 3.3 and 3.4).

First, Hellen Dawo conducts a systematic literature review of context and sustainable entrepreneurship scholarship – a first for the field. The chapter draws attention to the rapid rise in sustainable entrepreneurship scholarship in recent years and associated calls for more contextualised studies of the phenomenon. The chapter aims to catalogue, describe and analyse sustainable entrepreneurship research that considers context, through state-of-the-art literature reviewing techniques, incorporating 177 articles, published from 2006 to 2021. The analysis reveals six central themes in current context research, and that there are two broad perspectives applied: how sustainable entrepreneurship impacts contexts, and the impact of sustainable entrepreneurship on context. The chapter critiques existing research, making pertinent observations, such as the tendency to see context as a constant, rather than the dynamic and shifting factor that it often is, as well as the use of a narrow set of institutional theories.

The chapter by Lavlu Mozumdar, Kazi Shek Farid, Shatabdi Acharjee and Fatima Zannat Esha explores sustainable entrepreneurship in Bangladesh. The contextual element of this contribution goes beyond a Global South setting, to cover both online entrepreneurship and female entrepreneurship. The chapter explores different online businesses, from food to handicrafts, finding a range of different motivations and drivers, including the women's desires for self-identity through to more classic economic needs. The chapter also starts to explore the darker side of sustainable entrepreneurship, highlighting how cultural norms in Bangladesh in some instances question and challenge the female entrepreneurs. By highlighting these factors, the chapter draws our attention to the importance of the less tangible and more social elements of context – for instance, family and wider social support that are often critical for success.

Mmapatla Senyolo, Thomas B. Long, Vincent Blok and Onno Omta's chapter provides us with another case from the Global South. This time, the focus is on South Africa and the efforts of agri-tech entrepreneurs to provide smallholder farmers with the technological innovations they need to deal with the climate challenge. Many of these innovations are available, simple and effective, yet are not utilised due to a range of barriers. The chapter explores how agri-tech entrepreneurs attempt to overcome these barriers through business model innovation. The results show how the context influences the challenges faced by the entrepreneurs – in this case, insufficient resources and poor to non-existent financing options, rather than what we often find in a similar context, which is the limiting effects of the conservative opinions of farmers and a reluctance to try new approaches. This once again teaches us how different contexts challenge conventional wisdom and demonstrates the need for context-specific approaches and recommendations.

The final chapter is by Denise Speck and Thomas B. Long and provides another demonstration of the contextual nature of sustainable entrepreneurship, uncovering alternative forms and approaches within the setting of cocoa farming in Trinidad. The chapter directly engages with the contextual nature of sustainable entrepreneurship, uncovering alternative forms and approaches within the setting of cocoa farming in Trinidad. The chapter explores the application of a novel tool – digital storytelling – to empower existing sustainable entrepreneurs and, it is hoped, inspire the next generation to help reinstate what was once the thriving, but now a threatened Trinitario Cocoa industry. We learn, however, that to fully unlock the potential of the approach, that context must be placed front and centre. The chapter shows us a practical side to context – how becoming embedded within the cluster and understanding cultural nuances is critical to producing effective stories, and so critical also to the success of the sustainable entrepreneurship process.

References

Alvarez, S. A., Young, S. L., & Woolley, J. L. (2015), Opportunities and institutions: A co-creation story of the king crab industry. *Journal of Business Venturing*, *30*(1), 95–112. https://doi.org/10.1016/j.jbusvent.2014.07.011

Belz, F. M., & Binder, J. K. (2017). Sustainable entrepreneurship: A convergent process model. *Business Strategy and the Environment*, *26*(1), 1–17. https://doi.org/10.1002/bse.1887

Pacheco, D. F., Dean, T. J., & Payne, D. S. (2010), Escaping the green prison: Entrepreneurship and the creation of opportunities for sustainable development. *Journal of Business Venturing*, *25*(5), 464–480. https://doi.org/10.1016/j.jbusvent.2009.07.006

Pinkse, J., & Groot, K. (2015), Sustainable entrepreneurship and corporate political activity: Overcoming market barriers in the clean energy sector. *Entrepreneurship Theory and Practice*, *39*(3), 633–654. https://doi.org/10.1111/etap.12055

Hellen Dawo

10 Sustainable Entrepreneurship and Context: Mapping Research on the Nexus and Demarcating Future Research Directions

Abstract: The field of sustainable entrepreneurship has received considerable attention due to its potential to ameliorate grand challenges such as climate change and natural resource depletion. This rapid extension of knowledge in the field has necessitated a number of literature reviews in recent years, to guide its development. Consequently, there has been a call for contextualised studies of the sustainable entrepreneurship phenomenon in order to have a holistic understanding of how it occurs. The growing importance of context informed this particular study's election to focus on the nexus between sustainable entrepreneurship and context. This study aimed to catalogue how context has been problematised in sustainable entrepreneurship research to-date. It applies state-of-the-art techniques to collect and analyse 177 articles published in the English language, from the years 2006 to 2021. The study highlights both the nuanced and explicit role context has in sustainable entrepreneurship research, and how future studies can push this nexus forward.

Keywords: sustainable entrepreneurship, context, systematic literature review, entrepreneurial ecosystems

1 Introduction

The effects of climate change, such as rising sea level and global warming, have created an acute need for sustainability-oriented approaches for business. Adverse climatic effects, when coupled with the rapid depletion of natural resources, add to the myriad of challenges facing today's society, and by extension, to entrepreneurship. Sustainable entrepreneurship has been defined as 'the continuing commitment by businesses to behave ethically and contribute to economic development while improving the quality of life of the workforce, their families, local communities, the society, and the world at large, as well as future generations' (Crals & Vereeck, 2005: 174). This type of entrepreneurship provides an avenue for enterprises to not only provide solutions to prevailing ecological and socio-economic problems, but also play a role in

Hellen Dawo, University Utrecht School of Economics, Kriekenpitplein 21-22, 3584 EC, Utrecht, The Netherlands

https://doi.org/10.1515/9783110756159-013

regeneration of nature and/or culture heritage resources. Further, sustainable entrepreneurship occurs within context. The context determines when, how and why sustainable entrepreneurship is carried out (Goyal & Sergi, 2015; Korsgaard et al., 2022; Muñoz & Cohen, 2018b). Nevertheless, how context is explored in sustainable entrepreneurship literature remains subjective, despite repeated calls for a more contextualised study of the sustainable entrepreneurship process (Muñoz & Cohen, 2017).

The phenomenon of context has been explored to different extents in sustainable entrepreneurship research. Recent studies have highlighted the 'time' role of context by illustrating entrepreneurial synchronicity in facilitating sustainable entrepreneurship (Muñoz & Cohen, 2017). Other studies have examined the spatial context and its role in the sustainable entrepreneurial journey (Argade et al., 2021). In addition, the influence of institutional contexts (Pinkse & Groot, 2015; Thompson, Herrmann, & Hekkert, 2015) and social contexts (Bjerregaard & Lauring, 2015; Littlewood & Holt, 2015; Meek, Pacheco, & York, 2010) on sustainable entrepreneurship have been examined to varied extents. The variety of dimensions used to examine sustainable entrepreneurship and context warrant an organisation of the knowledge. This study provides the first consolidated examination of how context has been problematised in sustainable entrepreneurship research. It highlights the challenges and opportunities in this nexus (sustainable entrepreneurship and context), provides existing thematic categorisations and charts probable avenues to explore in future research.

Existing literature reviews on sustainable entrepreneurship have examined the field as a whole and; provided a conceptual basis for the sustainable entrepreneurship subdomain (Muñoz & Cohen, 2017); presented future research directions for ecological sustainability (Gast, Gundolf, & Cesinger, 2017); examined sustainable entrepreneurship and its potential to enable sustainability-as-flourishing (Schaefer, Corner, & Kearins, 2015); developed a demarcation of subfields in sustainable entrepreneurship, which could inform future research streams (Anand et al., 2021), among other developments in this field. Nonetheless, despite the wide application of context to demarcate or link sustainable entrepreneurship studies, a representative analysis of how the context lens is applied, based on rigorous methodology (Tranfield, Denyer, & Smart, 2003), is yet to be carried out. Further, how contextualised sustainable entrepreneurship research has, and can, inform transformations to counter grand challenges (such as climate change and natural resource depletion among others), is of great relevance in today's and future society.

The specific novel contributions of the review are as follows:

1. It provides a representative review of studies on sustainable entrepreneurship that includes context as one of the research parameters.
2. The study is the first to illustrate descriptively the studies on sustainable entrepreneurship that employ context both intentionally and unintentionally. Specifically, it highlights research trends and journals, illustrates the existing typologies of context employed and consolidates the methods applied by the existing studies.

3. The study includes a summary of current theoretical perspectives used in existing studies of sustainable entrepreneurship that include context, culminating in an inclusive conceptual framework of context in sustainable entrepreneurship research.
4. The systematic review allowed for development of research challenges to inspire future opportunities on the nexus of the two concepts (sustainable entrepreneurship and context).
5. The review informs sustainable entrepreneurs and policymakers as they encounter varied context, on challenges to pre-empt and opportunities to explore to develop bespoke solutions.

The paper is structured as follows. The next section describes the method applied during the review, including the research protocol applied by the study. It is followed by a results section where the descriptive and analytical results of the data analysis are presented. The key insights from the review are then presented in the discussion section and the study has a conclusion that summarises its key implications.

2 Method

This review combines bibliographic quantitative methodologies (Linnenluecke, Marrone, & Singh, 2020) with systematic qualitative methodologies (Anderson & Lemken, 2020) in order to yield a broad and representative understanding of the structure and specific characteristics of the nexus of sustainable entrepreneurship and context, in sustainable entrepreneurship literature. It followed four stages: i) preparation for the review, ii) conducting a data search, iii) analysis of the data and iv) presentation of the results (Tranfield, Denyer, & Smart, 2003). Each of these stages is explained in detail below.

2.1 Preparation for the Review

This entailed a scoping exercise that included defining the objectives of the review, and development of appropriate search terms through perusal of previous literature reviews and special issues. The objectives of the review were outlined using the following research questions:
1. How relevant is context to sustainable entrepreneurship research?
2. What theoretical constructs of context are used in existing literature, and where could future research concerning this nexus go?
3. What methodologies are currently applied in investigation of context within the sustainable entrepreneurship subfield, and how could this be advanced?

For the development of search terms, previous literature reviews on sustainable entrepreneurship and exemplar papers that investigated context and sustainable entrepreneurship were consulted. Particular attention was paid to terms most featured in these manuscripts that would enable a broad and representative collection of peer-reviewed publications. Another consideration was that the articles/book chapter should have investigated the two concepts (sustainable entrepreneurship and context) concurrently, either intentionally or inferred. This initial development exercise resulted in the search terms *'sustainable entrepreneur*'* and *'context'*. These two terms were used in the first data search. A further refinement of these search terms is described in the succeeding section.

2.2 Conducting the Data Search

For the review, the Scopus database was selected as the primary source of data. This is because compared to the Web of Science database, Scopus yielded a consistently larger number of results. An initial data search using the search terms *TITLE-ABS-KEY((("sustainable entrepreneur*") and ("Context"))) AND (LIMIT-TO (LANGUAGE, "English"))* resulted in 137 articles, published from 2006 to 2021. These articles were then analysed using biblioshiny (Sidhu, Singh, & Kumar, 2022), focusing on the key words. The analysis enabled a refinement of the search terms to include: (("sustainable entrepreneur*")) AND (("socio-ecological*" OR "Context" OR "setting*" OR "condition*")). This yielded 197 articles.

From these, the search was further refined by excluding literature reviews and books and articles published in 2022. This resulted in 177 articles from Scopus compared to 134 articles from Web of Science. The articles were extracted in Excel format. An initial content analysis was done, by reading the abstracts and checking if they were relevant to the review. That is making sure: i) they concerned sustainable entrepreneurship, ii) they addressed context and iii) the duplicates were removed. This last phase of data collection resulted in 160 articles. These articles were extracted from the Scopus database in various formats to facilitate analysis. After this wide-ranging search, the third stage of the process was initialised.

2.3 Analysis of the Data

In this stage the data was analysed in a step-wise manner in order to yield answers to our research questions as stated earlier.

1. How relevant is context to sustainable entrepreneurship research?
For this question, bibliometrics was used to provide a descriptive analysis of the data set including the trends in number of relevant documents published, and the

dominant journals where these articles were published (Linnenluecke, Marrone, & Singh, 2020).

2. What theoretical constructs of context are used in existing literature, and where could future research concerning this nexus go?
A scientific mapping exercise that entailed content analysis enabled identification of thematic clusters (Braun & Clarke, 2006). The analysis was strengthened by co-citation analysis (Anderson & Lemken, 2020) and bibliographic coupling (Linnenluecke, Marrone, & Singh, 2020), which enabled visualisation of network linkages.

3. What methodologies are currently applied in investigation of context within the sustainable entrepreneurship subfield, and how could this be advanced?
For this question, qualitative content analysis (Vaismoradi, Turunen, & Bondas, 2013) of the documents was conducted, which allowed a summary of the prevailing purpose of the studies, methodologies applied and findings. A summary of the review process is illustrated in Figure 10.1.

3 Results

3.1 Description of the Data Set

The 177 documents initially analysed consist of 143 articles, 17 book chapters, 15 conference papers, one editorial and one note. There are 22 mainstream management journals that host 87 of the total articles, representing 49% of the entire sample. These are depicted in Figure 10.2. The findings indicate a steady growth in prominence in the investigation of the nexus between sustainable entrepreneurship and context. Specifically, it indicates a 21.34% growth rate in publications from 2006 to 2021. This increase in articles that considered context as an important part of sustainable entrepreneurship research answers the first research question: how relevant is context to sustainable entrepreneurship research? The increased relevance of context in sustainable entrepreneurship research can be inferred by the increased number of studies that explicitly engage with it in recent years (Figure 10.3). The publication of these articles in high-quality business/management journals further emphasises the recognition of contextual influences on sustainable entrepreneurship (Figure 10.2).

3.2 Problematisation of Context

The first part of the second research question – what theoretical constructs of context are used in existing literature? – was answered qualitatively using content analysis of

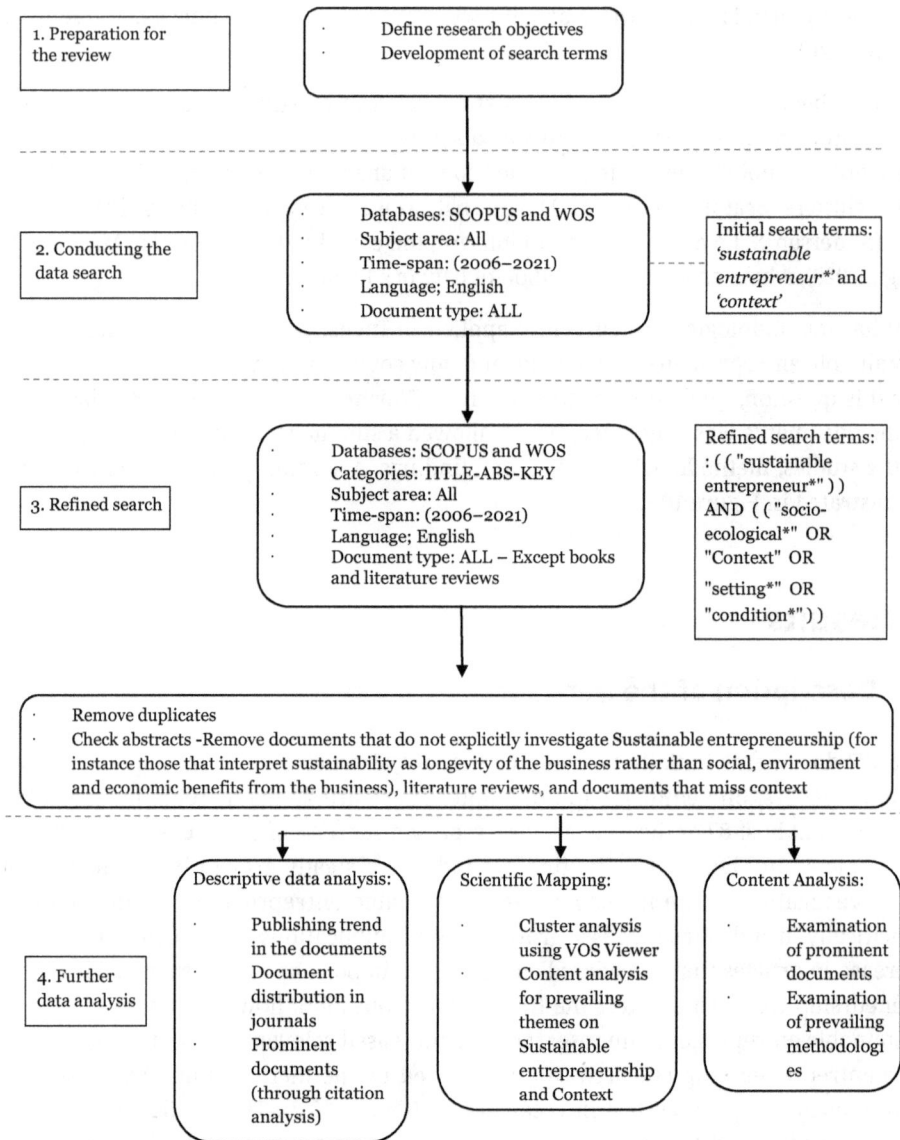

Figure 10.1: Summary of the review process.

the publications (Braun & Clarke, 2006), and quantitatively using co-citation and bibliographic coupling analysis (Linnenluecke, Marrone, & Singh, 2020).

From the content analysis of the abstracts of the documents, it emerged that there were five overarching dimensions used while investigating context in sustainable entrepreneurship literature. These were: spatial dimension of context, organisational dimension of context, institutional dimension of context, typology of

Sources of articles

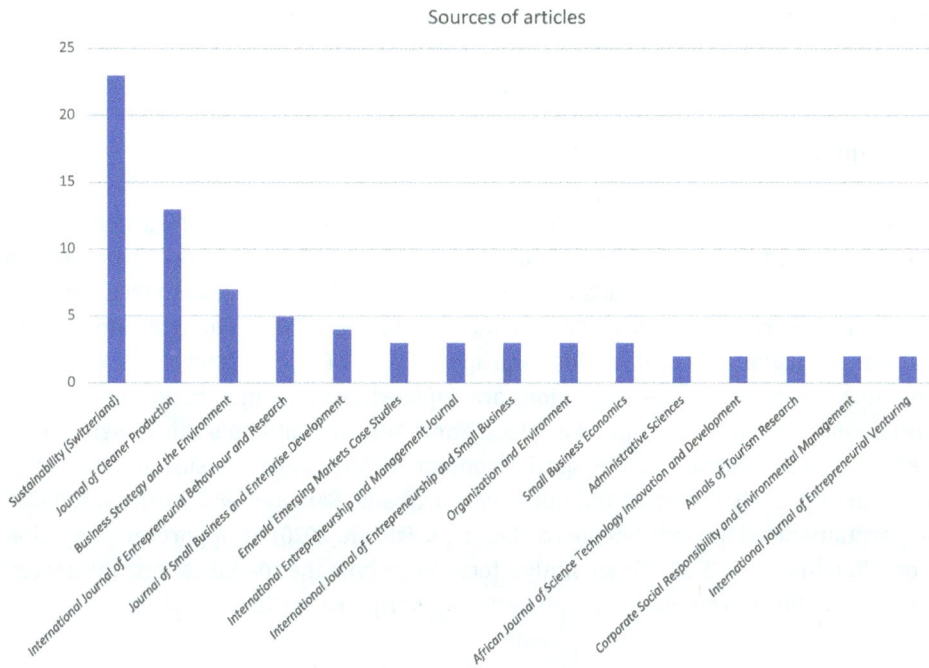

Figure 10.2: Graph depicting top 15 journals.

Trend in research production

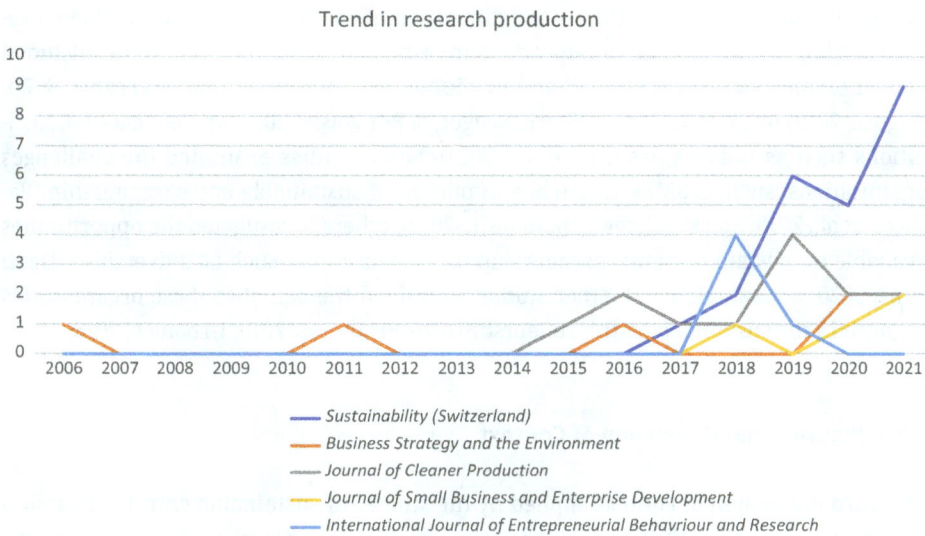

Figure 10.3: Increase in publications of sustainable entrepreneurship and context.

entrepreneurship dimension of context, and entrepreneurial characteristic dimension of context. These dimensions are illustrated below.

3.2.1 Spatial Dimension of Context

This is one of the more clearly applied dimensions of context used in sustainable entrepreneurship literature. The spatial dimensions entailed the investigation of the geographical location in which sustainable entrepreneurship takes place (Argade, Salignac, & Barkemeyer, 2021; Perez Nuñez & Musteen, 2020; Zhang & Song, 2020), such as particular countries, regions and specific areas (such as protected areas (Piñeiro-Chousa et al., 2021). These locations are depicted as the unique backdrop in which sustainable entrepreneurship takes place. Some studies that apply this dimension investigate the influence of the spatial context on the stages of sustainable entrepreneurship, such as opportunity discovery (Argade, Salignac, & Barkemeyer, 2021), opportunity development (Shepherd, Sattari, & Patzelt, 2020) or opportunity exploitation (Riandita et al., 2021). Other studies focused on how the spatial context influenced the sustainable entrepreneurship processes and/or journey (Kibler et al., 2015).

3.2.2 Organisational Dimension of Context

Organisational dimension is the second dimension of context used in sustainable entrepreneurship literature. The organisations investigated using this dimension included type of organisation such as small and medium-sized enterprises (SMEs) (Franco & Rodrigues, 2019) or manufacturing (Stark, Seliger, & Bonvoisin, 2017) and educational institutions such as universities (Agu et al., 2021). Some studies examined the challenges organisations, such as SMEs, face while in pursuit of sustainable entrepreneurship (Pacheco et al., 2018; Stark, Seliger, & Bonvoisin, 2017); others investigated the opportunities available for sustainable entrepreneurship for organisations, such as universities (Daub et al., 2020; Soukalova, 2016); other studies examined the activities these organisations engaged in for sustainable entrepreneurship (Bos-Brouwers, 2010; Urbaniec, 2018).

3.2.3 Institutional Dimension of Context

The third dimension of context applied by the studies of sustainable entrepreneurship analysed was the institutional dimension. In this instance the sustainable entrepreneurship literature examined institutional contexts such as sustainable entrepreneurship ecosystems (Tiba van Rijnsoever, & Hekkert, 2021), markets (Abdelnaeim, El-Bassiouny, & Paul, 2021; Cohen & Muñoz, 2017) and digital platforms (Brenner, 2018; Gregori & Holzmann, 2020; Saura, Palos-Sanchez, & Herráez, 2020). This is in addition to governance institutions such as local authorities and communities (Gasbarro, Rizzi, & Frey, 2018; Persaud, Nelson, & Satterfield, 2021) and regulations (Pacheco, Dean, & Payne, 2010; York, Hargrave, & Pacheco, 2016). These studies explored how actors in the institutional context enabled or hindered sustainable entrepreneurship.

3.2.4 Typology of Entrepreneurship Dimension of Context

The fourth dimension of the context that emerged from the documents was the application of the entrepreneurial typology, such as female entrepreneurship (Morgan & Winkler, 2020; Outsios & Farooqi, 2017), community entrepreneurship (Gurău & Dana, 2018; Masud et al., 2017) and rural entrepreneurship (Lang & Fink, 2019; Soleymani et al., 2021) as a context. These studies examined how sustainable entrepreneurship in these contexts contributed to the achievement of female empowerment (Morgan & Winkler, 2020), community resilience (Pallarès-Blanch, 2015), awareness or education (Subekti et al., 2019), sustainable development (Porter, Orams, & Lück, 2018) and nature conservation (Masud et al., 2017).

3.2.5 Entrepreneurial Characteristic Dimension of Context

The fifth dimension for investigation of the context within the sustainable entrepreneurship literature was the sustainable entrepreneurial characteristics, such as leadership (Kurucz et al., 2017), innovation (Pacheco et al., 2018) and cognitive attributes (Muñoz, 2018) as the context for investigation of sustainable entrepreneurship. This line of research examined how sustainable entrepreneurial characteristics influenced the successful implementation of the sustainable entrepreneurship process, through strategies such as business models for sustainability (Baldassarre et al., 2017).

The content analysis brought out the different ways in which the concept of context was handled by researchers in the sample. In the next analysis, the bibliometric techniques gave the overall analysis of the theoretical frameworks applied by the publications sampled.

3.3 Intellectual Structure of the Documents

The co-citation analysis (Vogel & Güttel, 2013) (using VOSviewer software) of the documents yielded the most historically influential documents in the data, by analysing which documents shaped the field of sustainable entrepreneurship. The findings were quite similar to an earlier literature review on the sustainable entrepreneurship field, specifically the study by Anand et al. (2021). The clusters that emerged were summarised as: sustainable business modelling, sustainable entrepreneurial ecosystems, sustainable business process (opportunity recognition, opportunity development and opportunity exploitation), enablers and challenges for sustainable entrepreneurship and theoretical frameworks for sustainable entrepreneurship. Due to the similarity to the earlier literature review (Anand et al., 2021), we will not delve into explaining the clusters that emerged from the co-citation analysis in this review. There are five clusters from the analysis.

Of importance for this review was the dimension of context applied in these influential documents. It was noted from the thematic content analysis of these clusters, through the lens of context, that context was often applied as a spatial dimension while examining sustainable entrepreneurship.

In order to identify current trends in the field, a bibliographic coupling analysis was carried out (Verbeek et al., 2002). A bibliographic coupling analysis is able to distinguish and identify current trends in the literature. This analysis yielded six thematic clusters from the data.

These clusters were thematically analysed (Braun & Clarke, 2006) by reading the documents in each cluster and outlining the topic, method applied and theoretical perspectives taken by the authors. This analysis partially provides answers for questions: ii) *What theoretical constructs of context are used in existing literature*, and where could future research concerning this nexus go? iii) *What methodologies are currently applied in investigation of context within the sustainable entrepreneurship subfield*, and how could this be advanced? The bibliographic coupling included documents that had at least five connections, therefore 90 documents were plotted. The overarching themes were identified as:

i) sustainable entrepreneurship business development and sustainable entrepreneurship education – the studies in this cluster examined the strategies applied by sustainable entrepreneurs for business development; and best practices for sustainable entrepreneurs or sustainable entrepreneurship education. For example, the study by Heilbrunn (2019) interrogated the practices employed by African refugees in a camp in Israel for proactive entrepreneurship, which enabled them to overcome stereotypes and ensure sustainable entrepreneurship in a minority setting, while another examined best practices in teaching environmental responsibility to students (inventors and innovators) at a university (Faludi & Gilbert, 2019). The documents in the cluster employed varied, but primarily, qualitative methods of analysis, such as conducting interviews (Faludi & Gilbert, 2019; Halberstadt et al., 2019) and case studies, some of which employ mixed methods (Panzer-Krause, 2019). Other studies administered surveys to get a consequential data set, for example, Ploum et al. (2018), in order to validate a competence framework for sustainable entrepreneurship. There were two (spatial and institutional) dimensions of context applied in this cluster. For instance, a study by Vlasov, Bonnedahl, and Vincze (2018) examined how embeddedness in place and in trans-local grassroots networks influenced development of social and sustainable entrepreneurship, applying the spatial dimension of context. Panzer-

Krause (2019) examined the role of networking in implementing green and/or degrowth for sustainable tourism, explicitly investigating the institutional context. From the 90 documents analysed, 28 were in this cluster (31%).

ii) sustainable entrepreneurship within specific geographical locations – the studies in this cluster examined either how location influenced specific sustainability processes, or how sustainable entrepreneurship practices influenced and/or changed locations. For instance, to investigate the entrepreneurial process of opportunity identification, the team of Argade, Salignac, and Barkemeyer (2021) investigated opportunity identification in a non-Western context (India). One of their conclusions was that motivational dynamics were influenced by contextual variations best summarised in a participant's quote 'there are many Indias' (Argade, Salignac, & Barkemeyer, 2021: 1). The cluster also included the evaluation of the specific impact of sustainability education through university courses or bespoke events. For example, the study by Agu's team examined drivers for sustainable entrepreneurial intention in ongoing students at Nigerian universities who had taken specific sustainability courses (Agu et al., 2021). The majority of studies in this cluster used quantitatively oriented methods for research. These included large-scale surveys like that employed by Fichter and Tiemann (2020) to determine if the integration of sustainability goals into generic business plan competitions (BPCs) had an effect on sustainability orientation of more than 1000 participants – similarly, a large data analysis to understand sustainable entrepreneurial behavioural intentions in the Italian context (Arru, 2020). The team of Eller et al. (2020) developed a model for sustainable opportunity identification using longitudinal and experimental evidence from more than 100 participants. The cluster also featured a few case studies such as Daub et al. (2020) who investigated how to introduce sustainability practices into the structure and processes of a business school with least resistance. The primary dimension of context applied in this cluster is spatial. From the 90 documents analysed, 21 were in this cluster (23%).

iii) start-ups or emerging sustainable enterprises within specific entrepreneurial ecosystems – these studies examine start-ups in relation to sustainable entrepreneurship. For instance, Leendertse, van Rijnsoever, and Eveleens, 2020 examine the influence of technology on achievement of climate performance, while Tiba, van Rijnsoever and Hekkert (2021) investigated the share of sustainable start-ups across different entrepreneurial ecosystems, with the aim of establishing the casual drivers of the differences in sustainability outcomes. The studies in this third cluster applied primarily quantitative approaches to analyse large data retrieval from credible websites (Tiba, van Rijnsoever, & Hekkert, 2021), or surveying specific accelerator programmes (Leendertse, van Rijnsoever, & Eveleens, 2020). In a few of the studies, case study-like approaches were applied; Gregori and Holzmann (2020) sampled participants in new venture competitions to yield insights into development of sustainable business models for digital technologies. Likewise, Bocken, Weissbrod and Tennant (2016) used five illustrative cases to show that large businesses can also benefit from experimentation for sustainable business model development. The cluster also included three documents conceptualising on the development of sustainable business models to facilitate sustainable transitions of companies and/or systems (Breuer et al., 2018; Schaltegger, Lüdeke-Freund, & Hansen, 2016). The studies in this cluster applied the institutional dimension of context. For instance, while examining climate-smart agriculture, Long, Blok and Coninx (2019) looked at how system-level factors influence sustainable entrepreneurial actions. From the 90 documents analysed, 14 were in this cluster (15.56%).

iv) how sustainable entrepreneurship is enacted (indicators, practices and impact of education) – the studies in this cluster are predominantly evaluative of the form and impact of sustainability practices. For instance, Soleymani et al. (2021) developed sustainable entrepreneurship indicators for a rural location in Iran, while Wagner et al. (2019) used three cases in Germany to determine the effect of support offered by university programmes on sustainable regional development. A study exemplifying the research on sustainable entrepreneurship practice by Muñoz and Cohen (2017) examines rhythmic patterns of sustainable entrepreneurship in relation to nature and society. Pinkse and Groot's (2015) study is a demonstration of how sustainable entrepreneurs face market barriers through political activism. The studies in this cluster used qualitative methods such as using the Fuzzy Delphi method to get expert opinions (Soleymani et al., 2021), a single case study of a collaborative innovation project in the demin industry (DiVito & Ingen-Housz, 2019), use of fuzzy-set qualitative comparison analysis to examine decision-making of 37 sustainable entrepreneurs (Muñoz, 2018) to develop a cognitive map in sustainable decision-making and conducting and analysing interviews to illustrate how sustainable entrepreneurs tackle institutional pillars (Gasbarro, Rizzi, & Frey, 2018). In this cluster there were also two conceptual reviews that review different forms of sustainable entrepreneurship. One presented a framework for culturally sustainable entrepreneurship (Swanson & DeVereaux, 2017), while the other looked at what is needed for sustainability-as-flourishing (Schaefer, Corner, & Kearins, 2015). The cluster employed both spatial and institutional dimensions of context, in order to explain prevalent sustainable entrepreneurship practices in their cases. From the 90 documents analysed, 14 were in this cluster (15.56%).

v) investigating sustainable entrepreneurship in varied organisational set-ups – the studies in this cluster used organisational structures such as small and medium-sized enterprises (SMEs), corporates or manufacturing as the backdrop for their investigation of the workings of sustainable entrepreneurship. For instance, Wahga, Blundel and Schaefer (2018) found that factors such as competitive advantage, (international) environmental regulations, industrial dynamism and reputation were consequential for sustainable entrepreneurial activities among SMEs situated in Pakistan, while Klewitz (2017) investigated sustainability-oriented innovations (SOIs) in SMEs, and how learning–action networks could condition an SME's strategic orientation for innovation. The studies in this cluster, logically, applied qualitative methods including interviews of the entrepreneurs in a specific industry (Salome, van Bottenbur, & van den

Heuvel, 2013) or organisation (Cantele, Vernizzi, & Campedelli, 2020). Case studies were used to examine the inner workings of the organisations under investigation, such as Rodgers (2010), who investigated three sustainable SMEs to determine their motivation and practices. One study in this cluster exemplified a mixed-method approach. Tarnanidis, Papathanasiou and Subeniotis (2019) investigated sustainable entrepreneurship in 150 Greek food manufacturing enterprises, through a combination of interviews, surveys and experimentation. The dimension of context applied in this cluster was organisational and it emerged that institutional logics were used to investigate this dimension. From the 90 documents analysed, 10 were in this cluster (11.11%).

vi) sustainability as a context – this was the smallest cluster and the studies in this cluster took a very unique stand by stating that sustainable entrepreneurship was a context. They looked at the influence of a particular type of entrepreneurship, such as female entrepreneurship (Bhardwaj, 2018), as an opportunity to achieve the goals of sustainable entrepreneurship within a community. The studies in this cluster applied a case study approach. The dimension of context applied was the typology of entrepreneurship. From the 90 documents analysed, 2 were in this cluster (2.22%).

The bibliographic coupling and content analysis yielded clusters that were similar to the initial content analysis of the whole data set, in which spatial dimension, organisational dimension, institutional dimension and typology of entrepreneurship dimension of studying context in sustainable entrepreneurship emerged. It is also notable that for all the clusters, studies on educational practices feature in one form or another. This underscores the relevance of knowledge development in the sustainable entrepreneurship subfield.

4 Discussion

Reflecting on the research questions – i) How relevant is context to sustainable entrepreneurship research? ii) What theoretical constructs of context are used in existing literature, and where could future research concerning this nexus go? and iii) What methodologies are currently applied in investigation of context within the sustainable entrepreneurship subfield, and how could this be advanced? – this study is both timely and insightful. The review gives evidence of the proliferation of 'contextualised' studies of sustainable entrepreneurship research in recent years. The theoretical constructs used to examine the nexus range from institutional logics (Persaud, Nelson, & Satterfield, 2021) to examining embeddedness (Dufays, 2016) or network (Panzer-Krause, 2019)-related theories. The studies were carried out at different organisational levels (Corbett & Montgomery, 2017) and types (Osborne et al., 2014) and using varied research methodologies (both qualitative and quantitative oriented). Thus, the nexus of sustainable entrepreneurship and context has gained relevance as a viable lens for the study of the phenomenon of sustainable entrepreneurship and has potential for further advancement. In this section we critically discuss how context has been problematised in sustainable entrepreneurship to-date. In the next section the future research agenda will be outlined.

There were two broad perspectives applied in problematising the sustainable entrepreneurship and context nexus: a) impact of context on sustainable entrepreneurship and b) impact of sustainable entrepreneurship on context.

a) Impact of context on sustainable entrepreneurship

Similar to mainstream entrepreneurship research (Ucbasaran, Westhead, & Wright, 2001), research on the nexus of sustainable entrepreneurship and context has examined the influence of external environments such as rural settings (Panzer-Krause, 2019) or a refugee camp (Heilbrunn, 2019) on sustainable entrepreneurship practices. The studies that investigated context using this frame mainly applied institutional and network logics. For example, de Lange (2017) examined how normative institutions, such as investors, rewarded sustainability in start-ups. The study by Gasbarro, Rizzi, and Frey (2018) examined how sustainable entrepreneurs address the regulative, normative and cultural-cognitive institutional pillars in a rural Italian setting. An example that applied network logic was Panzer-Krause (2019), who used network analysis to investigate features of a regional network of sustainable tourism enterprises that engaged in either green growth or de-growth strategies, within a rich institutional context in which the enterprises operated. De Lange (2016) examined a clean technology cluster to delineate the value of social capital for dynamism and long-term growth. Further, studies on development and implementation of sustainable entrepreneurial ecosystems (such as Leendertse, van Rijnsoever, & Eveleens, 2020; Tiba, van Rijnsoever, & Hekkert, 2021) examined the influence of these ecosystems on propensity for sustainable start-ups or enterprises.

These and other studies exemplify the frame that context is an environment external to the sustainable enterprise, and makes up the conditions from which sustainable practices arise. It represents the 'where' (Muñoz & Cohen, 2018b; Welter, 2011) of sustainable entrepreneurship and is the prevalent frame used in current sustainable entrepreneurship research.

b) Impact of sustainable entrepreneurship on context

Due to the proactive nature of sustainable entrepreneurship, it rationally follows that research on the nexus of sustainable entrepreneurship and context employed the frame that sustainable entrepreneurship influences the context in which it exists. For instance, sustainable entrepreneurship resulted in organisational changes including increase of sustainable innovation capacities (Klewitz, 2017) and implementation of sustainable business models (Gregori & Holzmann, 2020). Other studies examined how sustainable entrepreneurs could influence, and even change, normative institutional environment through such actions as political activism (Pinkse & Groot, 2015), or use of new technologies (Howells & Ertugan, 2019). The frame of sustainable entrepreneurship influencing context also applied to most studies on sustainable entrepreneurship education. Studies indicate that as early as 1996, Delft University, in the Netherlands, had introduced a subject on sustainable entrepreneurship and technology in two of their engineering programmes (Bonnet et al., 2006). Wagner et al. (2019) looked at evidence of the influence of universities' support programmes on development of sustainable enterprises for regional development using case studies. The theoretical lens used in this frame were mainly institutional and cognitive theories. Thompson et al.'s (2015) comparative case study of four sustainable entrepreneurs in the regulated biomass industry in the Netherlands aimed to determine how sustainable entrepreneurs change or create institutions. The cognitive theories were applied when examining the determinants of decision-making and other individual processes for sustainable entrepreneurship (Argade, Salignac, & Barkemeyer, 2021; Muñoz, 2018).

These studies typified the perspective that sustainable entrepreneurship had the potential to influence the context in which they emerged/existed. It presents the *'how'* (Muñoz & Cohen, 2018a; Tarnanidis, Papathanasiou, & Subeniotis, 2019) of sustainable entrepreneurship at varied contexts.

4.1 Summary of Current Field Application of Sustainable Entrepreneurship and Context Nexus

The review finds that the concept of 'context' is often assumed to mean a geographical location of a sustainable entrepreneurship action, and used to set studies apart from similar studies by planting them in a particular setting. The potential for contextual studies to contribute to generalisability of results from studies is less explored. This review identified five dimensions of context that are represented by the current body of work on sustainable entrepreneurship. The wide variety of dimensions adopted by researchers signals the lack of consolidation of definitions of context in the field, as well as how context is at times overlooked in order to achieve generalisability. In an effort to consolidate the manner in which contexts are investigated in sustainable entrepreneurship research, a conceptual framework has been developed. The conceptual framework depicted in Figure 10.4 maps out the current context-based studies for sustainable entrepreneurship. The purpose of the framework is not to offer specific factors for investigating context in sustainable entrepreneurship research; rather it serves to illustrate the complexity and variety of dimensions in which context can be investigated. Finally, an encouraging trend is that the more recent studies of sustainable entrepreneurship (Argade, Salignac, & Barkemeyer, 2021; Howells & Ertugan, 2019; Muñoz & Cohen, 2018a) exemplify an intentionality in examining contexts in

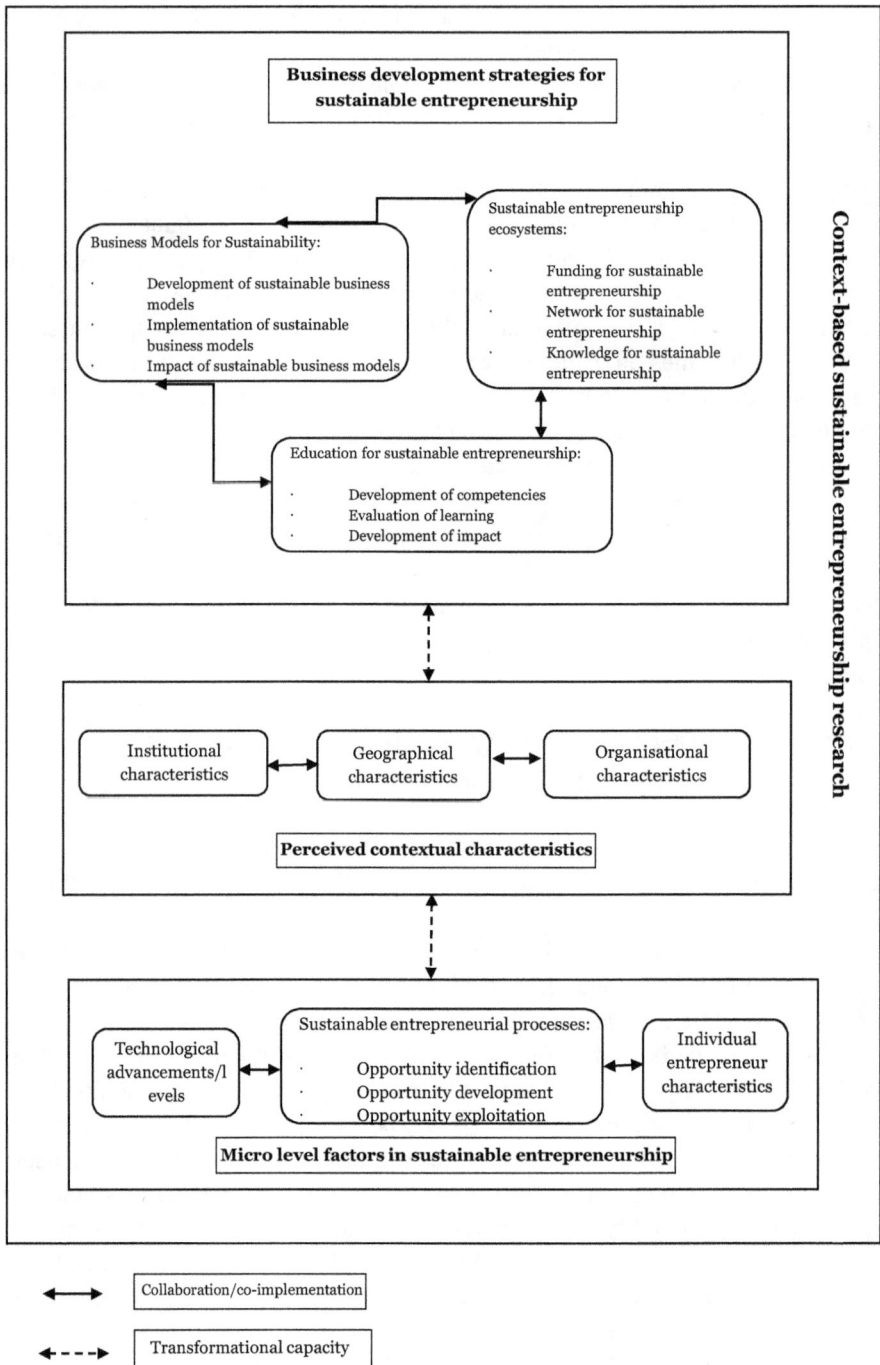

Figure 10.4: Conceptual framework for context-based sustainable entrepreneurship research.

sustainable entrepreneurship and incorporating its complexity and multi-level characteristics, which was lacking in earlier studies in this subfield.

5 Conclusions

In this section the gaps identified by the review are examined, and challenges for future research directions are presented.

a) From the review it was surmised that research examining varied context dimensions make up a significant number of studies in sustainable entrepreneurship. It illustrated six dimensions applied in sustainable entrepreneurship research, also highlighting that the dimensions were applied to varied extents by the sample (through percentage of total documents analysed – see Section 3.3). There was a variation in how researchers approached context, which came forth in the review. However, a definition of context/s was lacking. The variety of dimensions signifies the lack of construct clarity when examining context/s in sustainable entrepreneurship research.

Challenge 1: There is need for formulation of measurement of the influences of context to help guide future research in sustainable entrepreneurship. The measurements should capture the complexity of context with respect to varied levels of analysis, its evolution over time and varied dimensions it could entail.

b) While some studies explained concisely what context dimensions they were investigating and how they interact with the concept of sustainable entrepreneurship (Argade, Salignac, & Barkemeyer, 2021), there were many more studies that overlooked context. In many studies, context was kept behind closed doors during data collection, presentation of findings and discussion of results. In particular, studies situated in wealthier, more urban settings in the Global North tend to overlook cultural norms and prevailing socio-economic conditions. There is a pervasive lack of consideration of contextual influences throughout the research process, and its implications for the results of the study at the least, and research design and method at the most. This kind of approach downplays the institutional and financial infrastructure that enables certain approaches to implementation of sustainable entrepreneurship to succeed. In the wake of globalisation and the Internet of Things, contextualised studies could contribute to wider uptake of sustainable business practices, but only if a balanced approach to research, which includes depicting the context clearly, is applied. There is a great need to solve global challenges together, but there should be a greater realisation that the globe is not one, and local solutions and learnings should be encouraged.

Challenge 2: In future, research in sustainable entrepreneurship should explicitly consider and explain the context in which the study was carried out, in order to enable both theoretical and practical application of its findings.

c) The role of context in sustainable entrepreneurship research has been downgraded to either the context enabling sustainable entrepreneurship, or the context serving as an impediment to sustainable entrepreneurship. It is taken for granted that context remains constant throughout the study. However, context is dynamic and responds to stimuli from the entrepreneur, or other actors external (or internal) to the context. This dynamism is partially seen in studies that apply the institutional theoretical lens in examining sustainable entrepreneurship. Studies that apply institutional logics show changes and/or innovation in creating a favourable institutional environment (read context) for sustainable entrepreneurship. In addition, studies applying theories around networks also infer a change in the context through a change in relations and make-up of actors. The dynamic nature of context is seldom explored or captured in existing studies of sustainable entrepreneurship.

Challenge 3: Future studies need to explore existing methods that explicitly enable the capture of the changes in context during the sustainable entrepreneurship process and its implications.

d) Studies that examine context and sustainable entrepreneurship predominantly apply institutional and networking theories to examine this nexus. However, linking up to the previous comments, there is potential to explore other theoretical perspective, such as the theories of change, resource-based theories and a processual lens on sustainable entrepreneurship, to better investigate the role of context.

Challenge 4: Future research should investigate alternative theories for sustainable entrepreneurship, which better capture *how context changes* as a consequence of sustainable entrepreneurship.

References

Abdelnaeim, S. M., El-Bassiouny, N. M., & Paul, P. 2021. Up-fuse transforming plastic waste into innovative products: The case study of a sustainable Egyptian start-up. *Emerald Emerging Markets Case Studies,* *11*(1), 1–13.https://doi.org/10.1108/EEMCS-04-2020-0131

Agu, A. G., Kalu, O. O., Esi-Ubani, C. O., & Agu, P. C. 2021. Drivers of sustainable entrepreneurial intentions among university students: An integrated model from a developing world context. *International Journal of Sustainability in Higher Education, 22*(3), 659–680.https://doi.org/10.1108/IJSHE-07-2020-0277

Anand, A., Argade, P., Barkemeyer, R., & Salignac, F. 2021. Trends and patterns in sustainable entrepreneurship research: A bibliometric review and research agenda. *Journal of Business Venturing, 36*(3), 106092.https://doi.org/10.1016/j.jbusvent.2021.106092

Anderson, M. H., & Lemken, R. K. 2020. Citation context analysis as a method for conducting rigorous and impactful literature reviews. *Organizational Research Methods*, 1094428120969905.https://doi.org/10.1177/1094428120969905

Argade, P., Salignac, F., & Barkemeyer, R. 2021. Opportunity identification for sustainable entrepreneurship: Exploring the interplay of individual and context level factors in India. *Business Strategy and the Environment*, *30*(8), 3528–3551.https://doi.org/10.1002/bse.2818

Arru, B. 2020. An integrative model for understanding the sustainable entrepreneurs' behavioural intentions: An empirical study of the Italian context. *Environment, Development and Sustainability*, *22*(4), 3519–3576.https://doi.org/10.1007/s10668-019-00356-x

Baldassarre, B., Calabretta, G., Bocken, N. M. P., & Jaskiewicz, T. 2017. Bridging sustainable business model innovation and user-driven innovation: A process for sustainable value proposition design. *Journal of Cleaner Production*, *147*, 175–186.https://doi.org/10.1016/j.jclepro.2017.01.081

Bhardwaj, B. R. 2018. Can education empower women through entrepreneurial marketing: A model for upliftment of community services. *Journal of Enterprising Communities*, *12*(1), 19–31. Scopus. https://doi.org/10.1108/JEC-01-2017-0004

Bjerregaard, T., & Lauring, J. 2015. Socially sustainable entrepreneurship: A case of entrepreneurial practice in social change and stability. In *Handbook of Entrepreneurship and Sustainable Development Research*, Edward Elgar Publishing Ltd.https://doi.org/10.4337/9781849808248.00012

Bocken, N. M. P., Weissbrod, I., & Tennant, M. 2016. Business model experimentation for sustainability. *Smart Innovation, Systems and Technologies*, *52*, 297–306.https://doi.org/10.1007/978-3-319-32098-4_26

Bonnet, H., Quist, J., Hoogwater, D., Spaans, J., & Wehrmann, C. 2006. Teaching sustainable entrepreneurship to engineering students: The case of Delft University of Technology. *European Journal of Engineering Education*, *31*(2), 155–167. Scopus. https://doi.org/10.1080/03043790600566979

Bos-Brouwers, H. E. J. 2010. Corporate sustainability and innovation in SMEs: Evidence of themes and activities in practice. *Business Strategy and the Environment*, *19*(7), 417–435.https://doi.org/10.1002/bse.652

Braun, V., & Clarke, V. 2006. Using thematic analysis in psychology. *Qualitative Research in Psychology*, *3*(2), 77–101.https://doi.org/10.1191/1478088706qp063oa

Brenner, B. 2018. Transformative sustainable business models in the light of the digital imperative – A global business economics perspective. *Sustainability (Switzerland)*, *10*, 12.https://doi.org/10.3390/su10124428

Breuer, H., Fichter, K., Lüdeke-Freund, F., & Tiemann, I. 2018. Sustainability-oriented business model development: Principles, criteria and tools. *International Journal of Entrepreneurial Venturing*, *10*(2), 256–286.

Cantele, S., Vernizzi, S., & Campedelli, B. 2020. Untangling the origins of sustainable commitment: New insights on the small vs. Large firms' debate. *Sustainability (Switzerland)*, *12*(2), Scopus. https://doi.org/10.3390/su12020671.

Cohen, B., & Muñoz, P. 2017. Entering conscious consumer markets: Toward a new generation of sustainability strategies. *California Management Review*, *59*(4), 23–48.https://doi.org/10.1177/0008125617722792

Corbett, J., & Montgomery, A. W. 2017. Environmental entrepreneurship and interorganizational arrangements: A model of social-benefit market creation. *Strategic Entrepreneurship Journal*, *11*(4), 422–440. Scopus. https://doi.org/10.1002/sej.1250

Crals, E., & Vereeck, L. 2005. The affordability of sustainable entrepreneurship certification for SMEs. *International Journal of Sustainable Development & World Ecology*, *12*(2), 173–183.https://doi.org/10.1080/13504500509469628

Daub, C.-H., Hasler, M., Verkuil, A. H., & Milow, U. 2020. Universities talk, students walk: Promoting innovative sustainability projects. *International Journal of Sustainability in Higher Education*, *21*(1), 97–111. Scopus. https://doi.org/10.1108/IJSHE-04-2019-0149

de Lange, D. E. 2016. A social capital paradox: Entrepreneurial dynamism in a small world clean technology cluster. *Journal of Cleaner Production, 139,* 576–585.https://doi.org/10.1016/j.jclepro.2016. 08.080

de Lange, D. E. 2017.Start-up sustainability: An insurmountable cost or a life-giving investment? *Journal of Cleaner Production, 156,* 838–854. Scopus. https://doi.org/10.1016/j.jclepro.2017.04.108

DiVito, L., & Ingen-Housz, Z. 2019. From individual sustainability orientations to collective sustainability innovation and sustainable entrepreneurial ecosystems. *Small Business Economics,* Scopus. https://doi.org/10.1007/s11187-019-00254-6

Dufays, F. 2016. Embeddedness as a facilitator for sustainable entrepreneurship. In *Sustainable Entrepreneurship and Social Innovation,* Taylor & Francis. https://doi.org/10.4324/9781315748665

Eller, F. J., Gielnik, M. M., Wimmer, H., Thölke, C., Holzapfel, S., Tegtmeier, S., & Halberstadt, J. 2020. Identifying business opportunities for sustainable development: Longitudinal and experimental evidence contributing to the field of sustainable entrepreneurship. *Business Strategy and the Environment, 29*(3), 1387–1403. Scopus. https://doi.org/10.1002/bse.2439

Faludi, J., & Gilbert, C. 2019.Best practices for teaching green invention: Interviews on design, engineering, and business education. *Journal of Cleaner Production, 234,* 1246–1261. Scopus. https://doi.org/10. 1016/j.jclepro.2019.06.246

Fichter, K., & Tiemann, I. 2020. Impacts of promoting sustainable entrepreneurship in generic business plan competitions. *Journal of Cleaner Production, 267.* Scopus. https://doi.org/10.1016/j.jclepro.2020. 122076

Franco, M., & Rodrigues, M. 2019. Sustainable practices in SMEs: Reducing the ecological footprint. *Journal of Business Strategy,* https://doi.org/10.1108/JBS-07-2019-0136

Gasbarro, F., Rizzi, F., & Frey, M. 2018. Sustainable institutional entrepreneurship in practice: Insights from SMEs in the clean energy sector in Tuscany (Italy). *International Journal of Entrepreneurial Behaviour and Research, 24*(2), 476–498. Scopus. https://doi.org/10.1108/IJEBR-11-2015-0259

Gast, J., Gundolf, K., & Cesinger, B. 2017. Doing business in a green way: A systematic review of the ecological sustainability entrepreneurship literature and future research directions. *Journal of Cleaner Production, 147,* 44–56.https://doi.org/10.1016/j.jclepro.2017.01.065

Goyal, S., & Sergi, B. S. 2015. Social entrepreneurship and sustainability – Understanding the context and key characteristics. *Journal of Security and Sustainability Issues, 4*(3), 269–278. Scopus. https://doi.org/ 10.9770/jssi.2015.4.3(7)

Gregori, P., & Holzmann, P. 2020. Digital sustainable entrepreneurship: A business model perspective on embedding digital technologies for social and environmental value creation. *Journal of Cleaner Production, 272.* Scopus. https://doi.org/10.1016/j.jclepro.2020.122817

Gurău, C., & Dana, L.-P. 2018. Environmentally-driven community entrepreneurship: Mapping the link between natural environment, local community and entrepreneurship. *Technological Forecasting and Social Change, 129,* 221–231.https://doi.org/10.1016/j.techfore.2017.11.023

Halberstadt, J., Schank, C., Euler, M., & Harms, R. 2019. Learning sustainability entrepreneurship by doing: Providing a lecturer-oriented service learning framework. *Sustainability (Switzerland), 11*(5), Scopus. https://doi.org/10.3390/su11051217.

Heilbrunn, S. 2019. Against all odds: Refugees bricoleuring in the void. *International Journal of Entrepreneurial Behaviour and Research, 25*(5), 1045–1064. Scopus. https://doi.org/10.1108/IJEBR-10- 2017-0393

Howells, K., & Ertugan, A. 2019. Using smart technology in sustainable entrepreneurship in Island tourism: A preliminary research. In M. R. Dumay & J. Guthrie (Eds.), *Proceedings of the International Conference on Intellectual Capital, Knowledge Management and Organisational Learning, ICICKM,* (Vol. Vols, Vol. 2019December, pp,. (186–192). Academic Conferences and Publishing International Limited. https://doi.org/10.34190/IKM.19.045

Kibler, E., Fink, M., Lang, R., & Muñoz, P. 2015. Place attachment and social legitimacy: Revisiting the sustainable entrepreneurship journey. *Journal of Business Venturing Insights*, *3*, 24–29.https://doi.org/10.1016/j.jbvi.2015.04.001

Klewitz, J. 2017. Grazing, exploring and networking for sustainability-oriented innovations in learning-action networks: An SME perspective. *Innovation*, *30*(4), 476–503. Scopus. https://doi.org/10.1080/13511610.2015.1070090

Korsgaard, S., Wigren-Kristoferson, C., Brundin, E., Hellerstedt, K., Alsos, G. A., & Grande, J. 2022. Entrepreneurship and embeddedness: Process, context and theoretical foundations. *Entrepreneurship & Regional Development*, *34*(3–4), 210–221.https://doi.org/10.1080/08985626.2022.2055152

Kurucz, E. C., Colbert, B. A., Lüdeke-Freund, F., Upward, A., & Willard, B. 2017. Relational leadership for strategic sustainability: Practices and capabilities to advance the design and assessment of sustainable business models. *Journal of Cleaner Production*, *140*, 189–204.https://doi.org/10.1016/j.jclepro.2016.03.087

Lang, R., & Fink, M. 2019. Rural social entrepreneurship: The role of social capital within and across institutional levels. *Journal of Rural Studies*, *70*, 155–168.https://doi.org/10.1016/j.jrurstud.2018.03.012

Leendertse, J., van Rijnsoever, F. J., & Eveleens, C. P. 2020. The sustainable start-up paradox: Predicting the business and climate performance of start-ups. *Business Strategy and the Environment*, Scopus. https://doi.org/10.1002/bse.2667

Linnenluecke, M. K., Marrone, M., & Singh, A. K. 2020. Conducting systematic literature reviews and bibliometric analyses. *Australian Journal of Management*, *45*(2), 175–194.https://doi.org/10.1177/0312896219877678

Littlewood, D., & Holt, D. 2015. Social and environmental enterprises in Africa: Context, convergence and characteristics. In *The Bus. Of Soc. And Environmental Innovation: New Frontiers in Africa* (pp. 27–47). Springer International Publishing. Scopus https://doi.org/10.1007/978-3-319-04051-6_2

Long, T. B., Blok, V., & Coninx, I. 2019.The diffusion of climate-smart agricultural innovations: Systems level factors that inhibit sustainable entrepreneurial action. *Journal of Cleaner Production*, *232*, 993–1004. Scopus. https://doi.org/10.1016/j.jclepro.2019.05.212

Masud, M. M., Aldakhil, A. M., Nassani, A. A., & Azam, M. N. 2017. Community-based ecotourism management for sustainable development of marine protected areas in Malaysia. *Ocean & Coastal Management*, *136*, 104–112.https://doi.org/10.1016/j.ocecoaman.2016.11.023

Meek, W. R., Pacheco, D. F., & York, J. G. 2010. The impact of social norms on entrepreneurial action: Evidence from the environmental entrepreneurship context. *Journal of Business Venturing*, *25*(5), 493–509.https://doi.org/10.1016/j.jbusvent.2009.09.007

Morgan, M. S., & Winkler, R. L. 2020. The third shift? Gender and empowerment in a women's ecotourism cooperative. *Rural Sociology*, *85*(1), 137–164. Scopus. https://doi.org/10.1111/ruso.12275

Muñoz, P. 2018. A cognitive map of sustainable decision-making in entrepreneurship: A configurational approach. *International Journal of Entrepreneurial Behaviour and Research*, *24*(3), 787–813. Scopus. https://doi.org/10.1108/IJEBR-03-2017-0110

Muñoz, P., & Cohen, B. 2017. Towards a social-ecological understanding of sustainable venturing. *Journal of Business Venturing Insights*, *7*, 1–8.https://doi.org/10.1016/j.jbvi.2016.12.001

Muñoz, P., & Cohen, B. 2018a. Entrepreneurial narratives in sustainable venturing: Beyond people, profit, and planet. *Journal of Small Business Management*, *56*(S1), 154–176.https://doi.org/10.1111/jsbm.12395

Muñoz, P., & Cohen, B. 2018b. Sustainable entrepreneurship research: Taking stock and looking ahead. *Business Strategy and the Environment*, *27*(3), 300–322.https://doi.org/10.1002/bse.2000

Osborne, S. P., Radnor, Z., Vidal, I., & Kinder, T. 2014. A sustainable business model for public service organizations? *Public Management Review*, *16*(2), 165–172.https://doi.org/10.1080/14719037.2013.872435

Outsios, G., & Farooqi, S. A. 2017. Gender in sustainable entrepreneurship: Evidence from the UK. *Gender in Management*, *32*(3), 183–202.https://doi.org/10.1108/GM-12-2015-0111

Pacheco, D., de J, A., Caten, C., ten, S., Jung, C., Navas, F., V. G, H., & Cruz-Machado, V. A. 2018. Eco-innovation determinants in manufacturing SMEs from emerging markets: Systematic literature review and challenges. *Journal of Engineering and Technology Management*, *48*, 44–63.https://doi.org/10.1016/j.jengtecman.2018.04.002

Pacheco, D. F., Dean, T. J., & Payne, D. S. 2010. Escaping the green prison: Entrepreneurship and the creation of opportunities for sustainable development. *Journal of Business Venturing*, *25*(5), 464–480. https://doi.org/10.1016/j.jbusvent.2009.07.006

Pallarès-Blanch, M. 2015.Women's eco-entrepreneurship: A possible pathway towards community resilience? *Ager*, *18*, 65–89. Scopus. https://doi.org/10.4422/ager.2015.03

Panzer-Krause, S. 2019. Networking towards sustainable tourism: Innovations between green growth and degrowth strategies. *Regional Studies*, *53*(7), 927–938. Scopus. https://doi.org/10.1080/00343404.2018.1508873

Perez Nuñez, S. M., & Musteen, M. 2020. Learning perspective on sustainable entrepreneurship in a regional context. *Journal of Small Business and Enterprise Development*, *27*(3), 365–381. Scopus. https://doi.org/10.1108/JSBED-03-2020-0071

Persaud, A. W., Nelson, H. W., & Satterfield, T. 2021. Reconciling institutional logics within first nations forestry-based social enterprises. *Organization & Environment*, 10860266211042660.https://doi.org/10.1177/10860266211042659

Piñeiro-Chousa, J., López-Cabarcos, M. Á., Romero-Castro, N., & Vázquez-Rodríguez, P. 2021. Sustainable tourism entrepreneurship in protected areas. A real options assessment of alternative management options. *Entrepreneurship & Regional Development*, 1–24.https://doi.org/10.1080/08985626.2021.1872937

Pinkse, J., & Groot, K. 2015. Sustainable entrepreneurship and corporate political activity: Overcoming market barriers in the clean energy sector. *Entrepreneurship: Theory and Practice*, *39*(3), 633–654. Scopus. https://doi.org/10.1111/etap.12055

Ploum, L., Blok, V., Lans, T., & Omta, O. 2018. Toward a validated competence framework for sustainable entrepreneurship. *Organization & Environment*, *31*(2), 113–132.https://doi.org/10.1177/1086026617697039

Porter, B. A., Orams, M. B., & Lück, M. 2018. Sustainable entrepreneurship tourism: An alternative development approach for remote coastal communities where awareness of tourism is low. *Tourism Planning & Development*, *15*(2), 149–165.https://doi.org/10.1080/21568316.2017.1312507

Riandita, A., Broström, A., Feldmann, A., & Cagliano, R. 2021. Legitimation work in sustainable entrepreneurship: Sustainability ventures' journey towards the establishment of major partnerships. *International Small Business Journal*, 02662426211056799.https://doi.org/10.1177/02662426211056799

Rodgers, C. 2010. Sustainable entrepreneurship in SMEs: A case study analysis. *Corporate Social Responsibility and Environmental Management*, *17*(3), 125–132.https://doi.org/10.1002/csr.223

Salome, L. R., Van Bottenburg, M., & van den Heuvel, M. 2013. 'We are as green as possible': Environmental responsibility in commercial artificial settings for lifestyle sports. *Leisure Studies*, *32*(2), 173–190. Scopus. https://doi.org/10.1080/02614367.2011.645247

Saura, J. R., Palos-Sanchez, P., & Herráez, B. R. 2020. Digital marketing for sustainable growth: Business models and online campaigns using sustainable strategies. *Sustainability (Switzerland)*, *12*, 3. https://doi.org/10.3390/su12031003

Schaefer, K., Corner, P. D., & Kearins, K. 2015. Social, environmental and sustainable entrepreneurship research: What is needed for sustainability-as-flourishing? *Organization and Environment*, *28*(4), 394–413. Scopus. https://doi.org/10.1177/1086026615621111

Schaltegger, S., Lüdeke-Freund, F., & Hansen, E. G. 2016. Business Models for Sustainability: A Co-Evolutionary Analysis of Sustainable Entrepreneurship, Innovation, and Transformation. *Organization & Environment*, *29*(3), 264–289.https://doi.org/10.1177/1086026616633272

Shepherd, D. A., Sattari, R., & Patzelt, H. 2020. A social model of opportunity development: Building and engaging communities of inquiry. *Journal of Business Venturing*, 106033.https://doi.org/10.1016/j.jbusvent.2020.106033

Sidhu, A. S., Singh, S., & Kumar, R. 2022. Bibliometric analysis of entropy weights method for multi-objective optimization in machining operations. *Materials Today: Proceedings, 50*, 1248–1255. https://doi.org/10.1016/j.matpr.2021.08.132

Soleymani, A., Yaghoubi Farani, A., Karimi, S., Azadi, H., Nadiri, H., & Scheffran, J. 2021. Identifying sustainable rural entrepreneurship indicators in the Iranian context. *Journal of Cleaner Production, 290*.https://doi.org/10.1016/j.jclepro.2020.125186

Soukalova, R. 2016. The role of universities in the transfer of innovations in the creative industry in the Czech Republic. In K. S. Soliman (Ed.). *Proc. Int. Bus. Inf. Manag. Assoc. Conf. – Innov. Vis.: Reg. Dev. Sustain. Glob. Econ. Growth, IBIMA* (pp. 3166–3174). International Business Information Management Association, IBIMA; Scopus. https://www.scopus.com/inward/record.uri?eid=2-s2.0-84984598138&partnerID=40&md5=1c9efaffd56863d337c8e06390b063df

Stark, R., Seliger, G., & Bonvoisin, J. (Eds.). (2017). *Sustainable Manufacturing: Challenges, Solutions and Implementation Perspectives*. Springer International Publishing. https://doi.org/10.1007/978-3-319-48514-0

Subekti, P., Setianti, Y., Hafiar, H., Bakti, I., & Yusup, P. M. 2019. Environmental entrepreneurship education: Case study of community empowerment programs in Bandung Barat district, Indonesia. *International Journal of Entrepreneurship, 23*(2), Scopus. https://www.scopus.com/inward/record.uri?eid=2-s2.0-85070238351&partnerID=40&md5=9af6040eec31dfa30e35c752a5552fa6.

Swanson, K. K., & DeVereaux, C. 2017. A theoretical framework for sustaining culture: Culturally sustainable entrepreneurship. *Annals of Tourism Research, 62*, 78–88.https://doi.org/10.1016/j.annals.2016.12.003

Tarnanidis, T., Papathanasiou, J., & Subeniotis, D. 2019. How far the TBL concept of sustainable entrepreneurship extends beyond the various sustainability regulations: Can Greek food manufacturing enterprises sustain their hybrid nature over time? *Journal of Business Ethics, 154*(3), 829–846. Scopus. https://doi.org/10.1007/s10551-017-3443-4

Thompson, N. A., Herrmann, A. M., & Hekkert, M. P. 2015. How sustainable entrepreneurs engage in institutional change: Insights from biomass torrefaction in the Netherlands. *Journal of Cleaner Production, 106*, 608–618.https://doi.org/10.1016/j.jclepro.2014.08.011

Tiba, S., van Rijnsoever, F. J., & Hekkert, M. P. 2021. Sustainability startups and where to find them: Investigating the share of sustainability startups across entrepreneurial ecosystems and the causal drivers of differences. *Journal of Cleaner Production, 306*, 127054.https://doi.org/10.1016/j.jclepro.2021.127054

Tranfield, D., Denyer, D., & Smart, P. 2003. Towards a methodology for developing evidence-informed management knowledge by means of systematic review. *British Journal of Management, 14*(3), 207–222.https://doi.org/10.1111/1467-8551.00375

Ucbasaran, D., Westhead, P., & Wright, M. 2001. The focus of entrepreneurial research: Contextual and process issues. *Entrepreneurship Theory and Practice, 25*(4), 57–80.https://doi.org/10.1177/104225870102500405

Urbaniec, M. 2018. Sustainable entrepreneurship: Innovation-related activities in European enterprises. *Polish Journal of Environmental Studies, 27*(4), 1773–1779.https://doi.org/10.15244/pjoes/78155

Vaismoradi, M., Turunen, H., & Bondas, T. 2013. Content analysis and thematic analysis: Implications for conducting a qualitative descriptive study. *Nursing & Health Sciences, 15*(3), 398–405.https://doi.org/10.1111/nhs.12048

Verbeek, A., Debackere, K., Luwel, M., Andries, P., Zimmermann, E., & Deleus, F. 2002. Linking science to technology: Using bibliographic references in patents to build linkage schemes. *Scientometrics, 54*(3), 399–420.https://doi.org/10.1023/A:1016034516731

Vlasov, M., Bonnedahl, K. J., & Vincze, Z. 2018. Entrepreneurship for resilience: Embeddedness in place and in trans-local grassroots networks. *Journal of Enterprising Communities*, *12*(3), 374–394. Scopus. https://doi.org/10.1108/JEC-12-2017-0100

Vogel, R., & Güttel, W. H. 2013. The dynamic capability view in strategic management: A bibliometric review. *International Journal of Management Reviews*, *15*(4), 426–446.https://doi.org/10.1111/ijmr.12000

Wagner, M., Schaltegger, S., Hansen, E. G., & Fichter, K. 2019. University-linked programmes for sustainable entrepreneurship and regional development: How and with what impact? *Small Business Economics*, Scopus. https://doi.org/10.1007/s11187-019-00280-4

Wahga, A. I., Blundel, R., & Schaefer, A. 2018. Understanding the drivers of sustainable entrepreneurial practices in Pakistan's leather industry: A multi-level approach. *International Journal of Entrepreneurial Behaviour and Research*, *24*(2), 382–407. Scopus. https://doi.org/10.1108/IJEBR-11-2015-0263

Welter, F. 2011. Contextualizing entrepreneurship – Conceptual challenges and ways forward. *Entrepreneurship Theory and Practice*, *35*(1), 165–184.https://doi.org/10.1111/j.1540-6520.2010.00427.x

York, J. G., Hargrave, T. J., & Pacheco, D. F. P. 2016. Converging winds: Logic hybridization in the Colorado wind energy field. *Academy of Management Journal*, *59*(2), 579–610.https://doi.org/10.5465/amj.2013.0657

Zhang, H., & Song, M. 2020. Do first-movers in marketing sustainable products enjoy sustainable advantages? A seven-country comparative study. *Sustainability (Switzerland)*, *12*(2), Scopus. https://doi.org/10.3390/su12020450.

Lavlu Mozumdar*, Kazi Shek Farid, Shatabdi Acharjee,
Fatima Zannat Esha

11 The Untold Story of Women's Online Business in Bangladesh

Abstract: This study explores the different aspects of women's online businesses in Bangladesh. Data was collected from businesswomen using in-depth interviews and focus group discussions, and analysed through thematic analysis. Results reveal that women run online businesses, including clothing, beauty products, indigenous food, homemade bakery and handicraft products. They do this for self-identity, economic solvency, best time utilisation and creating social networks. They become empowered by doing this business, enabling them to develop business strategies effectively. They handle problems technically and love to do their businesses despite the challenge of triple burden. Sometimes, women face social restrictions and interruptions, but they follow social norms and regulations, and after being successful in their businesses, society praises and supports them. They need proper mental support from their family and society, and business management training from government and non-government organisations to run and sustain their businesses.

Keywords: online business, women entrepreneurs, business and family life, opportunities, challenges

1 Introduction

An enterprising e-venture requires the support of information and communication technologies (ICTs) in this era of a global village. The fast spread of ICTs in businesses has led to an online business revolution. It allows an entrepreneur to open up a virtual venture to operate various business activities. Moreover, an online business creates employment opportunities for anyone with access to the internet via a smartphone or a computer (Balachandran & Sakthivelan, 2013). E-marketing and electronic marketing of products through the internet have become vital for entrepreneurs to sustain their

---

*Corresponding author: Lavlu Mozumdar, Department of Rural Sociology, Bangladesh Agricultural University, Mymensingh, Bangladesh, e-mail: lavlu.rs@bau.edu.bd
Kazi Shek Farid, Department of Rural Sociology, of the Bangladesh Agricultural University, Mymensingh, Bangladesh
Shatabdi Acharjee, Department of Rural Sociology, Bangladesh Agricultural University, Mymensingh, Bangladesh
Fatima Zannat Esha, Department of Rural Sociology, Bangladesh Agricultural University, Mymensingh, Bangladesh

https://doi.org/10.1515/9783110756159-014

businesses because of technological advancements (Trainor, 2012). Another type of online business is social commerce or social media marketing, which allows entrepreneurs to start a business using their social media accounts (Malik & Mantas, 2021; Ukpere, Slabbert, & Ukpere, 2014). ICTs and social media provide the opportunity to do business and market products innovatively and effectively (Karakara & Osabuohien, 2020).

Women have been severely under-represented in accessing ICTs (Bhatnagar & Schware, 2000; Hafkin & Taggert, 2001; Huyer & Sikoska, 2003). Although women lack tech-related knowledge, ICTs can help them unlock their numerous potentials to achieve social and economic freedom. By ensuring a continuous flow of information to run their businesses, it can enable them to become breadwinners in their homes and take care of families and themselves (Gajjala, 1999; Huyer & Sikoska, 2003; Plant, 1997).

Social media has become an indispensable and alternate platform for women entrepreneurs to sell products online with little investment. Using this media, they can attract customers efficiently, and significantly boost their business performance (Irbo & Mohammed, 2020; Smits & Mogos, 2013). Ingress into social media, such as WhatsApp and Facebook, has become easier because of smartphone availability. Smartphone and internet connection has contributed to the rise of online businesses on these informal platforms. They have become vital to women's online businesses' advertising and marketing of products (Bresnahan & Trajtenberg, 1995). These have also made it more accessible for customers to view products and place orders (Ibrahim et al., 2014). ICTs have the potential to unlock a plethora of business initiatives and e-commerce ventures for women, which could be potential goldmines for women's empowerment in developing countries.

Currently, women in Bangladesh are encouraged to operate their business ventures by the promotion of entrepreneurial capabilities by the government and private organisations. By their entrepreneurial skills, women have the opportunities to become empowered and create employment for others. The environment of Bangladesh now supports women's online business activities. For instance, the Bangladesh government continuously encourages small and medium women entrepreneurs through various programmes, such as ensuring a continuous flow of financial aid and related necessary services (UNCTAD, 2019).

Businesses have recently evolved, based on Facebook, known as Facebook commerce (f-commerce), which provides wide-ranging entrepreneurial scope, with no entry barriers. Any woman with an entrepreneurial mindset and a smartphone can start a business in this virtual platform, with little investment and technical skills. Facebook works as an easily accessible medium for buyers and sellers to bargain and interact online (UNCTAD, 2019). Online business provides flexibility to balance family and work, based on society's perception, and it can be an excellent opportunity for Bangladeshi women to operate their businesses from their homes (Mukolwe, 2016).

Online-based business can be a crucial driver for eradicating poverty, improving livelihoods and achieving gender equity for women in Bangladesh. Moreover, online businesses can help create competencies for businesswomen to harness the necessary benefits for empowerment and better life functioning. However, evidence-based literature on women's online businesses in the Bangladesh context, which is different from the usual literature – that is, Western, online and female business – is missing. Therefore, this study explores the different aspects of women's online businesses in Bangladesh. This objective is assessed by the following research questions: (i) What is the nature of women's online businesses? (ii) Why do they come to these businesses? (iii) How do they manage and balance business and life? (iv) What impediments do they face in their businesses?

2 Women's Online Businesses in Bangladesh

Bangladeshi women face mobility constraints, and social and institutional barriers to creating their businesses in person because of the patriarchal nature of society (Mozumdar, 2018; Mozumdar et al., 2020). They have to prioritise taking care of all household responsibilities, bear lower socioeconomic status and are financially unstable (Mozumdar et al., 2019; Mozumdar et al., 2022). In this context, online business via social media could offer female entrepreneurs free rein by offering flexibility and possibilities for new entrepreneurship (Cesaroni, Demartini, & Paoloni, 2017). The number of online small and medium enterprises (SMEs) in Bangladesh has increased because of the development of ICTs. The majority of owners of these businesses are women. Hence, online business is trendy to be known as a business of women. Among all the Bangladeshi women entrepreneurs, a more significant percentage of young (67%) and higher educated women (69%) tend to capture the online business. After the COVID-19 pandemic, there has been a massive increase in women's online business, nearly 41% (ESCAP, UN, 2021). Because of the lockdown, the demand for online business has grown naturally. Most women entrepreneurs fall under the informal and micro-business categories. Women entrepreneurs are leading the expansion of e-commerce in this country (Islam et al., 2019).

Social media has become the vehicle for Bangladeshi women entrepreneurs to run their businesses. Among social media platforms, Facebook plays a crucial role in boosting online businesses (Sultan & Sharmin, 2020). A large number of women take advantage of live marketing using this media. Women's compatibility influences live marketing and ease of usage: a straightforward way of promoting and developing entrepreneurship potential of women. Online business has been possible because of social media's popularity, usefulness and brand creation, especially Facebook live marketing in this country.

Online business is the most suitable and accessible option for women entrepreneurs to manage their businesses in Bangladesh (Hossain, 2018). Some women-owned specific online businesses in this country are clothing, accessories and bakery stores.

ESCAP, UN (2021) reports that capital size, product quality, business plan, appropriate market drive and business integrity are the five key factors influencing women's social media-based online business growth and sustainability. Online-based business can play a significant role in women's lives because it can empower women by improving their financial situation and decision-making ability. This business also addresses gender disparity. Meanwhile, women's social status and management abilities can be upgraded through online business (Hossain & Sultana, 2014; Hossain, 2018).

F-commerce is becoming a shopping window or platform where customers can choose and order through Facebook pages with minimal risks. Moreover, women entrepreneurs of this platform do not need to invest money in setting up a physical store and do not have to pay or spend for rent and decoration. In many cases, women entrepreneurs are being used by wholesalers of clothing items, where women entrepreneurs obtain commission from these wholesalers. Later, businesswomen sell these clothing items through Facebook (Hossain & Sultana, 2014).

Despite the increased participation of women in online business, they encounter many barriers. In a gender-biased society, they are being harassed while buying industrial raw materials for being women. Some ignorant male customers tease them in their mail inboxes. There is a security issue since sometimes Facebook pages are hacked. Also, they face high competition when cheaper goods are imported. They are also confronted with other problems, such as financial issues, lack of technological expertise, customer relations, overall management know-how of e-businesses, supply chain management and family support (Amin, 2018; ESCAP, UN, 2021). Based on the above review, we propose our study's conceptual framework (Figure 11.1).

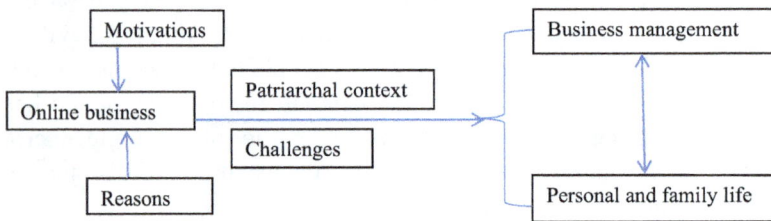

Figure 11.1: Conceptual framework.

3 Methodology

This exploratory research follows a qualitative approach. For collecting data, contacts were made following the snowball sampling technique with women entrepreneurs doing online business. Data was collected from 28 women entrepreneurs doing online businesses in Dhaka, Mymensingh, Gazipur, Bogura, Jamalpur and Sherpur districts of Bangladesh through 16 in-depth interviews (IIs) and two focus group discussions

(FGDs) (with 12 participants, six in each group) using a semi-structured II and FGD guide, respectively, from September 2021 to November 2021. The background characteristics of all participants are presented in Table 11.1.

In-depth interviews were conducted to get a thorough idea regarding women's online business, based on their perceptions. A pseudonym was assigned to all participants during data collection to ensure confidentially. Interviews were conducted in Bengali and recorded with a mobile phone, taking permission from the participants. It became easy for the participants to answer and share their stories in Bangla because it is their mother tongue. The interviewer took field notes during data collection, including the participants' non-verbal cues. Furthermore, FGDs helped to complement and validate the data collected through IIs.

The interviews and discussions were transcribed verbatim and translated into English. These translated transcripts were checked and modified accordingly if any inconsistency was found.

A thematic analysis was used to describe and interpret the data, which looks at patterns of meaning, involving reading through transcripts, getting a thorough overview of all the collected data and identifying meaning and patterns across the data. It enables researchers to generate issues, topics and concepts from data in the form of code through which a codebook (a list of all codes) was developed. Codes with similar characteristics are categorised as subthemes. Finally, themes are generated by identifying the patterns in the subthemes (Table 11.2). For example, the following transcript segment is connected to the code 'patriarchal attitude' under the subtheme 'social stigma', related to the theme of challenges in business.

'Our society does not want to accept any new things or creativity from women. Many neighbours said that as I am a teacher's wife, why do I choose this online business?'

Table 11.1: Background information of the participants.

Sl. no.	Name	Age	Education	Religion	Nature of business	Marital status	City
1	Anika	25	Masters (Ongoing)	Muslim	Handmade jewellery	Unmarried	Dhaka
2	Kotha	25	Degree	Hindu	Hair oil	Married	Gazipur
3	Tasnim	29	Masters	Muslim	Handicraft clothing	Married	Dhaka
4	Jerin	25	Masters (Ongoing)	Muslim	Bakery	Unmarried	Dhaka
5	Himo	27	Masters	Muslim	Monipuri clothing	Married	Mymensingh
6	Mathin	24	Masters (Ongoing)	Muslim	Multiple products	Unmarried	Dhaka

Table 11.1 (continued)

Sl. no.	Name	Age	Education	Religion	Nature of business	Marital status	City
7	Lopa	25	BSc	Muslim	Hair accessory	Unmarried	Dhaka
8	Munni	33	Master	Muslim	Clothing business	Married	Mymensingh
9	Jouty	21	BSc (Ongoing)	Muslim	Ladies' products	Unmarried	Bogura
10	Roksana	34	MPhil	Muslim	Indigenous food	Married	Mymensingh
11	Urmi	23	BCom	Hindu	Graphic design	Unmarried	Mymensingh
12	Oyshi	24	Masters (Ongoing)	Hindu	Jamdani saree	Unmarried	Dhaka
13	Tuli	23	Degree (Ongoing)	Hindu	Hand paint Clothing	Unmarried	Mymensingh
14	Saleha	23	BSc (Ongoing)	Muslim	Multiple products,	Married	Dhaka
15	Moutusi	25	Masters (Ongoing)	Hindu	Cosmetics and Jewellery	Unmarried	Gazipur
16	Bristy	25	BSc (Ongoing)	Muslim	Hand paint Clothing	Unmarried	Mymensingh
17	Nafisa	35	Bachelor	Muslim	Food delivery	Married	Mymensingh
18	khukumoni	28	HSC	Muslim	Clothing	Married	Sherpur
19	Nasrin	25	Masters (Ongoing)	Muslim	Clothing	Unmarried	Mymensingh
20	Sahana	30	Degree	Muslim	Indigenous food	Married	Sherpur
21	Suhagi	27	Bachelor	Muslim	Beauty product	Married	Sherpur
22	Suraya	23	Bachelor (Ongoing)	Muslim	Clothing and food business	Unmarried	Jamalpur
23	Nadira	32	Masters	Muslim	Clothing business	Married	Mymensingh
24	Susmita	21	HSC pass	Hindu	Beauty product	Unmarried	Mymensingh
25	Sadia	35	Dentist	Muslim	Clothing business	Married	Mymensingh
26	Samsunnahar	40	Degree	Muslim	Multidimensional	Married	Mymensingh
27	Songhita	31	Masters	Muslim	Handicraft	Married	Jamalpur
28	Asma	23	Bachelor	Muslim	Bakery food	Married	Mymensingh

Table 11.2: Identification of themes and subthemes from transcripts.

Themes	Subthemes
Causes of starting a business	Motivation, safe and convenience, economic independence and solvency, self-identity, skills and creativity, utilising time
Business management	Sources of capital, product delivery, product promotion, financial performance
Balancing business and family	Time management, prioritising family, prioritising business, family support
Challenges of business	Harassment, triple burden, family interruption, financial problem, business risk, managing customers, social stigma

4 Results and Discussions

4.1 Nature of Online Business

The field of entrepreneurship is considered solely a male domain (Ahl, 2006). Since women in developing countries usually hesitate to operate a business in the public arena (Danish & Smith, 2012; Jaim, 2020b; Roomi, Rehman, & Henry, 2018), the online platform provides women entrepreneurs with the opportunities to run a small business (Sandri & Hardilawati, 2019; Sudarmanti, 2019). Our women entrepreneurs run online businesses, such as clothing, beauty products, jewellery, female accessories, skincare, indigenous food, homemade bakery, handicraft products and graphic design businesses, firmly and happily from their homes. They sell various clothing items and beauty products, including cosmetics, makeup, skincare products, hair accessories, female accessories and lifestyle products. The participants sell different types of jewellery, such as handmade, gold plates, antic, traditional jewellery made from natural raw materials and city gold jewellery. They buy raw material from the market and make jewellery with their ideas. They use their skill in making jewellery with new designs. Nowadays, there is a tremendous demand for online-based bakery businesses. Women entrepreneurs sell homemade cake, pudding, sweet items, and traditional native cake items. In the graphic design business, which is a technical one, participants having relevant skills in this field sell graphic design, logos, banners and content. The indigenous food business is a new kind of online business. Indigenous products like brown sugar, rice, mountain turmeric powder, red chilli powder and date molasses are sold by participants who have the experience of living in an indigenous area where these kinds of indigenous products are available. Moreover, some entrepreneurs do multi-dimensional business, selling various items like cosmetics, handbags, jewellery, clothing, room decoration accessories, beauty products and skincare items. It is a trendy online business in the present era. Buyers can buy any kind of product they need from the entrepreneurs.

4.2 Causes for Starting an Online Business

There are many reasons for women entrepreneurs doing online business. Because of motivations from different sources and various perceived benefits of online business, women start such ventures.

4.2.1 Because of Motivations from Different Sources

A woman entrepreneur needs inspiration for starting anything new, such as an online business in the socio-economic context of Bangladesh, where women's involvement as entrepreneurs is not that visible. Inspiration to start a business comes from their willingness, family, friends and other entrepreneurs. Self decision-making and self-motivation are the first things a woman needs to start a business. Self-willingness, with a robust mindset, helps a woman start this type of business: 'You have to be self-motivated enough to start a business.' Again, if the family shows enough support and inspiration to a woman, her self-confidence increases significantly (Jaim, 2021a). While existing studies have identified diverse patriarchal problems for women operating businesses in Bangladesh (Jaim, 2019, 2020b; Roodman & Morduch, 2009), our study's findings show how family motivation can facilitate women to start a business.

In most cases, the family inspired women entrepreneurs to start an online business: 'My family inspired me from the beginning of this online business.' Siblings are a precious gift from God. They become friends and sources of inspiration for many women, as mentioned by one of the participants, 'I mainly got inspiration from my elder sister, and she always told me that I can get success by doing online business.' Friends also motivate women entrepreneurs by giving good ideas to start online businesses, especially during the corona pandemic when they were depressed. Women entrepreneurs are also motivated by other prominent entrepreneurs' success stories and business strategies. They meet with senior entrepreneurs through Women Entrepreneurship (WE), from whom they get ideas and inspiration: 'I was inspired by many entrepreneurs and by their success stories.'

4.2.2 It Is a Safe and Convenient Platform

Most women entrepreneurs consider online business the easiest, safest and most convenient platform, as they do not have to go outside to run this business. Doing something outside their home is not easy for women in Bangladesh because of their restricted mobility in this patriarchal setting (Coleman et al., 2019; Jaim, 2020b; Roomi, Rehman, & Henry, 2018). They can handle this business from their residence, with very few risks. They can conduct such business anywhere, without staying in a fixed place. In the words of our study participants: 'Obviously, it is a safe and comfortable business platform for women as we can operate it at our convenience.' This finding is supported by Fanggidae, Nursiani, and Angi (2019), who mentioned that one could do online business anywhere and anytime.

4.2.3 For Economic Independence and Solvency

Most participants generate employment opportunities for themselves and others by doing this business: 'As a self-dependent person, I can create employment opportunities for others.' Women in Bangladesh need to primarily depend on their husbands for economic needs. Many of the participants start an online business because of economic solvency. As they do not have any job, they choose this business to earn, meet their needs and achieve economic independence and solvency. Before starting this, some of the participants' families had financial crises. By doing online business, women entrepreneurs are financially capable and can meet their personal needs and contribute to their families. They feel pleased: 'I think most of my demands have been fulfilled through this online business. I can contribute to my family also.' This finding is comparable with Mozumdar (2018), who finds that women entrepreneurs have improved their living standards with increased income.

4.2.4 For Creating Own Identity

Creating self-identity is a big challenge nowadays. Some women become self-reliant and have created self-identity by conducting online business, which increases their self-confidence: 'I became self-reliant. Now I can drive myself and do not need anyone's help.' An online platform is a big platform for building good relationships. It creates a women's network with other entrepreneurs and customers: 'By doing online business, I could connect with many people living in Bangladesh's different parts.' By doing online business, women entrepreneurs find love and respect from their family, friends and relatives, which is evident in the study of Amin (2018). Through online business, they discovered that they could do something meaningful, which helped create their self-identity: 'I found a new world to work in . . . and got a lot of love and respect.' Anyone who wants to do social service could easily do this by earning from the business as it fulfils their desire to help others: 'I had a passion for social services. I could do so by conducting this business.' Online business refreshes women's minds, increases their activity and changes their psychological inception, which in turn increases their self-confidence. Doing something and earning something enhances their mental makeup: 'This online business refreshed my mind as I did something by myself.'

4.2.5 For Developing Skills and Creativity

A woman can develop her skill and creativity by doing online business. As an entrepreneur, she has many innovative and new ideas that help her to give her scope to explore herself in the outer world. Online business is a big platform to develop various skills, including communication skills. Women entrepreneurs started online business to develop their skills and potential, and eventually, their skills developed over time. As they meet with various people, face different situations and communicate with other entrepreneurs and customers, communication skill is developed by doing this business, as mentioned by the participants: 'My working skill developed, communication skill developed, and contact had grown.'

4.2.6 For Proper Utilisation of Time

More than half of our studied participants are married; the rest are unmarried and, usually, students. These women have some free time, which is one of the important reasons for starting a venture: 'The reason behind this business is I can use my time properly.' They can utilise their time effectively during the corona pandemic by doing this online business. As they had no work to do then, they chose to be a women entrepreneur and start an online business, resulting in the best use of their time.

In summary, women in this study do online business for different reasons, like being economically solvent, creating self-identity, contributing to their family, developing their knowledge and skills, improving creativity, mixing with various people and to gain social respect. Most of these causes are consistent with Fanggidae, Nursiani, and Angi (2019), who found that motivating factors of women's entrepreneurship through online business are unemployment, perceived rewards and opportunities – economic motives, self-actualisation, seeking busyness or filling free time and gaining experience.

4.3 Online Business Management

Numerous procedures are needed to operate and manage a business online. A business owner is in charge of handling various duties to ensure the efficient operation of the business.

4.3.1 Sources of Capital Investment

Women entrepreneurs invest money in their business from their savings, borrowing from their family or relatives or friends and taking loans from institutions like banks and non-governmental organisations (NGOs). As online business requires low investment at the starting point; most participants start their online business with their savings as a primary investment: 'My primary investment was from my savings (scholarship money I received for my academic achievement).' Participants borrow money from their families, including parents, relatives and close friends, and invest in their businesses. After using the money for the due purpose, the money would return to that person: 'I started the business by borrowing money from my father.' The study participants also took loans from banks and other financial institutions to invest money in their business: 'Sometimes, we take loan from banks or NGOs, if needed, to invest in our business.'

4.3.2 Product Delivery System

Women entrepreneurs use three systems of delivering their products to their customers: home, courier service and pickup van delivery. In the home delivery system, products are directly sent to customers' houses near their residences by the entrepreneurs and use couriers, if they are far. After taking the products, customers pay the bill. Customers prefer this system as an easy way to shop from home: 'I do home delivery in the country's districts, including Dhaka.' Courier service delivery systems now exist in all parts of the country, a smart way to send and receive products at reasonable times with a delivery charge. Women entrepreneurs must deliver using a courier service system if the product is sent to rural areas. In the pickup van delivery system, participants deliver the product to customers directly by the pickup van delivery system: 'If the buyers contact me, I carry the product to the road so that she could directly purchase the product from me.'

4.3.3 Product Promotion

Women entrepreneurs get different business promotional ideas from different sources and conduct their online business by opening online pages. They get ideas and techniques from their family, friends and relatives who know about business promotion. Women entrepreneurs have an extensive online platform, namely the Women in E-commerce forum or the WE group. The new entrepreneurs get business promotional ideas from that group and build networks with others. From this group, they can learn how to make product branding and create product profile so that customers become interested in ordering their product: 'I got business promotion ideas from the

WE group.' Facebook plays an excellent role for women entrepreneurs in providing business promotional ideas. As prominent entrepreneurs publish their different posts and motivational stories on Facebook, new and small entrepreneurs can quickly gain ideas and knowledge. Participants follow others' posts and see how others give discounts and sell, ideas that help them to promote their business: 'I took the business promotion ideas from Facebook pages.' Every prominent entrepreneur has an online platform. Women get a lot of business promotional ideas from the online platform of these prominent entrepreneurs. As many large entrepreneurs post their life stories and business strategies in the group, the participants can gain promotional ideas from these: 'I get different business promotional ideas from big entrepreneurs, other groups and the E-commerce forum.'

Branding of the product is an essential matter in the online business. Product branding refers to a product's symbol, name and design to create a recognisable identity for that item. It can be as simple as designing a logo and choosing a name and packaging colour. When a product is branded, there is high possibility to promote their business. By branding the product, women entrepreneurs could promote their business quickly, and customers can recognise them by their product branding, which makes them famous: 'I focus on branding of my products.' Photo shoot is an excellent part of business promotion nowadays. In an online business, a good product image helps promote the business. Customers always choose the best-picturised product that seems good to them. Women entrepreneurs emphasise photo shoots for the promotion of their products. They hire photographers and models for the photo shoot: 'I picturise my product with a model and a photographer. By this, I promote my online business.'

4.3.4 Financial Performance of the Online Business

Profit is the ultimate thing expected by any entrepreneur. Women entrepreneurs are satisfied with their business outcomes. They gain profit from their business and can fulfil their economic need. Some of them made a profit quickly by doing this online business. However, as they spend little time on the business, their profit is less significant. They would incur more profit if they could give their business more time, money and energy.

Online business has two types of outcomes. It can be successful or a failure. Most participants are satisfied with their business because they earn the expected profit, based on their invested time and money. Therefore, they think they are successful in their business and are happy to conduct it in the *long run: 'I think my business is successful because from the starting point I make a good profit.'* A business's success depends on *proper planning and the technique the entrepreneurs follow: 'By proper planning, I made my business successful and profitable.'*

A business may not be successful at the start, and an entrepreneur might not be satisfied with the initial outcome of the business. In the beginning, the entrepreneurs did not earn profit according to their expectations, and their businesses seemed to fail. However, later, they were able to make a profit. Moreover, as it was challenging to run the business during the corona pandemic, the women are satisfied with the outcome of their online business, and they consider it a profitable and promising business. As they start this business in a short period, they think they can gain more profit if they give it much time.

4.4 Ways to Balance Business and Family Together

Work–family balance is an inter-role phenomenon (Marks & MacDermid, 1996). It refers to how an individual is equally engaged and equally satisfied with her work and family roles (Greenhaus et al., 2003). Unbalanced work–family division implies more significant barriers to career progression and professional achievement for many women (Cross & Linehan, 2006). Managing an online business and the family together is a big challenge for them. As they have to give time to their family and study, sometimes it is difficult for them to manage both together. Managerial capacity is needed in managing family and business at the same time. However, they are happy because they can manage both their personal and business lives, though sometimes they have to make some sacrifices and have to take a lot of work pressure: 'Managing family life and business together is a very tough job. I start my family work early in the morning, and after completing the family task, I go for my business.'

Many married women and students work as women entrepreneurs nowadays. For balancing 'business and family' and 'business and study' together, women set a schedule for family and work-life and do their responsibilities accordingly: 'By proper scheduling, I could manage both family life and business life.' Most married women balance business and family by following the 'family first' rule. That means maintaining the family is their primary responsibility, which connotes almost similar findings of Ghouse et al. (2017) and Mehtap et al. (2017). They prioritise their family, and after completing their family tasks, they give time to their business: 'As the family is my priority and I do this business because of my family, I try to manage my family tasks first, and after completing them, I give time to my business.' As a result, women's family responsibilities substantially negatively impact their businesses (Ghouse et al., 2017; Mehtap et al., 2017), including financial losses (Chumra, 2020; Jaim, 2021a).

Moreover, those who are not married and started the business with a professional motive, spend as much time as possible trying to make their business successful. Every entrepreneur had to spend time to establish their business at the start. Once established, it needs less time. In addition, family support in the form of financial, social, mental and psychological support is very much essential to run a business successfully by balancing family and business life: 'I can balance my family life and business life. Of course, because of my family support, I could do this.' Amin (2018) found similar findings, who mentioned that the mental support of the family members is considered imperative for women entrepreneurs in developing countries.

4.5 Challenges of Online Business

Women entrepreneurs face a range of challenges in running online businesses. However, little is known regarding the problems of women engaged in online business in Bangladesh (Jaim, 2020a). This study has identified diverse challenges women face, including the patriarchal one, in operating a business in this country.

4.5.1 Harassments

Some harassment is associated with every business, especially with women entrepreneurs. In every case, they face new kinds of harassment. While women's restricted mobility is evident in patriarchal contexts (Jaim, 2020b; Roomi, Rehman, & Henry, 2018), hesitation of women in operating businesses outside has been recognised (Roomi, Rehman, & Henry, 2018), and sexual harassment in public places is not uncommon (Hossain & Sumon, 2013; Khatun, 2019); women doing business by residing within the four walls of their homes face harassment too. Sometimes, disturbing phone calls come, people send friend requests on Facebook, ask annoying questions and give unwanted messages and comments: 'Having our phone number on online pages causes much harassment. Some guys continuously call us over our phone without any reason. Some others make bad comments on our Facebook profile.' Nasty comments and bad reviews are a big problem in online business. Some fake people put nasty comments on their posts and live shows to damage the reputation of the women.

4.5.2 Triple Burden

Women entrepreneurs have a family, personal, study and business life. Many of our women entrepreneurs are students; some are married and have children. Their caregiving duties, family responsibilities, study and online business sometimes create extra pressure for them. Existing literature (Chmura, 2020; Ghouse et al., 2017; Mehtap et al., 2017) supports this. Sometimes, they fail to continue their business because of the patriarchal expectations of the society regarding their domestic duties (Roomi & Parrott, 2008).

4.5.3 Family Interruption

Family interruption causes mental stress to women entrepreneurs. Running a business is difficult if the family does not provide enough aid and support. Families often do not support women's online businesses at *the beginning. Some entrepreneurs hide their business activities from their families because they fear they will never support them if they know it: 'Family members interrupt me with their negative comments. They said this business is not as important as other jobs. They tried to break down my morale.'* In this patriarchal society, husbands sometimes interrupt and demotivate women entrepreneurs with negative comments and show disrespect to their businesses, which is also evident in the study of Jaim (2021a), although the support of the husband in operating a woman's business is very much crucial (Barragan, Erogul, & Essers, 2018; Constantinidis et al., 2019; Jaim, 2020b, 2021a).

4.5.4 Financial Problems

Financial problems are prevalent for every business holder (Orser et al., 2020), which include insufficient capital, low profit and unexpected loss during product delivery. During the early period of the business, the women struggled alone to establish the business as they often did not get any financial support from their families. Sometimes, they did not get the expected profit, according to the investment. Participants need more money to stock the product; however, they fail to do so because of capital shortage: 'For stocking the product, we need sufficient capital. However, we face problems in this respect.' The delivery company missed the product in a few cases, and then had to bear the costs.

4.5.5 Risk of the Business

There are many product variations, including fake and replica products. Fake product is a considerable risk in online business. Fake product has a lower price, and the customer does not differentiate between a real and a fake product. In this case, getting the product's actual price is a big challenge. When the price of the actual products seems high to the customers, they start bargaining for a lower price and feel reluctant to buy. Therefore, women entrepreneurs must convince their customers of the authenticity of the product: 'Many customers do not want to give the product's actual price. They bargain to lower the price. As the price of the real product is higher than the replica, it is tough to convince the customer.' Women entrepreneurs have to bear the risk if the government increases the amount of value-added tax (VAT): 'The Government has increased VAT for online business, which is a big problem for entrepreneurs.' Moreover, maintaining the quality of food is challenging. At the start of the business, women, because of inexperience, did not know how much to produce and stock. As a result, they had to bear financial loss because of producing and stocking large amounts. They failed to sell the product at the perfect time, and its quality deteriorated after a certain period.

4.5.6 Customer-Related Problems

Some customers sometimes cancel the product order just before the delivery. It creates problems for entrepreneurs, who must do many things before the product is delivered. As the entrepreneurs stock the product before selling, they had to bear the financial risk: 'After five days of discussion, one customer ordered the product. Just before the delivery day, he cancelled the order.' In a few cases, entrepreneurs had to bear double delivery charges when customers rejected the product after it reached them. Sometimes, customers do not notice the description or the actual colour of the product. After receiving it, they dislike the reality of it and return it, which results in financial loss for the entrepreneurs.

4.5.7 Social Stigma

Existent literature has confirmed that women entrepreneurs in developing countries face substantively diverse patriarchal problems (Ahmad, 2011; Bastian, Sidani, & Amine, 2018; Constantinidis et al., 2019; Jaim, 2020a, 2020c, 2021a, 2021b; Khatun, 2019; Naguib & Jamali, 2015; Xheneti, Karki, & Madden, 2019). People with stigmatised patriarchal attitudes create many hurdles. Participants always try to adhere to social norms and values, but sometimes people intentionally poke them. Society does not take entrepreneurship as a prestigious job, like others. Sometimes, businesswomen face religious problems: 'Society always demotivates us. Some senior citizens said that by doing this online business, we broke the religious belief.' This is already evident in the existing literature: women are discriminated against by religious customs (Roomi & Parrott, 2008). Religion binds women to involve close male relatives in outside activities (Danish & Smith, 2012).

5 Conclusions and Recommendations

This study uncovers the untold story of Bangladeshi women entrepreneurs who run their businesses using online platforms. It reveals that online businesses provide opportunities for women entrepreneurs to leverage their current circumstances to improve themselves. Based on customer needs, women find the right business idea to match the demand. Women can start their online businesses with the help of their families and friends. They are also motivated by the senior and prominent entrepreneurs' success stories. To start a business, women take money from their families, relatives and friends, and loans from banks and NGOs. They get ideas and techniques from their family, friends and relatives who know about business promotion.

Looking at how women entrepreneurs run their online businesses, Facebook plays an excellent role in providing business promotional ideas for them. Our study's women entrepreneurs consider online business the easiest, safest and most convenient platform as they do not have to go outside to run their businesses. It allows them to become self-reliant through financial solvency. This business allows women to find their true selves and create their own identities. They could utilise their time during the leisure and during the pandemic period by doing this online business. However, unmarried entrepreneurs are able to devote more time to business growth than married entrepreneurs.

While running an online business gives women much freedom, it also has drawbacks. Women entrepreneurs are sometimes the victims of online harassment. They find it challenging to run a business while caring for their families. They also experience financial difficulties, ranging from investment to maintenance of the business. The risk associated with the business is also a significant threat to its execution. Traditional social norms and values hamper and demotivate women entrepreneurs because society does not regard entrepreneurship to be as prestigious as other occupations. Development agencies and social and mass media operators can address this sociocultural challenge. Development and research agencies can support research into online abuse's root causes and dynamics. The journey of online businesswomen is still new. Their journey in this platform requires more technology training and awareness to make themselves skilled entrepreneurs, utilising the resources of ICTs. Through online business, e-commerce and f-commerce, platforms have the potential to play a significant role in combating the existing social disparities faced by Bangladeshi women entrepreneurs. These platforms enable female entrepreneurship, empowering them in developing countries' patriarchal societies.

This study contributes to the context – in terms of e-business being a new context, presenting new opportunities for female entrepreneurship, and also in the context of Bangladesh. These e-business aspects have taken place in an unusual context (i.e., Bangladesh, with specific cultures and societal norms, compared to the 'normal' context, often the United States and European Union), which has a vital role in shaping and sustaining female entrepreneurship.

References

Ahl, H. (2006). Why research on women entrepreneurs needs new directions. *Entrepreneurship Theory and Practice*, *30*(5), 595–621. https://doi.org/10.1111/j.1540-6520.2006.00138.x

Ahmad, S. Z. (2011). Evidence of the characteristics of women entrepreneurs in the Kingdom of Saudi Arabia. *International Journal of Gender and Entrepreneurship*, *3*, 123–143.

Amin, A. (2018). Women entrepreneurship and SMEs of online clothing business in Dhaka City. *Universal Journal of Management*, *6*(10), 359–372.

Balachandran, V., & Sakthivelan, M. S. (2013). Impact of information technology on entrepreneurship (e-entrepreneurship). *Journal of Business Management & Social Sciences Research*, *2*(2), 51–56.

Barragan, S., Erogul, M. S., & Essers, C. (2018). Strategic (dis)obedience: Female entrepreneurs reflecting on and acting upon patriarchal practices. *Gender, Work and Organization*, *25*, 575–592.

Bastian, B., Sidani, Y., & Amine, Y. (2018). Women entrepreneurship in the Middle East and North Africa. *Gender in Management: An International Journal*, *33*(1), 14–29.

Bhatnagar, S., & Schware, R. (2000). Information and communication technology in development. *Case Studies from India, World Bank Institute*, 1–192.

Bresnahan, T. F., & Trajtenberg, M. (1995). General purpose technologies' Engines of growth'?. *Journal of Econometrics*, *65*(1), 83–108.

Cesaroni, F. M., Demartini, P., & Paoloni, P. (2017). Women in business and social media: Implications for female entrepreneurship in emerging countries. *African Journal of Business Management*, *11*(14), 316–326. https://doi.org/10.5897/AJBM2017.8281

Chmura, M. (2020). Pandemic impacts entrepreneuring women at work and home, *Babson Thought & Action*.

Coleman, S. C., Orser, H. B., Foss, L., & Welter, F. (2019). Policy support for women entrepreneurs' access to financial capital: Evidence from Canada, Germany, Ireland, Norway, and the United States. *Journal of Small Business Management*, *57*(2), 296–322.

Constantinidis, C., Leb_egue, T., El-Abboubi, M., & Salman, N. (2019). How families shape women's entrepreneurial success in Morocco: An intersectional study. *International Journal of Entrepreneurial Behavior and Research*, *25*(8), 1786–1808.

Cross, C., & Linehan, M. (2006). Barriers to advancing female careers in the high-tech sector: Empirical evidence from Ireland. *Women in Management Review*, *21*, 28–39.

Danish, A. Y., & Smith, H. L. (2012). Female entrepreneurship in Saudi Arabia: Opportunities and challenges. *International Journal of Gender and Entrepreneurship*, *4*(3), 216–235.

United Nations Economic and Social Commission for Asia and the Pacific (ESCAP, UN) (2021). *Social media-based online businesses: Exploring challenges to start and scale for women entrepreneurs in Bangladesh*. Report, UN Social Development Division. URL: https://repository.unescap.org/handle/20.500.12870/4292

Fanggidae, R., Nursiani, N. P., & Angi, Y. F. (2019). *Women, entrepreneurs and online business (analysis of factors that motivate entrepreneurial women through online business)*. In *3rd International Conference on Indonesian Social & Political Enquiries (ICISPW 2018)* (pp. pp 199–203). Atlantis Press.

Gajjala, R. (1999). 'Third world' perspectives on cyberfeminism. *Development in Practice*, *9*(5), 616–619.

Ghouse, S., McElwee, G., Meaton, J., & Durrah, O. (2017). Barriers to rural women entrepreneurs in Oman. *International Journal of Entrepreneurial Behavior & Research*, *23*, 998–1016.

Greenhaus, J. H., Collins, K. M., & Shaw, J. D. (2003). The relation between work–family balance and quality of life. *Journal of Vocational Behavior*, *63*, 510–531.

Hafkin, N., & Taggert, N. (2001). *Gender, Technology, and Developing Countries: An Analytic Study*. Office of Women in Development, United States Agency for International Development.

Hossain, D., & Sultana, T. (2014). Clothing business on Facebook: Status of women in e-business. *ICT for Development Working Paper Series*, *4*(1), 47–66.

Hossain, K. T., & Sumon, M. S. R. (2013). Violence against women: Nature, causes and dimensions in contemporary Bangladesh. *Bangladesh EJournal of Sociology, 10*, 79–91.

Hossain, T. (2018). Empowering women through E-Business: A study on women entrepreneurs in Dhaka City. *Asian Business Review, 3*(3), 153–160.

Huyer, S., & Sikoska, T. (2003). *Overcoming the Gender Digital Divide. Understanding ICTs and Their Potential for the Empowerment of Women*. Santo Domingo: INSTRAW.

Ibrahim, J., Chee Ros, R., Sulaiman, F. N., Nordin, R. C., & Yuan, L. Z. (2014). Positive impact of smartphone application: WhatsApp & Facebook for online business. *International Journal of Scientific and Research Publications, 4*(12), 1–4.

Irbo, M. M., & Mohammed, A. A. (2020). Social media, business capabilities and performance: A review of the literature. *African Journal of Business Management, 14*(9), 271–277.

Islam, N., Ahmed, T., Mussarrat, M., Chowdhury, S. N., & Rahman, M. R. (2019). A multivariate analysis of the development of online women entrepreneurship in Bangladesh. *Think India, 22*(14), 10225–10237.

Jaim, J. (2019). *Patriarchal practices of male family members: Women business–owners in Bangladesh*. Paper presented in a Seminar of the Nottingham Trent University, Nottingham, 12 April.

Jaim, J. (2020a). All about patriarchal segregation of work regarding family? Women business-owners in Bangladesh. *Journal of Business Ethics, 175*(2), 231–245.

Jaim, J. (2020b). Bank loans access for women business-owners in Bangladesh: Obstacles and dependence on husbands. *Journal of Small Business Management, 59*(sup1), S16–S41. doi: 10.1080/00472778.2020.1727233

Jaim, J. (2020c). Does network work? Women business-owners' access to information regarding financial support from development programmes in Bangladesh. *Business Strategy & Development, 4*(2), 148–158.

Jaim, J. (2021a). Exist or exit? Women business-owners in Bangladesh during COVID-19. *Gender, Work and Organization, 28*(1), 209–226.

Jaim, J. (2021b). Problems of political unrest: Women in small businesses in Bangladesh. *Journal of Entrepreneurship*, https://doi.org/https://doi.org/10.1108/NEJE-01-2021-0004

Karakara, A. A. W., & Osabuohien, E. (2020). ICT adoption, competition and innovation of informal firms in West Africa: A comparative study of Ghana and Nigeria. *Journal of Enterprising Communities: People and Places in the Global Economy, 14*(3), 397–414.

Khatun, S. (2019). *Courage is the way: Rape and patriarchy in Bangladesh*. Paper Presented at Human Rights Actors' Conference, Ain o Salish Kendra, Dhaka, 5 December.

Malik, S., & Mantas, C. (2021). The adoption of social media platforms in informal home-based businesses in Kuwait. *Humanities and Social Sciences Letters, 9*(3), 273–287.

Marks, S. R., & MacDermid, S. M. (1996). Multiple roles and the self: A theory of role balance. *Journal of Marriage and the Family, 58*(2), 417–432.

Mehtap, S., Pellegrini Massimiliano, M., Caputo, A., & Welsh Dianne, H. B. (2017). Entrepreneurial intentions of young women in the Arab world: Socio-cultural and educational barriers. *International Journal of Entrepreneurial Behavior & Research, 23*(6), 880–902.

Mozumdar, L. (2018). *Entrepreneurship against the tide: Business performance of women entrepreneurs in a constrained environment. A survey in Bangladesh*. Doctoral Dissertation. Wageningen University and Research.

Mozumdar, L., Hagelaar, G., Materia, V. C., Omta, S. W. F., Islam, M. A., & van der Velde, G. (2019). Embeddedness or over-embeddedness? Women entrepreneurs' networks and their influence on business performance. *The European Journal of Development Research, 31*(5), 1449–1469. https://doi.org/10.1057/S41287-019-00217-3

Mozumdar, L., Hagelaar, G., Van der Velde, G., & Omta, S. W. F. (2020). Determinants of the business performance of women entrepreneurs in the developing world context. *Journal, 3*(2), 215–235. https://doi.org/10.3390/J3020017

Mozumdar, L., Materia, V. C., Hagelaar, G., Islam, M. A., Velde, G. V. D., & Omta, S. W. F. (2022). Contextuality of entrepreneurial orientation and business performance: The case of women entrepreneurs in Bangladesh. *Journal of Entrepreneurship and Innovation in Emerging Economies*, *8*(1), 94–120.

Mukolwe, E. (2016). Social media and entrepreneurship: Tools, benefits, and challenges. A case study of women online entrepreneurs on Kilimani Mums marketplace on Facebook. *International Journal of Humanities and Social Science*, *6*(8), 248–256.

Naguib, R., & Jamali, D. (2015). Female entrepreneurship in the UAE: A multi-level integrative lens. *Gender in Management: An International Journal*, *3*(2), 135–161.

Orser, B., Henry, C., Coleman, S., Potter, J., Halibisky, D., & Noël, É. (2020). Women enterprise policy and covid-19: Towards a gender-sensitive response. *Organisation for Economic Co-operation and Development (OECD) Webinar*, *9*, June 2020.

Plant, S. (1997). *Zeros and Ones. Digital Women and the New Technologies* (Vol. 4). London: 4th Estate.

Roodman, D., & Morduch, J. (2009). The impact of microcredit on the poor in Bangladesh: Revisiting the evidence. *Journal of Development Studies*, *50*(4), 583–604.

Roomi, M. A., & Parrott, G. (2008). Barriers to the development and progression of women entrepreneurs in Pakistan. *Journal of Entrepreneurship*, *17*(1), 59–72.

Roomi, M. A., Rehman, S., & Henry, C. (2018). Exploring the normative context for women's entrepreneurship in Pakistan: A critical analysis. *International Journal of Gender and Entrepreneurship*, *10*(2), 158–180.

Sandri, S. H., & Hardilawati, W. L. (2019). The womenprenenurs: Problem and prospect in digital era. *Jurnal Akuntansi Dan Ekonomika*, *9*(1), 93–98.

Smits, M. T., & Mogos, S. (2013). The impact of social media on business performance. In *Proceedings of the 21st European Conference on Information Systems (ECIS 2013) – article 125* (pp. 1–12).

Sudarmanti, R. (2019). The relationship between intensity usage of social media with women's small online business happiness. In *ICCSS 2019: Proceedings of the 2nd International Conference on Social Sciences, ICSS 2019, 5–6 November 2019, Jakarta, Indonesia* (p. 84). European Alliance for Innovation.

Sultan, M. T., & Sharmin, F. (2020). An exploratory investigation of Facebook live marketing by women entrepreneurs in Bangladesh. In *International Conference on Human-Computer Interaction* (pp. 415–430). Cham: Springer.

Trainor, K. J. (2012). Relating social media technologies to performance: A capabilities-based perspective. *Journal of Personal Selling and Sales Management*, *32*(3), 317–331. https://doi.org/10.2753/PSS0885-3134320303

Ukpere, C. L., Slabbert, A. D., & Ukpere, W. I. (2014). Rising trend in social media usage by women entrepreneurs across the globe to unlock their potential for business success. *Mediterranean Journal of Social Sciences*, *5*(10), 551–559.

United Nations Conference on Trade and Development (UNCTAD). (2019). *Bangladesh Rapid eTrade Readiness Assessment*.

Xheneti, M., Karki, S. T., & Madden, A. (2019). Negotiating business and family demands within a patriarchal society – The case of women entrepreneurs in the Nepalese context. *Entrepreneurship and Regional Development*, *31*(3), 259–278.

Mmapatla Precious Senyolo*, Thomas B. Long, Vincent Blok,
Onno Omta

12 Climate-Smart Agriculture Diffusion within Smallholder Agriculture Context: The Role of Business Models of Sustainable Entrepreneurs

Abstract: Climate-smart agriculture technological innovations (CSATIs) provide needed benefits within base-of-the-pyramid (BoP) contexts, where smallholder farmers are vulnerable to climate change. Yet, the diffusion of CSATIs is slowed by a range of barriers. Sustainable entrepreneurs can be catalysts for the enhanced diffusion of CSATIs. The business models they use drive their ability to diffuse CSATIs. While there is a good understanding of the role of business models in the diffusion of agri-technology in Western and developed economies, their role in BoP settings is less understood. This chapter takes an in-depth qualitative approach to explore factors that shape the ability of business models used by sustainable entrepreneurs to diffuse CSATIs within BoP contexts. The results indicate that adjustments to current business models could enhance the diffusion of CSATIs. While most sustainable entrepreneurs who participated in this study agree on the shortcomings of their current business models, they differed in how they addressed these shortcomings.

Keywords: business model, base-of-the-pyramid, smallholder farmers, climate-smart agriculture technological innovations

Acknowledgements: Authors are appreciative for the financial support offered by NUFFIC, NFP-PhD Programme, grant award CF9421/2014 and other support provided by Wageningen University (WUR) and the University of Limpopo that enabled the PhD research project upon which this chapter is based. We also thank the respondents of the study for their time and for sharing their insights with us. Reviewers' comments on earlier drafts are also appreciated.

*Corresponding Author: Mmapatla Precious Senyolo, Agricultural Economics Discipline, School of Agricultural and Environmental Sciences, Faculty of Science and Agriculture, University of Limpopo, South Africa, e-mail: mmapatla.senyolo@gmail.com
Thomas B. Long, Campus Fryslân Faculty, University of Groningen, Groningen, the Netherlands
Vincent Blok, Department of Social Sciences, Philosophy Subdivision, Wageningen University, the Netherlands
Onno Omta, Department of Social Sciences, Business Management and Organisation Subdivision, Wageningen University, the Netherlands

https://doi.org/10.1515/9783110756159-015

1 Introduction

Agriculture faces threats due to climate change, requiring increases in resilience to climate impacts and potential greenhouse gas (GHG) emission reductions (Arslan et al., 2015). Agriculture must also provide food security for growing populations in an environmentally sustainable way. These grand challenges are exacerbated in developing regions such as Africa, where smallholder farmers (SHFs) are often marginalised and vulnerable due to resource and knowledge constraints (Grainger-Jones, 2011). SHFs are an important group: they provide up to 80% of food for developing countries, manage sizeable areas of land (especially in sub-Saharan Africa and Asia) and constitute the largest share of the developing world's undernourished people (IFAD, 2013). SHFs are important within the South African context also (DAFF, 2012; Thamaga-Chitja & Morojele, 2014). However, these farmers face challenges that impede their growth and ability to effectively contribute to food security compared to large-scale commercial farmers. SHFs tend to have low adaptive capacity owing to several factors such as limited access to climate change information, low technological inputs and technical know-how, as well as shortages of other necessary farming resources (Kephe, Petja, & Ayisi, 2021). These challenges require a transition to a more sustainable agricultural system, to protect livelihoods and food security of SHFs.

Climate-Smart Agriculture (CSA) represents one solution: it aims to improve agricultural productivity while reducing greenhouse gas (GHG) emissions and adapting to climate impacts (FAO, 2010; Senyolo et al., 2018). Hence, CSA has been suggested as an integrative approach to both mitigate climate change and adapt to its impacts without compromising food security (van Wijk et al., 2020). CSA involves both new and established technological, policy and institutional interventions (Kaczan, Arslan, & Lipper, 2013). CSA technological innovations (CSATIs) include technologies that increase productivity while reducing GHG emissions and managing climate change impacts (FAO, 2010). Many of these technologies and practices already exist, such as water management (harvesting and saving), crop management, agroforestry and conservation agriculture.

Adoption of CSATIs by SHFs is slow however, regardless of their benefits (van Eck et al., 2017). Demand and supply factors affect the adoption and diffusion of CSATIs. Demand-side barriers can be traced back to inadequate understanding of user needs by those who design and provide innovations (Long, Blok, & Coninx, 2016). Supply-side barriers include lack of supporting partnerships and difficulty in reaching and convincing customers, leading to difficulty in providing impact (Long, Blok, & Poldner, 2017; Senyolo, Long, & Omta, 2021a). Supply and demand-side barriers are likely to interact, and so overcoming barriers to adoption of CSATIs must involve tackling both sides (Long, Blok, & Poldner, 2017).

Few studies explicitly explore the interrelations between supply and demand-side barriers (Blok et al., 2015; Long, Blok, & Coninx, 2016; Long, Blok, & Poldner, 2017). Yet, a business model approach could facilitate further exploration: the business model construct connects the supply and demand sides, and it explores and explains the core logic of a business while also allowing for reflection on how to capture value from providing new products and services that add value for the customer (Bocken et al., 2014; Teece, 2010). Business model innovation can improve technology diffusion through re-contextualisation of the company's purpose and the rationality of value creation, while rethinking value perceptions (Bocken et al., 2014).

This chapter aims to explore the factors that affect the ability of sustainable entrepreneurs to diffuse CSATIs to SHFs at the BoP, by examining their business models. The supply and demand interactions were explored using the business model as an analytical lens, by reflecting on the value propositions of sustainable entrepreneurs (i.e. technology providers) for their customers (i.e. farmers), and the value captured by their products and services (i.e. CSATIs). Low adoption rates among the SHFs, often found within BoP contexts, have been tackled through government and non-governmental organisations' (NGOs') initiatives, but with limited success. A business model perspective could facilitate private sector-led approaches to gain significant scale in tackling BoP markets. For any technology to succeed, an appropriate business model is necessary (Boons & Ludeke-Freund, 2013; Chesbrough, 2010). Hence, this study sought to answer what factors drive the ability of business models used by sustainable entrepreneurs in South Africa to diffuse CSATIs.

Exploring sustainable entrepreneurs' business models within the SHFs' context in South Africa, this chapter contributes to our understanding of the barriers to CSATIs' adoption, and the opportunities to enhance their adoption and diffusion. Yessoufou, Blok, and Omta, (2018) highlighted the specificities of BoP contexts, suggesting the need for private sector support in developing and delivering innovative technologies for BoP communities. Business models require adjustments to these contexts to be successful (Blok, Sjauw-Koen-Fa, & Omta, 2013; Chesbrough, 2010; Linna, 2012). For business models to be financially worthwhile, they need to develop over time to cope with the environmental threats and changing market opportunities (Gray et al., 2014). Appropriate business models should assist SHFs at the BoP to overcome adoption barriers and subsequently to adopt CSATIs. However, business models meant for the SHFs within BoP in general, particularly CSA contexts, have received inadequate attention in the literature.

2 Literature Review

2.1 Business Models and Technological Innovations

A business model explains how an organisation functions to deliver value to its target market while generating profit (Osterwalder & Pigneur 2004). All companies explicitly or implicitly employ business models. A business model comprises four pillars: product (value proposition), customer interface (target customer, distribution channel and relationship), infrastructure management (value configuration, core competency and partner network) and financial aspects (cost structure and revenue model). The business model concept helps us understand how firms do business (Bocken et al., 2014; Osterwalder, Pigneur, & Tucci, 2005), and the business model provides the broader perspective on the core activities of the company (organisational design, resource-based view, transacting structure, etc.).

Sustainable entrepreneurs can integrate sustainability into conventional businesses through the redesign of their business models, while in new businesses, they can pursue sustainable business models from the start (Bocken et al., 2014). Sustainable business models emphasise value creation and capture, while safeguarding that technological innovations generate socio-economic and environmental worth for clients and the general public (Bocken et al., 2014; Stubbs & Cocklin, 2008).

An effective business model is critical for technology adoption and diffusion (Teece, 2010). Without an appropriate business model, a good technology will flop (Chesbrough, 2010), as business models help technology providers in providing customer solutions to their perceived needs (Teece, 2010). Within this context, this meant that sustainable entrepreneurs develop technologies that were the 'best' from an engineering perspective, while also providing solutions for the socio-economic and environmental needs experienced by the farmers. There is demand for support for SHFs to achieve a 'normal way of doing businesses' (Senyolo et al., 2021a), and given that many CSATIs already exist, it is the business models that are needed for further diffusion and progress towards CSA.

2.2 Business Models at the Base-of-the-Pyramid

The potential of agribusinesses to support the adoption of CSA has received relatively little attention because businesses are often seen as part of the problem. Commercially orientated actors often pursue short-term gains at the expense of human development and the environment, and are perceived to focus on easier-to-reach segments and markets, requiring less business model adjustments and costs (Connolly & Phillips-Connolly, 2012). Gradually, many development actors and agribusiness leaders see that one of the strategic ways to achieve large-scale social impact is through commercially sustainable solutions. This means sustainable entrepreneurs within agricultural contexts are increasingly expected to deliver agricultural technologies to enhance productivity, while addressing sustainability aims such as climate mitigation and adaptation. The business models of entrepreneurs may have to be adjusted to fulfil these aims and provide new added value to farmers in BoP contexts (Blok, Sjauw-Koen-Fa, & Omta, 2013; Chesbrough, 2010; Long, Blok, & Poldner, 2017; Teece, 2010).

Modifications of business models by sustainable entrepreneurs could benefit SHFs in numerous ways (Agnihotri, 2013; Teece, 2010). Business models will have to take into account the limited access to extension, financing and other supporting services by

SHFs (Kephe, Petja, & Ayisi, 2021), as well as low productivity, high transaction costs, poor inputs and limited market access (Senyolo et al., 2021a). Despite the difficulties faced by SHFs, some case studies show the potential for business model innovation in providing a solution. However, these studies are conducted almost exclusively in Asia and Latin America, leaving an African context knowledge gap.

Our framework for answering the research question focuses on the business models of sustainable entrepreneurs. This allowed an exploration of how business models and key factors around them influence technology adoption for CSA. An abridged version of four interrelated components of the business model noted by Magretta (2002) to highlight key factors for business model for CSATIs (BM*f*CSATIs) was adopted (see Figure 12.1). Analysing the business models of agri-technology companies allows the identification of specific key issues and understanding of the business logic of the sustainable entrepreneurs. Subsequent subsections highlight how each aspect of the business model influences technology adoption and how these relate to enhancing the use of CSATIs among SHFs in BoP settings.

The value proposition describes how companies offer value to their customers, commonly through products and services (Gabriel & Kirkwood, 2016). A good value proposition has to tackle end-users' challenges (Long, Blok, & Poldner, 2017), as customers do not solely desire products but want solutions to their perceived needs (Teece, 2010).

The target customer defines the specific segment targeted by the sustainable entrepreneur. Our context focuses on the SHFs within BoP settings. SHFs face major disadvantages including low productivity, higher transaction costs, poor inputs, limited markets access, insufficient finances to purchase the required quantity of inputs, lack of technical know-how and skills and lack of storage and grinding technologies (Blok, Sjauw-Koen-Fa, & Omta, 2013; Kephe, Petja, & Ayisi, 2021; Senyolo, Long, & Omta, 2021a; Senyolo et al., 2021b). These challenges imply a high cost for servicing the SHF segment, with narrow profit margins (Karnani, 2007) or with potential profits only in the future. Moreover, the imperatives of services such as training, demonstrations and technical support in improving CSATIs' adoption particularly when working with SHFs, have been reiterated (Kephe, Petja, & Ayisi, 2021; Senyolo, Long, & Omta, 2021a; Senyolo et al., 2021b).

Value delivery focuses on how a business delivers the value it created while accounting for the resources and activities involved. This element informs us whether companies are engaged in 'once-off' sales, or whether they offer additional 'after-sale' services (Long, Blok, & Poldner, 2017). Customers–companies relationship is important for business models for sustainable innovations (BMfSI) as user-behaviour can be shaped through these forged relationships (Boons & Ludeke-Freund, 2013). Successful diffusion of sustainable innovations such as CSATIs would benefit from broader sustainability actions, market acceptance and limited rebound effects, which can be prompted through customer relationships (Long, Blok, & Poldner, 2017).

Companies require resources and partners to deliver the created value, reach targeted customers and retain relationships while earning the profits. Companies form partnerships to reduce risk, acquire resources and to optimise their business models. Access to a broader and heterogeneous network, comprising scientific, socio-economic, political and cultural linkages, is necessary for backing and encouraging sustainable innovations, particularly when they are radical (Ceschin, 2013).

Value capture is concerned with how companies seize the value they create in the form of profit. This component corresponds with all other elements (i.e., value proposition, value delivery and targeted customers) of the business model (Gabriel & Kirkwood, 2016). The rationale behind value capture is to maximise earnings through costs minimisation and competitive pricing as far as possible.

3 Methods: Data Collection and Data Analysis

This chapter sought to answer *what factors enable and hinder the ability of business models used by sustainable entrepreneurs in South Africa to diffuse CSATIs.* The research took an in-depth qualitative approach. This was thought to be an appropriate research design as (1) little was known of CSATI providers in the developing countries context, while (2) our research questions were of a 'why' and 'how' nature. The study relied on data from in-depth interviews with sustainable entrepreneurs, which were triangulated with the aforementioned literature in the fields of CSA, technological innovations and business models.

3.1 Data Collection

In order to identify respondents for this study, a non-probabilistic purposive sampling strategy was used, together with referrals from existing contacts and internet searches (see list of respondents on page 239). Ten face-to-face, in-depth semi-structured interviews were conducted, ranging from 45 min to 90 min. The lead author conducted the interviews during July and August 2017. Informed consent was obtained prior to each interview. Interviews were audio taped and transcribed by the interviewer, and where this was not the case, comprehensive notes were taken during the interview. The specific personal identifying information was removed during transcription to safeguard anonymity of the respondents.

The interviews were carried out using a flexible interview protocol that covered seven areas:

I. Interviewee background (e.g. respondent position and history, respondent's expertise, views about sustainability and role of technological innovations in offsetting the climate change impacts)

II. Company perspective (e.g. whether company has technology transfer component, established or required partnerships with other stakeholders and clients)
III. Information about the technology (e.g. what does the technology do and its value to end-users);
IV. Clients and adoption process (e.g. current or targeted customers, compatibility and applicability of the technology, existence of competitors)
V. barriers to dissemination of CSA technologies (e.g. challenges related to technology dissemination, areas where support is needed, perceived enabling and limiting factors)
VI. revenues or costs (e.g. costs charged for the technology and options for payment offered to farmers)
VII. policy environment (e.g., any policy or rules for the CSA technology in question and how it is thought to create opportunities or disturbances for adoption)

The following companies were interviewed:
- R1: Milling Company – Provide post-harvest storage and milling technologies. Sell seeds, agrochemicals and fertilisers on behalf of other companies
- R2: Agricultural Cooperative Company – Product ranges include irrigation, gardening, hardware, power tools, tractors and other farm implement spares and parts, animal feeds, seeds, fertilisers, animal health products, pet food, pet accessories, gardening chemicals and agricultural chemicals. Provide storage and milling technologies.
- R3: Milling Company – Provide post-harvest storage and milling and technologies. Sell seeds, agrochemical and fertilisers on behalf of other companies.
- R4: Seed Company – Buy, distribute and sell imported and local seeds.
- R5: Machinery Company – Manufacture, import and sell tractors, tractor parts, farming implements and trailers.
- R6: Fertiliser Company – Buy, distribute and sell fertilisers.
- R7: Seed Company – Produce and market seeds.
- R8: Fertiliser Company – Manufacture, blending, and supply of fertilisers.
- R9: Agricultural Cooperative Company – Product ranges include irrigation, gardening, hardware, power tools, tractors and other farm implement spares, animal feeds, seeds, fertilisers,, agricultural/gardening chemicals and fuel.
- R10: Seed Company – Produce, import, export and market seeds.

3.2 Data Analysis

Consistent with an in-depth qualitative approach, data analysis started with the production of interview transcripts. The data, in the form of transcripts, were coded in an iterative process. This involved reading and revision of the transcripts throughout the analysis as new questions and connections were identified. Statements and phrases relevant to the research questions were identified during this stage of the analysis. A preliminary set of themes were developed (e.g. 'Barriers to technology dissemination'), and then refined through further iterations. Following coding of initial themes, the transcripts were revised to identify relationships between themes identified during the preliminary stages of coding to place them into key categories. The categorisation involved several iterations to safeguard consistency within the developed categories.

4 Results

First, it was helpful to start with an inventory of our sample. There were five categories of agri-technology business in the study: Milling (x2), Fertiliser (x2), Seed (x3), Machinery (x1) and Agricultural cooperative (x2) companies. All these businesses were named after the key agri-technologies that they offer, and those named Agricultural cooperatives companies were characterised by a larger product service range, which included at least four of the products offered by the other sustainable entrepreneurs. Following the brief indication of the sampled sustainable entrepreneurs and presentation of the business model framework in Figure 12.1, we now show the four types of business models used by the respondent companies for targeting SHFs. The four types are 'Engagement', 'Limited service', 'Integrated package' and 'Sales and procurement'; they are summarised in Table 12.1 and illustrated by Figure 12.1.

The business model consists of four main components, namely value proposition, value delivery, value capture and target customer. Results of this study highlight that factors linked to the value proposition, value capture and target customer were the most important in terms of BoP contexts. The value delivery component was not identified as a distinguishing feature between the different business models, and so it was not examined within Table 12.1. Instead, we commented on it briefly after the presentation of the four categories of business models identified in this study.

4.1 'Engagement' Business Model

The main pillar of the 'Engagement' business model was the combination of targeted customers and the resulting value proposition (see Figure 12.1). The sustainable entrepreneurs in this category were milling companies, who responded to SHFs' demands regarding produce grinding, thereby raising its value and reducing post-harvest losses. The milling companies provided the storage and grinding technologies. In turn, these sustainable entrepreneurs' (R1 and R3) business models included buying the SHFs' produce. In this case, the SHFs benefited through increased production and better-quality maize/sorghum grains, thereby generating income and increased purchasing power.

Table 12.1: Summary of business model types and number of cases that supported the models.

	Engagement (2 cases)	Limited services (3 cases)	Integrated package (3 cases)	Sales and procurement (2 cases)
Value proposition	Handling, storage and grinding technology; Income and maize-meal for food security; Bringing inputs closer; Advisory services; Market for output	Products; Advisory services; Short-term credit; Limited support and training	Products; Advisory services; Short to medium-term credit; Integrated training and mentoring; Soil analysis; Precision agriculture; Maintenance; Netting houses	Products; Advisory services; Production loans; Integrated training and mentoring; Market for output
Target customer	SHFs as suppliers of raw material	SHFs as end-users of products plus limited packages	SHFs as end-users of products plus integrated packages	SHFs as end-users of products plus integrated packages and as suppliers of raw material
Value delivery				
Value capture	Reduced costs for ATPs; Increased volume and improved quality of grains brought by local SHFs	Reduced risks associated with credit defaults; Reduced financial and time costs associated with mentorship/ training	Increased sales resulting from successful farmers who received support, mentorship, and production loans; Increased willingness to pay	Increased sales resulting from successful farmers who received support, mentorship; Increased volume and improved quality of seeds or grains brought by SHFs

Source: Author's compilation from data.

Moreover, to safeguard the quantity and quality of the grains, the milling companies offered the targeted customers advisory and logistics services. Selling and delivering the agri-technologies, such as seeds and fertilisers, was the lever that these sustainable entrepreneurs used to facilitate their raw material sourcing processes. The rationale behind this model was to facilitate access to localised (where possible) and timely production inputs for SHFs, and consequently influence production to safeguard raw materials for the milling companies.

4.2 'Limited Services' Business Model

The second category of business model directly sold and distributed agri-technologies to customers. These sustainable entrepreneurs' main focus was to import, distribute and sell technologies to SHFs. The customer segment included large-scale commercial farmers, SHFs or government contractors (i.e. tender-preneurs) on behalf of the SHFs. The companies in this category had a value proposition largely focused on product sales and delivery, with limited packages of services such as advisory, training and short-term credit (see Figure 12.1). These businesses operated their sales within commoditised and bespoke systems. They operated through either on-demand supply (i.e. mail order) or via retail centres. The result was that businesses employing 'Limited services' business models became the link between the manufacturing and production companies and the farmers. SHFs were included in the formal economy by buying the agri-technologies at market price.

4.3 'Integrated Packages' and 'Sales and Procurement' Business Models

The third and fourth business model types both combine products with integrated services. The sustainable entrepreneurs who employed these business models seem to have gained additional strengths and were supportive of agricultural development. As a result, they employed a larger scale form of 'Engagement' and 'Limited services' business models. The customer segment included both large-scale commercial farmers and the SHFs or government contractors (i.e. tender-preneurs) on behalf of the SHFs. The value proposition in these business models were the product-service-based approach to agriculture.

The sustainable entrepreneurs were inclined to provide the value propositions that combine the activities of the businesses that employ 'Engagement' and 'Limited services' business models (see Figures 12.1). For instance, R2 noted that they provided production loans and mentorship to farmers as well as required production inputs accompanied by technical know-how. Another example is R5, who developed customised 'developmental packages' targeted specifically at SHFs, wherein their package included a tractor, conservation agriculture implements (e.g. no till implements), maintenance plans and training. In addition, R8 offered soil analysis together with recommendations of tailor-made products in a way that protected the environment. Other examples included the provision of medium-term credit and output market for customers (e.g. SHFs). While all these product-services were, in essence, value-creating elements, the common denominator was an increase in efficiency in everyday activities of the farmers.

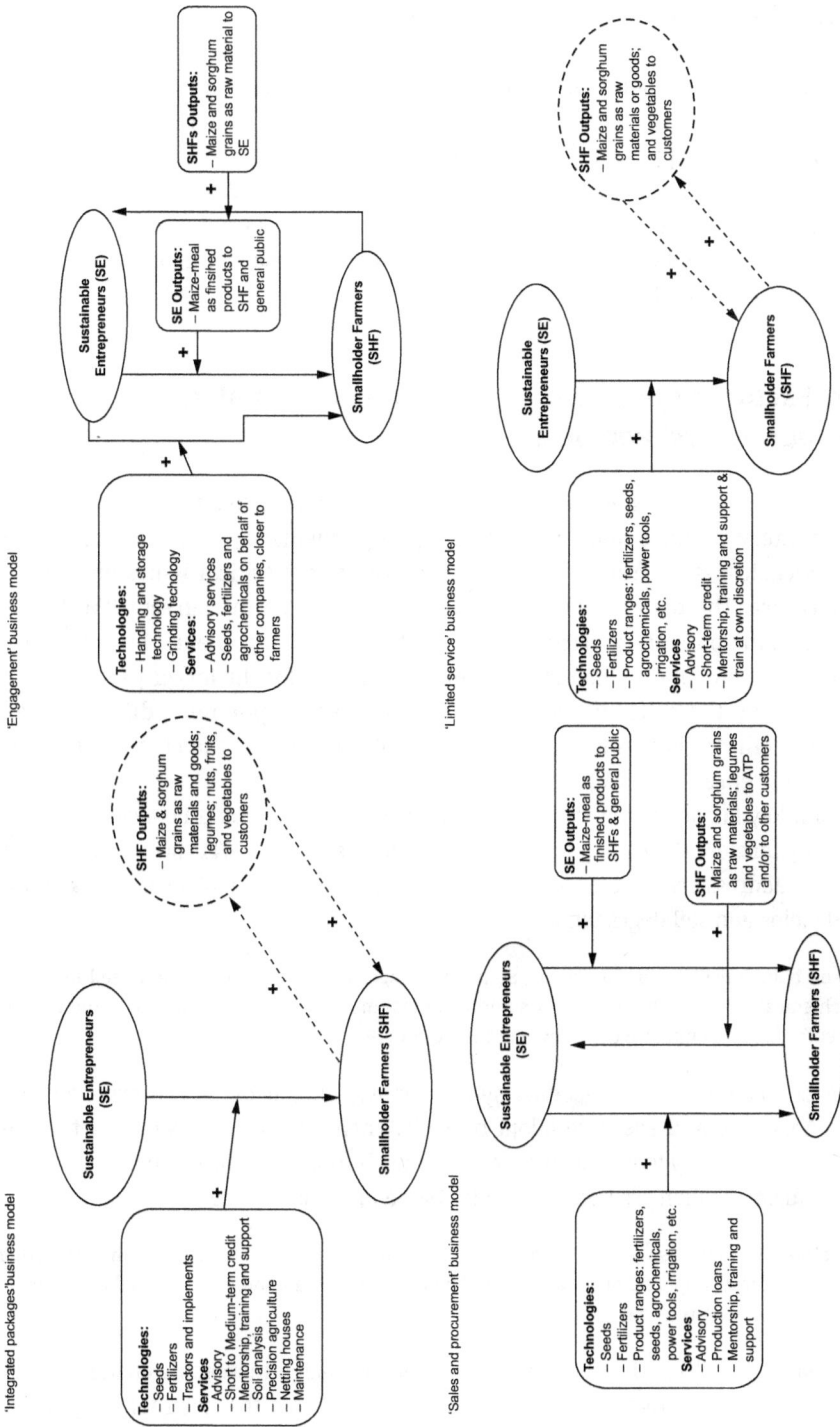

Figure 12.1: Overview of sustainable business models.

4.4 Value Delivery

Generally, the studied sustainable entrepreneurs applied similar means of communication for reaching their customers, regardless of business model types. The wider shift to service-based approaches in agriculture means that knowledge provision and sharing is more important. As such, farmers' information, field days, demos, exhibitions and internet-based solutions were often used to reach target customers. Hence, almost all business model included in the research used these channels, including R2, R10, R5, R1, R8, R7 and R9.

4.5 Key Factors of Business Models from Sustainable Entrepreneurs' Perspectives

To pinpoint the key factors of business models from sustainable entrepreneurs' viewpoints, the interview data collected from these respondents was studied through the BM*f*CSATI's critical issue framework, and compared to the critical issues highlighted in the literature. The data provides a supply perspective on the current BM*f*CSATIs, and highlights the possible shortcomings of sustainable entrepreneurs' business models. The results show that the perceived shortcomings are for the larger part mutually identified among the different respondents. However, respondents differ in their strategies to address those shortcomings. Figure 12.2 illustrates the critical issues for sustainable entrepreneurs' BM*f*CSATIs.

The first key factor related to the value proposition: there should be a clear demand for CSATIs by farmers. According to sustainable entrepreneurs, CSATIs potentially benefit SHFs as they address critical environmental and socio-economic challenges in relation to increased yields and soil degradation.

> The soil is no longer having nutrients. So it is no longer productive. So farmers need money to buy chemical fertilisers because it does not help them much if they have only seeds and they do not get fertilisers to nurture the growth of their crops. (R8)

Respondents noted that product-service system innovation is necessary to make technology more attractive and easier to adopt by SHFs. Their argument was largely that the provision of a seemingly 'good' technology alone might not be sufficient to address adoption and diffusion challenges; hence, a service-based approach would be more appealing.

> [W]e offer free mentorship, we do not charge those farmers for mentoring, and then the other thing is technical support that [farmers] get. The production loan, the planning and execution of the production loan is also the best for us. (R2)

It was revealed that SHFs (i.e. targeted customers) are facing increasing challenges due to climate change. Although sustainable entrepreneurs noted the need for adoption of

CSATIs to deal with climate change, they also perceived that SHFs lack the necessary knowledge, skills and financial capital to do so.

> I think [our CSATIs] is for both types of farmers, but some emerging and SHFs lack the finance for the technology. (R8)

Regardless of SHFs' challenges, some sustainable entrepreneurs saw providing CSATIs to SHFs as a business opportunity. There would be costs in understanding SHFs' needs and requirements. Nevertheless, SHFs represented a potentially profitable mass market. However, serving this segment would require a different approach, and one, which if successful, would increase technology adoption.

> I mean SHFs for me, represent an access to a market, which is untapped, because all our competitors are focusing on all big commercial farmers and neglect SHFs. What they do not realize is that it is really a huge market access. It is a huge market that is waiting to be tapped, but you cannot go there with standard rates (R5).

Respondents also noted several factors related to the value delivery component. First, sustainable entrepreneurs identified the importance of building relationships with their customers. Farmers value the service, probably because of the ability to ask questions and gain knowledge about the application, maintenance and/or marketing options. Respondents also noted that regular contact (although deemed costly) with customers was necessary to encourage their loyalty, mediating adoption and diffusion of CSATIs.

> There are lots of competitors . . . . [W]hat makes us tick is our feet on the farms. Our feet are physically on the farms, we have always believed that! (R6)

Second, sustainable entrepreneurs largely agreed that access to rural SHFs is difficult owing to their marginalised and isolated locations and underdeveloped infrastructures. New ways of reaching out to SHFs included the use of additional channels, such as village 'depots'. However, respondents considered this service costly for their businesses to maintain and noted it also raises potential conflicts with other businesses.

> [Company name] brings us these seeds, and you know that we have depots all over the provinces, so we take these seeds to the depots. Farmers can go there, when they go to buy maize meal, they also buy seeds. (R1)

Third, sustainable entrepreneurs noted that there was exploitation within the supply chain. For instance, government funds aimed at CSA were often absorbed by middlemen (e.g. tender-preneurs).

> and that is where the problem starts for the input of costs of farmers. Those people who are tendering . . . between the government, the buyers and our companies are making a lot of money. [Tender-preneurs] come and buy from us and that maize seed was 350,000 ZAR but the government pays [Tender-preneur] 1.5 million ZAR. The margin is so high and you see, the whole structure is a problem. (R10)

Fourth, good access to wider networks, including those related to policy, other suppliers and research was a requirement for sustainable entrepreneurs. It was important for key partners to understand the challenges faced by their targeted customers. For instance, while the government may have adequate financial resources and good intentions, SHFs lack appropriate farming skills, business mindsets, entrepreneurial and managerial skills, which may still jeopardise their prospects. These issues could be addressed through strategic partnerships among different stakeholders, such as private companies, researchers and government, to offer mentorship and training.

> The government have got resources, money, can offer these farmers training and everything . . . . [W]e do not have money that we can offer training, but the farmers that we work with are progressing far better than those working with government. [We] wish to help the government in mentoring those farmers to make sure they become sustainable in the system. (R2)

> There was [research institute, government department, four private companies], all these stakeholders are helping farmers. They are bringing different things. This one brings seeds, this one brings fertilisers, and this one brings agro-chemicals, etc., so that we can help the farmers. So we are working with all these stakeholders to help these entrepreneurs and farmers. (R1)

In terms of value capture, SHFs were not always able to afford CSATIs. While credit provision may enhance the value offering, it appeared that inflexibility in some business models, or rather their financial models, were an issue.

> Farmers have practiced farming for long time without fertiliser application and now have milked the whole nutrients on the soil. To get better and improved yields, they need to get fertilisers, but they do not always afford it. (R8)

A summary of the key results, underlining the specific barriers and modifications that could enhance CSATI's adoption and diffusion, is illustrated in Figure 12.2. Implications of these results are discussed in the following sections.

5 Discussion

In order to explore issues that affect the ability of the business models used by sustainable entrepreneurs to diffuse CSATIs within SHFs' context found in BoP, the theoretical backgrounds highlighted in Section 2 was was explored with empirical data collected from sustainable entrepreneurs. First, issues of business models for CSATIs that emerged from the empirical results are discussed. Second, the potential role of agri-technology companies in tackling the barriers to adoption of CSATIs by farmers is deliberated.

Value Proposition

Barriers:
– Mixed reaction regarding the extent of worth
– Convincing customers
Enablers:
– Further assessment and verification regarding CSATI impact
– Product-service system
– Information and support coordination towards customers

Value Delivery

1. Customer relationship and Channels
Barriers:
– Indirect relationship with SHF
– Reaching/accessing SHF
Enablers:
– Direct relationship with customers
– Shorten the chain
– Use of multiple channels to targeted customers
– Key resources and key partners
Barriers:
– Exploitation of supply chain leaving less or no resources for investment (e.g., market expansion, and servitisation)
– Limited supporting partnerships
Enablers:
– Access to policy and regulatory environment as well as networks
– Access to creditors
– Monitor the activities of chain actors for accountability

Target Customer

Barriers:
– SHF lack financial resources
– Mentoring and training need of SHF are not optional
– Poor access to input and output markets
– Standard rates of CSATIs are not appropriate for SHF
Enablers:
– Integrated tailored service packages
– Explore angle of quantity to compensate for relative cheaper prices needed by SHF

Value Capture

Barriers:
– Servitisation has cost implications
Enablers:
– Adjust business model or revenue models to improve value creation (e.g. to free resources for PSS)
– Secure strategic partnerships for the purpose of risk and cost sharing to service SHF

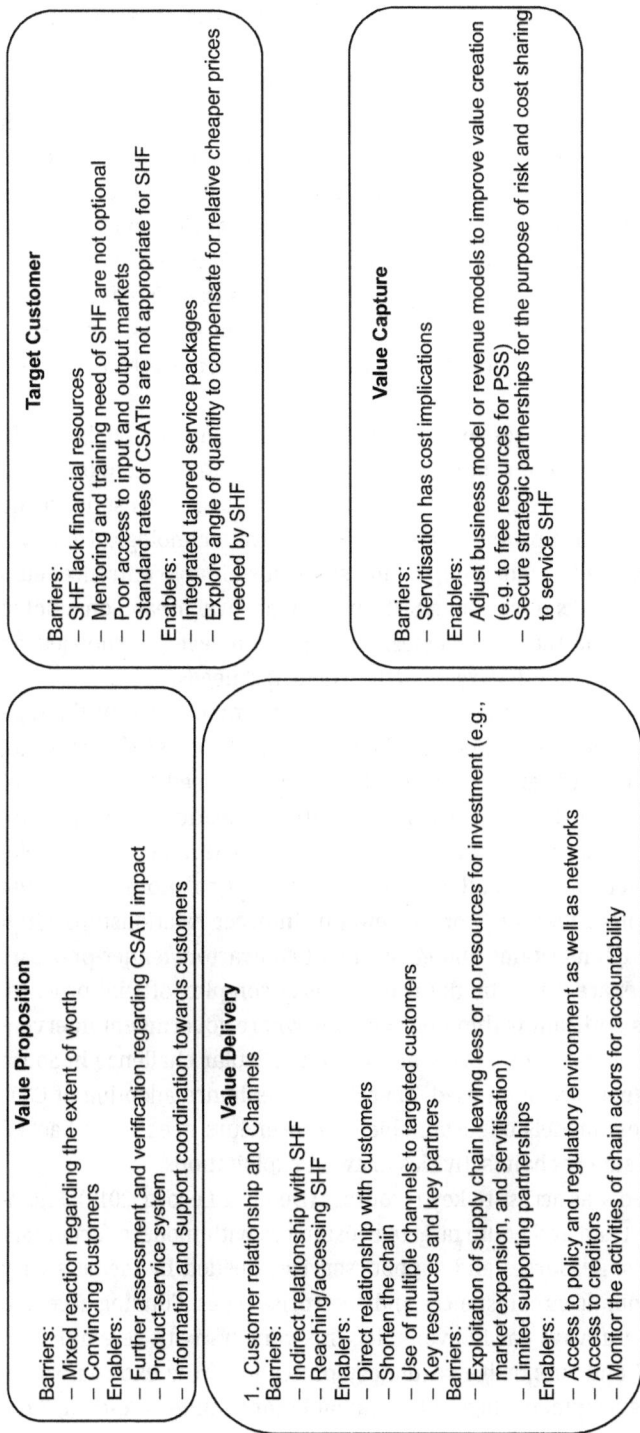

Figure 12.2: Overview of critical issues.

5.1 Integration of Issues for BMfCSATIs and Previous Research

The results revealed that the existing business models of the sampled sustainable entrepreneurs do not seem to be functioning optimally to diffuse CSATIs. Research showed that relevant and clearly articulated value propositions help overcome the sales and marketing difficulties. The sustainable entrepreneurs reported that product-service systems would boost adoption, implying that additional services such as training, mentoring and credit are needed to enhance provision of CSATIs. While end-users understand the benefits of CSATIs, we found that often the issue is affordability. This highlights the distinctiveness of the SHFs within the BoP context: they need credit access, which is often more than the proof of impact noted as key in Western contexts (Long, Blok, & Poldner, 2017).

These results tally with previous research that shows that business models should be understood as instruments for innovation and vital ways for enhancing adoption of technological innovations (Evans et al., 2017; Teece, 2010). Current results support the importance of customer relationships and channels in effective technological innovation diffusion (Boons & Ludeke-Freund, 2013). While some sustainable entrepreneurs emphasised the difficulty and risks of reaching SHFs in remote rural areas, some noted this as an opportunity to expand their businesses. The latter, however, acknowledged the need for adjustments of current offerings to better suit SHFs' needs.

The second critical issue regarding the value delivery component concerns the relationship with targeted customers and their marketing tactics (Gabriel & Kirkwood, 2016). According to ver Loren van Themaat et al. (2013), companies need modification of products/services to ensure that these are acceptable within specific customers' contexts. While our respondents recognised this factor, some reported having direct relationships with their customers whereas others reported indirect relationships. In the former scenario, respondents relied on word of mouth. Indirect relationships often meant higher costs due to high mark-ups that government contractors/tender-preneurs charged for their services, exacerbated by the use of overly complex official procurement systems. This issue is significant within BoP contexts, where government intervention is often a key driver in adoption of CSATIs, and it is a particular challenge in South Africa where tendering systems are often used. Therefore, to enhance adoption of CSATIs by SHFs, optimal business models of sustainable entrepreneurs need to be backed by high-level monitoring of supply chain activities to avoid exploitations.

The third key issue noted was access to key resources (Demil & Lecocq, 2010). Financial resources are needed to train and equip targeted customers with modern farm management and technical skills. Resources and support services needed by farmers vary according to their socio-economic circumstances and enterprise types. Funding access to provide such services is not always easily available. This concurs with research that cited the need for financial and supportive regulatory protection from external stakeholders during the initial development stages of sustainable innovations (Ceschin, 2013; Gabriel & Kirkwood, 2016). Literature further recognises the importance of tailor-made support provision (Gray et al., 2014) by interventionists to reduce the SHFs' barriers to adoption of CSATIs.

The fourth issue raised by respondents in relation to the value proposition was the need for low margins, especially in catering SHFs. Chesbrough (2010) also mentioned that lower initial margins may facilitate competition with reputable companies. Some CSATIs were felt to be too expensive for SHFs, suggesting higher margins. The proposed solution was to explore how sustainable entrepreneurs can make money while offering SHFs affordable products and services. These results are in accord with Teece (2010) that price systems are critical, because customers are inclined to buy only if the price is less than the utility yielded and producers will supply if price is at or above all costs, including return to capital. This suggests that to serve SHFs successfully, a higher number of products must be sold on a limited margin.

5.2 Sustainable Entrepreneurs' Potential to Tackle CSATIs' Adoption Barriers

SHFs need long-term production credit and finance access to buy CSATIs and/or pay for related services. Results revealed that sustainable entrepreneurs deliver a range of services to SHFs, which include provision of short- to medium-term credit. However, provision of relatively short-term credit is often inadequate for SHFs in BoP contexts. Long-term credit is thus necessary to enhance adoption of CSATIs by SHFs.

Results also revealed that the government may buy CSATIs from sustainable entrepreneurs on behalf of SHFs. This implies that government intervention was considered a driver to SHFs' adoption of CSATIs. Although sustainable entrepreneurs concurred that production credit was imperative for tackling some barriers to the adoption of CSATIs, some argued that risks are too high to bear, especially when dealing with SHFs. Hence, they emphasised that it is better to play by the book when lending money to farmers. This would mean that collateral will be required for production credit loan, consequently excluding many SHFs. These results corroborate previous research, suggesting that while product-service system innovation is a promising business model, it comes with noteworthy challenges for companies, customers and regulatory environments (Ceschin, 2013). This is because companies often find product-service system strategies complicated relative to traditional ways of delivering products alone.

In some instances, we found that sustainable entrepreneurs offered production loans for variable inputs, mentorship and training to farmers, conditional to them having basic infrastructures (e.g. tractors and irrigation waters) wherein in some cases, the government was often the provider of such infrastructures. This again suggests that government intervention in a multi-actor-based business model was a driver that can enable SHFs to buy and/or pay for CSATIs.

Results showed that sustainable entrepreneurs addressed SHFs' problems via specific business model formulations: 'Engagement', 'Integrated packages' and 'Sale and procurement'. For instance, milling companies in particular indicated that their inclination to help SHFs access technologies was strategic to ensure local SHFs produce enough quality produce, thereby eventually safeguarding their own supply of raw materials. Respondents' reasoning can be seen to be the economic and strategic driver behind their business logics in that they 'want to feed the cow they milk'. Nevertheless, the implication of this strategy is that these sustainable entrepreneurs have the potential to drive adoption of CSATIs if SHFs' obstacles are lack of input/output markets. However, where financial constraints are prevalent, collaboration between government and sustainable entrepreneurs would still be required to safeguard adequate adoption of CSATIs.

Results also highlighted that technology alone does not fully address SHFs' challenges. These farmers need additional support that includes use of product-service system strategies. By offering services such as soil analysis, maintenance plans, structured training and mentorship, these sustainable entrepreneurs' services can align to the principles of CSA. For example, one respondent noted that their company offered their customers two-year maintenance plans, indicating that this service can help improve the efficient use of technology and inputs, respectively, and importantly enhance agricultural productivity as well as reduce GHG emissions. This kind of service has major advantages with a product-service system strategy, including prolonging the life of capital (existing tractors through better care of these technologies). Life extension of the products, however, means reduced demand for replacement capital and additional sales. Therefore, lesser resources and materials would be needed when new tractors are designed and manufactured. Nonetheless, tractor maintenance service may to some degree substitute new tractors.

5.3 Study Limitations

Our study has a few limitations. Our analysis was based on a small study population of ten sustainable entrepreneurs. We also recognise the drawbacks of using the snowball approach to identify respondents. Where possible, we have corroborated results with internet searches to identify the agri-technology companies and/or respondents. Lastly, we concede that the business model does not permit all-inclusive detailed understanding of how these sustainable entrepreneurs' businesses run. Nonetheless, our study provides the first and important step in the right direction. Certainly, there are other factors, such as technology, ease of access, novelty, adaptability and self-drive, that are essential characteristics of agri-preneurial activity; these are not necessarily included in business model frameworks. Investigating these additional factors may enhance future research. Furthermore, future studies should seek to validate the above results by employing a larger sample covering other provinces of South Africa and other developing countries.

6 Conclusions

This study explored key issues for BMfCSATIs, by identifying barriers and enabling factors that could enhance adoption and diffusion of CSATIs. By pinpointing where in the business models of sustainable entrepreneurs these barriers and factors occur, we indicated how business models influence the adoption and diffusion of technological innovations in BoP contexts. We identified the shortcomings of the business models and suggested business model innovations.

Seeing that BMfCSATIs are non-optimal, it is conceivable to note them as one of the barriers to the uptake of CSATIs on smallholder farming within BoP contexts. This study revealed that SHFs have the potential to offer valuable opportunities for sustainable entrepreneurs that target them; however, their peculiar characteristics make them a difficult market to target. Nevertheless, if sustainable entrepreneurs that provide CSATIs with or without limited product-service system are able to advance to full product-service system and expand to accommodate SHFs through integrated services, these could help overcome some of the aforementioned business model shortcomings. Thus, if SHFs can access credit services with more structured training and mentorship or leniency towards their realities, then they may be motivated to be optimistic about their potential to contribute to the uptake of CSATIs within smallholder agriculture. This highlights a role for business model innovation, which may require additional understanding of the barriers that agri-technology companies face while targeting their market.

This research has contributed towards broader literature on business models and their associations with sustainable innovations. Although our empirical findings were largely consistent with key factors identified within literature, two additional issues peculiar to BoP contexts were identified. First, literature on the Western context indicated that relevant and clearly articulated value propositions concerning CSATIs would overcome their sales and marketing difficulties; however, current results indicated that within BoP, provision of 'good' CSATIs alone is not sufficient to enhance adoption. The product-service system could be a business model innovation that would help overcome barriers to the adoption of CSATIs. Second, these results indicated that the core requirement of SHFs within the BoP goes beyond proof of impact (as is the case in Western contexts), but includes a need for credit. The practical relevance of this study was to provide an input for future sustainable entrepreneurs concentrating on the SHFs' market or those intending to expand their market to cater to SHFs particularly concerning CSATIs. Furthermore, for policymakers aiming to enhance adoption of CSATIs, the results of this study could serve as a first step to identify areas of interventions.

References

Agnihotri, A. (2013). Doing good and doing business at the bottom of the pyramid. *Business Horizons*, *56*(5), 591–599. https://doi.org/10.1016/j.bushor.2013.05.009

Arslan, A., McCarthy, N., Lipper, L., Asfaw, S., Cattaneo, A., & Kokwe, M. (2015). Climate smart agriculture? Assessing the adaptation implications in Zambia. *Journal of Agricultural Economics*, *66*(3), 753–780. https://doi.org/10.1111/1477-9552.12107

Blok, V., Long, T. B., Gaziulusoy, A. I., Ciliz, N., Lozano, R., Huisingh, D., Csutora, M., & Boks, C. (2015). From best practices to bridges for a more sustainable future: Advances and challenges in the transition to global sustainable production and consumption: Introduction to the ERSCP stream of the Special volume. *Journal of Cleaner Production*, *108*, 19–30. doi: 10.1016/j.jclepro.2015.04.119

Blok, V., Sjauw-Koen-Fa, A., & Omta, S. (2013). Effective stakeholder involvement at the base of the pyramid: The case of Rabobank. *International Food and Agribusiness Management Review*, *16*(A), 39–44. https://edepot.wur.nl/298334

Bocken, N. M., Short, S. W., Rana, P., & Evans, S. (2014). A literature and practice review to develop sustainable business model archetypes. *Journal of Cleaner Production*, *65*, 42–56. doi: 10.1016/j.jclepro.2013.11.039

Boons, F., & Ludeke-Freund, F. (2013). Business models for sustainable innovation: State-of-the-art and steps towards a research agenda. *Journal of Cleaner Production*, *45*, 9–19. doi: 10.1016/j.jclepro.2012.07.007

Ceschin, F. (2013). Critical factors for implementing and diffusing sustainable product – Service systems: Insights from innovation studies and companies' experiences. *Journal of Cleaner Production*, *45*, 74–88. doi: 10.1016/j.jclepro.2012.05.034

Chesbrough, H. (2010). Business model innovation: Opportunities and barriers. *Long Range Planning*, *43* (2–3), 354–363. https://doi.org/10.1016/j.lrp.2009.07.010

Connolly, A. J., & Phillips-Connolly, K. (2012). *Can agribusiness feed 3 billion new people . . . and save the planet? A GLIMPsustainable entrepreneur™ into the future*. Managing wicked problems in agribusiness. doi: 10.22004/ag.econ.142306.

Department of Agriculture, Fisheries and Forestry (DAFF). (2012). *A Framework for the Development of Smallholder Farmers through Cooperatives Development*. In. Pretoria, South Africa: Department of Agriculture, Forestry and Fisheries, https://www.nda.agric.za

Demil, B., & Lecocq, X. (2010). Business model evolution: In search of dynamic consistency. *Long Range Planning*, *43*(2–3), 227–246. https://doi.org/10.1016/j.lrp.2010.02.004

Evans, S., Vladimirova, D., Holgado, M., Van Fossen, K., Yang, M., Silva, E. A., & Barlow, C. Y. (2017). Business model innovation for sustainability: Towards a unified perspective for creation of sustainable business models. *Business Strategy and the Environment*, *26*(5), 597–608. https://doi.org/10.1002/bse.1939

Food and Agriculture Organization of the United Nations (FAO) (2010). 'Climate-Smart' Agriculture. Policies, Practises and Financing for Food Security, Adaptation and Mitigation. Retrieved from Rome, Italy. http://www.fao.org/docrep/013/i1881e/i1881e00.pdf

Gabriel, C. A., & Kirkwood, J. (2016). Business models for model businesses: Lessons from renewable energy entrepreneurs in developing countries. *Energy Policy*, *95*, 336–349. doi: 10.1016/j.enpol.2016.05.006.

Grainger-Jones, E. (2011). *Climate-smart Smallholder Agriculture: What's Different* (ISBN 978-92-9072-282-3). Retrieved from Rome, Italy. https://www.donorplatform.org/files/content/Media/Agenda_2030/Lat est/SAFIN/IFAD_CSA.pdf

Gray, B. J., Duncan, S., Kirkwood, J., & Walton, S. (2014). Encouraging sustainable entrepreneurship in climate-threatened communities: A Samoan case study. *Entrepreneurship & Regional Development*, *26*(5–6), 401–430. https://doi.org/10.1080/08985626.2014.922622

International Fund for Agricultural Development (IFAD) (2013). *Smallholders, Food Security and the Environment*. Retrieved from Rome, Italy: International Fund for Agricultural Development. https://www.ifad.org/documents/38714170/39135645/smallholders_report.pdf/133e8903-0204-4e7d-a780-bca847933f2e

Kaczan, D., Arslan, A., & Lipper, L. (2013). *Climate-smart agriculture. A review of current practice of agroforestry and conservation agriculture in Malawi and Zambia. ESA working paper* (13–07). 10.22004/ag.econ.288985.

Karnani, A. (2007). The mirage of marketing to the bottom of the pyramid: How the private sector can help alleviate poverty. *California Management Review, 49*(4), 90–111. https://doi.org/info:doi/

Kephe, P. N., Petja, B. M., & Ayisi, K. K. (2021). Examining the role of institutional support in enhancing smallholder oilseed producers' adaptability to climate change in Limpopo Province, South Africa. *Oilseeds & Fats Crops and Lipids (OCL), 28*(14), 1–9. https://doi.org/10.1051/ocl/2021004

Linna, P. (2012). Base of the pyramid (BOP) as a source of innovation: Experiences of companies in the Kenyan mobile sector. *International Journal of Technology Management & Sustainable Development, 11*(2), 113–137. doi: 10.1386/tmsd.11.2.113_1

Long, T. B., Blok, V., & Coninx, I. (2016). Barriers to the adoption and diffusion of technological innovations for climate-smart agriculture in Europe: Evidence from the Netherlands, France, Switzerland and Italy. *Journal of Cleaner Production, 112*, 9–21. doi: 10.1016/j.jclepro.2015.06.044

Long, T. B., Blok, V., & Poldner, K. (2017). Business models for maximising the diffusion of technological innovations for climate-smart agriculture. *International Food and Agribusiness Management Review, 20* (1), 5–23. https://doi.org/10.22434/IFAMR2016.0081

Magretta, J. (2002). Why business models matter. *Harvard Business Review*, 1–8, May. https://hbr.org/2002/05/why-business-models-matter

Osterwalder, A., & Pigneur, Y. (2004). An ontology for e-business models. *Value Creation from E-business Models, 1*, 65–97. https://citeseerx.ist.psu.edu/viewdoc/download?doi=10.1.1.9.6922&rep=rep1&type=pdf

Osterwalder, A., Pigneur, Y., & Tucci, C. L. (2005). Clarifying business models: Origins, present, and future of the concept. *Communications of the Association for Information Systems, 15*(1), 1–43. doi: 10.17705/1CAIS.01601

Senyolo, M. P., Long, T. B., Blok, V., & Omta, O. (2018). How the characteristics of innovations impact their adoption: An exploration of climate-smart agricultural innovations in South Africa. *Journal of Cleaner Production, 172*, 3825–3840. doi: 10.1016/j.jclepro.2017.06.019

Senyolo, M. P., Long, T. B., & Omta, O. (2021a). Enhancing the adoption of climate-smart technologies using public – Private partnerships: Lessons from the WEMA case in South Africa. *International Food and Agribusiness Management Review, 24*(5), 755–776. https://doi.org/10.22434/IFAMR2019.0197

Senyolo, M. P., Long, T. B., Blok, V., Omta, O., & Van der Velde, G. (2021b). Smallholder adoption of technology: Evidence from the context of climate smart agriculture in South Africa. *Journal of Development and Agricultural Economics, 13*(2), 156–173. doi: 10.5897/JDAE2020.1191.

Stubbs, W., & Cocklin, C. (2008). Conceptualizing a 'sustainability business model'. *Organization & Environment, 21*(2), 103–127. doi: 10.1177/1086026608318042.

Teece, D. J. (2010). Business models, business strategy and innovation. *Long Range Planning, 43*(2–3), 172–194. https://doi.org/10.1016/j.lrp.2009.07.003

Thamaga-Chitja, J. M., & Morojele, P. (2014). The context of smallholder farming in South Africa: Towards a livelihood asset building framework. *Journal of Human Ecology, 45*(2), 147–155. https://doi.org/10.1080/09709274.2014.11906688

van Eck, L. C. J., Van der Hout Smith, P., & van den Bos Mba, A. J. (2017). *Climate Smart Agriculture: How Dutch Technology Can Add Value of the South African (Emerging) Farmers*. https://knowledge4food.net/wp-content/uploads/2018/01/171030_ScopingReportCSA_SouthAfrica_Final.pdf van Wijk, M. T., Merbold, L., Hammond, J., & Butterbach-Bahl, K. (2020). Improving assessments of the three pillars of climate smart agriculture: Current achievements and ideas for the future. *Frontiers in Sustainable Food Systems*, *4*(558483), 1–14. doi. 10.3389/fsufs.2020.558483.

Ver Loren van Themaat, T., Schutte, C. S., Lutters, D., & Kennon, D. (2013). Designing a framework to design a business model for the 'bottom of the pyramid' population. *South African Journal of Industrial Engineering*, *24*(3), 190–204. http://www.scielo.org.za/scielo.php?script=sci_arttext&pid=S2224-78902013000300016&lng=en&nrm=iso

Yessoufou, A. W., Blok, V., & Omta, S. (2018). The process of entrepreneurial action at the base of the pyramid in developing countries: A case of vegetable farmers in Benin. *Entrepreneurship & Regional Development*, *30*(1–2), 1–28. https://doi.org/10.1080/08985626.2017.1364788

Denise Speck*, Thomas B. Long

13 Sustainable Entrepreneurial Storytelling in the Caribbean: Digital Storytelling to Empower Trinidad and Tobago's Cocoa Sector

Abstract: Storytelling is essential to humankind, while globalisation and technological advancements are enabling the combining of both oral storytelling techniques and modern technologies, creating the medium of 'digital story telling'. In this chapter, we explore and elaborate on how digital storytelling can be combined with sustainable entrepreneurship to help empower communities and ultimately improve their environmental, social and economic welfare. We explore this phenomenon through the case of Trinidad and Tobago's cocoa sector. In doing so, the chapter highlights the contextual nature of sustainable entrepreneurship, uncovering alternative forms and approaches within the setting of cocoa farming in Trinidad.

Keywords: digital storytelling, cocoa, sustainable entrepreneurship, the Caribbean

1 Introduction

Storytelling is essential to humankind; its first traces are found in prehistoric cave engravings. However, globalisation and technological advancements stimulated the emergence of digital storytelling – combining both oral storytelling techniques and modern technologies (Rouhani, 2019). Digital storytelling is able to reflect personal narratives, historical events or specific themes (Robin, 2006). It is dynamic, cross-disciplinary, multi-levelled and transformative (Lambert & Hessler, 2018), stimulating co-creation, collaboration and awareness of issues within communities and beyond. These characteristics and traits make digital storytelling an interesting approach, especially when tackling societal challenges, such as climate change, food security or sustainability livelihoods. Sustainable entrepreneurship is a key process in the tackling of societal challenges, and this raises the question of what digital storytelling could mean for sustainability entrepreneurship and vice versa. Sustainable entrepreneurship is a process 'to discover, define and exploit opportunities' (Zahra et al., 2009: 519) and innovatively combine resources to address social needs to ultimately alter social.

***Corresponding author: Denise Speck,** Independent sustainable entrepreneur,
e-mail: bydenisespeck@gmail.com
Thomas B. Long, Campus Fryslân Faculty, University of Groningen, Groningen, the Netherlands

https://doi.org/10.1515/9783110756159-016

In this chapter we explore how *digital storytelling* can be combined with sustainable entrepreneurship to help empower communities and ultimately improve their environmental, social and economic welfare. The chapter highlights the contextual nature of sustainable entrepreneurship, uncovering alternative forms and approaches within the setting of cocoa farming in Trinidad.

There is little understanding about the linkages and strategic role of storytelling within entrepreneurship. Based on the premises of the StoryCenter (2021) approach and the Photovoice, the lead author previously conceptualised *digital* storytelling within sustainable entrepreneurship and explored the application of the practice (Speck, 2021). The results improved our understanding of *digital storytelling* and demonstrated how *digital storytelling* could be used by sustainable entrepreneurs to empower themselves and their communities. While some use storytelling as a marketing tool to boost business aims (Delgado-Ballester & Fernández-Sabiote, 2016), this previous research demonstrated *digital storytelling*'s potential as an empowerment tool to foster social and environmental value.

Based on the aforementioned interconnections, this practical case study of a cocoa cluster in Trinidad aims to test a recently developed *digital storytelling* approach (Speck, 2021) to better understand *how digital storytelling* dynamics function in different contexts.

1.1 The Case of Cocoa in Trinidad

Trinidad and Tobago, a twin island in the Caribbean, is situated 11 kilometres off the northern coast of South America, with approximately 1.4 million inhabitants (Figure 13.1 provides an impression of the landscape, the Trinidad cacao tree, and existing wildlife). Its tropical climate, proximity to the equator and history of human migrations presents the ideal cultivation space for cocoa. In fact, cocoa is deeply rooted in the history of Trinidad and Tobago; its first plants were seeded in the sixteenth century during Spanish colonisation and cocoa has since then left traces on the country's socio-economic development. A natural cross-pollination of Criollo and Forastero varieties gave rise to a special cocoa type – *Trinitario Cocoa*. In the early nineteenth century, Trinidad and Tobago was the third-largest producer of cocoa worldwide. But an interplay of events in the global cocoa market and the decline of cocoa prices increasingly shifted the nation's focus to its oil and gas industry. Due to these industrial developments, Trinidad and Tobago's agrarian system experienced a drastic change and the cultivation of cocoa decreased, endangering the future of *Trinitario Cocoa*. Within recent years, the government, with industry, implemented rehabilitation efforts to avoid the extinction of cocoa.

Today, a new generation of cocoa entrepreneurs promotes the excellence of *Trinitario Cocoa* in the global fine artisanal cocoa and chocolate niche market. One player is the Original Trinitario Cocoa and Chocolate (OTC) Foundation, a cluster that has been initiated by a selection of regional cocoa entrepreneurs – farmers, processors, chocolatiers, traders and agricultural consultants – to revive local cocoa industry collaborations, resources, and capabilities (Original Trinitario Cocoa and Chocolate Foundation, 2022).

Within this context, a *digital storytelling* approach was applied, intertwining both theory and practice. This paper provides insight into the storytelling approach identified in the project. It critically reflects upon the methodological challenges experienced and presents its key learnings and recommendations.

Literature is presented that outlines the approaches of *digital storytelling* and presents the main concepts that are at the root of this case study. This is followed by an explanation of methodological procedures, the results of the case study and finally a conclusion, providing limitations and recommendations for future research.

Landscape in Brasso Seco, Trinidad's Northern Range.

Ripe Trinitario Cocoa pods growing directly on the stem of the tree.

A hummingbird sitting on a branch.

Sunset at a remote beach in Tobago.

Figure 13.1: Images of Trinidad and Tobago (Speck, 2022).

2 Literature Review

2.1 Approaches to Digital Storytelling

There are two different pathways of *digital storytelling*: the StoryCenter approach and the Photovoice methodology.

The StoryCenter provides a guide to *digital storytelling*. A significant element of the StoryCenter approach is the Story Circle, which is limited to participants and facilitators and encourages sharing[1] (Rouhani, 2019; Lambert & Hessler, 2018) and listening (Matthews & Sunderland, 2017; Williams, Labonte, & O'Brien, 2003). According to Robin (2006) personal narratives are the most common motivations to create digital stories. They are a 'part of the oral storytelling tradition' and deal with personal experiences in which the teller regards himself/herself as the 'representative of the truth' (Stahl, 1977: 18). In the context of group settings, the sharing of personal narratives can serve multiple reasons: (1) it enhances empathy and awareness of others' situation, (2) it draws attention to shared issues and (3) it reduces distance to peers. Rouhani (2019) notes in her research that the Story Circle helps to collectively identify issues and share them with respective stakeholders to draw awareness to problems.

Photovoice is a tool for visual narratives where participants document and reflect on the community's concerns and strengths through photography. Dialogues about photographs enhance collective understanding about problems and facilitate access to policymakers (Wang & Burris, 1997; Romer, 2017) to strengthen disadvantaged communities[2] (Budig et al., 2018). Moreover, it enables individuals to share stories of their photographs, or as Romer (2017: 17) phrased it: 'It is through the eyes and voice of participants that others begin to see and learn what may not have been evident prior.' Photography serves as means for documentaries and artistic expressions on several levels[3] and can be tailored to specific contexts (Wang & Burris, 1997). This contextual and multi-levelled element appears relevant for the dynamic environment of sustainable entrepreneurship (de Bruin, Shaw, & Lewis, 2017). Furthermore, Wang and Burris (1997) acknowledge the importance of contextual embeddedness[4] and that the roles of participants and facilitators are not mutually exclusive; training locals to become facilitators strengthens community empowerment, encourages collaboration between community and organisation, improves the communities' infrastructure, legitimises the project within the community and

---

[1] In a case study of marginalised communities in New Zealand, it emphasised the skills of listening and being present with 'the emotional content' (Williams et al., 2003: 37) instead of judging underlying assumptions. In addition, participants were encouraged to listen emphatically to others' stories and share what the story has touched in them as a gesture of giving back to the creator.

[2] In a case study by Budig et al. (2018) about female empowerment in a Spanish community the *Photovoice* methodology strengthened both community and individual levels through increased awareness of their situations, perceptions about themselves and networking opportunities to policymakers.

[3] According to Romer (2017) the process of photographing tackles the individual level, whereas the photographs are interpreted by a collective.

[4] Within a participatory action research with village women in the Yunnan region in rural China, the women's contextual embeddedness was found crucial (Wang & Burris, 1997). The facilitators were required to be accountable, sensitive to politics, culture and ethics, acknowledge personal biases, be supportive, provide training on camera usage and enhance a dialogue within the community and stakeholders.

fosters grassroots workers' capabilities. In addition, returning photographs to the community expressed appreciation and respect.

Both constructs' methodologies entail several challenges. Most literature refers to technological challenges and the struggle to align the technical methodology (e.g., audiotapes) with reality. Facilitators' interventions and personal judgements may also influence outcomes, and prompts may further intensify interventions. Generally, ethics are essential in participatory approaches, and its consequences, visual images and confidentiality are the researcher's responsibility. Other challenges encountered are limitations in communication, transportation and finances (Rouhani, 2019).

2.2 Digital Storytelling for Sustainable Entrepreneurship

Why do sustainable entrepreneurs practise digital storytelling? What drives and motivates them? Most sustainable entrepreneurship practitioners see digital storytelling as a tool to raise awareness of key issues or verify business practices, using it at both the individual and collective level (Rouhani, 2019) as well as a connection (or ancient wisdom) across generations and time. By doing so, digital storytelling facilitates personal transformation (Rouhani, 2019; Lambert & Hessler, 2018; Matthews & Sunderland, 2017; Staley & Freeman, 2017) via improved understanding of oneself and the perceptions and behaviours of others. This, in turn, stimulates partnerships and enables under-developed regions and communities to access international markets. For instance, in the context of conflict areas, narratives have the potential to counter the media's unjust reports and invite more authentic perspectives, leading to more objective awareness and autonomous decision-making of communities and society at large (Speck, 2021).

2.3 Guiding Digital Storytelling: Strategies and Success Factors

Strategies for sustainable entrepreneurship practitioners on *how digital storytelling* can achieve more impact within marginalised communities are to (1) create awareness, (2) understand the context, (3) apply a variety of multimedia tools to enrich storytelling experiences, (4) draw out the relevancy of narratives, (5) stimulate dialogues within communities and the storyteller, (6) create positive narratives, (7) be wise in the process of storytelling within vulnerable groups and (8) focus on creating long-term impact instead of short-term intervention (Speck, 2021).

While the above points provide a clear route to impact and empowerment, sustainable entrepreneurs usually do not apply a specific methodology, and *digital storytelling* is often not applied as a specific strategy but rather approached as a marketing component (Speck, 2021). Creating awareness and understanding the context can be seen to be somewhat interlinked and interdependent. Being contextually embedded is critical in understanding the local culture and language, and to create sharing and listening environments (Romer, 2017). Particularly, dialogues are helpful to raise awareness, alter understanding and stimulate critical thinking capabilities of beneficiaries. Furthermore, responsibility and sensitivity of the storyteller are important when creating a digital story (Rouhani, 2019).

Applying a mix of multimedia tools and available approaches can improve impact. Both the StoryCenter approach and the Photovoice methodology (Lambert & Hessler, 2018; Wang & Burris, 1997) are validated approaches able to elevate the storytelling experience. And besides the 'usual suspects' of the digital space, such as photography and film, alternative approaches have been found to be effective, such as Ubuntu Friendship Circles, who has validated the power of Story Circles to enhance empowerment (Rouhani, 2019; Lambert & Hessler, 2018). Story Circles are a formal or informal setting where a collective is sitting in a circle, sharing stories of communal and intimate contexts, stimulated by prompts and reflection methods and without cross-talk.

To draw out the relevance of a narrative, they should be anchored to wider frameworks, such as the UN Sustainable Development Goals (SDGs). This helps to ensure value for a broader audience and measurable impact. Visual storytelling is a communication craft, and so structure is also important. The story should hold truth but is also mediated by a structured storyline (arch), a viewpoint (the storyteller) and a strategy to captivate the audience. Creating a positive narrative is seen as critical to increasing impact.

Speck (2021) also reveals that the storyteller's role is to prevent misinformation and manipulation. In other words, a participant shared that 'the story is the medicine; the storyteller is the shaman. So, [one must] understand that stories can be deeply nourishing, or they can cause a breakdown, depending on the wisdom of the storyteller.' Although referred to as wisdom, it appears necessary to ensure cultural, political and ethical appropriation and acknowledge personal bias (Rouhani, 2019; Wang & Burris, 1997). Lastly, the practice of cooperation and bringing together the right people is an essential role of the storyteller. The cooperation with a crew of professionals is relevant to creating a professional digital story while collaborating with brand ambassadors increased the story's reach.

2.4 Challenges

Storytellers can be hindered by technology, context, finances and ethics (Rouhani, 2019; Wang & Burris, 1997). In addition, Speck (2021) found that sustainable entrepreneurs often struggled to (1) reach a broader audience, (2) evaluate the performance of their storytelling activities and (3) develop content for their narratives. An overview of the research findings is provided in Table 13.1.

Table 13.1: Overview of Data Analysis Insights (Speck, 2021).

Digital storytelling drivers	Digital storytelling Activities	Digital Storytelling Challenges
1. Awareness	*Success factors:*	1. Context
2. Changing perceptions and behaviour	1. *Relevancy*	2. Finances
3. Connection	2. Structure	3. Technology
4. Understanding oneself	3. Sharing	4. Time
	4. Multimedia	5. Scale-up
		6. Performance measurement
	The role of the storyteller:	7. Content
	1. Contextual embeddedness	8. Ethics
	2. Sharing and listening	
	3. Cooperation	
	4. Responsibility	

3 The *Digital Storytelling* Approach and Research Design

The d*igital storytelling* initiative for the OTC is shaped in four stages: (1) planning, (2) realisation, (3) re-evaluation and (4) training (see Figure 13.2). The following will provide a more profound insight into the methodological approaches within each segment.

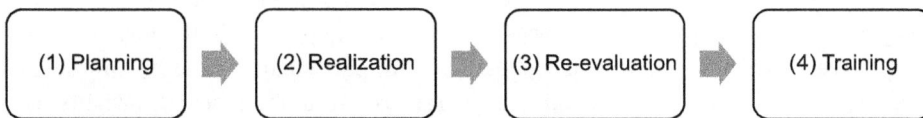

Figure 13.2: Stages of storytelling method.

Within the (1) planning stage, the storyteller is in close contact with the lead company to communicate the insights of his/her research for sustainable development, and to find potential pathways for realising this project. This is necessary to retrieve information about the specific context and prepare a detailed project plan to determine the scope and communicate to stakeholders. This extensive proposal is presented to the OTC committee members, and potential investors. Particularly, the budget sum presents a relevant element to communicate to potential sponsorship bodies and receive funding accordingly. Additionally, it entails information on the project objectives, the audience, the *digital storytelling* approach, the deliverables, the activity plan, the storyteller's role, the project materials and the budget.

The field trip to Trinidad and Tobago – (2) realisation – as herein referred to, was split into five categories: (a) acclimatisation, (b) content collection, (c) content creation, (d) feedback and (e) sharing. The initial weeks upon arrival are necessary to (a) acclimatise to the context – and, among other things, to get insight into the local culture, to get to know stakeholders and grasp the underlying culture respectively (see Figure 13.3).

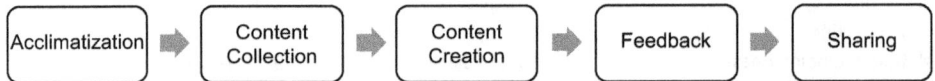

Acclimatization ➡ Content Collection ➡ Content Creation ➡ Feedback ➡ Sharing

Figure 13.3: Stages of participatory action research procedure.

For the (b) content collection, the participants receive a short description of the project and the storyteller, a code of ethics and informed consent. Then, members are contacted via phone to schedule introductory meetings. These in-person meetings are dedicated to sharing personal insights of the storyteller (who I am, what I am doing and what can be expected) as well as getting an insight into the context of the participants and their background, and receiving a tour of the estate or process facilities. Usually, these meetings are scheduled for approximately two to three hours; visits that are 'ice-breakers' enhance both comfort and trust towards the storyteller for upcoming, more focused storytelling visits. Subsequently, the participant and researcher schedule additional meetings to delve deeper into the participant's narrative. These agendas vary and are individualised to the participants' specific context. However, the Four Ps – product, place, people, process – methodology serves as the basic skeleton framework. Consequently, participants know to expect a content collection that is shaped around their product(s), process(es), people and place(s) in the form of photographs, recorded interviews and videos. Therein, participants must be approached non-judgmentally, or with a 'slate plate', as referred to in the research insights. This method decreases the researchers' bias and allows narratives to surge from the participants' unique insights and to understand patterns of common themes. More about this is on page 271, which tackles the storyteller's role to be wise.

The next step, (c) content creation, is initiated by creating a list of relevant themes, involving common or individual challenges and opportunities experienced in the space, such as workers' scarcity, low cocoa production, low involvement of younger generations, soil farming, permaculture, organic certification, diversification in crops and income as well as eco-tourism. Additionally, interviews are analysed and relevant statements regarding some of the above-mentioned themes are highlighted. This allows the storyteller to gain a better overview of what is happening on the ground and connect the dots of what has not been revealed or spoken about publicly before. Consequently, the themes and content are ordered, and articles, such as member profiles, blog posts, social media content and newsletter articles created with the respective photographs and video materials.

These materials are then shared with the respective participant to enhance (d) feedback streams, allowing members to express concerns and consent, and to provide inputs on areas that could be further refined or removed. Additionally, this step represents a necessary tool for self-development and increased empowerment, as it makes participants understand how they are perceived by others and more reflective about their enterprise. Consequently, the managerial team received revised versions of the content and gave final consent for publication.

Lastly, the content materials are (e) shared among respective organisations, such as the Inter-American Development Bank and the World Fair Trade Organization (WFTO) Europe, as well as the participants' channels themselves and Übergreen Organics platforms. Members with profound marketing expertise can track viewer engagement and provide insight into the reach of the respective post. This feedback helps to improve the content and points out the potential for future content creation.

The third step of the *digital storytelling* approach, (3) re-evaluation, has not been approached at this point. To do so, the storyteller must complete the main operations and hand in the content deliverables to the respective organisation and members. Consequently, it is planned to share feedback forms with participants that enable them to express their experiences and to share constructive criticism and their key learnings. This information will be relevant to further refine the *digital storytelling* approach and develop specific training manuals that target the participants' needs.

After analysing the feedback from the different stakeholders, (4) a virtual training session will be provided to participants to develop and sharpen storytelling competencies among the members. This session will include the following elements: the theoretical understanding of storytelling and its importance for sustainable entrepreneurs, a re-cap of the respective storytelling approach, a presentation of *digital storytelling* opportunities through a demonstration of participants' narratives, the participants' feedback, future suggestions for their enterprises and a template with different prompts and activities. This template serves to foster creative storytelling capabilities, sharpen skills to amplify their voices and create compelling, authentic narratives that empower participants and can be utilised to improve their marketing strategies.

3.1 Research Design – Participant Selection, Data Collection and Analysis

By applying the *digital storytelling* methodology through the case study, we are able to explore the storytelling approach (Speck, 2021) to better understand how *digital storytelling* dynamics function in different contexts, and to provisionally identify key dynamics and factors. We take a practical orientation and focus on the generation of tangible and usable knowledge. To achieve our aims, we drew primarily on qualitative research principles and approaches, drawing on our own observations and experiences in the case study, as well as those of others through semi-structured interviews. In the following section, we briefly highlight some of the key steps we took to generate our results and how we drew insights into the application of the *digital storytelling* approach.

The participants of this study were selected based on a 'convenience approach' whereby the coordinators of the cocoa project provided access to their network, through which 12 individuals participated in the research. These participants were all entrepreneurs actively involved in cocoa production and processing in Trinidad and Tobago and are part of the Original Trinitario Cocoa (OTC) Foundation. The OTC is a governing body that enables networking among cocoa entrepreneurs, skill development to alleviate poverty and the creation of a more sustainable future in the cocoa space. More precisely, the participants ranged from cocoa farmers, chocolatiers, cocoa traders and cocoa experts to entrepreneurs that create cosmetic products from cocoa butter. The recruitment of participants was arranged through the OTC manager who introduced the researcher's role and project and provided contact details to individually contact each participant. After an additional introduction email by the researcher, which informed participants about the researcher's background, the purpose and benefit of the study, and the date, appointments for personal meetings were scheduled via telephone. Thereafter, the researcher and participant scheduled a 1:1 meeting at the participants' location to plan further steps. The interviews were semi-structured, involving common themes. This was a helpful approach, since it allowed us to build an interview guide on specific themes, yet leaving enough flexibility to allow participants freedom to provide additional knowledge and experiences they thought were important. These themes were developed around the background of the participant's enterprise, contextual and wider challenges as well as experienced opportunities that enabled them to combat challenges. The semi-structured interviews were audio-visually recorded, and observations were noted. For analysis, the data were subjected to a process of abstraction and generalisation – a process that helped to detect common themes, wider challenges and solutions. In addition, the interview recordings, transcriptions and observations were helpful to evaluate the *digital storytelling's* approach based on the previously discussed drivers, activities and challenges, before, during and after the initiative.

4 Applying Digital Storytelling

After comprehending more about the implementation and practicality of *digital storytelling* to empower the cocoa community in Trinidad and Tobago, we find new insights in terms of (1) drivers, (2) activities and (3) challenges.

4.1 Drivers of Digital Storytelling

4.1.1 Creating Awareness

After spending time with the different actors, such as cocoa farmers, cocoa processors, chocolatiers and traders, and learning about their business, their background and the challenges and opportunities in the space, it became noticeable that the objective at a collective level was similar – to revive the local cocoa sector – although the individual level objectives were distinct.

Broadly defined, the *digital storytelling* project aimed to create awareness about *Trinitario Cocoa* – the product, the processes, the people and the place – on a national and international level. The aim was to increase demand for Trinitario cocoa products, thereby altering sales and export volumes and ultimately change global perception about the origin. More narrowly, farmers wanted to foster awareness about their farms, their regenerative agricultural practices and their 'bean-to-bar' processes. Thus, *digital storytelling* could enhance more than just livelihoods for their enterprise and families. Cocoa processors and chocolatiers relied on storytelling to secure competitive advantage by providing quality standards, justifying 'single origin' products and building trustworthy relationships with both suppliers and customers. Agricultural experts and consultants sought to increase awareness about regenerative practices and use storytelling as a tool to generate a broader reach and enable a movement for a more sustainable future for cocoa cultivation. And traders and international organisations aimed at reaching target markets overseas, such as Europe or the United States, increasing demand that ultimately alters national sales and export volumes and strengthens the local cocoa sector.

The specific understandings and objectives of awareness differed from stakeholder to stakeholder; however, creating awareness enabled the creation of value across different levels, actors and areas – environmental, economic and social.

4.1.2 Creating Connections

The processes involved in *digital storytelling* appeared – provisionally – effective in creating connections and dialogues among and between stakeholder groups. The networking efforts sparked conversations among farmers, chocolatiers, the managerial level and international organisations.

Storytelling contents, such as newsletters and blog posts, enabled knowledge about different subjects, such as the history of cocoa, the challenges and opportunities of cocoa and cocoa production in a particular area, such as Brasso Seco, to be shared with cluster members as well as international organisations, such as the Inter-American Development Bank (IDB), the World Fair Trade Organization–Europe (WFTO–Europe), and the European Business Chamber in Trinidad and Tobago (EUROCHAMTT). This type of information, however, mainly enabled a one-way dialogue without further feed-back streams.

4.2 Key Activities

4.2.1 Understanding the Context

The case study underlines the need for the storyteller to understand the context of cocoa cultivation in Trinidad and Tobago. Understanding culture, traditions, norms and language can take months if not years, or even a lifetime. Particularly, grasping the specifics of the cocoa industry across different parties and levels of expertise, including its processes, challenges and opportunities, is important to develop a cohesive and impactful narrative. Because how could one interpret the narratives and ask the right questions without a base of knowledge? To do so, the storyteller built relationships with locals and experts who were tightly connected to the communities, familiar with the theme of cocoa cultivation and seen as trustworthy individuals.

An agricultural consultant with close relationships with farmers played a crucial role in helping to adjust and acclimatise to the context. The consultant supported the storyteller by offering transportation to difficult-to-access rural areas, providing introductions and clarifying context-specific matters about the culture, the slang, cocoa and the local environments. This sensitivity was particularly important when communicating with more marginalised groups, such as farmers, some of whom experienced Western colonialism, slavery and oppression in their family lineages. Their insights were very personal and if not treated with care could have led to further harm. Hence, context is key and necessary to develop narratives that are authentic and close to the community's needs.

4.2.2 Drawing Out Relevancy

The experience of the cocoa case highlighted the importance of drawing out relevancy. To do this, the storyteller assessed the relevant themes of the UN Sustainable Development Goals, including: (1) SDG1: No poverty, (2) SDG8: Decent work and economic growth, (3) SDG10: Reduced inequalities, (4) SDG12: Responsible consumption and production, (5) SDG15: Life on land and (6) SDG17: Partnership for the goals. Using these anchor points helped to facilitate communication to external stakeholders, such as funding institutions. It gave the project more strength and created levelled communication that almost anyone could understand. It also helped to establish performance measurements for the project. This, however, was still in process and had not been refined at the time of writing.

4.2.3 Application of Multimedia Tools

The findings recommend the application of a variety of tools, such as audio recording, photography, video recording and paper note taking. This is not only useful to generate higher quality outputs tailored to certain target groups, but also to respond with sensitivity to individuals' participation in the project. It was noted that participants responded differently to a storyteller when in their own environment. Whereas some responded very openly about being recorded and photographed, others were more reluctant. Using a variety of tools created more compelling narratives, gave the storyteller flexibility and generated more trust. Hence, the methods needed to be adjusted individually, depending on the level of comfort one felt around certain tools. It was interesting to witness the interest of younger families and/or business members to improve their skills in handling a camera and other technical equipment. Hence, integrating the younger generation into the storytelling process might present a viable solution to promote leadership qualities and secure the industry's future development.

4.2.4 Structure

Multiple strategies were applied to ensure the structure of content collection and development. First, content themes and interview questions were designed around the Four Ps – product, people, process, place – of the respective participant (see Figures 13.4–13.6). One can easily lose guidance, being led by the many individual narratives and subjects of interest in their lives. Therefore, the Four Ps provided a clearly defined scope, via questions such as:

– What *products* is the business developing?
– Who are the *people* involved in this business?
– What are the *processes* of their business?
– Where is the *place* of the business, and what is unique about it?

In addition, the storyteller focused on themes around the individual challenges experienced in the space and what potential opportunities may overcome systematic hurdles (see Image 16.4). For example:

– What *challenges* is person *X*/business *X* experiencing that prevents them from achieving a sustainable business model?
– What *opportunities* are presented to overcome these challenges?

The data was utilised to create individual member profiles and analyse similarities and differences that allowed a generic understanding of *Trinitario Cocoa*'s presence in Trinidad and Tobago. Based on the results, the creation of stories began as photographic documentaries, blog posts, newsletters and/or short films. Key themes included: (1) bees as pollinators, (2) regenerative agriculture and intercropping practices, (3) 'made at origin' labelling to generate increased value at origin, (4) strengthening women-owned enterprises, (5) youth integration in the cocoa sector, (6) the evolution of a cocoa pod (see example), (7) cocoa farming in a special region and so on.

A structured storyline was very useful to create a shape for stories that allowed for consistency and professionality. The storyline generally consisted of four elements: introduction, problem, solution and call-to-action (see Table 13.2).

People: Cocoa farmer in the field.

Place: The farmer walks with cocoa pods on his shoulder through the family's cocoa estate.

Process: A cocoa pod being cracked with a machete after harvest.

Product: Tree-to-bar chocolate presented and sold at local markets.

Figure 13.4: Example photographs of Four Ps.

4.2.5 Sharing and Listening

Previous results suggest the use of sharing and listening environments in the form of Story Circles helps to develop authentic and empowering (collective) narratives. Naturally emerging Story Circles are mainly found within individual businesses. Therefore, different family members or business members are brought together to collectively reflect on and share the business' background, the challenges and the opportunities in the space. In most cases, this amplifies the storyteller's role of empathic listening to the participants' narratives and asking questions that prompt more profound insights without interfering with one's comfort zone. A two-way communication stream has good

People: Portrait of cocoa estate owner.

Place: Aerial view of the estate's grand house.

Process: Estate worker spreading cocoa pods on the drying beds.

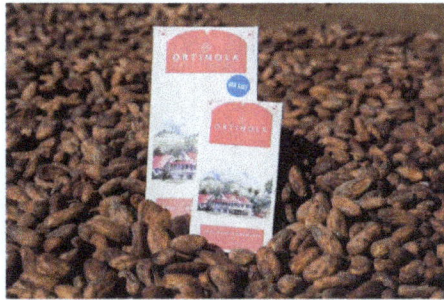

Product:'Bean-to-bar' chocolates surrounded by dried cocoa pods

Figure 13.5: Example photographs of Four Ps (Speck, 2022).

potential for impact, because not only does participants' information enhance authentic content collection and empowerment, but the storyteller also shares experience and insights. This creates a synergistic dynamic that enables participants to feel inspired and learn and triggers them to think further while creating a safe and comfortable space for them to open up.

In another instance, an agricultural trainer initiated regular meetings of the different farmers to exchange knowledge about current practices, challenges and good training methods in the form of Story Circles. What was initiated with in-person meetings transferred to the virtual spaces due to the advent of COVID-19. Generally, online meeting spaces are uncommon training spaces for farmers: most acquired the necessary skill to access virtual spaces rapidly and shared positive feedback about this form of knowledge exchange. Although virtual meetings are very beneficial for providing knowledge and saving commuting time to training locations, it also poses several challenges: it is less personal, it merely provides theory but less an experience, and it is difficult to organise with a large number of participants and, lastly, it reflects a rather one-sided feedback stream with one main moderator and a few extrovert members. Quiet and reluctant members are often restricted to the background and are not encouraged sufficiently to share their voices.

Cocoa flower: Cocoa flower that turns into a cocoa pod.

Cocoa pods: Ripe cocoa pods growing directly on the stem of a cocoa tree.

Cocoa bean harvest: A ripe cocoa pod that has been cracked with a machete to subtract the cocoa fruit.

Cocoa pod shells: Empty cocoa pods are left on the ground of the estate to mulch the ground and return nutrients to the soil (waste = Food Principle).

Figure 13.6: Evolution of a cocoa pod (Speck, 2022).

Table 13.2: Example of short film storyline.

(1) Introduction	Trinidad and Tobago is the birthplace of *Trinitario Cocoa. Trinitario Cocoa* is a very special variety, characterised by quality and fine flavour notes.
(2) Problem	The future of *Trinitario Cocoa* is endangered, because of changing climate patterns and a lack of successors.
(3) Solution	The solutions are sustainable farming methods and the integration of young people in family businesses.
(4) Call-to-Action	Inspire young Trinbagonians about the beauty of regenerative farming and living in harmony with nature.

But sharing also played a crucial role for the storyteller. After narratives have been identified with community members and different content created, the storyteller built and maintained relationships with partnering organisations – such as the local Cocoa Research Centre (CRC), the Inter-American Development Bank, and Compete Caribbean Programme, as well as the World Fair Trade Organization–Europe (WFTO–Europe) – to provide a channel to communicate storytelling outputs, to involve and update them in the storytelling process at origin and to generate possible strategic partnership for participants both locally and overseas. The impact, however, cannot be measured quickly and easily, and therefore it is so far unclear what impact these partnerships had on the cluster members' sustainable value creation.

4.2.6 Producing Positive Narratives

Positive narratives with a solution focus are critical to empowering the participant's voice, and a key tool to show goodwill and generate trust between the storyteller and the participants: marginalised communities are often affected by power imbalances, such as inequality or poverty, making them more reluctant and critical of external parties that enquire insights about their establishment.

For example, one farmer led a successful organic cocoa business that had been passed on from generation to generation. Increasing age and disinterest of younger generations to be involved in farming practices impeded the managerial operations of the estate and endangered the future of his heritage. He was very melancholic and disappointed and wished younger generations could understand the fulfilment of being a cocoa farmer. By interpreting this information, a storyteller has a degree of freedom in the narrative's journey while maintaining levels of authenticity. From an economic stance, it would not be wise to emphasise his struggles, turning his narrative into a melancholic story for consumers and businesses, about risky partnerships with Trinidadian farmers. From a social and environmental stance, it would be irresponsible to 'greenwash' the narrative and produce another profit-oriented campaign. Nonetheless, the struggle of increasingly ageing farmers is a prevalent issue, locally and globally, and should not be excluded from an authentic story about *Trinitario Cocoa*. It is, however, necessary and useful to focus on the positive aspects, the achievements, the pride, the quality and the characteristics that make his estate a special place. Such positive narratives will eventually present solutions to the generational gap that may lead to the loss of cocoa estates and Trinbagonian culture.

Hence, creating positive narratives is a delicate dance that requires a balance between authenticity and a solution focus, because reality is not always as positive as compared to commercial appeals, but should not be greenwashed either.

4.2.7 Role of the Storyteller

One question that became apparent is: who is the storyteller? A role that is certainly not exclusive, as the participant told his story, and the 'storyteller' re-framed his story in a written or oral medium to be shared publicly. Not only has the storyteller helped the participants to amplify their voices, but they helped to gain contextual understanding and to have a broader perspective of what is happening within Trinidad and Tobago's cocoa industry. Nonetheless, it has been crucial to practise responsible behaviour towards participants and listen emphatically without prejudice. Thereby, wisdom and openness were key by 'walking a humble path'. Therefore, communities were approached without a clear-set agenda, allowing the conversation and day to flow naturally and enable the participant to feel comfortable and in control. Hence, themes evolved naturally without merely projecting upfront theories and making participants fit within the given structure. These contents were re-distributed to members to provide feedback and approve statements accordingly. To gain value and awareness of the storytelling products, fostering and nurturing partnerships has been a crucial task of the storyteller.

4.3 Challenges

The *digital storytelling* initiative within the cocoa cluster in Trinidad and Tobago poses several challenges in terms of context, time, ethics, impact measurement, content and costs.

4.3.1 Context

The project posed challenges regarding language and the participant's context. Despite English being the native language of Trinbagonians, its command varies largely across the islands. Particularly, habitants of rural areas, such as cocoa farming communities, often speak with a heavy creole accent making it difficult for non-natives to grasp all nuances expressed while ensuring nothing gets lost.

Additionally, the socio-economic position of participants and their business was an important contextual factor. Participants of marginalised communities faced different challenges than well-established businesses. They lacked basic resources and capabilities for business modelling and marketing or even to set up *digital storytelling* training.

Context also played a crucial role in understanding the target audience. The storyteller had to be aware of whom the message was directed to and the objectives they aspired to. Hence, more partnerships mean more diverse target audiences, which means more time and costs to create individualised contents.

4.3.2 Time

The time limitation posed some unexpected challenges for the storyteller. Connecting with every member individually and allowing space and time for them to feel comfortable and open up on a deeper level was very time-intensive. In addition, farming communities often do not plan much in advance but guide their days in flow with nature, according to the principle '[I]t may be tomorrow or next week, it depends . . . we will let you know whenever the weather and time are right to harvest.' This bricolage behaviour has been very challenging and demanding within the entrepreneurial processes of the storyteller to structure meetings and deadlines efficiently.

Furthermore, the awareness-raising aims of the project were challenging within the project timeline. Outreach activities, individualised content preparation and partnership management required not only side activities, but also time and continuous efforts.

4.3.3 Ethics

Ethics were a critical aspect and were questioned multiple times before, throughout and after the project. The code of ethics and informed consent sheet increased the ethical quality of the field research; however, dealing with a large number of participants with different backgrounds and social classes required sharpened sensitivity and responsibility. This was especially true when dealing with personal stories and transforming them into a narrative that is then shared with a larger audience.

Interpreting narratives is subjective and what may be beneficial for one party might harm another. As such it is important to critically reflect on the participant's stories and turn the narrative into a potential solution. Sharing the written narratives in the form of a draft for final approval with the participants proved very helpful, too. It ensured the participant's integration and decision-making about the narrative composed about him/her.

4.3.4 Impact/Performance Measurement

The impact of content distribution both at the participants' as well as the audiences' levels was difficult to measure. Although the UN SDGs provided a clear and transparent guideline to communicate the project's desired impacts to stakeholders, it did not determine how to measure the performance of each separate activity, such as the content collection, content creation, distribution and training sessions. Since empowerment is considered an intrinsic element, it was perceived differently by each participant and could not be expressed within a predetermined time scope.

4.3.5 Cost

The time-intensity to obtain contextual sensitivity led to fairly high costs that individual organisations found hard to afford without the support of international organisations. Due to insufficient knowledge about general living costs in Trinidad and Tobago during the initial proposal development stage, and generally limited experience in the procedure of field trips, a realistic budget was difficult to estimate. Hence, additional products, such as exhibitions and short documentaries, that aimed at reaching a broader audience outside the industry-specific stakeholders of partnership organisations, were not covered sufficiently. Consequently, efforts were focused on acquiring additional funding to cover the latter costs respectively.

5 Conclusions

Based on previous research to investigate the drivers, activities and challenges of sustainable entrepreneurship to empower disadvantaged communities (Speck, 2021), this paper builds upon its conceptual recommendations. Through the case of the cocoa sector in Trinidad and Tobago, *digital storytelling* was practised in an agrarian context for six months. The project was still ongoing at the time of writing this chapter.

Trinidad and Tobago holds a secret of a culinary and cultural treasure that may be forgotten soon – *Trinitario Cocoa*. This special cocoa variety attracts national and international expert committees through its flavour profile and qualities (Leissle, 2018). Nonetheless, the cocoa industry faces tough challenges – the future of cocoa is endangered as young generations are not interested in continuing older farming legacy. While changing weather patterns, linked to climate change, increasingly challenge the growth of cocoa trees. The Original Cocoa and Chocolate Foundation (OTC) aims to revive the national cocoa industry by providing access and resources to a selected cluster of cocoa farmers, chocolatiers and traders. The field research and case presented here was applied in the context of the OTC members and aimed to tell the stories of individual members and collective themes that create more understanding of present contexts and aimed to empower the local cocoa sector.

The present field research replicates the *why, how* and *what* questions and supports the previous theoretical study. Therefore, the field research has been tested and evaluated by looking at the drivers, activities and challenges that enable one to better understand the dynamics and practicalities of *digital storytelling* within sustainable entrepreneurship (Speck, 2021).

As elaborated in previous literature, the field research emphasises that *digital storytelling* is context-dependent, multi-levelled and dynamic (Speck, 2021; Rouhani, 2019; Matthews & Sunderland, 2017). Therefore, differences in approaches were relevant for individual members within a similar context. Whereas literature focused on describing the storytelling procedures, information was scarce on the actual entrepreneurial process of setting up a storytelling project. Therefore, the actual *digital storytelling* is only a part of a bigger entrepreneurial process, consisting of planning, realisation, re-evaluation and training.

Generally speaking, the elements inherent to the drivers, activities and challenges are similar to previous research (Speck, 2021; Rouhani, 2019; Lambert & Hessler, 2018; Matthews & Sunderland, 2017). Thereby, this practice emphasises the perspective of the facilitator who is the external storyteller in contrast to storytellers inherent to the communities. Nonetheless, the roles and boundaries seem vague and difficult to differentiate clearly.

Furthermore, while previous theoretical insights were supportive and helpful in providing a base of knowledge and understanding they were also superficial and insufficient for creating a more profound *digital storytelling* practice. And one is able to foster sustainable development and challenge the replication of ideas.

5.1 Drivers

Nonetheless, the drivers to facilitate storytelling initiatives are obvious. *Digital storytelling* aims to create awareness about prevalent conditions at the origin that keep the audience informed and change the perceptions and behaviours of stakeholders. Creating awareness, however, was treated as a rather objective construct, as the concrete aim differed for every stakeholder involved. This, in turn, emphasises the importance of clearly defining the objectives and boundaries of such a *digital storytelling* initiative. Although *digital storytelling* sparked dialogues at individual and collective levels, most contents merely enabled a one-way dialogue without the possibility to give feedback. In contrast to Speck (2021), only little emphasis was placed on understanding oneself in the grand picture of cocoa agriculture. Storytelling within the cocoa sector in Trinidad and Tobago revealed the importance of creating connections across generations and time, so that ancient wisdom can be used to collectively protect cultural heritage and develop innovative solutions to global issues (Speck, 2021). This has been particularly relevant in family businesses, where older heads transmit stories and expertise to younger generations whereas younger generations have the skills and resources to create and share digital narratives.

5.2 Activities

Bearing in mind the drivers, it was aimed to better comprehend the activities of *digital storytelling*. Literature suggests an approach that intertwines elements of both the StoryCenter approach and the Photovoice methodology (Speck, 2021; Lambert & Hessler, 2018; Wang & Burris, 1997). The research acknowledged the storyteller's contextual embeddedness in understanding the local culture, and language and creating sharing and listening environments (Romer, 2017). It has been found particularly relevant to acquire a knowledge base that builds the foundation of a *digital storytelling* initiative upon which compelling stories are being created, as methodologies must be customised to the context of the industry as a whole and the individual participant.

Moreover, the findings approved the facilitators' emphatic listening skills to sensitively acquire information from participants (Romer, 2017). Particularly, in the context of working with marginalised groups, listening environments alter understanding and stimulate the critical thinking capabilities of beneficiaries (Speck, 2021) and are key to generating trust and dialogue to express narratives. Or, as referred to by Speck (2021), 'the story is the medicine; the storyteller is the shaman. So, [one must] understand that stories can be deeply nourishing, or they can cause a breakdown, depending on the wisdom of the storyteller.'

Next, relevancy was drawn out based on the UN Sustainable Development Goals to provide clear communication to stakeholders (Speck, 2021). In addition, it served to frame the scope of the initiative and communicate the project's objectives to external institutions that enabled funding for the project.

Also, the structure of *digital storytelling* became an apparent activity for the facilitator. '[V]isual storytelling is a communication craft. The story holds truth but is mediated by a structured storyline (arch), a viewpoint (the storyteller), and a strategy to captivate the audience' (Speck, 2021: 20). In line with this argument, the structure has been guided by four principles: introduction, problem, solution and call-to-action. This strategy helped to maintain uniform guidelines and define boundaries. Another element inherent to the structure of narratives is a solution focus (Speck, 2021). Positive narratives with a solution focus were important to creating empowering narratives that foster a positive impact at the origin and generate trust between the storyteller and the facilitator. Moreover, this research contributed to literature by further emphasising the dynamic nature of *digital storytelling*. Consequently, the *digital storytelling* approaches were not mutually exclusive; both oral and visual storytelling was essential to collect data, and the digital feature appeared necessary to target a broader audience.

The research also revealed novel contributions regarding activities to manage stakeholders, of the direct initiative as well as organisations to spread the word more broadly. Therefore, the facilitator needs to develop thorough planning to visit beneficiaries of the cluster and account for their rather flexible, last-minute mindsets. Similarly, networking played a crucial role in the activities of the facilitator to find the right connections to reach an audience and develop context-specific content materials. Therein, creating connections among beneficiaries enabled an interlinkage between generations and ancient wisdom (Speck, 2021). For instance, encouraging older heads to narrate stories and integrating younger generations' skill set to listen and capture narratives digitally presented an opportunity to create compelling and empowering stories. Consequently, the ancient wisdom of older farmers is protected and combined with the digital strength of younger participants.

After having gained insights regarding the drivers, and the key factors of a compelling story, the field research offered more knowledge about the challenges within *digital storytelling* in practice. Also, in this case, *digital storytelling* is analysed from the stance of an external facilitator. As referred to in literature, *digital storytelling* may be hindered by technology, context, finances and ethics (Rouhani, 2019; Wang & Burris, 1997). In addition, this research corresponds with previous studies that revealed practitioners' struggle to reach a broader audience, evaluate the performance of their storytelling activities and develop content for their narratives (Speck, 2021) that contain a positive narrative while retaining the authenticity of the context.

5.3 Future Research

The context-dependability and multifunctionality of *digital storytelling* for sustainable entrepreneurship through the example of Trinidad and Tobago's cocoa sector provides an array of future research pathways:

First, future research is needed to decipher more concrete boundaries and roles. Therefore, the research could frame *digital storytelling* by focusing on specific disciplines, such as brand marketing, folktale tradition or community empowerment, to better grasp the dynamics of *digital storytelling*. Additionally, research should decipher the roles of storytellers and entrepreneurs; distinguish who the storyteller and the entrepreneur are within the process; whether the roles are mutually exclusive; and whether the facilitator engages in consulting practices. This will help to establish more refined theories and provide tailored recommendations for practitioners.

Second, future research could investigate community empowerment and impact generation more comprehensively. This could be achieved by not only employing participatory action research (Rouhani, 2019) but with a longitudinal (Romer, 2017; Wang & Burris, 1997), comparative methodology within different entrepreneurial contexts and across different countries. This could yield richer insights and understand the what, how and why of change over time (Carduff, Murray, & Kendall, 2015) within different contexts.

Next, the study revealed implications for storytelling practitioners of different entrepreneurial stages. Thus, bricoleurs operate differently as more progressive and resource-available entrepreneurs and therefore require different approaches and practical guidelines for individual objectives of storytelling. Future research could investigate the impact of entrepreneurial stages on the objectives and practicality of *digital storytelling* and how to create interlinkages of different entrepreneurs to foster a level playing field.

Moreover, the study revealed the challenge to measure the success of the *digital storytelling* initiative, for individual participants as well as the collective. *Digital storytelling* is dynamic and complex and therefore challenging to measure constructively. Therefore, future research is recommended on determining how *digital storytelling* activities, their impact at origin as well as the broader impact on society, environment and economy can be measured.

Lastly, the research strengthened the importance of sharing circles (Speck, 2021; Rouhani, 2019; Lambert & Hessler, 2018). With increasing digitalisation, the facilitation of online environments has become more important than ever before. Thus, future research is recommended to investigate the effectiveness of online exchange platforms to stimulate collaboration and exchange and what elements and practices strengthen the success of a collaborative online environment.

References

Budig, K., Diez, J., Conde, P., Sastre, M., Hernán, M., & Franco, M. (2018). Photovoice and empowerment: Evaluating the transformative potential of a participatory action research project. *BMC Public Health, 18*, 1.https://doi.org/10.1186/s12889-018-5335-7

Carduff, E., Murray, S. A., & Kendall, M. (2015). Methodological developments in qualitative longitudinal research: The advantages and challenges of regular telephone contact with participants in a qualitative longitudinal interview study. *BMC Research Notes, 8*, 142.https://doi.org/10.1186/s13104-015-1107-y

de Bruin, A., Shaw, E., & Lewis, K. V. (2017). The collaborative dynamic in social entrepreneurship. *Entrepreneurship & Regional Development, 29*(7–8), 575–585. 10.1080/08985626.2017.1328902

Delgado-Ballester, E., & Fernández-Sabiote, E. (2016). 'Once upon a brand': Storytellingpractices by Spanish brands. *Spanish Journal of Marketing – ESIC, 20*(2), 115–131. https://doi.org/10.1016/j.sjme.2016.06.001

Lambert, J., & Hessler, B. (2018). *Digital Storytelling: Capturing Lives, Creating Community.* (5th edition.) Routledge. https://doi.org/10.4324/9781351266369

Leissle, K. (2018). *Cocoa.* Medford, MA: Polity Press.

Matthews, N., & Sunderland, N. (2017). *Digital Storytelling in Health and Social Policy: Listening to the Marginalized Voices.* (1st edition.) New York: Routledge.

Original Trinitario Cocoa and Chocolate Foundation – OTC (2022). *About.* https://www.otctt.org

Robin, B. (2006). The educational uses of digital storytelling. In C. Crawford, et al.(Ed.), *Proceedings of Society for Information Technology and Teacher Education. International Conference* (pp. 709–716). Chesapeake, VA: AACE.

Romer, R. (2017). *Photovoice: Community-based research in Bluefields, Jamaica.* Senior Honors Theses. 564. http://commons.emich.edu/honors/564

Rouhani, L. (2019). Using digital storytelling as a source of empowerment for rural women in Benin. *Gender Development, 27*(3), 573–586.

Speck, D. (2021). *Digital storytelling to empower disadvantaged communities within sustainable entrepreneurship.* MSc Sustainable Entrepreneurship. Campus Frylsân, University of Groningen.

Stahl, S. (1977). The personal narrative as folklore. *Journal of the Folklore Institute, 14*(1/2), 9–30. https://doi.org/10.2307/3814039

Staley, B., & Freeman, L. (2017). Digital storytelling as student-centered pedagogy: Empowering high school students to frame their futures. *Research and Practice in Technology Enhanced Learning, 12*(1), 1–17.

StoryCenter (2021). *StoryCenter,* retrieved 7 February 2021, https://www.storycenter.org

Wang, C., & Burris, M. A. (1997). Photovoice: Concept, methodology, and use for participatory needs assessment. *Health Education & Behavior: The Official Publication of the Society for Public Health Education*, *24*(3), 369–387.

Williams, L., Labonte, R., & O'Brien, M. (2003). Empowering social action through narratives of identity and culture. *Health Promotion International*, *18*(1), 33–40.

Zahra, S. A., Gedajilovic, E., Neubaum, D. O., & Shulman, J. M. (2009). A typology of social entrepreneurs: Motives, search processes, and ethical challenges. *Journal of Business Venturing*, *24*(5), 519–532.

Part IV: **Business Models**
Niels Faber

In Part IV, we explore the changes to the business model concept as a consequence of the pursuit of a sustainable development. The point of departure is that the business model concept describes the logic of value creation, using three generic building blocks: (1) value proposition, (2) organising model and (3) revenue model (Jonker & Faber, 2021; Teece, 2010). With the rising awareness of the need for sustainable societal development, consequentially the need for integrating sustainability thinking and acting into the business model concept grew. This resulted in what we now understand as sustainable business models. Similar to their traditional sibling, sustainable business models capture the logic of value creation, but now of a different nature. Sustainability has been conceptualised as a multi-dimensional concept that touches upon a variety of issues, including, among others, human well-being, global justice, inclusivity, preservation of natural resources and protection of biodiversity, which all are under pressure because of economic development (Wiedmann et al., 2020; WCED, 1987; Meadows et al., 1972).

Sustainable development fundamentally has challenged the way we conceptualise value in society and the economy. While these two have been separate matters for long, seemingly a convergence has taken place. Over time, more and more parts of society have been subjected to the workings of the economy, with market efficiency as the leading ideology and monetisation as its basis for valuation. Think, for instance, about the way energy production has gradually moved from being a public service to a fully privatised industry in many countries in Europe and elsewhere in the world. Similarly, the public provisioning of healthcare services is eroding, slowly but surely replaced by market dynamics that dictate what care is offered at what prices. Counterbalancing this development, the emergence of sustainable development provides us with a broader perspective on the notion of value, and showing us the negative effects of the 'market efficiency – monetisation' paradigm. The deliberate exclusion of matters that cannot be monetised, or cannot be directly ascribed to economic activity, as captured in the externalities concept (Coase, 1960; Buchanan & Stubblebine, 1962), is in the meantime counteracted. These external costs are deliberately taken on board from the sustainability perspective in the determination of the 'real costs' of human production and consumption. The adoption of such a different perspective on value requires a great many changes in organisations, demanding these to engage into a continuous mode of learning and adaptation to incorporate new insights and unlearn old habits.

The alternative approach towards value creation unfolds against the backdrop of the transitional role of business models in society. Because of its orientation on value creation, business models are considered to be the vehicles to change the rules of the game played by businesses and society (Bidmon & Knab, 2018). These rules of the game are a combination of formal policies, legislation and habits, laying down a specific regime on economic and societal actors (e.g., Geels & Schot, 2007). Going beyond being vessels for classical, economy-driven innovation, sustainable business models take an effort to en route also change the foundations of value itself, as also indicated above. The upcoming chapters build on the transitional abilities of sustainable business models.

Furthermore, we have shaped our chapters around the concept of the circular economy, which currently holds a central position in shaping a sustainable society. Building

https://doi.org/10.1515/9783110756159-017

on the principle of value preservation (Jonker & Faber, 2021), the circular economy on all accounts implies an economy of thriftiness and waste avoidance. The recognition that humankind no longer can afford continuous and growing exploitation of natural and biological resources lies at the foundation of this principle. Early warnings by Meadows et al. (1972) and novel insights that innovations for efficient material cannot keep pace with consumption growth (Wiedmann et al., 2020) strengthen the ambition to fundamentally reconstruct our economy and bring it in alignment with planetary boundaries and the pace of biological renewal. In the following chapters, we piggyback on the current interests into the circular economy, and shape our argument around it.

The four chapters in Part IV elaborate on the four topics identified above. In Chapter 14, the issue of sustainable value creation is addressed. The desire to adopt an alternative perspective on value time and again proves to be more difficult than expected. To shed some light on the challenges a shift from a pure economic perspective towards a multiple value creation brings to the fore, we elaborate these challenges from both theoretical and practical stances. Next, Chapter 15 addresses the learning implications for organisations when moving towards sustainability and circularity. Above all else, the realisation of a circular economy is a matter of discovering how to organise closed loops regarding materials, components and products. Chapter 16 elaborates on the various aspects of transformative learning that come into play when organisations engage with circularity. Subsequently, Chapter 17 focuses on the shaping of collaborations across organisations. Framing the move towards a circular economy as a matter of inter-organisational organising and coordination, this chapter presents an actionable method for the development of collaborative sustainable business models and elaborates on how these may accelerate transition. Lastly, Chapter 18 offers an outlook on the field of business models for sustainability, exploring new directions for the field. This last chapter of Part IV builds on insights obtained from research and emerging and upcoming developments that reshape or reset the stage, more and more pushing the issues of sustainability and circularity to the centre of the business model concept.

References

Bidmon, C. M., & Knab, S. F. (2018). The three roles of business models in societal transitions: New linkages between business model and transition research. *Journal of Cleaner Production, 178*, 903–916. https://doi.org/10.1016/j.jclepro.2017.12.198

Buchanan, J. M., & Stubblebine, W. C. (1962). Externality. *Economica, 29*(116), 371–384. https://doi.org/10.2307/2551386

Coase, R. H. (1960). The problem of social cost. *Journal of Law and Economics, 3*, 1–44.

Geels, F. W., & Schot, J. (2007). Typology of sociotechnical transition pathways. *Research Policy, 36*(3), 399–417. https://doi.org/10.1016/j.respol.2007.01.003

Jonker, J., & Faber, N. (2021). *Organizing for Sustainability: A Guide to Developing New Business Models.* Springer International Publishing. https://doi.org/10.1007/978-3-030-78157-6

Meadows, D. H., Meadows, D. I., Randers, J., & Behrens, W. W. I. (1972). *The Limits to Growth: Report for the Club of Rome's Project on the Predicament of Mankind*. New York: New American Library.

Teece, D. J. (2010). Business models, business strategy and innovation. *Long Range Planning*, *43*(2–3), 172–194. https://doi.org/10.1016/j.lrp.2009.07.003

World Commission on Environment and Development (WCED)) (1987). *Our Common Future*. New York: Oxford United Press.

Wiedmann, T., Lenzen, M., Keyßer, L. T., & Steinberger, J. K. (2020). Scientists' warning on affluence. *Nature Communications*, *11*(1), 3107. https://doi.org/10.1038/s41467-020-16941-y

Niels Faber, Bartjan Pennink

14 From Economic to Sustainable Value Creation

Abstract: This chapter discusses how the notion of sustainable value creation is currently understood in the business model discourse, and presents ways in which this discourse may develop in the future. The essence of value-creation is ill-understood at best, let alone what the underlying notion of value entails. The three questions what value is created from which sources, for whom is this value created and how is this value created signify the current search for further clarification. Additionally, clarity is needed regarding the types of values that are involved in sustainability and their specific, intrinsic features. In this chapter, we develop a conceptual lens that aims to unify these two clarifications, providing an analytical tool.

Keywords: sustainable value, value creation, actor–value matrix

1 Introduction

This chapter discusses how the notion of sustainable value creation is currently understood in the business model discourse, and presents ways in which this discourse may develop in the future. The business model concept roots in business studies, where it has been introduced as a vehicle to make sense of the process and logic of value creation in a specific context (Teece, 2010). As mentioned in the introduction, this logic takes shape in its three main building blocks (Jonker & Faber, 2021). The first building block, value proposition, explains what value is created for whom. Second, the organisation model describes the way the value proposition is organised. Lastly, the revenue model expresses who earns what from the realisation of the value proposition. Subsequently, the business model is an actionable concept, for it emphasises the importance of its context for the intended value creation (Lepak, Smith, & Taylor, 2007: 191), and provides footholds to determine how this context is shaped (Adner, 2017). How both value creation and context composition take their place in sustainable business models will be elaborated as part of our exploration.

Given its business studies roots, the business models concept has shaped around three principles from the start. First, the business model starts from the premise that a product or service is realised in a context that consists of a specific group of

Niels Faber, Campus Fryslân Faculty, University of Groningen, Groningen, the Netherlands
Bartjan Pennink, Faculty of Economics and Business, Department of Global Economics and Management, University of Groningen, the Netherlands

https://doi.org/10.1515/9783110756159-018

customers and business partners, leading to a specific form of transaction. This, for instance, is made explicit in the top three parts of the business model canvas (Oster-walder, Pigneur, & Clark, 2010). In other words, a business model may involve the making of shoes, cars, houses, insurances or haircuts. The product or service brought forth thus lies at the heart of a value proposition. Second, the business model has been considered as an organisation-centric concept. Hence, a business model chiefly still describes the value creation of a single organisation. This way, banks create business models around their various financial services, bakers around the breads they bake and car mechanics around the various repairs they may do to cars and motors alike. Third, the notion of value creation in terms of the actual value that is created has for long been limited to financial-economic value; the business model considered value in terms of costs and benefits, measured in currencies such as euros, dollars and yen, directly feeding into organisations' bottom lines.

With a rising societal awareness of, and need for, sustainable development (Meadows et al., 1972; WCED, 1987; WBCSD, 2015), the business model concept has been challenged on all three of its underlying principles. No longer is the business model exclusively about (1) generating monetary value, (2) bringing forth a product or service for a specific target audience and (3) being organisation centric. First and foremost, the sustainable development discourse has widened the perspective on values that a business model creates. The single-value focus on monetary earnings has gradually been supplemented by a multiple value perspective that encompasses among others environmental and social values. This widening of the scope on values complicates the concept of value creation in light of business models related to (i) the array of values that need to be addressed simultaneously (e.g., Elkington, 1997; Porritt, 2007; Gleeson-White, 2014) and consequently (ii) the variety of the types of values that are involved (e.g., Rockström et al, 2009; Raworth, 2017). Attempts to incorporate multiple value creation in the business model concept are among others the triple-layer business model canvas (Joyce & Paquin, 2016) or the strongly sustainable business model canvas (Kurucz et al., 2017).

Second, while still playing a role, products have become subservient to offering solutions to customers' problems. Instead, a business model's ability to create multiple values for multiple actors simultaneously is gradually complementing the customer value creation perspective. This may even imply the involvement of actors who are not immediately identifiable upfront, such as employees' family members, or future generations, who both may be indirectly affected by made choices. Hence, the question for whom value is created gains in relevance, but as indicated also has become more difficult to answer.

Third and last, along with this broader actor perspective, organisations came to realise that they can no longer muster the complexities that come along with the issue of multiple value creation by themselves. This has given rise to a more integrative approach to conceptualising business models spanning across organisational borders. Gradually, the business model perspective shifts from an organisation-centric to a network-centric or collective orientation (Jonker & Faber, 2021; see also Section 4.4). This development not only intensifies inter-organisational collaboration, but fundamentally changes the nature of these. Collaborating for multiple value creation implies integration on all three principles of a business model: (1) developing shared value propositions, (2) collectively organising value creation (see also Section 4.4) and (3) sharing in costs and benefits across all values created (Jonker, Stegeman, & Faber, 2018). The latter development brings to the fore the requirement for transparency regarding the way organisations collaborate, and how they create values and distribute costs and benefits. Amidst the described developments, new and sustainable business models aim to address these challenges on the underlying principles and bring forth novel ways to accommodate the addressing of multiple values, offering of solutions and inter-organisational collaborations simultaneously.

In the remainder of this chapter, we will take a closer look at the way multiple value creation is reconsidered in new and sustainable business models, and along the way touch on the intertwinedness of the challenges that come along. Against the backdrop of classical business models, we explore the consequences of enhancing the business model concept to include a multi-value and multi-actor perspective. In developing this perspective, we adhere to the importance of context in the business model concept, and built on the insights obtained in our research into regional and local economic development. The inclusion of multiple actors and multiple values simultaneously raises additional questions in relation to the business model, such as what values are created, who are the other actors and how do the involved actors relate to the created values. When taking this perspective on business models in the realm of sustainable development to its extreme, this may lead to the existential question whether a product or service should be produced at all, and if it should be what would be the benefits for society at large.

We proceed our discussion as follows. In Section 2, we elaborate on the way value creation in light of new and sustainable business models is developing. We present existing perspectives that aim to capture the concept of value creation, taking a closer look at various ways the notion of multiple values has been conceptualised. Next, we address the issue of multiple actor inclusion in the business model concept. Section 4 pushes the envelope, exploring the way multiple actor and multiple value perspectives may enrich sustainable and new business models, developing the actor–value matrix. This is seen as a means to keep the complexities in check that follow from widening the scope of sustainable and new business models when introducing multiple actors and values. We illustrate the way the actor–value matrix may be used, using an empirical case. The last section provides our final discussion and suggestions for further development of the concept of sustainable value.

2 Value Creation and Values

Despite its recognition at the core of the business model concept, the essence of value-creation is ill-understood at best (Lüdeke-Freund et al., 2020), let alone what the underlying notion of value entails. Implicitly value creation seems to be understood as a series of coordinated activities that brings forth something, that is, a good or service, that is considered to be of value to producer, customer and possibly other stakeholders. Ever since the emergence of the business model concept, this value is commonly expressed in monetary terms. Mazzucato (2019) even goes as far as to state that in our current economy value is completely determined by the price paid. Value creation thus reduces to any activity that is able to generate financial revenue.

Lüdeke-Freund et al. (2020) address three questions to shed some light on the issue of value creation in the context of business modelling in general and sustainable business models in particular. These are: (i) what value is created from which sources, (ii) for whom is this value created and (iii) how is this value created. The first addresses the values that are created, distinguishing a wide array of possible values that may be attributed to some created object, and where to obtain these values. The second question focuses on the actors for whom the object is of value. Lastly, question three aims to disclose the means through which this value is created. Together, Lüdeke-Freund et al. (2020) argue that the three questions give rise to a tentative theorisation of value creation in the realm of (sustainable) business models. This theorisation takes shape around these three questions, complemented by the question who eventually captures the value created. In answering the latter, they argue that this needs to be considered from the viewpoint of all stakeholders individually.

In their search for clarification of the concept of value, Lüdeke-Freund et al. (2020) first take a classical view on value creation and business models. This leads to explaining the matter of value from two perspectives: that of the customer and that of the producer. To customers, value is expressed in terms of the 'use value' or 'customer surpluses of a good or service', in line with elaborations of Bowman and Ambrosini (2000). The latter argue that something is considered to be of value when it either adds to the utility of the customer, or alternatively when the price paid is lower than the price the customer would have been willing to pay (i.e., the customer 'gained' value through a perceived discount). To the producer, the value of a good or service is expressed in terms of 'exchange value' or 'financial profit', making a direct reference to the difference between the revenue generated from the sale and the costs made for producing them (Bowman & Ambrosini, 2000). In this regard, value creation materialises in a transaction, that is, delivery of a good or service in exchange of a currency, in which both customer and producer come to determine its value. From this perspective, value is strictly monetised, and is temporal (the value is bound to the moment of the transaction) and subjective (only customer and producer are involved).

The scope of value creation in light of business models, however, is widening. This change is triggered by the growing importance of among others sustainable development (Meadows, et al., 1972; WCED, 1987), the emergence of the Sustainable Development Goals (SDGs) (United Nations, 2015), and the popularisation of the debate on economic change in writings such as Piketty (2014) and Raworth (2017). The latter give shape to a more fundamental consideration of the purpose and position of economy in society. Such developments have also inspired the emerging field of New Business Models, focusing on business models that target multiple value creation.

With the move towards sustainable development, value creation has started to include more values in addition to the economic value of profit. The renowned tripartite of people, planet and profit (Elkington, 1997) exemplifies this. The move to sustainable development, however, does not only imply *more* values. More particularly, it also involves the adoption of different sorts of values from separate domains as part of the business model discourse and practice, and rooted in fundamentally different paradigms. Given these paradigmatic differences, a closer look on how to deal with these additional values and how this can be included in the new business model concept seems to be in order.

Combining fundamentally different values for starters challenges the way economic value is perceived. The notions of use value and exchange value have a long lineage in economic thought, well before neoclassical economists arose (Gordon, 1964), feeding into the branch of subjective economic value theories. Value is hence determined from the individual perspective (i.e., use value) or from the worth of a commodity when subject to trade. The choice to stay close to contemporary, leading economic value theories unavoidably leads to the situation in which some values that come into play when enlarging the scope towards sustainable development may not be adequately addressed. This, for instance, is the case when considering environmental values. These values relate to the abilities of environmental systems towards flora and fauna alike, and seem irresponsive to subjective positions of producers and customers, and operate on a longer timescale than the instantaneous characteristics of economic transactions.

Alternative value theories are available, such as intrinsic theories of value (e.g., Korsgaard, 1983; Schroeder, 2005), which depart from the notion that goods and services have a value that is an inseparable part of them. As indicated in the previous paragraph, services rendered from natural and biological systems align with this notion of value. Their ecological values, intrinsic to these systems, follow from the various ways in which they support life (including human) on our planet (Rockström et al., 2009). In contrast, the ability to support life is not subject to individuals' preferences as is dictated by subjective economic theories of value. Instead, it is more appropriate to consider this ability as an intrinsic, absolute value of natural and biological systems; they exist with and without the presence of humankind, and are inert to a subjective way of value creation in transactions. However, individual and collective actions may cause actual damage to the environment, ultimately leading to its complete destruction and collapse of life support on Earth. Such collapse will occur, irrespective of individual or collective preferences, whether we like it or not. Concepts such as the circular economy seemingly build on the notion of intrinsic value of materials as the basis of value creation (e.g., Stahel, 1982). The ultimate aim of such a novel economic system is to maintain natural resources in the form of commodities, parts and products within the economy for as long as possible, at the highest quality as possible (e.g., Jonker & Faber, 2019). In a similar vein, a specific collection and level of social systems and services needs to be in place in order for civil society to function (Raworth, 2017; Fukuyama, 2011; McElroy, Jorna, & van Engelen, 2008). While social values are often subject to individual and collective preferences, and political debate, the common idea is that our societies do need, for instance, education, health care or some form of a functioning government to provide a necessary social infrastructure (Raworth, 2017). At the individual level, social values become manifest in the skills and knowledge an individual requires to function in society (Nussbaum, 2013; James, 2018). Fundamental to this part of the debate is the question how human and social welfare are achieved. Classical approaches, rooted in economics, take shape around utilitarian argumentation, making use of cost–benefit analysis to determine how social welfare is best served. Alternatively, Nussbaum (2013) suggests her capability approach. This approach builds on the idea that individuals should have a minimal level of capabilities to assure every individual is able to get the opportunities to survive and live a life with dignity. Also, with regards to social values, an intrinsic theory of value seems to be more fitting, or at least worth exploring further.

How to deal with a multitude of values of different kinds simultaneously, and across multiple future generations of stakeholders, has occupied the centre stage of the sustainable development debate from the start. Initially, the debate revolved around the trade-off between economic development and (negative) environmental impacts (e.g., IPCC, 2022; Meadows et al., 1972), feeding in to the fields of ecological economics (e.g., Boulding, 1966; Daly, 1977; Pearce, 1987) and environmental economics (e.g., Pearce, 2002). The addition of the societal component (WCED, 1987) led to the way sustainability is currently conceptualised. Besides Elkington's (1997) Triple P concept, alternatives are, for instance, the capital approaches by Porritt (2007) or Gleeson-White (2014). Both the latter provide a more detailed elaboration of Elkington's 'people' component. Yet, the Triple P and capital approaches differ fundamentally.

The absence of a clear value theory has brought controversy to the sustainability debate. A divide emerges between the fields of ecological and environmental economics. While related, they are fundamentally different schools of thought, particularly on how they conceptualise the issue of sustainable development. The distinction lies in the way they conceptualise the role of the economic system in relation to the environment and society. This is commonly referred to by the dichotomy of 'strong' versus 'weak' sustainability (Ayres, et al., 2001; Gutés, 1996). Environmental economics holds the relationship between economy, society and environment as one of balance. Hence, a sustainable development is one in which the right balance is found between economic growth, use of environmental resources and impacts on society. Theoretically, Solow (1986, 1993) has laid the basis for weak sustainability. The most accepted practical conceptualisation of this school of thought has been Elkington's (1997) Triple P, and it has found its ways towards policy in, among others, the United Nations Sustainable Development Goals (SDG), European Societal Challenges (ESG) and the 'Maatschappelijke Uitdagingen' (MU) of the Dutch government (Adviesraad voor wetenschap, technologie en innovatie, 2013).

In sharp contrast, strong sustainability advocates argue that the environment sets clear boundaries to how we may use our planet's physical and biological services. All of society's activities need to lie within the confines of these boundaries, including economic endeavours. The consequence of this line of argumentation is that economic development or growth is infeasible in the long run without permanently damaging services rendered by our planet's biological and physical systems (e.g., Rockström et al., 2009). Theoretical proponent of this school of thought, among others, has been Daly (1977). Conceptualisations offered in the capital approaches (Porritt, 2007; Gleeson-White, 2014) may also be considered part of the strong sustainability discourse. Both consider societal and economic systems as nested within natural systems, and reject the possibility to interchange values between these. The notion of strong sustainability also forms the foundations of Raworth's (2017) concept of the Doughnut Economy, in which she graphically captures the safe and just operating space for human action, and its economic systems.

Without choosing sides, in absence of a clear theory of value for sustainability, dealing with multiple values in the realm of business models is not a clear-cut endeavour. At least we may state is that business models and the economy in which they operate will need to be 'in tune' with the various characteristics of each type of values. Particularly, if a specific value type does not play by the rules of 'use value' and 'exchange value' that are so deeply embedded in the current economic fabric. Such considerations coincide with the call for profound reflections on the ways we have shaped our economy. This, for instance, has been addressed in economic concepts such as the Doughnut Economy (Raworth, 2017) and degrowth (Hickel, 2020). It also gave rise to more elaborate contemplations about the fabric of society and the way we have shaped current social contracts between civil society, the state and the market (Mintzberg, 2015). Finally, it inspired musings about the function of the economy within society, questioning whether it is a means to fulfil short-term needs through the delivery of goods and service, or it shares a higher goal in providing purpose to humankind (Handy, 1998). While working towards an integral value theory for sustainability, enriching the value creation logic of the business model concept with available insights might already be a place to start. We do so in the next section, continuing our exploration with the incorporation of additional stakeholders in value creation.

3 Including Outsiders

In the wake of the changing perspective on value creation, the necessity to include multiple actors within the business model concept looms. Traditionally, the business model concept embraces the notion of stakeholders, that is, actors that are involved in the realisation of the business model. Yet, it does so only to the point where a stakeholder contributes to the realisation of the intended value creation for producer and customer. How the business model may potentially affect other actors is not part of the consideration by design. Instead, a sharp distinction is made between the insiders and outsiders (e.g., Lindbeck & Snower, 2001). A possible explanation for this seems to be the way in which our economic fabric has been woven. For instance, Mazzucato (2019) emphasises the deliberateness with which some actors and their activities have been systematically put down as invaluable within the confines of the current economic system, and others have been privileged. Our dominant economic lens favours entrepreneurs, Schumpeterian heroes (Schumpter, 1934) or those with access to capital or other resources (Wernerfelt, 1984) and places them on the front stage. Meanwhile, the unfavoured are forced to lurk backstage finding themselves subject to social exclusion (Sirovátka & Mareš, 2008; Fervers & Schwander, 2015).

More recent developments, such as crowdfunding or crowdsourcing, have set a stage that allows traditional outsiders to take part in value-creating activities (Paredes, Barroso, & Bigham, 2018). Either through small donations, or through intellectually contributing to novel ideas, they have been able to develop or contribute to the realisation of new entrepreneurial activities. Besides these business-related instruments, classical outsiders also bring capabilities to the fore that enable them to create values for society at large (Nussbaum, 2013). This leads to forms of transactions within business models based on hybrid values, including time, money, energy and mobility (Jonker & Faber, 2021).

The involvement of other actors links to the social dimension of the discourse on sustainable development. Under the heading of social inclusion (Sirovátka & Mareš, 2008) or inclusivity (Jonker & Faber, 2021), the aim is to develop towards societies and economies that provide equal access to social, public and private goods and services to all people (Sirovátka & Mareš, 2008). This, for instance, includes jobs for people with a distance to the labour market, or to equate the rights of civic initiatives to those granted to companies. In short, inclusivity explicitly concerns access to social and economic opportunities for people who are marginalised because they either have no job or lack financial means.

However, inclusivity is not limited to the inclusion of human actors alone. The debate extends also to the inclusion of nature and ecosystems. Biodiversity and everything related to it is crucial as a basis for a liveable planet (Rockström et al., 2009) and a *healthy economy* (Raworth, 2017). Our business activities of the last century and a half have done considerable damage to nature and ecosystems (e.g., Czech, Krausman, & Devers, 2000). The pace at which biodiversity has been reduced in recent decades is increasing (Johnson et al., 2017). Hence, the question of what business is doing to restore it is finding its ways into corporate strategies (e.g., Smith et al., 2020; Wolff, Gondran, & Brodhag, 2018) and is supported by municipal and governmental plans (Hermoso et al., 2022). In light of the debate on business models, this implies that nature and related ecosystems are embedded in the stakeholder concept (Laine, 2010; Starik, 1995) and from the business model perspective take their place as actors in the issue of value creation right beside human actors, or at least be represented by them.

4 Actor–Value Matrix

The two expanding perspectives on multiple values and multiple actors, presented in the previous sections, challenge the issue of value creation. It unavoidably brings to the fore the need for a way to capture both expansions in light of the business model concept. Concerning creating new and sustainable business models, Jonker (2012) argues that collective collaboration and deliberately creating multiple values are crucial. Furthermore, new sustainable solutions often rely on collectively managed projects, which means that organisations need to adapt their business models to deliver value collectively, a phenomenon that research on new sustainable business models should address (Gauthier & Gilomen, 2016). Multi-actor involvement in economic development is widely recognised, for instance, in public–private partnerships (Gauthier & Gilomen, 2016; Reypens, Lievens, & Blazevic, 2016) or Open Innovation (Chesbrough, 2006). Multiple-value creation previously has been addressed as Shared Value Creation (Porter & Kramer, 2011), or the Triple-bottom Line (Elkington, 1997). However, how all these individual concepts come together in the issue of value creation in new and sustainable business models proves to be a complex undertaking and hence subject to ongoing research.

This was particularly the case in the work on local and regional economic development in less developed regions (Pennink, 2014). It was in these regions where we observed that stimulating local economies was not only a matter of economic value creation in the business model but also of creating trust between people (changing and enhancing the social fabric) and making the structures within which the business model operate transparently (strengthening the institutional structures, e.g., to overcome corruption). While developing business models, questions about *who* takes part or may contribute in discussions and *which values* where leading were raised in relation to the stimulation of the local economy. This work illustrates that business models are not only about economic value creation by an entrepreneur, but oftentimes also include the creation of other kinds of values (e.g., social values), and multiple actors. With regard to the involved actors, we note that it is relevant not just asking *for* whom the value is created (see Lüdeke-Freund et al. (2020) but also *by* whom.

The two initial questions, (1) which values are touched upon and (2) which actors are involved, we use for the construction of the 'actor–value matrix'. We use this as a simple model to gain insights into how actors and values are positioned in a specific context, in this case inspired on our research on regional and local economic development. The horizontal axis addresses the question of who is involved in the business model and on the vertical axis we position the question of which values are involved in the discussion. On the actors' axis, a variety of actors is identified among which are the business owner, employees and other actors who could be invited to take part in the creation of values. On the values axis we identify the values labelled as people, planet and profit values. Table 14.1 shows the resulting matrix.

Table 14.1: Actor–value matrix.

		Actors						
		Owner/ management	Employees	Customers	Local communities close to	Governmental actors	Civil society actors	Nature
Values	Economic	**Cell 1**						
	Ecological							
	Social						**Cell 2**	

The actor–value matrix gives us the options to analytically take a broader view of businesses and business models. In cell 1 situations (see Table 14.1) the discussion by owners or shareholders is focused on only economic value and how these may be created. When the scope of the discussion widens, and starts to include values such as people and planet, adopting Corporate Social Responsibility (CSR) in the traditional way (Carroll, 1979), the full extent of the first column will be covered. Other situations may also be analysed with the matrix, for example, crowdfunding in which next to the first column, economic values for civil society actors are included in the business model. For each of the discussions in the business model we start by answering the questions: (i) which actors take part in the business model discussion? and (ii) which values will be included? When these have been answered, we proceed by analysing the way the values are combined. For this, we answer the question (iii) in which way are the values combined into a *shared* value?

The latter provides us with the option to extend the discussion from how to create added value in an artificial vacuum to real local situations in which the business model takes shape. We argue that the various ways in which our questions are answered will contribute differently to a regional development and that certain combinations will contribute to a sustainable regional development more than other combinations. The last question, however, needs some additional explanation. We expect that for *sustainable* regional development combinations are needed that do not only cover cell 1 (see Table 14.1) activities. Instead, we argue that these always require the combination of more actors and more values. This will require more empirical research, focused on how these first expectations can be specified into hypotheses, making more explicit how we think a transition to a more *sustainable* regional development may materialise in practice.

Worthy to note is that the actor–value matrix does not only allow for the analysis of business activities, but also activities that take shape outside of the business realm (i.e., activities that are not focused on economic value). At the cross-section of social values and civil society actors, we envisage business models in which actors deliberate how they may create social values for society at large. We label this 'cell 2' (see Table 14.1). This encompasses social activities in a local situation such as football clubs or social activities that more explicitly try to create social cohesion in a local situation and are explicitly trying to contribute to regional sustainable development.

This way, the actor–value matrix provides the option to compare various combinations of value creation in business activities (cell 1) with non-business activities (cell 2), and determine which combinations of cell 1 and cell 2 activities contribute most to the transition to sustainable regional development.

The actor–value matrix enables the analysis of value creation in real-life situations. It reveals the variety of values from different fields that emerge from empirical enquiry, and identifies the variety of relevant actors that are involved. At the cross-section, the matrix clarifies how actors and values are related. Subsequently, Pennink (2004) provides footholds to determine how created values combine to create shared values, elaborating on how a shared image is created of a management problem. Pennink (2004) assumes that managers have formed images of the situation, the problem and also possible solutions. When they work together, they have to become aware that managers have their own individual images, giving rise to the possibility to create a shared image space. The shared image space may unfold in various ways. First, it can consist of the parts that all images have in common, thus forming an image of commonalities. Second, it can consist of creating a new shared image from all images, forming a combined image. Lastly, it can consist of the image of the one who takes or has the lead, leading to an imposed or coerced image. We think that describing 'creating value' with the help of images, differences in images and finding and creating a shared image space will help to shed light on 'creating value'.

The question now is what combinations of actors and values will contribute to the realisation of sustainable business models. This partly depends on what is valued by the actors included with regards to a sustainable development, and on the thresholds that are in play with regards to the values created. Different combinations will lead to sustainable development when the latter is explained in economic, social or ecological objectives.

Cell 1 activities are kept in check by the environmental and social values. Where entrepreneurial behaviour has been promoted as opportunity seeking almost without restrictions (see, for instance, Williamson, 1975, on the matter of opportunity seeking), environmental and social values reduce the degrees of freedom for economic activity.

5 Putting Things to Practice: The Case of Appingedam

In the Northern (North-East) part of Groningen a small city, Appingedam, is situated. Until 2021 this city was an independent municipality. In 2021 it became part of the larger Eemsdelta municipality, a merger of the former municipalities of Appingedam, Delfzijl and Loppersum. Here, we focus on the city of Appingedam.

In about 2017, the local entrepreneurs and the local government discussed the economic and social situation in the city centre of Appingedam. At that time, the number of shops was decreasing, the number of customers was at least not increasing and the number of visitors to the city centre was low. This asked for a new approach in order to (i) maintain what was present and (ii) to improve the local economy in terms of more entrepreneurs and more customers. A small group of entrepreneurs developed a new idea that focused on improving the living situation in the city centre. Their intention was to do something good for their city. The idea translated into 'The roadmap'. In this roadmap, the aim was to improve the level and number of shops and increase the number of visiting customers. This resulted in a loyalty-experience card. Customers were stimulated to use the card, by offering them participation in a lottery with the option to win a prize. In terms of business models, this solution is close to the classical business model in which only economic value is considered. In terms of our actor–value matrix, we observe a situation in which the actors are entrepreneurs and customers, and the values are centred on loyalty of the customer and the economic added value for the entrepreneurs. For the customer economic value materialises in the chance to win a prize. In spite of the good intentions of the entrepreneurs at the start and the ideas around which the roadmap was built, the business model did not develop further than 'just' a customer loyalty-experience card. Values such as 'development of the city of Appingedam' and improving the 'attractiveness of Appingedam' had not found their way in the final operation.

While the development of such a loyalty-experience card by local entrepreneurs is an interesting step, in the card's final form the focus is mainly on economic development in favour of mainly the local entrepreneurs. In this combination of values and actors the focus of the shared values is on economic development. However, for a sustainable regional development more is needed. Although the ideas of the roadmap have been well developed and attractive to several of the municipality's actors, the developments in Appingedam do need a new push because the number of shops is still decreasing, the number of visitors stagnates and buildings formerly used as shops are converted into housing facilities. The latter development is less attractive from the economic perspective.

From the perspective our actor–value matrix provides, next to economic, other values could become part of the roadmap. Similarly, also other actors might contribute to the development of the region. Not only entrepreneurs (of shops or restaurants) but also 'other' actors should have a say in this. We think that it might help to involve actors such as local government, tourists, non-governmental organisations (NGO), social welfare organisations, football clubs and church communities. By involving more stakeholders also more than economic values will be part of the discussions and can contribute to a broader understanding of the concept of development.

With the help of a group of Honours master's students we interviewed 13 people coming from a broad variety of organisations from the region (see Pennink, 2021).

Inspired by Pennink (2021), the extension of the idea of a loyalty-experience card with additional dimensions that will cover not only the entrepreneur–customer relation but also the relation of 'Appingedam–tourist', 'Appingedam–citizen' and 'Appingedam–citizen–NGOs in the region' has been proposed. In other words, we suggest increasing both the number of actors and the number of values as part of the question of how to stimulate the regional or local development of the city of Appingedam.

Based on conducted interviews we came up with the following extensions. First, the idea has been posited for an Inclusion experience card, in which organisations can show how many inhabitants of Appingedam are involved in the activities they organise. Second, we suggested a Tourist Experience card. This card may be used by tourists to find out about interesting places and get discounts by visiting them. The third suggestion is to offer a Cultural and Social involvement card. Appingedam inhabitants may use this card similar to the loyalty-experience card when participating in local activities, and receive discounts. Reversely, local organisations may use this card to show how many inhabitants of Appingedam visit events. Fourth, we suggested a Green card. Local organisations, entrepreneurs and inhabitants may use this card to make explicit how green they are. Fifth, the idea of an International (city) partnership card has been brought to the fore. This should enable local organisations, entrepreneurs and inhabitants to work out how they are connected to other parts of the world. And sixth and last, a Public Health card was suggested, allowing local organisations and Inhabitants of Appingedam to work out how their contribution to a healthier life can be made more visible. These extensions can also be seen as broadening the shared image space that started with the initial loyalty card that focused on economic value, to a card that incorporates social values. The new shared image space was created by the researcher who took the lead.

The provided suggestions show that a roadmap for the sustainable development of a (small) city is much more than to try to realise this centred on economic development of only local entrepreneurs. From the perspective of our actor–value matrix more actors such as inhabitants themselves and local organisations should be involved as well as the inclusion of a wider array of values to give substance to a sustainable development. The 'new' cards sketch the contours of which values that may be. This example is not perfect. It merely illustrates the start of a line of thinking on business models in a regional context. What we have been able to demonstrate with it is that focusing on entrepreneurs and their customers results in shaping a business model around return on investment will only result in added value for the entrepreneurs.

Taking into consideration the full potential of the actor–value matrix, it became a situation in which more stakeholders (the actors) and more 'cards' (the values) were involved, and the result of the value creation became directed to all regional actors instead of only the happy few.

Not all of the ideas are new. For example, the Tourist card does exist already (Leung, 2021). Besides, each of the ideas has to be worked out in detail, particularly concerning how the new card may work in practice and how we may convince organisations and inhabitants of Appingedam to use them. Yet, if we are able to develop this further, we are able to extend the scope of the roadmap to an economic *and* social regional *and* sustainable development. By extending the roadmap, according to the idea of the actor–value matrix, we should be able to create a map for the future of Appingedam as an attractive place to live. In terms of business models, we have shown that more actors and more values became part of the value creation process. How that creation process works requires further enquiry.

6 Discussion

The debate we presented in this chapter is by no means a neat, nor a finished debate. Partly we have been able to show where the debate on value creation and values in relation to business models currently stands. Yet, because these two topics touch upon many underlying issues and a wide array of disciplines, some close, some far, our narrative has been rough around the edges. This chiefly follows from the way value creation and value have been used in the business model concept. In this we share Lüdeke-Freund et al.'s (2020) observation that value-creation in the realm of business models is ill-understood. Too leniently has the concept built on the premise that the price paid for a good or service equals value. The attempts to turn the concept into a vehicle that enables a transition towards sustainable development have thus far only scratched the surface of what this means for the notion of value creation. That while the adaptation of business models for sustainability challenges it at its core, and demands a reconceptualisation of the meaning of value creation and value.

What we witness in the discourse on sustainable business models are two things. First, the way value creation is perceived has been moving from a single issue to what we have previously identified as multiple value creation. For instance, the Triple-P concept (Elkington, 1998) has been integrated in business model thinking (Joyce & Paquin, 2016), while the strongly sustainable business model canvas incorporates the notion of strong sustainability (Kurucz et al., 2017). Additionally, we see a widening of the scope of actors who are involved in the business model. Besides customers and producers, the wider stakeholder perspective is now commonplace in business model thinking (see, for instance, Jonker & Faber, 2021). The Appingedam case we presented provides some insights into the complexities that emerge from including multiple values and multiple actors, and how this requires a different way of thinking and co-ordination among all involved.

We presented the actor–value matrix as an instrument to unravel some of the complexities that originate from the pursuit of sustainability, and as such contribute to sustainable business modelling. The matrix in a systematic way helps to categorise values and actors, providing a framework for both analysis as well as design of business models. In analysis, the actor–value matrix provides a conceptual lens to frame reality and determine what values are created for and by whom. For design, the actor–value matrix offers a set of design parameters that guide choices to shape value creation among actors. On both analysis and design, the actor–value matrix makes the relations between values and individual actors visible, and how they may shape shared values. Regarding the latter, the matrix enables the forming of a shared image space. In order to assure the actor–value matrix is instrumental to the realisation of a sustainable business model, it helps to determine what actors create what values, and what values and actors are missing. This way the matrix makes the context of the sustainable business model, and in particular the value it intends to create, explicit.

In our discussion, we gave shape to the context of business models, making use of insights we have obtained in our earlier research on regional and local economic development. Because the notion of value creation lies at the core of both economic development and business models, this choice seems to fit. Furthermore, this has provided a clear geographical demarcation of which activities need to be taken into consideration and which not. Lastly, the notions of both value and actors underpin value creation in both concepts. Where we see a possible problem is the narrow focus of the regional and local economic discourse on traditional economic values. Taking this single value perspective may influence the choices made in determining the system boundaries taken into consideration. We think the widening of the scope using the combined multiple value and multiple actor perspective sufficiently lifts this possible limitation. More critical reflections and empirical enquires will be needed in future research to determine the robustness of the choices we made.

Despite its potential, the actor–value matrix does not resolve the understanding of value creation in the realm of business models. As said, it offers some support for modelling. Yet, where it comes to understanding value creation, we think a more in-depth insight into the adopted value perspective is in order. Currently, the actor–value matrix makes us of the Triple-P concept. This positions the matrix in the weak sustainability school of thought. This may for now provide sufficient footholds for business modelling. However, in order to develop the matrix into a more robust instrument for conceptualising value creation in a multiple value–multiple actor context, the adoption of a strong sustainability perspective may be more appropriate and thus requires further exploration.

Additionally, we see the need for an elaboration of the value theory around which our economic system and consequently business models take shape. This specifically is the case when the transition towards a sustainable development is desired. The concepts of 'use value' and 'exchange value', which currently dominate theorisation and practice, give shape to a sort of value creation that is in constant flux, determined at the moment a transaction takes place and a consequence of personal preferences. For example, a can of water may have a high value for a person who has walked through the desert for two days, finding himself/herself dehydrated, while at the same the can has a low value for a person standing in the rain. This gives shape to a market of transactions on which commodities easily exchange hands; at the moment seller and buyer agree on a price, the value is set. Yet, when taking a sustainability perspective, the question is whether a value theory that builds on contextuality and personal preference and is temporal provides a suitable basis for value creation with regards to environmental and social values. How do we meaningfully conceptualise the ability of natural and biological systems to sustain life such that it fits into a single transaction? Their value(s) transcend(s) that of their coincidental utility to humans, for they sustain life to all organisms on a permanent basis. Similarly, how do we translate various forms of social capital that sustain societies into measures that fit into the workings of current markets? Also here, the dynamics of social values seem to resonate on a longer time scale than markets allow for. Current value theory that favours the short term, and individual actors, seems rapidly to become obsolete and in need for a revision.

References

Adner, R. (2017). Ecosystem as structure: An actionable construct for strategy. *Journal of Management, 43*(1), 39–58.

Adviesraad voor wetenschap, technologie en innovatie (2013). Advies: Waarde creëren uit maatschappelijke uitdagingen. Adviesraad voor Wetenschaps- en Technologiebeleid. https://www.awti.nl/documenten/adviezen/2013/10/21/waarde-creeren-uit-maatschappelijke-uitdagingen-engels

Ayres, R., Van den Bergh, J., & Gowdy, J. (2001). Strong versus weak sustainability: Economics, natural sciences, and consilience. *Environmental Ethics, 23*(2), 155–168. https://doi.org/10.5840/enviroethics200123225

Boulding, K. E. (1966). The economics of the coming spaceship earth. In Jarrett, H. (Ed.), *Environmental Quality in a Growing Economy* (pp. 3–14). Baltimore, MD: Johns Hopkins Press.

Bowman, C., & Ambrosini, V. (2000). Value creation versus value capture: Towards a coherent definition of value in strategy. *British Journal of Management, 11*(1), 1–15. https://doi.org/10.1111/1467-8551.00147

Carroll, A. B. (1979). A three-dimensional conceptual model of corporate performance. *Academy of Management Review, 4*(4), 497–505. https://doi.org/10.2307/257850

Chesbrough, H. (2006). *Open Innovation: The New Imperative for Creating and Profiting from Technology.* Boston, MA: Harvard Business School Press.

Czech, B., Krausman, P. R., & Devers, P. K. (2000). Economic associations among causes of species endangerment in the United States. *BioScience, 50*(7), 593. https://doi.org/10.1641/0006-3568(2000)050[0593:EAACOS]2.0.CO;2

Daly, H. E. (1977). *Steady-state Economics.* Washington, D.C.: Island Press.

Elkington, J. (1997). The triple bottom line. *Environmental Management: Readings and CCases, 2,* 49–66.

Elkington, J. (1998). *Cannibals with Forks: The Triple Bottom Line of 21st Century Business*. Gabriola Island, Canada: New Society Publishers.

Fervers, L., & Schwander, H. (2015). Are outsiders equally out everywhere? The economic disadvantage of outsiders in cross-national perspective. *European Journal of Industrial Relations, 21*(4), 369–387. https://doi.org/10.1177/0959680115573363

Fukuyama, Y. F. (2011). *The Origins of Political Order: From Prehuman Times to the French Revolution*. New York: Farrar, Straus and Giroux.

Gauthier, C., & Gilomen, B. (2016). Business models for sustainability: Energy efficiency in urban districts. *Organization & Environment, 29*(1), 124–144.

Gleeson-White, J. (2014). *Six Capitals: The Revolution Capitalism Has to Have – Or can Accountants Save the Planet?*. Sydney, Australia: Allen & Unwin.

Gordon, B. J. (1964). Aristotle and the development of value theory. *The Quarterly Journal of Economics, 78*(1), 115. https://doi.org/10.2307/1880547

Gutés, M. C. (1996). The concept of weak sustainability. *Ecological Economics, 17*(3), 10. https://doi.org/10.1016/S0921-8009(96)80003-6

Handy, C. (1998). *The Hungry Spirit: Beyond Capitalism – A Quest for Purpose in the Modern World*. London: Arrow Books Limited.

Hermoso, V., Carvalho, S. B., Giakoumi, S., Goldsborough, D., Katsanevakis, S., Leontiou, S., Markantonatou, V., Rumes, B., Vogiatzakis, I. N., & Yates, K. L. (2022). The EU biodiversity strategy for 2030: Opportunities and challenges on the path towards biodiversity recovery. *Environmental Science & Policy, 127*, 263–271. https://doi.org/10.1016/j.envsci.2021.10.028

Hickel, J. (2020). *Less is More: How Degrowth Will Save the World*. Penguin Random House. https://www.penguin.co.uk/books/441772/less-is-more-by-jason-hickel/9781786091215

Intergovernmental Panel on Climate Change (IPCC) (2022). *Climate Change 2022: Mitigation of Climate Change. Contribution of Working Group III to the Sixth Assessment Report of the Intergovernmental Panel on Climate Change*. In Shukla, P. R., Skea, J., Slade, R., Alkhourdajie, A., Van diemen, R., McCollum, D., Pathak, M., Some, S., Vyas, P., Fradera, R., Belkacemi, M., Hasija, A., Lisboa, G., Luz, S., & Malley, J. (Eds.). Cambridge University Press. doi: 10.1017/9781009157926

James, P. (2018). Creating capacities for human flourishing: An alternative approach to human development. In Spinozzi, P., & Mazzanti, M. (Eds.), *Cultures of Sustainability and Wellbeing: Theories, Histories and Policies* (pp. 23–45). Abingdon: Routledge, Taylor & Francis Group.

Johnson, C. N., Balmford, A., Brook, B. W., Buettel, J. C., Galetti, M., Guangchun, L., & Wilmshurst, J. M. (2017). Biodiversity losses and conservation responses in the Anthropocene. *Science, 356*(6335), 270–275. https://doi.org/10.1126/science.aam9317

Jonker, J. (2012). *New Business Models: An Explorative Study of Changing Transactions Creating Multiple Value (s)*. Doetinchem, Netherlands: JAB Management Consultants BV.

Jonker, J., & Faber, N. (2019). Business models for multiple value creation: Exploring strategic changes in organisations enabling to address societal challenges. In Aagaard, A. (Ed.), *Sustainable Business Models: Innovation, Implementation and Success* Palgrave-MacMillan. https://www.palgrave.com/gp/book/9783319932743

Jonker, J., & Faber, N. (2021). *Organizing for Sustainability: A Guide to Developing New Business Models*. Springer International Publishing. https://doi.org/10.1007/978-3-030-78157-6

Jonker, J., Stegeman, H., & Faber, N. (2018). *The Circular Economy – Developments, Concepts, and Research in Search for Corresponding Business Models* [Working Paper]. Radboud University, Nijmegen School of Management. https://www.researchgate.net/profile/Niels_Faber/publication/313635177_The_Circular_Economy_-_Developments_concepts_and_research_in_search_for_corresponding_business_models/links/58a0b51645851598bab86654/The-Circular-Economy-Developments-concepts-and-research-in-search-for-corresponding-business-models.pdf

Joyce, A., & Paquin, R. L. (2016). The triple layered business model canvas: A tool to design more sustainable business models. *Journal of Cleaner Production, 135*, 1474–1486. https://doi.org/10.1016/j.jclepro.2016.06.067

Korsgaard, C. M. (1983). Two distinctions in goodness. *The Philosophical Review, 92*(2), 169. https://doi.org/10.2307/2184924

Kurucz, E. C., Colbert, B. A., Lüdeke-Freund, F., Upward, A., & Willard, B. (2017). Relational leadership for strategic sustainability: Practices and capabilities to advance the design and assessment of sustainable business models. *Journal of Cleaner Production, 140*, 189–204. https://doi.org/10.1016/j.jclepro.2016.03.087

Laine, M. (2010). The nature of nature as a stakeholder. *Journal of Business Ethics, 96*(S1), 73–78. https://doi.org/10.1007/s10551-011-0936-4

Lepak, D. P., Smith, K. G., & Taylor, M. S. (2007). Value creation and value capture: A multilevel perspective. *Academy of Management Review, 32*(1), 180–194. https://doi.org/10.5465/amr.2007.23464011

Leung, D. (2021). Tourists' motives and perceptions of destination card consumption. *Tourism Recreation Research, 46*(1), 39–51. https://doi.org/10.1080/02508281.2020.1801947

Lindbeck, A., & Snower, D. J. (2001). Insiders versus outsiders. *Journal of Economic Perspectives, 15*(1), 165–188. https://doi.org/10.1257/jep.15.1.165

Lüdeke-Freund, F., Rauter, R., Pedersen, E. R. G., & Nielsen, C. (2020). Sustainable value creation through business models: The what, the who and the how. *Tourism Recreation Research, 8*(3), 29.

Mazzucato, M. (2019). *The Value of Everything: Making and Taking in the Global Economy*. London: Penguin Books.

McElroy, M. W., Jorna, R. J., & van Engelen, J. (2008). Sustainability quotients and the social footprint. *Corporate Social Responsibility and Environmental Management, 15*(4), 223–234. https://doi.org/10.1002/csr.164

Meadows, D. H., Meadows, D.I., Randers, J., & Behrens, W. W. I. (1972). *The Limits to Growth: Report for the Club of Rome's Project on the Predicament of Mankind*. New York: New American Library.

Mintzberg, H. (2015). *Rebalancing Society: Radical Renewal beyond Left, Right, and Center*. Oakland: Berret-Koehlers Publishers.

Nussbaum, M. (2013). *Creating Capabilities*. Cambridge, MA: Belknap Press.

Osterwalder, A., Pigneur, Y., & Clark, T. (2010). *Business Model Generation: A Handbook for Visionaries, Game Changers, and Challengers*. New Jersey: Wiley.

Paredes, H., Barroso, J., & Bigham, J. P. (2018). All (of us) can help: Inclusive crowdfunding research trends and future challenges. In *2018 IEEE 22nd International Conference on Computer Supported Cooperative Work in Design ((CSCWD))* (pp. 796–801). https://doi.org/10.1109/CSCWD.2018.8465161

Pearce, D. (2002). An intellectual history of environmental economics. *Annual Review of Energy and the Environment, 27*(1), 57–81. https://doi.org/10.1146/annurev.energy.27.122001.083429

Pearce, D. W. (1987). Foundations of an ecological economics. *Ecological Modelling, 38*, 9–18.

Pennink, B. (2004). Samen managen met beelden: Het ontwikkelen van een model. PhD Thesis. University of Groningen. https://pure.rug.nl/ws/portalfiles/portal/13173522/thesis.pdf

Pennink, B. (2014). Dimensions of local economic development: Towards a multi-level, multi actor model. *Journal of Business and Economics, 6*(1), 249–256.

Pennink, B. J. W. (2021). *Regional (Sustainable) Economic and Social Development of Appingedam: From a 'Roadmap' to a 'City map'*. Internal report University of Groningen.

Piketty, T. (2014). *Capital in the Twenty-first Century*. Cambridge, MA: Harvard University Press.

Porritt, J. (2007). *Capitalism as if the World Matters*. London: Routledge.

Porter, M., & Kramer, M. R. (2011). The big idea: Creating shared value. *Harvard Business Review, 89*(1), 2.

Raworth, K. (2017). *Doughnut Economics: Seven Ways to Think Like a 21st-century Economist*. (1st edition.) UK: Penguin Random House.

Reypens, C., Lievens, A., & Blazevic, V. (2016). Leveraging value in multi-stakeholder innovation networks: A process framework for value co-creation and capture. *Industrial Marketing Management, 56*, 40–50.

Rockström, J, Steffen, W. L., Noone, K., Persson, Å., Stuart Chapin III, F., Lambin, E., Lenton, T. M., Scheffer, M., Folke, C., Schellnhuber, H. J., Nykvist, B., de Wit, C., Hughes, T., van der Leeuw, S., Rodhe, H., Sörlin, S., Snyder, P. K., Costanza, R., Svedin, U., Falkenmark, M., Karlberg, L., Corell, R. W., Fabry, V. J., Hansen, J., Walker, B., Walker, B., Liverman, D., Richardson, K., Crutzen, P., & Jonathan, F. (2009). Planetary boundaries: Exploring the Safe operating space for humanity. *Ecology and Society*, 14(2), http://pdxscholar.library.pdx.edu/iss_pub/64/

Schroeder, M. (2005). Cudworth and normative explanations. *Journal of Ethics, 3*, 28. https://doi.org/10.1093/acprof:oso/9780198713807.001.0001

Schumpeter, J. A. (1934). *The Theory of Economic Development*. Cambridge, MA: Harvard University Press.

Sirovátka, T., & Mareš, P. (2008). Social exclusion and forms of social capital: Czech evidence on mutual links. *Czech Sociological Review, 44*(3), 531–556. https://doi.org/10.13060/00380288.2008.44.3.05

Smith, T., Beagley, L., Bull, J., Milner-Gulland, E. J., Smith, M., Vorhies, F., & Addison, P. F. E. (2020). Biodiversity means business: Reframing global biodiversity goals for the private sector. *Conservation Letters, 13*(1), https://doi.org/10.1111/conl.12690

Solow, R. (1993). An almost practical step toward sustainability. *Resources Policy, 19*(3), 162–172.

Solow, R. M. (1986). On the intergenerational allocation of natural resources. *Scandinavian Journal of Economics, 88*(1), 141–149.

Stahel, W. R. (1982). The product-life factor. In Grinton Orr, S. (Ed.), *Inquiry into the Nature of Sustainable Societies: The Role of the Private Sector* (pp. 72–104). Geneva: HARC.

Starik, M. (1995). Should trees have managerial standing? Toward stakeholder status for non-human nature. *Journal of Business Ethics, 14*(3), 207–217. https://doi.org/10.1007/BF00881435

Teece, D. J. (2010). Business models, business strategy and innovation. *Long Range Planning, 43*(2–3), 172–194. https://doi.org/10.1016/j.lrp.2009.07.003

United Nations (2015). Sustainable development goals – United Nations. *United Nations Sustainable Development*. http://www.un.org/sustainabledevelopment/sustainable-development-goals/

World Business Council for Sustainable Development (WBCSD) (2015). Understanding the business contribution to society. WBCSD – World Business Council for Sustainable Development. http://www.wbcsd.org/work-program/development/measuring-impact.aspx

World Commission on Environment and Development (WCED) (1987). *Our Common Future*. New York: Oxford United Press.

Wernerfelt, B. (1984). A resource-based view of the firm. *Strategic Management Journal, 5*(2), 171–180. https://doi.org/10.1002/smj.4250050207

Williamson, O. E. (1975). *Markets and Hierarchies, Analysis and Antitrust Implications: A Study in the Economics of Internal Organization*. New York: Free Press.

Wolff, A., Gondran, N., & Brodhag, C. (2018). Integrating corporate social responsibility into conservation policy. The example of business commitments to contribute to the French National biodiversity strategy. *Environmental Science & Policy, 86*, 106–114. https://doi.org/10.1016/j.envsci.2018.05.007

Bart van Hoof, Sjors Witjes, Walter Vermeulen

15 Transformative Organizational Learning for Circular Economy

Abstract: Circular economy is used as a global language to advance solutions for sustainability consumption and production systems. The circular economy approach aims at improving resource efficiency and effectiveness through a variety of innovations based on the retention of the value of products and their resources. The circular economy approach adds a business model focus for scaling solutiongs to the field of corporate sustainability. Circular solutions require companies and entrepreneurs to acquire a strategic vision on how circularity can be best put into practice and to determine operational capacity to design and adopt circular practices. Translating corporate strategy on circularity into actions entails learning on the integration of sustainability criteria into business strategy and processes, comprehensively linking physical and social organizational dynamics. In this chapter, a learning cycle for *transformative change* is presented, balancing *physical and social impact creation, as part of the company's value creation practices.* To understand the feedback loops in detail, the adoption of the circular economy approach is analyzed at diverse scales, such as the business system context (macro), the value chain (meso), and the organization (micro). At every scale, mechanisms to adopt circular solutions are discussed and detailed questions for self-reflection are posed, as tools for organizations to translate corporate strategy on circularity into actions.

Keywords: transformative organizational learning, circular economy, feedback loop, transition

1 Corporate Sustainability and Circular Economy

The field of corporate sustainability (CS) studies the need for interpreting the consequential relation between company processes, and their impacts, by emphasizing the inter-relations of physical and social issues between individuals, the organization, the supply chain, and the wider society in a time perspective (Vermeulen & Witjes, 2016; Witjes & Lozano, 2016). Corporate sustainability includes Circular Economy (CE) as an

Bart van Hoof, School of Management, Universidad de los Andes, Bogotá, Colombia
Sjors Witjes, Department Business Administration, Radboud University, the Netherlands
Walter Vermeulen, Copernicus Institute of Sustainable Development, Utrecht University, Utrecht, the Netherlands

https://doi.org/10.1515/9783110756159-019

approach that has gained global acceptance to improve resource efficiency and innovation towards the use of circular and regenerative resources (Ellen MacArthur, 2015c). CE is characterized by minimizing or avoiding waste by adopting circularity through transforming linear economy systems by reducing, reusing, recycling, and recovering. CE contributes to sustainable development (e.g., the United Nations Sustainable Development Goals (UN SDGs)) by reducing burdens to the environment while stimulating business development (e.g. SDG 12), making it a cost-effective intervention to reduce waste and reduce greenhouse gas emissions (Schroeder, Anggraeni, & Weber, 2019).

Research on CE has evolved from understanding the outputs of impact on physical and social issues to understanding the process of business activities for transformative change of the organizational systems (Epstein & Widener 2010; Reike, Vermeulen, & Witjes, 2018). Understanding both output and process is essential for advancing and scaling the adoption of CE by companies. The process involves interaction levels of analysis of organizations of individual companies and the value chains they are embedded in, and structural changes are needed in how our production and consumption system functions (Rovanto & Bask, 2021). This calls for more than incremental technological improvements; for societal transformations in the sociological sense of changing institutions and structures of economic behavior (ISSC & UNESCO, 2013: 101; Sewell, 1992) both inside the firm and in the wider societal system: the dual and embedded nature of companies (Vermeulen & Witjes, 2016).

Taking the dual and embedded nature of companies as the starting point, we need to combine the knowledge developed from various disciplines to better understand how companies can adopt circularity and contribute to the sustainable development of wider society (Ruiz-Real et al., 2018). Taking a position on the circular economy requires an analysis of the physical dynamics inside the specific company about its full physical product life cycle, as well as an analysis of the social dynamics of the humans and their collaboration making the product life cycle possible. Both dynamics need to be addressed inside and outside the specific company. This includes the social impacts in the full product life cycle and the appropriateness of the economic practices in the transactions with various stakeholders throughout the value chain. For each element, separate tools are available to be applied in a systematically integrated way, such as environmental management systems that address the physical dynamics of the impact of corporate processes on the environment as well as the social processes ensuring the continuous improvement of, for example, reducing this impact.

Nevertheless, after two decades of using environmental management systems, many companies did get used to monitoring their progress, because – in principle – in applying ISO14001 and comparable systems they have signed up for continuous improvement. But, in practice, this monitoring of progress has a very limited application (Delmas, 2003: 38; MacDonald, 2005: 631). In the best cases, various key performance indicators on some of the physical dynamics are available to decision-makers in companies (Birkin, Polesie, & Lewis, 2009: 287; Boons & Lüdeke-Freund, 2013: 15; Yin &

Schmeidler, 2009). However, in contrast to that, retrospective self-reflection of the social dynamics inside the company and its connections with the outside world is hardly being practiced (Aguinis & Glavas, 2012: 955–957; Baumgartner, 2014: 259). Repetitive plan–do–check–act cycles tend to lose momentum and the level of improvement in each next cycle of continuous improvement reduces. Lack of internalization into the company's culture and value system and into communications with its societal stakeholders is often the core reason for this "jamming" of strategies for adopting demands on environmental issues and therefore also on CE. To enable significant change, companies need to make regular self-reflections of their dual and embedded nature, linking how they function in their social dynamics with what they achieve in their physical dynamics in their full production and consumption system.

2 Self-Reflection for Implementation of Circular Economy

Self-reflection can be defined as a temporary phenomenological experience of an individual to the higher mental function of sense-making (Gillespie, 2007). Self-reflection comes about when individuals acquire adequate information (Cyert & March, 1963), and analytical and communicative skills to make organizations learn (Argyris, 1996). A learning organization is created by individuals' ability to think of organizations as systems (Senge et al., 1999). Thus, it is individuals who acquire specific skills, information, and knowledge for organizations to learn. Within the CE context, self-reflection relates to the capacity to acquire the paradigmatic understanding of the physical and social dynamics for the adoption of CE in organizations as part of production and consumption systems.

For self-reflective analysis of CE, companies need to identify their room for innovation. For this process, search directions are needed. One might want to get such directions from governments, if they have formulated long-term targets, such as a 40% reduction of carbon emissions by 2030 (EU), 51% for Colombia, or 80% by 2050 (UK). Public policy targets and mechanisms such as regulation, incentives programs, information systems, and technical assistance, are examples to inspire both large and smaller firms.

Other motivations for self-reflection include value chain pressures by clients or innovation opportunities offered by suppliers, clients, and or neighboring firms, for example for the exchange of waste materials and or other symbiotic actions such as sharing facilities. In analyzing the adoption of CE and in supporting key actors in the field, a long-time perspective is required, not looking at short-term kick-off projects, but at enabling accelerating change processes, where each next cycle scales up its impact: transformative change. External change agents support companies to speed up CE adoption, to understand the essential dual and embedded nature of business; the key question is how an ongoing upward mechanism of transformative learning cycles can be achieved in practice.

The current practice of adopting CE, including the identification of key performance indicators (KPIs) and reporting on CE policies and outcomes often has a strong focus on the dynamics of the physical production processes in companies addressing and (in good cases) in their value chain. They may also address the social impacts of value creation (related to workers inside the company, the neighborhoods, and – if taken from a supply chain perspective – supplier companies). But in many cases, the three dimensions of environmental, social, and economic issues, and how these unfold across time, and place are addressed only partially. Simultaneously, however, the self-reflection on whether applied interventions work as expected is often limited. The social dynamics related to the social interventions aiming at reducing negative direct and indirect impacts are largely ignored and the analysis of the links between the social dynamics and physical dynamics are underexplored.

In transformative change, the learning cycle should be seen as a constantly rotating plan–do–check–act wheel, which should be riding up the sustainability ambitions quickly enough. Such transformative change can only be effective if it is a constant process of self-assessment by the company. In doing this, it is essential to explore the company's social intervention dynamics and their links to the level of success in affecting physical and social impact creation: the value creation practices. This finally needs to result in improving the effectiveness of efforts of reducing negative impacts and shifting toward positive effects in the three issue areas of environmental, social, and economic benefits, both here and there and both in the short term and the long term.

Circular economy theory of change for firms, embedded in societal systems, needs to explicitly link the social intervention dynamics as essential in the pathway from beliefs, values, needs, and motives via repetitive learning to successfully implementing social and technical innovations in the firm's societal systems. For companies, this implies a circular economy with permanent feedback between four elements:

a. ongoing goal re-orientation, addressing the three sustainable development dimensions (environmental, social and economic issues, time and place)
b. longitudinal analysis (retro- and prospective) of the general social dynamics in the firm and the social dynamics of introducing interventions
c. longitudinal analysis (retro- and prospective) of the physical and societal impacts of introducing interventions aiming at the triple issue fields (prosperity, people, planet)
d. linking the results of the analysis of social dynamics to the impacts in the physical and social realm, and translating this to goal re-orientation and adjusted social and technical strategies

These essential feedbacks are schematically represented in Figure 15.1. The feedback X refers to the reflection on whether social interventions applied in the organizational

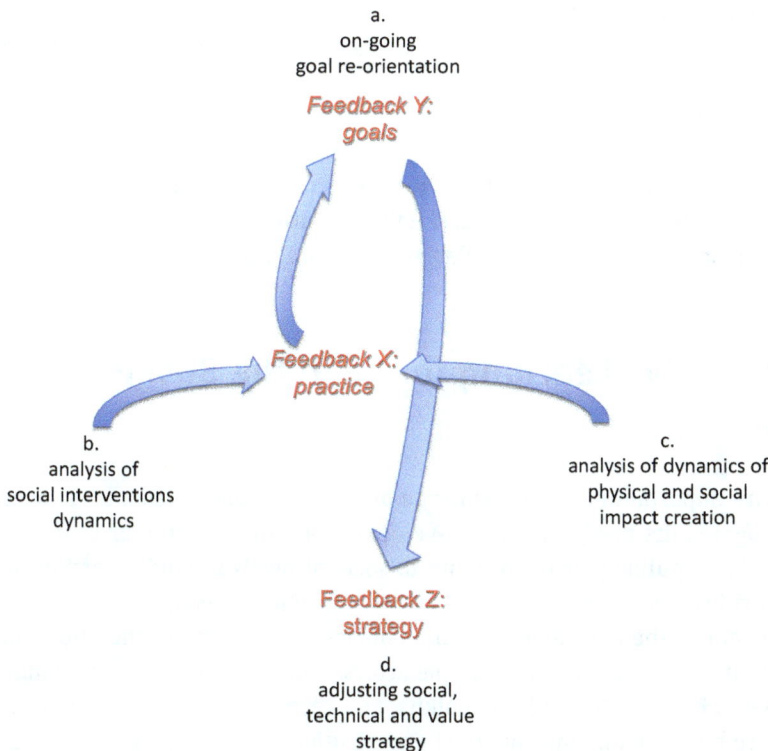

Figure 15.1: Permanent feedback between four elements of transformative change.
(Source: Vermeulen & Witjes, 2016).

structure and culture and the collaboration with value chain partners do result in the assumed effects on the performance in the physical and societal realm resulting from circular economy initiatives. Is the "theory of change" working and what other social interventions could be effective in the specific organization reviewed?

The feedback Y refers to the refining of the company's mission and goals in a circular economy based on the reflections under feedback X. At this stage, the required permanent monitoring of essential changes in the context of the company and the internal lessons learned on what works and what does not work need to be integrated. This can result in a reformulated, more challenging vision or mission document and needs to be translated into adjusted KPIs.

Feedback Z then refers to adjusted strategies both in terms of new circular economy projects enabling the attainment of the physical and social targets and the type of social interventions planned to achieve these. This includes making explicit assumptions about the "theory of change," which can be tested in the next phase.

Feedback X, Y, and Z are interdependent: the learning about the causal links between the social and physical dynamics (feedback X), the readjustment of corporate goals (feedback Y), and the integration of these first two learning cycles into the learning about interventions in the company's processes and its people to comply with the circular economy vision.

To understand the feedback loops in detail, the coming sections analyze circular economy at diverse scales, such as the business context (macro), the value chain (meso), and the organization (micro). At every scale, circular economy mechanisms are discussed, and detailed questions for self-reflection are posed, both as organizational tools for the implementation of circular economy practices.

3 Transformative Learning for CE in the Business Context

Public policies are important mechanisms for guiding and scaling systematic changes including paradigm shifts needed for the development of a more circular economy (Jänicke, 2002). These public policies respond to societal needs in guiding action by identifying priorities, setting goals, and implementing mechanisms that motivate stakeholders to change their behaviors. Public policies set a course in the mid- and long-term, triggering a critical mass of multiple actors, and contributing to systematic changes in society (Shove, 2010). Guides, toolkits, and recommendations for innovating regulation are published by international organizations such as the Ellen MacArthur Foundation and the Organisation for Economic Co-operation and Development (OECD) to enhance public policy development in the circular economy (Ellen MacArthur Foundation, 2015a, 2015b; OECD, 2020).

Diverse countries in the world have adopted public policy mechanisms to stimulate the scaling of circular economy transitions (McDowall et al., 2017). One of the first countries was Japan, in 2000 adopting the law for the promotion of effective utilization of resources. Following similar ideas, in 2005, Korea launched its national Eco-Industrial Park program, while China issued its Circular Economy promotion law in 2009 (Su et al., 2013). In 2015, the European Commission presented its Circular Economy package including mechanisms to finance research, technological innovation, and regulations (Kirchherr et al., 2018). In 2018, the Netherlands presented its national strategy to advance a circular economy in terms of phasing out the use of virgin resources by the year 2050 (Friant, Vermeulen, & Salomone, 2021), followed by a specific policy on circular agriculture by the Dutch Ministry of Agriculture. In Latin America and the Caribbean (LAC), various national and regional governments have adopted public policies setting priorities and objectives for the transition toward a circular economy (ECLAC, 2020). In 2020, the United Nations program launched a Regional Coalition Platform for circular economy to enhance collaboration among the national governments in LAC. One of the public policy approaches to scale CE in the region has been the adoption of Extending Producer Responsibility (ERP) Regulation as a type of regulation appointing producers a significant responsibility – financial and/or physical – for the treatment or disposal of post-consumer products. By setting takeback targets for disposed products and materials, EPR stimulated producers to innovate products design, as a circular economy alternative (Hickle, 2017). In LAC governments of Argentina, Bolivia, Chile, Colombia, Costa Rica Ecuador, and Honduras EPR regulations have been adopted, setting targets with industry to reduce waste streams related to electronic waste, tire waste, batteries, lightbulbs, packaging waste, pharmaceutical, and agrochemical packaging.

Existence of public policy and mechanisms such as EPR regulation, financial incentives, capacity building programs, information systems, and consumer awareness campaigns guide self-reflection for feedback strategy Y (see Figure 15.1), for goals setting for circular economy strategy. Business context mechanisms offer societal mid and long-term goals and develop mechanisms motivating circular economy developments, as presented in Table 15.1. Transformative learning in the business context involves understanding of societal needs, availability of incentive schemes, requirement for compliance, and/or certification schemes of standards, and availability of infrastructure that favors implementation of circular economy initiatives.

Table 15.1: Mechanisms of the business context favoring self-reflection for circular economy transformative learning.

Mechanism	Objective		Example	Stakeholders	
Public policy	–	Establishing priorities	National Strategy for Circular Economy of Colombia Dutch strategy on Circular Agriculture	–	National public institutions such as Ministries
	–	Orienting strategies for implementation		–	Presidential office
	–	Reaching out to stakeholders			
Innovation in regulation	–	Adjustment of existing regulation	Extended producer responsibility Regulation for reuse of treated sewages Innovation of public service tariffs	–	Environmental authority
	–	Development of new regulation		–	Commerce authority
	–	Sectoral guides		–	Public service authority

Table 15.1 (continued)

Mechanism	Objective	Example	Stakeholders
Incentives	– Provide financial resources for circular economy innovation – Public disclosure of circular economy advances	Credits, equity investment blended finance Grands Certifications	– Development Banks – Banks – Municipalities – Chamber of commerce – Business association
Capacity building and research	– Strengthen capacity for circular business model – Information dissemination – Legitimacy of circular business models	Circular economy courses Executive programs for circular economy Research programs on circular economy	– Universities – Research centers – Consultancies – Technical education
Information system	– Information on resources flows for decision-making – Material Flow Analysis (MFA) – Life Cycle Analysis (LCA)	Circularity gap – report PACE Resource outlook Holland Circular Hotspot	– Research centers – Statistical institution – International cooperation – Universities
Consumer awareness	– Paradigmatic change towards circularity – Sustainable consumption	Publicity campaign Certification	– Certification organization – Authorities – Consumer organizations
International cooperation	– Alignment of global trends – Experience exchange – Visibility of CE – Blended finance	Latin American alliance for Circular Economy	– Ministries – Cooperation agencies – Development banks – International institutions

Transformative learning for CE in the business context considers "feedback loop Y" in Figure 15.1, on ongoing goal orientation. As the business context is dynamic, new mechanisms motivating circular economy implementations are launched continuously. Therefore, the constant interaction of the firm with the stakeholders-network of the business context includes public institutions, universities, business associations, and consultancy firms. New trends in circular economy implementations and innovations in the regulatory framework provide inputs for ongoing goal orientation.

4 Transformative Learning for CE in the Value Chains

Circular economy emphasizes a systematic approach for the transformation of production and consumption systems, also recognized as value chains (Rovanto & Bask, 2021). Value chains link resource flows with product life cycles, through supply chain relationships among a diverse group of companies and individual consumers. Value chains also connect diverse complementary business models, from a business that designs, and supplies raw materials, to business models aggregating value through transformation, distribution, and/or service supply (Bolwig et al., 2010). The summary of the connected business models facilitates the use of a product and service throughout its lifetime. Some value chains consist of several complementary business models, while others integrate business models, known as vertical integration.

Value chains may cover diverse geographical scales. Global value chains extract materials in one country and process and transform raw materials in other countries while consumption occurs in other places, and even waste disposable and or treatment may occur in separate places (Hofstetter et al., 2021). Global dispersion of the diverse business models along the same value chain exists due to advantages and asymmetries, in the availability of resources, both physical raw materials, energy, and social resources such as labor and knowledge, and economic resources of market demands. Examples of global markets shown in many consumer goods such as electronics or the automotive industry where extraction and preparation of raw materials, transformation, production of parts, assembly, distribution, use, and disposition occur in diverse countries around the world (Rentizelas & Trivyza, 2022). Often, food and construction-related value chains are more concentrated geographically, where resources travel less around the globe.

Sustainable value chains consider environmental and social impacts related to suppliers of raw materials, products, services, and consumers, and other stakeholders such as governments and non-governmental organizations (NGOs) (Seuring & Muller, 2008). Impacts involve both direct operation such as waste generation, fair wages, and labor conditions, or broader local societal issues depending on the specific geographic locations, such as availability of infrastructure, resource conservation, and access to public services and collaborative governance. As part of sustainable value chains, circularity economy implementation at the meso level considers reflection on dissemination of internal company operations among suppliers, interfirm collaborations and with stakeholders and implementation in areas outside the immediate stakeholders (Rovanto & Bask, 2021).

The value chain approach distinguishes diverse circularity innovation models among resource recovery, recycling, recourse reuse, prevention, and circular design (OECD, 2019). The models consider diverse loops of resource efficiency and effectivity considering thermodynamics hierarchy (Korhonen, Honkasalo, & Seppälä, 2018), based on principles of regeneration, resource lifetime, and entropy. Energy recovery is considered short-loop circularity, followed by material recycling, re-manufacturing, repair, re-use, share, and circular design recognized as middle – and long loop circularity (Reike, Vermeulen, & Witjes, 2018). The diverse circularity models, interconnect, and connect, to specific stages and business models in the value chain. Design solutions are concentered often in anchor companies leading power relations among suppliers with interconnected business models in the value chain. Efficiency improvements such as re-manufacturing, and recycling, apply to most of the business models along the chain, while re-use and sharing circularity models apply to the user's stage (Bocken et al., 2014).

Circular economy implementation requires innovations affecting the transformative learning of diverse actors in the value chain. Innovations imply changes for the diverse supply chain stakeholders, which need to be technically viable and socially acceptable (Boons, 2002). The technical viability of the innovation depends on a range of factors, such as the maturity of the technology, technical capacity for implementation, or adaptability, (Rogers, Singhal, & Quinlan, 2014). Moreover, innovation-related challenges related to social acceptance is part of a legitimacy process and power relations and trust among the diverse value chain stakeholders. Often innovative circular value chains require newly established collaborative activities among stakeholders, to replace existing relationships developed through linear value chains. Collaboration among stakeholders and new partners requires capacities for information sharing, negotiation of costs and benefits, and flexibility for adjustments and integration of values (Van Hoof & Thiell, 2014). For example, waste recovering models require information on the quality and volume of waste streams and recycled materials, adjustments of supply procedures, cost–benefits negotiations, and alignment of new supply relationships.

Boons (2002) proposed a framework based on the value chain perspective, for analyzing how circular economy-related strategies impact diverse interconnected business models. He explains, for example, how resource efficiency in one business model affects material supply in another business model. Replacement of materials even might eliminate business models as part of the value chain, while recycling and waste recovery might add new business models to the value chain.

Suppliers of virgin materials, in all circular innovation models, reduce sales and might diversify their portfolios of products, including recovered materials; they also might become co-workers in the recycling process based on their expertise. Producers are impacted at diverse scales, pending on the circularity models. Often the use of re-cycled materials requires minor innovations regarding process adjustments, while the re-use of resources often implies technological innovations. Other models such as lifetime extension, sharing models, and service products change the whole production structure.

Distributors are affected by the opportunity of diversification of services for waste recovery in the case of recycling and reuse innovations. Other circularity models such as lifetime extension, sharing models, and service products, and completely new distribution services are required. All circularity models require the collaborative action of consumers representing the product or service demand within the value chains. Involvement of consumers in recycling, reuse, lifetime extension, sharing models, and service products requires social legitimacy through market acceptance. Marketing campaigns and behavioral experiments are the main instruments for transformative learning.

Recyclers are integrated into the value chain, only in one of the circularity innovation models. Disposal services are supported to disappear as one of the basic principles of the circular economy.

Transformative learning for CE adoption in the value chains considers "feedback loop Z" in Figure 19.1, on adjusting social, technical, and value strategy including reflections on sustainable supply function, marketing function, knowledge management, and communication with stakeholders. Value chain partners are main sources for establishing collaborations for CE adoption. Moreover, circular innovations affect existing relationships in the value chain, and therefore planning circular economy strategies requires adjustment to social, technical, and value strategies.

5 Transformative Learning at the Organizational Level

Circular solutions require companies' and entrepreneurs' transformative learning for acquiring a strategic vision, as well as operational capacity to design and implement circular practices. The learning involves the integration of physical and social criteria into project and business model design: organizational learning is a complex and dynamic process introduction changes on diverse levels in an organization (Argyris & Schon, 1997; Senge et al., 1999). The first level involves the individual organization member acquiring new knowledge and capabilities about what and how to identify, design, and implement sustainability alternatives such as circular economy models. On a second level, individual transformation is transferred to organizational structure when sustainability criteria make part of management decision-making and resources assigned to develop and implement sustainability-related business alternatives, such as circular economy models. The third level of learning aims at organizations acting as multipliers of sustainability management among their suppliers, clients, and other stakeholders. In literature, these levels of learning are recognized as single, double, and triple-loop learning (Scipioni, Russ, & Niccolini, 2021; Van Hoof, 2014). Each level describes a gradual approach of complexity, understanding single-loop learning as less complex, and triple-loop learning as the most complex stage affecting multiple stakeholders.

Organizational learning for CE adoption consists of a dynamic and complex process (Scipioni, Russ, & Niccolini, 2021). In the first place the dimension of complexity of learning as such, interrelated with advances in complexity of prevention-oriented circular economy strategies, such as cleaner production, industrial symbiosis, and sustainable business model development.

I. **Cleaner production** is recognized as a short loop circularity strategy to optimize resource efficiency in production processes, through the implementation of best practices in the adjustment of operation procedures, implementation of efficient technological applications, and valorization and reduction of production waste (Reike et al., 2018). Resource efficiency is directly related to economic gains. Organizational learning in cleaner production includes capacity building for identifying resource spills and identification of innovative pollution prevention alternatives. Moreover, cleaner production implementation implies the integration of resource efficiency and cost reduction.

Most of the cleaner production applications consist of innovation for process optimizations that only affect internal decision-making within the organization. Therefore, organizational learning in cleaner production is the first step in acquiring capacities and vision, for short-loop CE adoption. Reflective learning involves overcoming inertia, acquiring new knowledge, and adopting the vision of continuous improvement.

II. **Industrial symbiosis** involves resource exchanges among diverse firms, to convert waste streams and residual heat and water, into raw materials for another production process. Symbiosis is considered a middle loop circularity as it involves partnerships and scaling of circularity models (Reike et al., 2018). Industrial symbiosis requires firms to understand their resource flows and the ones of the potential symbiosis partners. Moreover, it requires the capacity to negotiate agreements with often non-traditional partners. Innovation consists of new technology required for resource recovery and exchange. The vision of linking economic and sustainability value is deepened.

In comparison to cleaner production, the industrial symbiosis strategy represents a more complex organizational learning capacity. Aside from the development of internal decision-making and capacities, symbiosis requires collaboration capacity with other firms, the development of a shared vision, and the creation of new business models (Scipioni, Russ, & Niccolini, 2021). Industrial symbiosis initiatives also may involve shared infrastructure to reduce operational costs and resource inefficiencies. Industrial symbiosis initiatives often complement core business activities (Chertow & Park, 2016).

III. **Circular product design** represents the full integration of sustainability criteria and innovations as part of product development for long-loop circularity (Reike et al., 2018). Business value is generated in the long term by environmental and social contributions to stakeholders, and the generation of economic revenues. Circular product design determines the strategic value proposition and operation structure of the business and its market.

In comparison to cleaner production and industrial symbiosis strategy, circular product design represents a more complex organizational learning capacity for long-loop circularity. Innovation consists in designing completely new value chains for a new product or service conceptualization. Innovation affects the complete group of stakeholders including clients and suppliers. Sustainable business development requires full integration of sustainability as part of management decision-making and core business activity.

Cleaner production, industrial symbiosis, and circular product design are related to CE by optimizing resource efficiency (less waste; short-loop circularity) and effectivity (longer lifetime; long-loop circularity). These strategies are diverse, complementary, and gradual, resulting from organizational learning, cleaner production being the less complex strategy for internal optimization, while industrial symbiosis requires additional interactions and capacity developments for interaction with stakeholders. Circular product design represents the highest complexity grade in organizational learning, as it requires full integration of sustainability criteria in core business activities. Figure 15.2 represents the grades of diverse strategies and operations of CE.

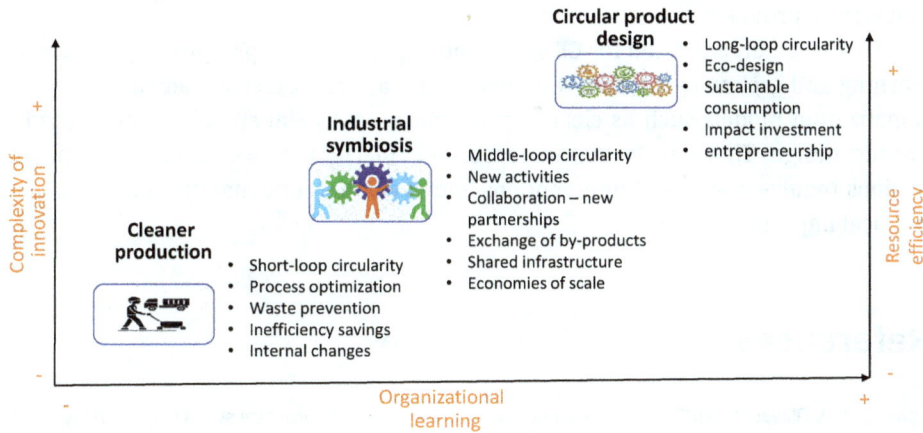

Figure 15.2: Strategies and operation of circular economy in firms.

Transformative learning for CE at the organizational level considers "feedback loop X" in Figure 19.1, on the operationalization of the circular practice. Capacity for organizational learning and technological innovation are the main resources, to advance circular economy implementation towards more complex transformation strategies. As an outcome, resource efficiency and effectivity improve scaling circular approaches such as cleaner production, toward symbiosis and circular product design.

6 Conclusions

Organizing for CE requires transformative learning on diverse levels of the business systems and considering periods. The mechanism for learning involves a constantly rotating plan–do–check–act wheel, as a constant process of self-assessment of the level of success of value creation through adjusted physical and social impact, both in the short term and the long term.

Feedback loops on the business context level consider permanent interaction with national and local CE networks, including public institutions such as environmental authorities, commerce- and industry-related authorities, universities, consultancies, international cooperation agencies, and business associations. This network provides mechanisms that orient goal setting and incentives for circular economy implementation, such as road maps, public policies, incentives, information systems, finance, and technical assistance.

As businesses are embedded in value chains, feedback loops for circular economy value strategy include resource recovery, recycling, recourse reuse, prevention, and circular design. The technical and social viability of these value strategies depends on value chain collaborations among suppliers, distribution channels, clients, consumers, and service providers.

Finally, an organization for CE shows the impact made in practice. Organizational learning and technological innovation are the main resources for advancing operationalization models such as cleaner production, industrial symbiosis, and circular product design. This way, feedback loops for circularity practice developed by organizations require analysis of interventions and evaluation of dynamics, and social and physical impacts.

References

Aguinis, H., & Glavas, A. (2012). What we know and don't know about corporate social responsibility: A review and research agenda. *Journal of Management, 38*(4), 932–968.

Argyris, C. (1996). Actionable knowledge: Design causality in the service of consequential theory. *The Journal of Applied Behavioral Science, 32*(4), 390–406.

Argyris, C., & Schön, D. A. (1997). Organizational learning: A theory of action perspective. *Reis: Revista Española de Investigaciones Sociológicas, 77/78*, (Jan.–Jun) 345–348.https://doi.org/10.2307/40183951

Baumgartner, R. J. (2014). Managing corporate sustainability and CSR: A conceptual framework combining values, strategies and instruments contributing to sustainable development. *Corporate Social Responsibility and Environmental Management, 21*(5), 258–271.

Birkin, F., Polesie, T., & Lewis, L. (2009). A new business model for sustainable development: An exploratory study using the theory of constraints in Nordic organizations. *Business Strategy and the Environment, 18*(5), 277–290.

Bocken, N. M., Short, S. W., Rana, P., & Evans, S. (2014). A literature and practice review to develop sustainable business model archetypes. *Journal of Cleaner Production, 65*, 42–56.

Bolwig, S., Ponte, S., Du Toit, A., Riisgaard, L., & Halberg, N. (2010). Integrating poverty and environmental concerns into value-chain analysis: A conceptual framework. *Development Policy Review, 28*(2), 173–194.

Boons, F. (2002). Green products: A framework for product chain management. *Journal of Cleaner Production, 10*, 495–505.

Boons, F., & Lüdeke-Freund, F. (2013). Business models for sustainable innovation: State-of-the-art and steps towards a research agenda. *Journal of Cleaner Production*, *45*, 9–19.

Chertow, M., & Park, J. (2016). Scholarship and practice in industrial symbiosis: 1989–2014. In R. Clift & A. Druckman (Eds.), *Taking Stock of Industrial Ecology* (pp. 87–116). Berlin: Springer.

Cyert, R., & March, J. G. (1963). *A Behavioral Theory of the Firm*. Englewood Cliffs, NJ: Prentice Hall.

Delmas, M. A. (2003). *In Search of ISO: An Institutional Perspective on the Adoption of International Management Standards*. Stanford University – Graduate School of Business. https://www.gsb.stan ford.edu/faculty-research/working-papers/search-iso-institutional-perspective-adoption-international

Ellen MacArthur Foundation (2015a). *Delivering the Circular Economy: A Toolkit for Policymakers*. Ellen MacArthur Foundation. https://ellenmacarthurfoundation.org/a-toolkit-for-policymakers

Ellen MacArthur Foundation (2015b). *Growth Within_ a Circular Economy Vision for a Competitive Europe*. Ellen MacArthur Foundation. https://emf.thirdlight.com/file/24/_A-BkCs_h7gRYB_Am9L_JfbYWF/Growth% 20within%3A%20a%20circular%20economy%20vision%20for%20a%20competitive%20Europe.pdf

Ellen McArtur Foundation (2015c). Towards a circular economy: business rationale for an accelerated transition, www.ellenmacarthurfoundation.org/publications

Ellen MacArthur Foundation (2023). *The Circular Economy: A Wealth of Flows: 2nd Edition*. London: Ellen MacArthur Foundation.

Epstein, M. J., & Widener, S. K. (2010). Identification and use of sustainability performance measures in decision-making. *Journal of Corporate Citizenship*, *40*, 43–73. https://doi.org/10.9774/GLEAF.4700.2010. wi.00006

Friant, M. C., Vermeulen, W. J., & Salomone, R. (2021). Analysing European Union circular economy policies: Words versus actions. *Sustainable Production and Consumption*, *27*, 337–353.

Gillespie, A. (2007). The social basis of self-reflection. In J. Valsiner (Ed.), *The Cambridge Handbook of Sociocultural Psychology* (pp. 678–691). UK: Cambridge University Press. https://doi.org/10.1017/ CBO9780511611162.037

Hickle, G. (2017). Extending the boundaries: An assessment of the integration of extended producer responsibility within corporate social responsibility. *Business Strategy and the Environment*, *26*(1), 112–124.

Hofstetter, J. S., De Marchi, V., Sarkis, J., Govindan, K., Klassen, R., Ometto, A. R., . . . Vazquez-Brust, D. (2021). From sustainable global value chains to circular economy – Different silos, different perspectives, but many opportunities to build bridges.. *Circular Economy and Sustainability*, *1*(1), 21–47.

International Social Science Council (ISSC) & United Nations Educational, Scientific and Cultural Organization (UNESCO) (2013). *World Social Science Report 2013*. OECD. https://doi.org/10.1787/ 9789264203419-en

Jänicke, M. (2002). *Capacity Building in National Environmental Policy; a Comparative Study of 17 Countries*. (Vol. 1) Berlin: Springer.

Kirchherr, J. (2018). Barriers to the circular economy: Evidence from the European Union (EU. *Ecological Economics*, *150*, 264–272. https://doi.org/10.1016/j.ecolecon.2018.04.028

Korhonen, J., Honkasalo, A., & Seppälä, J. (2018). Circular economy: The concept and its limitations. *Ecological Economics*, *143*, 37–46. https://doi.org/10.1016/j.ecolecon.2017.06.041

MacDonald, J. P. (2005). Strategic sustainable development using the ISO 14001 standard. *Journal of Cleaner Production*, *13*(6), 631–643.

McDowall, W., Geng, Y., Huang, B., Barteková, E., Bleischwitz, R., Türkeli, S., . . . & Doménech, T. (2017). Circular economy policies in China and Europe. Journal of Industrial Ecology, 21(3), 651–661.

Kirchherr, J. (2018). Barriers to the circular economy: Evidence from the European Union (EU. *Ecological Economics*, *150*, 264–272. https://doi.org/10.1016/j.ecolecon.2018.04.028

Organisation for Economic Co-operation and Development (OECD) (2019). *Business Models for the Circular Economy: Opportunities and Challenges for Policy*. Paris: OECD Publishing. https://doi.org/10.1787/ g2g9dd62-en

Organisation for Economic Co-operation and Development (OECD) (2020). *The Circular Economy in Cities and Regions: Synthesis Report, OECD Urban Studies*. Paris: OECD Publishing. https://doi.org/10.1787/10ac6ae4-en

Reike, D., Vermeulen, W. J., & Witjes, S. (2018). The circular economy: New or refurbished as CE 3.0? – Exploring controversies in the conceptualization of the circular economy through a focus on history and resource value retention options. *Resources, Conservation and Recycling, 135*, 246–264.

Rentizelas, A., & Trivyza, N. L. (2022). Enhancing circularity in the car sharing industry: Reverse supply chain network design optimisation for reusable car frames. *Sustainable Production and Consumption, 32*, 863–879. https://doi.org/10.1016/j.spc.2022.06.009

Rogers, E. M., Singhal, A., & Quinlan, M. M. (2014). Diffusion of innovations. In D. W. Stacks, M. B. Salwen & K. C. Eichhorn (Eds.), *An Integrated Approach to Communication Theory and Research* (3rd ed., pp. 432–448). Routledge. https://doi.org/10.4324/9780203710753

Rovanto, I. K., & Bask, A. (2021). Systemic circular business model application at the company, supply chain and society levels – A view into circular economy native and adopter companies. *Business Strategy and the Environment, 30*(2), 1153–1173.

Ruiz-Real, J. L., Uribe-Toril, J., De Pablo Valenciano, J., & Gázquez-Abad, J. C. (2018). Worldwide research on circular economy and environment: A bibliometric analysis. *International Journal of Environmental Research and Public Health, 15*(12), 2699.

Schroeder, P., Anggraeni, K., & Weber, U. (2019). The relevance of circular economy practices to the sustainable development goals. *Journal of Industrial Ecology, 23*(1), 77–95.

Scipioni, S., Russ, M., & Niccolini, F. (2021). From barriers to enablers: The role of organizational learning in transitioning SMEs into the circular economy. *Sustainability, 13*(3), 1021.

Senge, P., Kleiner, A., Roberts, C., Ross, R., Roth, G., & Smith, B. (1999). *The Dance of Change: The Challenges to Sustaining Momentum in Learning Organizations*. New York: Crown.

Seuring, S., & Müller, M. (2008). From a literature review to a conceptual framework for sustainable supply chain management. *Journal of Cleaner Production, 16*(15), 1699–1710.

Sewell Jr, W. H. (1992). A theory of structure: Duality, agency, and transformation. *American Journal of Sociology, 98*(1), 1–29.

Shove, E. (2010). Social Theory and climate change. *Theory, Culture & Society, 27*(2–3), 277–288. https://doi.org/10.1177/0263276410361498

Su, B., Heshmati, A., Geng, Y., & Yu, X. (2013). A review of the circular economy in china: Moving from rhetoric to implementation. *Journal of Cleaner Production, 42*, 215–227. https://doi.org/10.1016/j.jclepro.2012.11.020

United Nations Economic Commission for Latin America and the Caribbean (ECLAC) (2020). Natural resources in Latin America y de Caribbean, Economic Commission for Latin America and the Caribbean, Natural Resources Division, Bulletin 1 August, Santiago de Chile, retrieved on 30 July 2021, https://www.cepal.org/en/publications/type/natural-resources-latin-america-and-caribbean/1

Van Hoof, B. (2014). Organizational learning in cleaner production among Mexican supply networks. *Journal of Cleaner Production, 64*, 115–124.

Van Hoof, B., & Thiell, M. (2014). Collaboration capacity for sustainable supply chain management: Small and medium-sized enterprises in Mexico. *Journal of Cleaner Production, 67*, 239–248.

Vermeulen, W. J., & Witjes, S. (2016). On addressing the dual and embedded nature of business and the route towards corporate sustainability. *Journal of Cleaner Production, 112*, 2822–2832.

Witjes, S., & Lozano, R. (2016). Towards a more circular economy: Proposing a framework linking sustainable public procurement and sustainable business models. *Resources, Conservation and Recycling, 112*, 37–44.

Yin, H., & Schmeidler, P. J. (2009). Why do standardized ISO 14001 environmental management systems lead to heterogeneous environmental outcomes?. *Business Strategy and the Environment, 18*(7), 469–486.

Milou Derks, Rick Gilsing, Frank Berkers

16 Accelerating Transitions Through Business Model Thinking

Abstract: Sustainability transitions require deliberate collective action from multiple organisations, leading to the necessity to adopt new business models and re-design value networks. In both business model innovation and sustainability transition approaches the explicit activities needed to re-shape value creation and capture systems for organisations is largely unaddressed. Collaborative sustainable business modelling (CSBM) has been suggested in literature as a promising approach to fill this gap. We illustrate why CSBM can fill this gap and show how CSBM can support scaling, influence other value networks and create system change. However, existing CSBM approaches are not aimed at transitions and are unequipped to deal with transition dynamics. To fill this gap, we developed a CSBM for transitions approach, aimed at system change, enriched with four key aspects from transition studies. Through a case example we illustrate our approach, which consists of six phases. In all, we show that CSBM can be a fruitful approach to innovate and scale value networks and create the collective action needed for sustainability transitions.

Keywords: collaborative business modelling, sustainability transitions, value network, ecosystem, transition management

1 Introduction

A growing number of societal, ecological, economically complex and interdependent challenges, such as climate change and depletion of resources, require sustainability transitions to more sustainable forms of operation in numerous sectors. Businesses have an essential role to play in such sustainability transitions, since it is businesses that need to change their business model, reconfigure their supply chain, and corresponding value network to adopt and implement sustainability innovations (Sarasini & Linder, 2018; van Waes et al., 2018). Thus, to realise sustainability transitions, system-wide change requires change on the level of the value network, and the individual actor.

Note: This work is co-funded by the European Union (Ploutos - grant agreement No 101000594)

Milou Derks, Orange Corners, Prinses Beatrixlaan 2, 2595 AL, The Hague, The Netherlands
Rick Gilsing, TNO Vector, Anna van Buerenplein 1, 2595 DA, The Hague, The Netherlands
Frank Berkers, TNO Vector, Anna van Buerenplein 1, 2595 DA, The Hague, The Netherlands

https://doi.org/10.1515/9783110756159-020

On the level of the value network, transformation is required, since the implementation of sustainability innovations often requires collaboration among large groups of actors as well as interactions with new actors. Organisations cannot realise system change by themselves: collaboration and alignment are needed with other actors such as partnering businesses, non-governmental organisations (NGOs), financial institutions, research institutions, the government, and even customers or end-users. Only through a multi-actor reconsideration of the value network, understanding the needs and requirements of the individual actors of the network and how each actor should adapt its value creation logic, such systemic change can be fostered. Imagine, for example, the mattress system in the Netherlands. In the Netherlands in the region of 1.2 million old mattresses are discarded every year, and most of these are incinerated at relatively high cost. The pathway of mattress recycling is emerging, but requires the whole value network to transform. Mattresses need to be redesigned for efficient recycling, take-back infrastructure needs to be set up as well as a financing mechanism and favourable policy are necessary. This requires collaboration between mattress manufacturers, sales points, recyclers, local governments in charge of waste collection and willingness from end-consumers. The mattress case illustrates that a large number of partners is needed to develop an effective mattress recycle system (Aagaard, Lüdeke-Freund, & Wells, 2021).

On the individual actor level, transformation is required since the organisation needs to adapt its core activities in order to implement a sustainability innovation. Unfortunately, organisations are already facing a challenge besides the meta-level challenges of sustainability transitions: businesses in today's world have to deal with fast-changing markets and accelerated disruptions due to globalisation and digitalisation. Business model innovation can provide support in understanding, analysing and structuring the (renewal of) value creation and capture processes of organisations and help in aiding decision-making on how collaborations with other actors should be shaped. However, examining existing and often firm-centric business modelling as-usual approaches, we conclude that these are no longer appropriate to deal with the meta-level challenges of transitions, and the micro-level market disruptions stemming from globalisation and digitalisation, as has been highlighted by Derks, Berkers and Tukker (2022) and Gorissen, Vrancken and Manshoven (2016). Business modelling as-usual approaches tend to be organisation-centric, not taking into account required changes to other actors. Since effectively dealing with these meta and micro-level dynamics means that collaboration is required, transformation in the way the business is arranged and organised (i.e., the business model) is needed. A mode of business modelling that focuses on mobilising value networks, collaboration, inter-organisational value creation and reflexive capacity is thus required to coordinate business model adaptation for sustainability transitions.

Aagaard, Lüdeke-Freund and Wells (2021) and Gorissen, Vrancken and Manshoven (2016) identified collaborative sustainable business modelling (CSBM) as a potential powerful approach in integrating such a network-perspective to business modelling. CSBM is a structured and practical approach aimed at realising collaboration and multiple (e.g., financial, social, environmental) mutual value creation on a large scale. CSBM might therefore be a potentially powerful approach to accelerate sustainability transitions. CSBM entails a participatory process in which business models within the value network are adapted, leading to intertwined, aligned business models and long-term contracts for doing business within the value network (Rohrbeck, Konnertz, & Knab, 2013). CSBM is based on exploring and developing possibilities for cross-actor synergy through coordinated action. Its outcomes help in realising collaboration in mutually beneficial, aligned and intertwined business models, spanning the value network and connecting multiple actors from suppliers to customers. In turn, such business models have the potential to make systemic, sustainability-driven change.

Collaborative sustainable business models can be observed more and more in practice. Joint ventures emerge in which organisations work towards the development and deployment of innovative yet sustainable business solutions, often next to existing, ongoing business activities. In industrial settings, we see that collective facilities and services are established as a result of joint development based on shared actor needs. An example of this is the North Sea Energy programme, wherein 30 European parties are working together to develop collaborative business models to transform the North Sea into a pioneering region for the European energy transition. Such collaborative business models are needed since the transformation opportunities require extensive coordination to reconfigure existing value networks and sharing resources and finances. For example, the usage of gas and oil platforms to make green hydrogen and then transport it to shore requires coordination between the platform and pipeline exploiters, green hydrogen production companies, wind farm operators and onshore industry. Executing such opportunities will not only require change in the way each individual organisation does business, but also require costs and risks of usage of common infrastructure to be shared. It also calls for new ways of value creation and delivery that will require alignment of business models. The result of this will be profound changes in the way these actors have been doing business over the past decades.

CSBM is a relatively new field within business model literature. What the existing CSBM approaches, of relatively young maturity, have in common is the goal of building mutual beneficial value propositions while preventing contradictory incentives in the value network (Brehmer, Podoynitsyna, & Langerak, 2018; Mlecnik, Straub, & Haavik, 2019; Oukes, Berkers, & Langley, 2020). These approaches differ greatly in applicability and focus, offering only a general phase description of how CSBM takes place without explaining *how* each phase should be executed; tools or other practically applicable support is missing. Moreover, none of these approaches are aimed at realising sustainability transitions. Therefore, we have developed an approach to enhance the development and marketisation of sustainability initiatives through collaborative sustainable business models by combining insights from existing CSBM approaches with theory on transition management, into an actionable and practical approach. Enriching CSBM approaches with transition management can enable the application of

CSBM for transitions and give guidance to entrepreneurs wanting to contribute to sustainability transitions through their initiatives.

The chapter is organised as follows. The second section elaborates on why value networks can lead to sustainability transitions, justifying how CSBM – which influences the value network – can contribute to accelerating transitions. The third section identifies key concepts from transitions studies that are needed to realise system change through CSBM. The fourth section discusses the developed CSBM approach aimed at accelerating transitions, as well as its practical application to a case.

2 Sustainability Transitions as Ecosystem Changes

A business model describes how value is created and captured, whereas business modelling describes the process to develop a business model. Although conventional business model theory takes a rather organisation-centric perspective, interactions and transactions between different actors in the supply chain regularly take place to create value for end-users/customers. The value network illustrates the *links* between actors and shows tangible and intangible value transactions (e.g., the money flows, contractual information or other types of exchanges). It shows how companies and organisations are involved in the value-creation process. The business ecosystem naturally evolves from the value network and takes a more holistic approach including all relevant stakeholders, such as governmental actors, non-governmental actors, regulators and competitors, and often comprises several, potentially competing, value networks. Business modelling literature in principle considers the individual organisation, value network and business ecosystem as cascading systems of organisations, in which the organisation remains an integral and addressable.

Sustainability transitions focus on changing subsystems for the benefit of society (Kemp, Loorbach, & Rotmans, 2007). As such, in many sustainability transitions, organisations play an important role by changing their business models in order to change the subsystem: they need to adopt new practices and standards, implement new technologies, use different resources, change behaviours, meet new requirements and comply with new regulations, which almost always requires a change in their business model and their interaction with the value network. Although transition studies do not refer directly to the concept of (individual) organisations, it is clear that it is intended to promote change by guiding organisations to organise in a new way (Sarasini & Linder, 2018). These changing subsystems of organisations in sustainable transitions can thus be viewed as changing ecosystems, comprising all actors in landscape, regime and niche.

The value network is the critical level at which innovation in and between organisations can be shaped, and at which individual organisations can *influence* the wider system. The value network forms the bridge between the individual actor and the wider ecosystem. Scaling of such value networks, that is, aiming to replicate or expand the value network's value creation, can influence other value networks and eventually the whole ecosystem, for example, by means of standards, diffusion of technology, non-competitive collaborations and provisions, and thus bring about substantial change. Consequently, an ecosystem change can be induced by scaling value networks.

In order to deliberately change value networks, it is important to understand the processes through which these different system levels can be influenced. Organisations change through strategy-making processes and individual business model innovation (Latilla et al., 2020). Value networks change towards sustainability through individual and collaborative sustainable business modelling. Since CSBM focuses on redesigning value networks collaboratively it can thus be considered an actionable approach for shaping or accelerating sustainability transitions. Such value network approaches become especially useful when considering innovation for sustainability (Evans et al., 2017).

3 Integrating Key Transition Aspects in Collaborative Sustainable Business Modelling

Solely changing the value network through CSBM may not be sufficient to create change in the wider ecosystem. The business models in the value network may not always be scalable or there may be differences in terms of scaling potential between value network actors. For example, for some actors in the value network, business model scaling may entail a need to accommodate a minor increase production capacity, whereas for other actors it may call for significant investments into new equipment or factories. This may have significant implications for whom in the value network bears the investments and what this implies for how value is captured in the network. As a result, the financeability of the value network as well as scaling of the value network is a key concern to take into account. Furthermore, to achieve the targeted sustainability impact the cause–effect logic needs to be clear. Innovations often have unintended spill-over effects, challenging their sustainability potential. The impact logic should thus be clear to all parties involved. Additionally, most sustainability innovations aim to substitute existing fossil-fuel based structures, thereby replacing part of the business-as-usual for a more sustainable alternative. The incumbent regime will not always be enthusiastic towards innovations that might prove a risk to their business in the long run.

There are ways to increase the scalability potential of your value network. First, some collaborative sustainable business models may be highly disruptive in nature and break through the incumbent regime directly. In some cases, dominant regime actors are actively involved in a new collaborative sustainable business model, which requires this actor to deal with different value creation logics simultaneously. A CSBM for transitions approach can then assist in aligning the business models of other actors to fit within the new system surrounding the innovation. Second, some collaborative sustainable business models may not be as disruptive or may not be scaled sufficiently at first to challenge the regime directly. Increased adoption could be achieved by co-innovation of the business model, to adopt new practices or standards, implementing new technologies, using different resources and changing behaviours. If the collaborative sustainable business model specifies how new actors will benefit, then this can increase the adoption speed of other actors and help in reaching the scale needed for the innovation to make real impact (Bidmon & Knab, 2018). Other value networks that are not attracted immediately may be convinced by a clearly articulated value creation and capture logic.

Thus, a CSBM for transitions approach can support the pathways illustrated above, if the four themes identified above from transition studies as (i) impact logic, (ii) regime, (iii) scaling and (iv) financeability. The remainder of this section will discuss each of these four themes in more detail.

3.1 Impact Logic

Impact logic refers to the line of reasoning through which a collective of organisations or business initiatives expects to achieve its impact goals. These goals should be clearly defined such that one can measure or monitor when an initiative is successful. Additionally, monitoring of impact goals serves as the basis for communication, transparency and commitment among relevant actors. However, we often see that initiatives do not assess how impact goals should be achieved, how outputs lead to various desirable and undesirable outcomes and how those outcomes eventually lead to impact. Without a clear plan of action, initiatives may fail to reach the intended impact, as implicit assumptions were not validated, risks were overlooked or the cause–effect logic followed was not cohesive or comprehensive.

To foster continued involvement of different actors, it is important to also consider how achieving impact can be beneficial for each actor participating in the CSBM, and whether the overall impact goals align with or can exist next to individual businesses' goals. For example, it could happen that all actors participating in the CSBM are satisfied when their individual economic goals are achieved, but that these individual economic goals are actually at the expense of the overall environmental goals set for the initiative. Similarly, achieving overall social impact goals can put significant pressure on individual actors to achieve their economic goals, making it difficult for such individual actors to continue their participation. Therefore, impact logic calls for an explicit consideration of what impact is strived for, how and when this is achieved, and why this is relevant for the actors in the CSBM. Impact logic is sometimes also referred to as 'theory of change'.

3.2 Regime

Transformation of the regime refers to breaking down or shifting the dominant socio-technical, institutional and legal mode of thinking towards a more sustainable alternative. In general, a CSBM is driven by a form of innovation that emerges because of opportunities or challenges posed by the current business-as-usual, but as a result also challenges the business as usual. When transitioning to a new status quo, innovations increasingly replace existing solutions and form a new, novel regime.

For example, traditional central heating of households in the Netherlands is done via gas boilers, which are effective to control the temperature within a house but generate significant amounts of CO_2 in the process. Driven by the pursuit for green heating solutions and the emergence of new technologies such as heat pumps, we observe that the current regime is increasingly acknowledging the value of heat pumps and moving towards the adoption of heat pumps as the new business-as-usual for providing heating. This adoption represents a gradual process in which actors shift their current way of thinking and standardised practices (installing households with gas boilers versus ensuring insulated households equipped with heat pumps) to accommodate this phasing out and phasing in.

Such adoption can only be facilitated if one truly understands what the current regime is, that is, what are the current policies, perceptions, standards and norms that exist for the regime, and in what way does the proposed solution central to the CSBM go against these norms or standards? To generate impact through sustainability initiatives, such norms and standards have to be altered to generate sustainable impact. Accordingly, this calls for adoption of the sustainability innovation among actors in the regime, and the subsequent diffusion of the innovation over the regime to become the new dominant mode of thinking.

3.3 Scaling

Scalability refers to the capability of a CSBM to enhance, extend or increase the efforts conducted to increase the expected impact that is generated. Substantial scale is often key to achieving large-scale impact: projects generally start on a small scale or in pilot environments, allowing actors to maintain more control and allowing activities, technologies and practices to mature. Consequently, when the technologies or solutions have demonstrated their prowess, they can be scaled further. Since CSBMs built upon the contributions of, and exchanges between individual actors, who create significant dependencies, it is key to understand how scalability may impact the business network. Accordingly, if one has the intention to scale, one has to carefully understand what this means for the other actors involved, and what this means for their current way of working.

For example, scaling an energy trading platform requires the infrastructure on which the platform is constructed to be capable of supporting this. As a result, the decision to scale the platform has substantial ramifications for both the actors responsible for maintaining and developing the platform, as well as those on whom the infrastructure providers may rely. In addition, would scaling be beneficial to each actor (s)? Is their existing business strategy even suitable for scaling? Would these actors be able to capture value as a result of the scaling ambitions, or would the proposed scaling ambition create issues in capturing value? Before any scaling ambition can be made apparent, such reasons, dependencies and obstacles for the business network should be clarified. Failure to do so may place a major burden on the business network or individual actors in the network, resulting in resources being committed to scaling goals that are ultimately unfeasible.

3.4 Financeability

Financeability addresses the financial structure and related investments needed to support the execution of the intervention or solution. For CSBMs, this financial structure is generally more complex than for traditional, organisation-centric business models. Since compared to traditional business models (for which the responsibility lies with a single organisation), CSBMs depend on the investments and contributions of multiple stakeholders. CSBMs might require significant investments at their start to deploy and adopt an intervention. To be able to understand, monitor and control this need for investment, the investment landscape should be made explicit. Additionally, explicating the investment landscape can help in understanding what sources of finance, in general, are available, what concrete stakeholders can be leveraged to support the CSBM and what potential lock-ins exist (as stakeholders may partake in different or even conflicting projects or services) regarding these sources of finance.

Without a consideration of the investment landscape as well as how this affects actors within the CSBM, the risk of not possessing the necessary amount of equity to support the CSBM emerges. As a consequence, the CSBM may grind to a halt or be significantly delayed, and the proposed impact is not reached. This in turn would affect involved actors, creating conflict or decreased commitment within the business network. Furthermore, because of the novelty of value network oriented financial arrangements, financiers should be involved at an early stage and their propositions need to be aligned.

4 A Practical Approach for Collaborative Sustainable Business Modelling

The practical approach we have developed to support businesses and entrepreneurs willing to contribute to sustainability transitions through collaborative sustainable business modelling consists of six iterative phases. It is intended to support entrepreneurs in project consortia or collaborations that aim to achieve long-term impact through the realisation of sustainability innovations. Each phase is accommodated through tools that can be used to support their execution and builds upon the themes (i.e., *impact logic, regime, scalability, financeability*) relevant to transition management. The following phases are addressed:
- Phase 1: Scoping of the sustainability innovation
- Phase 2: Exploration and analysis of current and future business ecosystems
- Phase 3: Understanding the value creation process for the sustainability innovation
- Phase 4: Design of collaborative sustainable business model(s) supporting the innovation
- Phase 5: Evaluation and adaption of the collaborative sustainable business model
- Phase 6: Implementation, monitoring and scaling of the collaborative sustainable business model

In the following, we describe how the approach can be used to support the development of collaborative sustainable business models, elaborating on what each phase for the approach entails and what tools can be used to support each phase. To illustrate the applicability of the approach, we elaborate on how the approach has been applied to support collaborative sustainable business models for a case study drawn from the agricultural domain and what findings were obtained. In this case study, a European pilot consortium focused on introducing a platform-based service to support carbon sequestration by farmers in order to contribute towards more sustainable farming practices. The pilot consortium was led by a large farmers' association in the Netherlands, intending to provide this platform-based service to farmers in the Netherlands. To support the development, roll-out and adoption of the proposed service, relevant stakeholders such as an organic wholesaler, technology provider and knowledge providers/data analysts were involved. The goal was to understand and investigate under what conditions the service contributes towards long-term sustainable impact. Additionally, the consortium sought after solutions in terms of collaborative sustainable business models to support the adoption of the service. To this end, the collaborative sustainable business modelling approach was used.

4.1 Inclusion of Transition Aspects into the CSBM Approach

To adapt existing CSBM approaches to better suit the need to realise sustainability transitions, four key aspects from transition studies were identified: (i) impact logic: the importance of understanding how novel business models supporting sustainability innovations contribute to long-term impact and what scale of proliferation is needed to do so; (ii) regime: need for an explicit consideration of the ecosystem in which novel business models are to be positioned, and how as a result sustainability innovations depend on but also may impact ecosystem stakeholders; (iii) scalability: the scaling potential of each actor and the interdependence between actors regarding scaling; and (iv) financeability: the need for investigating the investment structure as well as the distribution of costs among value chain stakeholders to foster the development, roll-out and continued support for sustainability innovations.

In the following, we propose and demonstrate a practical approach to support collaborative sustainable business modelling, extending conventional CSBM approaches through integrating these transition studies' aspects.

Phase 1: Scoping of the Sustainability Innovation

The first phase of the approach concerns the *scoping of the sustainability innovation*. In this phase consortium stakeholders collaboratively discuss *what* the sustainability innovation entails and *why* it is relevant in the context of establishing *impact*. This phase focuses on fostering alignment between consortium stakeholders on how each stakeholder *perceives* the sustainability innovation and what each stakeholder intends to achieve by means of its deployment. The goal is to work towards and explicate shared ambitions on how the sustainability innovation will be deployed and what impact should be achieved through its deployment. Consortium stakeholders can have diverse motivations and drivers to participate in projects or pilot settings as well as different levels of engagement. It is important that commonalities among drivers are explored to stimulate long-term commitment of consortium stakeholders to participate. Any barriers or potential conflicts of interest should be addressed early on such that a stable collaboration climate can be facilitated.

To support the scoping phase, tools such as the ambition tool (Jacobs, Ubels, & Woltering, 2018) or methods such as Delphi or brainstorming techniques (Putman & Paulus, 2009) can be used. Use of the ambition tool forces stakeholders to list and rank a limited set of ambitions. These ambitions are collected and discussed jointly until a shared overarching ambition is agreed upon. Similarly, brainstorming can contribute to creative thinking and help in supporting the selection of a shared ambition to pursue. Additionally, it can aid thinking about solutions to barriers or challenges that emerge as part of this phase, which should be resolved before consortium stakeholders proceed with (investments for) the development of the sustainability innovation.

The scoping phase helped consortium stakeholders for the agricultural case study to explicate the drivers among project stakeholders and to find commonalities or shared ambitions. Additionally, it helped in ideating an initial plan in regards to how the platform-based service would be marketised. Through this exercise, stakeholders identified a shared ambition in terms of creating sustainable impact: both the farmers' association and organic wholesaler involved considered the solution as a means to contribute towards sustainability, either through helping farmers become sustainable or to reward farmers for sustainable business practices respectively. Next to this, the organic wholesaler would also be able to communicate a sustainable carbon-neutral story for its vegetables and fruits sold through deployment of the service if its own farmers used the platform-based service. For the technology provider involved, sustainability was also considered as an important driver; however, it was also indicated that this should be coupled to (financial) return on investments in regards to the development and deployment of sensors needed to support the service. A similar case was found for the knowledge provider/data analyst involved for the project consortium. Accordingly, the goal for the consortium was to find a collaborative structure in which the sustainable effects generated at the farmers could be coupled to financial returns to be distributed over the stakeholder network to take away any barriers related to lack of financial returns. To this end, opportunities to earn carbon credits through use of the service and to use the revenues generated through these credits to support financing of the business network was explored in more detail.

Phase 2: Exploration and Analysis of the Current Business Ecosystem

In the exploration and analysis phase of the approach, consortium stakeholders investigate how the sustainability innovation will impact incumbent stakeholders for the ecosystem in which the innovation is to be positioned, as well as their perceptions, drivers and attitudes towards the innovation. In addition, it also calls for understanding how the sustainability innovation is dependent on ecosystem stakeholders, for example in terms of legislation or as part of supply chain actions. This phase involves a mapping of the current status quo or regime for the ecosystem (Geels, 2002) and reflecting on how the regime is impacted as a result of the introduction of the proposed innovation. Such an investigation can help in unveiling barriers and challenges that may be posed by stakeholders towards the implementation and roll-out of the proposed solution, which should be addressed or mitigated to foster the impact that can be achieved by means of the innovation.

The exploration and analysis phase can be supported through tools such as (ecosystem-based) stakeholder analysis as well as ecosystem mapping. Stakeholder analysis can aid in gaining insights on the stakeholders' drivers, relationships and interactions and can support the understanding of *what motivates or drives* stakeholders (Gupta, 1995; Solaimani, Guldemond, & Bouwman, 2013). On the basis of this, potential challenges as well as their severity (in terms of the power of stakeholders for the regime) can be identified and can help in drafting mitigation plans or in further concretising the proposed innovation. Alternatively, ecosystem mapping or value network analysis can help in understanding what stakeholders exist for the ecosystem and what exchanges or interactions occur between stakeholders (Allee, 2008; Brehmer, Podoynitsyna, & Langerak, 2018). This can contribute to a better understanding of how the sustainability innovation may benefit, affect or even damage current value exchanges and what challenges or barriers as a result can be highlighted.

The exploration phase helped consortium stakeholders in the agricultural case study to identify important challenges towards the marketisation of the platform-based service. For example, the legality of carbon credits was indicated as an important challenge, as current legislation on carbon credits is still in development and that transparency on carbon credits is imperative. Although earning carbon credits was considered as an important incentive for both farmers and other stakeholders in the network, it emphasised that certification organisations would need to be involved, whereas lobbying should take place with national governments to support this aspect of the solution. The latter could also help in further supporting the financial feasibility of the proposed service through subsidisations.

Phase 3: Understanding the Value-Creation Process for the Sustainability Innovation

The next phase in this approach entails understanding the value-creation process for the sustainability innovation. In this phase, consortium stakeholders should investigate how end-users or customers create value through the proposed innovation and understand the value-creation process for the sustainability innovation. Questions should be posed regarding the changes imposed or introduced for end-users in order to use the sustainability innovation and what effect this may have on the value that is ultimately created for the end-user. This also should provide insights on what barriers towards adoption may still be present and how these can be resolved. Additionally, stakeholders should examine whether the value created aligns with the impact ambitions set for the sustainability innovation (whether using the innovation contributes to achieving this intended impact).

Customer journey mapping (Norton & Pine, 2013) can be used in this phase to help in visualising or describing the steps to be taken to *use* an innovation (as a solution). It presents a structured approach to map the steps an end-user or customer takes to create value as well as clarifies what value is created or destroyed as a result of this. This can be extended to also reflect on the roles or contributions of other stakeholders to support each step taken. This analysis can be complemented with user stories and scenarios to obtain an even deeper understanding of what value is created by means of the sustainability innovation. Alternatively, business process modelling tools such as Business Process Model and Notation (BPMN) or Event-driven

Process Chain (EPC) diagrams can help in understanding and mapping how activities for the value-creation process add value and what resources of stakeholders are needed to support this (Hotie & Gordijn, 2019).

Consortium stakeholders for the agricultural case study used customer journey mapping to better understand how farmers would use the platform-based solution and what values were generated as a result of this. This mapping is illustrated in Figure 16.1, colour coding the activities undertaken by various stakeholders as well as the activities introduced for farmers. The analysis made explicit that, even though farmers can use the platform-based service to (expectedly) improve the efficiency and effectiveness of farmland activities and can access carbon credits through use of the service, they are required to invest time in terms of data collection, are required to share this data, make efforts to integrate the advice for farming practices and invest and pay fees to make use of the service. Particularly the investments needed for the service were considered as a barrier to adoption in the face of uncertain expected benefits. To mitigate this, a solution was ideated to share the risk between the farmer and wholesaler, as the wholesaler is able to benefit through the sustainable efforts of the farmer (through being able to make carbon-neutral product claims). This solution entailed that the wholesaler would guarantee to purchase all carbon credits earned at a premium price to help farmers achieve quicker paybacks to account for the service investments to be made.

Phase 4: Design of Collaborative Sustainable Business Model(s)

In the next phase, the insights generated through the first phases serve as the input for the design of collaborative sustainable business model alternatives. In this phase, consortium stakeholders capture the business structure and value creation and capture logic needed to support the marketisation of the proposed sustainability innovation by means of collaborative sustainable business model design. Here, the value capture logic should ensure that mutual benefits are created for consortium stakeholders involved (Rohrbeck, Konnertz, & Knab, 2013). In addition to defining the business model structure (static), consortium stakeholders should also define the pathway to scaling, that is, how the business model is expected to evolve or be scaled over time (dynamic) and how this links to the goals set in terms of the impact that were set previously.

To support the design of collaborative sustainable business models, the Service-Dominant Business Model Radar (SDBM/R) can be used (Turetken et al., 2019). The SDBM/R offers a networked perspective on business models, emphasising the notion of value co-creation and mutual value creation. Given its networked perspective (as opposed to organisation-centric business model design tools such as the business model canvas) it enables stakeholders to map how value exchange between stakeholders takes place and visualise interactions needed. As the direct stakeholders are mapped for the business model design, it also becomes apparent how costs and

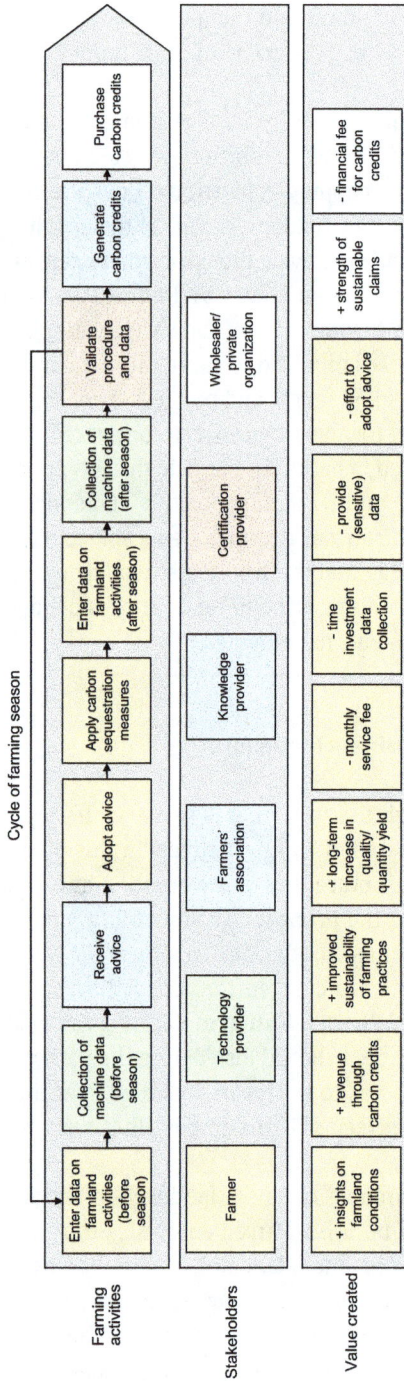

Figure 16.1: Case study: application of customer journey mapping to investigate the value creation process.

benefits are distributed: in case a stakeholder receives no benefits or incurs an excessive amount of costs, this could be a sign that mutual value creation is not achieved.

To support the analysis of the impact logic, programme theory (Funnell & Rogers, 2011) or benefits realisation mapping (Peppard, Ward, & Daniel, 2007) can be used. Both methods aim to clarify the 'fuzzy' process towards impact, starting from the deliverables (i.e., the sustainability innovation) towards outcomes on scale that link explicitly to the impact goals set, mapping the activities or business changes needed to facilitate this pathway towards impact. Use of this method can help in unveiling what assumptions or challenges underlie the business model design or selected scaling strategies.

Based on the collaboration form ideated in the previous phase, consortium stakeholders for the agricultural case study worked on the design of a collaborative sustainable business model (using the SDBM/R) in this phase. In this business model design, the farmers' association was considered as the orchestrator of the business model design, bringing together parties such as certification providers, data analysts and technology providers to provide on the one hand a platform-based service to farmers of the wholesaler involved and to ensure that the carbon credits generated through the service are bought by the wholesaler to compensate the farmer for its sustainable effort. To understand the operational nature of the business model design, the pathway to impact was mapped using benefits realisation mapping (Figure 16.2). Through this mapping, consortium stakeholders identified critical assumptions related to the roll-out of the business model design. For example, even though the farmer is rewarded through carbon credit sales (and therefore can over time compensate its investments) the initial investment costs still remain at the farmer. This can be a significant barrier for farmers to enter into the service or may discourage farmers who are not intrinsically motivated to adopt sustainable business practices. To scale the business model design further in terms of farmers involved, forms of financing (subsidisation, investors) should be incorporated as part of the business model to support this. Additionally, the amount of carbon credits that can be sold is limited to the amount of CO_2 reduction wholesalers need to justify carbon-neutral statements for its products sold. Although guarantees are offered to purchase a certain amount of carbon credits at a premium price, multiple wholesalers should be involved to increase the demand for carbon credits as the number of farmers using the service increases. This requires the farmers' association (orchestrator of the business model design) to scale its business activities and attract additional wholesalers or to collaborate with other (potentially competing) carbon sequestration service providers to gain access to additional wholesalers.

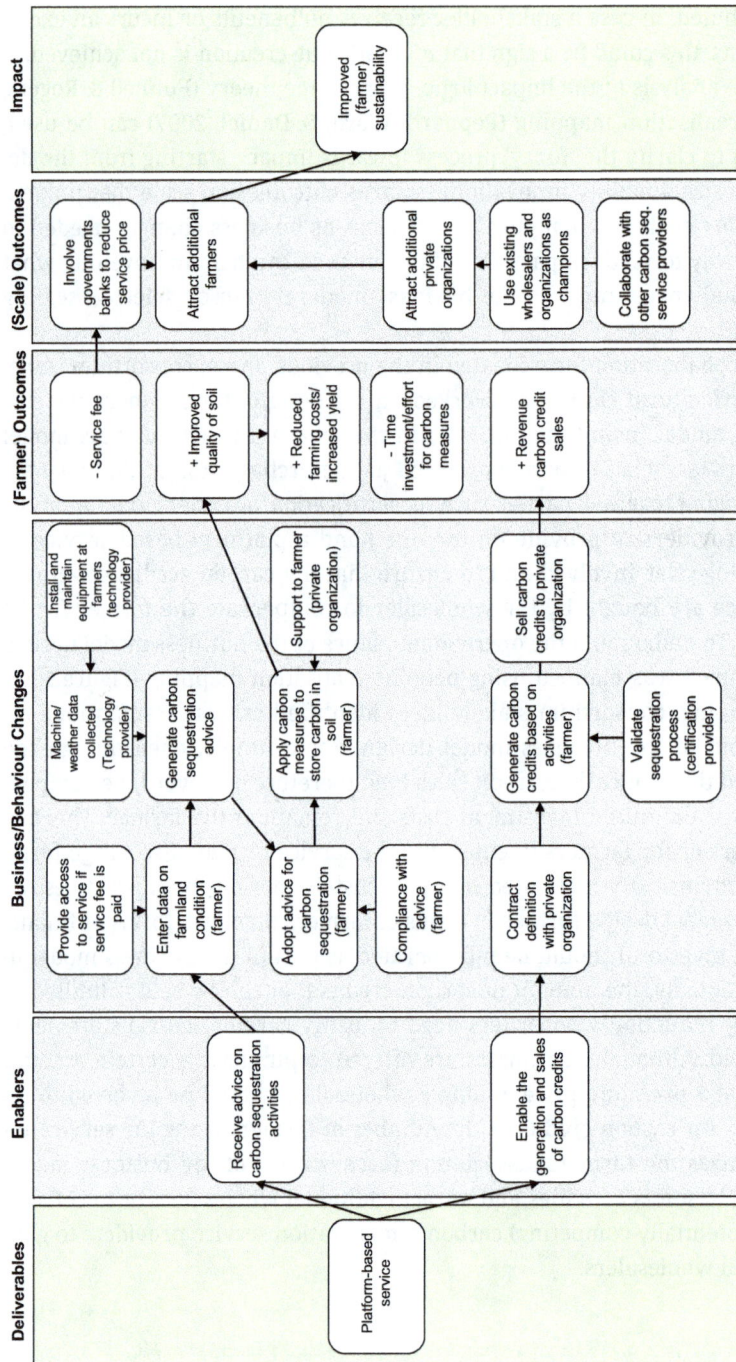

Figure 16.2: Case study: application of benefits realisation mapping to explicate the pathway to impact.

Phase 5: Evaluation, Adaptation and Selection of the Collaborative Sustainable Business Model

Before the sustainability innovation is implemented and marketised, formal evaluation of the collaborative sustainable business model design should take place. In this phase, the goal is to generate commitment of consortium stakeholders to dedicate resources towards the implementation and roll-out of the sustainability innovation. This calls for collaborative decision-making on whether the business model design should be pursued and should yield a *perceived* (i.e., in the eye of the beholder, depending on the strategy of each stakeholder involved) positive scenario for all stakeholders involved.

This phase can be supported through qualitative and quantitative means. For example, guiding questions or scorecards can be used to score business models on performance aspects (such as viability, feasibility, robustness or desirability) and make explicit on what the strengths and weaknesses of the business model design are (Gilsing et al., 2021). It can also drive the selection between business model alternatives. Similarly, techniques such as scenario analysis or stress testing can help in motiving the selection for a specific business model design, challenging assumptions towards long-term impact or the degree to which the collaborative sustainable business model can respond to internal and external changes (Bouwman et al., 2018; Tesch, 2016).

Additionally, quantitative evaluation support such as (sustainable) business casing can help in clarifying the financeability of the business model design and help in explicating how each consortium stakeholder is able to benefit through participation (Whelan & Fink, 2016).

The stakeholders in the agricultural case study used this phase to create commitment among the consortium to drive the roll-out of the business model design and to commit resources to its implementation. Both quantitative as well as qualitative means were used to support this phase. On the one hand, trial tests at farmers helped in validating the effectiveness of the platform-based service and testing whether the carbon models used to support the service were correct. On the basis of these efforts, initial carbon credits could be attributed to farmers, which consequently resulted in initial sales of these carbon credits to the wholesaler involved.

In addition to testing, the consortium stakeholders also used performance criteria to formally evaluate the business model design. As a result, some important considerations were identified. Even though these considerations did not prove to be show-stoppers, they did help in further clarifying assumptions made for the business model design. For example, farmers would require an intrinsic motivation to become sustainable in order to adopt the service. While in the context of the wholesaler this was not deemed problematic (as these farmers already focused significantly on becoming sustainable), this may pose an issue for attracting new farmers to participate. Additionally, carbon credit generation is a relative long-term process: it takes time for carbon to be stored for the soil. This means that farmers need to have a long-term commitment in order for the benefits to be reaped. Lastly, once farmers become increasingly sustainable, the expected benefits (through carbon credits sold) are expected to decrease (as less carbon credits over time are generated). This links to the need for (bolstering the) intrinsic motivation of farmers to participate.

In terms of feasibility, some legal barriers were identified. The definition of carbon credits on a European level is still fuzzy – it is not yet clear how long carbon should be stored for the soil to be considered as sustainable efforts (and thus equate to carbon credits earned). This could potentially impact the extent to which sustainable claims can be made based on carbon credits earned, as well as the price of carbon credits. In addition to legal barriers, it is technically also difficult to quantify the effect of carbon sequestration activities. Here, the consortium identified that there is need to visualise what sustainable activities have been conducted as part of the platform-based service; this can contribute to the sustainable claims made by private organisations and help in engaging governmental bodies for further funding.

Phase 6: Implementation, Monitoring and Scaling of the Collaborative Sustainable Business Model

Once commitment for the collaborative sustainable business model is achieved, roll-out and implementation can commence, marketising the solution. In this phase, consortium stakeholders focus on defining and executing implementation plans to support the roll-out of the collaborative sustainable business model. In this phase, tools such as road mapping (Phaal, Farrukh, & Probert, 2015) can help in structuring the implementation process and setting milestones for important business model deliverables. Depending on the performance of a collaborative sustainable business model in practice, consortium stakeholders should also consider to iteratively scale the business model in line with the impact objectives set.

In this phase, consortium stakeholders in the agricultural case study monitored the performance of the platform-based service in practice. In addition, the farmers' association (acting as the orchestrator of the business model design) sought after scaling opportunities to expand the current user base for the platform-based service. Through its own network, additional farmers were incorporated for use of the service. In parallel, the famers' association instigated collaborations with construction projects (such as the construction of energy windmills) that aimed to reduce their CO_2 footprint. Through this collaboration, such projects are to buy carbon credits through the platform-based service such that newly included farmers can be (financially) rewarded for their sustainable efforts. This helped in motivating more farmers to participate for the platform-based service.

5 Conclusions

The results of the application of our approach make explicit that, to support or accelerate sustainability transitions, it is not enough for entrepreneurs to solely consider how existing value networks should be adapted or changed to support the implementation and marketisation of new innovations: transitions require a holistic perspective on CSBM, considering the key transition concepts *impact logic, regime, financeability,* and *scaling.* For example, the case study illustrated that analysis of the impact logic and financeability of the proposed solution helped in supporting its adoption: identifying that farmers are required to make significant investments to adopt the solution and as a result may bear significant risks (as the potential outcomes can be uncertain), the consortium ideated by means of CSBM mechanisms to mitigate these risks. Additionally, analysis of the regime helped in identifying key stakeholders (such as certifiers) needed to achieve impact and helped in identifying how current laws and regulations in place could potentially challenge the intended impact of the solution, enabling consortium stakeholders to proactively seek collaborative solutions to address these concerns. Therefore, we advocate that the complementary use of CSBM and the key concepts for transition studies can help entrepreneurs to accelerate sustainability transitions.

References

Aagaard, A., Lüdeke-Freund, F., & Wells, P. (2021). *Business Models for Sustainability Transitions.* London: Palgrave Macmillan.

Allee, V. (2008). Value network analysis and value conversion of tangible and intangible assets. *Journal of Intellectual Capital, 9*(1), 5–24.

Bidmon, C. M., & Knab, S. F. (2018). The three roles of business models in societal transitions: New linkages between business model and transition research. *Journal of Cleaner Production, 178,* 903–916.

Bouwman, H., Heikkila, J., Heikkila, M., Leopold, C., & Haaker, T. (2018). Achieving agility using business model stress testing. *Electronic Markets, 28*(2), 149–162.

Brehmer, M., Podoynitsyna, K., & Langerak, F. (2018). Sustainable business models as boundary-spanning systems of value transfers. *Journal of Cleaner Production, 172*(20), 4514–4531. https://doi.org/10.1016/j.jclepro.2017.11.083

Derks, M., Berkers, F., & Tukker, A. (2022). Toward accelerating sustainability transitions through collaborative sustainable business modeling: A conceptual approach. *Sustainability, 14,* 7.

Evans, S., Vladimirova, D., Holgado, M., Van Fossen, K., Yang, M., Silva, E. A., & Barlow, C. Y. (2017). Business model innovation for sustainability: Towards a unified perspective for creation of sustainable business models. *Business Strategy and the Environment, 26*(5), 597–608.

Funnell, S., & Rogers, P. (2011). *Purposeful Program Theory: Effective Use of Theories of Change and Logic Models.* New York: John Wiley & Sons.

Geels, F. (2002). Technological transitions as evolutionary reconfiguration processes: A multi-level perspective and a case-study. *Research Policy, 31*(8–9), 1257–1274.

Gilsing, R., Turetken, O., Ozkan, B., Grefen, P., Adali, O. E., Wilbik, A., & Berkers, F. (2021). Evaluating the design of service-dominant business models: A qualitative method. *Pacific Asia Journal of the Association for Information Systems, 13*(1).

Gorissen, L., Vrancken, K., & Manshoven, S. (2016). Transition thinking and business model innovation – Towards a transformative business model and new role for the reuse centers of limburg, Belgium. *Sustainability (Switzerland), 8*(2).

Gupta, A. (1995). A stakeholder analysis approach for interorganizational systems. *Industrial Management & Data Systems, 95*(6), 3–7. https://doi.org/10.1108/02635579510091269

Hotie, F., & Gordijn, J. (2019). Value-based process model design. *Business Information Systems Engineering, 61*(2), 163–180.

Jacobs, F., Ubels, J., & Woltering, L. (2018). *The Scaling Scan: A Practical Tool to Determine the Strengths and Weaknesses of Your Scaling Ambition*. Mexico: PPPlab and CIMMYT.

Kemp, R., Loorbach, D., & Rotmans, J. (2007). Transition management as a model for managing processes of co-evolution towards sustainable development. *International Journal of Sustainable Development and World Ecology 14*(1), (2007): 78–91.

Latilla, V. M., Frattini, F., Franzo, S., & Chiesa, V. (2020). Organisational change and business model innovation: AN exploratory study of an energy utility. *International Journal of Innovation Management, 24*(4), https://doi.org/10.1142/S136391962050036X

Mlecnik, E., Straub, A., & Haavik, T. (2019). Collaborative business model development for home energy renovations. *Energy Efficiency, 12*(1), 123–138.

Norton, D., & Pine, J. (2013). Using the customer journey to road test and refine the business model. *Strategy & Leadership, 41*(2), 12–17. https://doi.org/10.1108/10878571311318196

Oukes, T., Berkers, F., & Langley, D. (2020). Collaborative business models in a Base-of-the-Pyramid context: A systemic literature review. *Proceedings 5th International Online Conference on New Business Models*. 5th International Conference on New Business Models, NBM 2020, Doetinchem.

Peppard, J., Ward, J., & Daniel, E. (2007). Managing the realization of business benefits from IT investments. *MIS Quarterly Executive, 6*(1).

Phaal, R., Farrukh, C., & Probert, D. (2015). Roadmapping for strategy and innovation. *Centre for Technology Management, 47*, 1–7.

Putman, V., & Paulus, P. (2009). Brainstorming, brainstorming rules and decision making. *The Journal of Creative Behavior, 43*(1), 29–40.

Rohrbeck, R., Konnertz, L., & Knab, S. (2013). Collaborative business modelling for systemic and sustainability innovations. *International Journal of Technology Management, 22*(63), 4–23.

Sarasini, S., & Linder, M. (2018). Integrating a business model perspective into transition theory: The example of new mobility services. *Environmental Innovation and Societal Transitions, 27* (August) 16–31.

Solaimani, S., Guldemond, N., & Bouwman, H. (2013). Dynamic stakeholder interaction analysis: Innovative smart living design cases. *Electronic Markets, 23*, 317–328.

Tesch, J. (2016). Discovering the role of scenario planning as an evaluation methodology for business models in the era of the internet of things (IoT). In European Conference on Information Systems (ECIS), pp. 1–17.

Turetken, O., Grefen, P., Gilsing, R., & Adali, O. E. (2019). Service-dominant business model design for digital innovation in smart mobility. *Business & Information Systems Engineering, 61*(1), 9–29.

van Waes, A., Farla, J., Frenken, K., De Jong, J., & Raven, R. (2018). Business model innovation and socio-technical transitions. A new prospective framework with an application to bike sharing. *Journal of Cleaner Production, 195*, 1300–1312.

Whelan, T., & Fink, C. (2016, October 21). The comprehensive business case for sustainability. *Harvard Business Review*. https://hbr.org/2016/10/the-comprehensive-business-case-for-sustainability

Niels Faber, Jan Jonker

17 A Long-Term Perspective on Sustainable Business Modelling Changing Value Creation, Actors and Scope in a Quest to Foster Transformation and Transition

Abstract: This chapter introduces, explores and discusses long-term perspectives on circular business models. We present a classification of seven archetypes of circular business models that have materialised over the past five decades, following various developments in the logic of value creation. These developments involve (1) a changing perspective on value creation from single to multiple value, (2) a change in the relevant unit of analysis, from organisation-centric to organising between organisations, (3) a change in the nature of collaboration across the three societal realms, (4) the rise of the internet of materials as a basis for procurement and exchange of materials and (5) the need for business models with a sustainable impact. Contrasting these developments against current practices, several conclusions are drawn. First, thus far these developments have not led to a fundamental change in the way value is perceived in the economic realm. Second, the need for intra-organisational collaboration is at odds with the increasingly shorter lifespan of organisations. Third, circularity and collectively organising for this requires a profound reconsidering of the social contract. Fourth, a fundamental change in the design of materials, components and products is required to give shape to a circular economy. Fifth, and last, knowledge about framing and measuring real impacts is yet to be developed.

Keywords: long-term perspective, sustainable business model, business modelling

1 Introduction

This chapter introduces, explores and discusses long-term perspectives on sustainable and circular business modelling. It identifies some foundational debates in this field, from a theoretical and conceptual perspective. In doing so, this does not mean that we disregard the practice of business modelling. On the contrary, we highly esteem the rich and abundant developments that unfold across organisations in a plethora of countries. While publications on business models have a track-record of more than

Niels Faber, Campus Fryslân Faculty, University of Groningen, Groningen, the Netherlands
Jan Jonker, Institute for Management Research, Radboud University, Nijmegen, the Netherlands

https://doi.org/10.1515/9783110756159-021

25 years (Osterwalder, Pigneur, & Tucci, 2005; Bocken et al., 2014), publications that deal with sustainability and circularity only started roughly a decade ago (Park, Sarkis, & Wu, 2010; Winkler, 2011). The debate we bring to the fore in this contribution starts by accepting this valuable history, without reiterating the past. Instead, we start our journey from the perspectives offered in the previous three chapters, namely with regard to sustainable value creation, organising sustainability, and collective and collaborative business models. The question we raise is, where do all insights and practices on the issues addressed in these chapters put us? This part's preceding chapters have provided the ingredients to understand the nature of business models and how these are linked to sustainability and circularity. Here we like to investigate what main challenges lie ahead. The observation is appropriate that we now have the ingredients to craft transition, yet our drive and knowledge to actually fully engage in this uncertain endeavour remains reluctant (*meestribbelen*). There are still too many restraining forces that protect the actual economic state of play and withhold effectuating significant and necessary changes. After decades of heralding the message on the inevitability to change, reality shows that this is incremental at best, moulded such that they do not endanger nor challenge the status quo. This leads to a permanently repeated broad social debate yet there is no real change.

A business model provides a logic for value creation and retention – a way in which and with whom an organisation, a chain or a loop of parties can organise value or value retention (Jonker & Faber, 2021). It consists of several building blocks: (1) the value proposition (the logic to value creation), (2) the organisational model including the parties involved and (3) the revenue model. In the process of value creation, several values are always created simultaneously for and by the parties concerned (the aforementioned 'multiple value creation'). We distinguish three forms of value creation: transforming, recycling and circularising (Jonker & Faber, 2021). Each of these three forms has its own goal or ambition: eco-efficiency, recovery and value retention. These forms of value creation do not exclude one another, but rather overlap. Value creation always takes place in a valuable social and ecological context. The process of value creation should at least respect this context and leave it intact, that is, not damage, exhaust or pollute it.

There is a wide variety of business models that enable sustainable value creation. Sustainability is about reduced use of raw/processed materials, fossil energy, water and the reduction of negative emissions and impact (environmental or otherwise), and so on during the process of making, functioning and disposal of a product, its components or raw or processed materials. Working on sustainability can be seen as working on improvements under the condition that production must take place within the production and absorption capacity of Earth. Sustainability can be implemented within the linear economy, but is just as much a part and task of the circular economy. To create some focus, we propose three basic or archetypal business models: the platform-, community-based- and circular economy models. Platform business models focus on sustainable impact and aim to make better and more efficient use of what we have through asset or performance management enabled by datafication and digitalisation. The second business model archetype refers to business models that are created around a community. It refers to the creation of multi-stakeholder thematic communities by citizens and/or public entities, together with companies related to healthcare, food, insurance, mobility or energy, for example. The main aim of the circular economy business model is to achieve value retention in and through organising loops, which require circular business and organisation models (Jonker & Faber, 2021).

On the basis of the distinction in three archetypes, Jonker, Faber, and Haaker (2022)elaborated a classification of seven types of business models. This classification is listed and briefly explained by way of introduction.

(1) *Resource models*: the essence of these models is the recovery of products, components and raw/processed materials at the end of the life cycle (discard phase).
(2) *Design models:* the essence of design models is to design products to fit within the logic of circularity. This includes: design for repair and maintenance, design for recovery and recycling and design for lifetime extension.
(3) *Lifetime extension models:* the essence of these models is to extend the lifetime of products, components and raw/processed materials.
(4) *Platform (sharing) models:* the essence of platform (sharing) models is to increase the use of the existing functional capacity of assets (products) that are already in circulation.
(5) *Product-as-a-service models:* these models focus on providing access to the function of a product to a user. The user no longer automatically becomes the owner of the product.
(6) *End-of-life models:* the essence of these models is that producers and importers retain responsibility for the collection and safe and appropriate processing of products they have made or imported at the end of the life cycle.
(7) *Lifecycle models:* the essence of these models is that producers retain ownership of the products they make throughout the entire lifecycle.

The above classification shows the development of the underlying logic of business models over the past five decades. Starting in the 1970s with the discovery of 'reduce– reuse– recycle', the focus predominantly has been on the use and reuse of materials and commodities. The 'resource model' is the leading category in this respect. Due to the activities of the Ellen MacArthur Foundation, the need for design models has been strongly propagated (Ellen MacArthur Foundation, 2012–2014). In line with the Zeitgeist, three types emerged from the principles of dematerialisation and servitisation (Vandermerwe & Rada, 1988; Tukker, 2004), resulting in lifetime extension, platform, and product-as-a-service models. Simultaneously, overarching developments such as the Internet of Things (IoT), Internet of Services (IoS), and more broadly datafication and digitisation, fuelled the latter models that take shape around principles of efficiency and efficacy. This leads in turn to concepts of access to functionalities, giving rise to performance concepts and thus to the performance economy (Stahel, 1982). The obligation to recollect products, components and materials at the end of their life cycle has a long-standing tradition in which producers bear the legal responsibility. Producers are obliged to maximise their efforts to collect their products at the end of the life cycle. This obligation has led to inter-organisational recollect structures. In recent years, this obligation has been revised, leading to the Extended Producer Responsibility (EPR) Directive (Academy of European Law, 2022). This directive dictates that producers are responsible for setting up and maintaining a network of collecting, transporting and responsible disassembly of any product they have brought to the market in the first place. The latest revision covers a broader scope of products, also including and redefining e-waste. The final model in this classification builds on most recent policies, especially fuelled by the Green Deal (European Commission, 2019) and related directives of the European Union (European Commission 2019, 2021a, 2021b; European Parliament, 2009). In spring 2022, the European Union launched the Sustainable Product Initiative (SPI) (European Commission, 2022), which proposes a life-cycle concept holding the producer responsible for all stages. As a consequence, a product is no longer sold, but its functionality is servitised and maintained by the producer or third parties operating under its authority. To make this work, material passports, either passive or interactive, become mandatory to track and trace every stage of the life cycle, for all materials involved. Finally, this also provides an overview of stocks and flows of materials in circulation, where they are, what their status is and when they will become available. This last type of business models lays the foundation to come to a circular economy in due course. Fostering the ambition of life-cycle models, a drastic change towards design models is necessary, to generate sufficient commodities within the economic system to realise a full-fledged circular economy roughly two decades in the future (Middelweerd, 2022).

Against the backdrop we described above, we distinguish five lines of development with regard to business modelling. These are (1) a changing logic of value creation, (2) reframing the unit of analysis – from organisations and integrated value chains, to networks and closed loops, (3) an investigation into the nature of collaboration to make sustainability work, (4) the rise of the Internet of Materials and (5) the debate on how to assess business model impact. We finish this chapter with the plea that a change of existing systems and institutions is inevitable.

2 Five Perspectives on the Development of Business Modelling

Over time, we observe that the nature of business modelling is in transition – from a perspective in which the way financial value is created towards one in which multiple values such as environmental and social impact are included, thus paying tribute to a changing role and position of businesses in society. In this way, the need for sustainable development has become embedded in business activities. Undeniably, these changes have not unfolded easily. Large organisations make abundant promises with regard to their financial, societal and sustainable contributions to these changes that are not always kept. The activity of greenwashing remains to dictate their agendas. Currently, the European Union has directives in the making to bring to a hold this freeriding phenomenon.

Below, we elaborate five ongoing changes of perspective that shape the business modelling landscape. These are a (i) changing perspective on value creation, (ii) debating the scope of a business model, (iii) the changing nature of collaboration in the value chain both horizontally and vertically, (iv) the rise and incorporation of novel phenomena such as the internet of materials and services and lastly (v) how to shape and determine the impact of business models in their social and environmental context. Each of these perspectives is concisely elaborated and practically illustrated with a case.

2.1 Changing Perspectives on Value Creation

Already in Chapter 18, the issue of value creation in the realm of business models was elaborated. In addition to this contribution, here we focus on how the nature of value creation is gradually changing in the light of societal and environmental demands. We stake the case that at present we fundamentally deviate from the Friedman Doctrine that 'the only responsibility of business is to increase its profits' (Friedman, 1970: 17). This doctrine has been embraced by businesses and governments around the globe, and has guided our own behaviours and has led to an unlimited, devastating effect of natural and social resources. Half a century later, we are confronted by the human impact driven by businesses, on a daily basis. Only recently, it has come to the fore what the profound consequences are and how this is linked to our way of thinking about value creation.

A change of perspective implies departing from a pure economic and societal fabric focused on consumption and growth, resulting in an anorexic perspective on monetisation, towards one in which concepts such as net-zero production (IEA, 2021), degrowth (Hickel, 2020), the doughnut economy (Raworth, 2017) and others give shape to the development of a new paradigm. This partially implies changing the rules of the industrial 'game', moving from a linear perspective on production, via recycling, towards an economy in which circularity, restoration and regeneration are leading values when it comes to production and consumption (Jonker & Faber, 2021). This leads towards an economic perspective based on purpose (Hurst, 2014) and multiple value creation (Jonker & Faber, 2019, 2021).

The amalgamation of these trends provides the foundations for a new theory of value that is fitting to new economic directions that accommodate a sustainable society (see, for instance, Jonker & Faber, 2021 on the various positions of value creation).

Part of this debate should be the position the economy holds in the debate: is the economy all-encompassing, including civil society (weak sustainability) (Ayres, van den Bergh, & Gowdy, 2001), or does the economy obey to limitations of the physical and natural environment and accommodate societal checks and balances (strong sustainability)? Last but not least, we should add to this much needed debate the EU frameworks in the making, since they shape step by step a long-term perspective on the future economy, making things practical and tangible (measuring CO_2, reducing water consumption, closing material loops, managing on value preservation, etc.).

A striking example of the ambition to create multiple values simultaneously is the case of Patagonia apparel company. This US retailer of outdoor sportswear was established in 1973 by Yvon Chouinard. From the start, this company was driven by the axiom that everything they make has an impact on the planet. This implies that materials, environmental and social programmes have been in place to ensure that products are made under robust environmental and animal welfare programmes, and to ensure that products are produced under safe, fair and humane labour conditions. This regime is enforced upon all their suppliers across the whole of the supply chain. At present, Patagonia is a multinational operating company across five continents in more than 100 countries. Most recently, the founder and other shareholders have donated all their stocks, with an estimated value of $3 billion, to a 'non-profit trust and a group of non-profit organisations' (CNBC, 2022).

2.2 Changing Unit of Analysis

From a bird's-eye perspective, we observe a movement from an institutionalised dominant organisation-centric perspective towards an amalgamation of various forms of organising. The classical linear value chain is complemented or replaced by horizontally and vertically integrated value chains, material loops and digital and social networks, all happening at the same time. These forms of organising find fertile grounds in the rapid and all-encompassing development towards digitisation and datafication, giving way to concepts such as Internet of Things (IoT), Internet of Service (IoS) and the promising but yet to be demonstrated Internet of Materials (IoM). Consequently, business models much more develop into an intra-organisational concept, involving an expanding array of stakeholders who bring along their particular, yet not always aligned needs and expectations. Given these empirical developments, the question arises what the implications are for the organisational scope of business models. A long track record exists when it comes to managing and coordinating within organisations. The body of knowledge on intra-organisational collaboration and coordination is significantly smaller. This fuels the need to develop concepts of intra-organisational coordination and the ramifications these have for legal, psychological and social contracts. Where business models were originally crafted around an organisation-centric logic of value creation, the outlined developments urge a perspective on intra-organisational collaboration. If, for example, a configuration of organisations set out to close a material loop, questions arise such as: (i) who is responsible for the governance? (ii) where does ownership of the different revenue models lie? and (iii) who is responsible for the maintenance of the loop 10, 20 or 30 years from now? It is these developments that need to be translated into a novel breed of concepts for business modelling. For instance, at present the circular economy is mainly forcibly crammed into conventional linear economic models, due to a lack of alternatives. In part, a possible answer is provided in the chapter on collective business models (see Chapter 20).

Mature examples of how this intra-organisational perspective operates in practice may be found in the Netherlands where it comes to the collection of wastepaper, consumer glass and plastics. Already for 25 years, there is a nation-wide collection and logistics structure in place, composed of hundreds of organisations. Businesses and consumers deposit locally, either at supermarkets or municipal garbage collection sites. The different waste streams are separated from the start and transported to dedicated waste and recycling sites. These operations are paid for by producer organisations (PROs). Consumers are stimulated to participate because they receive back their deposits when they return empty jars and bottles. This established system is currently able to process 90% of consumer glass (VNG, 2022) and paper has an 89% recycling rate (PRN, 2022). When it comes to plastics, the percentages are much lower, due to the variety of the composition of the waste, and the technical or mechanical (un)ability to separate this into mono-material waste streams; for the near future, expectations are high with regard to chemical recycling.

2.3 Changing Collaborations

The current fabric of society, including the economy, historically builds on a strict divide between the three realms of state, markets and civil society. This generally accepted divide has given way to functional rationalism. In turn, this has led to a transactional model that transfers responsibility in the various stages of the value chain. Consequently, there is no longer ownership of problems the realms have in common, such as drought, famine, depletion of natural resources, loss of biodiversity or economic asylum seekers.

Against the backdrop of the previous developments, the societal divide is fundamentally challenged. The logic and scope of value creation based on functional rationalism is changing, which has a fundamental impact on the nature of collaboration (see previous remarks on the changing nature of organising). This gives way to an integrated perspective on how problems collide; for example, water is linked to energy, is linked to mobility. This questions the scope, balances and boundaries between the three societal realms (Mintzberg, 2015) and how to address these conceptually, since single issue solutions no longer address the root causes.

In an attempt to address the growing importance of these issues, over the past decades, a variety of public–private collaborations (public–private partnerships (PPPs)) have taken shape across a broad array of domains. These PPPs fill the void between a purely commercial perspective on the one hand and a need for a public or common way of value creation on the other. The assumption is that commercial organisations are capable of public goods, without necessarily applying the economic principle of profit. In theory, this ambition sounds ideal, yet in practice involved that commercial organisations maintain 'the profit rules of the game'. To overcome this conflicting situation, it is with interest that the concept of the commons is revitalised, labelled under the header of the 'New Commons'. Debating this concept concurrently is a jump back in time, and a leap into the future – since, the concept of the commons dates back to the earliest of human settlements (e.g., Ostrom et al., 1999). The commons have had a key contribution in shaping a broad concept of welfare and well-being with long-standing historical roots. This meaning has been lost over the last six or seven decades (but we could even argue this loss of meaning already started at the beginning of the Industrial Revolution). It is intriguing that nowadays we find ourselves in the process of rediscovering and revitalising the possible applications of this concept, allowing us to shape the multiple value creation transition across a broader array of stakeholders and their needs (see also Chapter 18).

The island of Samsø, Denmark, is known for its transitional approach towards the development of a collective energy system. Samsø has completely transformed its energy system from fossil to renewable energy, even exporting its surpluses. This process has taken its little more than 3000 inhabitants over 25 years. They started this transformational process in 1977, winning the national competition for a plan to become 100% self-sufficient with renewable energies. Since then, they have made three 10-year Masterplans, of which the long-term objective has been to become an energy exporter by 2030. Taking a closer look, the technological challenge is much less important than engaging with the entire population. To make this happen, a step-by-step, person-by-person approach has been adopted, elaborated and refined offering value to all. All bases have been covered, including finance (loans), staying in pace with technological advancements, creating collective systems for harnessing and distributing energy and so forth. They are a living example of how a region-bound community, of considerable size, manages to give shape to a transition in 25 years.

2.4 The Rise of the Internet of Materials

We observe a tendency in which circular business models become en-vogue. This becomes visible in the adoption of servitisation models (Vandermerwe & Rada, 1988; the so-called Product as a Service), the rise of platforms (B2B as well as B2C) and laws underpinning extended product lifespan (including the Right to Repair; Chasson, 2020). This breed of business models is all based on (1) the material composition of products, (2) the function of those products during their life cycle including their reparability and (3) the quality and accessibility of their components and materials at the end of the products' life cycle. This can only be achieved if information about the materials, components and products is available at the different stages of the life cycle. This is where datafication comes into play.

Datafication of products and commodities enable tracking-and-tracing and creating material passports, which preludes a further implementation of the circular economy concept. Being able to determine stocks of materials, their quality and when these materials will be again available for processing into new products, shapes the backbone of circularity. At least that is the promise. How this will materialise in practice is still to be seen, for only small-scale experiments for specific niche markets have been conducted thus far. The real question is how this would work in an ongoing economy, in which a wide variety of materials are handled and used by an even larger variety of actors (producers and users alike) in various value-chains. The development leads to a rather massive storage of data, on products, their composition, their wear and tear, their whereabouts and their estimated end-of-life. The latter is important to determine the quality and availability of the stock of materials. In the wake of developments such as the Internet of Services (IoS) and the Internet of Things (IoT), we suggest labelling this development under the header of the Internet of Materials (IoM). We consider these three types of Internets as three closely intertwined systems. Fundamental issues related to privacy and (democratic) oversight of material availability and access are issues that yet are under scrutiny and need to be developed into safe and time-resistant systems. At this moment only broad questions on these matters are phrased, for we lack in-depth insight into the consequences of putting a datafied, circular economy into operation.

A striking example is the development of the European Battery Directive (European Parliament, 2006) and the consequential battery passport. The battery passport is a digital file that conveys information about all applicable ESG and life-cycle requirements based on a common definition of a sustainable battery. Each battery passport is linked to the digital battery passport platform (DBPP) offering digital information and data on the status and whereabouts of batteries. The ambition is to go beyond performance management of single batteries, and instead to offer insights into the life cycle of the industry's full value chain. This system under development leads to a global framework that governs the rules about measurement, auditing and reporting of parameters across the entire value chain. A digital identification (ID) for each battery contains data and descriptions concerning performance, production and provenance during the life cycle, and systems in place for advancing the battery's lifetime and fostering recycling. Information about development of the battery passport and the battery directive may be found at the website of the Global Battery Alliance (Global Battery Alliance, 2022).

2.5 Sustainable Impact of Business Models

Business models take shape based on a particular logic to create value. There is a multitude of logics available. The ambition to have a sustainable or circular impact is embedded in the wish to do good and create a better world. This raises the need to investigate the impact of a particular logic of a business model in light of the notion of sustainability. While this sounds easy, defining how impact in this respect is determined and measured is a complex matter in itself. Do we measure impact through impact reduction, for example, less carbon dioxide emissions? Do we measure impact based on material efficiency in production and use of products? Or, do we measure impact based on the easiness of disassembly at the end of the life cycle? Besides, we need to clarify the size of the impact landscape we should be looking at. What is the relevant scope at which impact is measured? Will that be at scope 2, 3, or are we already in need for a scope 4? And what are the trade-offs that emerge from choosing one over the other?

The ambitions and intentions to shape a new generation of business models look promising, however, at the end of the day impact is still predominantly measured on the basis of monetised indicators. Several frameworks, especially stimulated by the European Union, are currently in the making to establish a different mindset with regard to measuring impact. These frameworks deliberately step away from convention accounting, and take into consideration multiple values. Worthy to note is that monetisation is not the standard mechanism underpinning how these frameworks deal with these values. How does the concept of circularity fit into this discussion? Or more precisely, when may we consider something to be circular and thus making a 'circular impact'? Will this be after one round of reuse of commodities, components or products, or do only longer chains of repetitive uses come into play? It is still early days to fully move away from an economy that operates on the premises of a financially based form of impact accounting. We argue that many initiatives old and new are still needed to affect the mindsets of accounting professionals with regard to their established ways of working. What needs to be created and accepted across the accounting community is a language and standardised methodology to determine, measure and report on impacts.

While the above elaborates on the technical aspects of sustainable and circular accounting, in terms of relevant indicators and methodologies, the question of how this is reflected in a change of individual and collective behaviours remains unaddressed. The premise of value creation in a changing context that favours sustainability and circularity criticises simultaneously the taken-for-granted neo-liberal paradigm. This paradigm is so engrained in the fabric of society and economy that it is almost impossible to think outside its leading principle of continuous and unbounded economic growth. Searching for ways to make impact through business models inescapably demands a change in (consumptive) behaviour.

3 Conclusions

Despite the fact that we have been discussing the circular economy in conjunction with analogous developments towards sustainability, social inclusivity and biodiversity, it is still too early to observe conceptual and practical maturity. The debated five perspectives on business modelling are a clear witness of this argument. In common debates on economic transformation,[1] for example, political, business and societal, the suggestion is that the concept of circular economies will eventually cover the entirety of the whole economic system. In fact, the part of the economy that may be circularised is extremely limited, since it assumes no consumption takes place. Given the consumption of food, energy and a broad range of commodities, it will remain part of the economic fabric. Instead of pushing the notion of circularising to its extremes, it implies to invest in radical sustainification as is suggested by the European Commission (WEF, 2022). Against this backdrop, we draw the following five conclusions.

Conclusion 1

The new demands raised by the ambition to create a sustainable society, in part based on a circular economy, have not led to a critical, in-depth assessment of notions of value and value creation, that is, the foundations of business models. Often unnoticed is the fact that most business models fostering the circular economy are based on value creation over time. This stimulates the exploration of new theories of value that align with sustainable and circular business models. Secondary, these need to be linked to accounting principles and practices, to accommodate standardised impact measurement.

Conclusion 2

We tried to demonstrate that the classical business model perspective is organisation centric. The transition towards a more circular and sustainable economic system requires interorganisational collaboration. This needs to take shape in such a way that a collective perspective on collaboration and value creation is mandatory. This implies

---

1 We deliberately choose to use the term 'transformation' in this context. The common debate is often framed as a transition from a linear towards a circular economy. Taking a closer look, while the term 'transition' is continuously used, the actual measures taken to create change in this regard lead to a transformation of the existing economy, while keeping intact the underpinning notion of growth and the institutional arrangement that uphold this paradigm. In contrast, the actual meaning of transition would imply a system change, offering a perspective on concepts such as degrowth, collective value creation and an 'economy of enough'.

that conventional business models are replaced by ones that take shape around multi-actor models, enabling collective value creation. This places new demands on technical and organisational dimensions underlying these business models. The technical dimension will move towards an increase in digitisation, tracking-and-tracing, leading in its turn to questions related to governance over time. The organisational dimension is somewhat more complicated, for that involves the endurance and survival of organisations. Given the fact that organisations live shorter and shorter, this for sure creates a fundamental issue when it comes to issues such as responsibility, accountability and assurance.

Conclusion 3

At a fundamental level, working on collective business models for sustainability and circularity implies to re-discuss and redefine the nature of the social contract. As of the Industrial Revolution, the individual organisation is the cornerstone of a linear economy, shaped through organisation-centric business models and value chains. It goes without saying that within the economy as we know it, it operates on the basis of a variety of collaborative concepts, such as strategic alliances, joint ventures and industrial ecosystems. These collaborations are shaped on the premise of maximising financial value. When value creation becomes a collective effort over time, involving multiple values and multiple actors, the nature of collaborations and thus the nature of transactions radically changes. In this respect, actors will not be limited to organisations as we know them, nor to the roles of producer and consumer. Instead, they also involve non-organisational entities, including citizens, community-based initiatives and a variety of digital and social networks. This leads to inter-organisational hubs that form brokers between organisational and non-organisational functional entities, linked and driven in networks. Ultimately, this culminates in a re-exploration and redefinition of the scope and nature of the Commons.

Conclusion 4

A precondition to develop a flourishing circular economy after roughly 15–20 years from now is the investment in material (commodity), component and product design and their datafication in the light of value preservation. The pinnacle is that all designs of products, parts and materials incorporate the track-and-traceability of their compounding parts. Evidently, this leads to material passports at the most granular level possible. This may only come about if actual developments around the Internet of Things and the Internet of Services develop further and transform into the Internet of Materials.

At the same time, we observe a rapidly emerging discussion on the downsides of our societal addiction to data, particularly with regard to privacy issues. The stimulation of an Internet of Materials will result in an explosion of Big Data and an exponentially increasing Energy Footprint. This will on the one hand boost the actual debate on the consequences of data handling on energy use even further. On the other, life in its most minute details will be captured in data, only making the issue of privacy protection extremely relevant and urgent. In its turn this will raise issues such as the 'expiration date' of data, mandatory data destruction and the right to be deleted. It goes without saying that individuals, communities and networks may frame themselves as living datasets for sale, the commodification of the quantified self.

Conclusion 5

The whole transformation towards the circular economy is driven by the ambition to create impact, when it comes to CO_2 reduction, commodity use or energy production and use. The orphan of this discussion, however, is our limited knowledge on how to frame and measure impact. More in particular, we observe a debate where it comes to direct impacts (e.g., water use, land use, energy use) versus so-called hidden impacts (e.g., transporting products from one part of the globe to another, long-term effects of pollution, depletion of natural resources including loss of biodiversity). This raises again the issue of inter-generational responsibility; to what extent are we, the living, responsible for the effects of our present-day actions on generations to come. In essence, the circular economy is a concept of systematic reduction of such impacts, while safeguarding the conditions for a future-generation economy. Given that in itself the circular economy offers the promise of an actionable concept, it has not yet matured to that end. The above introduced discussions on the nature of value and value creation should be linked to this debate on impact. Only when the time perspective, value creation and impact are developed into an actionable vehicle will the circular economy materialise.

In hindsight, and despite our critical remarks on the status and development of the circular economy and in particular its business models, we consider this debate crucial in the actual process of transforming from an industrial civilisation towards a 'society of enough'. After 50 years of discussion, a changing economy, started through the introduction of the Performance Economy, the conclusion is inevitable that we have hardly scratched its conceptual surface. We like to abandon the polluting and resource-consuming linear economy. This implies the turn away from a (global) economy of scale in which volume is king, towards one in which local self-sufficiency is the leading principle, acting, living and economising within local natural boundaries. Yet, a clear and accessible alternative concept, commonly understood, is as yet not available. Perhaps rejuvenating the concept of the Commons could provide a stepping stone towards crafting a new economy.

References

Academy of European Law (2022). Extended producer responsibility (1/2). Waste Management: PPW, ELVs and WEES Directives. https://www.era-comm.eu/EU_waste_law/stand_alone/part_3/index.html

Ayres, R., van den Bergh, J., & Gowdy, J. (2001). Strong versus weak sustainability: Economics, natural sciences, and consilience. *Environmental Ethics, 23*(2), 155–168. https://doi.org/10.5840/enviroethics200123225

Bocken, N. M. P., Short, S. W., Rana, P., & Evans, S.(2014). A literature and practice review to develop sustainable business model archetypes. *Journal of Cleaner Production, 65*, 42–56.

Chasson, A. (2020, January 6). Major steps for durability and right to repair taken in France. Right to Repair. https://repair.eu/news/major-steps-taken-for-durability-and-right-to-repair-in-france/

CNBC (2022, September 14). Patagonia founder just donated the entire company, worth $3 Billion, to fight climate change. CNBC. https://www.cnbc.com/2022/09/14/patagonia-founder-donates-entire-company-to-fight-climate-change.html

Ellen MacArthur Foundation (2012). *Towards the Circular Economy Vol. 1: Economic and Business Rationale for an Accelerated Transition (P. 98)*. Ellen MacArthur Foundation.. https://www.ellenmacarthurfoundation.org/assets/downloads/publications/Ellen-MacArthur-Foundation-Towards-the-Circular-Economy-vol.1.pdf

Ellen MacArthur Foundation (2013). *Towards the Circular Economy Vol. 2: Opportunities for the Consumer Goods Sector (P. 112)*. Ellen MacArthur Foundation.. https://www.ellenmacarthurfoundation.org/assets/downloads/publications/TCE_Report-2013.pdf

Ellen MacArthur Foundation (2014). *Towards the Circular Economy Vol. 3: Accelerating the Scale-up across Global Supply-chains (P. 41)*. Ellen MacArthur Foundation. https://www.ellenmacarthurfoundation.org/assets/downloads/publications/Towards-the-circular-economy-volume-3.pdf

European Commission (2019, December 11). The European green deal sets out how to make Europe the first climate-neutral continent by 2050, boosting the economy, improving people's health and quality of life, caring for nature, and leaving no one behind. European Commission Press Release Database. https://ec.europa.eu/commission/presscorner/detail/en/ip_19_6691

European Commission (2021a). European climate law. European Climate Law. https://climate.ec.europa.eu/eu-action/european-green-deal/european-climate-law_en

European Commission (2021b, July 14). European green deal: Commission proposes transformation of EU economy and society to meet climate ambitions [European Commission Press corner]. EU Economy and Society to Meet Climate Ambitions. https://ec.europa.eu/commission/presscorner/detail/en/IP_21_3541

European Commission (2022). Sustainable products initiative. Law. https://ec.europa.eu/info/law/better-regulation/have-your-say/initiatives/12567-Sustainable-products-initiative_en

European Parliament (2006, September 26). *Directive 2006/66/EC of the European Parliament and of the Council of 6 September 2006 on Batteries and Accumulators and Waste Batteries and Accumulators and Repealing Directive 91/157/EEC (Text with EEA Relevance)* [European Union Law]. EUR-Lex. https://eur-lex.europa.eu/legal-content/EN/TXT/?uri=CELEX%3A32006L0066

European Parliament (2009). DIRECTIVE 2009/125/EC OF THE EUROPEAN PARLIAMENT AND OF THE COUNCIL of 21 October 2009 establishing a framework for the setting of ecodesign requirements for energy-related products (recast). Official Journal of the European Union. https://eur-lex.europa.eu/legal-content/EN/TXT/PDF/?uri=CELEX:32009L0125&from=EN

Friedman, M. (1970. September 13). A Friedman doctrine – The social responsibility of business is to increase its profits. *The New York Times*, 17.

Global Battery Alliance (2022). *Battery Passport*. Global Battery Alliance. https://www.globalbattery.org/battery-passport/

Hickel, J. (2020). *Less Is More: How Degrowth Will Save the World*. Penguin Random House. https://www.pen guin.co.uk/books/441772/less-is-more-by-jason-hickel/9781786091215

Hurst, A. (2014). *The Purpose Economy: How Your Desire for Impact, Personal Growth, and Community Is Changing the World*. Elevate.

International Energy Agency (IEA) (2021). *Net Zero by 2050: A Roadmap for the Global Energy Sector (IEA Publications)*. International Energy Agency. https://www.iea.org/reports/net-zero-by-2050

Jonker, J., & Faber, N. (2019). Business models for multiple value creation: Exploring strategic changes in organisations enabling to address societal challenges. In A. Aagaard (Ed.), *Sustainable Business Models: Innovation, Implementation and Success* Palgrave-MacMillan. https://www.palgrave.com/gp/book/9783319932743

Jonker, J., & Faber, N. (2021). *Organizing for Sustainability: A Guide to Developing New Business Models*. Springer International Publishing. https://doi.org/10.1007/978-3-030-78157-6

Jonker, J., Faber, N., & Haaker, T. (2022). *Circular Business Models: A Study to Classify Existing and Emerging Forms of Value Retention and Creation*. The Hague: Ministry of Economic Affairs and Climate Policy.

Middelweerd, H. (2022, April 25). Europese energietransitie in gevaar? onderzoek waarschuwt voor grondstoffentekort [news platform]. Change Inc. https://www.change.inc/energie/europese-energietransitie-in-gevaar-onderzoek-waarschuwt-voor-grondstoffentekort-38142

Mintzberg, H. (2015). *Rebalancing Society: Radical Renewal Beyond Left, Right, and Center*. Oakland: Berret-Koehlers Publishers.

Osterwalder, A., Pigneur, Y., & Tucci, C. L. (2005). Clarifying business models: Origins, present, and future of the concept. *Communications of the Association for Information Systems, 16*(1), 1.

Ostrom, E., Burger, J., Field, C. B., Norgaard, R. B., & Policansky, D. (1999). Revisiting the commons: Local lessons, global challenges. *Science, 284*(5412), 278–282. https://doi.org/10.1126/science.284.5412.278

Park, J., Sarkis, J., & Wu, Z. (2010). Creating integrated business and environmental value within the context of China's circular economy and ecological modernization. *Journal of Cleaner Production, 18*(15), 1494–1501. https://doi.org/10.1016/j.jclepro.2010.06.001

Papier Recycling Nederland (PRN) (2022). Papierrecycling. Papier Recycling Nederland. https://prn.nl/papierrecycling/

Raworth, K. (2017). *Doughnut Economics: Seven Ways to Think like a 21st-century Economist*. (1st edition.) Penguin Random House UK.

Stahel, W. R. (1982). The product-life factor. In S. Grinton Orr (Ed.), *Inquiry into the Nature of Sustainable Societies: The Role of the Private Sector* (pp. 72–104). Geneva: HARC.

Tukker, A. (2004). Eight types of product–service system: Eight ways to sustainability? Experiences from SusProNet. *Business Strategy and the Environment, 13*(4), 246–260. https://doi.org/10.1002/bse.414

Vandermerwe, S., & Rada, J. (1988). Servitization of business: Adding value by adding services. *European Management Journal, 6*(4), 314–324.

Vereniging van Nederlandse Glasfabrikanten (VNG) (2022). Recycling van glas. Vereniging van Nederlandse Glasfabrikanten. https://www.nederlandseglasfabrikanten.nl/duurzaamheid/recycling-van-glas/

World Economic Forum (WEF) (2022). (May 24). *Ursula von der Leyen's Speech to Davos 2022 in Full*. World Economic Forum. https://www.weforum.org/agenda/2022/05/ursula-von-der-leyens-speech-to-davos-2022-in-full/

Winkler, H. (2011). Closed-loop production systems – A sustainable supply chain approach. *CIRP Journal of Manufacturing Science and Technology, 4*(3), 243–246. https://doi.org/10.1016/j.cirpj.2011.05.001

Part V: **Performance and Impact**
Emma Folmer, Valerija Golubic

The chapters in Part V discuss a core element of sustainable entrepreneurship: the creation of positive impact. While there is considerable debate within the field about the precise definition of social and environmental entrepreneurship, there is broad consensus that its core goal is to generate positive impact. However, this consensus propels new questions, such as how this impact is defined, how it is measured and how we can optimise or scale it when we encounter it. Positive impact can be understood as the (innovative) solutions that social and environmental entrepreneurship produces to help solve societal problems (Vedula et al., 2022). These solutions can take the form of new products or services that restore and regenerate the environment, or improve the livelihoods of vulnerable groups in society. As such, positive impact can be societal or environmental value that benefits individuals, communities and wider societies (Stephan et al., 2016). These solutions that social and environmental entrepreneurs implement have been discussed in previous chapters in this volume. However, many questions remain unanswered with regard to the mechanisms that facilitate the impact creation process of social and environmental enterprises. How do we know when a solution is generating positive impact, and how can we optimally support these solutions? Beyond these practical questions, we need additional theoretical interpretation and conceptualisation of impact (Ebrahim and Rangan, 2014). A better understanding is needed of how leaders of social and environmental enterprises and other stakeholders see the role of impact and how organisational strategies are adapted in relation to impact creation. The chapters in Part V offer new perspectives on these matters.

The first chapter by Yew, Au and Drencheva (2022) very carefully describes the impact investment ecosystem in South-East Asia. It illustrates the variety of stakeholders that have an interest in positive impact creation. Alongside their various interests, they also have different expectations as to what impact is being created. The authors explore two broad conceptualisations of the goal, or the intention, of impact investment. The first is the 'Do no harm' principle. Impact investors who invest in organisations based on this principle are aiming to reduce negative externalities, and are avoiding investments in companies that are lacking environmental, social and governance (ESG) management. The second principle, 'Do Good', avoids harm like the first principle while in addition trying to allocate resources to companies that actively try to benefit the wider public and environment. This second principle is guiding impact investors that invest in social and sustainable enterprises that are mission-oriented. This chapter highlights the 'input' side of impact creation. The type of stakeholder that is providing investment as well as their intention behind investing plays an important role in how positive impact is conceptualised. The authors recognise that more work is needed to understand the side of the investee, and how they move forward to create and demonstrate impact once an investment has been made.

The second chapter in Part V by Ioan and Mateucci (2022) provides more insight into the impact creation process, and they propose and unpack the conceptualisation of impact as something that mainly involves 'mobilising others'. The authors argue that impact creation can be understood in terms of agency – to enable oneself and

https://doi.org/10.1515/9783110756159-022

others to create and exploit opportunities for change. The chapter illustrates eleven strategies – on the individual, community and ecosystem level – that social entrepreneurs use to develop agency in others. By doing so, the social entrepreneurs are creating a 'ripple effect' through empowering others to be social entrepreneurs and do the same. The first two chapters take a higher-level perspective on the field of social and sustainable entrepreneurship, the first sketching the 'input' side of this field, and the second providing an overview of the variety of actions social entrepreneurs take to create impact.

The third and the fourth chapters in Part V zoom in on more specific examples of social and sustainable entrepreneurship. Itani and Daou (2022) provide insight into what it means to be a social entrepreneur in an underdeveloped social entrepreneurial ecosystem. Specifically, they zoom in on the experiences of women social entrepreneurs in the technology sector. There is a direct link here to the second chapter, as the women entrepreneurs in Itani and Daou's (2022) account are aiming to empower and mobilise others to become change makers. Being women in tech in the Lebanese context is not self-evident, and the women in the sample are actively trying to shape the perception of what entrepreneurship is and can be. One of the findings that the authors present is that many of the social entrepreneurs in their sample are not aware that they are, and not labelling themselves as social entrepreneurs.

We should not forget that social entrepreneurship is an age-old practice, which received its label only several decades ago. It is therefore not surprising that some entrepreneurs, in some contexts, exercise social entrepreneurship as an understandable part of their entrepreneurial endeavours. However, the actual nature (definition), quality (measure) and quantity (scale) of impact achieved through such practices is rarely a point of attention. This raises the question whether awareness of social enterprise and entrepreneurship is needed in order to create (an overarching, scalable, systematic, targeted) impact. The answer might be yes if we consider the possibility of the aforementioned 'ripple effect', since scaling impact through investment may benefit from increased awareness and labelling of social entrepreneurship. Moreover, sustainable and social entrepreneurship stands a better chance of reshaping institutions – becoming the new norm – if it is recognised and acknowledged as such.

In the fourth and final chapter by Folmer, Johnson, Rebmann, van der Waal and Schneiders (2022) we see another instance of entrepreneurs who are (unintentionally) redefining entrepreneurship. The actors in this chapter engage in 'collective' or community entrepreneurship for positive impact. With entrepreneurship until now predominantly being seen and researched as an individual endeavour, the collective entrepreneurship process requires a new lens and raises new questions. In this final chapter the authors use the Theory of Change (ToC) model to illustrate the sequence of events through which groups of entrepreneurs create positive impact for their communities. Being a collective process with many stakeholders involved, this process is characterised by many contingencies, probably more so than 'traditional' individual entrepreneurship processes. The authors argue that while ToC models are mainly used by practitioners, there is value in theoretically embedding it in the social entrepreneurship literature since it can offer valuable insights – including attention to the temporal dimension and stakeholder interests – into the impact creation process.

The chapters in Part V provide us with insights into various aspects of positive impact creation by social and environmental enterprises. These insights can be summed up in the following conclusions, leading to promising areas of future research. First, these chapters show us that social and environmental entrepreneurship is seen and explained differently in different parts of the globe, and it even varies per region. The conditions for impact creation, the kind of impact that is being generated, as well as the way in which the impact can be supported and scaled up depend, thus, on the context where these enterprises operate. Our knowledge of impact creation is mainly based on research conducted in the Global North. Recognising context as one of the determinants of positive social and environmental impact suggests that we need more explanations on how this impact is achieved in different parts of the world, with the countries in the Global South being so far relatively unexplored and unexplained contexts. Second, the presented chapters draw attention to the importance of the communities and collective action for impact creation and scaling up. We have seen that communities can have different roles in impact creation. Communities can serve as a channel through which impact spills over to achieve a sustainable social change, or as agents in themselves who are capable of creating greater social impact. Getting a deeper insight into all the roles that communities (can) have in positive impact creation through some form of entrepreneurship is another promising avenue for future research. Finally, we see how a practitioner tool can skilfully be used in theory building for the purpose of supporting the understanding of the impact created. We encourage researchers to experiment with tools used by practitioners, in combination with rigorous research methodology, to bring new insights on how positive impact created by sustainable/social and environmental enterprises can be identified, measured, optimised and scaled up.

References

Ebrahim, A., & Rangan, K. (2014). What impact? A framework for measuring the scale and scope of social performance. *California Management Review, 56*(3), 118–141.

Stephan, U., Patterson, M., Kelly, C., & Mair, J. (2016). Organizations driving positive social change: A review and an integrative framework of change processes. *Journal of Management, 42*(5), 1250–1281.

Vedula, S., Doblinger, C., Pacheco, D., York, J., Bacq, S., Russo, M., & Dean, T. (2022). Entrepreneurship for the public good: A review, critique, and path forward for social and environmental entrepreneurship research. *Academy of Management Annals, 16*(1), 391–425.

Jian Li Yew, Wee Chan Au, Andreana Drencheva

18 Impact Investment in Southeast Asia: An Overview and Framework

Abstract: Aiming to finance solutions to various social and environmental challenges, impact investment is growing in importance in Southeast Asia. Acknowledging the unique aspects of the region, this chapter provides an overview of impact investment in Southeast Asia and offers a framework to present the decision principles, developments, dynamics and key participants of impact investment in the region. The framework highlights the diversity of impact investment activities and participants in Southeast Asia and offers a foundation for future research. It also helps individuals to identify opportunities to contribute to social and environmental change in different ways.

Keywords: impact investment, Southeast Asia, Sustainable Development Goals, social enterprise, social entrepreneurship

1 Introduction and Context

Globally, impact investment is gaining significant academic and practitioner interest because of its potential to contribute to the achievement of the United Nations Sustainable Development Goals (SDGs) and, more broadly, to systems change in capital flow and usage. Impact investing aims to deliver positive returns for both the investors' portfolios and society with social, economic, cultural and/or environmental benefits (Nicholls, 2010). According to a 2020 International Finance Corporation report, investments of USD 2.281 trillion could be considered impact investments under a broad definition, including those privately and publicly managed, and those with measured and intended impact (Volk, 2021). This is equivalent to about 2% of global assets under management (AUM). While still a small market niche, impact investment is becoming popular among asset managers, development finance institutions, family offices and foundations.

Impact investment is particularly growing in use and importance as an approach to contribute towards achievement of the SDGs in Southeast Asia (SEA): Indonesia, Malaysia, Philippines, Singapore, Thailand, Brunei, Vietnam, Lao, Myanmar, East Timor (also known as Timor-Leste) and Cambodia. In 2020, the total gross domestic product (GDP)

Jian Li Yew, Citrine Capital Selangor, Malaysia
Wee Chan Au, Newcastle University Business School Newcastle University, Newcastle-upon-Tyne, United Kingdom
Andreana Drencheva, King's Business School, King's College London, London, UK

https://doi.org/10.1515/9783110756159-023

of all members of the Association of Southeast Asian Nations (ASEAN)[1] amounted to approximately USD 3.08 trillion, and it is estimated that it will achieve a total of USD 4.47 trillion in 2025 (O'Neill, 2021). While these countries have progressed towards achieving the United Nations 2030 Agenda for Sustainable Development (e.g., the proportion of people living on less than USD 1.25 per day fell from one in two persons to one in eight persons in the last two decades (ASEAN, 2016)), the region still faces significant social and environmental issues, such as insufficient access to education and susceptibility to natural and human-induced disasters (ASEAN, 2016, 2020a). These challenges have been further amplified by the Covid-19 pandemic, which has had a significant impact on the societies and economies in the region with particularly devastating consequences for employment and income opportunities (ASEAN, 2020b; IMF, 2021; Morgan & Trinh, 2021; Viegelahn & Huynh, 2021). Thus, further progress towards the SDGs and post-pandemic recovery is likely to require increasing impact investment activities in the region.

While there is an acknowledgement of impact investment as locally embedded with regional differences (Zhao, 2020), there is little insight about the state of impact investment in SEA. The SEA region represents diverse formal and informal institutional arrangements with diverse social, cultural, economic and environmental issues in each country. To understand impact investment in the SEA region, it is essential to acknowledge that countries in the region have varied economic development stages and different maturity levels of business ecosystems. For example, in 2019, Cambodia's and Myanmar's Ease of Doing Business ranks were 144 and 165, respectively (World Bank, 2019). Comparatively, Malaysia's and Singapore's Ease of Doing Business ranks were 12 and 2, respectively (World Bank, 2019). To illustrate the diversity within the region further, as of 2017, only 27% and 48% of the population had a financial institution account in the Philippines and Indonesia, respectively, as compared to 98% in Singapore and 81% in Thailand (Demirgüç-Kunt et al., 2017).

The SEA countries represent a significantly different context from the countries usually examined in academic journals and books published in the Global North on the topic of impact investment. Such a regional focus is meaningful to gain a more nuanced understanding of impact investment and the ways it is performed with different intentions and outcomes. It is also beneficial for practitioners, educators and learners in gaining knowledge about how to navigate the field in this specific region. However, with the diversity within the region across social and environmental issues, institutional arrangements and types of investors, understanding the state of impact

---

[1] In this chapter, we follow convention in referring to Southeast Asia (SEA) as a geographic region and to the Association of Southeast Asian Nations (ASEAN) as a union of several countries within the region, to which East Timor is an observer, instead of a full member. Given the overlap between states in the region and members of the ASEAN, we use both terms in this chapter to refer to the region. Where data sources refer specifically to ASEAN states, thus excluding East Timor, we make this explicit, instead of using the broader SEA label.

investment in SEA remains challenging. This chapter contributes towards addressing this problem by introducing a framework for conceptualising the state of impact investment in SEA as an ecosystem that varies across countries and illustrating this framework with examples from the region.

This chapter is structured as follows. First, we explicate the foundation of impact investment based on two main principles: 'Do No Harm' and 'Do Good'. Next, we offer an overview of the impact investment market in SEA, with differences between countries and trends. Following, we provide a conceptual framework for understanding impact investment in SEA as an ecosystem based on 1) dynamics with the private, public and third sectors, 2) capital providers, managers and recipients as main participants in the field and 3) supporting organisations (refer to Figure 18.1 for details). Throughout the chapter, we provide examples to illustrate our conceptual framework based on publicly available data and our own experience in the field. Finally, we briefly outline the implications of this conceptual framework for research, offering suggestions for future research, and for practitioners.

2 The Meaning of Impact Investment

The term 'impact investing' has many meanings that differ across asset owners, fund managers, scholars and entities receiving such capital. Indeed, there is an unclear boundary between impact investing and related concepts, including socially responsible investing, ethical investing, sustainable investing, environmental, social, and governance (ESG) investing, responsible investing and social investing, among others. To amplify the complexity and confusion, concepts such as venture philanthropy, social finance, blended value and microfinance are also used in reference to impact investment. Instead of focusing on definitions and differentiating between different concepts, we aim to explore the principles behind these concepts as a common foundation for using investment towards relatively neutral and positive outcomes. Two distinct principles broadly underpin the different forms of investment approaches: 1) the intention to avoid any harm to society or the environment (i.e., the 'Do No Harm' principle) and 2) the intention to actively benefit society or the environment (i.e., the 'Do Good' principle). These principles focus on understanding the effects capital has on its investment recipients and how such impact cascades into the broader economy, society and environment.

2.1 'Do No Harm' Principle

The 'Do No Harm' principle considers both the direct and indirect, intended and unintended negative consequences of investment decisions. The primary purpose of the 'Do No Harm' principle is to prevent violation of investors' morals and values. This principle also aims to support the better management of risks, particularly sustainability risks, and generate long-term returns when such risks are mitigated or avoided.

The most common approach in applying the 'Do No Harm' principle is exclusionary or negative screening, through specific mandates and during the due diligence process, whereby investors select investments consistent with their particular value systems, such as the values of a specific religion, and avoid investments inconsistent with their value systems. This strategy usually excludes companies or industries that investors consider unsuitable for their goals, morally, ethically, religiously or otherwise. Historically, most negative screens have been designed to exclude companies in the 'sin' industries, such as tobacco, alcohol and weapons. However, through the years, investors have also increasingly avoided investments that support animal testing, child labour and other inhumane or damaging practices to society or the environment. Once investments have been made, investors may choose to actively monitor how well the recipients of their funds continue to adhere to the 'Do No Harm' principle beyond the initial investment decision as organisations may change their practices over time.

More recently, the 'Do No Harm' principle has been intertwined with ESG investment as investors are increasingly considering ESG factors alongside financial factors. In ESG investing, the ecological criteria include a company's use of energy sources, waste management, air and water pollution from operating activities and, fundamentally, its attitudes and actions towards climate. Environmentally, ESG promotes the conservation of the natural world. As for the social criteria, ESG covers internal and external stakeholder management, employment well-being, customer relationships, community management and, fundamentally, an organisation's stance on human rights. Socially, ESG promotes maintaining well-being. Finally, the governance criteria examine how a company is governed, including but not limited to executive compensation, board composition, whistle-blower schemes, bribery and corruption policies, reporting and disclosures and, fundamentally, an organisation's integrity and accountability. From a governance perspective, ESG sets the standards for running a company. In addition to this inside-out perspective (i.e., impact of companies on the sustainability factors in the outside world), some investors also co-currently adopt the outside-in perspective, where they assess the impact of sustainability factors in the outside world on their companies and investments. By integrating sustainability considerations, investors explicitly and systematically include ESG risks and opportunities into their considerations and practices, such as company-level investment analysis, wider-economy assessments and decision-making.

One of the leading global movements promoting the 'Do No Harm' principle is the United Nations Principles of Responsible Investment (UNPRI). As of 2021, there are 3826 signatories globally, representing USD 121.3 trillion assets under management. Of the total, only 83 signatories are headquartered in ASEAN states, as compared to 969 in the United States and 739 in the United Kingdom. Specifically, 60 signatories are from

Singapore, 13 signatories from Malaysia, 3 signatories from Indonesia, 3 signatories from Vietnam, 3 signatories from Thailand and 1 signatory from Brunei (UNPRI, 2022).

2.2 'Do Good' Principle

The 'Do Good' principle is the intention to and actions towards benefiting society and/ or the environment, stemming from either a moral obligation or moral ideals standpoint. While impact investment underpinned by this principle avoids harm, like investment underpinned by the 'Do No Harm' principle, it also actively seeks to benefit the wider public and natural world through strategic allocation of resources.

This approach allows for the mobilisation of capital to address societal and environmental challenges, whether on a local, national, regional or global level, in sectors such as healthcare, education, agriculture and finance. Investment with the 'Do Good' principle pursues explicit opportunities to generate positive societal or environmental impact while also generating financial returns and managing risks. It is an active process that requires active selection, portfolio construction, and management by investors, from both the economic and impact perspectives.

A prominent institution that promotes impact investment underpinned by the 'Do Good' principle is the Global Impact Investing Network (GIIN). According to GIIN, impact investments are any investments aiming to generate positive, measurable social and environmental impact alongside financial gains (GIIN, 2022). Thus, it promotes a hybrid approach that combines market goals driven by profitability and value capture with community goals that encourage collaboration and value creation (Roundy, 2019). The GIIN membership represents one of the largest communities engaging in impact investment, however, most of its members are from the Global North and only a handful are in SEA (e.g., UBS and Temasek in Singapore).

After this overview of the principles of impact investment, we turn to the impact investment market in SEA in particular.

3 The Impact Investment Market in Southeast Asia: An Overview

The impact investment market offers viable opportunities for investors to advance social and environmental solutions while also generating financial returns. This is evident in the tremendous growth of the impact investment market. In 2016, GIIN reported that impact assets grew from USD 25.4 billion to 35.5 billion from 2013 to 2015 (Mudaliar, Pineiro, & Bass, 2016). In 2020, GIIN reported that more than 1720 organisations managed USD 715 billion in impact AUM (Hand et al., 2020). As the market is growing, it is becoming more professionalised and robust. Progress can be seen in five main areas: 1) increasing research on market activity, trends, performance and practices; 2) sophistication of impact measurement and management practices; 3) growing numbers of professionals with relevant skills sets; 4) common understanding of definition and segmentation of the impact investing market; and 5) more data on investment products and opportunities (Hand et al., 2020). However, challenges, such as appropriate capital across the risk/return spectrum, suitable exit options and government support for the market, remain (Hand et al., 2020).

Looking closer, SEA is one of the fastest-growing regions for impact investment. The growth trajectory of impact investment in the region is witnessed through the quantum of impact capital (USD 6.7 billion) deployed in the two years from 2017 to 2019. This is more than half of the total amount (USD 11.3 billion) invested in the ten years from 2007 to 2016 (Prasad, Gokhale, & Agarwal, 2020). However, while a quarter of impact investors allocate to SEA, comparatively, only 3% of the total global impact AUM are allocated to the region (Hand et al., 2020), demonstrating both potential growth opportunities and challenges in attracting investments to the region.

To understand impact investment in SEA, it is essential to acknowledge that countries in the region vary across stages of economic development, political structures, maturity levels of business ecosystems and social development (such as Gini Coefficient, Human Development Index Rank, SDG Index Rank, Global Gender Gap Rank). These differences across the countries in the region create different opportunities for impact investment while also influencing the capital available for impact investment and the barriers that make it more difficult to channel capital towards positive impact for societies and the environment. To illustrate, Indonesia, Cambodia, the Philippines and Thailand received the highest amount of impact capital in the region. Specifically, Indonesia attracted the highest amount of impact capital, at USD 1,928.9 million, from 2017 to 2019, accounting for 31% of the total impact investment in the region (Prasad, Gokhale, & Agarwal, 2020). The vibrant ecosystem for impact investing in Indonesia, with impact-focused business support providers and large population base, contributed to its largest impact investing market status in ASEAN, both in terms of capital deployed and the number of deals (Prasad et al., 2018a). Cambodia, on the other hand, is not yet in the position to fully benefit from impact investment (Flynn, 2019), as it is transitioning from relying on international aid to address social and environmental issues. In line with the changing mantra of development from 'Funding Development' to 'Financing Development', the United Nation Development Program (UNDP) in Cambodia has been mobilising private sector resources to further the objectives of social development in Cambodia (Flynn, 2019). Being one of the poorest countries in the region, Myanmar's impact investment was gathering momentum with philanthropic institutions and impact investors (e.g., International Finance Corporation, Omidyar Network, Base of Pyramid Asia, Danish Investment Fund for Developing Countries, Insitor Impact Asia Fund of Insitor Management, and Asia Impact Investment Fund) steadily committing capital and expertise in specific social-economic impact sectors (Gaung, 2018) until the military coup in early 2021. The military coup has driven development funds and potential investment away, thus hindering the growth of the impact investment scene in Myanmar (Blenkinsop, 2021; Cornish, 2021; *The Jakarta Post*, 2021).

Furthermore, many investors who invest across SEA are not present in every country in which they invest, thus depending heavily on intermediaries and partners (Prasad *et al.*, 2018b). Although most investors are not present in their countries of investment, many are present in the region, often headquartered in Singapore, as a central financial hub in SEA with USD 2.9 trillion of AUM at the end of 2019 from 895 asset managers according to the Monetary Authority of Singapore (British Council, 2020b). Singapore is also known for its intermediaries that provide comprehensive support to social enterprises from business incubation to financial assistance (Watanabe & Tanaka, 2016). Indeed, Singapore is a hub of impact investment with international impact funds, such as Omidyar Network and LeapFrog Investments, as well as financial institutions, such as BNP Paribas, Credit Suisse and UOB Venture Management, providing options to (potential) SEA recipients of impact investment. Similarly, Indonesia is fast becoming a hub. In 2016, an estimated number of 25 foreign-based impact investors were looking to enter Indonesia, such as Garden Impact, Global Innovation Fund, Phi Trust and Melloy Fund by Rare, through operating with a remote team or by partnering with locals (UNDP, 2016). With contradictions, there are also at least four large investors who left the country, such as Grameen Foundation and LGT VP, due to common reasons including lack of investable pipelines fitting investment criteria and geographical focus on other regions.

Apart from international impact investors, many local impact funds are taking root. For instance, in Vietnam, Lotus Impact Fund provides seed capital and incubation support to seed-stage businesses, Dragon Capital's Mekong Brahmaputra Clean Development Fund invests an average of USD 5 million in environment-related causes and Evergreen Labs focuses on execution and scaling of existing positive impact solutions and business plans.

Much investment activities by private and public funds are driven by specific social outcomes areas (Castellas, Ormiston, & Findlay, 2018). In SEA, investors have primarily deployed capital to sectors that promote financial inclusion, expand access to basic services and create livelihoods through energy and infrastructure (Prasad et al., 2018b). In terms of private impact investments, the financial services sector, specifically microfinance, accounts for most impact deals and capital deployed in Cambodia, Myanmar and East Timor. In contrast, most capital deployed in Laos and Thailand has been in energy, whereas Vietnam and Singapore have most capital deployed in the information and communication technology (ICT) sector (Prasad et al., 2018b).

While these are 'hot' sectors for impact investment, these sectors may not necessarily match the needs on the ground. For instance, while East Timor faces a plethora of developmental challenges attributed to years of violence and instability, such as high under-nourishment and malnutrition (more than half of the children below the age of five demonstrate stunted growth (Sachs et al., 2021)) and poor healthcare (maternal mortality is at 215 per 100,000 live births (Sachs et al., 2021)), all impact investments in East Timor are only in the microfinance sector. Similarly, in Laos, all investment capital goes to financial services and infrastructure, while the country faces several developmental issues, including food security (e.g., one-fifth of the country's population consumes less than the minimum dietary requirements (ADB, 2021)) and poor healthcare (e.g., an under-five mortality rate of 86 per 1000 lives (ASEAN, 2017)). While these discrepancies between need and where capital is deployed highlight the challenges of impact investment in meeting social and/or environmental goals together with financial goals, they also demonstrate that some country-specific social entrepreneurship ecosystems are not mature enough or lack track record for investments in other sectors to occur. This level of ecosystem development consequently shapes the risk attitudes of investors and the required expertise to invest in industries without a prior track record. These discrepancies also showcase that the general market and its investment activities are often influenced by the strength and stability of institutions, as well as the economic environment and philanthropic traditions.

4 Impact Investment in Southeast Asia: A Framework

Impact investing challenges the traditional views that social and environmental issues should be addressed through state action and philanthropy, and that market investments should focus exclusively on achieving financial returns for shareholders. Indeed, impact investment can play an increasingly important role in addressing social and environmental challenges in ways that intersect with the public, private and third sectors, include diverse participants and gain support from other organisations. In this section, we offer an ecosystem framework of impact investment in SEA focusing on (1) the dynamics between impact investment with the public, private and third sectors; (2) capital providers, managers and recipients as the main participants in the ecosystem; and (3) the entities that provide support to the ecosystem to thrive.

4.1 Dynamics with Public, Private and Third Sectors

4.1.1 Dynamics with the Public Sector

Adopted by all 193 United Nations member states, the SDGs are a global effort to pursue an agenda for sustainable economic growth, social inclusion and environmental sustainability. Many of the SDGs are of a public service nature, such as health, education, basic infrastructure and public utilities, and within the remit of the public sector. The United Nations Conference on Trade and Development (UNCTAD) estimated the

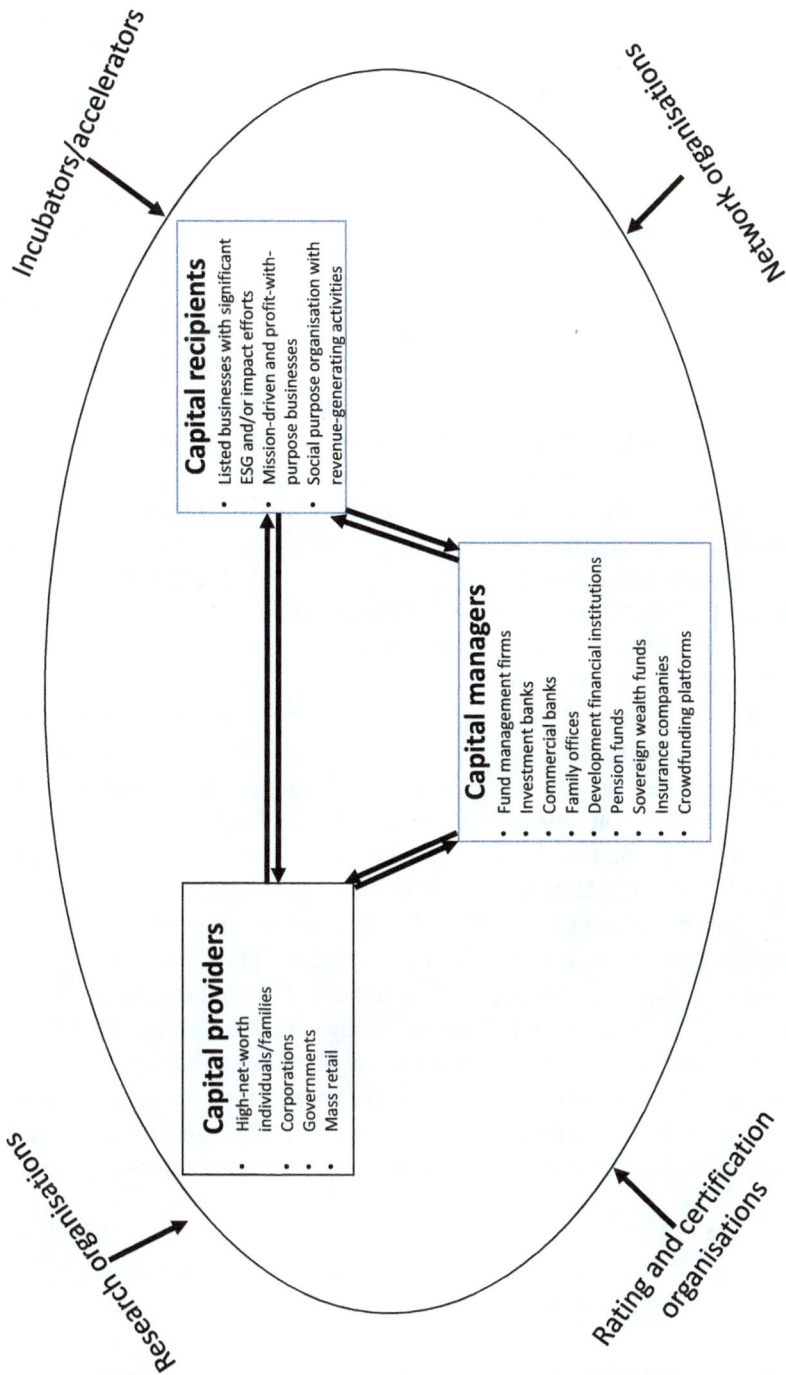

Figure 18.1: Impact investment ecosystem in Southeast Asia.

total investment needed in developing countries ranges from USD 3.3 trillion to USD 4.5 trillion per year for basic infrastructure, food security, health, education, climate breakdown mitigation and adaptation. Yet, there is an average annual funding short-fall of some USD 2.5 trillion (UNCTAD, 2014). Thus, while public sector action is required to meet the SDGs, it may be insufficient to meet demands across all SDG-related areas. Governments, especially of developing countries, have overwhelming responsibilities and chronic resource constraints and face debt crises (Harris & Lane, 2018; UNCTAD, 2019).

In this regard, impact investment is one way to support and finance the pursuit of the SDGs together with the public sector. For example, in the Philippines, despite the high allocation from the national budget to the education sector, the country suffers from the 'global learning crisis' where students have a low mastery of their subjects (Arowana Impact Capital Group, 2020). Subsequently, there are opportunities for impact investment in the education field, in complementing the government's efforts to establish an accessible, quality education system. Similarly, Malaysia faces the threat of a double burden in nutritional challenges, where 20.7% of children under five suffer from stunting and 12.7% of children are obese (UNICEF, 2019). To solve this challenge, it will take a multi-sectoral approach including education systems, health systems and water and sanitation systems, to which impact investment is in a good position to contribute in a collaborative manner.

However, SEA governments' outlook towards impact investment varies from country to country. In Singapore, the government has spearheaded multiple initiatives to foster the social entrepreneurship ecosystem, including the establishment of the Singapore Centre for Social Enterprises (raiSE) with funding from the Tote Board and the Ministry of Social and Family Development. In Thailand, the Social Enterprise Promotion Act was enacted in 2019, with establishments of the National Social Enterprise Promotion Committee, the Office of Social Enterprise Promotion (OSEP) and the Social Enterprise Promotion Fund (British Council, 2020a). Likewise, in the Philippines, the government has been proactive in supporting the social entrepreneurship sector, through the proposed Poverty Reduction Through Social Enterprise (PRESENT) Bill and Social Value Bill (18th Congress of the Republic of the Philippines, 2019). In contrast, in Cambodia, the government does not support social enterprises actively including legislation, funding, incubation or any other form (Mohan, Harsh, & Modi, 2017). In Myanmar, too, significant support from the government is lacking (British Council, 2013).

4.1.2 Dynamics with the Private Sector

Traditional capitalism promotes short-termism through unsustainable practices at the cost of the environment, communities, employees and future generations (Rayer, 2017). Companies have caused disasters, such as offshore oil spill incidents in Thailand

and Indonesia (Gokkon, 2019; *South China Morning Post*, 2022), disregarded human rights, such as one of the world's largest manufacturers of rubber gloves from Malaysia that used forced and indentured labour (Pattisson, 2021) and practised corruption and bribery, such as the illegal exploitation of jade mines in Myanmar (Heijmans, 2015).

As more and more of these cases get exposed by the media, they result in reputational damage and adverse litigation, thus leading to financial losses. Consequently, companies are encouraged to change their unsustainable practices. Profit maximisation in the short term is no longer an acceptable sole objective of businesses, but the optimisation of value that recognises the need for sustainability and impact considerations (Chandler, 2016; Pollman, 2021). At the same time, responsible companies have built-in advantages in targeting higher long-term profits by addressing sustainability risks and opportunities, thus boosting investors' confidence in such companies and putting pressure on traditional profit-maximising, cost-cutting entities to move towards more ethical and sustainable practices, as well as products and services that bring value. Indeed, businesses and investors increasingly view their ability to manage sustainability issues as material to their financial performance (Bugg-Levine & Goldstein, 2009). To facilitate this, Bursa Malaysia (Malaysia Stock Exchange) mandated sustainability reporting in 2006 and signed the Sustainable Stock Exchange's voluntary commitment to promote sustainability reporting in 2015 (*The Star*, 2015). Similarly in its neighbouring country, the Singapore Exchange (SGX) issued guidelines for companies to include sustainability reporting as part of annual reports on a 'comply or explain' basis in 2017 (PWC, 2016).

While corporate sustainability is slowly evolving to incorporate ESG practices and creating impact value, traditional corporate social responsibility (CSR) too furthers social entrepreneurship through various mechanisms. For instance, the Philippines Business for Social Progress (PBSP) is the largest and most influential corporate-led social development foundation, consisting of more than 250 large, medium and small-sized businesses. As of 2020, PhP 2329.54 millions were disbursed as grants and financial advances, and PhP 155 millions as development loans for micro small and medium enterprises (Philippine Business for Social Progress, 2020). In contrast, in Cambodia, CSR activity is at its infancy, thus capital from corporates is limited, while in Singapore, CSR among corporations is moving towards integrating ESG into respective business practices and operations. These examples illustrate the different pace of adoption and transition between CSR, ESG and impact investment (not mutually exclusive), in SEA. It is also important to note that many SEA economies are made of micro, small and medium-sized enterprises (MSMEs) with limited staff and capital. Thus, CSR at large scale with professionalised activities may be confined to only a few big corporations in certain SEA countries with more established economies. For instance, more than 93% of Vietnam's 500,000 businesses are small and medium-sized enterprises (SMEs) that have fewer than 30 staff and an average registered capital of USD 480,000 (Mohan, Harsh & Modi, 2017). Similarly, in Malaysia, there are 1,226,494

MSMEs in 2021, which account for 97.4% of overall establishments in Malaysia (SME Corp. Malaysia, 2021).

Moreover, the number of social enterprises is growing. As the legal definition of social enterprises differ from country to country, here, we broadly include registered businesses that embed societal missions in their offerings, revenue-generating non-governmental organisations (NGOs) that may have commercial arms registered separately, microfinance institutions and impact start-ups, all of which use market mechanisms to achieve specific social or environmental goals. Broadly defined, along the timeline of 2014 to 2017, there were approximately 100 entities in Malaysia, 92 entities in Cambodia, 400 entities in Singapore, 400 in Thailand, 454 entities in Indonesia, 645 entities in Myanmar, 1,000 entities in Vietnam and 30,000 entities in the Philippines (Mohan, Harsh, & Modi, 2017). Impact investment is a key mechanism to enable these businesses to achieve their missions. This is because social enterprises often face challenges in mobilising resources (Jayawarna, Jones, & Macpherson, 2020) and operate in environments where social and environmental issues, such as supporting refugees and indigenous population in Malaysia (Au, Drencheva, & Yew, 2022), are prominent (Mair, Martí, & Ventresca, 2012; Mair & Marti, 2009; Qureshi, Kistruck, & Bhatt, 2016).

4.1.3 Dynamics with the Third Sector

On the capital supply side, foundations have pioneered much of the work to develop the impact investing market, particularly through grants that fund impact investment pilots and studies in the early stage private equity and debt (Martin, 2013). Foundations can act as an exemplary investor, catalytic capital investor, intermediary developer, data provider, standard setter, network builder and thought leader (Wood, 2020). In SEA, foundations also play an important role in capacity building to support the impact investment ecosystem. For example, international foundations, such as ADM Capital Foundation and the Cambodia International Education Support Foundation, have been working extensively on changing the mind-set of social sector players to foster transparency, governance and effectiveness (Mettgenberg-Lemière, 2017). As the market grows, foundations will continue to play an increasingly important role in disseminating knowledge on best practice and capacity building. However, they too struggle to explicate their expectations of impact investments, such as whether or not they should take first-loss positions in order to catalyse participation of traditional investors and how much of a foundation's endowment should go into impact investments (Aggarwala & Frasch, 2017).

On the capital demand side, non-profit organisations (NPOs) are increasingly adopting business techniques to be more self-sustainable through revenue-generating activities. For example, many of Cambodia's 3600 NGOs have expanded into the social enterprise space with the aim to diversify their revenue streams as well as pursue alternative ways of achieving their missions (Lyne, Khieng, & Ngin, 2015), thus increasing the number of mission-driven ventures for impact investment opportunities. This situation is similar in other SEA countries, such as Malaysia and Indonesia (British Council Malaysia, 2018; UNDP, 2016).

Overall, impact investment can be at the intersection of addressing social and environmental challenges through interactions with the public, private and third sectors. It can aid governments funding solutions to these problems. It can support and encourage commercial businesses to respond to the demands of consumers and investors. It can provide the third sector with much needed resources.

4.2 Participants in Impact Investment

Impact investment has attracted a wide variety of participants, including fund managers, investment and commercial banks, family offices, foundations, development finance institutions, pension funds, sovereign wealth funds, religious institutions, insurance companies, crowdfunding platforms, individual investors and other intermediaries. While there are many participants in the impact investment space, we broadly categorise them into capital providers, capital managers and capital recipients to highlight the heterogeneity of participants and discuss their broad roles. We present each category on its own; however, it is also important to acknowledge the feedback loops that exist between capital providers, managers and recipients as they engage in the impact investment process, learn with and from one another, provide one another with feedback and use their experience to make different decisions in the present and in the future.

4.2.1 Capital Providers

The category of capital providers mainly includes high-net-worth individuals (HNWIs) and families, corporations, governments and retail investors. They are asset owners, with choices to either invest on their own or engage with capital managers to make investments on their behalf.

High-net-worth individuals represent the most active capital provider in the impact investment space (World Economic Forum, 2013). Indeed, a third (37.3%) of the portfolios of Asia-Pacific (excluding Japan) HNWIs are geared towards social investments, compared to only 31.6% for those globally (Capgemini, 2016). Private impact investors, who tend to focus on providing early stage capital, have been particularly active in Indonesia, the Philippines, Cambodia and Malaysia (Prasad, Gokhale, & Agarwal, 2020). At 45.8% of portfolio allocations towards social impact, Indonesia is a global leader in social impact investing from HNWIs, followed closely by Malaysia (43.6%) (Capgemini, 2016). Moving forward, the importance of HNWIs as impact investors will grow, as the investor community changes from baby boomers to millennials with expected intergenerational wealth transfer. This intergenerational wealth transfer, combined with their labour income, can have profound implications for financial markets if these new investors make different investment decisions aligned with their values, as already suggested by emerging data (Fort & Loman, 2016). For example, a 2019 survey found that 95% of millennials were interested in sustainable investing (Morgan Stanley, 2019).

Corporates also provide capital towards impact investment. For instance, in Indonesia, most funding for non-profits and social enterprises seems to come from multinational corporations. For example, Kopernik, a last-mile technology distribution enterprise, receives regular funds from ExxonMobil, Philips and Energia (Mohan, Harsh, & Modi, 2017). Similarly, Cellcard, a telecommunications company in Cambodia, has shifted from piecemeal projects to impact investments through funding platforms (Mohan, Harsh, & Modi, 2017).

Governments also own assets that can be invested purposefully. For example, as part of the government's effort to stimulate social innovation, the Malaysian government launched the MYR 3 million (USD 690,000) Social Outcome Fund through Agensi Inovasi Malaysia (ceased in 2020). The pay-for-success vehicle was designed to facilitate funding from various stakeholders into social enterprises and social purpose organisations. Social investments made were entitled to a reimbursement from the Fund if they resulted in cost savings for similar government interventions. Furthermore, the Malaysian Employees Provident Fund (national compulsory scheme) announced in mid-2021 its plan to have a fully compliant ESG portfolio by 2030 and a climate-neutral portfolio (with zero greenhouse gas emissions) by 2050, making it one of the first Asian pension funds to publicly commit to sustainability (Tan, 2022). However, these Malaysia-specific examples are not seen in many other SEA countries. For instance, the Cambodian government has not yet embraced the potential for ESG and impact investment as a force for economic growth and social improvement.

Retail investors also supply capital towards the impact investment space. To illustrate, a report by the Longitude and Rockefeller Foundation (2019) suggested that, while 77% of investors currently have 4 to 5% of their total portfolio invested in impact investing products, 55% of investors expect their allocation to impact investing funds to increase between 6 to 20% over the next two years. Similarly, Morgan Stanley (2017) reported that 75% of individual investors are interested in sustainable investing, 71% believe that companies with leading sustainability practices may be better long-term investments and 80% are interested in investments that can be customised to meet their interests and goals. These results showcase that more individual investors are interested and will likely increasingly allocate funds towards impact investment. Indeed, fund managers report that the amount of capital invested by retail investors has grown by 20% compound annual growth rate (CAGR) over five years (The Rockefeller Foundation, 2019).

4.2.2 Capital Managers

The capital managers category includes development financial institutions (DFIs), private and public fund managers, investment and commercial banks, family offices, crowdfunding platforms, among others.

Within SEA, DFIs remain the dominant players, accounting for 92% of the total impact investment (close to USD 11.2 billion) in the region (2007–2016) (Prasad et al., 2020), particularly in Indonesia, Thailand, Vietnam and Myanmar. For instance, Asian Development Bank (ADB) and Asian Infrastructure Investment Bank (AIIB) are development finance institutions that invest in the SEA countries. These institutions provide evidence of financial viability for private-sector investors while targeting specific social and environmental goals.

Other financial institutions, such as investment banks, are also gradually entering the impact investment market in what many see as an opportunity for profit over the long term and a response to clients looking to align investments with their personal values and goals (Hummels & Fracassi, 2016). For example, the Singapore-headquartered UOB Venture Management, a signatory to the Operating Principles for Impact Management, launched the Asia Impact Investment Fund (AIIF) in 2015 to invest in growth companies in SEA and China that improve the lives of lower income communities at the base of the economic pyramid. As of 2019, the fund has impacted more than 36,000 farmers, 700,000 micro-entrepreneurs and 10,000,000 young people from low-income households (UOB, 2019). From the sustainability perspective, in 2021 in Thailand, KBank Private Banking and Kasikorn Asset Management launched K-SUSTAIN-UI long–short fund that aims to generate profits from stocks that are positively or negatively affected by the transition towards sustainable business operations. While these are specific examples to emphasise the relevance of impact investment among financial institutions, generally, financial institutions are slow to adopt impact investment mechanisms.

There are also sovereign fund managers, who commit to the 'Do No Harm' and/or 'Do Good' principles. For instance, launched in 2015, Sukuk Ihsan is Malaysia's first social-impact bond (SIB) based on Islamic finance, and the first AAA-rated globally. It focuses on environmental causes, such as renewable energy, and social causes, such as education, and is managed by Khazanah Nasional Berhad, the Government of Malaysia's Investment Fund (Khazanah Nasional Berhad, 2015).

As discussed earlier, foundations are increasingly diversifying their asset allocations, thus contributing to the increasing size of impact investments. For instance, YCAB in Indonesia has evolved from being a non-profit foundation focused on sustainable development to a local impact investor, funding for-profit enterprises that offer products and services to emerging consumers. Similarly, religious funds are also laying the groundwork for impact investment. For example, Dompet Dhuafa and Rumah Zakat, the largest zakat collectors in Indonesia (home to the largest Muslim population in the world), invest in traditional charities and increasingly local small and micro enterprises in the education and health sectors (Chhina et al., 2014).

Moreover, crowdfunding, an intermediary between retail investors and entrepreneurs looking to raise capital through alternative financing mechanisms, is an emerging phenomenon. For instance, Kitabisa.co.id is a leading crowdfunding platform in Indonesia to facilitate investments in social enterprises and iGrow is an agricultural platform raising capital for farm inputs from urban social investors. In Singapore, there are several models: donation-based, rewards-based, lending-based, securities-based and equity crowdfunding. A few examples include FundedHere, Crowdo, Capital Match, Giveasia and Giving.sg. As these crowdfunding platforms reach out to a large audience, they have the potential to mobilise capital from the public and foster campaign capacity of fundraisers.

4.2.3 Capital Recipients

The capital recipients category includes businesses with sustainability and/or impact focus and social enterprises (broadly defined).

With the aim to achieve their social and/or environmental mission, social entrepreneurs utilise impact capital to establish and scale their businesses. They typically fundraise to grow their team size, enhance technological foundations or enter a new market. While they are recipients of impact investments, they face several hurdles. For example, many social enterprises in Vietnam encounter financing constraints, such as access to investors (45%) and small investment sizes (44%) (British Council, 2019). Conversely, in Indonesia, social enterprises face a small-ticket size funding gap. While more than 70% of social enterprises in Indonesia are in the pre-seed and seed stage (requiring USD 10,000 to USD 150,000 on average), most foreign impact investors come with a larger ticket-size offering (more than USD 1,000,000) (UNDP, 2016). These examples showcase the mismatch between the needs of capital recipients with the criteria of capital providers/managers. Having said that, there is undeniably growth in social enterprises accessing financing. For example, in Indonesia, investment in social enterprises was approximately USD 23 million in 2014, growing to USD 43 million in 2016 (UNDP, 2016). Listed businesses with sustainability and/or impact focus are also recipients of impact capital. They typically include businesses within certain fields, such as renewable energy, waste management, education and healthcare, to name a few. Increasingly, as more companies are transitioning from unethical practices to responsible and sustainable practices, while offering products and services of societal and environmental value, capital flows towards these companies.

As discussed earlier, traditional NGOs transitioning to social enterprises are also impact capital recipients. However, most of these transitioning NGOs lack several qualities, such as perceived good management, market fit and potential to scale (UNDP, 2016), thus making them not investment ready.

4.3 Support Organisations

Other players, such as network organisations and research institutions, provide support in various forms to capital providers, managers and recipients.

Network organisations, such as membership-based networks, offer resources and services to promote best practices, share data and information, and foster opportunities and collaborations. Asian Venture Philanthropy Network (AVPN) and Aspen Network of Development Entrepreneurs (ANDE) are among the most prominent international network organisations within the SEA context. While AVPN, a network that facilitates the flow of capital from around the world into the social sector in Asia, enables multi-sector collaborations in numerous philanthropic and investment initiatives, ANDE, a global network of organisations that propel entrepreneurship in developing economies, provides financial, educational and business support to growing businesses. An example of a local network is the Angel Investment Network Indonesia (ANGIN). Within Indonesia, it supports both investors and companies along the fundraising journey by providing sourcing, due diligence support and legal implementation to investors, while preparing companies to be investment ready.

There are also organisations that aim to promote accountability and credibility within the impact investment space through advocating and developing impact management and measurements tools. With regard to impact, globally accepted frameworks such as IRIS + and Social Return on Investments (SROI) are often used for impact reporting. However, time cost and financial cost are restraining factors for investees and investors to undertake impact assessments through upskilling internal stakeholders or third-party evaluators (Prasad, 2018). With regard to ESG, rating providers, such as Refinitiv, FTSE Russell, Sustainalytics and RepRisk, offer various services including but not limited to stock screening and research on specific sectors. For example, the FTSE4GOOD Bursa Malaysia Shariah Index (F4GBMS) launched by Bursa Malaysia and FTSE Russell aims to cater to investors' demand for ESG index solutions. Collectively, these measurement and rating organisations generally aim to provide an assessment of ESG risks and opportunities, as well as impact of companies' products and services, associated with an investment. While they continue to make progress in improving adaptation, they continue to face significant hurdles regarding fairness, accuracy and consistency, given that impact can be subjective, multidimensional and not always directly measurable with ceilings of accountability.

Incubators and accelerators provide mentorship and technical assistance to impact investment recipients. For example, in Cambodia, Impact Hub Phnom Penh has been contributing to the capacity building of start-ups, striving to solve problems in the country. In 2016, they partnered with USAID Development Innovations to launch Cambodia's first one-year social business incubation programme, providing support through business training, mentoring and access to prototyping budgets (Impact Hub Phnom Penh, 2016). Similarly, in Myanmar, incubators such as Opportunities Now and Phandeeyar are strengthening the pipeline for impact investment, through seed capital, hands-on mentoring support and access to networks and co-working spaces.

There are also institutions that fund and support impact-related research within the SEA context. For instance, the Lien Centre for Social Innovation based in Singapore offers thought leadership and evidence-to-action translation research, aiming to drive social consciousness and enable partnership-driven innovation. Similarly, the British Council also aims to promote the growth of social enterprise and impact investment in the region through research, policy dialogues, networking (e.g., Social Economy & Investment Conference, Social Investment Platform) and training (e.g., Business and Investment Readiness Programme, Skills for Social Entrepreneurs) (British Council, 2022).

Overall, these support organisations enable growth and professionalisation in the impact investment space through facilitating knowledge exchange among impact investors and increasing the supply of investment-ready impact capital recipients.

5 Discussion

5.1 Implications and Future Opportunities for Research

Our conceptual framework of impact investment in SEA offers a foundation for future comparative research. It shows an ecosystem with its dynamic interactions with the public, private and third sectors, diverse participants and support organisations. The examples and trends discussed in this chapter showcase the diversity of impact investment ecosystems in the region, instead of treating it as a single and homogeneous ecosystem. Based on the trends and examples provided in this chapter, one can assume that the impact investment ecosystems in higher income and more stable countries (e.g., Malaysia, Singapore) are more developed in comparison to lower income countries with recent or ongoing destabilising events, such as military coups, and weaker institutions (e.g., Myanmar, Cambodia), while data for some countries is severely limited (e.g., East Timor, Laos). However, robust and systematic research on the topic with comparable data across the region does not exist. Thus, it is not clear if these perceived differences are due to data availability, different levels of activity or different institutional configurations that make impact investment more or less appropriate and appealing for capital providers, managers and recipients. Thus, future research, that can use our framework as a foundation for comparison, is needed to investigate the differences across the countries in the region and the nuances in activities, mechanisms and outcomes of impact investment based on the configurations of formal (e.g., rule of law, legal recognition of social enterprises) and informal institutions (e.g., trust, legitimacy of social enterprises and impact investment).

It would also be particularly valuable for future research to differentiate impact investment underpinned by the 'Do No Harm' and 'Do Good' principles. Ultimately, the two principles prioritise different decision logics and goals, thus they are differently suited for the different types of capital investors, managers and recipients. Future research is required to investigate how impact investments with the two principles differ in prominence, frequency of use, challenges for recipients and social/environmental and financial returns across the SEA region.

Finally, our framework focuses on the organisational and institutional levels of analysis. However, within these organisations are individuals who make impact investment decisions (whether they are to provide or seek capital), interact with individuals from other sectors and with other roles in the ecosystem and reflect on their own values and experiences. Such individual level experiences and interactions are particularly useful for understanding the micro-foundations of the impact investment ecosystem and how it functions, grows and changes over time. Yet, our current understanding of individual level experiences and interactions within impact investment ecosystems in SEA is severely limited. Future research is required to investigate how, for example, individuals in capital receiving organisations build trust with impact investors and navigate business challenges, given the power dynamics at play.

5.2 Implications for Practice

For capital owners, this chapter provides a snapshot of the different players within the impact investment space, suggesting how they can set the standards for capital managers and recipients in investing and operating responsibly, sustainably and impactfully. For capital managers, this chapter showcases the ecosystem of impact investment in SEA, providing insights on challenges and opportunities throughout the region. This will support them in asset allocation, geography selection and other parameter-setting of funds, as well as setting reasonable goals to achieve by connecting capital to impact.

For capital recipients, this chapter provides an overview of the impact investment landscape in SEA, sharing valuable information about where they can turn to for financing new and scaling ventures. Importantly, the chapter highlights the push for incorporating sustainability factors (Tan, 2018) and shows the growing focus of investors towards financing mission-driven and sustainable businesses, as well as traditional commercial organisations with a good track record of ESG efforts and social responsibility. In this regard, the chapter brings attention not only to impact investment as a potential source of financing for mission-driven and sustainable enterprises, but also potentially to all types of investments underpinned by the 'Do No Harm' principle.

For individuals with an intention to get involved or are already part of the ecosystem, the chapter provides an overview of how they can actively contribute to achieving the SDGs. Beyond starting their own mission-driven and sustainable businesses, individuals have other options to support the achievement of the SDGs through impact investment. For example, they can consider career options in support organisations, such as membership bodies and research entities that support capital providers, managers and recipients by promoting best practices, sharing data and insights, and fostering opportunities for collaborations. On another hand, they can also use their capital for impact investment, for example, investing in impact investment funds and equity crowdfunding campaigns.

References

18th Congress of the Republic of the Philippines (2019). *An Act: Institutionalizing the Poverty Reduction through Social Entrepreneurship (Present) Program and Promoting Social Enterprises with the Poor as Primary Stakeholders* [Senate Bill No. 820]. https://legacy.senate.gov.ph/lisdata/3034527203!.pdf

Asian Development Bank (ADB) (2021). *Poverty: Lao PDR.* (Lao People's Democratic Republic) Asian Development Bank. https://www.adb.org/countries/lao-pdr/poverty

Aggarwala, R. T., & Frasch, C. A. (2017). The philanthropy as one big impact investment: A framework for evaluating a foundation's blended performance. *The Foundation Review, 9*(2), https://doi.org/10.9707/1944-5660.1370

Arowana Impact Capital Group (2020). *Education in the Philippines: Untapped Opportunity for Impact Investors.* https://arowanaimpactcapital.com/education-in-the-philippines/

Association of Southeast Asian Nations (ASEAN) (2016). ASEAN socio-cultural community blueprint 2025. The ASEAN Secretariat. https://www.asean.org/wp-content/uploads/2012/05/8.-March-2016-ASCC-Blueprint-2025.pdf

Association of Southeast Asian Nations (ASEAN) (2017). ASEAN statistical report on millennium development goals 2017. The ASEAN Secretariat. http://www.aseanstats.org/wp-content/uploads/2017/08/ASEAN_MDG_2017.pdf

Association of Southeast Asian Nations (ASEAN) (2020a). ASEAN sustainable development goals indicators baseline report. The ASEAN Secretariat. https://www.aseanstats.org/publication/asean-sdg-report-2020/

Association of Southeast Asian Nations (ASEAN) (2020b). 1st ASEAN policy brief: Economic impact of COVID-19 outbreak on ASEAN. The ASEAN Secretariat. https://asean.org/book/1st-asean-policy-brief-economic-impact-of-covid-19-outbreak-on-asean/

Au, W. C., Drencheva, A., & Yew, J. L. (2022). How do refugee entrepreneurs navigate institutional voids? Insights from Malaysia. In D. G. Pickernell, M. Battisti, Z. Dann & C. Ekinsmyth (Eds.), *Disadvantaged Entrepreneurship and the Entrepreneurial Ecosystem* (Vol. 14pp 121–144). Emerald Publishing Limited. https://doi.org/10.1108/S2040-724620220000014006

Blenkinsop, P.(20214March). *EU Suspends Development Funds for Myanmar after Army Coup.* Reuters. https://www.reuters.com/article/us-myanmar-politics-eu-idUSKBN2AW1EX

British Council (2013). Social enterprise landscape in Myanmar. British Council. https://www.britishcouncil.org/sites/default/files/burma_report.pdf

British Council (2019). Social enterprise in Vietnam. British council. https://www.britishcouncil.vn/sites/default/files/social-enterprise-in-vietnam.pdf

British Council (2020a). Global social enterprise: The state of social enterprise in Thailand. British Council. https://www.britishcouncil.org/sites/default/files/state_of_social_enterprise_in_thailand_2020_final_web.pdf

British Council (2020b). Global social enterprise – The state of social enterprise in Singapore. British Council. https://www.britishcouncil.org/sites/default/files/the_state_of_social_enterprise_in_singapore_0.pdf

British Council (2022). Social enterprise past programmes. British Council. https://www.britishcouncil.my/programmes/education/isp

British Council Malaysia (2018). The state of social enterprise in Malaysia. British Council. https://www.britishcouncil.org/sites/default/files/the_state_of_social_enterprise_in_malaysia_british_council_low_res.pdf

Bugg-Levine, A., & Goldstein, J. (2009). Impact investing: Harnessing capital markets to solve problems at scale. *Community Development Investment Review, 5*(2), 30–41.

Capgemini (2016). *Asia-Pacific Now Leads the World in High Net Worth Population and Wealth, Finds the Asia-Pacific Wealth Report 2016.* Capgemini: https://www.capgemini.com/news/asia-pacific-now-leads-the-world-in-high-net-worth-population-and-wealth-finds-the-asia-pacific/

Castellas, E. I.-P., Ormiston, J., & Findlay, S. (2018). Financing social entrepreneurship: The role of impact investment in shaping social enterprise in Australia. *Social Enterprise Journal, 14*(2), 130–155. https://doi.org/10.1108/SEJ-02-2017-0006

Chandler, D. (2016). *Strategic Corporate Social Responsibility: Sustainable Value Creation.* (4th edition.) SAGE. https://us.sagepub.com/en-us/nam/strategic-corporate-social-responsibility/book258527

Chhina, S., Petersik, W., Loh, J., & Evans, D. (2014). *From Charity to Change: Social Investment in Selected Southeast Asian Countries.* Lien Centre for Social Innovation, Singapore Management University. https://ink.library.smu.edu.sg/cgi/viewcontent.cgi?article=1010&context=lien_reports

Cornish, L. (2021, 15 February). *Donors Respond to the Myanmar Coup by Redirecting Funds.* Devex. https://www.devex.com/news/sponsored/donors-respond-to-the-myanmar-coup-by-redirecting-funds-99141

Demirgüç-Kunt, A., Klapper, L., Singer, D., Ansar, S., & Hess, J. (2017). *The Global Findex Database: Measuring Financial Inclusion and the Fintech Revolution.* World Bank Group. https://openknowledge.worldbank.org/handle/10986/29510

Flynn, G. (2019, 14 November). *How Does Cambodia Fit into the Global Trend of Impact Investing?* Capital Cambodia. https://capitalcambodia.com/how-does-cambodia-fit-into-the-global-trend-of-impact-investing/

Fort, A., & Loman, J. (2016). *Millennials & Impact Investment. A TONIIC Institute Report with Support from Bank of the West, Family Wealth Advisors.* http://www.pva-advisory.com/wp-content/uploads/2016/10/Millennials-Impact-Investment-May-2016.pdf

Gaung, J. S.(201818January). *Impact Investments in Myanmar Gather Momentum but Still to Scale Up.* DealStreetAsia. https://www.dealstreetasia.com/stories/impact-funds-for-myanmar-gather-momentum-but-still-way-to-scale-89207/

Global Impact Investing Network (GIIN) (2022). *What You Need to Know about Impact Investing.* Global Impact Investing Network (GIIN). https://thegiin.org/impact-investing/need-to-know/

Gokkon, B. (2019, 31 July). Indonesia investigates oil spill in java sea by state energy company. Mongabay Environmental News. https://news.mongabay.com/2019/07/indonesia-investigates-oil-spill-in-java-sea-by-state-energy-company/

Hand, D., Dithrich, H., Sunderji, S., & Nova, N. (2020). *GIIN Annual Impact Investor Survey 2020.* Global Impact Investing Network (GIIN). https://thegiin.org/assets/GIIN%20Annual%20Impact%20Investor%20Survey%202020.pdf

Harris, E., & Lane, C. (2018). *Debt as an Obstacle to the Sustainable Development Goals | UN DESA | United Nations Department of Economic and Social Affairs.* Department of Economic and Social Affairs, United Nations. https://www.un.org/development/desa/en/news/financing/debt-as-an-obstacle-to-sdgs.html

Heijmans, P. (2015, 23 October). The corruption of Myanmar's jade trade. Al Jazeera News. https://www.aljazeera.com/features/2015/10/23/the-corruption-of-myanmars-jade-trade

Hummels, H., & Fracassi, R. (2016). The institutional impact investing revolution. *Stanford Social Innovation Review*. https://ssir.org/articles/entry/the_institutional_impact_investing_revolution

International Monetary Fund (IMF) (2021). *Regional Economic Outlook for Asia and Pacific: Navigating Waves of New Variants, Pandemic Resurgence Slows the Recovery*. Washington, DC: International Monetary Fund.

Impact Hub Phnom Penh (2016). *The Launch of Something Epic!* Impact Hub Phnom Penh. https://phnompenh.impacthub.net/the-launch-of-something-epic/

Jayawarna, D., Jones, O., & Macpherson, A. (2020). Resourcing social enterprises: The role of socially oriented bootstrapping. *British Journal of Management, 31*(1), 56–79.

Nasional Berhad, K. (2015). *Khazanah Issues World's First Ringgit-Denominated Sustainable and Responsible Investment Sukuk*. Khazanah Nasional Berhad. https://www.khazanah.com.my/news_press_releases/khazanah-issues-worlds-first-ringgit-denominated-sustainable-and-responsible-investment-sukuk/

Lyne, I., Khieng, S., & Ngin, C. (2015). Social enterprise in Cambodia: An overview. *ICSEM Working Papers, No. 05, Liege: Liege: The International Comparative Social Enterprise Models (ICSEM) Project*. https://doi.org/10.13140/RG.2.1.1848.9449

Mair, J., & Marti, I. (2009). Entrepreneurship in and around institutional voids: A case study from Bangladesh. *Journal of Business Venturing, 24*(5), 419–435. https://doi.org/10.1016/j.jbusvent.2008.04.006

Mair, J., Martí, I., & Ventresca, M. J. (2012). Building inclusive markets in rural Bangladesh: How intermediaries work institutional voids. *Academy of Management Journal, 55*(4), 819–850. https://doi.org/10.5465/amj.2010.0627

Martin, M. (2013). *Status of the Social Impact Investing Market: A Primer, Prepared for the UK Cabinet Office*. Impact Economy. https://assets.publishing.service.gov.uk/government/uploads/system/uploads/attachment_data/file/212511/Status_of_the_Social_Impact_Investing_Market_-_A_Primer.pdf

Mettgenberg-Lemière, M. (2017). Social investment as a vehicle to achieve sustainable development goals. *Philanthropy Impact Magazine, 17*, 3–5.

Mohan, A., Harsh, S., & Modi, A. (2017). *Social Investment Landscape in Asia: Insights from Southeast Asia*. Asian Venture Philanthropy Network and Sattva. https://www.bosch-stiftung.de/sltes/default/files/publications/pdf_import/avpn_sociallinvestinglandscape_southeastasia.pdf

Morgan, P. J., & Trinh, L. Q. (2021). *Impacts of COVID-19 on Households in ASEAN Countries and Their Implications for Human Capital Development*. Tokyo, Japan: Asian Development Bank Institute (ADBI Working Paper 1226). https://www.adb.org/sites/default/files/publication/688271/adbi-wp1226.pdf

Stanley, M. (2017). *Sustainable Signals: New Data from the Individual Investors*. Morgan Stanley. https://www.morganstanley.com/pub/content/dam/msdotcom/ideas/sustainable-signals/pdf/Sustainable_Signals_Whitepaper.pdf

Stanley, M. (2019). *Sustainable Signals: Individual Investor Interest Driven by Impact, Conviction and Choice*. Morgan Stanley. https://www.morganstanley.com/pub/content/dam/msdotcom/infographics/sustainable-investing/Sustainable_Signals_Individual_Investor_White_Paper_Final.pdf

Mudaliar, A., Pineiro, A., & Bass, R. (2016). Impact investing trends: Evidence of a growing industry. Global Impact Investing Network (GIIN). https://thegiin.org/assets/GIIN_Impact%20InvestingTrends%20Report.pdf

Nicholls, A. (2010). The legitimacy of social entrepreneurship: Reflexive isomorphism in a pre–paradigmatic field. *Entrepreneurship Theory and Practice, 34*(4), 611–633. https://doi.org/10.1111/j.1540-6520.2010.00397.x

O'Neill, A. (2021). *ASEAN Countries GDP 2021*. Statista. https://www.statista.com/statistics/796245/gdp-of-the-asean-countries/

Pattisson, P. (2021, 30 March). US bars rubber gloves from Malaysian firm due to 'evidence of forced labour'. *The Guardian*. https://www.theguardian.com/global-development/2021/mar/30/us-bars-rubber-gloves-malaysian-firm-top-glove-evidence-forced-labour

Philippine Business for Social Progress (2020). *Fifty and Beyond: PBSP Towards a Better World, Annual Report*. https://assets.website-files.com/5ffe7acb1a4082165ba06c97/60af7f6d637b4879c5a8bf9e_AR20_DE SIGN_DRAFT_V12-compressed.pdf

Pollman, E. (2021). Corporate social responsibility, ESG, and compliance. *Faculty Scholarship at Penn Law*, (2568).

Prasad, M., Bauer, S., Gokhale, A., Borthakur, S., & Reddy, H. (2018a). The Landscape for Impact Investing in Southeast Asia – Indonesia. Global Impact Investing Network and Intellecap Advisory Services. https://thegiin.org/assets/Indonesia_GIIN_SEAL_report_webfile.pdf

Prasad, M., Bauer, S., Gokhale, A., Borthakur, S., & Reddy, H. (2018b). The Landscape for Impact Investing in Southeast Asia. Global Impact Investing Network and Intellecap Advisory Services. https://thegiin.org/assets/GIIN_SEAL_full_digital_webfile.pdf

Prasad, M., Gokhale, A., & Agarwal, N. (2020). *The Advance of Impact Investing in South East Asia – 2020 Update*. Australian Aid, Investing in Women, Intellecap. https://thegiin.org/research/publication/the-advance-of-impact-investing-in-south-east-asia---2020-update

PricewaterhouseCoopers (PwC) (2016) *SGX Sustainability Reporting Guide – Key Highlights*. PricewaterhouseCoopers (PwC). https://www.pwc.com/sg/en/publications/assets/sustainability-reporting-sgx-2016.pdf

Qureshi, I., Kistruck, G. M., & Bhatt, B. (2016). The enabling and constraining effects of social ties in the process of institutional entrepreneurship. *Organization Studies*, 37(3), 425–447. https://doi.org/10.1177/0170840615613372

Rayer, Q. (2017). Exploring ethical and sustainable investing. *The Review of Financial Markets*, 12, 4–10.

Roundy, P. (2019). Regional differences in impact investment: A theory of impact investing ecosystems. *Social Responsibility Journal*, 16. https://doi.org/10.1108/SRJ-11-2018-0302

Sachs, J., Kroll, C., Lafortune, G., Fuller, G., & Woelm, F. (2021). *Sustainable Development Report 2021: The Decade of Action for the Sustainable Development Goals*. Cambridge University Press. https://s3.amazonaws.com/sustainabledevelopment.report/2021/2021-sustainable-development-report.pdf

SME Corp. Malaysia (2021). *Profile of MSMEs in 2016-2021*. https://www.smecorp.gov.my/index.php/en/policies/2020-02-11-08-01-24/profile-and-importance-to-the-economy

South China Morning Post (2022, 26 January). Oil spill in Thailand threatens beaches as navy helps clean up. *South China Morning Post*. https://www.scmp.com/news/asia/southeast-asia/article/3164811/offshore-oil-spill-threatens-beaches-eastern-thailand-navy

Tan, C. C. (2022, 14 February). The rise of impact investing. *The Edge Malaysia*. http://www.theedgemarkets.com/article/rise-impact-investing

Tan, Z. Y. (2018, 24 June). Responsible investing: Looking for new ways to invest in social enterprises. *The Edge Markets*. http://www.theedgemarkets.com/article/responsible-investing-looking-new-ways-invest-social-enterprises

The Jakarta Post (2021, 11 March). ADB suspends funding for projects in Myanmar after military coup. *The Jakarta Post*. https://www.thejakartapost.com/seasia/2021/03/11/adb-suspends-funding-for-projects-in-myanmar-after-military-coup.html

The Rockefeller Foundation (2019)*The Individual Imperative: Retail Impact Investing Uncovered*. The Rockefeller Foundation. https://www.rockefellerfoundation.org/wp-content/uploads/FT_Focus-IMPACT_V10.pdf

The Star (2015, 18 May). Bursa Malaysia commits to sustainable stock exchanges initiative. *The Star*. https://www.thestar.com.my/business/business-news/2015/05/18/bursa-malaysia-commits-to-sustainable-stock-exchanges-initiative

United Nations Conference on Trade and Development (UNCTAD) (2014). Developing countries face $2.5 trillion annual investment gap in key sustainable development sectors, UNCTAD report estimates. United Nations Conference on Trade and Development. https://unctad.org/press-material/developing-countries-face-25-trillion-annual-investment-gap-key-sustainable

United Nations Conference on Trade and Development (UNCTAD) (2019). *Soaring Debt Burden Threatens Global Goals, Experts Warn.* United Nations Conference on Trade and Development. https://unctad.org/news/soaring-debt-burden-threatens-global-goals-experts-warn

United Nations Development Programme (UNDP) (2016). Overview of social finance in Indonesia. United Nations Development Programme.https://caps.org/content/other-research_doing-good&overview-social-finance-indonesia

United Nations Children's Fund (UNICEF) (2019). The state of the world's children 2019: Children, food and nutrition, growing well in a challenging World. United Nations Children's Fund (UNICEF). https://www.unicef.org/media/106506/file/The%20State%20of%20the%20World%E2%80%99s%20Children%202019.pdf

United Nations Principles for Responsible Investment (UNPRI) (2022). Signatory directory. United Nations Principles for Responsible Investment. https://www.unpri.org/signatories/signatory-resources/signatory-directory

United Overseas Bank (UOB) (2019). UOB annual report. United Overseas Bank. https://www.uobgroup.com/AR2019/

Viegelahn, C., & Huynh, P. (2021). COVID-19 and the ASEAN labour market: impact and policy response [Briefing note]. International Labour Organisation. http://www.ilo.org/asia/publications/issue-briefs/WCMS_816432/lang–en/index.htm

Volk, A. (2021). Investing for impact: The global impact investing market 2020. International Finance Corporation, World Bank Group. https://www.ifc.org/wps/wcm/connect/publications_ext_content/ifc_external_publication_site/publications_listing_page/impact-investing-market-2020

Watanabe, T., & Tanaka, Y. (2016). *Study of Social Entrepreneurship and Innovation Ecosystems in South East and East Asian Countries.* Inter-American Development Bank. https://publications.iadb.org/publications/english/document/Study-of-Social-Entrepreneurship-and-Innovation-Ecosystems-in-South-East-and-East-Asian-Countries-Country-Analysis-Republic-of-Singapore.pdf

Wood, D. (2020, July 13). Roles foundations play in shaping impact investing. *Stanford Social Innovation Review.* https://ssir.org/articles/entry/roles_foundations_play_in_shaping_impact_investing

World Bank (2019). *Ease of Doing Business Rank.* Doing Business Project World Bank. https://data.worldbank.org/indicator/IC.BUS.EASE.XQ

World Economic Forum (2013). *From the Margins to the Mainstream Assessment of the Impact Investment Sector and Opportunities to Engage Mainstream Investors.* A report by the World Economic Forum Investors Industries Prepared in collaboration with Deloitte Touche Tohmatsu. https://www3.weforum.org/docs/WEF_II_FromMarginsMainstream_Report_2013.pdf

Zhao, Y. (2020). A community-based theoretical framework for impact investment research. *Academy of Management Proceedings.* (p 19156). Briarcliff Manor, NY 10510: Academy of Management.

Alexandra Ioan, Alyssa Matteucci

19 Enabling the Agency of Others: The Ultimate Impact of Social Entrepreneurs

Abstract: Social entrepreneurs' impact has been a continuous source of debate and intrigue in the field. Issues such as how to document, attribute and measure impact are at the forefront of the discussion. In this chapter we focus on a specific dimension of impact that has been highlighted in the work of a particular group of social entrepreneurs: the Fellows elected by Ashoka, one of the largest networks of social entrepreneurs worldwide. We unpack Ashoka's vision and discuss 11 strategies that Fellows use to increase the agency of others towards social change. This analysis is based on the 2021 Ashoka Global Fellows Study, in which 817 Fellows were surveyed and 32 interviewed about how their work expands individuals' sense of agency. We argue that sustainable social change can be achieved by strengthening individuals' ability to contribute to their communities and that this is a primary way social entrepreneurs create impact.

Keywords: social impact, agency, social entrepreneurship, strategies

1 Introduction

Achieving the Social Development Goals (SDGs) requires stakeholders to track and understand their impact. But it is also clear that achieving the SDGs requires an acceleration of measures taken and solutions developed by a variety of stakeholders. Numerous initiatives, such as the 2030 Agenda Partnership Accelerator or Catalyst 2030, are focused on bringing stakeholders together for a more effective approach in the work towards achieving the SDGs. Core to these initiatives is collaboration, which multiplies efforts and effects, ultimately resulting in progress towards SDGs.

Social entrepreneurs are one of many stakeholder groups focused on achieving the SDGs (Littlewood & Holt, 2018). Whether through their own organisations and initiatives or through the spread of their systems-changing ideas, social entrepreneurs invent solutions that make advancements towards the achievement of the SDGs. Social entrepreneurs' impact reaches beyond their results in a specific field of work, such as healthcare, climate change or poverty reduction. In this chapter we will discuss social entrepreneurs' unique type of impact that contributes to the acceleration of ideas and solutions for achieving the SDGs. More specifically, we will discuss how

Alexandra Ioan, Practitioner and research in civil society, 5/5 Talgasse, 1150 Vienna, Austria
Alyssa Matteucci, Practitioner and researcher, 4809, Apt. 3F Beaumont Avenue, 19143 Philadelphia, USA

https://doi.org/10.1515/9783110756159-024

social entrepreneurs mobilise others – their target groups, communities, partners and more – and how they strengthen their agency to the point where individuals develop their own solutions to social problems, thus contributing to SDG efforts.

We will start the chapter with a brief background overview on the literature on social entrepreneurship and its impact, followed by a description of the methodology used to better understand the impact of the social entrepreneurs from the Ashoka network. We will continue with an overview of the history and specificities of the Ashoka Fellowship and then dive into the strategies we identified in the work of social entrepreneurs for how they enable the agency of others. We conclude with a discussion of how these findings contribute to the understanding of the impact of social entrepreneurship and its contribution to the achievement of the SDGs.

2 Background Literature on Social Entrepreneurship

In the past several years, the work of social entrepreneurs and social entrepreneurship has increasingly gained attention. They have been linked with addressing most (if not all) of the problems addressed by the SDGs and highly praised for their innovative solutions (Günzel-Jensen et al., 2020; SEFORIS, 2017; Catalyst 2030, 2022). At the same time, debates around tensions inherent in the work of social entrepreneurs and the risks they can pose for their integrity and mission achievement have also emerged (Giridharadas, 2019). The attention awarded to social entrepreneurship is also reflected in the complexity of defining it.

2.1 Definitions

Definitions in this field have been a source of debate. Is social entrepreneurship really something new and different from other types of social change work and initiatives throughout time? To what extent? Does the field of social entrepreneurship truly produce a distinctive impact? In trying to answer these questions, scholars differentiated between the concepts of social entrepreneurs (focusing on the individual person), social entrepreneurship (focusing on a social process) and social enterprises (focusing on organisations).

Thus, social entrepreneurs are:

> playing the role of change agents in the social sector by adopting a mission to create and sustain social value, recognizing and relentlessly pursuing new opportunities to serve that mission, engaging in a process of continuous innovation, adaptation and learning, acting boldly without being limited by resources currently in hand, and finally exhibiting a heightened sense of accountability to the constituencies served and for the outcomes created. (Dees, 1998: 4)

Social entrepreneurs are 'people with new ideas to address major problems who are relentless in the pursuit of their visions, people who simply will not take "no" for an answer, who will not give up until they have spread their ideas as far as they possibly can' (Bornstein, 2007: 1).

Social entrepreneurship has been defined as 'a process involving the innovative use and combination of resources to pursue opportunities to catalyse social change and/or address social needs' (Mair & Marti, 2006: 3). This process 'creates innovative solutions to immediate social problems and mobilises the ideas, capacities, resources and social arrangements required for sustainable social transformation' (Alvord, Brown & Letts, 2003: 137, 2004: 4).

Defining social enterprises has been a focus of management and organisational research as well. The term 'social enterprise' has been used as more of an 'umbrella construct' both in research and practice (Mair, 2010: 2; Mair & Marti, 2004; Battilana & Lee, 2014; Doherty, Haugh, & Lyon, 2014). Most of the definitions in the research field revolve around the innovative aspects of the social work of social enterprises (the way they approach an issue, the creative solutions they develop) or around their organisational setup (the way they operate and function, which in itself can be innovative).

In the first instance, social enterprises are perceived to find new and creative solutions to complex social problems compared to traditional providers of social services (Mair, 2010; Bornstein, 2007; Dey & Steyaert, 2012). Still, clearly establishing what is or what is not innovative has been a challenge, especially when embedding the work of social enterprises in different institutional contexts (Mair, 2010; Kerlin, 2013). Seelos and Mair (2017: 1) also specify that social enterprises 'often focus on problems that are not directly addressed by public sectors or businesses, and they provide products, services, or interventions by working with and also on behalf of their beneficiaries'. This intermediary role can also be considered a way through which social enterprises bring new approaches to social change processes.

When looking at the organisational setup, social enterprises are defined as organisations that focus primarily on a social mission while engaging also in commercial activities (Mair & Marti, 2006; Doherty, Haugh, & Lyon, 2014; Kerlin, 2010; Ebrahim, Battilana & Mair, 2014; Battilana & Lee, 2014). According to this view, it is these two different organisational goals, processes and structures that differentiate social enterprises from other organisations. This view has led to social enterprises being conceptualised and analysed as hybrid organisations (Battilana & Lee, 2014).

The difficulty in reaching consensus around a definition and categorisation of social enterprises also stems from the fact that social enterprises can take multiple organisational and legal forms – from non-profits, to limited liability companies and specific legal forms such as B-Corporations (in the US) or Community Interest Companies (in the UK) (Mair, Wolf, & Ioan, 2020). Hence, the 'umbrella construct' (Mair, 2010: 2) mentioned before is strongly rooted in a constantly evolving practice of social enterprises and social entrepreneurship.

2.2 Social Enterprises and Their Impact

Grasping the impact of social enterprises and social entrepreneurs has always been a key focus of both researchers and practitioners. Scholars have thought about how to define what this impact is and how to best conceptualise it (Ebrahim & Rangan, 2014; Maas & Liket, 2011; Rawhouser, Cummings, & Newbert, 2019; EC, 2014; OECD, 2015). They also conducted empirical work on the direct effects of social entrepreneurs' actions on target groups (Spear & Bidet, 2005; Davister, Defourny, & Gregoire, 2004; SE-FORIS, 2017), on the deeper institutional changes led by social entrepreneurs in communities (Mair, Wolf, & Seelos, 2016; Stephan et al., 2016) and on different scaling and diffusion models of impact (Seelos & Mair, 2017; Alvord, Brown, & Letts, 2004). Since the solutions that social enterprises develop for social problems are generally perceived as more innovative, there is also much interest in the scaling potential of these solutions (Seelos & Mair, 2017).

As a result of the tensions and challenges of pursuing social and economic goals simultaneously (Pache & Santos, 2013), scholars have also been interested in the conditions under which social outcomes of social enterprises might be negatively affected. The result of these multiple demanding organisational processes has been conceptualised as mission drift (Ebrahim, Battilana, & Mair, 2014; Mair, Wolf, & Ioan, 2020; André & Pache, 2016) – a process through which the social mission of the social enterprise is no longer primarily achieved.

Practitioners themselves have evolved in their understanding of the impact of social enterprises. They started with a focus on the effectiveness of the innovative solutions of social enterprises when it comes to target groups (Schwab Foundation for Social Entrepreneurship, 2020) or on the sustainable financial models that can support the activity of social enterprises (Yunus, 1998; Wilson & Post, 2013). This then continued with a focus on scaling and accelerating aspects of social enterprises and their ideas (OECD & EC, 2016) with the goal of expanding the social impact achieved. Lately, practitioner organisations working with social entrepreneurs have shifted their focus towards a degree of systemic change, which social entrepreneurs can or should pursue (Schwab Foundation & WEF, 2017; Ashoka, 2020). This can take the form of policy change, for instance, but also more fundamental market or industry changes (Wilf, 2018; Ashoka, 2020).

Parallels can be drawn between the way scholars – especially those focused on empirical work – and practitioners have looked at different levels of impact that social entrepreneurs and social enterprises generate. There is continuous dialogue between how organisations develop in practice and how researchers make sense of these developments.

2.3 Agency and Empowerment for Social Problem Solving

While perspectives vary when it comes to definitions and tracking impact, they all share a preoccupation with the role of agency in addressing social issues.

Classical literature has conceptualised agency as the result of one social actor delegating authority and power to another social actor in order to achieve goals on their behalf. This has been captured, for example, in the principal–agent theory in economics, political science and management (Shapiro, 2005; Eisenhardt, 1989; Mitnick, 1973). The questions in this approach revolve around issues of control, communication asymmetries, monitoring and competition.

The structure–agency debate in social sciences on the other hand (Connor, 2011) has been more focused on the relationship between social actors and their social environments – the tensions arising from this dynamic and the degree of constraints and opportunities for action for social actors. Questions along these lines are also reflected in the new institutionalism literature, specifically through aspects such as institutional entrepreneurship (DiMaggio, 1988; Mair & Marti, 2009; Hardy & Maguire, 2017; Weik, 2011) or community entrepreneurship (Peredo & Chrisman, 2006; Johannison & Nilsson, 1989). The effort to disentangle the interplay between the capacity of social actors to cause social change in a certain social setting, while being constrained at the same time by that setting, continues both in practice and in scholarly work.

There are many researchers who look at the issue of agency in connection to the idea of empowerment of people and communities (Ibrahim & Alkire, 2007; Samman & Santos, 2009). This appears mostly in the context of development studies, where the attention has shifted towards enabling disadvantaged groups and communities to actively take part in shaping the development of their communities and social contexts. In this area of work, agency is defined as 'what a person is free to do and achieve in pursuit of whatever goals or values he or she regards as important' (Sen, 1985: 203) or as 'an actor's or group's ability to make purposeful choices' (Samman & Santos, 2009: 3). Empowerment is defined as 'the process of enhancing an individual's or group's capacity to make effective choices, that is, to make choices and then to transform those choices into desired actions and outcomes' (Alsop, Bertelsen, & Holland, 2006: 1).

For the remainder of the chapter, we will focus on how social entrepreneurship contributes to issues of agency and empowerment in addressing social problems. We regard this as an additional avenue of understanding the long-term impact of social entrepreneurs beyond the concrete results they achieve in their fields of work. Moreover, looking into social entrepreneurs' strategies to increase agency can also contribute with empirical insights to the scholarly structure–agency debate. We will look at the social impact of both social entrepreneurs and social enterprises without differentiating between the role of individuals and organisations specifically. We acknowledge the fact that social entrepreneurs individually cannot achieve their social mission without appropriate team and organisational setups; therefore, we discuss the impact of the entrepreneurial endeavour overall. Due to the empirical sample on which the results of our analysis are based, the definition of social entrepreneurship we mostly rely on is the one related to the innovative aspects of the work of social entrepreneurs and social enterprises in addressing social problems – a key selection criterion for the social entrepreneurs in our sample.

3 Methodology

Every three years, Ashoka runs a global study in its network of more than 3700 social entrepreneurs (who are called Ashoka Fellows). This chapter is based on data gathered as part of the 2021 Ashoka Global Fellow Study conducted in partnership with the research team of the Management School at the Polytechnic of Milan. The mixed-methodology study consisted of a survey and in-depth qualitative interviews with Ashoka Fellows. The data collection was conducted between March and July 2021. Some first insights based on the study were included in the 2022 Ashoka global impact report (Ashoka, 2022).

3.1 Survey

We designed the survey to understand: (1) how Ashoka Fellows achieve impact in their communities directly, (2) how they contribute to systemic work such as policy or market changes and (3) how Ashoka contributes to their efforts in achieving social change. A total of 817 Fellows completed the survey, yielding a 26% response rate.

More than half of the sample identified as male (58%), which is representative of Ashoka's full Fellow population. This sample represents more than 80 of the 95 countries where Fellows have been elected. These Fellows work across a range of sectors, with the greatest number of Fellows working in education (23%), economic development (17%) and health (17%). Our sample was slightly skewed when considering election year. Most Fellows who responded were elected between 2010 and 2021 (60%).

3.2 Interviews

The purpose of the interviews was to understand how Ashoka Fellows achieve indirect impact by strengthening their communities and enabling the agency of others. We invited a stratified random sample of 32 Fellows to participate in one-and-a-half-hour interviews. Like the survey, most respondents identified as male (56%). Fellows again came from a range of sectors, with most working in education (22%), health

(22%), climate and planet (13%) and civic participation (13%). Our sample was slightly skewed, with most Fellows having been elected between 2010 and 2021 (59%).

The Polytechnic of Milan research team conducted an independent evaluation of survey and interview results. Throughout the process, they partnered with the Ashoka team to analyse survey responses for key trends and transcribe and code interview responses for key themes. Through an iterative process between the two teams, the main findings of the study emerged and were integrated in the 11 strategies presented in this chapter.

3.3 Research Background: Ashoka's History and Vision

For its first 20 years, Ashoka's theory of change held that there was no more powerful force for societal transformation than a system-changing idea in the hands of a social entrepreneur. By Ashoka's account, 'a social entrepreneur is an individual who conceives of, and relentlessly pursues, a new idea designed to solve societal problems on a very wide scale by changing the systems that undergird the problems' (Ashoka, 2020: 9). In the 1980s, Ashoka started selecting social entrepreneurs from around the world and supported them through financial and networking resources to accelerate the rate at which their solutions addressed seemingly intractable problems. Ashoka's selection process is focused on the individual social entrepreneur who may or may not belong to a specific organisation. The focus of Ashoka lies on the social entrepreneurial qualities of the individual and on the ideas they pursued, thus supporting the social entrepreneurship process as whole, regardless of the organisational perspective and form. Still, most Ashoka Fellows have founded organisations and together with their teams develop innovative solutions to social problems in many formats (nonprofits, for-profits, hybrid organisations, etc.).

By the late 1990s, Ashoka had built a strong network of top social entrepreneurs and contributed to establishing social entrepreneurship as a field for social change work. Together with the Ashoka Fellows, it developed an impact measurement framework for social entrepreneurship that focused not only on direct service provision but on progress in changing systems and mindsets to address the root causes of social problems (Ashoka, 2018).

Over the past 20 years, Ashoka observed that the Fellows focus a lot on enabling others to envision a better reality, build a team and take action. Across a wide range of geographies and sectors, Fellows engage those around them, inviting them to build something new and navigate challenges together. Ashoka recognises the profound effect this approach has had on Fellows' ability to shift whole systems and on individuals' abilities to lead change and bring about better realities. This is why the vision of Ashoka was reorganised and the focus shifted beyond exclusively supporting leading social entrepreneurs towards building a world in which 'everyone is a changemaker'.

The way to achieve this warranted more enquiry and the goal of the 2021 Ashoka Global Fellow Study was to spell out what Ashoka Fellows do to expand individuals' sense of agency and the ways in which they do this.

4 Strategies of Ashoka Fellows for Social Impact

What does building an 'Everyone a Changemaker' world look like in practice? How do Fellows generate positive social impact that serves both individuals and societies, leading to greater freedoms and opportunities for others to contribute? The findings from the Global Fellow Study revealed 11 strategies that Fellows use, which can be organised at three levels: individual, stakeholder and ecosystem.

At the individual level, Fellows are focused on developing an individual's skills and identity for engaging in social change work. At the stakeholder level, Fellows collaborate to engage more people in their effort. They partner, encourage replication and look to community members to lead.[1] At the ecosystem level, Fellows shape systems and create environments (cultural and physical) to support engagement and agency of numerous people and groups. See Table 19.1 for an overview of these strategies organised by this typology.

Table 19.1: Overview of the 11 strategies of the Ashoka Fellows.

Analysis level	Strategies
Individual	1. Create opportunities for individuals to contribute
	2. Encourage belief in individuals' own capacity to enact change
	3. Redefining personal 'weaknesses' as strengths
	4. Support the development of an identity of social engagement
Stakeholder	5. Build multiplier partnerships
	6. Facilitate so that communities find their own voices, goals and solutions
	7. Go beyond usually engaged people
Ecosystem	8. Generating change in policy and market systems
	9. Influence societal mindsets and cultural norms
	10. Foster supportive environments that enable personal and community agency
	11. Build ecosystems that sustain social engagement and agency

---

1 Replication: Ashoka Fellows frequently relinquish control and ownership of their ideas to see them spread as far as possible. To do this, they encourage organisations or institutions to take up their idea and bring it to an even larger scale, facilitating independent replication.

4.1 Individual-Level Strategies

1. Create Opportunities for Individuals to Contribute

The first step towards supporting the agency of the people and communities Ashoka Fellows work with is to create spaces and ways in which people can respond to concrete needs. As Fellows engage people as core contributors to their solutions, those contributors begin to see the world through the lens of possibilities rather than problems. Committed to the spread of this worldview, Fellows create opportunities for individuals to join their organisations as employees or volunteers, giving many the opportunity to practice social engagement. Specifically, 95% of Fellows in the survey sample provide employment opportunities and 87% provide volunteer opportunities.

2. Encourage Belief in Individuals' Own Capacity to Enact Change

Social entrepreneurs work on developing a core belief within people that they are capable of enacting changes in themselves and the larger world. The aim is to develop people's trust in themselves and to show them that even the smallest changes that they accomplish can make a difference and contribute significantly to their communities and the world. By encouraging problem-solving on a small scale, Ashoka Fellows foster people's ownership of a situation and agency in addressing that situation. The feeling of empowerment from acting – no matter how small the action – drives the more long-term desire for engagement and strengthens the belief around one's potential to influence social change.

> For me, it's the mindset and how you position yourself in the system – that you are not a subordinate, coordinated by the other. You are equal. – Ashoka Fellow, Indonesia

3. Redefining Personal 'Weaknesses' as Strengths

Social entrepreneurs look at what are traditionally considered people's strengths and weaknesses in a different way. They take stock of the skills and the expertise of people or groups (resulting most of the time from very diverse life experiences) and focus on putting them to action. More importantly, they look at what the broader society perceives as weaknesses – such as a disability, age, or socio-economic background – and convert these characteristics into strengths and into a basis on which people can contribute to their communities differently. This is known as 'asset framing', a concept coined by Ashoka Fellow Trabian Shorters, which is now used in a variety of contexts globally (Shorters, 2018). This approach capitalises on the different life experiences and perceptions that people can bring to the table and that in turn expand the pool of knowledge on which a solution to a social problem rests.

> If you really reach young people, it'll be something they can leverage as a strength, through empathy . . . . That changes their perspective to 'my parents do have a much harder time than I give them credit for' and that can easily shift into a leadership position where it becomes a strength. – Ashoka Fellow, Canada

4. Support the Development of an Identity of Social Engagement

Ashoka Fellows focus on developing long-term perspectives and changes in the people and communities they work with. For them, it is not most important for people to act on a certain cause for an indefinite period of time. Rather, people develop a new way of seeing themselves and expand their sense of possibility and agency that they then apply throughout their life in a variety of contexts and roles, facing a variety of problem-solving situations. Internalising this identity of 'changemaker' in Ashoka language, or the identity of someone who *can* and *will* make a difference, can have effects not only on how someone acts in their group, their community and their professional life, but also on their personal development and their life quality and satisfaction.

> I think the greatest challenge for me while working with young people is to generate this belief that they are valuable for themselves, for their families, for the communities. And I think wherever you go, interest young people. Every, every word just counts a lot. – Ashoka Fellow, Pakistan

4.2 Stakeholder-Level Strategies

5. Build Multiplier Partnerships

Social entrepreneurs know that their capacity of replicating a solution and even an idea themselves is limited and that it requires cumulative effort to solve a social problem. Therefore, they develop numerous multiplier partnerships in the hope that their partners will build on their original solution or generate their own. These partners can be individuals, communities, but also other organisations (funders, partners, other stakeholders, etc.).

Ashoka Fellows rely on a multiplier effect for their work in the sense that they develop peer leaders in the communities and organisations they partner with who can autonomously work with others towards solving the social problem. This multiplier strategy applies also to their own teams as well. Staff and volunteers gain ownership of the social issue and develop their own approaches to it. At the core of this strategy is the idea that Ashoka Fellows foster the ability to solve problems among the people they work with and encourage them to then advance in their mission. They aspire to develop leaders, not followers. This is significantly different than the more classical approach of multiplying a certain solution for a social problem with the help of partners.

> I think in a way, this festival gave them a platform to be more confident about themselves. Because they somehow get a position – even if they're volunteers – to do something . . . we try to cooperate with a lot of people and a lot of organisations as well. – Ashoka Fellow, Indonesia

6. Facilitate So That Communities Find Their Own Voices, Goals and Solutions

When working with communities and various stakeholders, Ashoka Fellows adopt the role of facilitators rather than of all-knowing leaders. Their purpose is to guide people towards their own objectives, wishes, and appropriate means for action. They operate from the power of influence (Battilana & Casciaro, 2021), rather than authority. They facilitate conversations and action, rather than decide for others. Ashoka Fellows do not address the communities solely as beneficiaries targeted by their own solutions and ideas, but rather they treat communities as experts and decision-makers for their own problems. This is where the development of solutions in cooperation with and driven by communities themselves emerges from.

> We don't believe that we are creators, we are only facilitators, we are showing the path. It's they who walk the path, not for us to lead them. – Ashoka Fellow, India

7. Go Beyond Usually Engaged People

Ashoka Fellows want to develop the engagement level of a large audience and not simply involve further the people who are already engaged and contributing to social problem solving. They do this through a broad range of activities – from communication campaigns to public events addressed to the broader public and designed in a way that can mobilise people towards social action. The broader audience approach can also take the form of going beyond professionals and experts in dealing with social problems and engaging laypeople as solution providers. Many Fellows mentioned efforts to engage the community beyond the inner circle of allies to garner wider engagement and deeper social motivation for change. This can lead to the emergence of 'unlikely allies' – actors who do not naturally encounter a certain social problem, but who can contribute to making significant progress on an issue through their interactions with other actors.

It's all about empowering people, you know, the strong belief that everybody has something to give, to contribute, everybody's talented somehow. And that if you want people to excel, you need to empower them. The level of being empowered in society is fundamental. We started doing this, focusing on street-connected children, so vulnerable kids, and youth. But we are doing this as well, in other layers of society. We do this as well in companies through our business ventures. – Ashoka Fellow, Belgium

4.3 Ecosystem-Level Strategies

8. Generating Change in Policy and Market Systems

Ashoka Fellows also work to change social or economic systems to benefit wider categories of population. Through these efforts, they go beyond providing services and products and they look to change the configuration of these markets and policy settings. This is in itself a way of changing the structural conditions that affect the ability of people to engage and enact change in their communities.

As evident in these discrete data points, our study found that, despite the COVID-19 pandemic and its corollary economic challenges, Fellows remained focused on their efforts to address policies and markets that perpetuated the very problems they were addressing. Thus, as Figure 19.1 shows, 66% of Fellows advised policymakers, 63% of Ashoka Fellows responding to the survey reported achieving legislative change

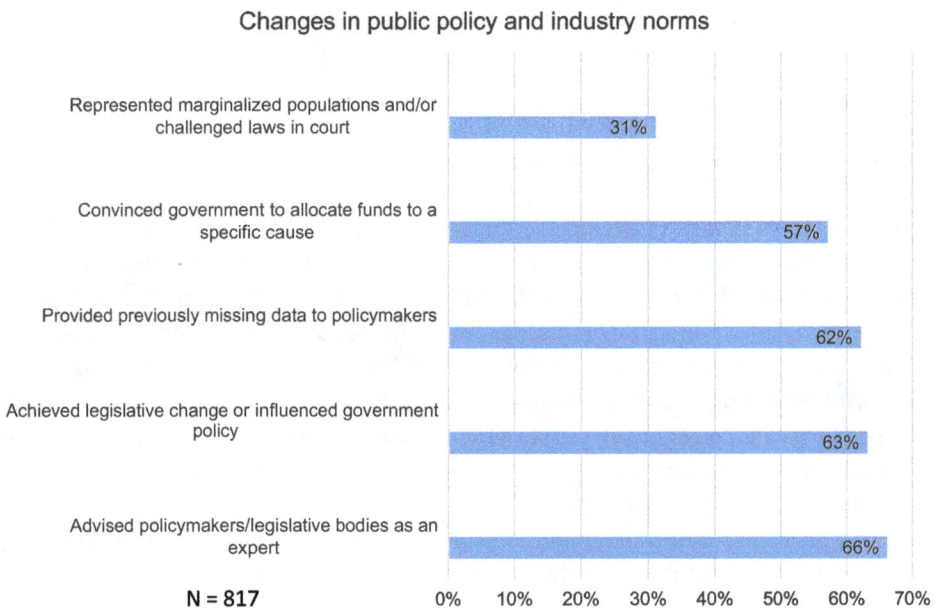

Changes in public policy and industry norms

Represented marginalized populations and/or challenged laws in court — 31%
Convinced government to allocate funds to a specific cause — 57%
Provided previously missing data to policymakers — 62%
Achieved legislative change or influenced government policy — 63%
Advised policymakers/legislative bodies as an expert — 66%

N = 817

Figure 19.1: Percent of Fellows who reported having made changes in public policy and industry norms.

or influenced government policy, 62% provided data and research to policymakers, 57% contributed to reallocation of funds by government, and 31% took legal action for policy change.

Regarding market dynamics, 52% of respondents worked with for-profit organisations to increase their inclusivity and respectively created a new market to facilitate access of people to a service or product. 51% of Ashoka Fellows report creating a service or product that previously did not exist and respectively created a change in the standards of an industry or large organisation, 42% facilitate access of some groups to a market and 41% influenced the flow of information in a specific market.

These changes pinpoint to the ultimate goal of increasing access and opportunities of engagement for various groups, constituencies and communities in order to foster agency.

9. Influence Societal Mindsets and Cultural Norms

Fellows understand that changing societal beliefs is necessary for sustainable social transformation. By influencing societal mindsets and cultural norms, they help others to see and act in accordance with social changes that benefit all (Mair, Wolf, & Seelos, 2016).

A total of 88% of survey respondents say they encourage people to think differently and they also work on influencing societal norms through campaigns (43%) and through their programmes (21%).

This type of work creates conditions more conducive to people realising that they can act as social change agents themselves. This work on a societal level complements the individual level focus on mindsets and contributes to the creation of new social standards.

10. Foster Supportive Environments That Enable Personal and Community Agency

Ashoka Fellows also develop environments that can foster social engagement and help people feel empowered. The key characteristics of these environments are that they are physically and emotionally safe, trustworthy, generally supportive and caring. They make certain that people are treated with dignity and feel accepted, establishing a strong foundation of trust needed to generate and sustain collective action. These types of environments can be physical spaces that can range from a simple classroom to a community centre or public square. What is more, the Ashoka Fellows also explicitly mention emotional and psychological spaces that they focus on creating, so that the groups they work with can tap into their capacity to contribute, feel comfortable to share their ideas, work with others and build something new. Often,

Fellows foster these environments within the walls of the organisations they run, creating an organisational culture of safety.

> One principle is a consistent engagement in a learning environment that is safe, trustworthy, non-judgmental, creative, caring, in a presence of a caring, compassionate adult, even physical and emotional spaces that are safe, and emotionally thriving. – Ashoka Fellow, India

11. Build Ecosystems That Sustain Social Engagement and Agency

Beyond the individual supportive environments that Ashoka Fellows create, they also build broader ecosystems that are in favour of people's engagement. Whether working with governments, with civil society organisations, funders, businesses, media companies or universities, social entrepreneurs work on reducing the barriers that prevent people from having agency more broadly in society. Each of these stakeholders can play a role in reducing barriers and making the engagement of individuals and communities easier. This implies working on systemic inequalities and addressing issues such as power and privilege in the interactions between different social actors.

> There are so many dynamics when it comes to system change. And for you to move the needle, you need to put in place certain activations or work with different stakeholders for sustainable impact. Because the initial sort of the first impact, if you've completed something successfully, does not mean it's a sustainable impact. – Ashoka Fellow, Ghana

5 Discussion and Conclusion

Through this chapter, we wanted to go beyond the impact the social entrepreneurs and social enterprises achieve in their respective fields of work and highlight the dimension of increased agency that they also foster through their activities. There is substantial literature on the way in which social enterprises mobilise resources and stakeholders for collective action in their own field. What we wanted to focus on here is how they strengthen the agency of others for social engagement overall, beyond their idea and their organisation.

By fostering increased engagement and problem-solving among their target groups, their communities, the many partners they work with, social entrepreneurs (and Ashoka Fellows in this case) contribute to the development of many agents of change who can in their own way contribute to social change. This is of particular importance in a global context that is more and more interconnected and in need of multiple solutions for complex problems such as those specified also by the Sustainable Development Goals (SDGs).

The 11 strategies identified above are deeply interconnected and build upon one another. In most cases, Ashoka Fellows employ several of these strategies simultaneously and they develop different combinations of approaches, depending on the field they work in, their specific local and national contexts as well as the level of development of their ideas and organisations. Over time, Ashoka Fellows can switch from one strategy to the other and create new combined models depending on the changes required by addressing the social problem.

This chapter contributes to the literature on social entrepreneurship, social change and agency by elaborating on the dimensions of indirect impact that can be achieved by social entrepreneurs. This illustrates the more fine-grained ways in which social entrepreneurs influence social change and raises questions about how to conceptualise the sustainability of the social change – in this case by ensuring the space and the skills of people to engage and act on a continuous basis.

The chapter also illustrates how the agency of social actors can be fostered in practice by social entrepreneurs and social enterprises starting from extensive empirical data. The global dataset used as the basis for this chapter complements similar extensive endeavours from other research projects (SEFORIS, 2017; ESEM, 2022; GEM, 2018), strengthening the empirical understanding of social entrepreneurs, their work and their impact.

Last but not least, the chapter also connects the perspective on agency in development work with the discussions around the impact of social entrepreneurs and social enterprises. The acknowledgement of the need for communities and individuals to be active contributors in the development processes they are part of speaks directly to the approach of social entrepreneurs in placing the agency of their target groups and stakeholders at the core of their work.

Future research could further investigate how enabling agency plays a role in the work of other social entrepreneurs, not only Ashoka Fellows, as these are a pre-selected group of social entrepreneurs. A future area of enquiry can be looking at whether the agency of social actors differs across work topics and fields and if some social problems are more accessible or attractive for engagement. On a similar note, further analysis could be conducted on the way in which specific local and/or regional contexts influence the capacity of social entrepreneurs to foster the agency of others and employ some strategies over others. Finally, it is useful to understand the dynamics and the ways in which social entrepreneurs make use of and combine multiple strategies identified in this chapter in order to strengthen agency. Variables such as organisational development level, organisational context, resources available, etc. can all serve as avenues of enquiry to further understand how these strategies are put into practice.

Overall, the 2022 Global Fellow Study data shows how mobilising and empowering others for social change is a long-term effect of the work of social entrepreneurs and how it lies at the core of developing solutions for social problems in any field of work. Addressing the Sustainable Development Goals requires such strategies due to the rapid pace of change and the high complexity of the issues addressed. Solutions can come from many places and social entrepreneurs are focused on expanding the pool of people with capacity for action.

References

Alsop, R., Bertelsen, M., & Holland, J. (2006). *Empowerment in Practice from Analysis to Implementation*. Washington, DC: World Bank. http://hdl.handle.net/10986/6980

Alvord, S. H., Brown, L. D., & Letts, C. W. (2003). Social entrepreneurship: Leadership that facilitates societal transformation. An exploratory study. Center for Public Leadership Working Paper Series;03–05. http://hdl.handle.net/1721.1/55803.

André, K., & Pache, A. C. (2016). From caring entrepreneur to caring enterprise: Addressing the ethical challenges of scaling up social enterprises. *Journal of Business Ethics*, *133*(4), 659–675. https://link. springer.com/article/10.1007/s10551-014-2445-8

Ashoka (2018). From social entrepreneurship to everyone a changemaker – 40 years of social innovation. *Social Innovations Journal*, 52. https://socialinnovationsjournal.org/editions/issue-52

Ashoka (2020). *Systemic and Empowering. Social Entrepreneurship in the Time of Philanthrocapitalism*. https://www.ashoka.org/en-us/files/systemic-and-empowering-social-entrepreneurship-time-philanthrocapitalismpdf

Ashoka (2022). *The Unlonely Planet 2022. How Ashoka Fellows Accelerate an Everyone a Changemaker World*. https://www.ashoka.org/en-us/unlonely-planet-2022?gclid=CjwKCAjw4ayUBhA4EiwATWyBriC myzmZ7x1IxXwwZvOdOrmpnCVX_WWA0t_bAoWotwNl6JpuObTBKRoClZAQAvD_BwE

Battilana, J., & Casciaro, T. (2021). *Power, for All: How It Really Works and Why It's Everyone's Business*. New York: Simon and Schuster.

Battilana, J., & Lee, M. (2014). Advancing research on hybrid organizing – Insights from the study of social enterprises. *Academy of Management Annals*, *8*(1), 397–441. https://doi.org/10.5465/19416520.2014. 893615

Bornstein, D. (2007). *How to Change the World: Social Entrepreneurs and the Power of New Ideas*. Oxford: Oxford University Press.

Catalyst 2030 (2022). Website: https://catalyst2030.net/

Connor, S. (2011). Structure and agency: A debate for community development?. *Community Development Journal*, *46*(suppl_2), ii97–ii110. https://doi.org/10.1093/cdj/bsr006

Davister, C., Defourny, J., & Gregoire, O. (2004). Work integration social enterprises in the European Union: An overview of existing models. *Revue Internationale de L'économie Sociale: Recma*, *293*, 24–50. https://orbi.uliege.be/bitstream/2268/90492/1/Work%20Integration%20Social%20Enterprises%20in% 20the%20European%20Union_An%20overview%20of%20existing%20models.pdf

Dees, J. G. (1998). *The Meaning of 'Social Entrepreneurship', Working Paper*. Stanford, California: Stanford University – Graduate School of Business. http://www.sogenc.org/dosyalar/6-TheMeaningofsocialEntrepreneurship.pdf

Dey, P., & Steyaert, C. (2012). Social entrepreneurship: Critique and the radical enactment of the social. *Social Enterprise Journal*, https://www.emerald.com/insight/content/doi/10.1108/17508611211252828/ full/html?fullSc=1

DiMaggio, P. J. (1988). Interest and agency in institutional theory. In L. G. Zucker (Ed.), *Institutional Patterns and Organisations: Culture and Environment* (pp 3–21). Cambridge, MA: Ballinger.

Doherty, B., Haugh, H., & Lyon, F. (2014). Social enterprises as hybrid organisations: A review and research agenda. *International Journal of Management Reviews*, *16*(4), 417–436. https://doi.org/10.1111/ijmr.12028

Ebrahim, A., Battilana, J., & Mair, J. (2014). The governance of social enterprises: Mission drift and accountability challenges in hybrid organisations. *Research in Organisational Behavior, 34*, 81–100. https://doi.org/10.1016/j.riob.2014.09.001

Ebrahim, A., & Rangan, V. K. (2014). What impact? A framework for measuring the scale and scope of social performance. *California Management Review, 56*(3), 118–141. https://doi.org/10.1525/cmr.2014.56.3.118

Eisenhardt, K. M. (1989). Agency theory: An assessment and review. *Academy of Management Review, 14*, 57–74. https://doi.org/10.5465/amr.1989.4279003

European Commission (EC) (2014). *Proposed Approaches to Social Impact Measurement*. https://ec.europa. eu/social/BlobServlet?docId=13401&langId=en

European Social Enterprise Monitor (ESEM) (2022). Website. https://euclidnetwork.eu/portfolio-posts/euro pean-social-enterprise-monitor-esem/

Giridharadas, A. (2019). *Winners take all: The elite charade of changing the world*. Vintage.

Global Entrepreneurship Monitor (GEM) (2018) Datasets. https://www.gemconsortium.org/data/sets?id=aps

Günzel-Jensen, F., Siebold, N., Kroeger, A., & Korsgaard, S. (2020). Do the United Nations' Sustainable Development Goals matter for social entrepreneurial ventures? A bottom-up perspective. *Journal of Business Venturing Insights, 13*, e00162. https://doi.org/10.1016/j.jbvi.2020.e00162

Hardy, C., & Maguire, S. (2017). Institutional entrepreneurship and change in fields. *The Sage Handbook of Organisational Institutionalism, 2*, 261–280.

Ibrahim, S., & Alkire, S. (2007). Agency and empowerment: A proposal for internationally comparable indicators. *Oxford Development Studies, 35*(4), 379–403. https://doi.org/10.1080/13600810701701897

Johannisson, B., & Nilsson, A. (1989). Community entrepreneurs: Networking for local development. *Entrepreneurship & Regional Development, 1*(1), 3–19. https://doi.org/10.1080/0898562890000000

Kerlin, J. A. (2010). A comparative analysis of the global emergence of social enterprise. *Voluntas: International Journal of Voluntary and Nonprofit Organisations, 21*(2), 162–179. https://link.springer.com/ article/10.1007/s11266-010-9126-8

Kerlin, J. (2013). Defining social enterprise across different contexts: A conceptual framework based on institutional factors. *Nonprofit Voluntary Sector Quarterly, 42*(1), 84–108. https://link.springer.com/chap ter/10.1057/9781137035301_5

Littlewood, D., & Holt, D. (2018). How social enterprises can contribute to the Sustainable Development Goals (SDGs) – A conceptual framework. In *Entrepreneurship and the Sustainable Development Goals* (pp 33–46). Bingley: Emerald Publishing Limited. https://doi.org/10.1108/S2040-724620180000008007

Maas, K., & Liket, K. (2011). Social impact measurement: Classification of methods. In *Environmental Management Accounting and Supply Chain Management* (pp 171–202). Dordrecht: Springer. doi: 10.1007/978-94-007-1390-1_8

Mair, J. (2010). Social entrepreneurship: Taking stock and looking ahead. In *Handbook of Research on Social Entrepreneurship* Edward Elgar Publishing. https://doi.org/10.4337/9781849804684.00007

Mair, J., & Marti, I. (2004). *Social Entrepreneurship: What are We Talking About? A Framework for Future Research*. (No. D/546). IESE Business School. https://ideas.repec.org/p/ebg/iesewp/d-0546.html

Mair, J., & Marti, I. (2006). Social entrepreneurship research: A source of explanation, prediction, and delight. *Journal of World Business, 41*(1), 36–44. https://doi.org/10.1016/j.jwb.2005.09.002

Mair, J., & Marti, I. (2009). Entrepreneurship in and around institutional voids: A case study from Bangladesh. *Journal of Business Venturing, 24*(5), 419–435. https://doi.org/10.1016/j.jbusvent.2008.04. 006

Mair, J., Wolf, M., & Ioan, A. (2020). Governance in social enterprises. In H. K. Anheier & T. Baums (Eds.), *Handbook on Advances in Corporate Governance: Comparative Perspectives* Oxford: Oxford University Press.

Mair, J., Wolf, M., & Seelos, C. (2016). Scaffolding: A process of transforming patterns of inequality in small-scale societies. *Academy of Management Journal, 59*(6), 2021–2044. https://doi.org/10.5465/amj.2015.0725

Mitnick, B. M. (1973). Fiduciary responsibility and public policy: The theory of agency and some consequences. *Annu. Meet. Am. Polit. Sci. Assoc., 69th* New Orleans: https://papers.ssrn.com/sol3/papers.cfm?abstract_id=1020859

Organisation for Economic Co-operation and Development (OECD) (2015). *Policy Brief on Social Impact Measurement for Social Enterprises.* https://www.oecd.org/social/PB-SIM-Web_FINAL.pdf

Organisation for Economic Co-operation and Development (OECD) and European Commission (EC) (2016). *Policy Brief on Scaling the Impact of Social Enterprises.* https://www.oecd.org/employment/leed/Policy-brief-Scaling-up-social-enterprises-EN.pdf

Pache, A. C., & Santos, F. (2013). Inside the hybrid organisation: Selective coupling as a response to competing institutional logics. *Academy of Management Journal, 56*(4), 972–1001. https://doi.org/10.5465/amj.2011.0405

Peredo, A. M., & Chrisman, J. J. (2006). Toward a theory of community-based enterprise. *Academy of Management Review, 31*(2), 309–328. https://doi.org/10.5465/amr.2006.20208683

Rawhouser, H., Cummings, M., & Newbert, S. L. (2019). Social impact measurement: Current approaches and future directions for social entrepreneurship research. *Entrepreneurship Theory and Practice, 43*(1), 82–115. https://doi.org/10.1177/1042258717727718

Samman, E., & Santos, M. E. (2009). *Agency and Empowerment: A Review of Concepts, Indicators and Empirical Evidence.* https://ora.ox.ac.uk/objects/uuid:974e9ca9-7e3b-4577-8c13-44a2412e83bb

Schwab Foundation and World Economic Forum (WEF) (2017). *Beyond Organisational Scale: How Social Entrepreneurs Create Systems Change.* https://www.weforum.org/reports/beyond-organisational-scale-how-social-entrepreneurs-create-systems-change/

Schwab Foundation for Social Entrepreneurship (2020). *Two Decades of Impact: How Social Entrepreneurs Have Improved 622 Million Lives.* https://www.weforum.org/reports/two-decades-of-impact

Seelos, C., & Mair, J. (2017). *Innovation and Scaling for Impact.* Redwood City: Stanford University Press.

SEFORIS. (2017). *Final Report Summary* https://cordis.europa.eu/project/id/613500/reporting

Sen, A. K. (1985). Well-being, agency and freedom. *The Journal of Philosophy, LXXXII,* 169–221. https://doi.org/10.2307/2026184

Shapiro, S. P. (2005). Agency theory. *Annual Review of Sociology, 31,* 263–284. https://www.jstor.org/stable/29737720

Shorters, T. (2018). *Asset Framing: The Other Side of the Story.* The Communications Network. https://www.comnetwork.org/resources/asset-framing-the-other-side-of-the-story/

Spear, R., & Bidet, E. (2005). Social enterprise for work integration in 12 European countries: A descriptive analysis. *Annals of Public and Cooperative Economics, 76*(2), 195–231. https://doi.org/10.1111/j.1370-4788.2005.00276.x

Stephan, U., Patterson, M., Kelly, C., & Mair, J. (2016). Organisations driving positive social change a review and an integrative framework of change processes. *Journal of Management, 42*(5), 1250–1281. https://doi.org/10.1177/0149206316633268

Weik, E. (2011). Institutional entrepreneurship and agency. *Journal for the Theory of Social Behaviour, 41*(4), 466–481. https://doi.org/10.1111/j.1468-5914.2011.00467.x

Wilf, S. (2018). How Ashoka fellows create systems change; new learnings and insights from the 2018 global fellows study. *Social Innovations Journal,* 52. https://socialinnovationsjournal.org/editions/issue-52/75-disruptive-innovations/2905-how-ashoka-fellows-create-systems-change-new-learnings-and-insights-from-the-2018-global-fellows-study

Wilson, F., & Post, J. E. (2013). Business models for people, planet (& profits): Exploring the phenomena of social business, a market-based approach to social value creation. *Small Business Economics, 40*(3), 715–737. https://link.springer.com/article/10.1007/s11187-011-9401-0

Yunus, M. (1998). *Banker to the Poor.* Haryana: Penguin Books India.

Mona Itani, Alain Daou

20 Breaking Boundaries: The Case of Women Tech-Entrepreneurs in Lebanon

Abstract: This chapter explores the case of women social entrepreneurs in Lebanon. In particular, it looks at women in technology and how they break the boundaries in a patriarchal context. Our findings are organised around three themes. First, we show how nascent the social entrepreneurship ecosystem in Lebanon is, as many of the women interviewed were unaware that they were social entrepreneurs; second, despite working in a male-dominated field, many of the interviewees use their feminine traits to advance their organisations' economic and social goals; finally, institutional boundaries of this highly masculinised sector of activity are being redefined and made more inclusive and impactful. Taking an institutional theory perspective, our findings shed light on the formation of women social entrepreneurship in a masculinised context and industry. We are contributing to expanding the definition of social entrepreneurship to include under-represented groups such as female tech-entrepreneurs in developing countries.

Keywords: social entrepreneurship, gender, tech-entrepreneurs, developing countries, institutional theory

1 Introduction

In the current entrepreneurship literature, there is agreement on the importance of contextualising entrepreneurship research, particularly when examining women entrepreneurs in under-developed countries, as well as the necessity to contextualise the gendered interpretation of entrepreneurial behaviour (Baughn, Chua, & Neupert, 2006; Welter, 2011; Zahra, 2007). Gender and location are particularly relevant in women's entrepreneurship research. The significance of studying this phenomenon in a developing country like Lebanon stems from the country's unique cultural makeup, which has long been known for combining Eastern and Western values, as well as the economic need for women's contributions due to high brain drain and unstable political conditions.

Even though patriarchy is a global issue, the Middle East is seeing a slower rate of change in changing conventional beliefs into more gender-equal attitudes (Jamali,

Mona Itani, Suliman S. Olayan School of Business, American University of Beirut, 1107 2020 Riad El Solh, 11-0326, Beirut, Lebanon

Alain Daou, School of Business, AUB-Mediterraneo, 65 Neophyto Nicolaides, 8011, Paphos, Cyprus

https://doi.org/10.1515/9783110756159-025

Sidani & Safieddine 2005). Patriarchy is prevalent in Lebanon, and despite its small size, it is extremely varied, with significant differences between cities based on religious and other influences, as well as between urban and rural areas, the latter being known to be far more conservative and stereotypical when it comes to their perceptions of the role of women in the home and society (Jamali, 2009). Despite the above-mentioned challenges, women entrepreneurs in Lebanon are playing a role in redefining boundaries and helping to enter a highly masculine space (Daou, Talbot, & Jomaa, 2022). We will be looking at women entrepreneurs in STEM (science, technology, engineering, mathematics), whereby we find that most women are social entrepreneurs and are unaware of their status or do not identify as such. This is especially true in contexts and industries where social entrepreneurship is still in its infancy, such as Lebanon and the technology sector. As a result, many social entrepreneurs go unrecognised in a context where there is no agreed-upon definition of social entrepreneurship and no legislative framework to support it. This is even more salient in areas like STEM, where social business models are not the norm and where there is little understanding and awareness of the issue (Gupta et al., 2020). Hence, our research question is: what can we learn about social entrepreneurship from women tech-entrepreneurs, given their entrepreneurial and gender identity in a patriarchal context?

Our findings are organised around three main themes. First, many of the women interviewed were unaware that they were social entrepreneurs; second, despite working in a male-dominated field, many of the interviewees use their 'feminine traits' to advance their organisations' economic and social goals; finally, we will show how they redefine the institutional boundaries of this highly masculinised sector of activity. The rest of the chapter is organised by first introducing the context of Lebanon and the challenges women in general and women entrepreneurs in particular face; Section 3 discusses the literature review around institutional theory and women entrepreneurship, women entrepreneurs in technology, and women in social entrepreneurship, leading to our research question. Section 4 presents our qualitative methodology and the sampling, followed by Section 5 discussing the results around three key themes. Finally, Section 6 presents the discussion and conclusion.

2 Context

Our study is in Lebanon, a Middle Eastern country plagued with socio-economic and political problems. The religious (both Christian and Muslim) influence is prominent in all aspects of life, leading to 'traditional patriarchal dynamics and archaic paternalistic legislative frameworks' (Afiouni & Karam, 2019: 74). From a gender perspective (see Table 20.1), Lebanon ranks 132 out of 156 countries on the Global Gap Index; 112th out of 156 countries in political empowerment; 156th in economic participation and opportunity; and STEMS attainment is 18.03% for women versus 30.34% for men (WEF, 2021).

Table 20.1: Key gender gap indicators for Lebanon.

Indicator	Rank (women/men)
Global gender gap	132/156
Economic participation and opportunity	139/156
Educational attainment	113/156
Political attainment	112/156
Labour force participation	144/156
STEMS attainment	18% vs. 30.34%

Source: WEF 2021

As for the entrepreneurship ecosystem, Lebanon has a small market. Out of the 2.8$ billion raised by start-ups in 2021 in the MENA (Middle East and North Africa) region, Lebanese start-ups only raised 42$ million (Wamda Research Lab, 2022). This nascent ecosystem was initially supported by initiatives such as the Lebanese Central Bank through Circular 331, the European Union and the World Bank, among other entities (Daou, Talbot, & Jomaa, 2022). Some of the programmes targeted women to empower them and bridge the gap. In a patriarchal context where businesswomen are considered too sentimental and have more challenges than their male counterparts in gaining legitimacy, the Lebanese League of Women in Business (LLWB) created in 2017 the Lebanese Women Angel Fund (LWAF) with the support of the World Bank as a gender-investing initiative that trains qualified women on how to become seed investors and support women entrepreneurs (Daou, Talbot, & Jomaa, 2022).

As for the social entrepreneurship ecosystem in Lebanon, it faces even more challenges since it is misunderstood. People still equate it with not-for-profits or see it as a strategy for for-profits to access grants from donors. Moreover, social entrepreneurship in Lebanon does not have an agreed-upon definition, and social enterprises do not have a legal framework, having to register either as for-profits or not-for-profits, adding to the confusion. Despite rising awareness, a couple of donor-led programmes to support social entrepreneurs and the Lebanese Social Enterprise Association (LSE) creation, a lot needs to be done. However, from a gender lens, a recent impact assessment of Lebanese social enterprises showed that women lead 37% of social enterprises in Lebanon. Moreover, women board members make up 48% of total board members in Lebanese social enterprises, compared to only 14% in traditional private sector firms (Daou, 2022). Hence, despite all the challenges faced by the social entrepreneurship ecosystem in Lebanon and its nascent nature, it has proved so far that it is much more inclusive than the private or public sectors, and women play a crucial role in its formation and development.

3 Literature Review

3.1 Institutional Theory and Women Entrepreneurship

Institutional theory is an adequate theoretical framework for understanding women entrepreneurship, as explained by Bastian, Sidani and Amine (2018) and as interpreted from Baughn, Chua and Neupert (2006), where the previous research studies on the topic were criticised due to ignoring institutional aspects of entrepreneurship. Institutional theory in entrepreneurship research looks at socially constructed (Thornton & Ocasio, 1999) institutional arrangements for gaining legitimacy, as it is composed of cognitive, normative and regulative pillars (Bruton, Ahlstrom, & Li, 2010). The accepted beliefs, and actions in a particular context (religion, profession, etc.) that shape the cognitive pillar are important to us. Hence, depending on the society we are embedded in and the sector of activity, women entrepreneurs might face challenges in entering this highly masculine space and developing to their full potential. This is even truer in a patriarchal society such as Lebanon and in a sector of activity that is dominated by men, such as the technological one, under study in this chapter (Daou, Talbot, & Jomaa, 2022). In this Middle Eastern context, both formal institutions, such as laws and regulations, but also informal institutions, such as religion, patriarchy and family centrality (Afiouni, 2014), play a role in constraining women entrepreneurship. As entrepreneurship is socially constructed, contextual and gendered (Marlow & Swail, 2014), institutional logics in this field might evolve as society or groups evolve (Ocasio, Mauskapf, & Steele, 2016). For instance, the Lebanese League of Women in Business (LLWB) supports STEM projects for girls in underprivileged communities. It is supporting young women entrepreneurs to break the glass ceiling and enter this highly gendered sector, hence playing an enabling role (Yunis et al., 2019), and encouraging women entrepreneurs to venture into this space. This study is aligned with previous ones using institutional theory to investigate the dynamics related to entrepreneurship in the Middle East and Lebanon in particular (Bastian, Sidani, & Amine, 2018; Daou, Talbot, & Jomaa, 2022). Moreover, this chapter extends previous studies by looking at a highly masculinised sector within entrepreneurship, that is, tech-entrepreneurship, and by looking at a particular set of women entrepreneurs, that is, social entrepreneurs, as they differ from others in their motivations, and the business model they adopt.

3.2 Women Entrepreneurship in Technology

As entrepreneurship is a gendered space (Marlow & Swail, 2014), some sectors within this space are even more gendered, such as technology-driven start-ups. Regarding research on women entrepreneurship, the majority focused on the traditional sectors such as retail and services, which are traditionally female-dominated sectors (Anna et al., 2000; Brush & Cooper, 2012), leaving women tech-entrepreneurship as an under-researched field. According to a literature review by Poggesi et al. (2020) on women entrepreneurship in STEM fields, little research has been done on this topic, with research questions focusing on networking, financing, performance, and gender barriers. Moreover, the authors call for a more thorough understanding of context, social norms and culture that can help gain a more granular understanding. For instance, Ezzedeen and Zikic (2012) find that some of the challenges women starting STEM start-ups face relate to resistance in financing, male clients and male subordinates. Hence, given the nature of the technology field, women entrepreneurs are expected to portray masculine norms to be taken seriously (Marlow & McAdam, 2012).

3.3 Women in Social Entrepreneurship

The rising interest in social entrepreneurship arises from its critical role in tackling social issues and its impact on community service (Zahra et al., 2009). In social entrepreneurship, the founders' values are often aligned with the firm's core social values. These values play a motivational role in their journey of building and growing the business venture since balancing the social and economic dimensions is often a tricky matter. Lewis and Gasealahwe (2017) show that young women entrepreneurs described their businesses as an extension of themselves and an augmentation of their identities and self-worth. Despite the numerous challenges women encounter, the beneficial impact women entrepreneurs have on society through the values they bring to the table is noteworthy. Women-led organisations also stress the role of gender in prosocial factors like compassion and nurture (Bampton & Maclagan, 2009; Hechavarria et al., 2016), and are governed by an ethics of care (Humbert & Roomi, 2018; Jaffee & Hyde, 2000; Stephan & Pathak, 2016). Hence, women tend to positively impact their communities by bringing attention to social and environmental issues like education, children, women's health and prejudice against particular groups of people (Mailloux, Horak, & Godin, 2002). Without them knowing it or doing it intentionally, many of the women-led ventures could fit the definition of social entrepreneurship without formally being so.

Zahra et al. (2009) offer three typologies of social entrepreneurs, respectively. The first typology based on Hayek (1945) considers the social entrepreneur to be a 'Social Bricoleur' who is someone engaged in creating 'social bricolage' since s/he is knowledgeable in the local environment and has adequate resources and knowledge to solve specific problems on the local scale, which sometimes might be of limited scope. The second typology is based on Kirzner's (1973) emphasis on entrepreneurs' constant alertness to opportunity and new information and their ability to introduce systemic changes. This typology considers the social entrepreneur to be a 'social constructionist' who exploits social needs and opportunities that are not typically addressed by the existing institutions and creates ventures that address those social needs thus creating social wealth. The difference between this typology and the former is that it doesn't rely on the importance of the entrepreneur's local knowledge or contextual information (Hayek, 1945) but rather relies on their opportunity recognition and inno- vativeness in tackling those opportunities. Moreover, the second typology tackles ven- tures that have a broader scope and can go international, unlike the first typology where ventures will be limited in size and scope. The third typology based on Schum- peter (1934) considers the social entrepreneur to be a 'social engineer' where s/he has the ability to work on complex social problems and disrupt the current system to offer solutions that are not possible to have within the existing institutions. The main difference between this type of social entrepreneurs and the former two is that they bring revolutionary change to the current system and introduce dramatic changes to the social sphere similar to what Schumpeter's (1942) innovative entrepreneurs do to the business world.

Most often social entrepreneurs are not aware of being so, or do not identify as so. This is particularly true in contexts and sectors where social entrepreneurship is still nascent such as in Lebanon and in sectors such as STEM. Social entrepreneurs, according to Drayton (2002: 123), 'have the same core temperament as their industry- creating, commercial entrepreneur contemporaries'. Hence, in a context where there is no agreed upon definition of social entrepreneurship, no legal framework support- ing it, in sectors of activity such as technology where social business models are not the standard, and little knowledge and awareness on this topic, many social entrepre- neurs go unnoticed, thus depriving the field from the attention it deserves and limit- ing the opportunities that it provides. Given the disconnect in the research between technology-based entrepreneurship and social entrepreneurship, this chapter tries to tackle this issue, leading to our research question: 'What can we learn about social entrepreneurship from women tech-entrepreneurs given their entrepreneurial and gender identity in a patriarchal context?'

4 Methodology

The research presented in this book chapter is based on Itani's (2021) doctoral thesis. The results under focus are only a subset of the entire research and mainly tackle the relationship between women technology entrepreneurs and social entrepreneurship. The methodology used in this study is qualitative. The aim of the study is to investi- gate the dynamics of women technology entrepreneurs in Lebanon and relating it to social entrepreneurship. In-depth semi-structured interviews with the women entre- preneurs themselves served as the main tool of data collection. The data collection process was very iterative, and each interview created learnings that enriched the fol- lowing interview. A reflexive qualitative data analysis approach was used while ap- plying elements from grounded theory. Semi-structured interviews with 15 female tech-entrepreneurs in Lebanon were conducted to answer the above-mentioned research question using an interview guide that was prepared prior to the interviews and based on the literature review. The sample utilised was purposive, given Lebanon's embryonic (social) entrepreneurship ecosystem and the fact that few women tech-entrepreneurs fit the required criteria. The interview questions were not asked passively but interactive reflection was attempted and made during the interview to enhance the gained understanding of the interviewees' experiences.

The interviews varied between 50 and 90 min and were all recorded and transcribed. Analysis of the transcribed interviews was an iterative process, which part of is shown in this chapter. To preserve the anonymity of the interviewees, all participants were given pseudonyms and quotes were generalised. Table 20.2 summarises the key attributes of the interviewed women entrepreneurs.

Table 20.2: Interviewee summary.

Dimension	Categories	Frequency
Age	20–29	4
	30–39	10
	40–49	1
Background	Engineering	6
	Design or similar	5
	Business or similar	4
Years in operation	<2 years	6
	2–5 years	7
	>5 years	2
Marital status	Single	10
	Married with no kids	1
	Married with kids	3
	Divorced with kids	1
Religion	Christian	8
	Muslim	7
Geographic location	Beirut and vicinity	13
	Outside Beirut	2

It is notable that five of the entrepreneurs were running online platforms including e-commerce platforms, four of them were offering technology education services in different formats and two of them provided creative and graphic design services that are high-tech in nature. The remaining entrepreneurs were distributed in the automotive, facility management, gaming and cybersecurity industries. One of the latter also had a gaming academy, so she was also active in the technology education space.

Like grounded theory, the analysis focused on categorising and sorting data themes that appear in the statements of the interviewees. Formulation of general expressions of categories was performed and reviewed iteratively. After data saturation was reached and determined the completion of the data collection, a theoretical reflection of the relationships and interconnectedness of the different categories took place using coding of the interviews' transcripts. Since this chapter revolves around the social aspect of the interviewed entrepreneurs' work, Table 20.3 shows their pseudonyms and the type of their work and impact.

Table 20.3: Interviewee impact.

Pseudonym	Industry	Considers herself a social entrepreneur?	Business has a clear social impact?
Aya	E-commerce	No	No
Carla	Technology education	No	Yes
Caroline	E-learning	No	Yes
Christy	Automotive	No	No
Dina	Creative content and animation	No	No
Fatima	E-coaching	Yes	Yes
Josiane	Cybersecurity	No	Yes
Lea	Digital services	No	No
Rima	Creative content and animation	No	Yes
Rola	Gaming	No	Yes
Sabrine	Technology education	No	Yes
Siham	Digital services	No	No
Suha	Facility management	No	No
Tala	Technology education	No	Yes
Yara	Digital crowdsourcing	Yes	Yes

5 Results

As the objective of this chapter is to look at the women social entrepreneurs in technology, our results can be grouped under three key themes: First, many of the women interviewed did not know that they fit the criteria of social entrepreneurs; second, despite being in a male-dominated field, many of the interviewees use their 'feminine traits' to advance their organisations' economic and social objectives; and finally, we will discuss how they redefine the institutional boundaries of this highly masculinised sector of activity.

Theme 1: Being Social Entrepreneurs Without Knowing It

Our results show that although very few of the interviewed entrepreneurs identified as social entrepreneurs, social impact was part of their social motivation and it reflected clearly in their mission, hence they fit the criteria of social entrepreneurs as per Zahra et al.'s (2009) typology. Even though they do not identify themselves as social entrepreneurs, they could be counted as so. This applies well to the STEM academies that several of the interviewees were running. Carla is someone who rejects the title 'social entrepreneur' because of her misunderstanding of what social entrepreneurship is as she equates it with philanthropy. Nevertheless, Carla had ambitions to not only transform the mentality of her academy pupils but also to shape the entire Lebanese curriculum and offer the latest technology to Lebanon's public schools, as one of the early pioneers in education technology.

> I would like to be a dramatic voice of change in terms of the national curriculum, it is directly related to my business. I started with the parents, and they loved it, then we went to the private schools and we were approved, and the students love what we do, now it is time to spread to governments. It is time to leave our marks wherever and however I can, because I believe that I can change the method of teaching in the country. (Carla)

Given her high faith in her ability to instil change, she refers to herself as a dramatic voice of change and aims to make substantial changes in her country. Carla is disrupting and altering the face of the educational institution, with clear objectives to uplift the antiquated teaching methods currently utilised in Lebanon.

Based on the three typologies of social entrepreneurs proposed by Zahra et al. (2009), and based on the analysis of the qualitative interviews, the majority of the interviewed entrepreneurs would fit in one social entrepreneurship typology, although only two of them have identified themselves as social entrepreneurs. Specifically, Rima and Sabrine can both be considered to be 'social bricoleurs' because they are putting their knowledge and expertise in use to solve problems of local nature to bring about social impact and social good. In addition, Fatima, Tala and Yara can all be considered as 'social constructionists' where they are making use of the social opportunities in the market to create ventures with a potential of growth. Finally, the growth-seekers and social change agents who are Carla, Caroline and Rola can be considered to be the 'social engineers', since their ventures show significant innovation as they are changing the game not just on a local level but also on a regional and international level.

Theme 2: Displaying Feminine Traits Despite Operating in a Male-Dominated Field

One important finding from the conducted qualitative research is how female entrepreneurs demonstrate an empathetic understanding towards their customers, beneficiaries and the wider community. Most importantly, they showed a clear vision of their entrepreneurial endeavours that extended beyond their personal or business success to serve the largest possible number of stakeholders.

Once again, the entrepreneurs running STEM academies such as Tala, Yara, Rola and Carla were striving through their proactive activities to foster innovation and creativity, with the objective of building a better future for future generations. They are aware that their mission should be inclusive and must involve the public schools and the less-privileged groups in society. For them, they are pushing to mainstream and integrate twenty-first-century STEM skills in the educational curriculum as they believe that these skills are vital for everyone. Therefore, they are aware that they need to involve the public sector in this endeavour even if that is difficult and not straightforward in a country such as Lebanon, which is characterised by a high level of bureaucracy and lack of transparency when it comes to governmental procedures and institutions. It is notable that this is an unconventional way to do and view business, as typically profit-making aspirations tend to dominate the business thinking. For example, business metrics would entail an increased market share, a greater number of customers and the like. On the contrary, Tala exhibited a greater degree of wisdom when she showed that she has given the situation a good amount of thinking and knew that even if schools created their self-running makerspaces, she would not run out of business. This is her vision, and this is what she wants to achieve and providing support for those schools that will always need guidance and training from experts like herself. Thus, women tech-entrepreneurs in this context show that despite being highly skilled and capable, they are not solely into their businesses for the commonly known goals of profit and power but rather for achieving a specific mission that has a wider social angle.

> I would love to have several [centres] spaces crowded with kids who come to work and share and help each other, same concept of makerspace for older people. They are full of creative and innovative ideas and it is their makerspace. I would love to have this outside the schools just to have the opportunity for people in underprivileged zones because they have a lot of potential and can solve needs that we do not know of. I would also love if we reach the day where schools

have their own makerspace where students can use over the break or use it to do anything they think of. They should do projects to satisfy themselves and what they are passionate about. . . . I cannot cover all the schools in Lebanon. If you believe what you are doing is a right for everyone, and it is the job of the public sector, then make it available for the teachers. (Tala)

Tala operates in the education sector and has developed a centre to provide the children and youth with the makerspace facilities they need to be creative and productive. She sees success as her vision spreading across schools where they will start to adopt and integrate the hands-on STEM skills that she is working hard to introduce into the curriculum even if she was not directly managing this under her company. She does not have monopolistic tendencies because she genuinely believes in the mission and the impact of realising it. She would be satisfied with being a support for those schools that are willing to advance in their students' twenty-first-century learning. She also wants to extend this work beyond private schools to reach all the segments of the community as she acknowledges them to have equal potential and rights as the more privileged youth in the private schools who are currently her customers.

Theme 3: Breaking Boundaries and Redefining the Institutional Space

A major emphasis in the literature is made on entrepreneurship's economic contribution (e.g., Landstrom, 2008). Our results show that women entrepreneurship contributes to the economy in direct and indirect ways. By creating job opportunities for themselves and others through their ventures in addition to creating a volume of business, women entrepreneurs are contributing directly to enhance the economy. For example, Suha and Yara stress in their interviews the fact that they are contributing in their best capacity to lessen the unemployment problem and lack of good opportunities to the Lebanese youth, and that creating employment opportunities and opening some of these to the less privileged is part of their mission. However, equally importantly, the work that women entrepreneurs do inside and outside of their enterprises also contributes to the development of the economy in less direct ways. For example, Suha, in contributing towards providing a better life by emphasising the well-being of her employees, is contributing to having more productive and healthier employees who would shape the whole workplace positively.

Josiane wanted to stay in the entrepreneurship space but expressed her desires and plans to have more power and more say about how things happen within that space. According to her, entrepreneurship has changed and is not the same as it used to be and this is why more room should be made for the more relevant and younger generation like herself to take a more effective role in it. She is using her second start-up, which provides training and coaching to entrepreneurs on pitching, to stay relevant in the field and to be in close contact to entrepreneurs and start-ups. She also mentioned how she convinced several of her friends to take on the entrepreneurial path and how her journey has inspired them and encouraged them to take the leap of faith. Her plans and actions reinforce correlating entrepreneurship with her identity and achieving this identity with her long-term success. For her, she is not attached to her current start-ups as she mentioned but seems to be very much attached to the field of entrepreneurship itself.

> I want to keep running the companies that are going to succeed and move into the venture capital investor space. I want to be the one who is making decisions in these investments and mentor entrepreneurs of start-ups because I am doing it myself. I am sick and tired to hear from old farts. People who are 60 years old telling us how it is to be an entrepreneur. It is a new environment. Don't talk to me about entrepreneurship today you don't know and you're not in it.

Josiane is disrupting and changing the face of the entrepreneurial institution. Just like Carla is disrupting the face of the educational institution Carla stated that she would often offer the same robotics training completely for free to a male customer's sister after she sees resistance and hesitation from the parents, and more particularly mothers, to enrol her in her programmes. Both being international award winners, Rola and Carla were also doing their share in acting as women in technology role models and disseminating this message on a local, regional and even a global scale as they are often invited to speak as keynote speakers or panellists in conferences. Rola openly acknowledges her role as a girls' advocate in the interview, as shown in the following quote.

> I try to influence all women that I meet hoping to bring positive change. Let us start with the women around us. I have a mission, officially because I am the advocate for women; even if it annoys some – but I do not care.

Many of the interviewees showed a deep understanding of the under-representation problem of women in technology-related fields. For instance, when discussing with Sabrine, Rola and Carla, they emphasise greatly the importance of empowering young girls and women to enter STEM. As for Josiane, she went a step further by not just wanting to give her time in talking to girls and empowering them as a role model so that they have a better future, but she also connected this to having a better qualified and more productive female workforce in technology. Based on her experience, she concluded that women need to believe that they can perform in high-tech jobs equally well as their male counterparts. She also realised that she had a role to play to lessen the negative influences of the cultural stereotypes that surround young women and make them value their capabilities. She was eager and willing to give her time to support a cause she believed in, to empower many girls around her and make them not only benefit from her experience but also stop doubting themselves. She was also willing to go through continuous arguments with her male co-founder who would blame her for her continuous insistence on recruiting women coders despite some bad experiences with some women recruits.

6 Discussion

This chapter examines the role of women tech-entrepreneurs in Lebanon and how they use social entrepreneurship to break through institutional barriers. Despite having business models and characteristics of social entrepreneurs, many of the women tech-entrepreneurs we interviewed did not identify as such. Women tech-entrepreneurs in Lebanon apply social problem-solving to entrepreneurship, and they use the elements of social entrepreneurship when they talked about giving back, desired social impact and the goal of creating real change on a large scale. Although a handful of the questioned entrepreneurs recognised themselves as social entrepreneurs, the definition offered by Zahra et al. (2009) is appropriate and may be applied to many of the interviewees since they were adopting creative business models to have a bigger social effect. A key contrast between sustainability entrepreneurs and social entrepreneurs, according to Makhlouf (2011: 2), is that the latter must 'see themselves and behave as social enterprises primarily pursuing a social mission'. As a result, it is critical to emphasise that we are not trying to rename or categorise women tech-entrepreneurs as social entrepreneurs because that is something they can only do, but rather that we are highlighting their role in making a positive impact in society and how that impact is inherent in their entrepreneurial behaviours.

Women entrepreneurs have an influence on a wide range of stakeholders, including family members and close friends, consumers and benefactors, workers and business partners, and the larger circle of women in society, whether directly or indirectly. Women entrepreneurs act as motivational role models and change agents, supporting in the creation of new women entrepreneurs and inspiring young girls to pursue careers that have previously been considered the realm of males, such as STEM in this case. Giving back as part of their professional work, which many corporations would classify as corporate social responsibility, was not an afterthought, as it is for many other businesses, but an integral part of why and how these women tech-entrepreneurs do business, and in many cases even played a role in defining their success, without them being fully aware of it. By promoting feminine traits such as caring and giving as a vital component of the entrepreneurial process, they were promoting unconventional values in a highly masculine sector. Those traits were used to show how they cared about their community and linked their job to a wider social effect, shattering preconceptions, shifting attitudes and redefining what entrepreneurship is and how it should be done.

Another important conclusion is how Lebanon's women tech-entrepreneurs break institutional barriers. Entrepreneurship should be considered as an institution, according to Tolbert and Coles (2018), since it incorporates the behavioural patterns of institutions and their corresponding social understandings, which are also context-dependent, such as geographic location and time. By adopting this logic, our interviewees can be classified as actors who are working to establish new institutions that they deem adequate, and who have the power and resources to shape the character of these institutions and enact institutional change (Garud, Hardy, & Maguire, 2007; Thornton & Ocasio, 2008; Weik, 2011). As a result, women tech-entrepreneurs in Lebanon are change agents (Dacin, Dacin, & Matear, 2010), as they are destroying long-held standards and dictating new business practices by enforcing more humane leadership and genuine collaboration with other stakeholders. This feature of forming collaborative relationships to create social value and effect is typically critical for success, particularly in social enterprises (Pearce & Doh, 2005).

We are contributing to expanding the definition of social entrepreneurship to include under-represented groups such as female tech-entrepreneurs in developing countries. On the one hand, they are disrupting the common understanding of technology-based entrepreneurship as a masculine, purely profit and commercial-oriented activity and transforming into a more social and purposeful mission with high-impact results on their local and extended community. On the other hand, since they do not refer to themselves as social entrepreneurs, one of the conclusions is that the concept of social entrepreneurship is still misunderstood and limited to a not-for-profit like notion of social work. This research opens the door to many questions related to entrepreneurship in general and social entrepreneurship in particular. For instance, it would be interesting to compare women tech-entrepreneurs in different developing countries to identify the similarities and differences or between developed and developing countries as well. Moreover, despite women being trailblazers in social entrepreneurship in Lebanon, we could have a deeper dive into why women tech-entrepreneurs in Lebanon shy from embracing social entrepreneurship nomination and what is it about this sector that makes it different.

References

Afiouni, F. (2014). Women's careers in the Arab middle east: Understanding institutional constraints to the boundaryless career view. (pp. 314–336Ed) *Career Development International, 19*(3), https://doi:10.1108/CDI-05-2013-0061

Afiouni, F., & Karam, C. M. (2019). The formative role of contextual hardships in women's career calling. *Journal of Vocational Behavior, 114*, 69–87.https://doi:10.1016/j.jvb.2019.02.008

Anna, A. L., Chandler, G., Chandler, G., & Mero, N. P. (2000). Women business owners in traditional and non-traditional industries. *Journal of Business Venturing, 15*(3), 279–303. https://doi:10.1016/S0883-9026(98)00012-3

Bampton, R., & Maclagan, P. (2009). Does a 'care orientation' explain gender differences in ethical decision making? A critical analysis and fresh findings. *Business Ethics: A European Review, 18*(2), 179–191. https://doi:10.1111/j.1467-8608.2009.01556.x

Bastian, B. L., Sidani, Y. M., & Amine, Y. E. (2018). Women entrepreneurship in the middle east and North Africa: A review of knowledge areas and research gaps. *Gender in Management, 33*(1), https://doi:10.1108/GM-07-2016-0141

Baughn, C. C., Chua, B. –. L., & Neupert, K. E. (2006). The normative context for women's participation in entrepreneurship: A multicountry study. *Entrepreneurship Theory and Practice, 30*(5), 687–708. https://doi:10.1111/j.1540-6520.2006.00142.x

Brush, C. G., & Cooper, S. Y. (2012). Female entrepreneurship and economic development: An international perspective. *Entrepreneurship & Regional Development, 24*(1–2), 1–6. doi: 10.1080/08985626.2012.637340

Bruton, G. D., Ahlstrom, D., & Li, H. –. L. (2010). Institutional theory and entrepreneurship: Where are we now and where do we need to move in the future?. *Entrepreneurship Theory and Practice, 34*(3), 421–440. https://doi.org/10.1111/j.1540-6520.2010.00390.x

Dacin, P. A., Dacin, M., & Matear, M. (2010). Social entrepreneurship: Why we don't need a new theory and how we move forward from here. *Academy of Management Perspectives, 24*(3), 37–57. https://doi:10.5465/AMP.24.3.37

Daou, A. (2022). Social entrepreneurship in Lebanon impact assessment 2019–2020. *Lebanese Social Enterprise Association*, 1–36.

Daou, A., Talbot, D., & Jomaa, Z. (2022). Redefining boundaries: The case of women angel investors in a patriarchal context. *Entrepreneurship & Regional Development, 34*(1–2), 137–157. https://doi:10.1080/08985626.2022.2037164

Drayton, W. (2002). The citizen sector: Becoming as entrepreneurial and competitive as business. *California Management Review, 44*(3), 120–132. https://doi:10.2307/41166136

Ezzedeen, S. R., & Zikic, J. (2012). Entrepreneurial experiences of women in Canadian high technology. *International Journal of Gender and Entrepreneurship, 4*(1), 44–64.

Garud, R., Hardy, C., & Maguire, S. (2007). Institutional entrepreneurship as embedded agency: An introduction to the special issue. *Organisation Studies, 28*(7), 957–969. https://doi:10.1177/0170840607078958

Gupta, P., Chauhan, S., Paul, J., & Jaiswal, M. P. (2020). Social entrepreneurship research: A review and future research agenda. *Journal of Business Research, 113*, 209–229.https://doi.org/10.1016/j.jbusres.2020.03.032

Hayek, F. A. (1945). The use of knowledge in society. *American Economic Review, 35*, 519–530.

Hechavarría, D. M., Terjesen, S. A., Ingram, A. E., Renko, M., Justo, R., & Elam, A. (2016). Taking care of business: The impact of culture and gender on entrepreneurs' blended value creation goals. *Small Business Economics, 48*, 225–257.https://doi:10.1007/s11187-016-9747-4

Humbert, A. L., & Roomi, M. A. (2018). Prone to 'care'? Relating motivations to economic and social performance among women social entrepreneurs in Europe. *Social Enterprise Journal, 14*(3), 312–327. https://doi:10.1108/SEJ-11-2017-0058

Itani, M. S. (2021). How women entrepreneurs disrupt the traditional culture and economy: The case of women technology entrepreneurs in Lebanon. PhD Thesis. University of Leicester.

Jaffee, S., & Hyde, J. S. (2000). Gender differences in moral orientation: A meta-analysis. *Psychological Bulletin, 126*(5), 703–726. https://doi:10.1037/0033-2909.126.5.703

Jamali, D. (2009). Constraints and opportunities facing women entrepreneurs in developing countries: A relational perspective. *Gender in Management: An International Journal, 24*(4), 232–251. https://doi:10.1108/17542410910961532

Jamali, D., Sidani, Y., & Safieddine, A. (2005). Constraints facing working women in Lebanon: An insider view. *Women in Management Review, 20*(8), 581–594. https://doi:10.1108/09649420510635213

Kirzner, I. (1973). *Competition and Entrepreneurship*. Chicago: The University of Chicago Press.

Landstrom, H. (2008). Entrepreneurship research: A missing link in our understanding of the knowledge economy. *Journal of Intellectual Capital, 9*(2), 301–322. https://doi:10.1108/14691930810870355

Lewis, C., & Gasealahwe, B. (2017). *Lowering Barriers to Entrepreneurship and Promoting Small Business Growth in South Africa*. OECD Economics Department Working Papers. (Vol. 1449 1–46). https://doi:10.1787/d60e254f-en

Mailloux, L. D., Horak, H. C., & Godin, C. (2002). Motivation at the margins: Gender issues in the Canadian voluntary sector. (Statistics Canada, for the Voluntary Sector Initiative Secretariat.) March 31, 2002

Makhlouf, H. H. (2011). Social entrepreneurship: Generating solutions to global challenges. *International Journal of Management & Information Systems (IJMIS)*, *15*(1), 1–8. https://doi:10.19030/IJMIS.V15I1.1589

Marlow, S., & McAdam, M. (2012). Analyzing the influence of gender upon high-technology venturing within the context of business incubation. *Entrepreneurship Theory and Practice*, *36*(4), 655–676. https://doi:10.1111/j.1540-6520.2010.00431.x

Marlow, S., & Swail, J. (2014). Gender, risk and finance: Why can't a woman be more like a man?. *Entrepreneurship & Regional Development*, *26*(1–2), 80–96. https://doi:10.1080/08985626.2013.860484

Ocasio, W., Mauskapf, M., & Steele, C. W. (2016). History, society, and institutions: The role of collective memory in the emergence and evolution of societal logics. *Academy of Management Review*, *41*(4), 676–699. https://doi:10.5465/amr.2014.0183

Pearce, J., & Doh, J. (2005). The high impact of collaborative social initiatives. *MIT Sloan Management Review*, *46*, 30–39.

Poggesi, S., Mari, M., Vita, L. D., & Foss, L. (2020). Women entrepreneurship in STEM fields: Literature review and future research avenues. *International Entrepreneurship and Management Journal*, *16*, 17–41.https://doi:10.1007/s11365-019-00599-0

Schumpeter, J. A. (1934). *The Theory of Economic Development*. Cambridge, MA: Harvard University Press.

Schumpeter, J. A. (1942). *Capitalism, Socialism, and Democracy*. New York: Harper and Brothers.

Stephan, U., & Pathak, S. (2016). Beyond cultural values? Cultural leadership ideals and entrepreneurship. *Journal of Business Venturing*, *31*(5), 505–523. https://doi:10.1016/J.JBUSVENT.2016.07.003

Thornton, P. H., & Ocasio, W. (1999). Institutional logics and the historical contingency of power in organizations: Executive succession in the higher education publishing industry, 1958–1990. *American Journal of Sociology*, *105*(3), 801–843. https://doi:10.1086/210361

Thornton, P. H., & Ocasio, W. (2008). Institutional logics. In R. Greenwood, C. Oliver, R. Suddaby & K. Sahlin (Eds.), *The SAGE Handbook of Organizational Institutionalism* (pp. 99–128). London: SAGE Publications Ltd. https://doi:10.4135/9781849200387.n4

Tolbert, P. S., & Coles, R. (2018). Studying entrepreneurship as an institution. In *Knowledge and Institutions* (Vol. 13pp. 271–299). Springer. https://doi:10.1007/978-3-319-75328-7_13

Wamda Research Lab (2022). *2021 Year in review – Investments in Mena*.

Weik, E. (2011). Institutional entrepreneurship and agency. *Journal for the Theory of Social Behaviour*, *41*(4), 466–481. https://doi:10.1111/j.1468-5914.2011.00467.x

Welter, F. (2011). Contextualizing entrepreneurship – conceptual challenges and ways forward. *Entrepreneurship Theory and Practice*, *35*(1), 165–184. https://doi:10.1111/j.1540-6520.2010.00427.x

World Economic Forum (WEF) (2021). *Global Gender Gap Report 2021*. Washington DC: World Economic Forum.

Yunis, M. S., Hashim, H., & Anderson, A. R. (2019). Enablers and constraints of female entrepreneurship in Khyber Pukhtunkhawa, Pakistan: Institutional and feminist perspectives. *Sustainability*, *11*(1), 1–20. https://doi:10.3390/su11010027

Zahra, S. A. (2007). Contextualizing theory building in entrepreneurship research. *Journal of Business Venturing*, *22*(3), 443–452. https://doi:10.1016/j.jbusvent.2006.04.007

Zahra, S. A., Gedajlovic, E., Neubaum, D. O., & Shulman, J. M. (2009). A typology of social entrepreneurs: Motives, search processes and ethical challenges. *Journal of Business Venturing*, *24*(5), 519–532. https://doi:10.1016/j.jbusvent.2008.04.007

Emma Folmer, Anna Rebmann, Charlotte Johnson,
Esther van der Waal, Alexandra Schneiders

21 Mapping Change in Local Energy: Community Energy Groups and Their Theory of Change

Abstract: While social and environmental entrepreneurships have often been studied separately, in this chapter we study entrepreneurs who integrate social and environmental goals. Specifically, we study community enterprises in the local energy sector. Acknowledging the complexity of simultaneously creating social and environmental impact, this chapter uses the Theory of Change (ToC) model to unpack how these community enterprises are aiming to create change. We compare two community enterprises in the local energy sector and observe that their impact trajectory differs as they are differently embedded in their respective communities. This chapter provides avenues for future research, using ToC or other process tools, to get a better understanding of the impact creation process.

Keywords: community entrepreneurship, Theory of Change, energy sector, impact creation

1 Introduction

Entrepreneurship literature has tended to focus either on environmental entrepreneurs or on social entrepreneurs as separate categories, with few papers looking at those enterprises that have both environmental and social goals (Vedula et al., 2022). This represents an important gap in the literature, as many environmental grand challenges also present social challenges among them and many social challenges are exacerbated by environmental ones. For entrepreneurship to help to solve our most pressing grand challenges we will need approaches that integrate both social and environmental goals (Vedula et al., 2022; Johnson & Schaltegger, 2019). There is also little research that looks in depth at the impact that social and environmental enterprises make and how these connect to the activities and processes of these enterprises

Emma Folmer, Campus Fryslân Faculty, University of Groningen, Groningen, the Netherlands
Anna Rebmann, King's Business School, King's College London, London, UK
Charlotte Johnson, University College London, UCL Institute for Sustainable Resources, London, UK
Esther van der Waal, University of Groningen, Groningen, the Netherlands
Alexandra Schneiders, University College London, London, UK

https://doi.org/10.1515/9783110756159-026

(Vedula et al., 2022). In this chapter we argue that sustainable entrepreneurship 'focuses on creating products and ventures that address environmental, social and economic market failures simultaneously' (Schaefer, Corner, & Kearins, 2015: 396). We provide insights into change processes, outcomes and impacts in social and environmentally focused enterprises using the example of community energy groups and their aims to enable the transition to a just energy system.

The transition to a decarbonised energy system represents a grand challenge that presents both environmental and social challenges. Decarbonisation is essential to reduce the impacts of climate change, but at the same time there are already huge inequalities in the energy system that are being perpetuated and potentially exacerbated by the transition to clean energy (Carley & Konisky, 2020). Community energy initiatives are community-based social enterprises that are working to deliver community-led renewable energy, energy demand reduction and energy supply projects, which can be wholly owned and/or controlled by communities or through partnership with commercial or public sector partners (Community Energy England) with the aim to enable a more just energy transition. The transition to renewable energy has opened up new opportunities for community energy initiatives.

Increasing renewable energy production is accompanied by a shift to a more decentralised energy system, in which smaller renewable energy assets are developed closer to sources of energy demand. The increasing amount of distributed generation from renewable sources is not without its challenges. Existing distribution networks can struggle to balance electricity demand with supply. The distribution networks were designed to supply end-users with power from remote centralised sources that could ramp up electricity production when needed, rather than receive power from many decentralised renewable sources that do not necessarily produce electricity at the time it is demanded. Thus, the transition to renewables puts a strain on the existing electricity grid infrastructure that networks manage in part by limiting the amount of renewable energy generation that can be built and operated in different locations. However, new opportunities are opening up, driven by the need to reduce such challenges and speed up the low carbon transition by matching local renewable energy supply to local demand. Local energy systems can increase low carbon generation and storage while also stimulating flexibility in supply and demand to optimise the use of these assets. This shift to local energy creates a growing role for community enterprises because community enterprises innovate solutions and business models to tackle local issues and progress their social mission.

Our research is situated in the field of local energy and focuses on innovations that are being driven by community energy groups. The need for local and flexible energy production and use drives innovation across technical, financial and legal spheres. We are interested in ways that communities are engaged in these innovation processes and how their entrepreneurial engagement can shape outcomes. Our interest is in line with the increasing awareness that the scale of transformation required to meet climate targets requires societal not just technological transformation (National Grid, 2020). Our research is also aligned with the call for mission driven innovation that delivers societal value, rather than only growth for growth's sake (Mazzucato, 2018, 2016; Schot & Steinmueller 2018).

Local energy is sometimes associated with increased participation leading to a more democratic energy sector and more empowered consumers (Burke & Stephens, 2018). This builds on previous research on ways local ownership of energy assets produces local economic benefits, as well as empowering communities and producing social impacts beyond energy usage (Walker & Devine-Wright, 2008; Walker et al., 2007; Seyfang, Park, & Smith, 2013). However, mutually beneficial relationships between local energy infrastructure and social outcomes are not technologically determined. They must be created. Critical scholarship shows that processes of conceiving and implementing local energy systems are highly political, enabling some actors and materialising some futures, while constraining others. Focusing on the UK, Devine-Wright (2019) has argued that local energy initiatives are not synonymous with community energy initiatives. In general, the projects are highly technical and lack the participatory processes, non-market ethics and place attachment that define community energy. He cautions that by removing these, local energy innovations may not produce the 'long-term societal transformation' required to meet climate targets.

Critical analysis of the processes of innovation is required to understand the potential for local energy initiatives to deliver social and environmental benefits to the communities involved. In this chapter we compare two community energy initiatives from different legal and institutional contexts (UK–NL) and we map the processes that they are setting up to initiate change in the energy system. We look at both the environmental and social outcomes that they achieve. The research question is: what change processes do community energy groups initiate to generate impact?

The chapter is structured as follows: in the next section we provide a brief overview of relevant research on community entrepreneurship as well as a brief history of community energy in the UK and the Netherlands. These respective contexts may influence the change processes community energy groups choose to initiate. We then introduce our research approach, and elaborate on the selected case studies. We provide a mapping of the Theories of Change (ToCs) of two community energy projects. The last section provides implications for our understanding of community energy initiatives as change agents in the transition to a more flexible, more equitable and lower carbon electricity system.

2 Literature

2.1 Community Energy as a Form of Sustainable Entrepreneurship

Critical scholars have emphasised the importance of broad participation from various stakeholders in the transition to a more distributed, decarbonised electricity system. Without civic engagement and broad support from the public it is unlikely that climate targets will be accomplished. Community energy initiatives represent a form of community-based sustainable entrepreneurship. They are seen as important in bringing local communities on board for the changes needed to transform the energy system (Devine-Wright, 2019). Community energy groups offer participatory processes, non-market ethics and place attachment that enable societal transformation to meet climate targets and to be a fair transition (Walker & Devine-Wright, 2008; Seyfang et al., 2013; Devine-Wright, 2019).

Looking more narrowly at the definition of a community energy initiative, the community energy initiative is often characterised as a social business. For instance, Becker et al. classify a community energy initiative as a social business if it meets the following conditions:

> organisations involved at least to some extent in the market, with a clear social, cultural and/or environmental purpose, rooted in and serving primarily the local community and ideally having a local and/or democratic ownership structure (one-member-one- vote rather than one-euro-one-vote). (Becker et al. 2017: 26)

They describe how these groups create value for their communities through, among other things, contributing to regional development, addressing climate change, the overall reduction of energy consumption, the protection of biodiversity, sustainable agriculture, a transition town agenda or social justice and the empowerment of disadvantaged social groups (Becker, Kunze, & Vancea, 2017). Given that community energy initiatives have both social and environmental goals while aiming for economic viability, we argue that they meet the definition of sustainable enterprises (as given by Schaefer et al. 2015).

While sustainable enterprises per definition address social needs and feature a social investment component, there is a considerable difference in the extent to which returns are invested in social purposes and are oriented to serve the local community. Some local energy initiatives are more investment-oriented and mostly serve a local or supra-local community of interest formed by the investors (Becker, Kunze, & Vancea, 2017). Others are explicitly focused on the social aspect by earmarking revenues of energy projects for local purposes, reducing the cost of energy through lowering the tariff or insulation measures or making investment in or co-ownership of renewable energy accessible for people with less disposable income or savings (Burke & Stephens, 2018).

2.2 Understanding Impacts of Sustainable Enterprises by Mapping Their Theory of Change

The envisioned impact(s) of a community energy initiative as well as its trajectory towards achieving those impacts can be represented by a Theory of Change. A Theory of Change is a story of how and why a desired change is expected to happen (Weiss, 1995). It describes a series of actions that are leading to an expected outcome. A commonly used model for the Theory of Change is the so-called 'logic model' (Ebrahim & Rangan, 2014). This model describes the activities of a mission-driven organisation, and consequently its outputs, outcomes and impacts. It is important to make a distinction between output, outcomes and impact because these describe different 'levels of change' as a result of the organisations' activities. Output refers to 'tangible' products from the organisation's activities, typically represented by 'count data', such as the number of people who attended a workshop, or the metric tons of CO_2 emissions that have been saved. Outcomes refer to sustained impact on the level of the beneficiary group, such as increased opportunity, motivation or ability. Impacts refer to system-level changes on the level of a community or society and are the most difficult to achieve and to demonstrate.

Making credible causal links between activities on the one hand, and outcomes and impacts on the other is very difficult, due to intervening variables, situational factors and unintended effects (Ebrahim & Rangan 2014; Nicholls, 2018). Yet, a ToC provides useful insights into the actions and processes by which a sustainable enterprise is working to create impact. At the same time, it can be a reflective tool, allowing for critical reflection on the envisioned and realised impacts, as well as the assumptions that link the activities to the outputs, outcomes and impacts (Weiss, 1995). By studying the ToC of sustainable enterprises we can begin to understand more about the change process they use to create both social and environmental change and how these processes may interact or not with one another.

3 Research Approach

In our study, we take a case study approach, developing two case studies of community energy groups developing new local energy opportunities. Case studies are best suited to understand the change processes that these community energy groups initiate. We require a 'deep dive' through various data sources to gauge their change processes, outcomes and impacts in both the social and environmental dimension.

We present two case studies of community energy groups, one based in England and one based in the Netherlands innovating in local energy through the installation of electric vehicle (EV) charging infrastructure. The community energy groups presented here are part of the 'Social Entrepreneurship at the Grid Edge' project on community energy initiatives. This research project (funded by CREDS[1]) was set up to understand various dimensions of community energy groups, including their entrepreneurial processes, their governance and their impacts. Both community groups meet the following criteria: they operate in urban communities, they operate in the renewable energy sector and their projects actively involve or are initiated by community partners. Each community energy group may be engaged in multiple projects simultaneously. Therefore, we focus on one project (or two closely related projects) as the unit of analysis within each of the case studies.

We selected urban community energy groups as these have been little studied. The focus in research on both community energy and community entrepreneurship has been on rural-based communities where there are already strong community identities. There is a question as to how applicable findings in rural areas are to urban areas where community boundaries are less clear cut and people do not need to rely so much on neighbours and resources in their immediate locality. Additionally, while there may be greater opportunities for local energy initiatives because demand is higher, the existing built environment and governance bodies in urban areas can constrain the development of local energy assets and initiatives.

The selection of the projects was a two-stage process. In the first stage we compiled a database of urban community energy projects in the UK and the Netherlands that have the aim to increase the collective consumption of renewable energy. Projects have been identified through a thorough search of: the grey literature, funding sources for community energy organisations and local energy innovation, intermediary and support groups as well as academic data sources (UKERC). Once projects have been discovered, we have identified the lead partner, other project partners, the technologies involved, size and state of implementation. In the second stage, we selected projects that provided variation on several theoretical dimensions, that is, technology, implementation phase, successfulness and community involvement.

For the selected projects we will present the Theory of Change, and map how these projects are aiming to create value. Generally speaking, community-based enterprises are aimed at meeting local needs, which can be economic (jobs, economic growth), social (strengthening a sense of community), cultural (preserving local culture and identity), environmental or political. For community energy groups it makes sense to include all these needs as potential ways to create value for the local community. While unpacking the value created by community energy groups, we link this to the Theory of Change to understand at what levels the projects are meeting local needs.

The ToC mapping is based on multiple data sources. For each project we interviewed a range of stakeholders (project initiators, community members, local authorities, etc.) to

---

1 Centre for Research into Energy Demand Solutions – Funded by UK Research and Innovation, Grant agreement number EP/R035288/1.

get a multi-dimensional perspective of project development and impacts as well as how the regulatory environment has affected these. The main source of initial data will be retrospective accounts of projects that have already been implemented to some extent. The use of multiple interviews per case study will allow us to triangulate data. We will also access archival data to triangulate with interview data. This archival data is sourced from documents such as: annual reports, strategic planning documents, grant applications, crowdfunding campaigns, presentations, newspaper articles, web articles, meeting minutes, social media posts and public interviews.

Before we move on to a mapping of the ToCs of the selected cases, the next section will provide information on the context in which these community enterprises operate.

3.1 Community Energy Initiatives in the Dutch and UK Contexts

Both England and the Netherlands had a presence of grassroots activism in the field of renewable energy in the 1970s. This period was characterised by the initial development and implementation of alternatives to the oil-based economy and energy system more generally. In the Netherlands, this resulted in a steady development of local renewable energy cooperatives throughout the 1980s and 1990s. In England, this development was less pronounced as there was less regulatory space for local ownership of energy generation. At the turn of the millennium both countries committed to a more pro-market orientation of the energy market, resulting in increased liberalisation. This did not result immediately in more community-based energy initiatives, due to regulatory uncertainty and a lack of support schemes for small- and medium-sized projects.

However, in the UK during the first decade of the twenty-first century, climate change and community energy entered the public spotlight and began to draw the attention of a wide range of civil society actors, including non-governmental organisations (NGOs), schools, hospitals and sports clubs. Established intermediaries in the social enterprise sector, such as Co-operative UK, began to develop strategies to support members interested in pursuing renewable energy projects (Conaty & Mayo, 2012).

In this same period in the Netherlands, a wave of pioneers operating on the liberalised energy market came up. They had a broad focus and a local approach to energy sustainability. These cooperatives opted for low-risk and relatively simple projects that could yield short-term, visible results, including resale of green electricity, collective purchase of privately owned solar panels and information provision on energy saving and production. Enabling factors were the 2008 net metering regulation that allowed household energy producers to deduct the energy they produced from their energy bill, and the dropping prices of solar panels due to rapid technological development.

In the last decade community energy has boomed in the UK and the Netherlands. In the UK, the establishment of the Feed-In-Tariff in 2009, providing subsidies for the generation of renewable energy, encouraged a diversity of new national programmes and networks to emerge to support and finance community renewable energy. The number of community energy organisations has increased to approximately 300 in 2020. The majority of community energy projects being rural, this period saw the first urban cooperatives. Following successful projects, community organisations evolved from being groups of non-specialist volunteers to established and staffed organisations with substantial expertise, running multiple renewable energy projects at a time. A small service sector of intermediaries emerged, networked in community energy coalitions at both Scotland and UK level. Financial resources for community energy diversified with the increasing willingness of commercial banks to provide debt for larger community energy projects, as well as the establishment of several social investment funds and crowdsourcing platforms dedicated to community energy.

Similarly, in the Netherlands the number of community energy initiatives grew from 40 in 2009 to more than 500 today. Also, an extensive network of organisations supporting the community energy movement developed, including national knowledge exchange platform HIER opgewekt (2014), regional support organisations (e.g., GREK, Us Kooperaasje, and Drentse Kei), cooperative energy supplier Energie VanOns (2014), cooperative project developer Bronnen VanOns (2019) and the merger of various community and sustainable energy lobby groups Energie Samen (2018).

The Netherlands is prioritising community energy groups as new market players; for example, the 2019 climate agreement goal aimed at 50% of local ownership of renewable energy assets and the Regional Energy Transition Strategies have been developed involving community energy organisations. Previously, a Crown Decree offered front running energy communities the opportunity to apply for experimentation with new business models normally impeded by the Electricity Act, in anticipation of the extended support for prosumers in its successor the Energy Act. In terms of financial support, community energy groups can make use of two subsidy schemes, both functioning as a feed-in-tariff and capped in terms of annual budget. The SDE++ scheme (Stimulering Duurzame Energie) is allocated via a highly competitive auction model open to all prospective energy generators, whereas the SCE (Subsidy Cooperative Energy) is a dedicated support mechanism for community energy groups and only open to homeowner associations and cooperatives with participants from a certain postal code area.

Recently, the UK has become a less supportive regulatory and policy context for community energy groups than the Netherlands. The UK has been prioritising innovation by licence holders (commercial businesses and start-ups). Support available for community energy groups has been dramatically reduced since 2016 and finally the closure of the feed-in-tariff scheme in April 2019. There was limited replacement by the Smart Export Guarantee in January 2020, which obliges suppliers to offer a payment tariff to small-scale generators of energy but there are no guarantees on price or length of contract, which limits its value as a support mechanism due to low financial returns and uncertainty. Consequently, there is now no longer subsidy support for electricity generation at local scales relevant to the community energy sector.

From 2016 to 2018 there has been a significant decline in community energy activity in the UK with new electricity generation capacity and annual investment into the sector falling by 80% as well as an 81% fall in the formation of new community energy organisations (Community Energy England, 2020).

3.2 Case study Descriptions

3.2.1 Brighton Energy Coop (UK): EV charging project

In 2010, the feed-in-tariff had just been launched in the UK. There were already some existing community energy groups around the country. The co-founders of Brighton Energy Coop (BEC) saw the opportunity available to launch a community energy group in Brighton and Hove. The mission of BEC is broadly to work towards the sustainable energy transition through a community-based effort. BEC also advocates for the community energy sector in a broad sense. BEC developed a business model to crowdfund investment to install solar energy systems in the Brighton and Hove area. BEC owns the installations. The sites get the photovoltaics (PV) on their roofs for free and BEC gives them a discount on the electricity generated by the solar PV. Money from selling the solar electricity generated by these systems gets distributed back to the BEC investors and to projects in the local community through BEC's Community Fund. The leases run for 20–25 years and at the end of the lease BEC plans to gift the arrays to the sites. As BEC is a Community Benefits Society, a specific UK legal organisational form for organisations wishing to create benefit for a wider community, beyond its specific members, and any profits must be used to benefit the wider community. Thus, any surplus after paying investors and the running costs of BEC is put into a community benefit fund. Most recently this fund has been channelled into schools to their further decarbonisation but also the education of pupils around energy savings and decarbonisation. The first installation by BEC took place on Hove Enterprise Centre in 2012, followed by City Coast Church. By 2020, BEC had installed 80 solar arrays on 39 sites, creating a large portfolio of solar assets. BEC developed from an initial concept in 2010 to now having 2.5 full-time equivalent (FTE), 3 part-time freelancers, 5 non-executive directors and 450 + members.

One of the BEC founders had been considering the possibilities for EV charging, as it was clear to him that the shift of transport from fossil fuels to electrification was a big growth area and would require more demand for low carbon electricity. Therefore, it would make sense to place charge points where there are renewable energy generation assets. It also could be a potential new opportunity for revenue generation from BEC-owned solar panels, helping to ensure that as much electricity as possible is consumed onsite, that is, a form of collective self-consumption. Thus, the deployment of EV chargers to booster the community energy business model was an idea BEC wanted to explore further.

BEC applied for grant funding to find out what level of electric vehicle (EV) charging usage will provide sufficient additional income to make community owned solar PV viable after the abolition of the Feed-in-Tariff (FIT). The project was financed by a grant from Power to Change, a charity focused on promoting and developing community businesses. The grant was part of Power to Change's Next Generation Community Energy Programme, looking to support community energy groups searching for post-Feed-in-Tariff business models. BEC's project was mostly knowledge- and research driven, and BEC did not expect this initial project for exploring EV charging to be commercially viable. Because of this, they did not want to risk its members' investments for the project.

In the project, BEC has piloted the installation of EV charge points linked to their existing solar arrays to learn about the potential for linked PV and EV investments to generate extra revenue that will enable greater financial viability at future sites. BEC placed 10 EV charging points at different locations, to provide a variety of use cases to analyse. All locations were chosen because they were sites where BEC had already installed a PV array, as the EV chargers needed to be connected to the same network. All EV chargers were installed over the course of 2021.

3.2.2 Vrijstad Energie (NL): Shared EV Charging Hub

Vrijstad Energie (VE) is a cooperative located in Culemborg, a commuter town 30 kilometres from the city of Utrecht. Vrijstad Energie was founded in 2016 with the mission of providing local solutions to the energy transition. Their goals are to reduce energy usage and take ownership of energy production and manage it democratically. The idea of a solar roof construction on top of a neighbourhood parking lot had been developing separately, yet parallel to the founding of VE. The idea was first pitched in 2015 by a local architect who had moved into the community, and a small group of local residents continued to work on this idea. When this idea gained momentum and support, the project group decided to subsume it under the umbrella of VE. Several members of the project group then also joined the board of VE.

The project initially consisted of a construction with a solar roof that would be built above the neighbourhood parking lot. The neighbourhood 'EVA-Lanxmeer' is a so-called 'ecological' neighbourhood and the houses do not have individual parking spaces. Soon after developing the idea of the solar roof, the project was extended with the plan to install 12 EV-chargers. The addition of the EV infrastructure rendered the business case for the project viable. The electricity generated by the solar roof is partially used for EV charging and the remainder is sold to a regional sustainable energy company. Members of the collective are eligible for a discount when charging their car. The project was partially financed by municipal and provincial subsidies, yet the majority of the financing came from cooperative members.

Soon after the project's realisation in 2018, VE applied for additional funding tied to a national sandbox experiment around smart charging hubs. This additional funding was used to install one 'vehicle-to-grid' charger that allows EVs to deliver energy back to the grid, and to hire a developer who developed a smart charging application for the charging hub. With the app, users can indicate when their car needs to be fully charged. On the basis of this data, the charging and discharging of vehicles can be handled flexibly at times when the load capacity of the grid and energy prices are most favourable and allowing for a slower, more sustainable charging compared to fast-charging processes. VE has just over 200 members, consists of 20 volunteers (including 6 board members) and 3 paid freelance staff members.

4 Findings

Figures 21.1 and 21.2 show the Theory of Change modelled as a 'logic model' for each of the two cases. The logic model (Ebrahim & Rangan, 2014) describes the activities of a mission-driven organisation, and consequently its outputs, outcomes and impacts. We composed these ToCs based on the various sources of data we collected about these cases: interviews with founders, stakeholders and documents such as business plans, websites and reports.

We can observe that many of BEC's activities are driven by their operational model. The operational model of BEC required that they involve various different stakeholders as each of the planned sites for the installation of EV chargers was owned and operated by a different stakeholder. Therefore, one of the main activities for BEC was to find the sites that would commit to the project. Another set of activities are focused on generating and analysing the economic implications of this new business model. For BEC, it was important that the EV chargers were labelled as 'community energy' on EV charging network maps and apps as they thought it might be a source of competitive advantage, attracting EV drivers to charge at their charging points rather than others in the increasingly competitive EV charging market. Also, BEC wanted to collect the usage data from the charging points to increase their understanding of the viability of the combination of PV panels and EV chargers.

Another set of activities are primarily driven by BEC's mission. These activities contribute to their mission to widen awareness of community energy to benefit the community energy sector and are not necessarily required for the business model to be operational. These include disseminating knowledge to the community energy sector about the business model, but also the labelling of EV chargers as a community energy plays a role in widening public awareness about community energy.

The ToC distinguishes between mid-term outcomes and long-term impacts. In the mid-term, the activities of BEC have contributed to improving the EV charging infrastructure. Also, from the outcomes it is clear that BEC has gained leverage for future

Project activities	Outputs	Project outcomes	Longer term impacts
Apply and get funding	Grant application and business plan		
Work with energy consultancy – to help with business modelling	Next Generation grant funding		Sustaining the community benefit fund
Find and sign contracts for EV charging sites	Consultancy report one site	BEC – deploy knowledge in next projects: EV chargers part of ERDF grant and discussions in future solar PV projects	Enables transition to electric vehicles and decarbonisation of transport that will lower air pollution and CO_2 emissions
Tender for EV charger supplier	Eight sites signed up		BEC – developing additional revenue streams to business model to help it adapt to the post-feed-in-tariff environment
Installing EV chargers	Contract with EV charger manufacturer	BEC gains market knowledge – understanding usage patterns of their EV chargers, revenue potential and when EV chargers can complement solar PV	
Get EV chargers labelled as community energy on EV charging network maps and apps	Ten EV chargers installed		
	EV chargers labelled as community energy	Share knowledge & modelling tool with community energy groups	Strengthen community energy by raising awareness among EV drivers
Mapping and researching stakeholders	Survey data		Strengthen the community energy sector – other CEG groups are able to harness learnings to add to their business models
Collect usage data	Usage data		
Develop modelling tool	Modelling tool		
Disseminate learnings to community energy groups	Next gen video and report, talks		

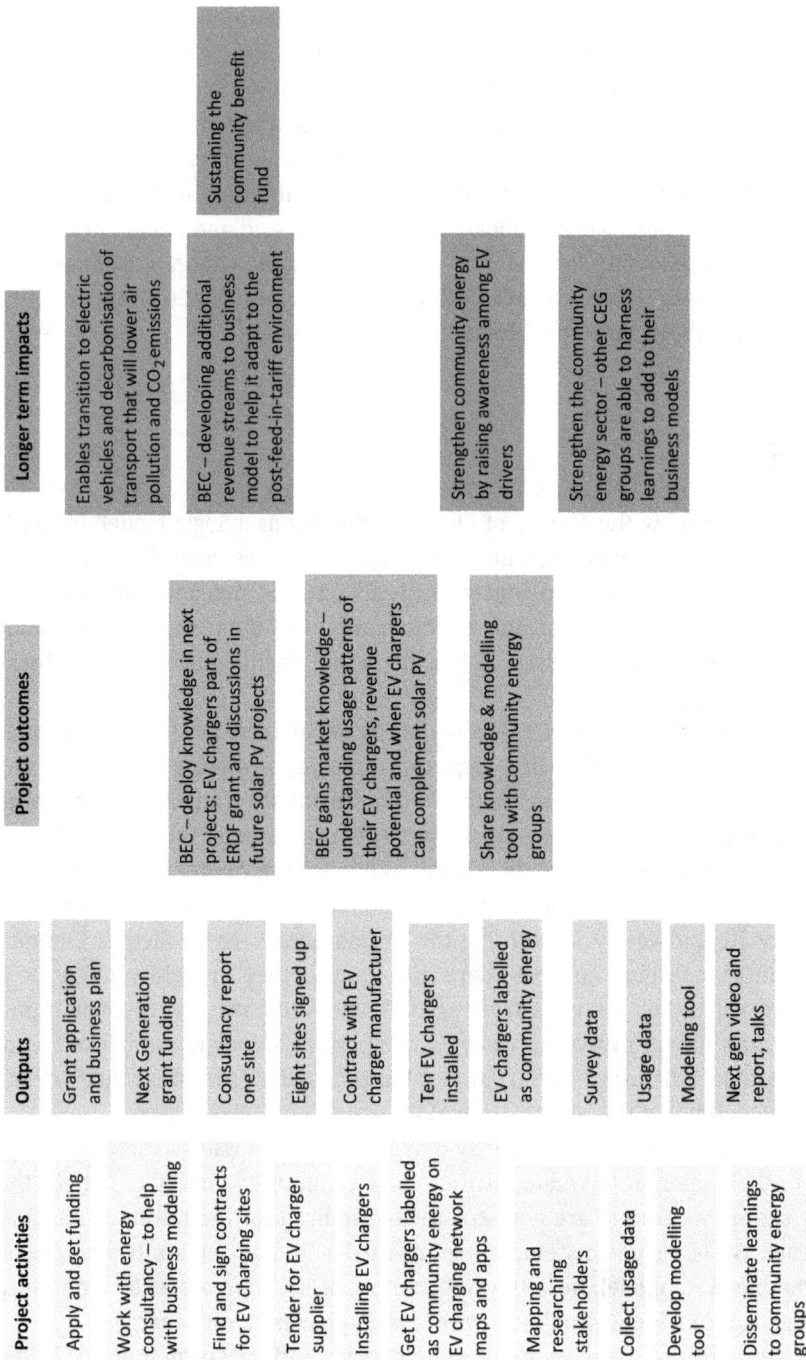

Figure 21.1: Theory of Change Brighton Energy Coop: EV charging project.

Project activities	Outputs	Project outcomes		Longer term impacts
Apply and get funding	Municipality subsidy funding	VE – gains legitimacy for future projects		Community and municipality: CO_2 neutral neighbourhood
Set up community crowd funding	SDE subsidy obtained			
Request building permit	70 per cent of investments are from local residents	VE – gains knowledge about complex project	VE – learning about how to deploy new technologies for decarbonisation	VE – participating in H2020 project on sustainable digital energy services
Series of project meetings with community residents	Building permit obtained	Community – shared sense of ownership		Enables transition to electric vehicles and decarbonisation of transport that will lower air pollution and CO_2 emissions
Install solar roof construction over parking lot	Community concerns are addressed	Community – increased social safety on parking lot	Community – being a frontrunner in CO_2 neutral neighbourhoods	
Install lighting and cameras on parking lot	784 solar panels + construction built	Multifunctional usage of space: solar, EV charging		Community – facilitating electric driving
Install EV chargers on parking lot	Improved lighting and surveillance	Residents – access to EV charging infrastructure		
Collect usage data	12 EV chargers installed		Share knowledge and experience with experiment stakeholders	Society – providing knowledge and inspiration around sustainable energy innovations
Develop smart charging application – experiment 'smart charging squares'	Smart charging application developed	App developer – building knowledge of smart charging applications		

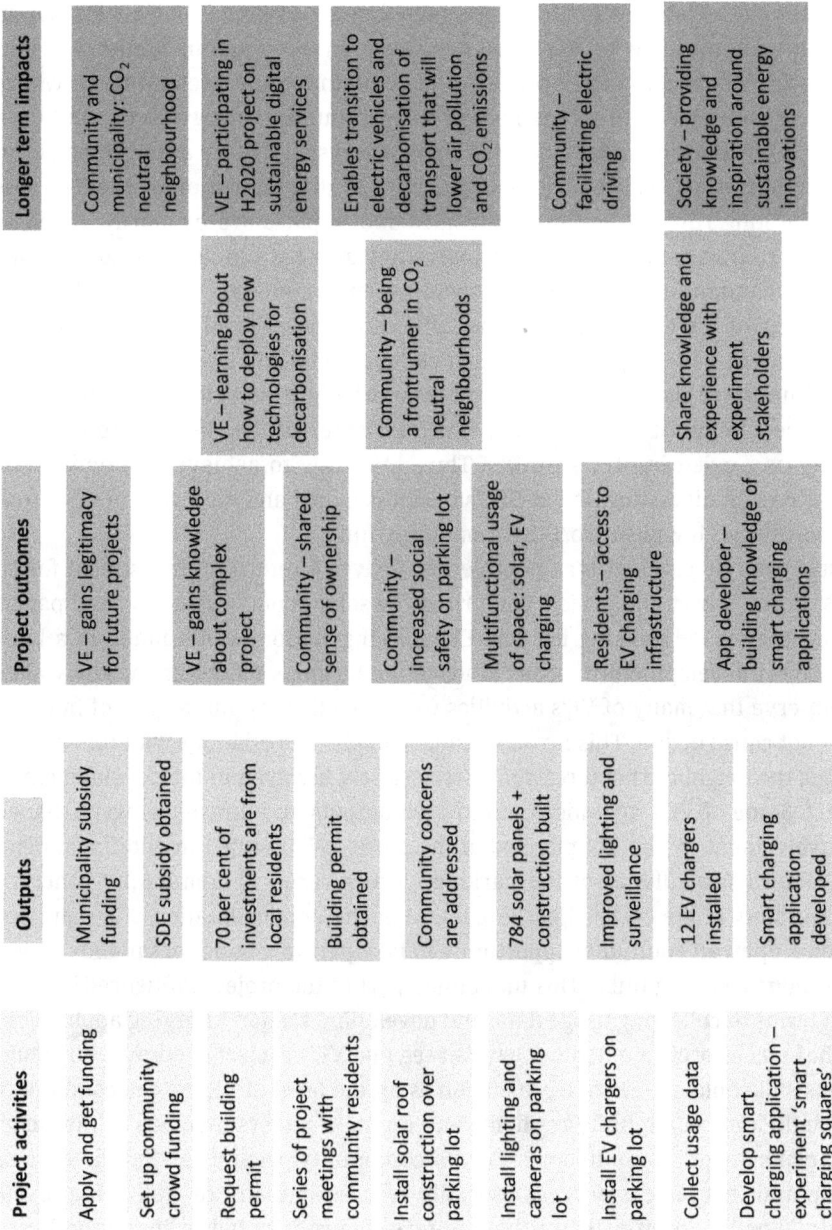

Figure 21.2: Theory of Change Vrijstad Energie: shared EV charging hub.

projects through the knowledge they have gained in the project. Their dissemination activities and outputs have led to shared knowledge in the community energy sector. The longer-term impacts mainly concern the community and societal level, where BEC's project contributes to strengthening the community energy sector and on a wider level contributes to a decarbonised transport system. There are also long-term benefits for BEC itself, as the project contributes to diversification of the business model in the long run. While these outcomes and impacts are primarily aimed at meeting environmental and economic goals, they also help to achieve social goals whereby the community energy groups want to ensure energy transition does not leave the parts of the community behind. This can be seen in BEC's model through their engagement with organisations such as local museums and small businesses that would not have the funding to install renewable technologies themselves. Furthermore, the community benefit fund, which provides further benefits to the local community, is funded by BEC's profits. Thus, by trying to achieve economic goals through successful diversification of BEC's business model and discovery of new profitable opportunities it will support the community fund.

Vrijstad Energie planned for the project to deliver a return on investment for its members. At the outset, the project comprised the solar roof construction and panels on the neighbourhood parking lot. The EV charging stations were added in a later stage of project development in order to make the business model financially viable. We can observe that many of VE's activities were aimed at the initial goal of building the solar roof construction. This involved some complex negotiations with the municipality. Also, the neighbourhood residents were closely involved in the development of the project. Some of VE's activities (and in turn outputs and outcomes) were shaped by this involvement. While not planned at the outset, VE invested in additional lighting and camera surveillance of the parking lot as a result of community concerns around the safety of the covered parking lot. After the implementation of the project, VE stumbled upon an additional opportunity to take part in a national sandbox experiment on smart charging hubs. This unplanned part of the project influenced VE's activities in terms of collecting usage data, and developing a smart charging application.

On the level of project outcomes, we can see that VE's project generated outcomes for various stakeholders. There were outcomes on the level of VE, on the community level, for individual community residents and for stakeholders involved in the smart charging experiment. The outcomes for the community, such as a shared sense of ownership and increased safety, are socially focused and add to well-being of the community. For VE specifically, in the mid-term the project led to increased legitimacy and learnings for future projects, which will deliver impacts in the long term. Currently, VE is involved in a H2020 project on sustainable digital energy services. Similar to BEC, one of the long-term impacts on a society level is that VE contributes to decarbonised transport system. These impacts are focused on achieving environmental goals but through the close involvement of neighbourhood residents, social outcomes and impacts can be achieved as well.

5 Discussion and Implications

The purpose of this chapter was to demonstrate the type of projects and actions that community energy initiatives pursue to reach their goal of transforming the energy system. The chapter has also demonstrated how a Theory of Change model can be used to increase our understanding of change processes. The two cases discussed in this chapter are examples of community energy groups that have developed entrepreneurial projects with benefits for local communities and for the wider society, which are both environmental and social. Through the achievement of environmental goals, both organisations achieve social outcomes as well. Some of these social goals are intended and planned for, but others such as community safety in the VE case, emerge from the development of the project. The legal organisational forms of both enterprises, a Community Benefit Society (CBS) for BEC and a coop for VE, are a consequence of founders wanting to ensure that community benefits are achieved. The CBS ensures all extra profits go to the wider community, whereas the coop form ensures that the members (who are local residents) are beneficiaries.

Linked to this, the two projects show differences in the beneficiary groups that they aim to serve. BEC is benefiting the general EV driving community by improving the EV charging infrastructure and the community energy sector more generally by sharing knowledge about the feasibility of EV charging to boost community energy's financial returns. Through boosting financial returns, their project should indirectly benefit other organisations and individuals through the community benefit fund. VE was founded by members of the Culemborg neighbourhood of 'EVA-Lanxmeer', and its beneficiary group is closely aligned with this neighbourhood community. VE aims to provide economic benefit to its (community) members by providing them with a return on their investment. VE also wants to improve the EV charging infrastructure locally, to help community members make the transition to electric vehicles. In contrast to BEC, VE is thus bound to a smaller geographic scale – the neighbourhood community – whereas BEC is happy to work across a much wider region. This makes the stakeholders that BEC works with more varied, but also while their partner sites are very involved in the projects, BEC's shareholders are not as involved in the development of BEC's projects as VE's shareholders. In the interviews with VE board members, they stated that their members often visit them at home when they have a question or query. This may mean that the type of unplanned social outcomes that we see in the VE case may be more difficult to achieve for BEC due to less intensive involvement of the wider shareholder community. Despite these differences, both projects intend to contribute to the development of the community energy sector, by collecting and sharing data and information.

The ToC models contributed to our understanding of the type of actions community energy initiatives take in order to facilitate change in the energy system. While their actions may be – to a more or lesser extent – geographically bound, we can also observe that the outcomes and impacts of their actions reach beyond local communities.

Modelling the ToC also provides insight into the type of actions that community energy initiatives deploy. While some of these are more pragmatic, that is, closely linked to making the project operational, others are more mission-centric, that is, closely linked to the mission of the project. In the case of VE, we also observed that some of the actions were unplanned for, and were the result of processes early in the project. While modelling and studying a ToC can support our understanding of what it is that community energy initiatives do, and how they aim to facilitate change, there are also clear limitations. A ToC does not allow establishing causal links between activities on the one hand, and outcomes and impacts on the other, due to intervening variables, situational factors and unintended effects (Ebrahim & Rangan, 2014, Nicholls, 2018). By collecting data from a multitude of sources and triangulating the information about the projects, we were able to contextualise the actions of the community energy initiatives. Mapping the other cases in the 'Social Entrepreneurship at the Grid Edge' project will increase our understanding of how the actions of community energy initiatives can contribute to positive social and environmental changes in the energy system.

References

Becker, S., Kunze, C., & Vancea, M. (2017). Community energy and social entrepreneurship: Addressing purpose, organisation and embeddedness of renewable energy projects. *Journal of Cleaner Production, 147*, 25–36.

Braunholtz-Speight, T., Mander, S., Hannon, M., Hardy, J., Mclachlan, C., Manderson, E., & Sharmina, M. (2018). *The Evolution of Community Energy in the UK*. UKERC working paper.

Burke, M. J., & Stephens, J. C. (2018). Political power and renewable energy futures: A critical review. *Energy Research & Social Science, 35*, 78–93. https://doi.org/10.1016/j.erss.2017.10.018

Carley, S., & Konisky, D. M. (2020). The justice and equity implications of the clean energy transition. *Nature Energy, 5*(8), 569–577.

Community Energy England (2020) State of the Sector Report 2020 https://communityenergyengland.org/news/state-of-sector-report-2020.

Conaty, P., & Mayo, E. (2012). Towards a co-operative energy service sector. *Journal of Cooper Studies, 45*, 46–55.

Devine-Wright, P. (2019). Community versus local energy in a context of climate emergency. *Nature Energy, 4*(11), 894–896. https://doi.org/10.1038/s41560-019-0459-2

Ebrahim, A., & Rangan, K. (2014). What impact? A framework for measuring the scale and scope of social performance. *California Management Review, 56*(3), 118–141.

Johnson, M., & Schaltegger, S. (2019). Entrepreneurship for sustainable development: A. *Review and Multilevel Causal Mechanism Framework. Entrepreneurship Theory and Practice, 44*(6), 1141–1173.

Mazzucato, M. (2016). From market fixing to market-creating: A new framework for innovation policy. *Industry and Innovation, 23*(2), 140–156. http://www.tandfonline.com/doi/full/10.1080/13662716.2016.1146124

Mazzucato, M. (2018). Mission-oriented innovation policies: Challenges and opportunities. *Industrial and Corporate Change, 27*(5), 803–815. https://academic.oup.com/icc/article/27/5/803/5127692

National Grid (2020) Future Energy Scenarios https://www.nationalgrideso.com/document/173821/download.

Nicholls, A. (2018). A general theory of social impact accounting: Materiality, uncertainty and empowerment. *Journal of Social Entrepreneurship, 9*(2), 132–153. DOI 10.1080/19420676.2018.1452785

Schaefer, K., Corner, P. D., & Kearins, K. (2015). *Social, Environmental and Sustainable Entrepreneurship Research: What Is Needed for Sustainability-as-Flourishing?* https://doi.org/10.1177/1086026615621111

Schot, J., & Steinmueller, J. E. (2018). Three frames for innovation policy: R&D, systems of innovation and transformative change. *Research Policy, 47*(9), 1554–1567. https://linkinghub.elsevier.com/retrieve/pii/S0048733318301987

Seyfang, G., Park, J., & Smith, A. (2013). A thousand flowers blooming? An examination of community energy in the UK. *Energy Policy, 61*, 979–989.

Vedula, S., Doblinger, C., Pacheco, D., York, J., Bacq, S., Russo, M., & Dean, T. (2022). Entrepreneurship for the public good: A review, critique, and path forward for social and environmental entrepreneurship research. *Academy of Management Annals, 16*(1), 391–425.

Walker, G., & Devine-Wright, P. (2008). Community renewable energy: What should it mean? *Energy Policy, 36*(2), 497–500. https://doi.org/10.1016/j.enpol.2007.10.019

Walker, G., Hunter, S., Devine-Wright, P., Evans, B., & Fay, H. (2007). Harnessing community energies: Explaining and evaluating community-based localism in renewable energy policy in the UK. *Global Environmental Politics, 7*(2), 64–82. https://doi.org/10.1162/glep.2007.7.2.64

Weiss, C. H. (1995). Nothing as practical as good theory: Exploring theory-based evaluation for comprehensive community initiatives for children and families. In J. Connell, A. Kubisch, L. Schorr & C. Weiss (Eds.), *New Approaches to Evaluating Community Initiatives: Concepts, Methods and Contexts* (pp 65–92). New York: Aspen Institute.

List of Figures

https://doi.org/10.1515/9783110756159-027

List of Tables

https://doi.org/10.1515/9783110756159-028

Index

https://doi.org/10.1515/9783110756159-029